LITTLE MUSEUMS

Over 1,000 Small

(and Not-So-Small)

American Showplaces

Lynne Arany and Archie Hobson

An Ink Projects Book

An Owl Book
Henry Holt and Company   New York

Henry Holt and Company, Inc.
Publishers since 1866
115 West 18th Street
New York, New York 10011

Henry Holt® is a registered
trademark of Henry Holt and Company, Inc.

Published in Canada by Fitzhenry & Whiteside Ltd.,
195 Allstate Parkway, Markham, Ontario L3R 4T8.

Library of Congress Cataloging-in-Publication Data
Arany, Lynne.
Little museums : over 1,000 small and not-so-small American
showplaces / by Lynne Arany and
Archie Hobson.—1st ed.
p.   cm.
"An Ink Projects book."
"An Owl book."
ISBN 0-8050-4823-5 (alk. paper)
1. Museums—United States—Guidebooks.   2. Popular culture—
United States—Guidebooks.   3. United States—Guidebooks.
I. Hobson, Archie, 1946–   .   II. Title.
AM11.A73   1998   97-9406
069'.0973—dc21

Henry Holt books are available for special promotions
and premiums. For details contact: Director, Special Markets.

First Edition 1998

Designed by Betty Lew

Printed in the United States of America
All first editions are printed on acid-free paper. ∞

1   3   5   7   9   10   8   6   4   2

Contents

Acknowledgments xxv • Introduction xxvii • A Few Things to Know xxx

....

ALABAMA

Cullman Ave Maria Grotto 1 • Fairfield Alabama Historical Radio Society/Don Kresge Memorial Museum 2 • Fairhope American Bicentennial Museum 2 • Marietta Johnson Museum 2 • Florence W. C. Handy Home, Museum, and Library 3 • Fort McClellan U.S. Army Chemical Corps Museum 3 • Georgiana Hank Williams, Sr., Boyhood Home and Museum 4 • Hartselle Tomb of Mystery Museum 4 • Hurtsboro Museum of Ordinary People (MOP) 4 • Mobile Eichold–Heustis Medical Museum of the South 5 • Montgomery F. Scott and Zelda Fitzgerald Museum 5 • George and Lurleen Wallace Center for the Study of Southern Politics 6 • Salem Lunchbox Museum 6 • Selma National Voting Rights Museum and Institute 6 • Tuscaloosa Ma'Cille's Museum of Miscellanea 7 • Paul W. Bryant Museum 7

....

ALASKA

Anchorage Alaska Aviation Heritage Museum 8 • Fairbanks Dog Mushing Museum 9 • University of Alaska Fairbanks Museum 9 • Homer Miller Comb Museum 9 • Pratt Museum 9 • Ketchikan Totem Heritage Center 10 • Kodiak Baranov Museum 10 • Nome Carrie M. McLain Memorial Museum 10 • Sitka Sheldon Jackson Museum 11 • Skagway Klondike Gold Rush National Historical Park 11 • Wasilla Museum of Alaska Transportation and Industry 11

....

ARIZONA

Bisbee Shady Dell RV Park and Campground 13 • Cordes Junction Arcosanti 14 • Dos Cabezas Frontier Relics Museum 14 • Dragoon Amerind Foundation 14 • Florence Pinal County Historical Museum 15 • Green Valley Titan Missile Museum 15 • Hackberry International Bioregional Old Route 66 Visitors Center and Preservation Foundation 15 • Mesa Champlin Fighter Aircraft Museum 16 • Page John Wesley Powell Memorial Museum 16 • Phoenix Arizona Mining and Mineral Museum 16 • Hall of Flame Museum of Firefighting 17 • Medical Museum 17 • Sylvia Plotkin Judaica Museum of Greater Phoenix 17 • Prescott Bead Museum 17 • Phippen Museum of Western Art 18 • Smoki Museum 18 • Sacaton Gila River Cultural Center 18 • Saint Johns Raven Site Museum/White Mountain Archaeological Center 18 • Scottsdale Fleischer Museum 19 • Second Mesa Hopi Cultural Center 19 • Springerville Casa Malpais 19 • Tucson Arizona–Sonora Desert Museum 20 • University of Arizona Mineral Museum 20 • Wickenburg Desert Caballeros Western Museum 20 • Willcox Rex Allen Arizona Cowboy Museum 21 • Window Rock Navajo Tribal Museum 21 • Yuma Century House Museum (Sanguinetti House) 21

ARKANSAS

Bauxite Bauxite Museum 22 • Bentonville Wal-Mart Visitor Center 22 • Eudora Henry and Rubye Connerly Museum 23 • Eureka Springs Frog Fantasies Museum 23 • Hammond Museum of Bells 24 • Miles Musical Museum 24 • Fort Smith Patent Model Museum 24 • Hot Springs Fordyce Bathhouse Visitor Center 25 • Tiny Town 25 • Pine Bluff Band Museum 25 • Pine Ridge Lum 'n' Abner Museum and Jot 'Em Down Store 26 • Pottsville Potts Inn Museum 26 • Smackover Arkansas Oil and Brine Museum 26 • Van Buren Bob Burns Museum 27

CALIFORNIA

Northern California

Donner Summit Western SkiSport Museum 29 • Santa Rosa Church of One Tree/Robert L. "Believe It or Not!®" Ripley Memorial Museum 29 • Truckee Emigrant Trail Museum 30 • Woodland Hays Antique Truck Museum 30

San Francisco/Bay Area

Burlingame Burlingame Museum of Pez Memorabilia 31 • Palo Alto Barbie Hall of Fame 31 • Museum of American Heritage 32 • San Francisco Hello Gorgeous!! 32 • Musée Mécanique 32 • Museum of Ophthalmology 33 • Tattoo Art Museum 33 • San Jose Winchester Mystery House/Winchester Products Museum/Winchester Historic Firearms Museum 33 • Sunnyvale Lace Museum 34

Central California

Big Sur Henry Miller Memorial Library 34 • Montecito Lotusland 34 • Santa Cruz Santa Cruz Surfing Museum 35

Los Angeles Area

Altadena Banana Museum 36 • Culver City Museum of Jurassic Technology 36 • Hollywood Hollywood High School Museum 37 • Hollywood Studio

Museum 37 • L. Ron Hubbard Life Exhibition 37 • Lingerie Museum 38 • Science-Fantasy Preserves 38 • Los Angeles Carole and Barry Kaye Museum of Miniatures 38 • Museum of Neon Art 39 • Southern California Institute of Architecture (SCI-Arc) 39 • Watts Towers of Simon Rodia 39 • Malibu Malibu Lagoon Museum and Historic Adamson House 40 • Newhall William S. Hart Museum 40 • Pasadena Mini Cake Museum 40 • Simi Valley Ronald Reagan Presidential Library and Museum 41

Outer Los Angeles Area

Boron Twenty-Mule Team Museum 41 • Helendale Exotic World Burlesque Museum and Hall of Fame 42 • Victorville California Route 66 Museum 42 • Roy Rogers–Dale Evans Museum 43

San Diego Area

Escondido Lawrence Welk Museum 43 • La Mesa Computer Museum of America 44 • Oceanside California Surf Museum 44 • San Diego Museum of Death 44 • Museum of the American Presidency 45

COLORADO

Burlington Kit Carson County Carousel 46 • Cañon City Colorado Territorial Prison Museum 46 • Colorado Springs John May Museum Center 47 • Museum of the American Numismatic Association 47 • World Figure Skating Museum and Hall of Fame 47 • Denver Black American West Museum and Heritage Center 48 • Denver Museum of Miniatures, Dolls and Toys 48 • Trianon Museum and Art Gallery 48 • Dolores Anasazi Heritage Center 49 • Fort Morgan Fort Morgan Museum 49 • Genoa Wonder View Tower (Genoa Tower) 49 • Golden Buffalo Bill Memorial Museum and Grave 50 • Colorado Railroad Museum 50 • Grand Junction Museum of Western Colorado 50 • La Junta Koshare Indian Kiva Museum 50 • Leadville National Mining Hall of Fame and Museum 51 • Tabor Opera House 51 • Manassa Jack Dempsey Museum 51 • Montrose Ute Indian Museum 52 • Pueblo Fred E. Weisbrod Aircraft Museum/International B-24 Museum 52 • Sterling Overland Trail Museum 52 • Trinidad A. R. Mitchell Memorial Museum of Western Art 53 • Vail Colorado Ski Museum–Ski Hall of Fame 53 • Victor Lowell Thomas Museum 53

CONNECTICUT

Bridgeport Barnum Museum 55 • Bristol American Clock and Watch Museum 56 • New England Carousel Museum 56 • Canterbury Prudence Crandall Museum 56 • Danbury Danbury Scott-Fanton Museum/Charles Ives House 56 • Essex Connecticut River Museum 57 • Farmington Hill-Stead Museum 57 • Hartford Harriet Beecher Stowe Center 57 • Kent Sloane-Stanley Museum/Kent Furnace 58 • Newington American Radio Relay League/Museum of Amateur Radio 58 • Old Lyme Nut Museum 58 • Riverton Hitchcock Museum (John Tarrant Kenney Hitchcock Museum) 59 •

Terryville Lock Museum of America 59 • Washington (Washington Green) Institute for American Indian Studies 59 • Waterbury Mattatuck Museum 60 • West Hartford Museum of American Political Life 60 • Willimantic Windham Textile and History Museum 60 • Winchester Center Winchester Center Kerosene Lamp Museum 61

DELAWARE

Dover Delaware Agricultural Museum and Village 62 • Johnson Victrola Museum 62 • Fort Delaware State Park Fort Delaware 63 • Georgetown Treasures of the Sea Exhibit 63 • Oak Orchard Nanticoke Indian Museum 63 • Wilmington Kalmar Nyckel Foundation and Shipyard 64

DISTRICT OF COLUMBIA

Washington, D.C. Folger Shakespeare Library 65 • House of the Temple Library/Museum 66 • Labor Hall of Fame 66 • National Building Museum 66 • National Gallery of Caricature and Cartoon Art 66 • National Jewish American Sports Hall of Fame/B'nai B'rith Klutznick National Jewish Museum 67 • The Textile Museum 67 • U.S. Chess Hall of Fame and Museum 67

FLORIDA

Apalachicola John Gorrie State Museum 68 • Chokoloskee Smallwood Store Museum 68 • Cross Creek Marjorie Kinnan Rawlings State Historic Site 69 • Delray Beach Morikami Museum and Japanese Gardens 69 • Estero Koreshan State Historic Site 69 • Fort Pierce UDT-SEAL Museum 70 • Fort Walton Beach Indian Temple Mound Museum 70 • Gainesville Devil's Millhopper State Geological Site 70 • Fred Bear Museum 71 • Jacksonville Karpeles Manuscript Library Museum 71 • Key West East Martello Museum and Gallery 71 • Melbourne Beach McLarty Treasure Museum 72 • Miami American Police Hall of Fame and Museum 72 • Miami Beach The Wolfsonian (formerly Collection of Decorative and Propaganda Arts) 72 • Mulberry Mulberry Phosphate Museum 73 • Naples Teddy Bear Museum of Naples ("Frannie's") 73 • Ocala Don Garlits Museum of Drag Racing and International Drag Racing Hall of Fame 73 • Ormond Beach Hungarian Folk Art Museum 74 • Panama City Beach Museum of Man in the Sea 74 • Perry Forest Capital State Cultural Museum 74 • Saint Augustine Lightner Museum 75 • Oldest Store Museum 75 • Sanibel Island Bailey-Mathews Shell Museum 75 • Tampa Ybor City State Museum 76 • White Springs Stephen Foster State Folk Culture Center 76 • Winter Haven Water Ski Museum–Hall of Fame 76 • Winter Park Charles Hosmer Morse Museum of American Art 77

GEORGIA

Atlanta Center for Puppetry Arts 79 • Johnny Mercer Museum 79 • Robert C. Williams American Museum of Papermaking 79 • Telephone

Museum 79 • William Breman Jewish Heritage Museum 80 • Buena Vista Pasaquan 80 • Columbus Gertrude Pridgett "Ma" Rainey House 81 • Dahlonega Dahlonega Courthouse Gold Museum 81 • Dalton Crown Gardens and Archives/Bedspread Museum 81 • Eatonton Uncle Remus Museum 82 • Elberton Elberton Granite Museum and Exhibit 82 • Fort Gordon U.S. Army Signal Corps Museum 82 • Savannah Juliette Gordon Low Girl Scout National Center 83 • Summerville Paradise Garden 83

HAWAII

Hawaii (The Big Island)

Captain Cook Royal Aloha Coffee Mill and Museum 84 • Kamuela Parker Ranch Visitor Center and Museum 85 • Kealakekua Kona Historical Society Museum 85 • Kohala Coast Eva Parker Woods Cottage 85

Maui

Lahaina Wo Hing Temple Museum 86 • Puunene Alexander and Baldwin Sugar Museum 86 • Wailuku Bailey House Museum (Maui Historical Society Museum) 87

Oahu

Ewa Hawaiian Railway Society 87 • Honolulu Damien Museum and Archives 87 • Japanese Cultural Center of Hawaii 88 • Judiciary History Center 88

IDAHO

Arco Experimental Breeder Reactor #1 89 • Blackfoot Idaho's World Potato Exposition 89 • Boise Basque Museum and Cultural Center 90 • Old Idaho Penitentiary/History of Electricity in Idaho Museum 90 • Bonanza Yankee Fork Gold Dredge 90 • Hailey Blaine County Historical Museum 91 • Idaho City Boise Basin Museum 91 • Moscow Appaloosa Horse Club Museum 91 • Rexburg Teton Flood Museum 92 • Rigby Farnsworth TV Pioneer Museum (Jefferson County Historical Society) 92 • Weiser National Oldtime Fiddlers Hall of Fame 92

ILLINOIS

Arcola Louis P. Klein Broom and Brush Museum 93 • Chicago American Police Center and Museum 94 • Feet First 94 • International Museum of Surgical Science and Hall of Immortals 95 • Museum of Holography 95 • Peace Museum 95 • Des Plaines McDonald's Museum 95 • Edwardsville Louis H. Sullivan Architectural Ornament Collection 96 • Evanston Dave's Down to Earth Rock Shop and Prehistoric Life Museum 96 • Glenview Hartung's License Plate and Automotive Museum 97 • Lemont Cookie Jar Museum 97 • McLean Dixie Truckers Home and Route 66 Hall of Fame 97 • Metropolis Super Museum 98 • Moline Deere & Co. Administrative Center 98 • Mount Vernon Wheels Through Time Museum 99 • Park Ridge Museum of

Anesthesiology 99 • Quincy Valentine Museum 99 • Rockford Time
Museum 100 • Springfield Parks Telephone Museum 100 • Teutopolis
Teutopolis Monastery Museum 100 • Wadsworth Gold Pyramid House 101 •
Wauconda Curt Teich Postcard Exhibit and Archives 101 • West Frankfort
National Museum of Coal Mining 102 • Woodhull Max Nordeen's Wheels
Museum 102

INDIANA

Angola General Lewis B. Hershey Museum 103 • Auburn Auburn-Cord-
Duesenberg Museum 103 • Bloomington Elizabeth Sage Historic Costume
Collection 104 • Carmel Museum of Miniature Houses and Other Collections 104
• Crawfordsville Old Jail Museum 104 • Elkhart RV/MH Heritage
Foundation/Hall of Fame/Museum/Library 105 • Fairmount Fairmount Historical
Museum/James Dean Exhibit 105 • Fountain City Levi Coffin House State Historic
Site 106 • Geneva Limberlost State Historic Site 106 • Greentown Greentown
Glass Museum 106 • Huntington Dan Quayle Center and Museum 107 •
Indianapolis Indiana Medical History Museum 107 • Jeffersonville Howard
Steamboat Museum 107 • Kokomo Elwood Haynes Museum 108 • Madison
Dr. William D. Hutchings Office and Hospital 108 • Mitchell Virgil I. Grissom
Memorial 108 • Muncie Academy of Model Aeronautics/National Model Aviation
Museum 108 • Ball Corporation Museum 109 • Nashville John Dillinger
Historical Wax Museum 109 • Peru Circus City Festival Museum 109 • South
Bend Studebaker National Museum 110 • Terre Haute Eugene V. Debs Home 110
• Wakarusa Bird's Eye View Museum of Miniatures 110

IOWA

Cedar Falls Ice House Museum 111 • Cedar Rapids National Czech and Slovak
Museum and Library 111 • Charles City Floyd County Historical Society
Museum 112 • Chester Hayden Prairie 112 • Clarinda Nodaway Valley
Historical Museum 112 • Clear Lake Surf Ballroom 113 • Council Bluffs
Squirrel Cage Jail (Pottawattomie County Jail) 113 • Dyersville National Farm Toy
Museum 114 • Elk Horn Danish Immigrant Museum 114 • Indianola National
Balloon Museum 114 • Keokuk Keokuk River Museum/George M. Verity 115 •
Knoxville National Sprint Car Hall of Fame and Museum 115 • Lucas John Lewis
Mining and Labor Museum 115 • Mason City Van Horn's Antique Truck Museum
and Circus Room Display 115 • Missouri Valley Steamship Bertrand Display 116
• Mount Pleasant Midwest Old Threshers Heritage Museum and Museum of
Repertoire Americana 116 • Newton Jasper County Historical Society
Museum/Maytag Exhibit 117 • Okoboji Higgins Foundation/National Bank Note
Museum and Library 117 • Pella Pella Historical Village Museum 117 •
Princeton Buffalo Bill Cody Homestead 118 • Quasqueton Cedar Rock/The Walter
Residence 118 • Spillville Bily Clock Museum/Antonin Dvořák Exhibit 118 •
Van Meter Bob Feller Hometown Exhibit 119 • Winterset Birthplace of
John Wayne 119

KANSAS

Abilene *Museum of Independent Telephony* 120 • Atchison *Amelia Earhart Birthplace* 121 • Chanute *Martin and Osa Johnson Safari Museum* 121 • Coffeyville *Dalton Defenders Museum* 121 • Ellis *Walter P. Chrysler Boyhood Home and Museum* 122 • Florence *Harvey House Museum* 122 • Goessel *Mennonite Heritage Museum* 122 • Goodland *High Plains Museum* 123 • Greensburg *Big Well and Celestial Museum* 123 • La Crosse *Kansas Barbed Wire Museum* 123 • Lawrence *Ryther Printing Museum* 124 • Lucas *Garden of Eden and Cabin Home* 124 • Marysville *Original Pony Express Home Station No. 1 Museum* 124 • Meade *Dalton Gang Hideout* 125 • Medicine Lodge *Carry A. Nation Home* 125 • Norton *Gallery of Also-Rans* 125 • Sedan *Emmett Kelly Historical Museum* 126 • Wellington *Chisholm Trail Museum* 126 • West Mineral *Big Brutus* 126

KENTUCKY

Bardstown *Oscar Getz Museum of Whiskey History* 128 • Benham *Kentucky Coal Mining Museum* 129 • Berea *Berea College Appalachian Museum* 129 • Bowling Green *National Corvette Museum* 129 • Clermont *Jim Beam American Outpost* 129 • Corbin *Colonel Harland Sanders Cafe and Museum* 130 • Danville *McDowell House and Apothecary Shop* 130 • Elizabethtown *Schmidt Coca-Cola Memorabilia Museum* 130 • Fort Mitchell *American Museum of Brewing History and Arts* 131 • Vent *Haven Museum* 131 • Henderson *John James Audubon Museum and Nature Center* 131 • Hopkinsville *Pennyroyal Area Museum* 132 • Lexington *American Saddle Horse Museum* 132 • Headley-Whitney Museum 132 • Louisville *Colonel Harland Sanders Museum* 132 • *Museum of the American Printing House for the Blind* 133 • Murray *National Scouting Museum* 133 • Owensboro *International Bluegrass Music Museum* 133 • Paducah *Museum of the American Quilters Society* 134

LOUISIANA

Avery Island *McIlhenny Co.* 135 • Baton Rouge *Center for Political and Governmental History* 135 • Carville *John R. Trautman Carville Museum* 136 • Eunice *The Eunice Museum* 136 • Gibsland *Bonnie and Clyde Festival* 136 • Jennings *W. H. Tupper General Merchandise Museum & Louisiana Telephone Pioneer Museum* 137 • Lawtell *Matt's Museum* 137 • Marthaville *Louisiana Country Music Museum* 138 • Monroe *Emy-Lou Biedenharn Foundation* 138 • New Orleans *Germaine Cazenave Wells Mardi Gras Museum* 138 • New Orleans *Historic Voodoo Museum* 139 • *New Orleans Pharmacy Museum* 139 • Old U.S. Mint: *New Orleans Jazz Collection and Carnival Exhibit* 139 • Oil City *Caddo–Pine Island Oil and Historical Society Museum* 140 • Opelousas *Jim Bowie Museum* 140 • Plaquemine *Gary J. Hebert Memorial Lockhouse* 141 • Sulphur *Brimstone Museum* 141

MAINE

Bath Maine Maritime Museum 142 • Brunswick Peary-MacMillan Arctic Museum 142 • Bucksport Northeast Historic Film 143 • Caribou Nylander Museum 143 • Farmington Nordica Homestead Museum 143 • Island Falls John E. and Walter D. Webb Museum of Vintage Fashion 144 • Kennebunkport Seashore Trolley Museum 144 • Kingfield Stanley Museum 144 • Owls Head Owls Head Transportation Museum 144 • Patten Lumberman's Museum 145 • Pemaquid Point (Bristol) Pemaquid Point Lighthouse and Fisherman's Museum 145 • Rangeley Wilhelm Reich Museum 145 • Rockland Shore Village Museum (The Lighthouse Museum) 146 • Sabbathday Lake (New Gloucester) Shaker Museum 146 • Sebago (Douglas Hill) Jones Museum of Glass and Ceramics 146 • Southwest Harbor Wendell Gilley Museum 147 • Thorndike Bryant's Museum (Bryant's Stoves and Music, Inc.) 147 • Wiscasset Musical Wonder House 147

MARYLAND

Annapolis Banneker-Douglass Museum 148 • Baltimore American Visionary Art Museum 149 • Babe Ruth Birthplace and Baseball Center 149 • Baltimore Museum of Industry 149 • Baltimore Public Works Museum 150 • Dr. Samuel D. Harris National Museum of Dentistry 150 • Eubie Blake National Museum 150 • H. L. Mencken House 151 • Lacrosse Hall of Fame Museum 151 • Mount Vernon Museum of Incandescent Lighting 151 • Fort George Meade National Cryptologic Museum 152 • Frederick National Museum of Civil War Medicine 152 • Glen Echo Clara Barton National Historic Site 152 • Linthicum Historical Electronics Museum 153 • New Carrollton Museum of Menstruation (MUM) 153 • Ocean City Ocean City Life-Saving Station Museum 153 • Silver Spring George Meany Memorial Archives 154

MASSACHUSETTS

Boston Boston Athenaeum 155 • Computer Museum 156 • Brookline Frederick Law Olmsted National Historic Site 156 • Cambridge Mount Auburn Cemetery 156 • Dalton Crane Museum 157 • Dedham Museum of Bad Art 157 • Fall River Fall River Historical Society 158 • Marine Museum at Fall River 158 • Fiskdale Saint Anne Shrine 158 • Harvard Fruitlands Museums 158 • Leominster National Plastics Center and Museum 159 • Lincoln DeCordova Museum and Sculpture Park 159 • Lowell American Textile History Museum 159 • Boott Cotton Mills Museum 160 • New England Quilt Museum 160 • Northampton Words and Pictures Museum of Fine Sequential Art 160 • North Easton Shovel Museum/Arnold B. Tofias Archives 161 • Onset Porter Thermometer Museum (Dick Porter—Thermometer Man) 161 • Orleans French Cable Station Museum 161 • Petersham Fisher Museum of Forestry 162 • Rockport Paper House 162 • Sandwich Sandwich Glass Museum 162 • Thornton W. Burgess Museum 163 • Springfield Indian Motocycle Museum and Hall of Fame 163 • Springfield Armory National Historic Site 163 • Titanic Museum 163 • Waltham Charles River Museum of Industry 164 • Watertown Blindiana/Tactual Museum/Museum on the

History of Blindness 164 • Weston Cardinal Spellman Philatelic Museum 165 • Williamstown Sterling and Francine Clark Art Institute 165 • Worcester American Sanitary Plumbing Museum 165 • Higgins Armory Museum 166

MICHIGAN

Acme Music House 167 • Ann Arbor Kelsey Museum of Archaeology 168 • Baraga (Askel) Hanka Homestead Ulkomuseo (Living Outdoor Museum) 168 • Bloomfield Hills Cranbrook Art Museum 168 • Farmington Hills Marvin's Marvelous Mechanical Museum 169 • Flint Labor Museum and Learning Center of Michigan 170 • Gaylord Call of the Wild 170 • Hanover Lee Conklin Antique Organ Museum 170 • Holland Holland Museum (formerly the Netherlands Museum) 171 • Iron Mountain Cornish Pumping Engine and Mining Museum 171 • Ishpeming U.S. National Ski Hall of Fame and Ski Museum 171 • Lansing Michigan Museum of Surveying 172 • Marshall American Museum of Magic 172 • Midland Herbert H. Dow Historical Museum 172 • Monroe Monroe County Historical Museum 173 • Muskegon Muskegon Museum of Art 173 • Negaunee Michigan Iron Industry Museum 173 • Novi Motorsports Hall of Fame of America 174 • Petoskey Little Traverse Regional Historical Museum 174 • Plymouth Plymouth Historical Museum 174 • Roscommon Civilian Conservation Corps Museum/Higgins Lake Nursery 174 • Saint James Beaver Island Historical Society/Mormon Print Shop Museum and Marine Museum 175

MINNESOTA

Alexandria Runestone Museum 176 • Austin First Century Museum (the Hormel Museum) 177 • Chisholm Minnesota Museum of Mining 177 • Ely International Wolf Center 177 • Eveleth United States Hockey Hall of Fame 178 • Grand Rapids Judy Garland Historical Center in the Central School Heritage and Arts Center 178 • Hibbing Greyhound Bus Origin Center 178 • Hinckley Hinckley Fire Museum 179 • International Falls Grand Mound Interpretive Center 179 • Koochiching County Historical Museum/Bronko Nagurski Museum 179 • Le Sueur Le Sueur Museum 180 • Little Falls Charles A. Lindbergh House 180 • Minneapolis–Saint Paul American Swedish Institute 180 • Museum of Questionable Medical Devices 181 • The Bakken: A Library and Museum of Electricity in Life 181 • Moorhead Heritage Hjemkomst Interpretive Center 181 • Northfield Northfield Historical Museum 182 • Pipestone Pipestone County Historical Museum 182 • Sauk Centre Sinclair Lewis Boyhood Home 182 • Shoreview American Museum of Asmat Art/Bishop Sowada Gallery 183 • Winona Polish Cultural Institute/Polish Museum 183

MISSISSIPPI

Belzoni Catfish Capitol Museum 184 • Ethel Wright Mohamed Stitchery Museum ("Mama's Dream World") 185 • Biloxi Mardi Gras Museum 185 • Bovina Earl's Art Gallery 185 • Clarksdale Delta Blues Museum 185 • D'Iberville Warren L. Fuller Breweriana Collection 186 • Greenwood Prayer Museum 186 •

Holly Springs Graceland Too 187 • Lucedale Palestinian Gardens 187 • Meridian Jimmie Rodgers Museum 187 • Mississippi State Templeton Music Museum and Archives 188 • Petal International Checker Hall of Fame 188 • Piney Woods Laurence C. Jones Museum 188 • Ruleville American Costume Museum 189 • Valley Park Valley Park Shortline Railroad/Agriculture/Historic Museum (C. B. "Buddie" Newman Museum) 189 • Vaughan Casey Jones Museum 189 • Vicksburg Corner Drug Store 190

MISSOURI

Des Peres American Kennel Club Museum of the Dog (formerly the Dog Museum) 191 • Fort Leonard Wood U.S. Army Engineer Museum 191 • Fulton Winston Churchill Memorial and Library in the United States 192 • Hazelwood Museum of Western Jesuit Missions 192 • Independence Leila's Hair Museum 193 • National Frontier Trails Center 193 • Kansas City Black Archives of Mid-America 193 • Negro Leagues Baseball Museum 193 • Thomas Hart Benton Home and Studio State Historic Site 194 • Toy and Miniature Museum of Kansas City 194 • Kearney Jesse James Farm and Museum 194 • Kirksville Still National Osteopathic Museum 194 • Mansfield Laura Ingalls Wilder–Rose Wilder Lane Home and Museum 195 • Mexico American Saddlebred Horse Museum 195 • New Madrid New Madrid Historical Museum 196 • Poplar Bluff Margaret Harwell Art Museum 196 • Saint Joseph Albrecht-Kemper Museum of Art 196 • Glore Psychiatric Museum 196 • Patee House Museum/Jesse James House Museum 197 • Saint Louis Bowling Hall of Fame and Museum 197 • Mercantile Money Museum 197 • Museum of Cosmetology Arts and Sciences 198 • National Video Game and Coin-Op Museum 198 • Scott Joplin House State Historic Site 198 • Stanton Jesse James Wax Museum 198

MONTANA

Billings Moss Mansion 200 • Oscar's Dreamland 201 • Bozeman American Computer Museum 201 • Broadus Mac's Museum 201 • Chinook Blaine County Museum 202 • Circle Montana Sheepherders Hall of Fame 202 • Helena Montana Historical Society Museum 202 • Livingston International Fly Fishing Center 203 • Miles City Range Riders Museum and Huffman Pictures 203 • Missoula Smokejumper and Aerial Fire Depot 203 • Philipsburg Ghost Town Hall of Fame 204 • Polson Montana Fiddlers Hall of Fame 204 • Shelby Marias Museum of History and Art 204 • Virginia City Thompson-Hickman Memorial Museum 205 • Wolf Point Louis Toav's John Deere Collection 205 • Worden Huntley Project Museum of Irrigated Agriculture 205

NEBRASKA

Alliance Carhenge 207 • Aurora Plainsman Museum 208 • Bancroft John G. Neihardt Center 208 • Boys Town Boys Town Hall of History 208 • Chadron Museum of the Fur Trade 208 • Cozad Robert Henri Museum and Historical Walkway 209 • Dannebrog National Liars Hall of Fame 209 • Elm Creek

Chevyland U.S.A. 210 • Holdredge Phelps County Historical Museum 210 • Lincoln National Museum of Roller Skating 210 • Minden Harold Warp Pioneer Village 211 • Omaha Great Plains Black Museum 211 • University of Nebraska Medical Center Library 212 • Royal Ashfall Fossil Beds State Park 212

NEVADA

Boulder City Boulder City/Hoover Dam Museum 213 • Caliente Caliente Railroad Boxcar Museum 214 • Eureka Eureka Sentinel Museum 214 • Genoa Genoa Courthouse Museum 214 • Las Vegas King Tut's Tomb and Museum 215 • Liberace Museum 215 • Magic and Movie Hall of Fame 215 • Overton Lost City Museum 216 • Rachel Little A'Le'Inn/Area 51 Research Center 216 • Reno Liberty Belle Antique Slot Machine Collection 217 • Searchlight Searchlight Historical Museum 217 • Tonopah Central Nevada Museum 217 • Virginia City Fourth Ward School Museum 218 • Julia C. Bullette Red Light Museum 218 • Virginia City Radio Museum 218 • Winnemucca Buckaroo Hall of Fame and Heritage Museum 219

NEW HAMPSHIRE

Allenstown Museum of Family Camping 220 • Bethlehem Crossroads of America 221 • Cornish Saint-Gaudens National Historic Site 221 • Enfield Museum at Lower Shaker Village 221 • Franconia New England Ski Museum 221 • Laconia Carpenter Museum of Antique Outboard Motors 222 • Manchester Lawrence L. Lee Scouting Museum and Max I. Silber Library 222 • Portsmouth Red Hook Brewery 222 • Wolfeboro Wright Museum of American Enterprise 223

NEW JERSEY

Atlantic City Atlantic City Historical Museum 224 • Kentucky Avenue Museum 225 • Far Hills Golf House/USGA Museum and Library 225 • Fort Monmouth United States Army Communications-Electronics Museum 225 • Franklin Franklin Mineral Museum 226 • Haledon American Labor Museum/Botto House National Landmark 226 • Lyndhurst Trash Museum/Hackensack Meadowlands Development Commission Environment Center 226 • Margate City Lucy the Margate Elephant 227 • Menlo Park (Edison) Thomas A. Edison Memorial Tower and Museum 227 • Montclair Montclair Art Museum 228 • Morristown Macculloch Hall Historical Museum 228 • Neshanic Doyle's Unami Farms/Corn Maze 228 • Newark Institute of Jazz Studies 229 • Oceanville Noyes Museum of Art 229 • Parsippany Craftsman Farms/Gustav Stickley Museum 229 • Paterson Paterson Museum/Rogers Mill 230 • Rahway Herman Abrams, Archaeologist of Himself 230 • Somerville United States Bicycling Hall of Fame 230 • Tenafly African Art Museum of the S.M.A. Fathers 231 • Teterboro Aviation Hall of Fame and Museum of New Jersey 231 • Tuckerton Barnegat Bay Decoy and Baymen's Museum 231 • West Trenton New Jersey State Police Museum and Learning Center 232 • Wildwood George F. Boyer Museum and National Marbles Hall of Fame 232

New Mexico

Abiquiu Georgia O'Keeffe House 233 • Albuquerque American International Rattlesnake Museum 234 • Food Museum (aka Potato Museum) 234 • Meteorite Museum 235 • National Atomic Museum 235 • Capitan Smokey Bear State Historical Park 235 • Fort Sumner Billy the Kid Museum 236 • Gallup Navajo Code Talkers Room 236 • Las Vegas City of Las Vegas Museum and Rough Riders Memorial Collection 237 • Los Alamos Los Alamos Historical Museum 237 • Nageezi Chaco Culture National Historical Park 238 • Nambe Liquid Paper Museum 238 • Organ Space Murals Museum 238 • Portales Bill Dalley's Windmill Collection 239 • Quemado The Lightning Field 239 • Roswell International UFO Museum and Research Center 240 • UFO Enigma Museum 240 • Sandia Park Tinkertown Museum 241 • Santa Fe Bataan Memorial Military Museum and Library 241 • Indian Arts Research Center 242 • Taos Harwood Foundation 242 • Truth or Consequences Geronimo Springs Museum 242

New York

New York City

The Bronx Judaica Museum 244 • Wave Hill 245 • Brooklyn Coney Island Museum and Sideshows-by-the-Seashore 245 • Green-Wood Cemetery 246 • Manhattan Eldridge Street Synagogue 247 • First National Church of the Exquisite Panic 247 • Forbes Magazine Galleries 247 • Glove Museum 248 • Joe Franklin's Office 248 • Maidenform Museum 248 • Museum at the Fashion Institute of Technology 248 • Museum of American Financial History 249 • Museum of Postal History 249 • Rose Museum at Carnegie Hall 249 • Skyscraper Museum 250 • Tamiment Institute Library/Wagner Labor Archives 250 • Queens Isamu Noguchi Garden Museum 251 • Staten Island Garibaldi and Meucci Museum of the Order Sons of Italy in America 252 • Jacques Marchais Museum of Tibetan Art 252

Upstate New York

Ballston Spa National Bottle Museum 253 • Bolton Landing Marcella Sembrich Opera Museum 253 • Brewster Southeast Museum 254 • Clayton Antique Boat Museum 254 • Corning Rockwell Museum 254 • Croghan American Maple Museum 255 • Deansboro Musical Museum 255 • East Aurora Elbert Hubbard Roycroft Museum 255 • Eden Original American Kazoo Company Factory and Museum 256 • Elmira National Soaring Museum 256 • Hammondsport Wine Museum of Greyton H. Taylor 256 • Hastings-on-Hudson Newington Cropsey Foundation Gallery of Art and Cultural Studies Center/Ever Rest 257 • Ilion Remington Firearms Museum and Country Store 257 • LeRoy Jell-O Museum (LeRoy House) 257 • Liverpool Salt Museum 258 • Mountainville Storm King Art Center 258 • North Chili Victorian Doll Museum and Chili Doll Hospital 258 • North Tonawanda Herschell Carrousel Factory Museum 259 • Orchard Park Burgwardt Bicycle Museum 259 • Palmyra Alling Coverlet

Museum 259 • Paul Smiths White Pine Camp 260 • Purchase Neuberger Museum of Art 260 • Whitehall Skenesborough Museum/Whitehall Urban Cultural Park Visitor Center 260

Long Island

Bridgehampton Bridgehampton Historical Museum 261 • Cold Spring Harbor Cold Spring Harbor Whaling Museum 262 • East Hampton Home, Sweet Home Museum 262 • Pollock-Krasner House and Study Center 262 • Huntington Station (West Hills) Walt Whitman Birthplace State Historic Site 262 • Locust Valley John P. Humes Japanese Stroll Garden 263 • New Hyde Park American Guitar Museum 263 • Upton Brookhaven National Laboratory (BNL) Science Museum 263

NORTH CAROLINA

Asheville Thomas Wolfe Memorial 265 • Aurora Aurora Fossil Museum 265 • Bailey Country Doctor Museum 265 • Belhaven Belhaven Memorial Museum 266 • Fayetteville John F. Kennedy Special Warfare Museum 266 • Fuquay-Varina Marvin and Mary Johnson's Gourd Museum 266 • High Point Furniture Discovery Center and the Furniture Hall of Fame 267 • Kannapolis Fieldcrest Cannon Textile Exhibition 267 • Kill Devil Hills Wright Brothers National Memorial 268 • Lake Junaluska World Methodist Museum 268 • New Bern New Bern Civil War Museum 268 • Randleman Richard Petty Museum 269 • Smithfield Ava Gardner Museum 269 • Stanfield Reed Gold Mine State Historic Site 269 • Waxhaw Museum of the Alphabet 270 • Winston-Salem R. J. Reynolds Tobacco 270

NORTH DAKOTA

Belcourt Turtle Mountain Heritage Center 271 • Dickinson Dakota Dinosaur Museum 272 • Fargo Roger Maris Museum 272 • Hatton Hatton-Eielson Museum 272 • Jamestown National Buffalo Museum 273 • Makoti Makoti Threshers Museum 273 • New Town Three Affiliated Tribes Museum 273 • Rugby Geographical Center Pioneer Village and Museum 274 • Strasburg Ludwig and Christina Welk Homestead/Lawrence Welk Birthplace 274

OHIO

Akron Goodyear World of Rubber 275 • Bainbridge Dr. John Harris Dental Museum 275 • Barnesville Barbara Barbe Doll Museum 276 • Bellevue Post Mark Collectors Club Museum 276 • Cambridge Degenhart Paperweight and Glass Museum 276 • Centerville International Women's Air and Space Museum 277 • Cincinnati Stowe House 277 • Circleville Ted Lewis Museum 278 • Cleveland Cleveland Police Historical Society, Inc., and Museum 278 • Dittrick Museum of Medical History 278 • Columbus Thurber House 279 • Dayton Paul Laurence Dunbar State Memorial 279 • Delphos Museum of Postal History 279 • Dennison Dennison Railroad Depot Museum 280 • Dover Warther Museum 280

• East Liverpool Museum of Ceramics 280 • Granville Granville Life-Style Museum (H. D. Robinson House) 281 • Greenville Garst Museum (Darke County Historical Society Museum) 281 • Kent Kenneth W. Berger Hearing Aid Museum and Archives 281 • Kenton Dougherty House–Victorian Wedding Museum 282 • Marietta Campus Martius: The Museum of the Northwest Territory/Ohio River Museum 282 • Marion Wyandot Popcorn Museum 283 • Newark National Heisey Glass Museum 283 • Ohio Indian Art Museum/Moundbuilders State Memorial 283 • North Canton Hoover Historical Center 284 • Norwich National Road/Zane Grey Museum 284 • Plain City Select Sires Bull Hall of Fame 284 • Sandusky Merry-Go-Round Museum 285 • Vandalia Trapshooting Hall of Fame and Museum 285 • Vermilion Inland Seas Maritime Museum (formerly the Great Lakes Museum) 285 • Wapakoneta Neil Armstrong Air and Space Museum 286 • Westerville Motorcycle Heritage Museum 286 • Wilberforce National Afro-American Museum and Cultural Center 286 • Youngstown Youngstown Historical Center of Industry and Labor 287

OKLAHOMA

Anadarko National Hall of Fame for Famous American Indians 288 • Ardmore/Marietta Landing Mom-Pop's Grocery Store 289 • Bartlesville Bartlesville Museum in the Price Tower/Shin'enKan 289 • Chickasha Muscle Car Ranch 289 • Claremore J. M. Davis Arms and Historical Museum 290 • Clinton Oklahoma Route 66 Museum 290 • Coyle Gerald Johnson Free Museum 291 • Dewey Tom Mix Museum 291 • Enid Mr. and Mrs. Dan Midgley Museum 291 • Erick 100th Meridian Museum 292 • Foyil Totem Pole Park 292 • Gage Jim Powers Junk Art Museum 293 • Gene Autry Gene Autry Oklahoma Museum 293 • Goodwell No Man's Land Historical Museum 293 • Guthrie National Lighter Museum 294 • Hominy Marland Station Wall of Memories 294 • Lawton Percussive Arts Society Museum 294 • Oklahoma City Lee Way Motor Freight Museum 295 • Pawnee Pawnee Bill Museum 295 • Shattuck Shattuck Windmill Museum and Park 295 • Stillwater National Wrestling Hall of Fame and Museum 296 • Sheerar Museum 296

OREGON

Brownsville Living Rock Studios 297 • Cottage Grove Cottage Grove Museum 298 • Florence Fly Fishing Museum 298 • Hood River Luhr Jensen Fishing Tackle Museum 298 • John Day Kam Wah Chung and Company Museum 299 • Monmouth Paul Jensen Arctic Museum 299 • Newberg Gabe Self-Cleaning House/Business Building Authority 299 • Pendleton Pendleton Round-up Hall of Fame 300 • Port Orford Prehistoric Gardens 300 • Portland American Advertising Museum 301 • 24-Hour Church of Elvis 301 • UFO Museum 301 • Vacuum Cleaner Museum 301 • Redmond Petersen Rock Gardens 302 • Saint Benedict Mount Angel Abbey Museum 302 • Seaside Seaside Museum and Historical Society 302 • Sisters World Famous Fantastic Museum 303 • Union Cowboys Then and Now Museum 303

PENNSYLVANIA

Allentown *Lock Ridge Furnace Museum* 305 • *Saylor Cement Museum* 305 • Beaver Falls *Air Heritage Museum and Aircraft Restoration Facility* 305 • Bethlehem *Kemerer Museum of Decorative Arts* 306 • Biglerville *National Apple Museum* 306 • Boothwyn *Real World Computer Museum* 306 • Columbia *Watch and Clock Museum of the National Association of Watch and Clock Collectors* 307 • Custer City *Penn-Brad Oil Museum* 307 • Doylestown *Fonthill Museum* 307 • Easton *Canal Museum* 308 • Erdenheim *Business Card Museum* 308 • Exton *Thomas Newcomen Library and Museum in Steam Technology and Industrial History/James R. Muldowney Printing Museum* 309 • Harmony *Harmony Museum* 309 • Kennett Square *Mushroom Museum at Phillips Place* 310 • Kutztown *Cut and Thrust Edged Weapons Museum/Co-op Gallery* 310 • Lackawaxen *Zane Grey Museum* 310 • Lancaster *Lancaster Newspapers Newseum* 311 • Lititz *Candy Americana Museum* 311 • Merion *Barnes Foundation* 311 • Middletown *Three Mile Island Visitors Center* 312 • Mifflinburg *Mifflinburg Buggy Museum* 312 • Nazareth *Martin Guitar Company* 312 • Northumberland *Joseph Priestley House* 313 • Orrtanna *Mister Ed's Elephant Museum* 313 • Philadelphia *American Swedish Historical Museum* 314 • *Center for the History of Foot Care and Foot Wear (The Shoe Museum)* 314 • *Fabric Workshop and Museum* 314 • *Historic Bartram's Garden* 315 • *Mario Lanza Museum* 315 • *Mummers Museum (New Year's Shooters and Mummers Museum)* 315 • *Museum of Nursing History* 315 • *Mütter Museum, College of Physicians of Philadelphia* 316 • *Rosenbach Museum and Library* 316 • *Wanamaker Museum* 316 • Pittsburgh *James L. Kelso Bible Lands Museum* 317 • *Mattress Factory* 317 • *Stephen C. Foster Memorial* 318 • Pleasantville *Otto Cupler Torpedo Company's Nitroglycerin Museum* 318 • Pottstown *Streitwieser Foundation Trumpet Museum* 318 • Towanda *French Azilum* 319 • University Park *Frost Entomological Museum* 319 • White Mills *Dorflinger Glass Museum* 319 • York *Harley-Davidson Motorcycle Plant and Museum (Rodney C. Gott Museum)* 320 • *Weightlifting Hall of Fame* 320

RHODE ISLAND

Bristol *Haffenreffer Museum of Anthropology* 321 • *Herreshoff Marine Museum/America's Cup Hall of Fame* 321 • Newport *International Tennis Hall of Fame and Museum* 322 • *Museum of Yachting* 322 • *Rhode Island Fisherman and Whale Museum* 322 • *Touro Synagogue* 322 • Pawtucket *Slater Mill Historic Site* 323 • Providence *American Diner Museum* 323 • *Culinary Archives and Museum at Johnson and Wales University* 323

SOUTH CAROLINA

Aiken *Aiken Thoroughbred Racing Hall of Fame and Museum* 324 • Charleston *Macaulay Museum of Dental History* 324 • Columbia *South Carolina Criminal Justice Hall of Fame* 325 • Darlington *NMPA Stock Car Hall of Fame/Joe*

Weatherly Museum 325 • Georgetown Rice Museum 325 • Greenville Bob Jones University Art Gallery and Museum 326 • Laurens World's Only Ku Klux Klan Museum 326 • Parris Island Parris Island Museum 326 • Rock Hill Museum of York County 326 • Saint Helena Island York W. Bailey Museum 327 • Spartanburg George E. Case Collection of Antique Keyboards 327

SOUTH DAKOTA

Chamberlain Akta Lakota Museum and Cultural Center 328 • Old West Museum 329 • Deadwood Adams Memorial Museum 329 • Huron Cheryl Ladd Room 329 • Lake Norden South Dakota Amateur Baseball Hall of Fame 330 • Lemmon Petrified Wood Park and Museum 330 • Mitchell Corn Palace 330 • Murdo Pioneer Auto Show 331 • Sioux Falls Sioux Empire Medical Museum 331 • Spearfish National Fish Culture Hall of Fame and Museum 332 • Saint Francis Buechel Memorial Lakota Museum 332 • Sturgis National Motorcycle Museum and Hall of Fame 332 • Vermillion Shrine to Music Museum 333

TENNESSEE

Adamsville Buford Pusser Home and Museum 334 • Chattanooga International Towing and Recovery Hall of Fame and Museum 335 • National Knife Museum 335 • Crossville Homesteads Tower Museum 335 • Dayton Scopes Museum/Rhea County Courthouse 335 • Grand Junction National Bird Dog Museum and Field Trial Hall of Fame 336 • Hendersonville House of Cash 336 • Johnson City Museum of Ancient Brick 336 • Memphis National Civil Rights Museum 337 • National Ornamental Metal Museum 337 • Pink Palace Museum 337 • Sincerely Elvis 338 • Millersville (Goodletsville) Museum of Beverage Containers and Advertising 338 • Nashville Hank Williams, Jr., Family Tradition Museum 338 • Museum of Tobacco Art and History 339 • Norris Lenoir Museum 339 • Oak Ridge American Museum of Science and Energy 340 • Pigeon Forge Carbo's Smoky Mountain Police Museum 340 • Trenton Trenton Teapot Museum 340 • Vonore Sequoyah Birthplace Museum 341 • Waverly World o' Tools Museum 341

TEXAS

Albany Old Jail Art Center 342 • Arlington Smith's Sewing Machine Museum 343 • Beaumont Babe Didrikson Zaharias Museum 343 • Eye of the World Museum 343 • Canton Brewer's Bell Museum 344 • Corpus Christi International Kite Museum 344 • Corsicana Lefty Frizzell Country Music Museum (Pioneer Village) 344 • Crowell Gafford Family Museum 344 • Dallas Celebrity Shoe Museum 345 • The Conspiracy Museum 345 • Mary Kay Museum 345 • Olde Fan Museum 346 • Denton World's Only Pecan Art Museum 346 • Dublin Dr. Pepper Bottling 346 • El Paso Billie Sol Estes Museum 347 • U.S. Border Patrol Museum 347 • Fort Worth American Airlines C. R. Smith Museum 347 • Fredericksburg Bauer Toy Museum 348 • Gish's Old West Museum 348 • Glen Rose Creation Evidences Museum 348 •

Greenville American Cotton Museum 349 • Houston American Funeral Service Museum 349 • Beer Can House 349 • The Orange Show 350 • Marfa Chinati Foundation/La Fundación Chinati 350 • El Paisano Hotel 350 • McLean Devil's Rope Museum and Route 66 Museum 351 • Nederland Windmill Museum/Tex Ritter Museum 351 • Pharr Old Clock Museum 351 • Smitty's Juke Box Museum 351 • Plano Cockroach Hall of Fame 352 • JCPenney Historical Museum and Archives 352 • Port Arthur Museum of the Gulf Coast 352 • San Antonio Barney Smith's Toilet Seat Art Museum 353 • Buckhorn Hall of Horns, Texas History, Fins, Feathers and Boar's Nest 353 • Church of Anti-Oppression Folk Art 353 • Hangar 9/Edward H. White II Memorial Museum 354 • Hertzberg Circus Collection and Museum 354 • Magic Lantern Castle Museum 354 • Shiner Edwin Wolters Memorial Museum 354 • Turkey Bob Wills Museum 355 • Hotel Turkey 355 • Waco Loud Cry Museum 355

UTAH

Delta Great Basin Museum 356 • Eureka Tintic Mining Museum 356 • Grantsville Donner-Reed Pioneer Museum 357 • Green River John Wesley Powell River History Museum 357 • Lehi John Hutching's Museum of Natural History 357 • Moab Hole N' The Rock 358 • Monument Valley Goulding's Museum 358 • Provo Earth Science Museum at Brigham Young University 358

VERMONT

Bennington Bennington Museum 359 • Burlington Williams Hall Art Museum of Kitsch Art (WHAMKA) 359 • Glover Bread and Puppet Museum 360 • Huntington Birds of Vermont Museum 360 • Manchester Village American Museum of Fly Fishing 360 • Pittsford New England Maple Museum 361 • Proctor Vermont Marble Exhibit 361 • Saint Johnsbury Fairbanks Museum and Planetarium 361 • Shelburne National Museum of the Morgan Horse 362 • Windsor American Precision Museum 362 • Woodstock Vermont Raptor Center 362

VIRGINIA

Alexandria Adams Center for the History of Otolaryngology—Head and Neck Surgery 364 • George Washington Masonic Memorial 364 • Arlington U.S. Patent and Trademark Museum 365 • Chincoteague Oyster Museum 365 • Dumfries Weems-Botts Museum 365 • Mount Solon National Jousting Hall of Fame 366 • New Market Bedrooms of America 366 • Paeonian Springs American Work Horse Museum 366 • Petersburg U.S. Slo-Pitch Softball Association Hall of Fame Museum 367 • Richmond Black History Museum 367 • Edgar Allan Poe Museum 367 • Money Museum 368 • Virginia Beach Old Coast Guard Station Museum 368 • Waverly First Peanut Museum in U.S.A. 368 • Winchester Patsy Cline at the Kurtz Cultural Center 369

WASHINGTON

Bellingham Roeder Home 370 • Bickleton Whoop-n-Holler Museum 371 • Castle Rock Castle Rock Exhibit Hall 371 • Cle Elum Cle Elum Historical Telephone Museum 371 • Concrete Camp Seven Museum 372 • Electric City Gehrke Windmill Garden 372 • Forks Hoh Rain Forest Visitors Center 372 • Friday Harbor/San Juan Island Pig War Museum 373 • Goldendale Maryhill Museum of Art 373 • Grayland Furford Cranberry Museum 373 • Long Beach Marsh's Free Museum 374 • World Kite Museum and Hall of Fame 374 • Neah Bay Makah Cultural and Research Center 374 • Port Gamble Of Sea and Shore Museum 375 • Pullman Smith Soil Monolith Collection 375 • Richland Columbia River Exhibition of History, Science, and Technology 376 • Seattle General Petroleum Museum 376 • Memory Lane Museum at Seattle Goodwill 376 • Saint Charles Archery Museum 377 • Thorniley Collection of Type 377 • Vintage Telephone Equipment 377 • Wing Luke Asian Museum 378 • Spokane Bing Crosby Library 378 • Steilacoom Bair Drug and Hardware Co. Living Museum 378 • Steilacoom Tribal Cultural Center and Museum 379 • Stevenson Don Brown Rosary Collection 379 • Toppenish American Hop Museum 379 • Wenatchee North Central Washington Museum 380 • Yakima World Famous Fantastic Museum 380

WEST VIRGINIA

Berkeley Springs Homeopathy Works 381 • Museum of the Berkeley Springs 382 • Clifftop Camp Washington-Carver 382 • Grafton International Mother's Day Shrine 382 • Huntington Museum of Radio and Technology 383 • Moundsville Prabhupada's Palace of Gold 383 • West Liberty Women's History Museum 383 • White Sulphur Springs Presidents Cottage Museum 384

WISCONSIN

Appleton Outagamie Museum and Houdini Historical Center 385 • Ashippun Honey of a Museum 386 • Augusta Dells Mill Water-Powered Museum 386 • Baraboo Circus World Museum 386 • Bayfield Hokenson Brothers Fishery 387 • Clear Lake Clear Lake Historical Museum 387 • Couderay The Hideout 387 • Fort Atkinson Dairy Shrine/Hoard Historical Museum 388 • Lac du Flambeau George W. Brown, Jr., Ojibwe Museum and Cultural Center (formerly Lac du Flambeau Chippewa Museum and Cultural Center) 388 • Milton Milton House Museum 388 • Milwaukee America's Black Holocaust Museum 389 • International Clown Hall of Fame and Research Center 389 • Mount Horeb Mount Horeb Mustard Museum 389 • Neenah Bergstrom-Mahler Museum 390 • Oneida (De Pere) Oneida Nation Museum 390 • Phillips Wisconsin Concrete Park 390 • Platteville Rollo Jamison Museum/Mining Museum 391 • Prairie du Chien Fort Crawford Medical Museum 391 • Shell Lake Museum of Woodcarving 391 • Watertown Octagon House/America's First Kindergarten 392 • Wisconsin Dells H. H. Bennett Studio Foundation Museum 392 • Woodruff Doctor Kate Museum 392

WYOMING

Cheyenne *Cheyenne Frontier Days Old West Museum* 394 • Cody *Buffalo Bill Historical Center* 394 • Diamondville *Stolen Bell Museum* 395 • Evanston *Uinta County Historical Museum* 395 • Green River *Sweetwater County Historical Museum* 396 • Jackson *Jackson Hole Museum and Historical Center* 396 • Laramie *American Heritage Center* 396 • *Geological Museum* 397 • Rawlins *Wyoming Frontier Prison Museum* 397 • Sheridan *Don King's Western Museum* 397 • Thermopolis *Hot Springs County Historical Museum and Cultural Center* 398

VIRTUAL MUSEUMS 399

Big Sources for Museum Data 399 • *Other Places to Visit* 399 • *Roadside Sources* 403

INDEX BY CATEGORY 405

Acknowledgments

Among many who offered suggestions, information, and big enthusiasm, LA would especially like to thank longtime cohorts in travel Ron Perfit, Joelle Hertel, Charles M. Haecker, Jane Kepp, Jane Treuhaft, Cathy Cameron, Michael Lekson, Debra Heft, Tom Pechar, and Stephen Myles. Thanks are due as well to special informants and contributors Jean and David Kelsay, Michael Kernan, Joanne Arany, and Gilbert Brovar.

AH would like to thank particularly Marc Miller, Paul Lagassé, David Diefendorf, Bill Stott and his electronic correspondents in Texas, Barbara Britton, Fred Cisterna, Bill and Ruth Botzow, Ferris Cook and Ken Krabbenhoft, and, for a thousand reasons, Verna Hobson and Susan Lacerte. He also salutes the happy memory of Judith Wragg Chase, longtime curator of the Old Slave Mart Museum (Charleston, South Carolina).

We are grateful to cyberwizard Jim Angus at the Los Angeles Museum of Natural History for sharing on the virtual end, and for the continuous interest of Jack Judson of the Magic Lantern Castle Museum (San Antonio, Texas), Gaylord Kubota of the Alexander and Baldwin Sugar Museum (Maui, Hawaii), and Mike Howard of the Museum of Ordinary People (Hurtsboro, Alabama), and our new friend, Bob Oliver, at the Baltimore Area Visitors Center. We can't imagine the depth of this project without the committed correspondents on the Museum-L, the Popular Culture and Libraries, and the Roadside Internet mailing lists, and in particular, A. J. Wright and Allen Ellis.

And our heartfelt thanks go as well to generous and eagle-eyed "roadsiders" Chuck Woodbury, publisher of *Out West: The Newspaper That Roams*; Paul Taylor, publisher of *Route 66* magazine; Jamie Jensen, author of *Road Trip USA*; Susanne Theis at The Orange Show (Houston, Texas); Nancy Neiger, publisher, *Yesterday's Highways*; Bob Phillips, the *Texas Country Reporter*; Brett Leveridge, the *Roadside* mailing list and website majordomo; muralist Gary Sweeney; Harriet Baskas and Adam Woog, authors of *Atomic Marbles*; Rachel Epstein, author of *Mailbox, U.S.A.*; and Laura Bergheim, author of *Weird Wonderful America* and *An American Festival of World Capitals*.

And, finally, we offer profuse thanks to those whose help was invaluable in the production of the book: Debbra Lupien, Karen Van Craenenbroeck, Fran Pak, and Leah Gonzalez, and of course to the folks at Henry Holt, past and present: Paula Kakalecik, Alessandra Bocco, Betty Lew, Dominique D'Anna, Audrey Melkin, Kathleen Fridella, and Emily Brown.

Introduction

America is a land full of museums. Some are huge and known to all, like the Metropolitan Museum of Art, or the National Air and Space Museum, or the Rock 'n' Roll Hall of Fame. And then, descending in familiarity from the less well known through the esoteric to the completely unheard of, there are Little Museums.

What are Little Museums? Who creates them? In this book we tell you about more than 1,000 places you *must* see. They and their masterminds are quite a mix. Think you've visited every kind of museum there is? We'll bet there are places here unlike any you've ever seen.

America Is Little Museums Country

Why? Well, for one thing, people here have almost any kind of background you can name; we've brought a lot with us from the rest of the world, and we've been Americanizing it in many different ways. We also have a lot of disposable wealth, which helps do things like open museums. We don't have a National Academy directing our intellectual affairs, and we do have a governmental system that is quite tolerant, on the whole, of that brand of deviance called imagination. We live all over a vast country, sometimes developing our own culture and sense of history in isolation from almost everyone else. Our transportation system—that is to say, the private automobile—favors the spread of little museums; you can't take a plane or train or even a bus to some of the places we describe.

All this is tantamount to saying that this is a great country for individual expression. And it's the individuals behind a lot of the museums we describe who took our heart at the beginning, and caused us to write this book. Sometimes several of them have banded together, but often a museum is the mission of a possessed loner. Whatever the object of their attentions, be it the record of a declining industry, the life of a local historical figure, the practice of a rarefied art form, or bottle caps, their love makes *them*, as much as their displays, the museum. Their explanation for this is often quite modest; the quest of Bettie B. Gafford of Crowell, Texas, began simply enough on that fateful day years ago when she traded her fancy cowboy boots for her first china cabinet; while she tells us she still misses those boots, she wouldn't quite trade off her niche as the local repository for all things worthy yet unwanted by their original owners. Jack Judson says of his more formal Magic Lantern Castle Museum in San Antonio: "I collect . . . so as to share this little-known subject with those who do not know of it, and to have a complete resource for researchers of pre-cinema. I own all the collection and where it is housed, and fund all from my own resources. I charge nothing to come and see or research."

But you've been thinking, this is all a matter of definition. What do you mean little? And who says it's a museum?

What's Little?

In some cases, even very well known museums are just plain small—physically. Maybe they don't want to be larger, or have severely limited their focus, or occupy a small site and can't expand. You'll find some of them here.

But we're talking, for the most part, about museums that are *little* because not that many people go to see them. Physically, they may be huge or tiny—this doesn't concern us. What matters is that they are not On the Beaten Path. These museums may be out of the mainstream for various reasons. They may be hidden in the shadow of better-known museums. They may not do much to promote themselves. They may like the idea of being visited by twenty rather than two thousand people a day. They may hew faithfully to the vision of a founder or benefactor who did not want The Big Museum. Their creators may appreciate life in some remote corner of the Plains. The object of their focus may be arcane, or their approach eccentric.

We'd like to send you to museums where you can experience some intimacy—with the institution itself, with what it shows, with the people who show it. We'd like you to not find yourself several layers of plate glass and three guards away from everything. We'd like you to not feel rushed or crowded. We remember what it was like trying to get a feeling for King Tut's jewels in fifteen seconds, over the top of six heads.

What's a Museum?

This is a topic of heated debate. Some people feel that *museum* is a word not just anybody should be able to use. We note, though, that the first place called a museum (in Alexandria, Egypt, a few years back) came closest, in modern terms, to today's "living museum"; it was actually concerned with teaching about the natural world. The museum tradition further grew and developed from the 16th- and 17th-century *Wunderkammern*, or wonder-cabinets, that were notable for their juxtaposition of the natural with the arcane (and were perhaps the first repositories that raised the question of whether irony was in the eyes of the beholder or the curator). We also note that a *museum*, in European and much English-speaking usage, is what would otherwise be called an art gallery. And at root, the word honors the Muses, those nine goddesses whose bailiwick embraced almost any kind of knowledge or expression. We think all this opens the door to the Museum World fairly wide.

A collection alone, of course, isn't a museum. No matter how complete, no matter how aesthetically devastating, no matter how fastidiously organized your sand dollar collection is, it isn't a museum if no one but you ever sees it. And it isn't a museum just because you invite Cousin Darlene and Uncle Fred over. It has to be offered to a larger public.

Ah yes, but what *is* being shown? And how do we distinguish the Curator from the Sideshow Barker or the Crafty Salesman? Is it Museum Professional or Mountebank we see before us?

Dear Reader, all we're going to say is that we regard every place in this book as a museum. What *kind* of a museum is another question, and one we think you'll answer for yourself. There's no accounting for taste, some sage has declared—a statement clearly off the mark today, as there's an entire industry devoted to accounting for taste. But *we're* not going to be part of it. In the pages that follow you'll find such varied phenomena as

archaeological sites	folk art	roadside attractions
architectural wonders	halls of fame	sculpture parks
archives	hideouts	ships
ballrooms	homes	spare rooms
basements	hotels	storefronts
birthplaces	lighthouses	studios
botanical gardens	mills	summer camps
breweries and distilleries	mines	temples
carousels	natural wonders	theaters
dentists' offices	power plants	walkways
factories	prisons	wildlife centers
failed utopias	restaurants	windmills
farms	restorations	workshops

not to mention some gargantuan machines, a maze, an RV park, several holes in the ground, a grotto or two, and at least one elephant.

Does a Little Museum need an imprimatur? How should it conduct its business? There are no prescriptions in our book. Many of these places are accredited by the American Association of Museums, but some of them haven't even heard of the AAM. As for the manner in which they show their stuff, it may be thoroughly correct; enthusiastic but not so correct; haphazard; idiosyncratic; bizarre; commercial; reverential; ironic, even sardonic; downright zany; and a few others we've forgotten.

Before you rush off to our selections, we want to insist on the following:

1. Any time you're in a college town, check out the campus museums. We've included a lot of special ones here, but there are many, many more.
2. And if you *really* love museums, don't forget local historical societies. We've included a lot of these, too, but who knows what gems lie behind other, unopened doors?

A Few Things to Know

Admissions: You should assume that museums will be closed on major holidays, and it is always wise to call ahead to confirm hours. Where "fee" is listed, there are often discounts—for children, persons over 65, or others. "Donation" means that there isn't an admission charge and that donations are accepted; in some cases there is a suggested donation, which is essentially a fee. Unless, of course, you're at a spot like Connecticut's Nut Museum, in which case the medium of exchange *is* a nut.

By Appointment Only: We can't stress this enough. If we say "By Appointment Only," please respect the museum's wishes and do not show up unannounced.

Tours: These often require a call ahead to confirm or reserve. This is especially true if you're part of a "group"—in the case of our littlest museums this can mean more than two. Also, many places that do not offer formal tours will be glad to show you around if you phone ahead.

Handicapped Accessibility and Services: Little Museums vary widely in their ability to offer wheelchair access, etc.; again, calling ahead is wise.

Kids: Check out our Index by Category at the back. We've made a selection of Little Museums that we feel are particularly attractive to kids. We were by no means comprehensive, though, so we suggest you browse through and consider what your child likes. Our blurbs often mention if a museum is particularly child-friendly, and we made every effort to say when we knew the museum was not.

Websites/Area Codes: Perhaps obvious . . . but while we've made every effort to update area codes through '98, if a number doesn't work, it may just be the area code that's defunct. And it won't be news for those who have wandered in cyberspace that websites are only as certain as your Internet service.

ALABAMA

Alabama is especially rich with the work of folk artists and visionaries. It's also home to some of the more remarkably unique collections we've encountered. A rare mix of fearless individualism and exuberance, a history that at times seems locked to the Confederate era, and an economy dependent on a few key resources—Alabama and its museums express all of that, and provide ample opportunity for both fun and reflection.

What's Big: The towering Vulcan statue presides over Birmingham, where "what's big" also includes the Birmingham Civil Rights Institute, and Tuxedo Junction. In Enterprise you have the Boll Weevil Monument, a tribute to the demise of King Cotton and the future of peanuts; in Huntsville, the U.S. Space and Rocket Center. Montgomery, home of the First Capital of the Confederacy, and where Rosa Parks began the first bus boycott, is now the site of Maya Lin's Civil Rights Memorial. Finally, in Tuskegee, you'll find the Carver Museum; and in Tuscumbia, right near Muscle Shoals, the Alabama Music Hall of Fame.

BIRMINGHAM

In Dora, northwest of town on US 78, is the Alabama Mining Museum, which does a great job of covering the coal-mining years in this area and serves as a quieter— yet key—counterpoint to the roaring iron and steel industry museums at Sloss Furnaces and the Tannehill Ironworks to the southwest in McCalla. The industrial sandstone and found-objects work of folk artist Lonnie Hollie may be found over by the Municipal Airport. *While you're in the area, see also*: Fairfield, Tuscaloosa.

CULLMAN

Ave Maria Grotto   Brother Joseph Zoettl spent his entire adult life serving as a Benedictine monk in the Saint Bernard Abbey here in Cullman. His youth was

spent exclusively in his Bavarian homeland. Yet the astonishing detail and rich-
ness of texture in the miniature replicas of historic sites and shrines he constructed out of found bits of marble, seashells, glass, and jewels would have you
believe he'd been a world traveler. All taken from the mind's eye—and aided by
photos and drawings—the structures have been carefully tended by the resident
monks since Brother Joseph's death in 1961.

📷 205 734-4110 • Saint Bernard Abbey, Cullman, AL 35055

🚗 About 50 miles north of Birmingham. Take I-65 to US 278/Hwy 74, then east 1 mile.

🕐 Mon.–Sun. 7 A.M.–dusk. Fee.

FAIRFIELD

Alabama Historical Radio Society/Don Kresge Memorial Museum
When Don Kresge died in 1992, he left behind a personal collection of rare radios
and their technical documentation—and a dream that a museum would be
founded to share and preserve radio history. Well, it's here now. Besides the endlessly surprising variety of shapes and sizes of the radios themselves—and we're
talking all pre-transistor here—there's real attention paid to the development of
the technology and its pioneering wizards, from the days of early crystal sets to
modern television.

📷 205 631-6680 • Fairfield Civic Center, 6509 E. J. Oliver Blvd., Fairfield, AL 35260

🚗 On the west side of Birmingham, take I-59/20 to Exit 118.

🕐 Mon.–Fri. 9 A.M.–4 P.M. Tours by appointment. No fee.

FAIRHOPE

American Bicentennial Museum   If you were around in 1976, we're sure
you'll remember all those hand-painted fire hydrants, and if you were really lucky
you got to see Operation Sail float into New York Harbor. Mary Douglas Foreman
and her daughter Michelle May are dedicated to keeping the spirit—and the
kitsch—alive. Red, white, and blue hula hoops, Uncle Sam beverage containers,
license plates. There were 64,384 Bicentennial events, and a healthy selection of
items commemorating them has made it to Morphy Ave.

📷 334 928-7160/2546/7681 • 357 Morphy Ave., Fairhope, AL 36532

🚗 Twenty miles east of Mobile. Take I-10E and exit onto US 98S.

🕐 Wed.–Fri. noon–4 P.M. Call for appointment. No fee.

Marietta Johnson Museum   Marietta Johnson, a contemporary of single-
taxer Henry George, made her mark in progressive early-20th-century thinking with
her philosophy of organic education. Based on the premise that a child is a product of his or her environment and that education must be "life-giving to body,

mind, and spirit," the arts, music, and dance were equally emphasized along with traditional academic coursework. Pix, artifacts, literature, and videos are on hand in her 1907 classroom to explain her successful program. *Publications, Library*

■ 334 990-8601 • 440 Fairhope Ave., Fairhope, AL 36532

🚗 Twenty miles east of Mobile. Take I-10E and exit onto US 98S.

🕒 Mon.–Fri. 1 P.M.–5 P.M. No fee.

FLORENCE

In the northwest corner of the state, in the Muscle Shoals area, Florence is where you'll find Wilson Dam (aka the "Grandfather of all TVA Dams"). On a smaller scale, in size if not accomplishment, nearby Tuscumbia is home to Ivy Green, the birthplace/museum of Helen Keller.

W. C. Handy Home, Museum, and Library W. C. Handy's tunes were *called* blues ("Memphis Blues," "St. Louis Blues," etc.) but their innovative use of breaks, as well as their incorporation of other musical traditions from gospel to tango, popped him out of the traditional blues mold and set him apart as a composer at the front edge of jazz. Here in his log cabin birthplace you'll find his piano and cornet, original music scores, and memorabilia from a career that spanned the turn of the century to the early days of rock 'n' roll. *Tours, Library*

■ 205 760-6434 • 620 W. College St., Florence, AL 35630

🚗 Muscle Shoals area. Just off US 72 and west of downtown, at Marengo St.

🕒 Tues.–Sat. 10 A.M.–4 P.M. Fee.

FORT MCCLELLAN

U.S. Army Chemical Corps Museum Nerve gas, mustard gas, sarinen— why, these are only the modern-day chemical and biological warfare weapons of choice. Back in biblical times a goodly dose of skunk cabbage or a decomposing body or two served the same purpose and, we suspect, might have as easily backfired, though perhaps not so lethally. While the Corps has its roots in World War I and the displays emphasize the two world wars, there are over 4,000 artifacts that cover the whole spectrum, from deterrence to protective gear (check out the well-known but most unusual Disney-approved use of Mickey in the for-kids-only gas mask) to attack poisons and equipment, right on up through the Persian Gulf war. While you're on the base, don't miss the Women's Army Corps Museum (205 848-3512). While it could leave you thinking only clothes make the (military) woman, we know better. And those government-issue undergarments are worth the trip. *Gift Shop, Library*

■ 205 848-4449/6550 • Building 2299, Fort McClellan, AL 36205

🚗 Northeastern Alabama, just east of Anniston. From I-20 take the Oxford exit onto Hwy
21N about 10 miles to the Fort McClellan Galloway or Baltzell Gates.

🕐 Mon.–Fri. 9 A.M.–3 P.M. No fee.

GEORGIANA

Hank Williams, Sr., Boyhood Home and Museum   This museum is a
local effort to preserve the memory of one of country music's brightest and most
enduring stars. While some of his more glitzy performing effects are in the Hank Jr.
Family Museum in Nashville, this is where you'll find his entire discography including all the 78s and early album covers, the marquees and posters from his shows,
and even the church bench he stood on to sing as a child.

■ 334 376-2555 • 127 Rose St., Georgiana, AL 36033

🚗 About 60 miles south of Montgomery. Take I-65 Exit 114 (Georgiana-Starlington) onto
Hwy 106E into town.

🕐 Mon.–Sat. 10 A.M.–5 P.M., Sun. 1 P.M.–5 P.M. Fee.

HARTSELLE

Tomb of Mystery Museum   Magic and celebrity paraphernalia collector John
Reed is especially partial to the illusions that make young women vaporize or at
best (or worst) leaves them with head and feet, but no torso in sight. A major Houdini fan, he prizes the trick handcuffs and other magician and music memorabilia
he's collected for years, from Elvis to Elton. But can he conjure up the King himself?

■ 205 773-8517/7143 • Hartselle, AL 35640

🚗 Hartselle is about 13 miles south of Decatur on US 31.

🕐 Owner John Reed expects to reopen in a new location in the near future. Call for an
update.

HURTSBORO

Museum of Ordinary People (MOP)   "One day there will be a place where
art, junk, memorabilia, and a living artist will combine to make up a truly ordinary
place to visit." Fluxus artist Mike Howard has long envisioned a place where you
can see art "the way it's supposed to be seen—in the environment of junk, bad
lighting, and screaming kids." Mike has in mind a sort of *Tony 'n' Tina's Wedding* of
the art world, and welcomes you to sit down in his cozy home and studio in rural
Alabama and have a cup of coffee with the artists. The twist is, like Tony 'n' Tina,
Mike and wife Mary will be brought to you from Central Casting.

■ 334 667-0481/718 488-8740 • PO Box 311, Hurtsboro, AL 36860

🚗 In eastern Alabama, about 30 miles west of Phenix City, Alabama/Columbus, Georgia. Take US 431S to Hwy 26, then west for 15 miles.

🕐 By appointment only. No fee.

MOBILE

While you're in the area, see also: Fairhope

Eichold–Heustis Medical Museum of the South   Eichold–Heustis, covering over 200 years of medical history, houses the largest collection of medical artifacts in the southeast at the first medical college in the state. And the artifacts and photos here are indeed quite a blend of the claimed "obsolete and the proven, the primitive and the innovative, the bizarre and the commonplace." You'll find pharmacological potions, 1859 papier-mâché anatomical models from Paris, guides to "proper" bloodletting techniques, early X-ray tubes, cardiographs, eyeglasses, and much more. *Tours, Food, Library*

📱 334 434-5055 • 1504 Springhill Ave., Mobile, AL 36604

🚗 Located in the lobby of the Lafayette St. entrance of the University of South Alabama, Springhill Avenue Campus.

🕐 Mon.–Fri. 8 A.M.–5 P.M. Tours by appointment. No fee.

MONTGOMERY

The Hank Williams Memorial here is gone (go down to Georgiana for a Hank fix), but in Prattville, just northwest of town, along Highway 31S, you'll find a worthy stop at Mr. Rice's Trailer Court. Mr. Rice has set up camp in an abandoned drive-in movie theater, and his past as a Fundamentalist Baptist preacher provides the message for his sculptures, which use the wreckage of discarded appliances, crashed cars, and telephone poles to complement his commentary.

F. Scott and Zelda Fitzgerald Museum   Oddly enough, this former Fitzgerald home is the only museum we know of dedicated to either Scott or Zelda, and while they only lived in Zelda's hometown briefly in the early '30s, they did do quite a bit of writing (*Save Me the Waltz*; *Tender Is the Night*) here. A number of original letters, early book editions, pix and newsclips, Zelda's paintings, and their typewriters are joined by other period artifacts. (If you're on a literary tour, about 160 miles southwest, in Monroeville, the Monroeville Courthouse and Museum has memorabilia of local writers Harper Lee and Truman Capote.)

📱 334 264-4222 • 919 Felder Ave., Montgomery, AL 36106

🚗 Just southeast of downtown.

🕐 Wed.–Fri. 10 A.M.–2 P.M., Sat.–Sun. 1 P.M.–5 P.M., and by appointment. Donation.

George and Lurleen Wallace Center for the Study of Southern Politics   The Wallaces each served as this state's governor, and while George had the greater notoriety and certainly left his mark during his campaign for the presidency, Lurleen quite handily took over the management of the state. Exhibits feature personal memorabilia from both regimes and their personal lives, as well as from other significant Southern politicians. *Tours*

🔲 800 556-1972/334 834-1972 • Monroe and Decatur Sts., Montgomery, AL 36130

🚗 Downtown.

🕐 Mon.–Fri. 9 A.M.–5 P.M. No fee.

SALEM

Lunchbox Museum   We tracked this down from its former home just across the border in Columbus, Georgia. Greatly expanded into a stuffed-to-the-rafters mural-embellished cotton warehouse in an 1832 antique village, all the items on display are for sale, no matter how rare, so what you'll get to see may change over time. Over 2,000 lunchboxes—from the rare Hometown Airport dome-style models to the turn-of-the-century early lithographed (trains, picnics, sport themes) lunch pails and the characters we know so well, like Roy Rogers, Batman, Zorro, and Dr. Doolittle; and their compatriot Thermoses (over 1,500), TV trays, and pop-art wastebaskets. A bonus here is the comprehensive Southern pottery collection from the 1800s, old radios, and Coca Cola items, which include a 1934 Bakelite radio in the shape of a Coke bottle. Next door is the Dr. A. D. McLain Drugstore and Doctor's Office Museum, open by appointment only. Ask about it here.

🔲 888 OLD SALEM [657-2536] /334 749-1925 • Old Salem Antiques and Collectibles, 50 Lee County Rd. 175, Salem, AL 36874

🚗 In eastern Alabama about 15 miles west of Phenix City, AL/Columbus, GA, off US 280/431.

🕐 Mon.–Sun. 10 A.M.–6 P.M. No fee.

SELMA

National Voting Rights Museum and Institute   On March 7, 1965, Martin Luther King, Jr., led black and white civil rights workers on the pivotal freedom march across the Edmund Pettus Bridge from Selma to Montgomery, leading to the Voting Rights Act later that year. Through photos and artifacts, this museum chronicles an era when a federal law was necessary to override individual states' rights to discriminate on the basis of race. The nearby Old Depot Museum also covers some of this territory, then works its way back to Selma's critical role in the Civil War.

🔲 334 418-0800 • 1012 Water Ave., Selma, AL 36702

About 49 miles west of Montgomery, off US 80 and Hwy 22, near the foot of the Edmund Pettus Bridge.

Mon.–Fri. 10 A.M.–5 P.M., Sat. 1 P.M.–5 P.M., Sun. by appointment. Fee.

TUSCALOOSA

In Tuscaloosa, you'll also want to check out Greenwood Cemetery with its unique headstones dating back to the early 1800s. Worth a trip nearby are the Kentuck Museum (folk art and traditional American crafts) in Northport and Moundville Archaeological Park with its evidence of an advanced culture residing here from A.D. 1000 to 1500. And not too far afield to the west is the Aliceville Museum and Cultural Arts Center, with its World War II German POW camp exhibit and locally ubiquitous Coca-Cola artifacts. A jot farther, to the north, in Fayette, visit with painter Jimmy Lee Suddeth. Painting with natural pigments (grass, leaves, berries) and discarded house paints on found scrap wood, his themes are American icons—such as horses, houses, and the Statue of Liberty. Another sort of American icon may be taken in at the only U.S. Mercedes-Benz Visitors Center and factory plant in nearby Vance. While *you're in the area, see also*: Birmingham.

Ma'Cille's Museum of Miscellanea   Ma'Cille's place is a wonder of surrealistic ruin. Ancient bottles cover the rambling tin-roofed sharecropper's home that holds most of the collection of "one of's" and way more than one of household, farm, and personal items that Lucille House tucked away in her quest to have "one of everything." If she didn't acquire it or get it as a donation, she was apt to have made it. She even learned taxidermy along the way, contributing such items as a now quite frayed checker-playing pair of possums to the overflow of other odds and ends like hatboxes, old stamps, old portraits, matchbook covers, a one-room schoolhouse, bags of oats, cotton gins, and bottles, zillions of bottles.

205 758-7588 • Tuscaloosa Chamber of Commerce, Tuscaloosa, AL 35402

West-central Alabama.

Ma'Cille's is temporarily closed and is scheduled to reopen in 1998.

Paul W. Bryant Museum   The smaller, privately run "Bear Hall No. 1," last heard about in nearby West Blocton, is currently missing in action, so we'll have to go with this grander-scale celebration of college football's legendary Crimson Tide. Led by Coach Paul "Bear" Bryant from 1958 through 1982, University of Alabama's playing history is documented here from its first team in 1892, with all manner of pix and artifacts, and Mr. Bryant's trademark houndstooth porkpie hat, of course.
Tours, Gift Shop, Library, Screenings

205 348-4668 • 300 Paul W. Bryant Dr., Tuscaloosa, AL 35487

On the University of Alabama campus. From I-59, exit onto I-359 and take the 35th St. exit to 10th Ave. Turn left and proceed to Bryant Dr., then turn right.

Mon.–Sun. 9 A.M.–4 P.M. Fee.

ALASKA

Few of you have come to Alaska with museums in mind; everything we describe here is, therefore, according to our thinking, "little." But don't expect *too* little. There are times when a small Alaska museum can be The Biggest Thing in Town—as when, on the Inside Passage, you and everyone else on the boat end up in the same "quiet" room for the same few moments. Welcome to "The Last Frontier"!

What's Big: The land—not just because it *is* big, but because that's what everyone came here for. Put into a museum, a crowd like the one you're likely to find at the foot of one of Alaska's glaciers would be something *really* big.

ANCHORAGE

Alaska Aviation Heritage Museum   Next to the world's busiest seaplane base, this museum details the history of the bush pilots, aviation pioneers, and military fliers. All of the two dozen planes you'll see have flown in Alaska, and they range from 1920s mail planes through a World War II Catalina Flying Boat to a 1960s Iroquois helicopter. There are displays on Carl Ben Eielson (*see also* Hatton, North Dakota's Hatton-Eielson Museum), Wiley Post, and other major figures, models, photos, Japanese military artifacts, and much more. Gift Shop, Programs, Screenings

🏛 907 248-5325 • 4721 Aircraft Dr., Lake Hood, Anchorage, AK 99502

🚗 Aircraft Dr. runs along the south side of Lake Hood, southwest of downtown and just north of the International Airport. Take Lake Hood exit right from International Airport Rd. Tour buses from the city and shuttles from the airport come to the museum.

🕐 Mon.–Sun. 9 A.M.–6 P.M. Fee.

FAIRBANKS

Dog Mushing Museum   You know about the Iditarod (*see also* Nome's Carrie M. McLain Museum), but in Alaska dogsleds are more than one big race. This museum, with displays in more than one location, will show you sleds and apparatus, the kind of gear you would need to survive behind your dogs, and, of course, much on the dogs themselves.

🔲 907 456-6874 • Fairbanks, AK 99708

🚗 The Fairbanks Community Museum is downtown, at Cushman and 5th, in the Old City Hall. Call for other places and hours.

🕐 Fairbanks Community Museum: Wed.–Sat. noon–4 P.M. No fee.

University of Alaska Fairbanks Museum   Our friends are much impressed with the presentation of varied materials at this museum, which offers geographical, natural, and cultural exhibits. There are Russian, gold, and animal displays, including a 36,000-year-old bison found in the permafrost, as well as video programs on the aurora and other Alaska phenomena. *Gift Shop, Screenings*

🔲 907 474-7505 • University of Alaska, Fairbanks, AK 99775

🚗 The university is in College, northwest of downtown Fairbanks, at the corner of University Ave., College Rd., and Farmers Loop Rd.

🕐 June–Aug.: Mon.–Sun. 9 A.M.–7 P.M. Hours slightly reduced rest of year. Fee.

HOMER

Miller Comb Museum   Here's a truly unusual museum: It has over 3,000 combs, pieces of hair art, and related items, and it travels! The Millers leave Arizona for Alaska each spring, taking the goodies with them. They began collecting in the 1950s, and the combs go back 2,500 years. The materials and artistry extend to almost anything imaginable, and the Millers will talk the history of hair ornamentation with you.

🔲 907 235-8819 • Homer, AK 99603

🚗 Homer is at the southwest tip of the Kenai Peninsula. Call the Millers for directions and an appointment.

🕐 May–Sept. by appointment only. No fee.

Pratt Museum   This is a general local history and nature museum, one with an excellent reputation. There are Russian and native artifacts, regional artworks, and plant and animal displays including an imposing whale skeleton.

🔲 907 235-8635 • 3779 Bartlett St., Homer, AK 99603

🚗 It's right in the middle of town, near the junction with Pioneer Ave.

🕐 May–Sept.: Mon.–Sun. 10 A.M.–6 P.M. Reduced hours rest of year. Closed Jan. Fee.

KETCHIKAN

Totem Heritage Center   The center is famous for its 33 Tlingit and Haida totem poles and house posts, the largest such collection. A third local people, the Tsimshian, are also represented in exhibits and activities, which include classes and workshops on native arts and crafts. *Tours, Programs*

🏠 907 225-5900 • 601 Deermount St., Ketchikan, AK 99901

🚗 Ketchikan, in the extreme southeast, is an Inside Passage stop; you'll probably be using a walking map. The Totem Heritage Center is northeast of the town center.

🕐 Mid-May–Sept.: Mon.–Sat. 8 A.M.–5 P.M., Sun. 9 A.M.–5 P.M. Rest of year: Tues.–Fri. 1 P.M.–5 P.M. Fee.

KODIAK

Baranov Museum   This was once Russian America, and the museum preserves samovars, icons, and a variety of trade items in an 1808 warehouse building used by Aleksandr Baranov. There are also native and local historical items, including a 26-foot skin kayak. Visit the Russian Orthodox Church and seminary nearby to further your sense of the pre-American period. *Gift Shop*

🏠 907 486-5920 • 101 Marine Way, Kodiak, AK 99615

🚗 Kodiak is on Kodiak Island; you'll come by plane or by the Alaska Marine Hwy. The museum is in the Erskine House, downtown, across from the ferry terminal.

🕐 May–Labor Day: Mon.–Fri. 10 A.M.–4 P.M., Sat.–Sun. noon–4 P.M. Reduced hours or by appointment other times of year. Closed Feb. Fee.

NOME

Carrie M. McLain Memorial Museum   Nome is at the end of the Iditarod Race, and just about at the end of the continent, and the museum has displays on dog racing and on the life of the peoples of the area and the Bering Sea. Ivory carvings, gold rush memorabilia and artifacts, and a large collection of photographs and records form a research base as well as museum.

🏠 907 443-2566 • Public Library Bldg., 200 E. Front St., Nome, AK 99762

🚗 You won't miss it; it's front and center, on the water.

🕐 June–mid-Sept.: Mon.–Sun. 9 A.M.–6 P.M. Reduced hours rest of year. No fee.

SITKA

Sheldon Jackson Museum   Named for an 1890s missionary, the oldest museum in Alaska is now state run. Its collections focus on the Aleut, Inuit, Athabaskan, and Northwest Coast Indian cultures; there are baskets, clothing, and woven items, kayaks, beadwork, masks, totem poles, ivory and wood carvings, and varied goods used in trade by Europeans. Also in Sitka are the Isabel Miller Museum (907 747-6455), in the Centennial Building, with historical displays; the Sitka National Historical Park, with the 1842 Russian Bishop's House and fort, commemorating the period of Russian-native trade; and the Alaska Raptor Rehabilitation Center (907 747-8662), a short walk from downtown on Sawmill Creek Rd., where you may see the work of rehabilitating injured bald eagles and other birds of prey. *Gift Shop, Programs*

🏠 907 747-8981 • 104 College Dr., Sitka, AK 99835

🚗 Sitka is on Baranov Island, in the Panhandle. The museum is just east of the center of town, on the Sheldon Jackson College campus.

🕐 Mid-May–mid-Sept.: Mon.–Sun. 8 A.M.–5 P.M. Rest of year: Tues.–Sat. 10 A.M.–4 P.M. Fee.

SKAGWAY

Klondike Gold Rush National Historical Park   This is not simply a museum, or the city as museum, but an entire district as museum: The 1897–98 Klondike gold rush poured through Skagway and neighboring Dyea and up the White Pass and Chilkoot trails, leaving uncounted artifacts and memories. Today, you can tour Skagway's historic buildings, take the White Pass and Yukon Railroad, or even—be prepared—avoid the crowd and hike the trail, to walk where the goldbugs walked. Skagway's Visitors Center has over 200,000 artifacts, and tours of other sites start here. You might want to look in at the Trail of '98 Museum at City Hall (907 983-2420) also. *Tours, Programs, Screenings*

🏠 907 983-2921 • http://www.gov/klgo • Skagway, AK 99840

🚗 Skagway is in the Panhandle, on Lynn Canal off the Inside Passage. The visitors center is at 2nd and Broadway, just up from the ferry terminal.

🕐 Tours and programs at the Visitors Center, mid-May–mid-Sept. Call or write for information. No fee.

WASILLA

Museum of Alaska Transportation and Industry   In indoor and outdoor exhibits, the museum displays vehicles from trucks and tractors to snow machines, planes, boats, and rail and construction equipment, all involved in the development of Alaska. You'll also find a Bush Pilot Hall of Fame, sleeper cars that carried World War II troops, the unique Chitina Auto Railer, and many other specialized machines. *Gift Shop*

🔲 907 376-1211 • http://www.alaska.net~rmorris/mati1.htm • 3800 West Neuser Dr., Wasilla, AK 99687

🚗 The museum is 0.75 mile off the Parks Hwy (Route 3) at Mile 47, just northwest of the Wasilla airport.

🕐 May–Sept.: Mon.–Sun. 9 A.M.–6 P.M. Oct.–Apr.: Tues.–Sat. 9 A.M.–5 P.M. Fee.

$\blacktriangle$RIZONA

It started with the Hohokam, who built a series of canals so they could live comfortably and farm in what is now the Phoenix area. A little while later (say, a thousand years or so), Americans caught on, and now the desert has sprouted bluegrass turf and Arizonans live in suburbs too. Not everyone, of course: Some of these museums lie along lonely roads from There to There. Arizona's dry climate accounts for the museums that focus on desert-thriving flora like cacti, or aircraft; others are the natural result of an expanding and diversifying economy and culture.

What's Big: Another state full of big scenery, that's what. The Grand Canyon is a showcase of zillions of years of rock deposits, curated, as it were, by the Colorado River, which has laid all this history open for your eyes. Or if it's the human scene you want, they say that the New Cornelia Tailings Dam, down near Ajo, is the biggest in the world—biggest dam or biggest mine dump, take your pick. There are some vast military reservations; a lot of the things people in New Mexico think are UFOs come from one base or another here. Museums? Sure: There's Tucson's Pima Air and Space Museum; Flagstaff's Museum of Northern Arizona; Yuma's Territorial Prison; or maybe even the Meteor Crater at Winslow (created by those pesky aliens?).

BISBEE

Shady Dell RV Park and Campground   If you go to Bisbee you'll be getting a load of mine and labor history, or else you'll be checking out the art scene. Here's a different idea: Rent one of the classic trailers at the Shady Dell. Then you'll be staying *in* a museum. How about a 1949 Airstream? a 1948 Silver Streak? a 1950 Spartanette (sounds strenuous)? Period decor, big-band cassettes, and assorted memorabilia will enhance the mood. But call Ed Smith or Rita Personett before you go; they say weekends, especially, are busy.

$\blacksquare$ 520 432-3567 • 1 Douglas Rd., Bisbee, AZ 85603

🚐 Bisbee is in extreme southeastern Arizona, on Hwy 80. The RV park is 1.5 miles east of historic Bisbee on 80, 0.5 block off the traffic circle.

🕐 Call for information and reservations.

CORDES JUNCTION

Arcosanti   Arcosanti is the working out of the vision of architect Paolo Soleri, a new city being created according to principles of arcology ("architecture and ecology as one integral process"). The building is being done by participants in workshops, some of whom may be among the 7,000 residents ultimately envisioned, in an energy-efficient "urban laboratory." If you're in the Scottsdale area, you may want to visit the Cosanti Foundation, Soleri's headquarters in Paradise Valley (602 948-6145), to learn more about the concept and see more of Soleri's structures. *Tours, Gift Shop, Food, Programs*

📱 520 632-7135 • http://www.arcosanti.org • Cordes Junction, AZ 86333

🚐 It's an hour north of Phoenix. Take I-17 to Exit 262 at Cordes Junction and follow signs.

🕐 Mon.–Sun. 9 A.M.–5 P.M. Tours begin at gallery on the hour, 10 A.M.–4 P.M. Fee for tour.

DOS CABEZAS

Frontier Relics Museum   This is the "found" museum of Orville Mickens, who retrieved most of its contents from "in, around, and under" Arizona's forts and ghost towns. Mickens has everything organized, with information on what someone else might call *provenance*, and is ready to tell you about it all. Truly a personal museum.

📱 520 384-3481 • Dos Cabezas, AZ 85643

🚐 Dos Cabezas is in far southeastern Arizona. Exit from I-10 at Willcox and follow Route 186 for about 14 miles, going toward the Chiricahua National Monument.

🕐 Mon.–Sat. 9 A.M.–5 P.M. Call to confirm. Fee.

DRAGOON

Amerind Foundation   Archaeologist William Fulton created the Amerind Foundation in 1937, and his former residence now houses an important museum of American cultures—primarily of the Southwest, but also from the Arctic through Central America. There is also a collection of artworks by both Indian and white painters and sculptors. The surroundings are spectacular. *Gift Shop*

📱 520 586-3666 • Texas Canyon, Dragoon, AZ 85609

🚐 Dragoon is in southeastern Arizona, an hour east of Tucson on I-10. Take Exit 318 and go 1 mile southeast on Dragoon Rd., looking for signs.

🕐 Sept.–May: Mon.–Sun. 10 A.M.–4 P.M. Rest of year: Wed.–Sun. 10 A.M.–4 P.M. Fee.

FLORENCE

Pinal County Historical Museum   There's something for almost everyone here—purple glass items and glass insulators, farm machinery, all sorts of artifacts from frontier households, dentists' tools, cactus furniture, a telephone switchboard, and on and on. But there are some special collections too. Barbed wire, for one thing—many types. Prison relics, including nooses, hangman's trapdoor, and a gas chamber seat. And a splendid collection of bullets. *Tours, Library*

■ 520 868-4382 • 715 S. Main St., Florence, AZ 85232

🚗 Florence is in south-central Arizona, about 50 miles southeast of Phoenix, on Hwy 79 and Hwy 287. The museum is central, near the Pinal County Visitors Center.

🕐 Apr.–July 15 and Sept.–Nov.: Wed.–Sun. noon–4 P.M. Dec.–Mar.: Wed.–Sat. 11 A.M.–4 P.M., Sun. noon–4 P.M. Donation.

GREEN VALLEY

Titan Missile Museum   Want to relive the Cold War? This is the only remaining Titan intercontinental missile silo; they preserved one so we could savor those days. From the 1960s into 1987, there was always a crew here, and a missile, waiting, waiting. Now you can walk through the complex, look down on Titan, check out the control panels. We won't ask why you've come. *Tours, Gift Shop*

■ 520 625-7736 • Green Valley, AZ 85622

🚗 Green Valley is a half-hour south of Tucson via I-19. Take Exit 69W (Duval Mine Rd.).

🕐 By tour only. Nov.–Apr.: Mon.–Sun. 9 A.M.–4 P.M. Rest of year: Closed Mon., Tues. Fee.

HACKBERRY

International Bioregional Old Route 66 Visitors Center and Preservation Foundation   On one of the few remaining stretches of fabled Route 66, artist Bob Waldmire has settled into a former general store and created a museum devoted first to the highway and next to preservation of the older way of life—plant, animal, and human—that the superhighways bypass. Waldmire has received international media attention, but still, this isn't Times Square, and you'll get a chance to relax too. *Gift Shop, Library*

■ 520 769-2605 • Hackberry, AZ 86411

🚗 Hackberry is on old Route 66, 25 miles northeast of Kingman, in northwestern Arizona. Get off I-40 onto 66 between Seligman (east) and Kingman (west).

🕐 Year round, seven days a week "by chance or appointment." Fee.

MESA

Champlin Fighter Aircraft Museum   The focus here is on fighters from World War I (Fokker, Sopwith, Nieuport) and World War II (Spitfire, Focke-Wulf 190, P-40 and P-51, Yak-9), although there are some Vietnam-era jets. There's also what claims to be the most complete collection of aircraft machine guns in the world. The neighboring Confederate Air Museum (602 924-1940) specializes in World War II planes. *Tours, Gift Shop*

■ 602 830-4541 • Falcon Field, 4636 Fighter Aces Dr., Mesa, AZ 85215

🚗 Mesa is a southeastern suburb of Phoenix. Take US 60E from I-10 to Higley Rd. (Exit 186). Go north 5 miles to McKellips Rd., and turn left. Falcon Field Dr. will be on your right, leading to Fighter Aces.

🕑 Mon.–Sun. 10 A.M.–5 P.M. Fee.

PAGE

John Wesley Powell Memorial Museum   A long way downstream from the Powell museum in Green River, Utah, this one illustrates the Major's adventures in the Glen Canyon (now Lake Powell) and Grand Canyon areas, has such items as the bed he died in, and also includes a large collection of Anasazi and other Southwestern arts and crafts and artifacts. There are also fluorescent minerals, ethnographic exhibits, and materials on the history of the Page area. *See also* the Sweetwater County Historical Museum in Green River, Wyoming. *Tours, Gift Shop, Library*

■ 520 645-9496 • http://www.pagehost.com/lakepowell/info.htm • 6 N. Lake Powell Blvd., Page, AZ 86040

🚗 Page is in extreme northern Arizona, on US 89. Take Business Loop 89 into town. The museum is at the corner of N. Navajo Dr. and Lake Powell Blvd. (the main street).

🕑 Apr.–Oct.: Mon.–Sat. 8 A.M.–6 P.M., Sun. 10 A.M.–6 P.M. Slightly reduced hours off-season. Closed mid-Dec.–mid-Feb. No fee.

PHOENIX

While you're in the area, see also: Mesa, Scottsdale

Arizona Mining and Mineral Museum   Copper comes in many colors, and this museum is noted for its spectacular ore samples. There's also gold, a huge chunk of the thing that made the hole at Meteor Crater, and a collection of mining tools. Fluorescent rocks and lapidary displays add to the interest. Perhaps you'll get excited enough to buy a gold pan. *Gift Shop*

■ 602 255-3791 • Arizona Dept. of Mines & Mineral Resources, 1502 W. Washington St., Phoenix, AZ 85007

🚗 In downtown Phoenix. Exit from I-10 onto 7th Ave. south, then turn right (west) on Washington, and go to 15th Ave.

🕐 Mon.–Fri. 8 A.M.–5 P.M., Sat. 1 P.M.–5 P.M. No fee.

Hall of Flame Museum of Firefighting   Magnificent restored fire trucks and their predecessors, going back to the early 18th century, are the key to this collection. There are also thousands of pieces of gear and other artifacts, books, and pictures; an interactive safety exhibit; and a display of fire-safety systems. *Tours*

📞 602 275-3473 • 6101 E. Van Buren St., in Papago Park, Phoenix, AZ 85008

🚗 It's across the street from the Phoenix Zoo and next to Phoenix Municipal Stadium.

🕐 Mon.–Sat. 9 A.M.–5 P.M., Sun. noon–4 P.M. Guided tours at 2 P.M. Fee.

Medical Museum   Dr. Robert Kravetz has been collecting medical items of all sorts—old instruments, quack remedies, scales, leech jars, pillmaking equipment, doctors' bags—for years, and he has twelve display cases of them here. Lydia Pinkham's Vegetable Compound, bone saws, ear trumpets . . . what are you waiting for?

📞 602 242-2555 • 6025 N. 20th Ave. (Phoenix Baptist Hospital Lobby), Phoenix, AZ 85015

🚗 The hospital is at Bethany Home Rd. and 20th Ave., north of downtown. Take I-17 to Exit 204 and proceed east on Bethany Home.

🕐 Mon.–Sun. 8 A.M.–9 P.M. No fee.

Sylvia Plotkin Judaica Museum of Greater Phoenix   A re-created Tunisian synagogue, with authentic artifacts, is central to a collection that includes sculpture, furniture, devotional items, and archives. The museum has a strong educational mission and presents a variety of programs, video presentations, and other activities. *Tours, Gift Shop, Programs, Screenings*

📞 602 264-4428 • Temple Beth Israel, 3310 N. 10th Ave., Phoenix, AZ 85013

🚗 Just north of downtown, at the corner of 10th Ave. and W. Osborn Rd.

🕐 Tues.–Thurs. 10 A.M.–3 P.M., most Suns. noon–3 P.M., after Fri. evening services. Closed Jewish and national holidays. Tours at other hours by appointment. No fee.

PRESCOTT

Bead Museum   Southwestern peoples have produced beads for centuries, but this museum is about beads from all over the world: huge, heavy African beads, beads made from human bone, beads as currency, glass beads, Hubbell trade beads, and many other varieties, ancient or created yesterday. It's a small, full space, in which you'll sense the ubiquity and importance of this form of body ornamentation. *Gift Shop, Library*

📞 520 445-2431 • http://www.ariz.com/beads • 140 S. Montezuma, Prescott, AZ 86303

🚌 Prescott is about 2 hours north-northwest of Phoenix via I-17 to Cordes Junction, exiting onto Hwy 69. In town, 69 becomes Gurley St.; turn left onto Montezuma.

🕐 Mon.–Sat. 9:30 A.M.–4:30 P.M. Sun. by appointment. Donation.

Phippen Museum of Western Art   This is a center for Western (particularly what is called Cowboy) art, with paintings, bronzes, and sketches celebrating the open spaces. There is also a collection of photographs and artifacts on the topic. Contemporary as well as 19th-century artists are featured. *Gift Shop*

📞 520 778-1385 • 4701 Hwy 89N, Prescott, AZ 86301

🚌 About 6 miles northeast of downtown, on the way to the airport.

🕐 Mon., Wed.–Sat. 10 A.M.–4 P.M., Sun. 1 P.M.–4 P.M. Fee.

Smoki Museum   Opened in 1935, in a building designed to approximate a pueblo, the Smoki Museum exhibits artifacts and artworks of Southwestern peoples, as well as Plains tribes. Photographs, paintings, and writings of Kate Cory, noted early-20th-century student of the Hopi, are central to the collection. *Tours, Gift Shop, Library*

📞 520 445-1230 • 147 N. Arizona St., Prescott, AZ 86304

🚌 On entering town on Hwy 69, look for Arizona Ave. on the right.

🕐 May–Sept.: Mon.–Tues., Thurs.–Sat. 10 A.M.–4 P.M., Sun. 1 P.M.–4 P.M. Oct.: Fri., Sat., Sun. only. Other times by appointment. Fee.

SACATON

Gila River Cultural Center   Here's a good place to learn about cultures of Arizona from the ancient Hohokam to today's Pima, Maricopa, Apache, and Tohono o'Odham (Papago). Outdoors there are traditional structures of the various peoples. Indoors is an arts and crafts center. *Gift Shop, Food, Programs, Publications*

📞 520 963-3981 • Casa Blanca Rd., Sacaton, AZ 85221

🚌 Sacaton is an hour southeast of downtown Phoenix via I-10. The cultural center is at Exit 175, just off the highway.

🕐 Mon.–Sun. 8 A.M.–5 P.M. No fee.

SAINT JOHNS

Raven Site Museum/White Mountain Archaeological Center   Visit an archaeological work in progress: Raven Site is a town of 800 years ago being rediscovered, its contents studied, catalogued, and preserved, by James and Carol Cunkle and a host of helpers. The museum displays what has been found so far, including a large collection of earthenware vessels. There are petroglyph and ethnobotany hikes. Down the road is Casa Malpais in Springerville. *Tours, Gift Shop, Hands-on, Programs*

📱 520 333-5857 • Saint Johns, AZ 85936
🚙 Raven Site is in east-central Arizona, 16 miles south of St. Johns and 12 miles north of Springerville, off US 180/191; follow signs.
🕐 May–mid-Oct.: Mon.–Sun. 10 A.M.–5 P.M. Tours on the hour. Fee.

SCOTTSDALE

Fleischer Museum   At the end of the 19th century, California, its light and landscapes, attracted American painters as Provence had attracted the French, and the California School of Impressionists developed. Fashion passed them by in mid-century, but today they are celebrated again. The Fleischer Museum, in elegant surroundings, displays their work, along with sculptures and paintings of Soviet Impressionists. *Tours*
📱 602 585-3108 • The Perimeter Center, 17207 N. Perimeter Dr. (Pima and Bell Rds.), Scottsdale, AZ 85255
🚙 Scottsdale is on the east side of Phoenix. The Perimeter Center is at the intersection of Pima and Bell Rds., near the Scottsdale Municipal Airport. From downtown, take I-17N, and exit onto Bell Rd. (Exit 212); continue about 12 miles east.
🕐 Mon.–Sun. 10 A.M.–4 P.M. Closed holidays. Tours by appointment. No fee.

SECOND MESA

Hopi Cultural Center   In the spectacular and historically rich Hopi country, this is a center for anyone visiting the pueblos. There are displays of jewelry, weaving, kachina dolls, and other Hopi crafts, as well as info on the people's history, and the Center periodically presents dances and other events. *Gift Shop, Food, Programs*
📱 520 734-6650 • Second Mesa, AZ 86043
🚙 Second Mesa is on the Hopi Indian Reservation, northeast of Flagstaff, in northeastern Arizona. Take Hwy 87N from Exit 257 (near Winslow) for just over 60 miles, to the junction with Hwy 264, and proceed west on 264 for 5 miles.
🕐 Jan.–Dec.: Mon.–Fri. 8 A.M.–5 P.M., Sat.–Sun. 9 A.M.–3 P.M. Call to confirm hours in winter and for information on dances and other programs. Fee.

SPRINGERVILLE

Casa Malpais   Casa Malpais was home to the mysterious Mogollon (the Hopi and Zuni both claim kinship) from about 1200 to about 1400, when, for reasons not yet known, they abandoned it. Excavation here did not begin until 1990. Now you may visit this ongoing archaeological project and see in its museum artifacts recovered to date. *Tours*

🏠 520 333-5375 • 318 Main St., Springerville, AZ 85938
🚗 Springerville is in east-central Arizona. Casa Malpais is on Main St., aka US 60/180.
🕐 June–Sept.: Mon.–Sun. 9 A.M.–5 P.M. Rest of year: closed Sun. Fee.

TUCSON

Arizona–Sonora Desert Museum   This living museum displays, in a series of distinct habitats, the animal and plant life and terrain of the huge Sonoran Desert, which stretches across the U.S.-Mexico border. From mountain animals like cougar and wolves to grassland and water dwellers, you'll find them among 1,300 kinds of desert plants in a spectacular setting. This could be an all-day visit, and in summer, you should be prepared for the climate! *Gift Shop, Food*
🏠 520 883-2702 • 2021 N. Kinney Rd., Tucson, AZ 85743
🚗 The museum is in Tucson Mountain Park, 14 miles west of the city. From downtown, take Speedway Blvd. west, continuing on Gates Pass Rd. until it joins Kinney. Or take Ajo Way west, turning right onto Kinney.
🕐 Mar.–Sept.: Mon.–Sun. 7:30 A.M.–6 P.M. Rest of year: Mon.–Sun. 8:30 A.M.–5 P.M. Fee.

University of Arizona Mineral Museum   The mineral collection here in-cludes over 14,000 specimens, focusing on Arizona's big three—copper, gold, and silver—but including examples of almost anything found in the state, as well as much from elsewhere, even from space: the meteorite collection is extensive. Flandrau Center itself has many programs geared to kids.
🏠 520 621-4227 • at the Flandrau Science Center, University Blvd. and Cherry St., Uni-versity of Arizona campus, Tucson, AZ 85721
🚗 The campus is in the center of Tucson. Exit from I-10 onto E. Speedway Blvd. Turn right on Cherry St. after about 2 miles.
🕐 Mon.–Fri. 9 A.M.–5 P.M., Sat.–Sun. 1 P.M.–5 P.M. Also Wed.–Sat. evenings. No fee.

WICKENBURG

Desert Caballeros Western Museum   In Dude Ranch country, the Desert Caballeros Museum displays a mix of Indian artifacts and arts, period rooms depicting life in the area a century ago, and a black-light mineral room. There is also a gallery with 19th-century landscapes including the work of Albert Bierstadt and Western art from Remington and Catlin through contemporary painters and sculptors. *Tours, Gift Shop, Programs, Library*
🏠 520 684-2272 • 21 N. Frontier St., Wickenburg, AZ 85358
🚗 Wickenburg is about 70 miles northwest of Phoenix. Museum Park is at the junction of Hwys 93/89 and 60. The museum is around the corner on Frontier St.
🕐 Mon.–Sat. 10 A.M.–4 P.M., Sun. 1 P.M.–4 P.M. Fee.

WILLCOX

Rex Allen Arizona Cowboy Museum   In the West, it's hard to tell the cowboys from the cowboy actors. Rex Allen, from these parts, sang and played guitar, and parlayed his talents into movies and TV, where he also became the "Frontier Doctor." Here's a collection of memorabilia. Nearby, you can also get a look at local history and Apache lore at the Cochise Visitor Center (520 384-2272).

■ 520 384-4583 • 155 N. Railroad Ave., Willcox, AZ 85643

🚗 Willcox is in southeastern Arizona, east of Tucson, at Exit 340 of I-10. Railroad Ave. parallels the highway; go southeast from the exit.

🕐 Mon.–Sat. 10 A.M.–4 P.M. Fee.

WINDOW ROCK

Navajo Tribal Museum   The Navajo, who moved into the area in the 13th century, are now the largest Indian nation in the Four Corners area, their reservation the largest in the country. Here you'll see historical artifacts and displays (some on their predecessors in the area, including the Anasazi) as well as contemporary arts like weaving and silversmithing. A short distance west, at Saint Michael's Mission, you may visit a small museum devoted to the history of Catholicism's approach to the Navajo; call 520 871-4171. And about 50 miles north on Route 12, in Tsaile, you could try another Navajo showplace, the Hatathli Museum, at Navajo Community College; call 520 724-6654 for information.

■ 520 871-6673 • Navajo Arts and Crafts Bldg., Hwy 264, Window Rock, AZ 86515

🚗 Window Rock is in northeastern Arizona, near the New Mexico line, at the junction of Routes 264 and 12. From I-40, take Exit 357 (Lupton) and go 25 miles north on 12.

🕐 Apr.–Oct.: Mon.–Sat. 8 A.M.–6 P.M. Rest of year: Mon.–Fri. 9 A.M.–6 P.M. Donation.

YUMA

Century House Museum (Sanguinetti House)   There's a lot to see in Yuma, particularly at the Territorial Prison State Historic Park. What we're suggesting here is a break from heat and history. This building does have a history, of course, and there are displays on Yuma's; but we think you might like just being in this fine Sonoran-style house, and especially in its gardens, noted not only as a horticultural oasis but for their birds. *Tours, Gift Shop, Food, Programs, Library*

■ 520 782-1841 • 240 Madison Ave., Yuma, AZ 85364

🚗 It's in central Yuma, near the river. Take the Giss Pkwy exit off I-8; Madison Ave. crosses Giss 4 blocks west of the highway.

🕐 Tues.–Sat. 10 A.M.–4 P.M. Closed legal holidays. No fee.

ARKANSAS

Perhaps you've come for the waters. Native Americans in the area certainly did, and Hernando de Soto came all this way in 1541 to partake. And while Arkansas conjures up all kinds of small-town images—yes, even more than a bit backwoodsy, from Li'l Abner to Lum 'n' Abner—it's got a broad and rich economic history from its unusual natural resources beyond the remedial hot springs: diamonds and oil, bauxite and brine. As you may know, it's also a fine place to grow spinach and raise young presidents.

What's Big: In Murfreesboro, the Crater of Diamonds; in Hot Springs, the Mid-America Museum and the Arkansas House of Reptiles.

BAUXITE

Bauxite Museum   A company town if ever there was one, Bauxite had its start in 1887 with the discovery of extensive ore deposits. From bauxite comes aluminum, and the museum reflects the history of that industry (Alcoa, Reynolds, etc.)—and particularly its contribution to the World War II effort—as much as the changes in home life in a town still tied into bucks from bauxite. In nearby Benton is the unique all-bauxite-built Gann Museum (1893), with a nice local history collection.
- 501 557-5318/2997 • PO Box 242, Bauxite, AR 72011
- About 15 miles southwest of Little Rock. Take I-30S to Exit 123 (Bryant-Bauxite), following Hwy 183 through Bryant into town. It's behind the post office.
- Wed. 10 A.M.–2 P.M., or by appointment. No fee.

BENTONVILLE

Wal-Mart Visitor Center   The simple WALTON'S 5–10 lettering above the red and white awning wouldn't tip you off that this little variety store was to become the cornerstone of a retailing dynasty. But you'll learn all about the Sam Walton story when you come to what's now the Wal-Mart Visitor Center. See his original office; photos, mementos, and '50s and '60s merchandise; and an exhibit on his plan to "Buy American" from a company that has changed the way to sell American. While we're on things American, you might also want to look into the Daisy International Air Gun Museum, at the factory here in Bentonville. *Gift Shop*

🏠 501 273-1329 • 105 N. Main St., Bentonville, AR 72712

🚗 About 25 miles north of Fayetteville. Take US 71 or 71B north to Hwy 72 (Central Ave.). It's downtown on the west side of the square.

🕐 Mar.–Oct.: Mon.–Fri. 9 A.M.–5 P.M. Nov.–Feb.: Tues.–Sat. 9 A.M.–5 P.M. No fee.

EUDORA

Henry and Rubye Connerly Museum   Way over in about as far southeast Arkansas as you can get is the old Henry Connerly Grocery and Feed Store that Henry and Rubye left behind to be turned into a microcosm of yesteryear. As they say, the store itself is a museum, but you might also enjoy poking around the selection of period stuff from ladies' shoes to cotton-picking sacks.

🏠 501 355-4633 • 1453 Duncan St., Eudora, AR 71640

🚗 In southeastern Alabama, at US 65 and Hwy 8. It's 0.5 block north of City Hall.

🕐 Shown by appointment only by calling Mrs. Harold Hart. No fee.

EUREKA SPRINGS

You're in the heart of Ozark country here, and also the home of not only the Anita Bryant Theater—Ms. Bryant has a stage act these days—but also the Wonderful World of Tiny Horses. If that's not enough, besides our listings below, you might want to venture a few miles east to Berryville for the Saunders Memorial Museum. Over in the "Turkey Capital of Arkansas" Col. C. B. (no, not *that* colonel) Saunders has an eclectic assortment that includes an Arabian sheik's tent and Annie Oakley's and Pancho Villa's sidearms. Onyx Cave, also out this way, is a sort of throw-back pre–theme park "attraction." If buttons are your thing, the Gay Nineties Button and Doll Museum at the cave entrance is a definite stop.

Frog Fantasies Museum   They could call this Frogs-R-Us and not be too far off the lily pad. As Louise Mesa will tell you, it took only one for her family to get started. Now she and her husband Pat have over 6,000 of the critters—ceramics from Japan, necktie and umbrella prints, old pull-toys, salt-and-pepper shakers, Frog Light beer bottles, Indonesian temple frogs, archaic frog pipes, blue frogs, pink frogs, and frogs in little outfits. The joint, indeed, is jumping. . . . *Gift Shop*

🏠 501 253-7227 • 151 Spring St., Eureka Springs, AR 72632

🚙 About 60 miles northeast of Fayetteville. Take US 62 into the historic district.
🕐 Mon.–Sun. 10 A.M.–5 P.M. Fee.

Hammond Museum of Bells   Tintinnabulists Anonymous has Curtis and Lenore Hammond as their charter members, but even if you think it's just so much ringing in your ears, there's a lot to be learned here about the making and the history of bells, chimes, and carillons. Thousands of 'em, all shapes, all sizes, archaeologically ancient to artsy and avant-garde. *Tours, Gift Shop*
🏠 501 253-7411 • 2 Pine St., Eureka Springs, AR 72632
🚙 See Frog Fantasies, above. It's across Spring St. at the post office trolley stop.
🕐 Apr.–Nov. 15: Mon.–Sat. 9:30 A.M.–5 P.M., Sun. 12:30 P.M.–4 P.M. Fee.

Miles Musical Museum   This is a wondrous collection of all manner of music-making machines that Floyd C. Miles has brought together. Huge fantastically painted dance hall organs, hurdy-gurdys, calliopes, skating-rink Wurlitzers, or a Coinola Nickelodeon are apt to be turned on at any time. The robust and enthusiastic presentation also includes a good assortment of circus stuff, a collection of animated figures from the 1904 Saint Louis World's Fair, and a few other surprises. *Tours, Gift Shop*
🏠 501 253-8961 • US 62, Eureka Springs, AR 72632
🚙 About 60 miles northeast of Fayetteville, it's right on US 62W.
🕐 May–Oct.: Mon.–Wed., Fri.–Sun. 9 A.M.–4 P.M. Fee.

FORT SMITH

Besides a number of perhaps more apparent civic virtues, Fort Smith has renown as the home of the World's Largest Mr. Peanut. It's also within spitting distance of Alma, the "Spinach Capital of the World," and a statue of our pal Popeye. While you're in the area, see also: Van Buren.

Patent Model Museum   Inventors are a fascinating lot, and when you get a close look at these patent models you can often feel the surge of genius in someone like Da Vinci when he was developing his flying machines. And you can imagine how nutty the neighbors might have thought their visionary neighbor. There are 85 of these miniature (required specs were 12-inch square, max) working models of patents applied for between 1835 and 1881—from the Rube Goldbergesque combo fold-down bed, wardrobe, and bureau to a round refrigerator from 1876 to a floating bed fitted with oars from the same year—and blueprints and drawings of a bunch more. When you're in the Washington, D.C., area you might want to stop at the U.S. Patent and Trademark Museum in Arlington, Virginia, for more about the original patent office, and more models. *Tours*
🏠 501 782-9014 • 400 N. 8th St., Fort Smith, AR 72901

🚙 Downtown historic district, off Garrison Ave.

🕐 Mon.–Fri. 10 A.M.–4 P.M. No fee.

HOT SPRINGS

Fordyce Bathhouse Visitor Center   Suffering from "social or business fatigue"? A stroll back in time to the 1920s hot springs heyday may be just what the doctor ordered. The pre-penicillin era when people could come for a few weeks "to take a cure" is wholly evoked in this tour through exotic-sounding facilities—vapor cabinets, needle showers, Sun-ray cabinets, hydrotherapy treatments like a Scotch douche for that nagging sciatica, and electro and mechano therapies. The 1915 Spanish Renaissance Revival Fordyce Bathhouse has been completely restored to its original marble and terra cotta glory. *Tours, Gift Shop*

📞 501 623-1433 • Hot Springs National Park, 369 Central Ave., Hot Springs, AR 71902

🚙 Downtown, on Hwy 7N (Central Ave.) following signs to "National Park Visitor Center," it's in the middle of "Bathhouse Row."

🕐 Mon.–Sun. 9 A.M.–5 P.M. No fee.

Tiny Town   This brings to mind the *Twilight Zone* episode where the humans turn out to be giants. We don't know why Americans like tiny things—stuffing ships into bottles, knitting picayune hats—but they do. And this family affair is an entire miniature mechanical Wild West–era town and Indian village, all to one-quarter scale.

📞 501 624-4742 • 374 Whittington Ave., Hot Springs, AR 71901

🚙 Downtown, 3 blocks off Hwy 7N.

🕐 Mar.–Nov.: Mon.–Sun. 10 A.M.–4:30 P.M. Fee.

LITTLE ROCK

While you're in the area, see: **Bauxite**

PINE BLUFF

Band Museum   Seventy-six trombones (at least) and hundreds of other instruments, some dating back as far as the early 1700s, all of them with a past playing in a band.

📞 501 534-4676 • 423 Main St., Pine Bluff, AR 71601

🚙 Downtown, about 4 blocks from the Jefferson County courthouse.

🕐 Mon.–Fri. 10 A.M.–5 P.M. No fee.

PINE RIDGE

Lum 'n' Abner Museum and Jot 'Em Down Store   If you've ever listened to Garrison Keillor's A *Prairie Home Companion* radio show, you can begin to get an idea of what Chester "Chet" Lauck and Norris "Tuffy" Goff (aka Lum Eddards and Abner Peabody) were up to on their hugely popular *Lum 'n' Abner* radio show of the '30s and '40s. Started as a one-shot performance, their "old country storekeepers" routine took off, rivaling Amos and Andy, and eventually making movie stars of themselves as well. So here in this speck-on-the-map town is the Dick Huddleston store and original inspiration for the show, jammed full of memorabilia of the local good ole boys made good. *Tours, Gift Shop*

🏠 501 326-4442 • Hwy 88, PO Box 38, Pine Ridge, AR 71966

🚗 About 55 miles west of Hot Springs on Hwy 88.

🕐 Mar. 1–Nov. 15: Tues.–Sat. 9 A.M.–5 P.M., Sun. noon–5 P.M. Rest of year by appointment. No fee.

POTTSVILLE

Potts Inn Museum   One hundred years of ladies' hats tucked into a restored antebellum home that was once a major stop on the Butterfield Overland Stage route. Many of the chapeaux in question are the 1920s feathered and furred creations of Marshall Fields' designer Michael McLain, and they decorated the do's of the likes of Queen Marie of Romania and Warren G. Harding's ever-fashionable first lady. *Tours, Programs*

🏠 501 968-1877 • Town Square, Hwy 247, Pottsville, AR 72801

🚗 About 78 miles northwest of Little Rock, near Russelville, just off I-40 and US 64.

🕐 Tues.–Sat. 10 A.M.–5 P.M., Sun. 1 P.M.–5 P.M. Fee.

SMACKOVER

Arkansas Oil and Brine Museum   The cotton and timber markets were looking pretty bleak down here when Busey No. 1 well near El Dorado blew in in January of '21 to begin one of the wildest booms in the nation's history. While the exciting times waned pretty quickly, they've left a great legacy. Here's the period machinery and the stories of those who experienced the black gold boom—and the bromine, or brine, discovery that followed. *Gift Shop, Programs, Publications, Library*

🏠 501 725-2877 • 3853 Smackover Hwy, Smackover, AR 71762

🚗 In south-central Arkansas, it's 10 miles north of El Dorado on Hwy 7.

🕐 Mon.–Sat. 8 A.M.–5 P.M., Sun. 1 P.M.–5 P.M. No fee.

VAN BUREN

Bob Burns Museum   Tucked into the cuted-up restored Victorian historic district of this 1818 settlement town, in the old original railroad depot, is a collection of pix and memorabilia that celebrates another one of Arkansas' big radio stars of the 1930s and '40s, Bob "Bazooka" Burns—aka the Arkansas Traveler. This good ole Van Buren homeboy's claim to fame was also funning on his razorback kinfolk—and while he made quite a name for himself in a movie career as well, like our friends Lum 'n' Abner, it's the memory of the musical instrument he invented to accompany himself that sticks even harder. Created from a length of gas pipe, it seems it inspired those World War II boys to call their newly issued shoulder-held rocket launchers by the same name—bazooka.

● 800 332-5889/501 474-2761 • http://www.vanburen.org • 813 Main St., Van Buren, AR 72956

🚗 Just east of Fort Smith, in the Old Frisco Depot at the intersection with Hwy 59.

🕐 Mon.–Sat. 9 A.M.–5 P.M. No fee.

CALIFORNIA

It's a real challenge to say something about the state of California that doesn't seem like it's been said way too many times before. It's big, it's diverse—culturally, geographically, and economically—it's loaded with history, and can be as conservative as it is cutting edge. It's a pumped-up slice through the United States, and its museums tell that story as well as anything.

What's Big: In a state of some truly unique cultural enterprises like drive-in religious services and drive-through redwoods, the sultanate of swap meets, a land of pet cemeteries, surfing, Spanish missions, the latter-day source of Pyramid Power, and a place always under the influence of the threat of natural disasters, what's big is truly subjective and perhaps best addressed by state section, so please read on.

NORTHERN CALIFORNIA

Our definition of Northern California, arbitrary as it may be, is everything north and northeast of the immediate Bay Area. So you'll find some spots here, and throughout this section, that are just a hop away from the bay. Starting with nearby Fairfield, we wouldn't want you to miss J. Frank Webster and his Hot Dog Hall of Fame. Call the Hot Dog Hot Line (707 426-4618) to find out how to see his collection until he gets his own space. In Saint Helena, there's the Silverado Museum for Robert Louis Stevenson fans; in Sacramento, the Towe Ford Museum of Automotive History (small compensation for the loss of Warren Harris's Thermometer Museum formerly based near here, but it will have to do); in the way north, in Weaverville, there's the J. J. "Jake" Jackson Memorial Museum; and finally, we'd like to send you to Paradise—for the Gold Nugget Museum. Starting from the Shrine of the Unknown Tourist in Bolinas, there's a lot to see in Northern California. We see it as a place to fit in a museum or two as you enjoy the forests and the shore and savor a glass of wine or two on the way. *While you're in the area, see also*: San Francisco/Bay Area.

DONNER SUMMIT

Western SkiSport Museum   Just *schuss* on over between runs to get a taste of the sport from the early gold rush days when skis, introduced to North America by Nordic miners, were known as "Norwegian snowshoes" or "snow skates." Then a necessity for survival—and the only way the mail could get through during the rugged winters—the now-archaic 14-foot-long sticks rapidly became a source of sport and diversion. Besides more on the story of the gliding mid-19th-century trans-Sierra letter carrier, John "Snowshoe" Thompson (*see also* the Genoa Courthouse Museum in Genoa, Nevada), you'll find equipment, photos, and film footage marking great moments in ski history from the opening of the West and the gold rush in the 1800s through World War II heroics and the daredevil athletes of today.
Tours, Programs, Library, Screenings
🔲 530 426-3313 • Boreal Ski Area, Donner Summit, CA 95728
🚗 Lake Tahoe area. I-80, Castle Peak exit, 15 miles west of Truckee.
🕐 Dec. 1–end of ski season: Tues.–Sun. 10 A.M.–4 P.M. Rest of year: Wed.–Sun. 10 A.M.–4 P.M. No fee.

SACRAMENTO

While you're in the area, see: Woodland

SANTA ROSA

Church of One Tree/Robert L. "Believe It or Not!®" Ripley Memorial Museum   That's IN-CRED-I-BLE! Almost exactly one century after the good people of Santa Rosa set out to build a Baptist Church completely from the timber of just one (giant) redwood, the good folks of the very same town decided to pay homage to their itinerant native, Robert Leroy Ripley. What better location than that very same church. So here it is. While the stuff on display here covers Ripley the man—his safari hat and many-stickered suitcase, original cartoons, and the garb he wore while penning them—his story would not be complete without a two-headed calf or fur-bearing trout. Curator John Hacku is also on hand to provide further tales of a man who was perhaps as odd as the things he collected. You better believe it. *Screenings*
🔲 707 524-5233 • http://www.sfnet.net/kp/ripley • 492 Sonoma Ave., Santa Rosa, CA 95401
🚗 About 40 miles north of San Francisco. From US 101 take 3rd St. exit (downtown), turning right to Santa Rosa Ave., then right to Sonoma Ave., then right again.
🕐 Apr.–Oct.: Wed.–Sun. 10 A.M.–4 P.M. Fee.

TRUCKEE

Emigrant Trail Museum We'll get right to the point. While this museum covers some of the more romantic aspects of Western history, you're undoubtedly here for the most infamous evidence of an era that was also fraught with peril. Unlike Colorado's Alferd Packard, the 89-member Donner Party were not happy cannibals, but cannibals they were, nevertheless. Artifacts and a movie provide all the gory details of how it went for the 47 survivors of that distressing winter of 1846–47 in the snowbound Sierras. Alas, old Snowshoe was about ten years late with his mail route—surely he would have gotten both the mail *and* the Donners through. . . .

🏠 530 582-7892 • Donner Memorial State Park, 12593 Donner Pass Rd., Truckee, CA 96161

🚗 Lake Tahoe area. I-80, Donner State Park exit, about 0.5 mile west of Truckee.

🕓 Mon.–Sun. 10 A.M.–4 P.M. Fee.

WOODLAND

Hays Antique Truck Museum A. W. "Pop" Hays couldn't resist taking his career in the trucking business one step further when he hit retirement. Looks like he went full tilt, and full scale. With over 200 trucks-for-all-purposes dating from 1903 to 1954, all restored or in original condition, and with all the big and little manufacturers represented, this is a great glimpse into the hauler's world before CB and the deluxe cabs of today. *Gift Shop*

🏠 530 666-1044 • 2000 E. Main St., Woodland, CA 95776

🚗 Sixteen miles northwest of Sacramento. Take I-5; it's just off the Road 102 exit.

🕓 Mon.–Sun. 10 A.M.–4 P.M. Closed Wed. Nov.–Mar. Fee.

SAN FRANCISCO/BAY AREA

Those of you have been here know what a swell place the San Francisco/Bay Area is (we're including Silicon Valley in that assessment and in our listings for this section). Those who haven't, well, you've a treat in store—our eclectic list of museums should give you some idea of the spirit and diversity to be found. Before we tell you what's big here, we'd like to tip you off that the Museum of Modern Mythology is rumored to be close to finding a new home since its last was condemned after the '89 quake; we also hope that Mickey McGowan will have found a place to reopen his Unknown Museum in the near future. Until then, big places we like to visit include San Francisco's Mexican Museum, the Center for the Arts in Yerba Buena Gardens, and the Palace of the Legion of Honor (a foggy evening's a particularly good time to see it). Also not to be missed in S.F. are the Galeria de la Raza in the Mission district (and while you're in the

Mission, in an entirely different vein, you might want to meander over to the Good Vibrations storefront and their small but intriguing display of historic sexual arcana and boudoir toys) and the NAMES Project Gallery in the Castro district, housing the AIDS quilt collection. In Berkeley, stop at the Hearst Museum of Anthropology; in Sausalito, the San Francisco Bay Model Visitors Center; in Danville, the Behring Hoffman Museum (cars, medieval art, and a copy of Lucy's bones!); and in San Jose, the Rosicrucean Egyptian Museum. *While you're in the area, see also*: Northern California: Santa Rosa.

BURLINGAME

Burlingame Museum of Pez Memorabilia   Are Pez dispensers *still* around, you ask? Indeed they are, and Nancy and Gary Doss have the largest collection we know of—over 300 of the cartoon-character topped plastic dispensers, nicely set out in a back room of their computer store. A 1968 Psychedelic Eye Pez, a 1962 Bullwinkle Pez, a rare 1955 full-bodied Space Trooper, Popeye, and Mickey too. All of them inspired by the ingenuity of an Austrian food exec, Eduard Haas, who had sold adult breath mints (Pez is short for *Pfefferminz*, peppermint in German) since 1927 but came to fame only in 1949 with his American patent for an "automatic candy dispenser" and the fruit flavors more suited for kids. *Tours, Gift Shop, Hands-on*

■ 650 347-2301 • http:www.spectrumnet.com/pez • 214 California Dr., Burlingame, CA 94010

🚗 Take US 101S, Broadway/Burlingame exit, then left onto California Dr.

🕐 Tues.–Sat. 10 A.M.–6 P.M. No fee.

PALO ALTO

Barbie Hall of Fame   The Barbie machine has been busy since Mattel cofounder Ruth Handler—using her daughter and a racy German doll of the era, named Lilli, as models—created her in 1959, and collector Evelyn Burkhalter knows precisely which (very few) of the permutations of an over 16,000-item empire she is missing. You won't notice, however. This place is a Barbie Sens-U-Round and, politically correct issues aside, you're apt to be overwhelmed by the thoughtful, chronologically arranged tableaux, from pouty Barbie with demure Di-style side-glance eyes to the Jackie-O bubble-do era, the day-glo sixties, and the careerist eighties (Barbie astronaut, with bubble-head). Look for the Midge with teeth. And Ken still looks like a wimp to us. *Gift Shop*

■ 650 326-5841 • The Doll Studio, 433 Waverly St., Palo Alto, CA 94301

🚗 About 30 miles south of San Francisco. Take US 101S, Palo Alto exit into downtown.

🕐 Tues.–Fri. 1:30 P.M.–4:30 P.M.; Sat. 10 A.M.–noon, 1:30 P.M.–4:30 P.M.; and groups by appointment. Fee.

Museum of American Heritage   In the process of expansion and relocation to the historic 1907 Williams House, the Museum of American Heritage is a fitting contribution to a town that sits on the cutting edge of modern technology, here in the heart of Silicon Valley. Dedicated to the curation of technically ingenious electrical and mechanical devices of the past century or two, here's some stuff you may have to explain to your children for a change—like early crystal radio sets, music box discs vintage 78 rpm, and telephones that Mr. Bell could still relate to. *Hands-on, Programs*

🏛 650 321-1004 • 351 Homer Ave., Palo Alto, CA 94301

🚗 Take US 101S, Palo Alto exit onto University Ave., then left on Middlefield, and left again for 3–4 blocks on Homer.

🕐 Fri.–Sun. 11 A.M.–4 P.M. No fee.

SAN FRANCISCO

Hello Gorgeous!!   Ken Joachim is just crazy about Barbra (Barbra Streisand, that is), crazy enough to put his house in hock, doggedly pursue recalcitrant Realtors, and put it all on the line to build this shrine to the redoubtable vocalist. "Hello Gorgeous!!," the memorable opening line from *Funny Girl*, is the apt name of this spot that features memorabilia, posters, portraits, costumed mannequins, wigs, and a general assortment of tasteful Barbra-stuff, particularly focusing on her film career. *Gift Shop*

🏛 415 864-2628/2678 • 549-A Castro St., San Francisco, CA 94114

🚗 Off Market St., between 18th and 19th Sts. MUNI: #24 Divisadero, #35 Eureka.

🕐 Mon.–Thurs. 11 A.M.–7 P.M., Fri.–Sat. 11 A.M.–8 P.M., Sun. 11 A.M.–6 P.M. Fee.

Musée Mécanique   The Musée Mécanique is a delightful historical collection of arcade games, from whimsical early contraptions, like a toothpick amusement park and carnival fortune-tellers, to the latest sensory-assaulting computer games. Most may be activated for your entertainment pleasure. But there are things to see outside also. Don't miss the Victorian *camera obscura*, a giant darkened dome, that "magically" projects the view outside onto a screen inside. And while this is a stop on every tourist's checklist, and you won't see as many fat and happy lounging seals on the rocks below here anymore (they've been meandering down to the wharf area), the view (and path) to the Sutro Baths ruins and Lands End is just as wonderful as ever.

🏛 415 386-1170 • Cliff House, 1090 Point Lobos Ave., San Francisco, CA 94121

🚗 On the coast, just beyond Golden Gate Park. It's underneath the Cliff House Restaurant. MUNI: #18 46th Ave., #38 Erie.

🕐 Mon.–Fri. 11 A.M.–7 P.M., Sat.–Sun. 10 A.M.–8 P.M. No fee.

Museum of Ophthalmology   Only a tiny portion of the museum's holdings of over 10,000 eye-related objects may be seen by the public in the third-floor lobby display cases. But what's shown is a fascinating selection that may include a clay votive eye from 200 B.C., Japanese ivory netsuke figures wearing spectacles c. 1850, all manner of corrective eye gear, delicate pre-1900 surgical instruments, and Chinese spectacle cases made of sharkskin or silk, dating from the 1700s. Exhibits change regularly, and while they're most known for their traveling "suitcase" exhibits to schools, they are glad to accommodate those with special interests by appointment. *Library, Programs*

🏛 415 561-8500 • http://www.eyenet.org • 655 Beach St., San Francisco, CA 94109

🚗 Across from the Cannery at Fisherman's Wharf, it's on the 3rd floor of the American Academy of Ophthalmology headquarters. MUNI: #32 Embarcadero.

🕐 Mon.–Fri. 9 A.M.–5 P.M., and by appointment. No fee.

Tattoo Art Museum   Tattoos may have gone mainstream but Lyle Tuttle goes way back, and this museum/tattoo parlor reflects his deep commitment to this historically controversial craft. Skin decoration is, of course, nothing new, and Tuttle's collection includes "flip racks" (sort of like picking a wallpaper pattern) dating back to 1898, ancient manual and early electric tattooing tools, and an anthropological selection of photos and prints showing how cultures from Africa to Polynesia have used pigment and other processes to permanently embellish their bodies. You're just a few blocks from the North Beach Museum (in the Eureka Federal Savings Bank; 415 626-7070), which covers this area's history quite nicely. And that icon to Beat eras past, City Lights Bookstore.

🏛 415 775-4991 • 841 Columbus Ave., San Francisco, CA 94133

🚗 In the North Beach area, just south of the intersection of Mason and Greenwich Sts. MUNI: #30 Stockton.

🕐 Mon.–Thurs. noon–9 P.M., Fri.–Sat. noon–10 P.M., Sun. noon–8 P.M. No fee.

SAN JOSE

Winchester Mystery House/Winchester Products Museum/Winchester Historic Firearms Museum   Sarah L. Winchester thought she would die if her house was ever completed, so she built it, and kept building it, with halls and stairways to nowhere, at all kinds of angles, with all kinds of nooks and crannies and details that she felt could always use just a bit more work. Well, the reaper called anyway, but she left behind this Victorian wonder, as well as an impressive collection of Tiffany and other art glass and the Winchester rifles (and other company products from the 1920s like flashlights and roller skates) that were her birthright. *Tours, Gift Shop, Food*

🏛 408 247-2101 • 525 S. Winchester Blvd., San Jose, CA 95128

🚗 About 50 miles south of San Francisco. Take US 101S to I-280 into San Jose, turning north onto S. Winchester Blvd.

🕐 Mid-June–Sept.: Mon.–Sun. 9 A.M.–8 P.M. Oct.–mid-June: 9 A.M.–5 P.M. Fee.

SUNNYVALE

Lace Museum   As intricate and delicate as the microscopic etching on a silicon chip, and even more fantastic since the work, of course, is done entirely by hand. We're talking about the finest of lacemaking as seen in vintage apparel, antique cloths, and linen work. *Tours, Gift Shop, Programs, Library*

📞 408 730-4695 • 525 S. Murphy Ave., Sunnyvale, CA 94086

🚗 About 35 miles south of San Francisco. I-280 to the Saratoga–Sunnyvale Rd. exit, staying on Sunnyvale Ave., then left onto El Camino Real, and right onto S. Murphy.

🕐 Tues.–Sat. 11 A.M.–4 P.M. Tours and other hours by appointment. No fee.

. . . .

CENTRAL CALIFORNIA

From Santa Cruz south to Santa Barbara. While you're meandering through (we're assuming you're on Route 1, and not the dreaded I-5), some big and not-so-big spots you might want to add to your list are: the Famous Voices Museum in Monterey, the Shakespeare Press Museum in San Luis Obispo, the Santa Barbara Mission, and, as you get down into the Los Angeles mountains, the Union Oil Museum in Santa Paula. And don't forget about Castroville's giant artichoke (this is the Artichoke Capital of the World, after all).

BIG SUR

Henry Miller Memorial Library   Henry Miller (and Ansel Adams, and just about anyone who's had the opportunity to drive along this dramatic coast for that matter) found the Big Sur area a soothing and inspirational retreat when he lived here during the '50s. The library (and bookstore) has a collection of his rare editions as well as a number of his original watercolors and pen-and-ink drawings.

📞 408 667-2574 • http://www.henrymiller.org • Hwy 1, Big Sur, CA 93920

🚗 About 10 miles south of the village of Big Sur, before the Julia Pfeiffer Burns State Park, right on Hwy 1.

🕐 Summer: Mon.–Sun. 11 A.M.–5 P.M., though may vary. Hours vary rest of year. No fee.

MONTECITO

Lotusland   Madame Ganna Walska, a diva to the core, never had the voice to go with her aspirations, but she did know how to marry rich (we know, this story sounds awfully *Kane*-ish, but make no mistake, she was a force in her own right). So while the Polish soprano's career faltered, and her various marriages didn't quite work out, this "enemy of the average," a possessor of a finely tuned inner voice, seemed to find expression, and ulitmately the public adulation she sought, in her garden. Once she bought (in 1941) the pink stucco California Mission house and land she was to name Lotusland, she began developing the turn-of-the-century gardens. Restored since her death in 1984 at 97, they are a phantasmagoric, singular vision using cacti of all kinds, succulents, and the rare and unusual, in a display as excessive—and compelling—as Walska's personality. Lotusland can handle a very limited number of visitors—you will need to reserve space well ahead of your visit.

🖼 805 969-9990 • 695 Ashley Rd., Montecito, CA 93108

🚙 Just east of Santa Barbara. Call for directions.

🕐 Feb. 15–Nov. 15, tours by reservation only: Wed.–Sat. 10 A.M. and 1:30 P.M. Fee.

SANTA BARBARA

While you're in the area, see: Montecito

SANTA CRUZ

Santa Cruz Surfing Museum   Pix, videos, and chomped-up boards tell the tale of this wet and wild sport that goes back to the '30s in the shark-infested waters that seem only to enhance the thrill of surfing the great waves that curl up around Santa Cruz. You're apt to find some of the old-timers on hand to share tales of the early glory days hereabouts. *Gift Shop*

🖼 408 429-3429 • Mark Abbott Lighthouse, West Cliff Dr. at Lighthouse Point, Santa Cruz, CA 95062

🚙 About 60 miles south of San Francisco, off Hwy 1. Off the harbor, west of downtown.

🕐 Mon., Wed.–Sun. noon–4 P.M. Donation.

· ·

LOS ANGELES AREA

While the Museum of the Modern Poodle is gone, Dr. Blyth's Weird Museum is no longer with us, and the quintessential little museum, the Max Factor Museum of Beauty, has been shut down (pieces of its displays may be found at the mega–Hollywood Entertainment Museum, but it's just not the same), surely you can find solace in some of the other little offerings here. As for big, get thee to the Getty (now that the Los Angeles location is open, the Malibu site is being restored. Call ahead.). Or the Griffith Park Observatory (the Tesla Coil exhibit is memorable), Forest Lawn Memorial Park (yes, there are museums at both the

Glendale and Hollywood Hills locations; but don't forget the unrelated Pet Memorial Park in nearby Calabasas), Crystal Cathedral in Garden Grove, the Central Library branch (downtown) of the Los Angeles Public Library, the Japanese-American National Museum, the Petersen Automotive Museum, the Los Angeles subway, the celebrity photo exhibit at the Roosevelt Hotel, and the contrarian Rose Bowl–antidote Doo-Dah parade in Pasadena. And don't forget to stop at the County Coroner's Department gift shop before you leave town. See for yourself if there's valet parking. We Love L.A. *While you're in the area, see also*: Central California: Montecito, Santa Barbara; Outer Los Angeles Area.

ALTADENA

Banana Museum   Self-proclaimed "Top Banana" Ken Bannister is, well, bananas about bananas. He sees a smile in every one, and his enthusiasm is totally infectious. Which goes a long way in explaining how 9,000 members of his Banana Club, founded in those early smiley-face '70s, have contributed over 17,000 banana items, with nothing "lewd, crude, or lascivious" in the bunch. So what's he got? A German banana warmer (zips the fruit right in); banana telephone; a 45-year-old wind-up fruit; banana slippers; and even a petrified banana. You don't need us to tell you who he was for in the Clinton-Dole election.

■ 818 798-2272/900 BANANAS [226-2627] • http://www.banana-club.com • 2524 N. El Molino Ave., Altadena, CA 91001

🚗 From Pasadena at Colorado and Lake Ave., head north on Lake 3 miles to Mariposa St., turn left 1 block, then right onto El Molino. It's across from the fire station.

🕐 By appointment only. Fee.

CULVER CITY

Museum of Jurassic Technology   First, let's make one thing perfectly clear. This museum is dedicated to the study of the *lower* Jurassic. We clarify, since after that, things may seem a bit, ummm, inscrutable. Some say science, some say art, some say tongue planted firmly in cheek. We say appearances aren't everything, so the complex exhibits, vitrines, and dioramas—intended to demonstrate (emphasis on *intended*; some don't quite work as expected) all manner of scientific principles and sociological experience—might best be enjoyed with a totally open mind, and a firm appreciation for museum director David Wilson's brand of creative thought. *Gift Shop*

■ 310 836-6131 • http://www.mjt.org • 9341 Venice Blvd., Culver City, CA 90232

🚗 Just east of the intersection of Bagley Ave. (4 blocks west of Robertson Blvd.) and Venice Blvd., on the north side of the street.

🕐 Thurs. 2 P.M.–8 P.M., Fri.–Sun. noon–6 P.M. Donation.

HOLLYWOOD

Hollywood High School Museum   *It's all happening at the high school.* . . . Former Secretary of State Warren Christopher ('42), Nobel Prize winner William Shockley ('29; he invented the transistor), Ken Handler ('61; son of Mattel's Ruth, and her model for the Ken doll). See, not everyone was off being tutored on the set. Some of the other alum are of course more predictable, like: Frances Gumm, James Baumgarner, and Joe Yule, Jr. You may know them better as Judy Garland, James Garner, and Mickey Rooney, but they're here with snaps and memorabilia, the way they were.

🏠 213 461-3891 • 1521 N. Highland Ave., Hollywood, CA 90028
🚗 Downtown Hollywood, at Highland Ave. and Sunset Blvd.
🕐 Mon.–Fri. 8:30 A.M.–3 P.M., by appointment only. No fee.

Hollywood Studio Museum   Known as "The Barn," this simple structure was literally just that when Cecil B. DeMille made his first trip West, looking for studio space to shoot *The Squaw Man* in 1913. In partnership with the East Coast–based Jesse L. Lasky Feature Play Co. (another partner was Lasky's brother-in-law Samuel Goldfish . . . that's Goldwyn to you), DeMille set up shop, and the rest, of course, is history. While it's been moved a few times it's not far from its original site, and restoration from recent fire damage should be complete by the time you read this. Early projectors and cameras, Valentino's shirt, the furniture from the atmospheric Egyptian Theatre, set models, the Ben-Hur chariot (1926 and 1959), and all kinds of pix, artifacts, and memorabilia from the careers of the stars and the film companies behind them. Check with the museum on the status of the long-awaited excavation of DeMille's *The Ten Commandments* set, just up the coast. While you're near the Bowl, though, the recently renovated Hollywood Bowl Museum (213 850-2058) has an exhibit on the venue's history—the musical artists who played there and the artists who were feted there, film clips of movies shot there, programs, and posters. *Tours, Gift Shop, Programs, Library, Screenings*

🏠 213 874-BARN [2276] • 2100 N. Highland Ave., Hollywood, CA 90068
🚗 Across the street from the Hollywood Bowl, at Highland and Odin St. It's at the south end of the parking lot.
🕐 Sat. 10 A.M.–4 P.M., Sun. noon–4 P.M. and by appointment. Fee.

L. Ron Hubbard Life Exhibition   L. Ron (that's Lafayette Ronald) as in Eagle Scout (America's youngest); L. Ron the screenwriter (*Battlefield Earth*); L. Ron, *National Geographic* photographer; L. Ron aka "Flash," the '30s barnstorming aviator; L. Ron, drug detox expert; L. Ron among the Blackfeet Indians in his Montana childhood home; L. Ron . . . Oh yes. He's the one who brought the world Scientology. An arguable contribution to the universe, but he goes to the head of the class—clearly a marketing genius. Housed fittingly in a restored 1924 bank building, his life and philosophy are presented here for you. Don't miss the 1929

Pantages Theater, an Art Deco–Renaissance wonder, just two blocks east at Argyle Ave. *Tours*

■ 213 960-3511 • http://www.lronhubbard.org • 6331 Hollywood Blvd., Hollywood, CA 90028

🚐 At the corner of Hollywood and Ivar Ave., 1 block west of Vine.

🕐 Mon.–Sun. 10 A.M.–10 P.M. Five scheduled tours each day. Fee.

Lingerie Museum   While Frederick's may conjure up a, shall we say, over-the-top image of lingerie styling, catering to the needs of Hollywood's celebs is serious business. And so here's where you'll find some of the most dazzling of understuff of the stars, from Mae West to Loretta Young, Madonna, Zsa Zsa—and Tony Curtis (*Some Like It Hot*) and Milton Berle—and four decades' worth of lingerie history, from the "missiles and snowcones" of the '40s and '50s to the innerwear as outerwear of the last decade.

■ 213 466-8506/213 957-5953 • Frederick's of Hollywood, 6608 Hollywood Blvd., Hollywood, CA 90028

🚐 Downtown Hollywood, 2 blocks east of Highland Ave.

🕐 Mon.–Thurs. 10 A.M.–6 P.M., Fri. 10 A.M.–9 P.M., Sat. 10 A.M.–6 P.M., Sun. noon–5 P.M. No fee.

Science-Fantasy Preserves   This 18-room "movie star mansion" has more than a few unusual inhabitants, and former horror movie magazine editor Forrest J Ackerman will be glad to introduce you to them, disembodied though most of them may be. Life masks of Boris Karloff, Bela Lugosi, Lon Chaney, Jr., and Vincent Price are joined by a reproduction of the robotrix from Fritz Lang's 1927 silent classic *Metropolis*, Lugosi's *Dracula* cape and ring, slews of stills, fantasy films, set models, posters, and books—over 300,000 sci-fi items collected over 70 years . . . you may never leave. . . .

■ 213 MOON FAN [666-6326] • http://www.scifi.com/pulp/4SJ • http://www.best.com/~4forry • 2495 Glendower Ave., Hollywood, CA 90027

🚐 From the Los Feliz Blvd. and Vermont Ave. entrance to Griffith Park, follow Vermont into the park 2 blocks to Cromwell Ave. At stop sign, continue onto Glendower Ave.

🕐 Sat. 11 A.M.–1 P.M., and by appointment. No fee.

LOS ANGELES

Carole and Barry Kaye Museum of Miniatures   Tiny, tiny, tiny versions of some really big things, like a completely furnished Fontainebleau (France, not Florida), an early Roman banquet hall, and a French Empire Salon with a less-than-Lilliputian-size cut-crystal chandelier. Nothing is larger than $\frac{1}{12}$ scale, and the opulence of these specially commissioned pieces from artisans around the world is only rivaled by the original sites themselves. Even the more plebeian themes like Peter Brown's Soda Shoppe or a Parisian artist's garret, which appears better-appointed than real life, were spared no economy of detail, no expense in construction. *Gift Shop, Library*

- 213 937-MINI [6464] • http://www.museumofminiatures.com • 5900 Wilshire Blvd., Los Angeles, CA 90036
- Just east of Fairfax Ave., across from the Los Angeles County Museum of Art.
- Tues.–Sat. 10 A.M.–5 P.M., Sun. 11 A.M.–5 P.M. Fee.

Museum of Neon Art   Historic and contemporary neon and electric art collection gives Las Vegas a run for its money. L.A. has always been a neon kind of town and the vintage pieces are some of the best of their kind. The old theater marquees are particularly wonderful: take note of the '50s Fox Venice and the Melrose Theater lady from the '20s. Animated signs like a tail-wagging-calf dairy sign and one with a woman diving into a pool are pure liquid light artistry. *Tours, Gift Shop, Library, Programs*

- 213 489-9918 • 501 West Olympic Blvd., Los Angeles, CA 90015
- Downtown LA. Take I-110 (Harbor Fwy) Exit 9th St. East. Continue east on 9th to Grand Ave., then turn right. It's next to Grand Hope Park. Enter on Hope St., at Olympic.
- Wed.–Sat. 11 A.M.–5 P.M., Thurs. 11 A.M.–8 P.M., Sun. noon–5 P.M. Fee.

Southern California Institute of Architecture (SCI-Arc)   The gallery at SCI-Arc houses changing exhibitions of the architectural kind. SCI-Arc sees its mission as a mandate to teach this discipline as a fusion of aesthetic, social, and cultural concerns; the cutting-edge solutions to building a "foundation for an unpredictable future" may be seen in projects that explore themes from alternative bicycle design to an investigation of the work of Rem Koolhaas to issues that concern the immediate L.A. urban experience.

- 310 574-1123 • http://www.sciarc.edu • 5454 Beethoven St., Los Angeles, CA 90066
- Just north of LAX. From I-405 (San Diego Fwy) exit onto Jefferson Blvd., then turn west 3 miles to Beethoven.
- Mon.–Sun. 9 A.M.–6 P.M. No fee.

Watts Towers of Simon Rodia   The Towers of Simon (Sabato) Rodia may not be available for touring due to restoration work, but you can still get a really good look at this wondrous web of seashells, glass, pottery shards, and tiles on a base of concrete-coated rebar, created over 33 years by the late tilesetter. Reminiscent of Antonio Gaudi's La Sagrada Cathedral in Barcelona, the eight soaring towers preside over the neighborhood. You can see the upper portions of the towers from inside the Watts Towers Art Center (213 485-1795) next door; it also has Rodia-related and African and contemporary art exhibits. *Tours*

- Info: 213 847-4646/Curator: 213 485-4580 • 1765 E. 107th St., Los Angeles, CA 90002
- In the Watts section, go east on 103rd St. to Wilmington Ave., turn right to 108th St., then right again 1 block to Willowbrook Ave., then right onto 107th St. to the end of the block.
- Mon.–Sun. dawn to dusk. Tours: Sat. 10 A.M.–4 P.M., Sun. noon–4 P.M. Donation.

MALIBU

Malibu Lagoon Museum and Historic Adamson House   Elite Malibu has a true treasure tucked away for the hoi polloi. Built in 1929 for Rhoda Rindge Adamson and her family by Stiles O. Clements, this fabulous "Moorish-Spanish Colonial Revival" home dazzles with its rich and colorfully vibrant Malibu tile (the Rindges established this influential pottery that thrived in the Deco era) applied seemingly everywhere, and offers an unparalleled beachside setting for the museum's collections on local history, with photos and artifacts from the original Chumash Indian settlers to the Spanish California ranching days and the early days of the Malibu movie colony. *Tours, Gift Shop*

- 📞 310 456-8432/1770 • 23200 Pacific Coast Hwy, Malibu, CA 90265
- 🚗 Right off the Pacific Coast Hwy (Hwy 1), on the Malibu Lagoon State Beach.
- 🕐 Tours: Wed.–Sat. 11 A.M.–3 P.M. (last tour at 2 P.M.), and Tues. by appointment only. Fee.

NEWHALL

William S. Hart Museum   William S. "Two Gun Bill" Hart began his film career in 1914 when he was well into his fifties, following a Midwest pioneer childhood and a New York stage career that reached its peak with Western roles in shows like *The Squaw Man* and *The Virginian*. But the West itself was calling, and so he came out and launched a hugely successful silent film career, as actor, writer, and director. He's left behind his collection of Navajo textiles and Western Americana and costumes and memorabilia from the days of the silents. *Tours, Library*

- 📞 805 254-4584 • http://www.smartdocs.com/~mmetters/hart.html • William S. Hart County Park, 24151 San Fernando Rd., Newhall, CA 91321
- 🚗 In the Valley. I-405N (San Diego Fwy) to I-5N (Golden State Fwy) exiting onto Hwy 14. Take the first exit (San Fernando Rd.), going under the freeway. It's about 1.5 miles to the park.
- 🕐 Mid-June–mid-Oct. Tours: Wed.–Sun. 11 A.M.–3:30 P.M. Rest of year: Wed.–Fri. 10 A.M.–12:30 P.M., Sat.–Sun. 11 A.M.–3:30 P.M. Donation.

PASADENA

Mini Cake Museum   Frances Kuyper *is* "The Cake Lady" and she's been baking and decorating cakes since 1950. Recently retired from teaching and demonstrating, she's now made a dream come true with this confection of a museum in her home. Models of decorating wizardry are on display (tell the food inspectors not to worry, they're all done with Styrofoam and Perma-ice), and they're as zingy as the exuberant Ms. Kuyper's personality. *Tours, Library, Programs*

- 📞 818 793-7355 • 432–434 N. Lola Ave., Pasadena, CA 91107

🚙 From I-210 exit onto Altadena Dr. North, then left onto Villa, and left again onto Lola. Her 5-tiered wedding-cake mailbox is the tip-off.

🕐 By appointment only. No fee.

SIMI VALLEY

Ronald Reagan Presidential Library and Museum   The Great Communicator and former president of the Screen Actors Guild provides a soothing setting for you to stroll through and reflect on the era of his '80s White House stint. Featured are a Prosperity Gallery, a selection of Head of State gifts, and the First Lady's Gallery. The irony of his voting record may be explored in the Voices of Freedom Gallery; a stelae-like section of the dismantled Berlin Wall is also on hand. Changing exhibits have recently included shows like an oddly homogenized (or should we say, pasteurized?) take on the sixties. A nice counterpoint might be the Thousand Oaks Library (805 497-6282) about 15 miles to the south. It has an interesting little archive on the history of radio and early TV. A stop at the nearby but rapidly decaying Bottle Village, the tile, textile, and bottle–constructed masterwork of Tressa "Grandma" Prisbrey, may also be in order. *Tours, Library*

🏛 805 522-8444 • 40 Presidential Dr., Simi Valley, CA 93065

🚙 US 101N (Ventura Hwy) to Hwy 23N (Moorpark-Fillmore). Exit east on Olsen Rd. and proceed to Presidential Dr. and follow signs.

🕐 Mon.–Sat. 10 A.M.–5 P.M., Sun. noon–5 P.M. Fee.

OUTER LOS ANGELES AREA

Outer Los Angeles pretty much means out-in-the-desert, a stark yet compelling landscape—preferably experienced just after a late afternoon thunder shower when the desert flowers are in bloom. Big out here is relative (space is what's big), but the place that does it best is Joshua Tree National Monument. Elvis is big here too. If you find yourself idling in Palm Springs, ask if the Honeymoon Hideaway (guess who spent his here) has opened its doors yet.

BORON

Twenty-Mule Team Museum   On the edge of Edwards Air Force Base, the town of Boron has a history that traverses the desert frontier to the frontier of space. Exhibits cover the early-20th-century discovery of borates in the area, which led to its distinction as the "Borax Capital of the World." You'll also find mining lore, Santa Fe Trail memorabilia, a mural of a twenty-mule team pulling borax-laden wagons across the desert (you might recall the scene from TV's *Death*

Valley Days, at one time hosted by none other than Ronald Reagan), an early beauty shop, and the space shuttle. And the surreal fields of energy-producing high-tech wind machines at Tehachapi are just about 40 miles to the west, off Hwy 58.

📞 760 762-5810 • 26962 Twenty Mule Team Rd., Boron, CA 93516

🚗 About 55 miles north of San Bernardino. Take I-15N to US 395N to Hwy 58, then 6 miles west.

🕐 Mon.–Sun. 10 A.M.–4 P.M. Donation.

HELENDALE

Exotic World Burlesque Museum and Hall of Fame   Looming a bit like a desert mirage, the tall wrought-iron gate to Exotic World stands ajar, beckoning. Once you're inside, you're in the hands of Dixie Evans, former burlesque star and Marilyn impersonator, who will regale you with anecdotes (Why a "G" string? Because it's the thinnest string on a violin. What was Knute Rockne's inspiration for the Four Horsemen's Back Shift field maneuver? Well, we'll leave that one to your imagination) and show off the costumes, fans, photos, and props donated by the likes of Tempest Storm, Sally Rand, and Gypsy Rose Lee. *Gift Shop*

📞 760 243-5261 • 29053 Wild Rd., Helendale, CA 92342

🚗 Take I-15N from San Bernardino, exit D St. in Victorville, turning left onto National Trails (Route 66), then go 17 miles to Vista Rd. and turn left. Proceed to Helendale Rd. and turn right, and right again onto Wild Rd.

🕐 Most days 10 A.M.–4 P.M., and by appointment. Fee.

VICTORVILLE

California Route 66 Museum   The stretch of old Route 66 that goes through Victorville rests on a legacy of Mojave Desert travelers dating back to local Indian tribes, then Spanish missionaries, then later the Mormons. While lately the romance and the spirit of the route have captured the attention of Europeans and Asians seeking to find the "real" America, the museum of course serves to preserve and protect—with pix, cars, and highway artifacts—an almost vanished era of small towns linked and kept alive by the automobile. This one's in a swell old bank building from 1918, and is not too far from a collection in Rancho Cucamonga, the Route 66 Territory Museum (800 JOG-RT66 [564-7866]). *Gift Shop, Library*

📞 760 951-0436/261-US66 [8766] • 16849 D St., Victorville, CA 92393

🚗 I-15N from San Bernardino, exit D St. It's at 6th and D St. (Route 66) in Old Town.

🕐 Apr.–Oct.: Thurs.–Sun. 10 A.M.–4 P.M. Nov.–Mar.: Thurs., Sat.–Sun. 10 A.M.–4 P.M. No fee.

Roy Rogers–Dale Evans Museum   Yes, yes, it's true. Stuffed Trigger, Trigger Jr., Buttermilk, and Bullet are all here. But so is a lifetime of memorabilia saved up by the King of the Cowboys and his wife and co-star, Dale, like early TV promo items (Post Toasties), Pat Brady's Jeep Nellybelle, Sons of the Pioneers record covers, costumes, and stills from the silver screen. *Gift Shop, Screenings*

■ 760 243-4547 • http://www.royrogers.com • 15650 Seneca Rd., Victorville, CA 92392

🚗 I-15N from San Bernardino, exit onto Roy Rogers Dr. Turn left on Civic Dr., then right onto Seneca Rd.

🕐 Mon.–Sun. 9 A.M.–5 P.M. Fee.

SAN DIEGO AREA

San Diego's a relaxed sort of place. And while we know it has a venerable place in our nation's military history, we think its main industry these days is leisure activity. But lest you think San Diego culture is solely synonymous with Sea World, other big and noteworthy things here are the San Diego Zoo, of course; the new and wonderful Mingei Folk Art Museum; the San Diego Railroad Museum and the San Diego Model Railroad Museum (as well as the beautifully restored Union Station); the Spanish Colonial "Gaslamp Quarter" and historic Coronado Island; and if you're out by Campo—and if trains are your thing, this is definitely a destination for you—stop in at the Gaskill Brothers Store Museum. *While you're in the area, see also*: Yuma, Arizona.

ESCONDIDO

Lawrence Welk Museum   Champagne-music schmaltzmeister Welk left behind this big resort and golf course (one of his other pastimes) along with geriatric memories of an accordion player who held an audience from the day he left home in North Dakota in 1924 through over two decades on national TV on *The Lawrence Welk Show*. His distinctive hand-chopping motions while conducting, the bubble-maker in the background, well, you might not remember all that, but there's a complete lifesize bandstand and TV set-up to help re-create it for you, as well as photos, memorabilia, and the world's largest champagne glass. *See also* the Ludwig and Christina Welk Homestead in Strasburg, North Dakota. *Gift Shop*

■ 760 749-3448 • 8860 Lawrence Welk Dr., Escondido, CA 92082

🚗 North of San Diego take I-15N exit Deer Springs/Mountain Meadow Rd. and turn right, then left onto Champagne Blvd. for 2.5 miles to Lawrence Welk Dr.

🕐 Mon. 9 A.M.–5 P.M.; Tues., Thurs. 9 A.M.–1 P.M., 4 P.M.–7 P.M.; Fri.–Sat. 9 A.M.–7 P.M.; Sun., Wed. 9 A.M.–1 P.M. No fee.

LA MESA

Computer Museum of America   Seven decades of computer technology. Over 100 historic devices on display, photos of many more, and they're getting smaller all the time. Some fascinating for their "mad scientist" or futuristic appearance alone, others so huge, like ENIAC, that you can't imagine what's going on inside the box. But it's the obsolete-in-our-lifetime (or more like, since your last cup of coffee) factor that is perhaps most fascinating. Your 1977 Commodore PET 2000-8 is immortalized right there along with the earliest vacuum tube and punch-card models. Bring your own last-year's-model and make a donation.

■ 619 465-8226 • http://www.computer-museum.org • Coleman College, 7380 Parkway Dr., La Mesa, CA 91942

🚐 About 10 miles east of San Diego. Take I-8 exit Lake Murray Blvd./70th St. and turn east onto Parkway Dr. It's within the concourse of the college.

🕑 Mon.–Thurs. 9 A.M.–5 P.M., Fri.–Sat. 9 A.M.–4 P.M. No fee.

OCEANSIDE

California Surf Museum   Shrine and archive, who would argue it's a "totally awesome, rad, righteous, bodacious, and rippin' " tribute to surfing's greats, and their tools of the trade? The search for the perfect wave on the West Coast can be traced back to Duke Kahanamoku and the resurgence of surfing in Hawaii in the 1890s, and it was only a matter of moments before developers dreamed up surfing exhibitions to lure residents to turn-of-the-century So. Cal. Funky and appealing exhibits include: a range of boards from the 150-pound simple redwood planks of yesteryear to the ultra-light, finned boards of today, each with their story; great moments in surf history (captured with some astonishing shots due to impressive innovations in waterproof photography); and changing exhibits on stars like hollow-board inventor Tom Blake and local boy Phil Edwards, first to take the "impossible" Banzai Pipeline in 1962. *Tours, Gift Shop, Programs*

■ 760 721-6876 • http://www.surfart.com/casmhmpg.htm • 223 N. Coast Hwy, Oceanside, CA 92054

🚐 Near the Oceanside pier. From I-5 take the Mission Ave. exit (Oceanside). Head west on Mission for about 1 mile (3 lights) to the Coast Hwy, then turn right. It's 1 block down, on the left, at 3rd St.

🕑 Mon.–Sun. 10 A.M.–4 P.M. Donation.

SAN DIEGO

Museum of Death   No metaphor, the Museum of Death is definitely dedicated to the dark side. From the relatively mundane antique mortician apparatuses and life-size execution devices, to the ever more grisly items of used electric chair clothing, graphic videos and photos of "heinous death," and a special feature of *art brut*—the artwork of serial killers—all in a satin-lined basement space that at one time may have been used to store bodies from an upstairs mortuary. As an antidote you might visit the Museum of Creation and Earth History in nearby Santee (619 448-0900). *Gift Shop*

■ 619 338-8153 • 548 5th Ave., San Diego, CA 92101

🚗 Hwy 163 into 10th Ave. South to Island Ave., turn right to 5th Ave., and turn right again. It's downstairs in the Rita Dean Gallery.

🕑 Tues.–Sun. noon–10 P.M. Fee.

Museum of the American Presidency   Social Science teacher Jim Fletcher had a personal collection of Richard Nixon memorabilia he'd been hoarding since he was a teen, as well as a Big Idea on how to get his students interested in both American history and entrepreneurship. So they began this museum, and now have the largest collection of items presidential west of the Mississippi. Campaign buttons galore (featuring mainly those who made it; runners-up need not apply), a "Click with Dick" noisemaker, "Rough Rider" cigarettes, a Woodrow Wilson pocket knife, and Nancy Reagan's rose-colored sunglasses are among the items, some dating back to the 1800s. Of course, if you haven't had enough, you can head up north a bit to the Nixon Library in Yorba Linda. *See also* West Hartford, Connecticut.

■ 619 270-0694 • http://www.geocities.com/capitolhill/3065 • Clairemont High School, 4150 Ute Dr., San Diego, CA 92117

🚗 Just north of San Diego from I-5, exit Balboa. At first light after the exit ramp, turn east onto Balboa, continue on to Clairemont Dr., turn right, then it's 1 short block to Ute, and turn right again.

🕑 By appointment only, Mon.–Fri. 7:30 A.M.–3:30 P.M. No fee.

COLORADO

The Rockies have been holy to people from the Utes to the Beats, magnetic to visitors from men with pickaxes to women with snowboards. At their feet, along the Front Range, lies Metropolis, stretching from federal (bureaucracy) and cosmopolitan Denver to federal (military) and conservative-Christian Colorado Springs—with the space between fast disappearing into suburbs. The high plains, to the east, and the mountains, to the west, are still largely frontier vastnesses. Some of the most fascinating sites, or sights, in Colorado are abandoned, from Mesa Verde to the mineshafts of the Cripple Creek district; in this sense, the state's "museums" include many you'll find for yourself, by chance.

What's Big: Denver's Art Museum, U.S. Mint, Museum of Western Art, and Museum of Natural History; the Pro Rodeo Hall of Fame in Colorado Springs; Mesa Verde's visitors center.

BURLINGTON

Kit Carson County Carousel   Carousel fans, rejoice! This one is in such good shape, with the original paint, that it has been designated a National Landmark. Drop by on your way across the High Plains and ride this museum.

🏠 719 346-8070 (Burlington Chamber of Commerce) • Kit Carson County Fairground, Burlington, CO 80807

🚙 Burlington is in east-central Colorado, near the Kansas line, on I-70. Take Exit 435.

🕐 Memorial Day–Labor Day: 1 P.M.–8 P.M. Write for private tour off-season. Fee.

CAÑON CITY

Colorado Territorial Prison Museum   This prison, with over 120 years' history, has seen many executions, much violence, and the enforced residence of numerous "characters," including the notorious cannibal Alferd Packard. The promotional term for such a museum is "colorful." *Gift Shop*

🏠 719 269-3015 • 1st and Macon, Cañon City, CO 81212

🚗 Cañon City is in south-central Colorado, an hour west of Pueblo on US 50. The prison and museum are on the southwest side of town; follow signs.

🕐 May–Aug.: Mon.–Sun. 8:30 A.M.–8 P.M. Rest of year: Wed.–Sun. 9 A.M.–4 P.M. Fee.

COLORADO SPRINGS

John May Museum Center   Thousands of bugs, including some large and menacing jungle species. Spiders, centipedes, other creepy customers, but also butterflies and moths. It's a strange place to find oneself doing some serious entomological sightseeing. For a change of pace, there's also a space museum (flying things?). *Gift Shop*

🏠 719 576-0450 • 1710 Rock Creek Canyon Rd. (SR 115), Colorado Springs, CO 80926

🚗 Take Route 115 (Nevada Ave.) south from I-25 Exit 140, passing Fort Carson and looking for signs including a giant beetle.

🕐 May–Sept.: Mon.–Sun. 8 A.M.–8 P.M. Fee.

Museum of the American Numismatic Association   This is the headquarters of the largest of coin clubs, but the museum has more than coins. You'll also see paper money, medallions, art objects created by numismatic engravers, and other memorabilia and artifacts of the world of money. Ever wondered what a $100,000 bill looks like? What "shoe money" is? The ANA is a serious collectors' organization, but the museum makes this arcane world accessible.

🏠 719 632-2646 • 818 N. Cascade Ave., Colorado Springs, CO 80903

🚗 The museum is on the campus of Colorado College. Take Exit 143 (Uintah St.) off I-25, go east, and turn right on Cascade Ave.

🕐 Mon.–Fri. 8:30 A.M.–4 P.M. Sat. also in summer. No fee.

World Figure Skating Museum and Hall of Fame   The U.S. Figure Skating Association here presents the history of the sport, in skates and other equipment, costumes, medals and trophies, posters, and other memorabilia, and in art based on the theme (including works by Brueghel, Homer, and Warhol). There are both international and U.S. Halls of Fame, with salutes to the greats, and an archive of records and references. *Library*

🏠 719 635-5200 • 20 1st St., Colorado Springs, CO 80906

🚗 It's on the southwest side of the city. Take Exit 140 off I-25 onto Nevada Ave. (Hwy 115) south. Turn right on Lake Ave. toward the Broadmoor Resort, then right on 1st St.

🕐 Mon.–Fri. 10 A.M.–4 P.M. In summer, Sat. also (in winter, first Sat. of month). No fee.

DENVER

Even if you're not flying in, you'll want to take a look at the new airport. If you really need an excuse, go to see Gary Sweeney's artpiece "America Why I Love Her," which pinpoints some of the country's more unusual little museums on two grand-scale maps. *While you're in the area, see also*: Golden.

Black American West Museum and Heritage Center In the home and office of the first black woman doctor in Colorado, this museum was begun by Paul Stewart, who as a child always had to play the Indian because "there was no such thing as a black cowboy." Surprise: Nearly a third of all cowboys were black. Covered wagons, the gold rush, San Juan Hill—the artifacts, records, and memorabilia here tell a story long overlooked. *Tours, Gift Shop*
- 303 292-2566 • The Dr. Justina Ford House, 3091 California St., Denver, CO 80205
- The museum is at the corner of California Ave., 31st St., and Downing St., just northeast of downtown Denver; drive out Stout St. and turn right on 31st.
- May–Sept.: Mon.–Fri. 10 A.M.–5 P.M., Sat.–Sun. noon–5 P.M. Rest of year: Wed.–Fri. 10 A.M.–2 P.M., Sat.–Sun. noon–5 P.M. Fee.

Denver Museum of Miniatures, Dolls and Toys On the second floor of the Pearce-McAllister Cottage, a Victorian landmark, you'll find a world of little people, little houses, little bears, little furniture, a little circus—how little can you get? Many of the intricate pieces could fit in your hand. Some reproduce the large (a Newport mansion), some the regional (a Santa Fe adobe). *Gift Shop*
- 303 322-1053 • 1880 N. Gaylord St., Denver, CO 80206
- The museum is east of downtown, just west of City Park and the Denver Zoo, on Gaylord near the corner of 18th Ave. From I-25, take Exit 205 and follow University Ave. north to 18th Ave.; turn left and then right onto Gaylord.
- Tues.–Sat. 10 A.M.–4 P.M., Sun. 1 P.M.–4 P.M. Fee.

Trianon Museum and Art Gallery Decor, did you say? Here's a place with an unimaginable collection of furniture, porcelain, bronzes, clocks, rugs, mirrors, lamps, silk robes, and paintings by people like Watteau and Poussin. It comes from France, Italy, Imperial Russia, China, and even America. For some reason there's a sizable gun collection among it all, including an original 1877 Gatling. This is Betty Metzger's place, and she'll show you around it, in detail. *Tours*
- 303 623-0739 • 335 14th St., Denver, CO 80202
- It's downtown, at 14th and Tremont, just northwest of the civic center and capitol.
- Mon.–Sat. 10 A.M.–4 P.M. Fee.

DOLORES

Anasazi Heritage Center   In this part of the country, you're going to see a lot of signs of the Anasazi, whose cliff dwellings were built around 700 to 1,000 years ago. The Heritage Center has a huge collection of artifacts, and its displays and activities make the life of these mysterious people, as well as the practice of archaeology, vivid. *Gift Shop, Hands-on, Programs, Library, Screenings*

🔲 970 882-4811 • 27501 Colorado Route 184, Dolores, CO 81323

🚗 Dolores is in extreme southwestern Colorado, 10 miles northeast of Cortez and the entrance to Mesa Verde National Park. From the east side of Cortez, take Hwy 145N, then turn onto 184W, following signs.

🕐 Mon.–Sun. 9 A.M.–5 P.M. No fee.

FORT MORGAN

Fort Morgan Museum   This quiet museum in a quiet town out in the open spaces has a number of things to offer, from the story of a nearby prehistoric campsite to Plains tribal artifacts to materials on white settlement. Two displays on 20th-century popular culture may catch your attention, though—the reconstructed 1920s Hillrose Soda Fountain and the Glenn Miller Exhibit, devoted to the early life of the bandleader. *See also* the Nodaway Valley Historical Museum in Clarinda, Iowa. *Gift Shop*

🔲 970 867-6331 • 414 Main St., Fort Morgan, CO 80701

🚗 Fort Morgan is in northeastern Colorado, on I-76. Take Exit 80 onto Main St. and go south to City Park.

🕐 Mon.–Fri. 10 A.M.–5 P.M., Sat. 11 A.M.–5 P.M. Also Tues.–Thurs. 6 P.M.–8 P.M. No fee.

GENOA

Wonder View Tower (Genoa Tower)   This is Jerry Chubbuck's collection of arrowheads, bottle caps, a two-headed cow and other freaks, glass insulators, camel nose rings, and hundreds of items almost or totally inexplicable. The 87-step tower, built in the 1930s, claims to be the highest point between the Mississippi and the Rockies (take that, Black Hills!) or, variously, between New York and Denver. See six states for a buck! *Gift Shop*

🔲 719 763-2313 (Genoa Town Hall) • Genoa, CO 80818

🚗 Genoa is on I-70, just east of Limon and 90 miles east of Denver, in the High Plains of east-central Colorado. Take Exit 371; the tower is along the frontage road.

🕐 Mon.–Sun. 8 A.M.–8 P.M. Fee.

GOLDEN

Buffalo Bill Memorial Museum and Grave   The icon of the Wild West, one of the most famous Americans of them all (*see also* Buffalo Bill museums in Princeton, Iowa, and Cody, Wyoming), is buried in this spectacular setting. The museum, a few steps from the grave, contains posters, photographs, paintings, dime novels, costumes, saddles—memorabilia of the man and of those who spent time around him (like Sitting Bull and Annie Oakley). *Gift Shop, Food*

🏠 303 526-0747 • 987 ½ Lookout Mountain Rd., Golden, CO 80401

🚗 Take I-70W from Denver to Exit 256 and follow signs. Or take 6th Ave. west to Golden to Lariat Trail (19th St.) and follow scenic route.

🕐 May–Oct.: Mon.–Sun. 9 A.M.–5 P.M. Rest of year: Tues.–Sun. 9 A.M.–4 P.M. Fee.

Colorado Railroad Museum   Railroads in Colorado have had special challenges in serving mines and towns high in the mountains. Narrow and standard gauge rolling stock can be seen here, along with snow-removal machinery, gear and other artifacts, and memorabilia. There's also an intricate HO layout illustrating some of the Mountain State's challenges. *Gift Shop*

🏠 800 365-6263 • 17155 W. 44th Ave., Golden, CO 80402

🚗 From Denver take I-70 12 miles west to Exit 265 and follow signs on Hwy 58 to 44th Ave. If traveling east on I-70, use Exit 266 and go 3 miles west on 44th.

🕐 June–Aug.: Mon.–Sun. 9 A.M.–6 P.M. Rest of year: 9 A.M.–5 P.M. Fee.

GRAND JUNCTION

Museum of Western Colorado   If you're coming into the Western Slope and would like an introduction to its prehistory, history, and natural attributes, this is a good place to go. The collection includes artifacts of ancient (Fremont culture), less ancient (Mimbres), and recent (Ute) native groups, and displays on recorded history, also. Nearby (at 4th and Main) is Dinosaur Valley, whose animated reptiles will thrill your kids while you take in the paleontology.

🏠 970 242-0971 • 248 S. 4th St., Grand Junction, CO 81501

🚗 Grand Junction is in west-central Colorado, on I-70. Take Business 70 approaching the city and exit onto Ute Ave. downtown; the museum is at the corner of Ute and S. 4th.

🕐 Memorial Day–Labor Day: Mon.–Sat. 10 A.M.–5 P.M. Rest of year: Tues.–Sat. Fee.

LA JUNTA

Koshare Indian Kiva Museum   This unique museum grew out of the activities of Boy Scouts. Troop 232, the Koshare Indian Dancers, still uses it as a base.

They organized in 1933, and in 1949 the Ceremonial Round Room (Kiva) was built. As the Dancers gained in reputation, the museum gained in collections; it now has a wide range of Southwestern and Plains costumes and artifacts, along with Western paintings, pottery, and more. Dances are held on summer Friday and Saturday evenings, and there are many other programs. *Gift Shop, Programs*

- 800 693-KIVA [5482] • 115 W. 18th St. (at Otero Junior College), La Junta, CO 81050
- La Junta is in southeastern Colorado, 60 miles east of Pueblo. From US 50, head south on Colorado Ave. to 18th St., then west on 18th; the museum faces the campus.
- Mon.–Sun. 10 A.M.–5 P.M. Fee.

LEADVILLE

National Mining Hall of Fame and Museum   This elegant new (1987) museum has walk-through hard rock and coal "mines," dioramas and a model railroad illustrating Western mining history, a Hall of Fame with plaques honoring giants of the industry, and eye-popping gold and crystal displays. Almost everything you can think of (except diamonds) has been mined in or near Leadville. *Tours, Gift Shop, Publications, Library*

- 719 486-1229 • 120 W. 9th St., Leadville, CO 80461
- Leadville is 2 hours west-southwest of Denver, high in the Rockies. Take I-70 to Exit 171 (Dowds Junction), then Route 24S.
- May–Oct.: Mon.–Sun. 9 A.M.–5 P.M. Rest of year: Mon.–Fri. 10 A.M.–2 P.M.; weekend group tours by appointment. Fee.

Tabor Opera House   If you can imagine finding yourself all alone on Broadway, you have an idea what walking through the Tabor Opera House is like. This was one of the hot spots of the West, where Houdini as well as headline singers entertained the miners at the height of the boom. Now you may be the only person in the building, a remarkable experience whether you're up in the nosebleed section of the balcony or down examining the cramped dressing rooms used by legends. The whole place remains as in the old days, its plush furniture and scenery slowly gathering dust.

- 719 486-1147 • 308 Harrison Ave., Leadville, CO 80461
- Harrison Ave. is Leadville's main drag (Hwy 24). You can't miss the Opera House.
- Memorial Day–Sept.: Daily except Sat. 9 A.M.–5:30 P.M. Fee.

MANASSA

Jack Dempsey Museum   This boyhood-home museum provides about as stark an example as you can find of the contrast between humble beginnings and world fame. The "Manassa Mauler" left here while still a teenager, but kept in touch. The museum displays memorabilia of his early life and exhibits on some of his boxing triumphs.

📷 719 843-5207 • 410 Main St., Manassa, CO 81141

🚗 Manassa is in south-central Colorado, south of Alamosa. From US 285 turn east on Hwy 142. The museum is between 4th and 5th Sts. on Main St. (Hwy 142).

🕐 May–Sept.: Mon.–Sat. 9 A.M.–5 P.M. Fee.

MONTROSE

Ute Indian Museum   The Ute were the most prominent people in Colorado before whites arrived. This museum, on land once farmed by the noted leader Ouray, and where his wife Chipeta is buried, details the life and culture of the Ute, in exhibits and in regular festivals and programs. There is also a display on the pioneering 1776 Dominguez-Escalante expedition, and a native plants garden. *Gift Shop, Programs*

📷 970 249-3098 • Montrose, CO 81402

🚗 Montrose is in west-central Colorado, some 60 miles southeast of Grand Junction via US 50 and 550. The museum is 3 miles south of Montrose on 550; follow signs.

🕐 Mon.–Sat. 10 A.M.–5 P.M., Sun. 1 P.M.–5 P.M. Call for off-hours appointment. Fee.

PUEBLO

Fred E. Weisbrod Aircraft Museum/International B-24 Museum
The special feature of this museum, which has two dozen military aircraft, including a B-29 and a B-47, outdoors, is the display room on the role of the B-24 "Liberator" in World War II, with memorabilia of the bombers' crews and missions.

📷 719 948-9219 • at Pueblo Memorial Airport, Pueblo, CO 81001

🚗 Pueblo is in south-central Colorado, on I-25. The airport is just east, on Business US 50.

🕐 Mon.–Fri. 10 A.M.–4 P.M., Sat. 10 A.M.–2 P.M., Sun. 1 P.M.–4 P.M. Fee.

STERLING

Overland Trail Museum   After gold was found farther west, and until the continental railroad opened in 1869—less than a decade later—the valley of the South Platte River, now followed by I-76, became the Overland Trail, the road of fortune seekers, speculators, and pioneers. This museum holds memories of those who made the trip and of those whose land they crossed. In addition to the relics of travelers, there are such treasures as a large number of branding irons and, outside, a sample of prairie grasses.

📞 970 522-3895 • 21053 County Rd. 26½, Sterling, CO 80751

🚗 Sterling is in northeastern Colorado, on I-76. Take Exit 125 onto Hwy 6, heading west.

🕐 Apr.–Oct.: Mon.–Sat. 9 A.M.–5 P.M., Sun. 10 A.M.–5 P.M. Rest of year: Tues.–Sat. 10 A.M.–4 P.M. Donation.

TRINIDAD

A. R. Mitchell Memorial Museum of Western Art   Arthur Roy Mitchell (1889–1977) was a noted Western artist and illustrator. This museum has more than 250 of his paintings, and also shows the work of a number of other regional painters; a century of images, detailing Trinidad history, from the local Aultman Studio; a collection of Hispanic religious folk art; and other artifacts and artworks. *Gift Shop*

📞 719 846-4224 • 150 E. Main St., Trinidad, CO 81082

🚗 Trinidad is in south-central Colorado, near the New Mexico border, on I-25. Take Exit 13B onto Main St. and proceed east past the intersection of Commercial.

🕐 May–Sept.: Mon.–Fri. 10 A.M.–4 P.M. Call for off-season hours. No fee.

VAIL

Colorado Ski Museum–Ski Hall of Fame   This is, of course, one of America's best-known ski resorts, and here you have a hall saluting more than 100 major figures in Colorado skiing, and galleries depicting the 130-year history of what began as transportation but quickly became sport. You'll see 19th-century skis and a range of equipment and memorabilia, some relating to the 10th Mountain Division, which trained here during World War II and whose veterans were key in Vail's development. *Gift Shop*

📞 970 476-1876 • 231 S. Frontage Rd. East, Vail, CO 81658

🚗 Vail is in central Colorado, 80 miles west of Denver, on I-70. Take Exit 176. The museum is in the Vail Transportation Center, just east of the exit.

🕐 Year-round except May and Sept.: Tues.–Sun. 10 A.M.–5 P.M. No fee.

VICTOR

Lowell Thomas Museum   Early in the 20th century, Victor was one of the boomingest mining centers in Colorado, part of the renowned Cripple Creek district. Here you'll see artifacts and memorabilia of those days, while at the same time glimpsing the boyhood of journalist Lowell Thomas (*see also* the Garst Museum, Greenville, Ohio), who started his career with a newspaper route here.

🏠 719 689-3307 • 3rd and Victor, Victor, CO 80860

🚗 Victor is in south-central Colorado, about 20 miles (but a good 2 hours) west-southwest of Colorado Springs. Take US 24W from Colorado Springs and turn south on Hwy 67 at Divide, passing through Cripple Creek.

🕐 Memorial Day–Labor Day: Mon.–Sun. 9 A.M.–5 P.M. Fee.

CONNECTICUT

An amazing amount of what we think of as American comes from, or began in, Connecticut. Is it because Connecticut itself began as an outpost of 17th-century Massachusetts, and outposts have a way of attracting the adventurous and creative? Is it because this isn't very good farming country, but with its rivers and mineral resources was ideal for early industry? Whatever the reason, Connecticut and its children cooked up a lot of "American stuff."

What's Big: In New Haven, Yale's Center for British Art and University Art Gallery, as well as the noted Peabody (natural history) Museum; in Hartford, the Wadsworth Atheneum, a monument to the city's (and state's) longtime cultural prominence; Gillette Castle, a magnificent whim in Haddam; Mystic Seaport, a preservation-and-restoration mecca in Mystic; Groton's Submarine Force Museum and U.S.S. *Nautilus*; and of course, those museums to folly, the Foxwoods and Mohegan Sun casinos, which seem on the way to becoming the most-visited sites in human history.

BRIDGEPORT

Barnum Museum   If Phineas T. Barnum could turn his American Museum of 1841 into a career as "the World's Greatest Showman," we think you owe it to him to visit this institution, which is devoted to that career. Jumbo, Tom Thumb, Jenny Lind, the Cardiff Giant, the original Siamese Twins—that's Show Business! The museum also has displays on Bridgeport's industrial history, which was fantastic in its own way. *Tours, Gift Shop, Programs*

🏛 203 331-1104 • 820 Main St., Bridgeport, CT 06604

🚗 It's off Exit 27 on I-95 (follow signs), and within walking distance of the train station.

🕐 Tues.–Sat. 10 A.M.–4:30 P.M. Sun. noon–4:30. Open Mon. in July and Aug. Fee.

BRISTOL

American Clock and Watch Museum   Clocks and watches (think of names like Seth Thomas) are a historic Connecticut product. Here you'll find more than 3,000 timepieces—some, like the 1825 Planetary Clock from Paris, aren't Connecticut-made—in their splendor. There's also a sundial garden. Plan to be here on the hour! *Gift Shop, Library*

🏠 860 583-6070 • 100 Maple St., Bristol, CT 06010

🚗 Bristol is southwest of Hartford. Take Exit 38 off I-84 and follow Route 6 for 9 miles, to junction with Route 69; Maple St. runs left from junction. Or take Exit 31 from I-84 and go north on Route 229 for 5.5 miles, then left on Woodland St. for 1 mile.

🕐 Apr.–Nov.: Mon.–Sun. 10 A.M.–5 P.M. Fee.

New England Carousel Museum   The painted ponies, dipping and rising to the festival music, are part of many memories. Here's a place devoted to the artistry and mystique, with a miniature circus as well, and special events for children of all ages. It has a branch in Mystic also: call **860 536-7862**. *Tours, Programs*

🏠 860 585-5411 • 95 Riverside Ave., Bristol, CT 06010

🚗 Take eastbound Exit 31 off I-84; follow Route 229N, then Route 72W (Riverside Ave.). Or take westbound Exit 33 to Route 72W.

🕐 Apr.–Nov.: Mon.–Sat. 10 A.M.–5 P.M., Sun. noon–5 P.M. Closed Mon.–Wed. rest of year. Fee.

CANTERBURY

Prudence Crandall Museum   This fine house, built in 1805, became the scene in 1833 of Prudence Crandall's effort—the first in New England—to educate black girls. By September 1834, racist mobs had forced the school's closing, and Crandall continued her teaching elsewhere. Today you may contemplate this history in dignified and quiet surroundings. *Gift Shop, Programs, Library*

🏠 860 546-9916 • Canterbury Green, Jct. of Routes 14 and 169, Canterbury, CT 06331

🚗 Canterbury is in eastern Connecticut, northeast of Norwich. Exit from I-395 onto either Route 14W or Route 169N.

🕐 Feb.–mid-Dec.: Wed.–Sun. 10 A.M.–4:30 P.M. Fee. Library by appointment only.

DANBURY

Danbury Scott-Fanton Museum/Charles Ives House   Danbury was once the "Hat Capital of the World," and the displays at the Dodd Shop, part of the museum complex, detail the technology, ancillary industries, and labor conditions of the period. The Rider House exhibits carpenters' and joiners' tools and other items from the area's working past. But for something completely different (we think), you may visit (by appointment) the home of Charles Ives, America's most unusual composer. *Library*

🔲 203 743-5200 • 43 Main St., Danbury, CT 06810

🚗 Danbury is in western Connecticut, on I-84 and Route 7. The museum is just south of the center of town, near the intersection with South St. (Route 53).

🕐 Wed.–Sun. 2 P.M.–5 P.M. Donation.

ESSEX

Connecticut River Museum   Boat and steam train rides draw many visitors to Essex. The museum offers displays on the life of the river and local maritime history from the 17th century. The replica of the 1775 *Turtle*, the first American submarine, is an important attraction. *Gift Shop*

🔲 860 767-8269 • Steamboat Dock, 67 Main St., Essex, CT 06426

🚗 Essex is on the Connecticut River in southeastern Connecticut. Take Exit 69 off I-95. Follow Route 9N to Exit 3, and follow signs.

🕐 Tues.–Sun. 10 A.M.–5 P.M. Closed major holidays. Fee.

FARMINGTON

Hill-Stead Museum   Theodate Pope, pioneering female architect, more or less began her career in 1901 by telling Stanford White, then the lion of the profession, how she wanted this house built for her father and his art collection. You must come here to see the masterpieces by Manet, Degas, Monet, and others, because they are never loaned out. And if you come, you'll be rewarded by a sunken garden by Beatrix Farrand and other visions of earthly paradise. *Tours, Programs*

🔲 860 677-4787 • 35 Mountain Rd., Farmington, CT 06032

🚗 Farmington is a western suburb of Hartford. Take I-84 to Exit 39, and follow Route 4W, then turn left (south) on Route 10, and left on Mountain Rd., following signs.

🕐 May–Oct.: Tues.–Sun. 10 A.M.–5 P.M. Nov.–Apr.: same days, 11 A.M.–4 P.M. Fee.

HARTFORD

While you're in the area, see also: Farmington, Newington, West Hartford

Harriet Beecher Stowe Center   The last (1873–96) home of the most popular 19th-century American writer (*see also* the Stowe House, Cincinnati, Ohio) is a fine example of a style of domestic architecture—the "villa" or "cottage" located in a "rustic" part of a city, in this case the Nook Farm neighborhood. There is much

Stowe memorabilia, here, in the research library, and in the adjacent Day House. The Mark Twain House is a step away. *Tours, Gift Shop, Library*

🖾 860 522-9258 • http://www.hartnet.org/stowe • 77 Forest St., Hartford, CT 06105

🚗 Take Exit 46 from I-84, and go right onto Sisson Ave., right on Farmington Ave., and right on Forest St.

🕐 Tues.–Sat. 9:30 A.M.–4 P.M., Sun. noon–4 P.M. Open Mon. June–Columbus Day and in Dec. Fee.

KENT

Sloane-Stanley Museum/Kent Furnace   Eric Sloane, writer and painter, was also a collector of handmade tools, and his collection established this museum in 1969, with the backing of the Stanley company of New Britain. After Sloane's death in 1985, his studio was reconstructed here, and you can see his artworks, books, and other collections including weathervanes, almanacs, and hats. Kent Furnace was an important 19th-century pig iron producer; its ruins surround the museum. *Gift Shop, Publications*

🖾 860 927-3849 • Route 7, Kent, CT 06757

🚗 Kent is in extreme western Connecticut, about 45 minutes north of Danbury. The museum is 1 mile north of town on Route 7.

🕐 Mid-May–Oct.: Wed.–Sun. and holidays 10 A.M.–4 P.M. Fee.

NEWINGTON

American Radio Relay League/Museum of Amateur Radio   This is Ham Headquarters. If you've ever been interested in amateur radio, you'll find a display of artifacts including Admiral Byrd's receiver from the 1935 Arctic expedition, and items dating back to 1921, the dawn of the radio era. Station W1AW, next door, may also be toured. There is a full range of membership services. *Tours*

🖾 860 594-0200 • http://www.arrl.org • 225 Main St., Newington, CT 06111

🚗 Newington is just southwest of Hartford. Main St. runs north from Route 175 in the center of town. Go about a mile, and the museum's antennas will be on your left.

🕐 Mon.–Fri. 8 A.M.–5 P.M. Tours on the hour or by appointment. No fee.

OLD LYME

Nut Museum   In the quarter century since Elizabeth Tashjian created this shrine to nuts, it has been both celebrated on national television and studiously ignored by the Connecticut tourism authorities (perhaps a state nicknamed for its pedlars' bogus nutmegs feels the whole idea cuts a little close to the skin). When you find it, you'll see all manner of n-u-t-s, as well as Miss Tashjian's nut-based art. You'll learn all manner of nutology. You may hear nut music, too.

🏠 860 434-7636 • 303 Ferry Rd., Old Lyme, CT 06371

🚗 It's in a mansion surrounded by nut trees. Call for directions, or follow the squirrels.

🕐 May–Oct.: Wed., Sat.–Sun. 1 P.M.–5 P.M. Other times by appointment; call to confirm. Fee, including one nut per person.

RIVERTON

Hitchcock Museum (John Tarrant Kenney Hitchcock Museum)   Lambert Hitchcock, the great chairmaker, began business here in 1818, and the village became known as Hitchcocksville. Company showrooms nearby may still be visited. In 1972 John Tarrant Kenney established this museum to display the "fancy chairs" so common in American homes.

🏠 860 738-4950 • Old Union Church, 1 Robersville Rd., Riverton, CT 06065

🚗 Riverton is in northwest Connecticut. Take Route 44W from Hartford to New Hartford and follow signs. From I-84, take Route 8N from Waterbury and exit onto Route 20 for Riverton.

🕐 Apr.–Dec.: Thurs.–Sun. noon–4 P.M.

TERRYVILLE

Lock Museum of America   Locks are typical of the kind of hardware Connecticut grew rich on, and here you'll see the most complete collection anywhere of locks, keys, knobs, bolts, padlocks, safes, and other elements of the early security industry.

🏠 860 589-6359 • 130 Main St., Terryville, CT 06786

🚗 Terryville is in west-central Connecticut, just west of Bristol. Take Exit 38 off I-84 and follow Route 72; go left on Main St. to the museum.

🕐 May–Oct.: Tues.–Sun. 1:30 P.M.–4:30 P.M. Fee.

WASHINGTON (WASHINGTON GREEN)

Institute for American Indian Studies   Formerly the American Indian Archaeological Institute, this small center, hidden in the Connecticut forest, offers a reconstructed Algonkian village and surrounding plant trails as part of its focus on Eastern Woodland peoples. You may participate in IAIS archaeological work, and there are contemporary arts displays. *Tours, Gift Shop, Hands-on, Programs, Publications, Library*

🏠 860 868-0518 • Off Route 199, Curtis Rd., Washington (Washington Green), CT 06793

🚗 Washington is in east-central Connecticut, northeast of Danbury. From I-84, take Exit 15 and follow Route 67, then Route 199N. Watch for IAIS signs.

🕐 Apr.–Dec.: Mon.–Sat. 10 A.M.–5 P.M., Sun. noon–5 P.M. Jan.–Mar.: closed Mon., Tues. Fee.

WATERBURY

Mattatuck Museum   The Mattatuck presents 18th- and 19th-century regional painters, contemporary artists, decorative arts, furniture, and historical artifacts. Its displays on the chief local industry are special, however; Waterbury was long the Brass City, and the museum details its rise and heyday. *Gift Shop, Food*

🏛 203 753-0381 • 144 W. Main St., Waterbury, CT 06702

🚗 Waterbury is in southwestern Connecticut, on I-84. Take Exit 21 and go right onto Meadow and right onto W. Main. Fork left at 2nd light; museum is on left.

🕐 Tues.–Sat. 10 A.M.–5 P.M. Sun. noon–5 P.M. No fee.

WEST HARTFORD

Museum of American Political Life   This is a huge trove of everything from buttons worn at George Washington's inaugural to the ones your children will wear in future Ross Perot campaigns. There's Goldwater-Edsel-Mets material ("Back a real loser"); an 1896 Full Dinner Pail; FDR for vice president (remember 1920?); and other curiosities. There are also presentations on expansion of the franchise and main themes throughout the history of presidential campaigns. *See also* San Diego, California, for the Museum of the American Presidency.

🏛 860 768-4090 • University of Hartford, 200 Bloomfield Ave., West Hartford, CT 06127

🚗 Bloomfield Ave. is Connecticut Route 189, which runs north from US 44 about 2 miles northwest of downtown Hartford.

🕐 Tues.–Sat. 11 A.M.–4 P.M. Fee.

WILLIMANTIC

Windham Textile and History Museum   Willimantic was a cotton, then a silk, town, one of many textile centers in this "forgotten" part of New England. The world's largest mill was once here. Now the museum, also a research center, recalls the history of the American Thread Company and the lives of its workers. *Tours, Gift Shop, Programs, Library*

🏛 860 456-2178 • 157 Union-Main St., Willimantic, CT 06226

🚗 Willimantic is in east-central Connecticut, on Routes 66 and 32. The museum is at the east end of Main St., where it joins Union.

🕐 Fri.–Sun. 1 P.M.–5 P.M. Tours other times by appointment. Fee.

WINCHESTER CENTER

Winchester Center Kerosene Lamp Museum   Here's an example of an enthusiasm that grew into a museum: the collection of George and Ruth Sherwood. Kerosene lamps were ubiquitous in American households before electricity took hold in the 1880s, and here you'll see hundreds. A look at the forgotten.

■ 860 379-2612 • 100 Old Waterbury Tpke (Route 263), Winchester Center, CT 06094

🚗 Winchester Center is north of Torrington, in northwest Connecticut. Take Route 8 to Exit 46 and follow signs.

🕐 Sat.–Sun. and holidays 9:30 A.M.–4 P.M. No fee.

DELAWARE

Unless you've made a trip *to* Delaware, you may think the whole thing is a series of highways passing around Wilmington and through its suburbs. Did you know that the other two-thirds of the state is largely tranquil, agricultural, and Southern? That it has little towns where the sharp smell of the sea makes the strongest demand on your senses? Delaware may be small, but some of it is actually remote.

What's Big: Winterthur, Hagley, and Nemours, keys to the complex of museums and gardens (some of them in Chadds Ford and Kennett Square, Pennsylvania) north and northwest of Wilmington. Winterthur is now home to the fabled Campbell soup tureen collection (late of Camden, New Jersey), in case you were wondering.

DOVER

Delaware Agricultural Museum and Village   Here you'll find exhibits on just about everything having to do with farming in the Delmarva region. There are farm machines and a crop-dusting biplane, the first broiler-chicken house, peach sorting equipment, wagons, bottles, tools, a re-created village with shops and other buildings, and a noted folk art collection. *Gift Shop, Hands-on, Programs*

- 302 734-1618 • 866 N. DuPont Hwy, Dover, DE 19901
- It's on Route 13, north of Dover and just south of Delaware State University.
- Jan.–Mar.: Mon.–Fri. 10 A.M.–4 P.M. Apr.–Dec.: Tues.–Sat. 10 A.M.–4 P.M., Sun. 1 P.M.–4 P.M. Fee.

Johnson Victrola Museum   In a 1920s Victrola dealer's store, this is a memorial to Delaware's own Eldridge Reeves Johnson, the inventor who founded the Victor Talking Machine Company in 1901. It's about him and it's about his machines, which changed our lives; you won't find more Victor items anywhere else. Nipper is here too, in oils. Nearby are the 1792 Delaware State House and the two Meeting House Galleries—Gallery 1 focuses on archaeology, particularly items from the

Island Field site near Bowers Beach; Gallery II emphasizes early-20th-century Delaware life. *Gift Shop, Library*

🔲 302 739-4266 • Bank Lane and New St., Dover, DE 19903

🚗 Take the Governor's Ave. exit from Route 13 and follow State Museums signs.

🕐 Tues.–Sat. 10 A.M.–3:30 P.M. No fee.

FORT DELAWARE STATE PARK

Fort Delaware   Our great-grandfather did a year here as a Confederate prisoner, so we can't resist sending you on a boat ride to this 1859 fort. There's a designated museum with Civil War memorabilia, but the whole place is a sort of museum to national folly.

🔲 302 834-7941 • on Pea Patch Island, in the Delaware River near Delaware City, Fort Delaware State Park, DE 19706

🚗 You must take a boat (they leave every 30 minutes) from the dock on Clinton St. in Delaware City, on Route 9 south of Wilmington.

🕐 Mid-June–Labor Day: Wed.–Fri. 11 A.M.–4 P.M.; Sat., Sun., and holidays 11 A.M.–6 P.M. Reduced hours Apr.–mid-June and Sept. Fee.

GEORGETOWN

Treasures of the Sea Exhibit   Sunken treasure! Gold, silver, cannons! Mel Fisher found it on the N*uestra Señora de* A*tocha,* and now you can see it in this quiet setting. There's a video presentation on the search, and they say you can even buy some of the goodies in the gift shop. *Tours, Gift Shop*

🔲 302 856-5700 • Delaware Technical and Community College, Georgetown, DE 19947

🚗 Georgetown is in southern Delaware. The college is on Route 18/404, just west of the junction with Route 113. The exhibit is in the library building.

🕐 Mon.–Tues., Fri.–Sat.; call to verify hours and fees.

OAK ORCHARD

Nanticoke Indian Museum   The Nanticoke tribe operates this museum as an act of self-preservation. You'll see bead, feather, and bone work, regalia, baskets, and other artifacts. The library has books, videos, and photographs for researchers. Events include an autumn powwow. *Tours, Gift Shop, Library*

🔲 302 945-7022 • Routes 24 and 5, Oak Orchard, DE 19966

🚗 Oak Orchard is east of Millsboro, in southeastern Delaware. Take Route 24 east from Millsboro for 7 miles, or west from Route 1 for 12 miles.

🕐 Summer: Tues.–Fri. 9 A.M.–4 P.M., Sat. 10 A.M.–4 P.M., Sun. noon–4 P.M. Reduced hours in winter. Fee.

WILMINGTON

While you're in the area, see also: Fort Delaware. *In Pennsylvania, see*: Boothwyn, Kennett Square

Kalmar Nyckel **Foundation and Shipyard**

The *Kalmar Nyckel* brought the first Swedish settlers to this area in 1638. Today a replica is being constructed at this shipyard, and there are displays on the Swedes in America and on the history behind that first immigration. Shipbuilding artifacts, paintings, and other educational materials contribute to the story. Nearby, at 606 Church St., is Old Swedes (Holy Trinity) Church, active since 1698. *Tours*

🏠 302 429-7447 • 1124 E. 7th St., Wilmington, DE 19801

🚗 It's on the Christina River at Swedes Landing, southeast of downtown.

🕐 Mon.–Fri. 10 A.M.–4 P.M., Sat. 11 A.M.–3 P.M. Fee.

DISTRICT OF COLUMBIA

D.C., of course, is the home of the ultimate marble-monolith museums. You can see most everything you can imagine in the vast repositories of ournationscapital. D.C. is a paradox of Southern small-town demeanor stirred up with a mix of international intrigue, political machinations, tourists in madras, and urban zeitgeist.

What's Big: Everything. And we've included quite a few of them. But we do want to mention a few other favorites and must-sees: the Phillips Collection, of course, the Smithsonian's National Museum of African Art and National Museum of American History, the deco-moderne U.S. Department of the Interior Museum, the collection and gardens at Dumbarton Oaks, the National Postal Museum, and the freshly restored Thomas Jefferson Building of the Library of Congress. Rumor has it that New York's Black Fashion Museum has relocated here, so look for that too.

WASHINGTON, D.C.

While you're in the area, see also: Fort George Meade, MD, Glen Echo, MD, New Carrollton, MD, Silver Spring, MD, Alexandria, VA, Arlington, VA, Dumfries, VA

Folger Shakespeare Library The home of the First Folio of Shakespeare—from 1623—this beautiful museum and library is renowned for its extensive collection of rare Renaissance books and manuscripts as well as the world's largest collection of Shakespeare's printed works. You'll also find exquisite changing exhibits on such things as medieval book arts, artifacts pertaining to Shakespearean works, and period musical presentations. *Tours, Gift Shop, Library*

📖 202 544-4600 • http://www.folger.edu • 201 E. Capitol St. SE, Washington, DC 20003
🚗 Between 2nd and 3rd Sts. SE. Metro: Blue, Orange/Capitol South.
🕐 Mon.–Sat. 10 A.M.–4 P.M. No fee. Group tours by appointment: 202 675-0365.

House of the Temple Library/Museum   Even if you have no interest in seeing J. Edgar Hoover's baby shoes—or a re-creation of his entire office for that matter—you might want to stop here for a guided tour of some pretty remarkable architecture. You'll get a peek at a nice collection of Robert Burns memorabilia too, and a sense of the broad and mysterious reach of freemasonry. The National Museum of American Jewish Military History (202 265-6280) is nearby on R Street. *Tours*

■ 202 232-3579 • Supreme Council of the Scottish Rite of Freemasonry, 1733 16th St. NW, Washington, DC 20009

🚗 Between R and S Sts. NW. Metro: Red/Dupont Circle.

🕐 Guided tours only. Mon.–Fri. 8 A.M.–2 P.M. Sat. by appointment. No fee.

Labor Hall of Fame   From Samuel Gompers to Frances Perkins to A. Philip Randolph, leaders of American labor history are celebrated with photos, artifacts, and memorabilia. The fascinating, mostly untold, stories of the men and women who made a difference in the lives of America's workers are capped by a filmed interview with Mother Jones on her 100th birthday. *Tours*

■ 202 371-6422 • 200 Constitution Ave. NW, Washington, DC 20201

🚗 At 3rd St. NW. U.S. Dept. of Labor Frances Perkins Building lobby. Metro: Red/Judiciary Square.

🕐 Mon.–Fri. 8:30 A.M.–4 P.M. No fee. Group tours by appointment.

National Building Museum   The theme is American achievements in the building arts, and you'll find all kinds of architecture-related special exhibits here, like a history of the Brooklyn Bridge, Tools as Art, or a display on the rebuilding of Oklahoma City after the bombing of the federal building. But no matter what's up—and it's always interesting—the star of this show is the Pension Building that houses the museum. Designed by General Montgomery C. Meigs for pension distributions following the Civil War, it was way ahead of its time for its engineering details, especially in its use of light and ventilation. The vast interior space, with its eight colossal Corinthian brick columns hand-painted in trompe l'oeil to resemble marble, the tiled floor and stairwells, and fabulous arches and skylights make this a magical place. *Gift Shop, Tours, Hands-on*

■ 202 272-2448 • 401 F St. NW, Washington, DC 20001

🚗 Between 4th and 5th Sts. Metro: Red/Judiciary Square.

🕐 Mon.–Sat. 10 A.M.–4 P.M., Sun. noon–4 P.M. Group tours by appointment.

National Gallery of Caricature and Cartoon Art   Frivolous? Hardly. Cartoons can be serious business. And this museum is just the place to go for an in-depth, yet concise, overview of the history of caricature and cartoon art, from the earliest days of the form's use as a political saber to the delight found in the most whimsical comic strips. The permanent exhibit has items dating back to 1747; special exhibits further enhance our understanding of the role freedom of expression has in making this such a powerful art form in America. Housed in the 1887 Baltimore Sun Building, Washington's first skyscraper.

🏛 202 638-6411 • 1317 F St. NW, Washington, DC 20004

🚗 Between 13th and 14th Sts. Metro: R/B/O/Metro Center.

🕐 Tues.–Sat. 11 A.M.–4 P.M. No fee.

National Jewish American Sports Hall of Fame/B'nai B'rith Klutznick National Jewish Museum Art, history, and ethnography are melded together here in this comprehensive display of art and artifacts taken from all aspects and periods of Jewish culture and history. The ethnographic dimension is further explored through the Sports Hall of Fame, tracing the too little known contributions of Jews to American athletic accomplishment. *Gift Shop*

🏛 202 857-6583 • 1640 Rhode Island Ave. NW, Washington, DC 20036

🚗 At 17th St. NW. Metro: Red/Farragut North.

🕐 Sun.–Fri. 10 A.M.–5 P.M. Donation.

The Textile Museum Textiles and carpets dating back to 3,000 B.C. and from all corners of the globe and traditions from Coptic to pre-Columbian, from China to the American Southwest. Fragility dictates that the exhibits change frequently, but there is always something exotic and inspiring on display. *Tours, Gift Shop, Library, Publications*

🏛 202 667-0441 • 2320 S St. NW, Washington, DC 20008

🚗 Between 23rd and 24th Sts. NW. Metro: Red/Dupont Circle.

🕐 Mon.–Sat. 10 A.M.–5 P.M., Sun. 1 P.M.–5 P.M. Fee.

U.S. Chess Hall of Fame and Museum The history of American chess and its players, going all the way back to 1492. Photographs, chessboards, and a wide variety of pieces, as well as the very first commercial chess computer, are showcased here. You'll note the late hours—that's when the games (for newcomers and diehards alike) begin. And chess reminds us of Checkers, who reminds us of the late Richard Milhous Nixon. What better way to close out D.C. than to tell you you can now stay in the infamous lookout room in the former Howard Johnson's (now the Premier Hotel; 800 965-6869 X7954) and enjoy the view across to the Watergate while you peruse the break-in memorabilia that enhances the room's decor. *Library*

🏛 202 857-4922 • 1501 M St. NW, Washington, DC 20005

🚗 Between 15th and 16th Sts. NW. Metro: Red/Farragut North.

🕐 Mon.–Thurs. 5:30 P.M.–11 P.M., Sat. noon–9 P.M., Sun. noon–6 P.M. No fee.

FLORIDA

Caveat: Nothing in Florida is "little." There are simply too many visitors and too many pursuing recreation to allow anything to remain undiscovered. All right, we're over-stating. But the explosion of theme parks, re-creations (of places far from here, or places nowhere in history), and similar tourist objectives has left large parts of Florida paved with attractions. The state's Division of Parks and Recreation has actually taken to promoting its (relatively unknown) sites as "the Real Florida," a reminder that there were people, and there was nature, before the onslaught. We find it ironic that the Tupperware Museum and Xanadu have not survived in one Florida or the other.

What's Big: Leaving aside all the film studio–created hoopla, there are places like Lakeland's Sun 'n' Fun Air Museum, the Art Deco District of Miami Beach (an example of the city as museum), Miami's Museum of Contemporary Art, Daytona USA, and, taken as a whole, the tour routes in Key West and St. Augustine.

APALACHICOLA

John Gorrie State Museum   John Gorrie was one of those people who do a little of everything. By the time yellow fever struck in 1841, he had been Apalachicola's mayor and held various other posts. The epidemic spurred him into becoming one of the pioneers of refrigeration, and by extension, air conditioning.

■ 904 653-9347 • 46 6th St., corner of Ave. D, Apalachicola, FL 32329

🚗 Apalachicola is a port at the beginning of the Florida Panhandle, southwest of Talla-hassee, on US 98/319. Look for Gorrie Square.

🕙 Thurs.–Mon. 9 A.M.–5 P.M. Fee.

CHOKOLOSKEE

Smallwood Store Museum   In a quiet fishing town on the edge of the Ever-glades, this little museum will give you an idea of what a general store and trading post was like early in the 20th century. Ask the staff about the outlaw days in Chokoloskee. *Gift Shop*

■ 941 695-2989 • Mamie St., Chokoloskee, FL 33925

🚙 Chokoloskee is in extreme southwestern Florida, southeast of Naples, in the Everglades National Park. Take Route 29S from US 41 (the Tamiami Trail) past Everglades City, to the end.

🕐 Mon.–Sun. 10 A.M.–4 P.M. In winter, open to 5 P.M. Fee.

CROSS CREEK

Marjorie Kinnan Rawlings State Historic Site   Small tour groups here may visit the rural home of the author of *The Yearling* and *Cross Creek*. The house is typical "Cracker" architecture and with the surrounding citrus grove and marsh represents a part of Florida fast disappearing. Rawlings' grave is nearby. *Tours*

■ 904 466-3672 • Cross Creek, FL 32640

🚙 Cross Creek is about 20 miles southeast of Gainesville and north of Ocala, on Route 325. If you are traveling south on US 301, exit west at Island Grove.

🕐 Grounds: Mon.–Sun. 9 A.M.–5 P.M. House: Oct.–July: Thurs.–Sun. 10 A.M.–11 A.M. and 1 P.M.–4 P.M. Fee.

DELRAY BEACH

Morikami Museum and Japanese Gardens   Before this part of Florida hit its tourist stride, early in the 20th century, the Yamato Colony was hard at work farming. Here's a chance to get a good look at Japanese culture in an unlikely place: The museum celebrates the colony (and aspects of Japan many tourists miss when they travel there), and there are 200 acres of parks and gardens. *Tours, Programs, Library*

■ 561 495-0233 • 4000 Morikami Park Rd., Delray Beach, FL 33446

🚙 Morikami Park is southwest of downtown Delray Beach. Take Exit 41 (Linton Ave.) west off I-95, go 3 miles, and turn left on Jog Rd., following signs.

🕐 Tues.–Sun. 10 A.M.–5 P.M. Fee.

ESTERO

Koreshan State Historic Site   The Koreshan Unity was a communal religious movement founded by Dr. Cyrus Teed, who hoped that in Estero the New Jerusalem would rise. Teed died in 1908, and the community gradually declined, but you can visit the remains; the buildings and landscaping speak of an embracing vision of life, as the Koreshans saw it, within the earth. There's also the Koreshan Unity Foundation, a library-museum deriving from the movement, just across Route 41; call 941 992-2184 for information on lecture tours. *Tours, Programs*

■ 941 992-0311 • US 41 and Corkscrew Rd., Estero, FL 33928

🚗 Estero is in southwestern Florida, south of Fort Myers. From I-75, take Exit 19 and go west 2 miles, to the corner of Corkscrew Rd. and US 41.

🕐 Park: Mon.–Sun. 8 A.M.–dusk. Historic settlement: Mon.–Sun. 8 A.M.–5 P.M. Fee.

FORT PIERCE

UDT-SEAL Museum   The Navy's Underwater Demolition Teams were first trained here during World War II. In 1962, their role was redefined and they were renamed the SEALs (for sea, air, and land). The museum details their history, with displays including landing craft, boats, and rafts, diving gear and uniforms, weapons and demolition apparatus, and varied memorabilia. *Gift Shop*

■ 561 462-3597 • 3300 N. State Rd. A1A, N. Hutchinson Island, Fort Pierce, FL 34949

🚗 Fort Pierce is in east-central Florida, about 90 miles southeast of Orlando. From Route 1, take A1A (via the North Beach Causeway) onto the island. Museum is on the right (ocean side) at about 2.9 miles.

🕐 Tues.–Sat. 10 A.M.–4 P.M., Sun. noon–4 P.M. Fee.

FORT WALTON BEACH

Indian Temple Mound Museum   The Mississippian culture flourished in these parts from about 600 to 1,000 years ago. We know it largely from its mounds, ceremonial structures built in the middle of villages. The one at Fort Walton Beach has a base 223 feet by 178 feet, and today stands next to a museum exhibiting stone, bone, shell, and pottery items revealing the artistry of the ancient inhabitants, as well as artifacts from the period when whites arrived.

■ 904 243-6521 • 139 Miracle Strip Pkwy, Fort Walton Beach, FL 32548

🚗 Fort Walton Beach is in the western Panhandle, a half-hour east of Pensacola. The museum is right in town, at the junction of US 98 and State Route 85.

🕐 June–Aug.: Mon.–Sat. 9 A.M.–4 P.M. Rest of year: Mon.–Sat. 11 A.M.–4 P.M. Fee.

GAINESVILLE

Devil's Millhopper State Geological Site   Why are we sending you to this odd outdoor site? First, it's a spectacular example of the sinkhole, a phenomenon common in Florida's soft rock. Second, it has been a research asset, and in the interpretive center you'll see some of the materials recovered here, and learn what they mean about Florida's history. Third, if botany interests you, you'll see, as you descend into the Millhopper, species you won't see elsewhere in Florida.

📷 352 392-1721 • 4732 Millhopper Rd. (Route 232), Gainesville, FL 32606

🚗 Just northwest of Gainesville, on Route 232 (otherwise NW 53rd Ave. or Millhopper Rd.).

🕐 Apr.–Sept.: Mon.–Sun. 9 A.M.–dusk. Rest of year: 9 A.M.–5 P.M. Fee.

Fred Bear Museum Fred Bear traveled around the world bowhunting for decades; this museum displays large mounted animals and animal heads, but also Inuit and African artifacts, ancient weapons, Mastodon ivory, tools, charms, and other items Bear picked up along the way. There's also an archery pro shop. *Gift Shop*

📷 352 376-2327 • I-75 at Archer Rd., Gainesville, FL 32608

🚗 The museum is on Gainesville's southwest side. Exit from I-75 onto Archer Rd. (Route 24); Fred Bear Dr. is just west of the Interstate.

🕐 Wed.–Sun. 10 A.M.–6 P.M. Fee.

JACKSONVILLE

Karpeles Manuscript Library Museum This is one of several Karpeles museums around the country. Their mission is to collect, preserve, and exhibit items like the Emancipation Proclamation, a draft of the Bill of Rights, or treatises of Galileo or Darwin, in order to teach the importance of original manuscripts in the study of history. Displays rotate among the museums, which are generally in larger, older buildings with a quiet atmosphere suitable to perusing documents. *Programs, Publications, Library*

📷 904 356-2992 • http://www.rain.org/~karpeles/ • 101 W. 1st St., at Laura St., Jacksonville, FL 32206

🚗 It's in downtown Jacksonville. Call for precise directions.

🕐 Mon.–Sun. noon–4 P.M. No fee.

KEY WEST

East Martello Museum and Gallery In Key West, you'll probably go on the tour of famous houses and the Wreckers' and Mel Fisher museums. We think you shouldn't miss this place, because it will give you a sense of the community's whole history, through a large collection of historical and maritime artifacts. The artworks include those of well-known local Mario Sanchez.

📷 305 296-3913 • 3501 S. Roosevelt Blvd., Key West, FL 33040

🚙 South Roosevelt Blvd. is State A1A, on the south side of the island.
🕐 Mon.–Sun. 9:30 A.M.–5 P.M. Fee.

MELBOURNE BEACH

McLarty Treasure Museum   One of the Spanish fleets that took gold from the Caribbean was wrecked near here in 1715. Although clues were found early in this century, it took a 1950s hurricane to reveal that this survivors' campsite was key to the story. The museum displays worked gold items, a Spanish saddle, a ship's bell, and other evidence of a fleet much of which is still somewhere out there. *Programs*
■ 951 589-2147 • Sebastian Inlet State Recreation Area, 9700 South A1A (Ocean Blvd.), Melbourne Beach, FL 32951
🚙 The Sebastian Inlet SRA is midway between Melbourne (north) and Vero Beach (south) on Route A1A, which runs along the barrier island on Florida's east-central coast.
🕐 Mon.–Sun. 10 A.M.–4:30 P.M. Fee. Interpretive group programs by reservation.

MIAMI

While you're in the area, see also: Miami Beach

American Police Hall of Fame and Museum   This museum is now quite "big," but we think it's unusual enough to merit a visit. You want to sit in an electric chair? In a gas chamber? You get the idea: It's touristic. But it has 10,000 items of all sorts, from a guillotine to Harrison Ford's *Blade Runner* car, and a hall dedicated to all American cops who have died in the line of duty since 1960; the organization conducts outreach programs for survivors. This is a bewildering mix of dead serious and hey-look-at-this! *Gift Shop, Programs, Publications, Screenings*
■ 305 573-0070 • http://www.aphf.org • 3801 Biscayne Blvd., Miami, FL 33137
🚙 Biscayne Blvd. is US 1. The museum's just north of the intersection with I-195.
🕐 Mon.–Sun. 10 A.M.–5:30 P.M. Fee.

MIAMI BEACH

The Wolfsonian (formerly Collection of Decorative and Propaganda Arts)   Mitchell Wolfson, Jr., has spent years collecting thousands of objects produced in Europe and America in the years 1885–1945, the period in which machine production replaced hand production. His collection contains works of all sorts, including posters, furniture, appliances, ceramics, books, sculpture, prints, and glassware, selected for changing exhibits. *Gift Shop, Programs, Publications*

■ 305 531-1001 • 1001 Washington Ave., Miami Beach, FL 33139

🚗 It's on (north-south) Washington Ave. at 10th St., in the Art Deco District.

🕐 Tues.–Thurs. 10 A.M.–6 P.M., Fri. 10 A.M.–9 P.M., Sun. noon–5 P.M. Fee.

MULBERRY

Mulberry Phosphate Museum   We tend to forget that anything like mining goes on in Florida, but here's a reminder: Mulberry is "the Phosphate Capital of the World." In the course of extraction, many evidences of ancient life have come to light, and you'll see a 10-million-year-old baleen whale fossil and Ice Age plants, among other things. You'll learn about the phosphate industry in the area too. *Tours*

■ 941 425-5492 • Mulberry, FL 33860

🚗 Mulberry is in central Florida, an hour southwest of Orlando. The museum is downtown, 1 block south of Hwy 60, on Hwy 37.

🕐 Tues.–Sat. 10 A.M.–4:30 P.M. Donation. Call 941 425-2823 to arrange tours.

NAPLES

Teddy Bear Museum of Naples ("Frannie's")   If you think your kids already have enough teddy bears, we'd advise you to avoid this museum! There are thousands of them, and some are for sale. Others are taking part in animated displays or being played with by visiting children. There are classes in making bears. There's a Li-bear-y. Enough! The spirit of whoever invented the teddy bear must be hiding in the pines around here somewhere. *Gift Shop, Hands-on, Programs, Publications, Library*

■ 800 681-2327 • 2511 Pine Ridge Rd., Naples, FL 33942

🚗 Naples is in far southwestern Florida. Take Exit 16 off I-75 onto Pine Ridge Rd., and go 1.75 miles west.

🕐 Dec.–Apr.: Mon., Wed.–Sat. 10 A.M.–5 P.M.; Sun. 1 P.M.–5 P.M. Rest of year: also closed Mon.; call to confirm hours. Fee.

OCALA

Don Garlits Museum of Drag Racing and International Drag Racing Hall of Fame   "Big Daddy" Garlits and wife Pat founded this museum in 1976, after a quarter century of drag racing. Here you'll see 75-odd cars covering the sport's history, memorabilia of the greats, and also Garlits' collection of antique and classic cars. *Gift Shop*

■ 352 245-8661 • 13700 SW 16th Ave., Ocala, FL 34473

🚗 Ocala is in north-central Florida, an hour northwest of Orlando. Take I-75 to Exit 67 (County Rd. 484); the museum is just east of the exit.

🕑 Mon.–Sun. 9 A.M.–5:30 P.M. Fee.

ORMOND BEACH

Hungarian Folk Art Museum   One of several organizations in the Casements, John D. Rockefeller's winter home, this museum displays a wide array of folk arts—embroidery, costumes, porcelain, woodcrafts, and others—and is ready to expound on the history and culture of Hungary and the Hungarians. Nearby there's a Boy Scout exhibit, and a collection of Rockefellerana.

■ 904 767-4292 • 25 Riverside Dr., Ormond Beach, FL 32174

🚗 Ormond Beach is in northeastern Florida, just north of Daytona Beach. The museum is in the Casements, now a cultural center. From I-95, take Route 40 (Granada Blvd.) east across the Halifax River, and turn left on Riverside Dr.

🕑 Mon.–Fri. 9 A.M.–5 P.M., Sat. 9 A.M.–noon.

PANAMA CITY BEACH

Museum of Man in the Sea   Here is a museum devoted to the whole history of diving and underwater exploration and salvaging. There are dioramas, hands-on shallow-water displays, old diving equipment, submersibles, and a variety of other artifacts, written records, and illustrations. *Tours*

■ 904 235-4101 • 17314 Back Beach Rd. (US 98), Panama City Beach, FL 32413

🚗 Panama City Beach is west of Panama City, on US 98. The museum is just west of the junction with Route 79.

🕑 Mon.–Sun. 9 A.M.–5 P.M. Fee.

PERRY

Forest Capital State Cultural Museum   Forest products were long the base of Florida's economy. Here you will see, on 13 acres, aspects of this history. The turpentine industry is detailed in a diorama and exhibits. There's a map of Florida's 67 counties, each cut from a different native wood. And there's a mid-19th-century Cracker homestead, illustrating the life of early settlers. *Gift Shop*

📷 904 584-3227 • 204 Forest Park Dr., Perry, FL 32347

🚗 Perry is in north Florida, an hour southeast of Tallahassee. The museum is 1 mile south of town on US 19/98.

🕐 Mon., Thurs.–Sun. 9 A.M.–5 P.M. Fee.

SAINT AUGUSTINE

Lightner Museum   This is a good place to get a sense of the life of the wealthy for whom Henry Flagler intended to develop Florida's east coast. The Alcazar was a very grand hotel, and now the Lightner Museum exhibits the kinds of decorative items that graced affluent homes (as well as hotels) at the end of the 19th century.

📷 904 824-2874 • City Hall Complex, 75 King St., Saint Augustine, FL 32085

🚗 If you're headed south on Route 1, turn left at King St. The museum is in the former Hotel Alcazar, at the corner of Cordova St. (From A1A southbound, turn right on King.)

🕐 Mon.–Sun. 9 A.M.–5 P.M. Fee.

Oldest Store Museum   It's not as old as Saint Augustine, but it's a 19th-century general store (C. F. Hamblen's). The presentation is touristic, but you can get a sense of what was sold (and how it was sold) and done in such an emporium. You'll find some familiar items, and many we've all forgotten about. *Tours*

📷 904 829-9729 • 4 Artillery Lane, Saint Augustine, FL 32084

🚗 Artillery Lane is the next street south from King St. (*see* Lightner listing). The museum is between Saint George and Aviles streets, behind the Trinity Episcopal Church.

🕐 Mon.–Sat. 9 A.M.–5 P.M., Sun. noon–5 P.M. Fee.

SANIBEL ISLAND

Bailey-Mathews Shell Museum   Sanibel has been the Shell Capital of the World for a long time, but this museum is new to the scene. Not just the local shells, but beauties from all over the world are here—tree snail shells, fossil shells, traditional artworks made with shells, shells worked into valentines—two million shells in all. Displays are educational as well as eye-popping. *Gift Shop, Programs, Library*

📷 941 395-2233 • http://www.coconet.com • 3075 Sanibel-Captiva Rd., Sanibel Island, FL 33957

🚗 Sanibel is in southwestern Florida, southwest of Fort Myers via Route 867, which, on the island, becomes the Sanibel-Captiva Rd. The museum is 0.7 mile west of the Tarpon Bay–Palm Ridge Rd. intersection.

🕐 Tues.–Sun. 10 A.M.–4 P.M. Fee.

TAMPA

Ybor City State Museum   From the 1880s, when it was designed as a company town, until the Depression, Ybor City was the "Cigar Capital of the World," a community of Cuban, Spanish, Italian, and other workers. This was the original center of Florida's Cuban community. Much of what you'll see is in the old Ferlita bakery; nearby is La Casita, a typical cigarmaker's "shotgun" house of the period.

🏠 813 247-6323 • 1818 E. 9th Ave., Tampa, FL 33605

🚗 Ybor City is northeast of downtown Tampa. Take Exit 1 off I-4 and go south on 22nd St., right on Palm Ave., left on 19th St., and right on 9th Ave.

🕐 Museum: Tues.–Sat. 9 A.M.–5 P.M. La Casita: Tues.–Sat. 10 A.M.–3 P.M. Fee.

WHITE SPRINGS

Stephen Foster State Folk Culture Center   This site on the Suwanee River opened as a memorial to the composer (*see also* the Stephen C. Foster Memorial in Pittsburgh, Pennsylvania) in 1950. There's a Stephen Foster Museum and Carillon Tower, with what are said to be the world's largest tubular bells. It's also a folk culture center, and in addition to vernacular buildings and crafts displays, there's a Memorial Day festival. *Gift Shop, Programs*

🏠 904 397-2733 • US 41N, White Springs, FL 32096

🚗 White Springs is in northern Florida, northwest of Lake City on I-75. Exit onto Route 136 and go 3 miles east to the Center, which is also on US 41N.

🕐 Grounds: Mon.–Sun. 8 A.M.–sunset. Museum: Mon.–Sun. 9 A.M.–5 P.M. Fee.

WINTER HAVEN

While you're in the area, see also: Mulberry

Water Ski Museum–Hall of Fame   The first water skis ever made are here, along with boats and motors and a large collection of memorabilia and photographs. The Hall of Fame celebrates the introducers of skiing's styles, including barefoot and jumping. And if you're looking for current action, Cypress Gardens is one mile away. *Library*

🏠 941 324-2472 • 799 Overlook Dr. SE, Winter Haven, FL 33884

🚗 Winter Haven is in central Florida, an hour southwest of Orlando. From I-4, take Hwy 27S for about 16 miles, and turn right on SR 542 (Dundee Rd.). At stoplight, turn left on Carl Floyd Rd., then right on Overlook.

🕐 Mon.–Fri. 10 A.M.–5 P.M. No fee.

WINTER PARK

Charles Hosmer Morse Museum of American Art   There is more of the work of Louis Comfort Tiffany, the great artist in glass, in this museum than anywhere else in the world. There are stained-glass windows, blown glass, and lamps, along with furniture, jewelry, pottery, and other decorative arts. American painters of the turn of the century are also well represented. *Tours*

■ 407 645-5311 • 445 Park Ave. North, Winter Park, FL 32789

🚗 Winter Park is on the northeast side of Orlando. Take the Fairbanks exit off I-4E to Park Ave., and go left for 4 traffic lights.

🕓 Tues.–Sat. 9:30 A.M.–4 P.M., Sun. 1 P.M.–4 P.M. Fee. Call for tour reservations.

GEORGIA

Peaches, presidents, peanuts, pecans, plantations, paper pulp . . . and Pogo. To us, Georgia always makes us think of that wonderful character and his political friends out in the Okefenokee Swamp. Which you too can visit, way down in Waycross.

What's Big: Civil War artifacts are everywhere; one of the most intriguing museums is Kennesaw's Big Shanty Museum, which features the story of the great locomotive chase; there's also the Confederate Naval Museum in Columbus, the Museum of Aviation in Warner Robins; the National Prisoner of War Museum in Andersonville; and Atlanta's Civil War Cyclorama. Up in Calhoun is the New Echota State Historic Site—the remains of the last Cherokee Nation capital in Georgia and the start of the Trail of Tears. Folk art is also big, and besides Finster and Pasaquan, there's the Georgia Guidestones in Nuberg, and Mrs. Pope's Museum in Cairo. And finally, in the not-too-distant future, we hear a right proper peanut museum will be opening in Ashburn.

ATLANTA

The town once known as Terminus, then Marthaville, is not just Coke and CNN. The capitol building is quite remarkable, and while we cover the Uncle Remus Museum in Eatonton, The Wren's Nest, Remus author Joel Chandler Harris' Atlanta home, is a good stop too. The carefully restored Fox Theatre offers tours of one of the last great movie palace "atmospherics." There's also the special Michael C. Carlos Museum at Emory University, the APEX African-American Museum, and a CNN tour that features memorabilia from its classic MGM films archive. And, a few miles south in Jonesboro, the Pope-Dickson Funeral Home (770 478-7211) keeps an odd and rare collection of Egyptian embalming instruments. You must call first for location though, since viewing is limited to Mr. Baxter Bedell's traveling lectures.

Center for Puppetry Arts   Not just for kids. Over 200 puppets—including ancient ceremonial clay puppets from Mexico, traditional Indonesian shadow puppets, Italian rod marionettes in battle armor, and electronically animated figures—provide a terrific glimpse of a global form of art and communication. Punctuated by live performances, hands-on exhibits, and videos with both an adult and kid bent, there's fun here for all. *Tours, Hands-on, Programs, Library, Screenings*

■ 404 873-3391 • 1404 Spring St. NW, Atlanta, GA 30309
🚗 In midtown, Exit 102 from I-75/85. It's between Peachtree St. and I-75/85 at 18th St. MARTA: N-S/Arts Center.
🕐 Mon.–Sat. 9 A.M.–4 P.M. Fee.

Johnny Mercer Museum   Mr. "Moon River" himself is celebrated with memorabilia from his life and career as lyricist for over 640 tunes, with at least one immortalized by Andy Williams.

■ 404 651-2477 • Georgia State University, Pullen Library/Special Collections Dept., 8th Floor, 103 Decatur St., Atlanta, GA 30303
🚗 Downtown, 1 block from the World of Coca-Cola. MARTA: E-W/GSU.
🕐 Mon.–Fri. 9 A.M.–5 P.M. No fee.

Robert C. Williams American Museum of Papermaking   The ancient art of papermaking is represented by artifacts dating back to 2000 B.C. along with early papermaking machinery. Over 20,000 unique watermarks are in this collection, as are samples of materials that served as precursors to the primarily fiber-based paper we know today. Particularly appealing is the selection of decorated and marbled papers on display. *Tours*

■ 404 894-7840 • http://www.ipst.edu/amp/ • Institute of Paper Science and Technology, 500 10th St. NW, Atlanta, GA 30318
🚗 In midtown, Exit 101 from I-75/85, heading west on 10th St. It's just past Hemphill Ave. on the left. MARTA: N-S/10th St.
🕐 Mon.–Fri. 8:30 A.M.–5 P.M. Donation. Request tours in advance.

Telephone Museum   This is a well-thought-through history of telephones from Mr. Bell's first experiments through the wonder of fiber optics. "Electric Toys" to Western Union at the beginning, the units on display date back to 1876. Vintage switchboards and modern switching units are displayed along with exhibits on the history of the service industry itself. *Tours, Hands-on*

■ 404 223-3661/Tours: 404 529-0971 • BellSouth Center, 675 W. Peachtree St. NE, Atlanta, GA 30375
🚗 In midtown, Exit 100 from I-75/85. It's next to the Fox Theatre, between 3rd St. and Ponce de Leon Ave., on the 2nd floor (Plaza Level) of the shorter of BellSouth's 2 buildings. MARTA: N-S/North Ave.
🕐 Mon.–Fri. 11 A.M.–1 P.M. Additional tour hours by appointment. No fee.

William Breman Jewish Heritage Museum   Part of what's different about this museum is the Door Number One/Door Number Two choice as you enter. That is, while both sections coalesce into the larger picture of Atlanta's Jewish heritage, you may begin with the Holocaust and its effect on local families, or with the first Jewish immigrants to the area in 1845, and trace how that community grew and changed over time. The approach results in a rich and varied picture of a lively and thriving minority culture. *Gift Shop, Hands-on, Programs, Library*

● 404 873-1661 • The Selig Center, 1440 Spring St. NW, Atlanta, GA 30309

🚗 In midtown, Exit 102 from I-75/85. It's adjacent to the Center for Puppetry Arts at 18th St. MARTA: N-S/Arts Center.

🕐 Mon.–Thurs. 10 A.M.–5 P.M., Fri. 10 A.M.–3 P.M., Sun. 1 P.M.–5 P.M.

BUENA VISTA

Pasaquan   While Buena Vista no longer has the draw of the questionably lamented Elvis Presley Collection, the work of Saint EOM (aka Eddie Owens Martin) is still here for all to see. A sharecropper's son and former NY street hustler turned visionary, he came to believe, among other revelations about the future of the universe, that "hair was a spiritual antenna" and tried to grow his straight up. The four-acre complex of hand-built concrete, carved wood, and hammered aluminum pagodas, temples, and serpentine walls—all brightly hued with the best of Sherwin-Williams in swirling patterns and mystical symbolism—is based on the late artist's vision that we must learn the ways of the "ancients" if we are to survive into the future.

● 912 649-9444 • http://www.shockoestudios.com/steom.htm • County Rd. 78, Buena Vista, GA 31803

🚗 About 30 miles east of Columbus. Take Hwy 137N from Buena Vista Town Square, taking the left fork at Moon's Mini-Mart. Then take the second paved road (County Rd. 78) on your right after the fork. Pasaquan is a half-mile up on the right.

🕐 Sat. 10 A.M.–6 P.M., Sun. 1 P.M.–6 P.M., and by appointment. Fee.

COLUMBUS

Columbus has a lot going for it besides having been the site of the '96 Summer Olympics' exciting Women's Fast Pitch Softball games. We should note, however, that one of our favorite spots—The Lunchbox Museum—has moved just over the Alabama border, to Salem. In the Columbus area, don't forget about FDR's "Little White House" in Warm Springs; Plains, Georgia, home of Jimmy, Rosalyn, and Billy Carter, is not far to the southeast. And, yes, Billy's service station is still there. *While you're in the area, see also*: Buena Vista. *In Alabama, see*: Hurtsboro, Salem.

Gertrude Pridgett "Ma" Rainey House   "Mother of the Blues" Ma Rainey's home when she died in 1939. She is known as much today for opening doors in the recording industry to other black performers as for her powerful blues and gospel vocal style. Until the city raises funds for a complete rehabilitation, you can look at the deteriorating house from the outside only. Just a few blocks away at 821 8th Ave. is the Liberty Theater, where, from 1925 through the entire era of segregation, black luminaries like Duke Ellington, Marian Anderson, and Ella Fitzgerald might be found in performance. It's well into the process of restoration as a performing arts center, and a memorabilia exhibit is part of the design plan.

■ 800 999-1613 (Visitor Bureau) • 805 5th Ave., Columbus, GA 31901
🚗 Between 8th and 9th Sts.
🕐 24-hour access to exterior only.

DAHLONEGA

Dahlonega Courthouse Gold Museum   Well, the gold is pretty much gone now, and chicken-raising seems to be the thing to do, but there's still plenty to ponder at the site of one of our nation's earliest gold rushes. Like, the irony of de Soto's fruitless search in these parts just three centuries earlier, or the role the 1828 discovery had in the removal of the Cherokee. It is fascinating to learn about the strikes here in the east (*see* Reed Gold Mine in Stanfield, North Carolina also), when we more likely think of them being a western thing. Lots of mining apparatus, gold nuggets and dust, and a how-to film, 19th-century style, housed in an 1838 Greek Revival courthouse. About 20 miles to the northeast is the ersatz Bavarian burg of Helen.

■ 706 864-2257 • Public Square, Dahlonega, GA 30533
🚗 From Atlanta, take Route 19N about 60 miles.
🕐 Mon.–Sat. 9 A.M.–5 P.M., Sun. 10 A.M.–5 P.M. Fee.

DALTON

Crown Gardens and Archives/Bedspread Museum   The story is, young Catherine Evans made a hand-tufted bedspread and thus revived a century-old craft. The next thing you know, Dalton is the "Carpet Capital of the World." Oh yes, the technology, while no longer used in bedspreads, is still the rage in floor coverings. So here, tucked in the old offices of the Crown Cotton Mills, is the Bedspread Museum, to tell us about the origin and growth of this industry. Civil War stuff here too. *Publications, Library*

■ 706 278-0217 • 715 Chattanooga Ave., Dalton, GA 30720

🚗 About 90 miles northwest of Atlanta. Take I-75 to Exit 136, go east on Walnut Ave. to Thornton, turn left to Tyler, turn right, then turn left onto Chattanooga.

🕐 Tues.–Fri. 10 A.M.–5 P.M., Sat. 9 A.M.–1 P.M. Donation.

EATONTON

Uncle Remus Museum   Joel Chandler Harris grew up here (as did Alice Walker) and became steeped in the trickster and wisdom stories imparted through his friendship with George Terrell, a former slave. Harris developed these tales from black and African folklore during his journalism career, using the voices of Uncle Remus and Br'er Rabbit and preserving both dialect and oral tradition in the process. The museum, built from former slave cabins, re-creates a home where these stories might have been told; original editions and carvings of the characters are on display.

📱 706 485-6856 • Hwy 441S, Eatonton, GA 31024

🚗 About 80 miles east of Atlanta. Take I-20 to US 129/441S into Eatonton, then go 3 blocks south on 441 to Turner Park.

🕐 Mon.–Sat. 10 A.M.–5 P.M. (closed 1 hour at lunchtime), Sun. 2 P.M.–5 P.M. Sept.–May: Closed Tues. Fee.

ELBERTON

Elberton Granite Museum and Exhibit   Everything granite, and you'll definitely want to make this your first stop if your plan is to visit the nearby mysterious Georgia Guidestones, just one of America's answers to Stonehenge. A film and special display explain it all for you, but do take a look at the rest of this austere museum's exhibits—this is a *big* industry here, and the historical tools and quarrying photos are worth a look too.

📱 706 283-2551 • One Granite Plaza, Elberton, GA 30635

🚗 Thirty-six miles east of Athens, museum is a half-mile west of town on Route 72/17. For the Georgia Guidestones, go all the way into town and turn north on Route 77 for about 7 miles.

🕐 Jan. 15–Nov. 15: Mon.–Sun. 2 P.M.–5 P.M. Hours vary rest of year. No fee.

FORT GORDON

U.S. Army Signal Corps Museum   Think about how important communications are in any military endeavor, and you'll get an idea why the army has put special effort into the preserving and cataloguing of these items that each represent an accomplishment in communication development and design. Have a look at the Wig-Wag flags used in the Civil War, early telegraph keying mechanisms,

Navajo code talker displays, and the sophisticated microwave equipment used in Vietnam. Items of "foreign design" are represented by a cache of captured equipment from the Iraqis in Desert Storm. *Library*

🏛 706 791-3856/2818 • Building 36305, Fort Gordon, Fort Gordon, GA 30905

🚗 About 10 miles southwest of Augusta, take I-20S onto Bel Air Rd. Enter Fort Gordon at Gate 1; it's at 37th St. and Ave. of the States.

🕐 Tues.–Fri. 8 A.M.–4 P.M., Sat. noon–5 P.M. No fee.

SAVANNAH

Juliette Gordon Low Girl Scout National Center All that early Girl Scout stuff—the badges, the stars, the uniforms—is collected here, along with a nice overview of the quite remarkable founder of the U.S. Scouts. *Tours*

🏛 912 233-4501 • 142 Bull St., Savannah, GA 31401

🚗 Take I-16E into Savannah. I-16E will go right into Montgomery St. Get in the right lane, go past the Civic Center, then turn right onto Oglethorpe Ave. to Bull St.

🕐 Mon.–Tues., Thurs.–Sat. 10 A.M.–4 P.M.; Sun. 11 A.M.–4:30 P.M. Fee.

SUMMERVILLE

Paradise Garden The 800 number is a tip-off, and by now, many have heard about Paradise Garden and its creator, the visionary artist and mechanic-preacher Rev. Howard Finster. But all the attention of the press, and all the placement of his *objets* (there were over 36,000 items in the now-diminishing collection at last count) in museums monolithic, doesn't seem to have affected his work, nor his message. And the Garden—with its intricate constructions of painted and adorned busted machines and street finds—is full of messages. Take your bifocals, and be prepared to experience the divine and sacred as filtered through the hands of Mr. Finster.

🏛 800 FINSTER [346-7837] • Route 2, Box 113, Rena St., Summerville, GA 30747

🚗 Northwest Georgia. Follow I-75N to Exit 128, turning left onto Hwy 140W. At the end, turn right onto US 27N for about 14 miles to Summerville, then continuing on about 3 more miles into Pennville. Look for the Smile gas station, then take the 3rd right, at the Paradise Garden sign.

🕐 Mon.–Sun. 10 A.M.–6 P.M. Fee (except on Tues.). Note: Howard Finster is on-site every Sun. 2 P.M.–5 P.M.

HAWAII

Unless you live here, it seems pretty likely that the first thing on your mind when planning a trip is not what museums you should be trying to fit into your itinerary. No, this tropical paradise, land of surf, sun, and an exotic blend of cultures, more likely beckons for other reasons. But, hey, while you're in the neighborhood, perhaps when there's just a tiny bit of cloud cover, you'll have an urge to prowl indoors, and what rich rewards you have ahead of you. More than just Gidget and the Big Kahuna.

What's Big: Pineapples (the entire island of Lanai is owned by Dole) and the sugar industry. Hop over to Molokai for the restored 1878 R. W. Meyer Sugar Mill. And volcanoes. Geology and state-of-the-art seismology exhibits are the focus at the Jaggar Museum near Hawaii's still quite active Kilauea volcano, where you can also visit the goddess Pele. For a review of the history and royal ancestry on Hawaii, see the Lyman Museum/Mission House and the Huliheʻe Palace, and on Oahu, the ʻIolani Palace. And big in theme if not size is the new North Shore Surf and Cultural Museum in Honolulu.

HAWAII (THE BIG ISLAND)

CAPTAIN COOK

Royal Aloha Coffee Mill and Museum   More mill than museum, but their 1906 beautiful old coffee roaster is still on daily duty. And while you're appreciating the aroma, or a cup or two, take a quick tour of the other old mill equipment, historic photos, and a bottle and artifact collection dating back to the 1860s. The gen-u-ine snake oil bottle, complete with snake, is a highlight. Down the road a bit is the Saint Benedict Painted Church, known for its vibrant, biblically themed murals in tropical colors.

▪ 800 KONA BOY [566-2269]/808 328-9851 • 160 Napoopoo Rd., Captain Cook, HI 96704

🚙 Southwest coast. Traveling on Route 11, between mile markers 110 and 111 in Captain Cook, turn off toward the ocean onto Napoopoo Rd. It's about 3.5 miles, on the right.

🕐 Mon.–Sun. 9 A.M.–6 P.M. No fee.

KAMUELA

Parker Ranch Visitor Center and Museum   We know you think Texas when you think ranch, but think again. Parker Ranch—one of the largest and still fully operational in the United States—was founded by John Palmer Parker, a Massachusetts sailor who jumped ship in 1809, managed King Kamehameha I's fish ponds, came into two acres of Mauna Kea land when he married the king's granddaughter, and kept on going. The displays celebrate the life and times of the *paniolo*, or island cowboys. The original 1800s tack room has been moved here, and a video with footage from 1947 shows you ranch action. There are also slices of home life, with a spectacular selection of antique quilts and family Bibles. *Tours*

💼 808 885-7655 • Parker Ranch Shopping Center, Kamuela, HI 96743

🚙 North-central. At the junction of Routes 19 and 190.

🕐 Mon.–Sun. 9 A.M.–5 P.M. Fee. No ranch visitors, but tours of related sites available.

KEALAKEKUA

Kona Historical Society Museum   Here in Kona coffee country, visit this small local-history museum, steeped in the coffee industry dating back to the late 1820s. Try to schedule a visit so you can tour nearby Uchida Coffee Farm, now being turned into a living history museum. *Tours*

💼 808 323-2005 • Mamalahoa Hwy, Kealakekua, HI 96750

🚙 Southwest coast. Near Captain Cook, in the historic Greenwell Store on the makai (ocean) side of Route 11, between mile markers 111 and 112, next to Greenwell Farms.

🕐 Museum: Mon.–Fri. 9 A.M.–3 P.M. Tours by reservation only: Tues., Thurs. 9 A.M. Fee.

KOHALA COAST

Eva Parker Woods Cottage   This restored 1920s cottage has been filled with artifacts that are meant to evoke the deeply felt *Kalahuipua'a*, or "spirit of place," attributed to the ancient Hawaiians. Samples of *tapa*, a ti-leaf cape, fishhooks, and feather leis are on display, along with replicas of items from A.D. 1200–1700 made by local artisans. But a far more complete picture is to be found on a tour of the area with the resident historian, who will show you remarkable archaeological remains and an extensive petroglyph preserve, the 2,300-year-old freshwater fish ponds, and native flora that have played key roles in medicine and religion besides as a foodstuff, throughout local history.

🏠 808 885-4830 • Mauna Lani Bay Hotel, One Mauna Lani Dr., Kohala Coast, HI 96743
🚗 On the Kohala (northwest) Coast, near Puako off Route 19 (Queen Kaahumanu Hwy).
🕐 Tues. 3 P.M.–4:30 P.M., Wed. 2:15 P.M.–4:15 P.M., Thurs. 9 A.M.–10 A.M. Tours: Tues.–Thurs., Sat. No Fee.

MAUI

LAHAINA

Wo Hing Temple Museum   Before the missionaries and the whalers even, just ten years after James Cook's 1778 "discovery" of the islands, the Chinese established themselves as a vital component of life in Maui. Employed in the plantations and sugar mills, as tunnel-builders and workers on the island irrigation systems, they maintained strong ties to their homeland. The Wo Hing Society, and its temple, served to support those ties and the local community. That history and community are evoked through early Thomas Edison films from 1898 and 1906 and the restored altar room, art, and antiquities on display. *Tours*

🏠 808 661-5553/3262 • 858 Front St., Lahaina, HI 96761
🚗 Northwest coast. About 2 blocks from the harbor area, just past Lahainaluna Rd.
🕐 Mon.–Sun. 10 A.M.–4 P.M. Walking tour of area available.

PUUNENE

Alexander and Baldwin Sugar Museum   Sugar, while not the power-house it used to be, is still king—at least of the agricultural sector of Hawaii's economy. Built into the former plantation superintendent's house, just down the road from the still-working mill, this award-winning six-room museum brings to life—through carefully conceived groupings of historic photos, clothing, and arti-facts like lunch pails and labor contracts—a picture of a multi-ethnic workforce and the complex industry it supported. *Gift Shop*

🏠 808 871-8058 • 3957 Hansen Rd., Puunene, HI 96784
🚗 North-central, 10 minutes from the Kahului airport, at the intersection of Puunene Ave. (Route 311/350) and Hansen Rd., a half-mile from Dairy Rd. (Route 380).
🕐 July–Aug.: Mon.–Sun. 9:30 A.M.–4:30 P.M.; Sept.–June: Mon.–Sat. 9:30 A.M.–4:30 P.M. Fee.

WAILUKU

Bailey House Museum (Maui Historical Society Museum)   Featuring pre-contact artifacts including tapa (barkcloth), feather articles, and shell implements, this former female seminary from 1833 also houses the stuff that comprised the pioneer's life of a 19th-century missionary. They also have on hand one of the great duke's (Kahanamoku, that is) redwood surfboards and a few other surprises.

🏛 808 244-3326 • 2314-A Main St., Wailuku, HI 96793

🚌 Northwest, at the junction of Routes 320 and 30.

🕐 Mon.–Sat. 10 A.M.–4 P.M. Fee.

OAHU

EWA

Hawaiian Railway Society   Ride in an open gondola or a covered car in this ex–U.S. Navy 45-ton Whitcomb diesel locomotive straight to the crashing surf at the water's edge. The train lines here—converted from narrow gauge during World War II—date back to 1890, served the sugar mills and plantations, then carried troops and military supplies before closing down in 1947. The narrated historic tour takes you through island ghost towns, and ends with a chance to look at some unique rolling stock in the process of restoration. *Gift Shop*

🏛 808 681-5461 • http://www.nmc.csulb.edu/users/trains • 91-1001 Renton Rd., Ewa, HI 96706

🚌 Southwest coast. Take H-1 west, Exit 5A, drive south 2.5 miles, turn right onto Renton Rd., and go 1.5 miles to end.

🕐 1.5-hour round trips depart Sun. 12:30 P.M. and 2:30 P.M. Weekday schedule varies. Fee.

HONOLULU

Damien Museum and Archives   Tucked behind a Catholic Church, a short hop away from the glitz and pizzazz of Waikiki, is this small tribute to the life of Father Damien, a man remembered for his work and devotion in easing the lives of victims of Hansen's Disease (leprosy), a community exiled to the island of Molokai by the Hawaiian government in 1864.

🏛 808 923-2690 • 130 Ohua Ave., Honolulu, HI 96815

🚌 In Waikiki, between Kuhio and Kalakaua Aves., 3 blocks from the Honolulu Zoo.

🕐 Mon.–Fri. 9 A.M.–3 P.M., Sat. 9 A.M.–noon. Donation.

Japanese Cultural Center of Hawaii   The history of the Japanese in Hawaii from the first immigration in 1868 through the 1960s is explored through artifacts and photographs of daily home, work, and religious life. A video on the Japanese-American men in the 442nd and 100th Battalions complements the permanent exhibit; a teahouse and martial arts *dojo* round out the picture. *Food*

🏠 808 945-7633 • 2454 S. Beretania St., Honolulu, HI 96826

🚗 In downtown Honolulu, heading toward Waikiki.

🕐 Wed.–Sun. 10 A.M.–4 P.M. Fee.

Judiciary History Center   Tells the story of the unique transition of Hawaiian judicial history from the days under a monarchy to its change to a western legal system in 1893. Special exhibits focus on topics like the extreme effects on daily life in Hawaii under martial law during World War II. *Tours*

🏠 808 539-4999/548-3163 • Ali'iolani Hale, 417 S. King St., Honolulu, HI 96813

🚗 Between Mililani and Punchbowl Sts., across from the 'Iolani Palace.

🕐 Tues.–Thurs. 10 A.M.–3 P.M. Tours available Mon.–Fri. No fee.

IDAHO

▼▼

Until the Snake River Valley got irrigated (making those "famous potatoes," among other things, possible), Idaho was p-r-e-t-t-y sparsely populated. Gold rushers built their mad cities, but those boomed and died in the midst of an awful lot of Nowhere. Today there's still a lot of Nowhere, but it is attracting Nowhere Seekers—and not just survivalists and Rapture-awaiters, but the kind of people who've always headed for the exurb. So Idaho is becoming Somewhere. Look at the Boise area: The people you saw in California last year are probably here now. How do its museums reflect Idaho? If you can make sense of this variety, let us know.

What's Big: Nothing, yet—but don't wait too long!

ARCO

Experimental Breeder Reactor #1   This is *really* the middle of Nowhere, and for that reason was chosen after World War II for the development of nuclear reactors. EBR-1 became the first reactor in the world to produce usable electricity, Arco the first town to use it. You may tour the site; see and have explained to you the "pioneer" phase of the nuclear age. *Tours*

🏛 208 526-0050 • at the Idaho National Engineering Laboratories, Arco, ID 83213

🚗 It's about 20 miles east of Arco, in south-central Idaho, along Route 20/26; look for signs. Or take Route 20W from Idaho Falls.

🕐 June–Aug.: Mon.–Sun. 8 A.M.–4 P.M. Rest of year: by appointment. No fee.

BLACKFOOT

Idaho's World Potato Exposition   Some Idahoans may wish they'd never heard of potatoes, but not these folks: This is russet country. At the Exposition, you'll see tools and equipment used in growing spuds, examples of potato products (including the World's Largest Potato Chip), and other exhibits on the industry and the life of potato farmers. *Tours, Gift Shop, Screenings*

🔌 208 785-2517 • 130 NW Main St., Blackfoot, ID 83221

🚗 Blackfoot is in southeastern Idaho, midway between Idaho Falls and Pocatello, on I-15 and Routes 26 and 91. The Exposition is right in the center.

🕐 June–Labor Day: Mon.–Sat. 9 A.M.–7 P.M., Sun. 10 A.M.–5 P.M. May, Sept., and Oct.: closed Sun. Fee.

BOISE

While you're in the area, see also: Idaho City

Basque Museum and Cultural Center   The Basques, those mysterious people of the Pyrenees, first arrived in Idaho late in the 19th century, when men were recruited for the lonely job of sheepherding. Boise became their urban resort. The museum details their music, dance, sports and games (there's a *fronton*), and work and family lives in America. *Tours, Gift Shop, Programs, Library*

🔌 208 343-2671 • 611 Grove St., Boise, ID 83702

🚗 The museum is in central Boise, 5 blocks from the capitol. Take the Vista Ave. exit off I-84 and go up Capitol Blvd., turning right on Grove.

🕐 Tues.–Fri. 11 A.M.–4 P.M., Sat. 11 A.M.–3 P.M. Donation.

Old Idaho Penitentiary/History of Electricity in Idaho Museum   This popular site held Idaho's bad guys and gals from 1870 until 1973, and you can get an idea of what life (and in some cases, death) was like in this place at that time. Balls and chains, "the hole," gallows, rogues' gallery, tattoo art, etc. One building houses the History of Electricity in Idaho Museum, which, despite what you were thinking, is all about turning on the current *outside* these walls. *Tours*

🔌 208 368-6080 • 2445 Old Penitentiary Rd., Boise, ID 83701

🚗 Old Penitentiary Rd. is 2 miles southeast of downtown, via Warm Springs Ave.

🕐 Memorial Day–Sept.: Mon.–Sun. 10 A.M.–6 P.M. Rest of year: Mon.–Sun. noon–5 P.M. Fee.

BONANZA

Yankee Fork Gold Dredge   If you want to see what eventually became of the gold rush, visit the Yankee Fork Dredge, which operated until the early 1950s. Dredging caused enormous damage, visible along many western rivers. At the Interpretive Center outside Challis, you may see video and other exhibits on the mines and history of this remote area. *Tours*

🔌 208 879-5244 • Bonanza, ID

🚗 The dredge is just northeast of Bonanza and southwest of Custer, on the Yankee Fork Rd., in the Challis Natl. Forest, deep in central Idaho. The Land of the Yankee Fork Historic Area Interpretive Center is just south of Challis, at the Route 93/75 junction.

🕐 Interpretive Center open year-round. Call for hours and for Yankee Fork Dredge tour information. No fee for Interpretive Center; fee for Dredge tour.

HAILEY

Blaine County Historical Museum   This little museum has a typical range of local historical materials but also, surprisingly, is home to the Joe Fuld Political Button Collection, with items from the 1840s on. There's also an exhibit on a notorious native, the poet Ezra Pound.

■ 208 788-4185 • Main St. and Galena, Hailey, ID 83333

🚗 Hailey is in south-central Idaho, south of Sun Valley. Main St. is Route 75; the museum is at the north end of town.

🕐 June–Sept.: Mon., Wed.–Sat. 11 A.M.–5 P.M. Other times by appointment.

IDAHO CITY

Boise Basin Museum   In 1863 Idaho City was the largest city in the Northwest—because thousands of placer miners had just arrived looking for the Boise Basin's gold. The museum tells the story of those days, and there are walking tours of the town, which, having failed to become Idaho's capital, became a sort of museum itself. *Tours*

■ 208 392-4550 • Montgomery and Wall Sts., Idaho City, ID 83631

🚗 Idaho City is 38 miles northeast of Boise up Route 21. Turn left onto Montgomery St.

🕐 Memorial Day–Labor Day: Mon.–Sun. 11 A.M.–4 P.M. In May, weekends only. Fee.

MOSCOW

While you're in the area, see also: Pullman, WA

Appaloosa Horse Club Museum   This little museum is dedicated both to the Appaloosa horse and to the Nez Perce, the people of the Oregon/Washington/Idaho border who developed the breed. If you visit in summer, some Appaloosa themselves may be seen outside.

■ 208 882-5578 • Hwy 8, Moscow, ID 83843

🚗 It's on Hwy 8 west of Moscow, on the Washington border.

🕐 Mon.–Fri. 8 A.M.–5 P.M. No fee.

REXBURG

Teton Flood Museum   The June 5, 1976, flood occurred when a newly completed dam upstream on the Teton River failed, inundating Rexburg and vicinity. The museum also has pioneer life exhibits. *Gift Shop, Publications, Screenings*

🏛 208 356-9101 • 51 N. Center, Rexburg, ID 83440

🚗 Rexburg is in southeastern Idaho, northeast of Idaho Falls, on Route 20.

🕐 June–Aug.: Mon.–Sat. 10 A.M.–5 P.M. Rest of year: Mon.–Fri. 11 A.M.–4 P.M. Donation.

RIGBY

Farnsworth TV Pioneer Museum (Jefferson County Historical Society)   Much of American culture seems to be television inventing the West. To stand all that on its head, here's a museum that shows the West inventing television. Philo T. Farnsworth (1906–71) grew up in this small town, and he, kids, is the guy who brought electronics into the business of transmitting pictures.

🏛 208 745-8423 • 118 W. 1st South, Rigby, ID 83442

🚗 Rigby is in southeastern Idaho, between Rexburg and Idaho Falls on US 20.

🕐 Tues.–Sat. 1 P.M.–5 P.M. or by appointment. Fee.

WEISER

National Oldtime Fiddlers Hall of Fame   Weiser is host each year (in June; call 208 549-0450) to the National Old-Time Fiddlers Contest. If you're not here then, drop by the Hall of Fame and see pictures and memorabilia of past winners, and some of the instruments used. You'll enjoy walking downtown too.

🏛 208 549-0452 • 10 E. Idaho, Weiser, ID 83672

🚗 Weiser is northwest of Boise, on the Oregon border. Exit from I-84 onto Route 95N through Payette. The Hall of Fame is downtown, next to the Chamber of Commerce.

🕐 Mon.–Fri. 9 A.M.–5 P.M. No fee.

ILLINOIS

Illinois is a surprising state. Sometimes we think of it as the state of Chicago: that toddlin' town with its urban energy, architecture unparalleled thanks to the likes of Louis Sullivan and Frank Lloyd Wright, the blues of course, Carl Sandburg, muckraking, political machines, 1968, the Untouchables, and Union Station. But there's the other Illinois, the proverbial "Land of Lincoln," the world of rolling prairies and rich farmlands, the Mississippi River, Mormon settlements, Lewis and Clark, Marquette and Joliet, Route 66, and a protected bit of small-town America.

What's Big: Big and getting bigger all the time is the attention paid to the remnants of old Route 66, which ran through the state from Chicago on its way to L.A. And Illinois is full of roadside remnants, like a giant ketchup bottle. In Chicago not to be missed are the architectural boat tours along the lakeshore, a visit to Frank Lloyd Wright's Oak Park, a stroll through the University of Chicago campus, the Museum of Science and Industry, the Art Institute of Chicago, and the Field Museum. In Batavia, just outside of Chicago, the Fermi National Accelerator Lab is the place to go; in Monmouth is Wyatt Earp's Birthplace; in Collinsville (just across from Saint Louis), head to Cahokia Mounds; in Nauvoo is the Joseph Smith Historic Center; and in Union, there's the Illinois Railway Museum.

ARCOLA

Louis P. Klein Broom and Brush Museum   If the Fuller Brush man had had some of these goodies in his kit bag, perhaps he would never have given up the business. English vanity brushes with delicate carving, Palmer method (think penmanship) pen-tip cleaner brushes in animal shapes, Civil War horse brushes, and even a yak tail from Tibet. While the labeling's a bit weak, the myriad shapes and forms of the brushes and brooms on display are impressive enough. The bonus here, in the "Broom Corn Capital of the World," is that this was also the home of Raggedy Ann's creator, Johnny Gruelle, and you'll find Raggedy's original

1915 patent application sketches here along with Ann and Andy dolls and books. Come here in September—the annual Broom Corn Festival parade features Arcola's own "Lawn Rangers," a precision power lawn mower drill squad.

📷 217 268-4530 • Arcola Depot Welcome Center, 135 N. Oak, Arcola, IL 61910

🚌 In east-central Illinois. Take I-57 Exit 203, onto Route 133W about 1 mile into town.

🕓 May–January: Mon.–Sun. 9 A.M.–5 P.M.

CHICAGO

Alas, the International Cinema Museum is gone (perhaps to resurface somewhere in the Southwest, we're told), but leave some time to visit the fine DuSable Museum of African-American History (312 947-0600) and the Chicago Historical Society (312 642-4600). The Billy Graham Center (630 752-5909) in Wheaton and the Motorola Museum of Electronics (847 576-6559) in Schaumburg are in the vicinity. And the Tooth Fairy Museum (847 945-1129) is just to the north side, in Deerfield. *While you're in the area, see also*: Des Plaines, Evanston, Glenview, Lemont.

American Police Center and Museum   In 1968 the whole world *was* watching, it seemed, and in the years following the Democratic National Convention antiwar protest tumult, the Chicago police began to feel it was time to counter the media—and the Walker Report—image of "rampant police brutality." Retired officer Joe Pecoraro founded the museum in 1974, and its collections span the Prohibition-era gangster years through modern drug and DNA-dependent investigations, as well as those Yippie years when Mayor Richard Daley the elder ruled the Windy City roost. *Tours, Programs, Library, Screenings*

📷 312 431-0005 • 1717 S. State St., Chicago, IL 60616

🚌 At 17th St. in the South Loop, near Chinatown. Bus: #29 State.

🕓 Mon.–Fri. 8:30 A.M.–4:30 P.M. Donation.

Feet First   There really was a Dr. Scholl, and this is where you can find out all about him and the wooden-soled shoes that made him famous. From the low-tech of one of the early ubiquitous fitting devices, a shoe fluoroscope, as well as antique shoes, photos, old catalogues, and memorabilia from the life of William Scholl and his company, to a high-tech computer offering the latest on modern foot surgery. Also features kids and seniors hands-on programs, we imagine leading to lots of future happy feet. *Tours, Hands-on, Programs*

📷 312 280-2487 • http://scholl.edu • College of Podiatric Medicine, 1001 N. Dearborn, Chicago, IL 60610

🚌 River North area, 3 blocks south of Division. Bus: #70 Division.

🕓 Mon., Tues., Fri. 9 A.M.–4 P.M.; Wed., Thurs. 9 A.M.–7 P.M. No fee.

International Museum of Surgical Science and Hall of Immortals

Sometimes it's hard to distinguish ancient torture devices from instruments dedicated to the craft of healing. This historic mansion is packed with a global range of equipment and treatments for you to consider: ancient Peruvian trephination tools, artifacts and illustrations of Eastern medicine's surgical pioneers, battlefield amputation devices, the clever collapsible wooden stethoscope-in-a-top-hat designed by Dr. Theophile Laennec in the 1800s, handmade X-ray tubes and the Victorian X-ray-proof underwear that went with them, an iron lung (the cornerstone of "modern" medicine from the 1950s), and a plethora of cure-alls like Karnak Stomachachic Tonic, and our favorite, Dr. Schiffman's Cigarettes "guaranteed to relieve bronchial distress." *Tours, Programs, Publications, Library*

■ 312 642-6502 • 1524 N. Lake Shore Dr., Chicago, IL 60610

🚗 Between Burton Pl. and North Ave., it's half a block south of the North Ave. exit from Lake Shore Dr. Bus: #151 Sheridan.

🕐 Tues.–Sat. 10 A.M.–4 P.M., Sun. 11 A.M.–5 P.M. Donation.

Museum of Holography
These days, with holograms even on your Master-Card, the edge is off this laser-generated special effects trick. Nevertheless, there's still room to be impressed by the range of projection devices and 3-D imagery on display here.

■ 312 226-1007 • http://www.museumofholography.com • 1134 W. Washington St., Chicago, IL 60607

🚗 From downtown, it's 11 blocks west of State St. Bus: #20 Madison.

🕐 Wed.–Sun. 12:30 P.M.–5 P.M. And by appointment for large groups. Fee.

Peace Museum
A museum about peace is also one about war, human rights, social justice, and change, and the people who have dedicated their lives to these issues. Represented by artifacts reflecting historic attempts to resolve conflict in nonviolent ways, the exhibits are strong on the role of music—one of John Lennon's guitars is here along with a topical music collection—and art, with a powerful group of 20th-century antiwar posters. *Gift Shop, Programs*

■ 312 440-1860 • 314 W. Institute Pl., Chicago, IL 60610

🚗 River North. Half a block north of W. Chicago Ave., between Franklin and Orleans Sts. "El": Ravenswood (Brown)/Chicago Ave.

🕐 Tues.–Sat. 11 A.M.–5 P.M. Fee.

DES PLAINES

McDonald's Museum
Raise your hand if you can remember a world before the Golden Arches. Hmmm. You'd be remembering a world where potatoes were freshly peeled, the burgers—and buns—were grilled, and the Coke and root beer were drawn from barrels. Why, just like the brothers McDonald (Dick and Maurice,

that is) did it in their innovative self-service "Speedee"-logoed operation out in San Berdoo back in 1948. And as you all know from McD 101, Ray Kroc bought them out (in '55), and things have changed a bit. This Des Plaines site was Ray's first (down in Oak Brook at the MickeyD "campus" is the official, invitation-only, Ray Kroc Museum and archive); and while this vintage-looking store is actually a re-creation, it is built to blueprint and loaded with original equipment and memorabilia. You'll have to go to Downey, California, to see a recently restored actual original.

■ 847 297-5022 • 400 N. Lee St., Des Plaines, IL 60016

🚗 Just north of O'Hare Airport. Heading north, take I-294N Dempster West exit onto US 14W (Dempster), then turn right onto Lee.

🕐 Mid-Apr.–mid-Oct. only. June–Aug.: Wed.–Sat. 10 A.M.–4 P.M., Sun. 1 P.M.–4 P.M. Other times closed Mon., Tues., Thurs. No fee.

EDWARDSVILLE

Louis H. Sullivan Architectural Ornament Collection   Southern Illinois University at Edwardsville is no slouch in its preservation and presentation of its impressive art, architectural, and ethnographic collections. But what's unique here are the salvaged Louis Sullivan architectural details. The beautiful terra cotta façade ornaments and treatments in other materials are found on display in buildings throughout the campus, but the heart of the collection is in Lovejoy Library and Classroom Building II.

■ 618 692-2996 • The University Museum, Southern Illinois University at Edwardsville, Edwardsville, IL 62026

🚗 About 25 miles east of St. Louis, Missouri. From I-270, take I-55N and exit onto Route 143W.

🕐 Lovejoy Library: Mon.–Thurs. 8 A.M.–11:30 P.M., Fri. 8 A.M.–9 P.M., Sat. 9 A.M.–5 P.M., Sun. 1 P.M.–9 P.M. No fee.

EVANSTON

Dave's Down to Earth Rock Shop and Prehistoric Life Museum   Like most people's basements, this one is full of some really old stuff, but in this case it's all been identified and labeled, and in fact, you'll even find some rare fossil specimens that have been named after the shop and museum's owner, Dave Douglass. He and wife Sandra, a rock hound herself, have a grand and growing, small but distinctive collection of items from the fossil record, including a sauropod femur, a 1.5-billion-year-old algae colony, a 60-million-year-old butterfly, a six-inch shark, and the semi-eponymous giant scorpion, *Titanoscorpio douglassi*.

■ 847 866-7374 • 704 Main St., Evanston, IL 60202

🚐 At the north end of Chicago, half a block west of Chicago Ave.

🕐 Mon., Tues., Thurs., Fri. 10:30 A.M.–5:30 P.M.; Sat. 10 A.M.–5 P.M. No fee.

GLENVIEW

Hartung's License Plate and Automotive Museum Lee Hartung is the license plate king, and while you might happily browse his motorcycle collection dating back to 1901, or the wide range of generally rolling types of items on display—bikes, autos, trucks, and tractors among them—he's proudest of the plates. And why not? He's got them for all 50 states and most of Canada too, starting from first issue to present years. But do be sure to leave time for the radiator caps, spark plugs, hood ornaments, and car nameplates as well.

🏠 847 724-4354 • 3623 W. Lake Ave., Glenview, IL 60025

🚐 About 20 miles north of Chicago. Off I-94, Exit 34B-C, west onto Lake Ave.

🕐 Mon.–Fri. hours vary, Sat.–Sun. usually 10 A.M.–4 P.M. Donation.

LEMONT

Cookie Jar Museum Who stole the cookies from the cookie jar? No matter, you're bound to be distracted anyway by the bounty of shapes and forms found in this changing collection of some 2,000 hand-painted biscuit and cookie jars from around the world, a few dating as far back as the 1880s. Owner Lucille Bromberek has fun setting them out in tableaux (like keeping the lions with the lambs), and she's quite convincing when she conjures up the secret night life of her favorite "party animals" for you.

🏠 630 257-5012 • 111 Stephen St., Lemont, IL 60439

🚐 About 20 miles southwest of Chicago. I-55 Exit 271A-B (Lemont S), 3 miles into town.

🕐 Mon.–Sun. 10 A.M.–2 P.M. Fee.

MCLEAN

Dixie Truckers Home and Route 66 Hall of Fame McLean is tucked along one of the remaining bits of Route 66 and the Dixie Truckers Home truck stop has been serving up road food staples to a trucking—and a wandering—crowd since 1928. The Hall of Fame here is dedicated to Illinois people who have helped make the Mother Road a living memory. They may be no-names to you and me—a 75-year-old waitress or a veteran gas station owner, for instance—but they and the lost buildings and landmarks shown in the photographs on display here really do the job of evoking a time when travel wasn't just one generic interstate turnout after another. The long-awaited Route 66 Depot Museum, located opposite the Dixie, should be open by now. *Gift Shop, Food*

🖼 309 874-2323 • McLean, IL 61754

🚗 Forty-eight miles northeast of Springfield, at I-55 and US 136.

🕐 Mon.–Sun. 24 hrs/day. No fee for exhibits.

METROPOLIS

Super Museum   Metropolis may be the last place in America with an actual phone booth. But where else would Superman change his clothes? They've also got a newspaper called the *Metropolis Planet*, and a 15-foot-tall statue of the Supe himself. If all that isn't enough to tell you this town takes its name heritage seriously, then get over to the museum, where Jim Hambrick shares his collection of items from the life and times of the man of steel. Especially strong on the '50s TV show (and George Reeves' costumes and baggy tights), there's tons of stuff going back to the first *Action* comic in 1938, the '40s radio show, various movie series, on up to the modern TV version. Beware the lingering effects of kryptonite as you depart. For those who prefer to travel on land, don't miss the world's longest truss span bridge, crossing the Ohio River into Kentucky. Or, while you're still on the Illinois side, you might want to check out a new museum dedicated to a more earthly mineral, fluorspar. About 50 miles to the northeast, the American Fluorite Museum (618 287-3192) is on an old mining site in Rosiclare.

🖼 618 524-5518 • 517 Market St., Metropolis, IL 62960

🚗 In southern Illinois, at the Kentucky border. I-57S, to I-24 Exit 37 (Metropolis).

🕐 Mon.–Sun. 9 A.M.–9 P.M. Fee.

MOLINE

Deere & Co. Administrative Center   Moline calls itself the "Farm Implement Capital of America" and owes it all to John Deere. Mr. Deere, a blacksmith originally from Vermont, saw a lot of banged-up iron plows. With one of those blinding flashes of insight he saw that plows must be made from steel instead, to withstand the dense loamy soil of Illinois, and with that he changed the course of American farming. Early Deere farm tools date back to 1837, and you can see them here along with the most high-tech modern industrialized farming equipment, housed in the surprising and equally modern Eero Saarinen–designed administrative center. *Tours, Gift Shop, Library*

🖼 309 765-4793/4235 • John Deere Rd., Moline, IL 61265

🚗 In northwest Illinois, across from Davenport, IA, on Route 5 (John Deere Rd.), on the south side of town. Call for exact directions.

🕐 Mon.–Fri. 9 A.M.–4:30 P.M. Video shown at 10:30 A.M. and 1:30 P.M. No fee.

MOUNT VERNON

Wheels Through Time Museum   There was a time, around World War I, when the military might have selected Harley-Davidson's three-wheeled motorcycle prototype as its utility vehicle. That contract went to the Jeep, though that didn't stop Harleys (and Indians and other early bike manufacturers) from claiming their spot in the history and lore of American motorcycling. One hundred thirty of the rarest American motorcycles and associated memorabilia, advertising, and art. *Tours, Gift Shop*

■ 618 244-4116/4118 • Route 1, Veterans Memorial Dr., Mount Vernon, IL 62864

🚗 South-central Illinois. I-57 Exit 95 (Mount Vernon). Go east on Route 15 to Veterans Memorial Dr. Turn south and follow road 2.75 miles. Museum is located behind Dale's Harley-Davidson dealership.

🕐 Mon.–Tues., Thurs.–Fri. 9 A.M.–5 P.M.; Sat. 9 A.M.–4 P.M. Wed. by appointment. No fee.

PARK RIDGE

Museum of Anesthesiology   There's a lot to know about getting numb, and here's the place to start. Housed in a small medical museum and library is a variety of anesthesiology equipment, medical history, manuscripts, and a video oral history collection, all of which shows us we've mercifully come a long way since the days of biting a bullet. *Publications, Library*

■ 708 825-5586 • Wood Library, 520 Northwest Hwy, Park Ridge, IL 60068

🚗 Just northeast of O'Hare Airport. I-294N exit onto Touhy Ave. east, to Northwest Hwy.

🕐 Mon.–Fri. 9 A.M.–4:45 P.M. No fee.

QUINCY

Valentine Museum   The whole show is all of two glass cases, but that's because a number of these sweet and saucy valentines are tucked between the covers of old albums. Run by tenants of this 1933 landmarked former hotel, the collection spans from the early 20th century to the last decade or so, and includes the frilliest—and sappiest—of lace-ornamented cards, along with a number of the wittier ones printed in postcard format. A smattering of hand-mades and historic birthday and calling cards rounds out the collection. Almost next door is the far more formal Gardner Museum of Architecture and Design (217 224-6873), which does a bang-up job of preserving Quincy's rich architectural heritage.

■ 217 224-3355 • Lincoln Douglas Apts., 101 N. 4th St., Quincy, IL 62301

🚗 West-central Illinois, off Route 24, on the northwest corner of 4th and Maine Sts.

🕐 Mon.–Fri. 1 P.M.–6 P.M. and some Sat.; by appointment only. Donation.

ROCKFORD

Time Museum Starting with a circa 1567–1200 B.C. Egyptian funerary stone depicting sunrise, the history of tracking time is chronicled here with a most remarkable collection of horological devices. We're especially fascinated by a French (Rebillier, 1860) "skeletonized" watch that kind of looks like a Man Ray print, and a 1964 Norwegian timepiece, described as a "spectacularly complicated mechanical astronomical clock"—it certainly looks so. *Gift Shop, Programs*

🔊 815 229-4199/398-6000 • Clock Tower Resort, 7801 E. State St., Rockford, IL 61125

🚗 I-90 exit at Business 20 (Rockford). It's on the lower level of the Clock Tower Resort and Conference Center, near the Convention Center entrance.

🕐 Tues.–Sun. 10 A.M.–5 P.M. Fee.

SPRINGFIELD

If Illinois is the "Land of Lincoln," then Springfield is Lincoln's county seat. Honest Abe's roots here reach far and wide, and you won't step too far without encountering something with a tie to our nation's 16th president. And, as with elsewhere in Illinois, Frank Lloyd Wright too has left his mark. His Dana-Thomas House here is an early Prairie-style home and is full of his originally designed furniture and art glass.

Parks Telephone Museum This little telephone museum focuses on its Illinois connection. Not too surprising, since Alexander Graham Bell and his pal Mr. Watson made the invention's big breakthrough in Chicago. Oliver Parks, a latter-day lineman for Illinois Bell, hoarded most of the equipment here that neatly tells the story of the instrument's changing technology and the people who keep it going, through an array of historic photos and wonderful old phones from the first crank-types to World's Fair future phones.

🔊 217 789-5303 • 529 S. 7th St., Springfield, IL 62701

🚗 I-55, 6th St. exit in Springfield. It's at the corner of 7th and Edwards, with its own entrance in the Ameritech building.

🕐 Mon.–Fri. 8 A.M.–5 P.M. No fee.

TEUTOPOLIS

Teutopolis Monastery Museum Essentially a pioneer-museum-in-a-monastery, with a few special twists. While the friars are gone now, they've left behind the items that got them (and some townfolk) through the days in the 1800s when the monastery was founded to meet the spiritual needs of the German

Catholic settlement—molds used to make altar bread; a demonstration of the 62-spool cord machine used to make the monks' cincture, or waist tie; ladies' curling irons; and the wooden shoes that were all the rage back then. *Tours, Gift Shop, Library*

- 217 857-3328 • Saint Francis Church, 110 S. Garrott St., Teutopolis, IL 62467
- South-central Illinois, at US 40 and S. Garrott St.
- Apr.–Nov.: Open first Sunday of month 12:30 P.M.–4 P.M. Fee.

WADSWORTH

Gold Pyramid House   The Onan family took the 1970s' dalliance with "pyramid power" very seriously, and so they cornered the gold market and built the 17,000-square-foot, six-story pyramid, coated it with 24-karat gold leaf, and called it home. These days the tip has seen a bit of tornado damage, so it's not quite as gold as it once was, but the inside remains a wonder and contains apparently authentic reproductions of King Tut's chariot (472 ounces of gold) and his tomb, rivaled only by the original and perhaps the Luxor Hotel's tribute in Las Vegas.

- 847 662-6666/Group tours: 847 244-7777 • 37921 N. Dilleys Rd., Wadsworth, IL 60083
- North of Chicago, 7 miles south of the Illinois–Wisconsin line. I-94 to Hwy 132, turn east 1 block to Dilleys Road, then north 2.5 miles.
- Apr.–Oct.: By appointment only. Fee.

WAUCONDA

Curt Teich Postcard Exhibit and Archives   No one produced more picture and advertising postcards than The Curt Teich Company, even in the cards' heyday early in the 20th century. And this lucky museum has the entire works, all 350,000, prints and negatives. While your purpose must be research to access the archive, there's a permanent exhibit featuring a cross-section of all types and times—hand-tinted, giant fruits, slick beach scenes, old main streets, politics, natural wonders—and another one on Route 66 and "America's Love Affair with the Road" that also features cards and memorabilia from the Teich collection. *Tours, Gift Shop, Programs, Publications, Library, Screenings*

- Museum: 847 526-7878/Archives: 847 526-8638 • Lake County Museum, Route 176 and Fairfield Rd., Wauconda, IL 60084
- 45 miles northwest of Chicago. I-94N, Route 176W to Lakewood Forest Preserve.
- Museum: Mon.–Sat. 11 A.M.–4:30 P.M., Sun. 1 P.M.–4:30 P.M. Fee, except Mon. Research: By appointment only.

WEST FRANKFORT

National Museum of Coal Mining   No re-creations here. Don your safety hat and descend 600 feet below ground into the Old Ben Coal Mine No. 25 and the real world of an American coal miner. Big bucks have been spent to make the mine safe for tours, but you'll get a real feel for the risks and dangers of this disappearing occupation from guides who are all former miners themselves. There are also 415 acres of surface facilities to explore, running the gamut from reclamation and coal preparation to environmental remediation and shipping to market, and featuring some of those surreally large coal scooping machines. *Tours, Gift Shop*

● 618 YES-COAL [937-2625] • Mine 25, Route 37N, West Frankfort, IL 62896

🚗 South-central Illinois. From I-57 (Exit 65 at West Frankfort) travel east on Hwy 149 6 miles to Logan Rd. Turn right on Logan and go 1 mile.

🕐 Mon.–Sun. 9 A.M.–5 P.M. Fee.

WOODHULL

Max Nordeen's Wheels Museum   Like Elvis, John Deere has left his mark, particularly out here in farm country. Inveterate collector Max Nordeen is the proud owner of Mr. Deere's death notice. But, of course, that's not all. In a state that seems to have a disproportionate number of museums with the word "wheels" in their names, Max's place really stands out—as much for him as for the stuff he can't wait to show you. The expected vintage cars and other rolling stock are joined by a special assortment of World's Fair souvenirs, antique nude photographs, a World War I–vintage naughty key chain collection direct from Paris, toys, clocks, and, truly, finds of all kinds.

● 309 334-2589 • Woodhull, IL 61490

🚗 Northwest Illinois, about 20 miles south of Moline. I-74S to Route 17E, then turn north (onto N. Division St.) just before the water tower. Go through town and continue north for about 2 miles. It's on the 100-acre farm just to the east.

🕐 June–Aug.: Tues.–Sun. 9 A.M.–4 P.M.; May, Sept.–Oct.: Sat.–Sun. 9 A.M.–4 P.M. Fee.

INDIANA

Unless you're a car-racing or basketball fan, you may tend to forget about Indiana when you think of the Midwest. Say "agriculture" and Iowa or downstate Illinois comes to mind; say "industry" and it's Ohio or Michigan. The funny thing is that, as its museums reveal, Indiana has been involved in just about every kind of Midwestern, and American, activity. There's the auto industry and related endeavors. There are pioneers and inventors. There are entertainers, artists, and public figures. And there is fun, idiosyncracy, and controversy.

What's Big: A number of museums in the Indianapolis area, including the one at the Speedway, the Children's Museum, and the Eiteljorg Museum of Western Art; the Minnetrista Centers in Muncie.

ANGOLA

General Lewis B. Hershey Museum   For those of you who don't remember, Lewis B. Hershey ran the Selective Service System (the draft) for three decades, and up through the Vietnam War his was a household name. Here is a collection of his memorabilia and materials on the draft since its earliest days in the Civil War.
- 🏠 219 665-4103 • Tri-State University, 300 S. Darling, Angola, IN 46703
- 🚗 Angola is in the northeast corner of Indiana, on US 20 just east of I-69 and south of the Indiana Toll Road (I-80/90). Tri-State University is southwest of downtown.
- 🕐 Call for information and directions.

AUBURN

Auburn-Cord-Duesenberg Museum   These three names have become legend. The cars were built in Auburn, and the museum is in the old factory showroom and administration building, an Art Deco delight. *Gift Shop, Food, Library*
- 🏠 219 925-1444 • 1600 S. Wayne St., Auburn, IN 46706

🚗 Auburn is at the intersection of I-69 with SR 8, in northeastern Indiana, 20 miles north of Fort Wayne and 30 miles south of the Indiana Toll Road (I-80/90).

🕐 Mon.–Sun. 9 A.M.–5 P.M. Fee.

BLOOMINGTON

Elizabeth Sage Historic Costume Collection   Among Indiana University's museums and collections, this one intrigues us, and we list it even though you have to be a researcher to get to see it; we figure some of you are probably that serious. The Sage Collection has over 14,000 items, everyday as well as high-fashion. There are publications and plates as well as the costumes themselves. *Library*

📧 812 855-4627 • http://www.fa.indiana.edu/~sage/ • Memorial Hall East 232, Indiana University, Bloomington, IN 47405

🚗 Bloomington is southwest of Indianapolis on Route 37; call for directions.

🕐 The collection is open for research only by appointment; call also for information on appearances of its materials at other regional institutions.

CARMEL

Museum of Miniature Houses and Other Collections   One of two miniature-enthusiast sites in Carmel, this museum has a number of complete dollhouses and partial houses, rooms, settings, and other items; the display changes periodically. Special displays include such things as log cabins and election memorabilia. One block west, at 130 North Range Line Rd., is the national headquarters of the National Association of Miniature Enthusiasts (NAME); call 317 571-8094 for information.

📧 317 575-9466 • 111 E. Main St. (131st), Carmel, IN 46032

🚗 Carmel is immediately north of the Indianapolis city line. From I-465 take Keystone exit north to 131st (Main St.) and turn right. If coming south into area on US 31, take US 431 (east branch) and turn west (right) at 131st.

🕐 Wed.–Sat. 11 A.M.–4 P.M., Sun. 1 P.M.–4 P.M. Closed early January. Donation.

CRAWFORDSVILLE

Old Jail Museum   Built in 1881–82, the Old Jail is the first (and last operational) of the "Seven Sisters"—the only seven rotary jails built in the United States. It held prisoners, mostly overnight as drunks or "tramps" or on charges like "possession of a live raccoon," until 1973. John Dillinger never stayed here. Today this oddity houses local history and arts and crafts exhibits. The Labor Day Breakout is an annual highlight. While you're in Crawfordsville, you might also want to stop by the Ben-Hur Museum, on Wallace Ave., and see the study where Lew Wallace, Civil War general and minister to Turkey, wrote the popular novel; displays pertain to the Broadway and movie versions, as well as inventions and Civil War memorabilia. Call 317 362-5769 for information. *Tours, Gift Shop*

■ 765 362-5222 • 225 N. Washington St., Crawfordsville, IN 47933

🚗 Crawfordsville is an hour northwest of Indianapolis on I-74. Exit onto US 231S. The Old Jail is on the highway, on the north side of downtown.

🕐 June–Aug.: Wed.–Sat. 10 A.M.–4:30 P.M., Tues. and Sun. 1 P.M.–4:30 P.M. Apr.–May and Sept.–Oct.: Wed.–Sun. 1 P.M.–4:30 P.M. Fee only for large groups or off-hours tours.

ELKHART

RV/MH Heritage Foundation/Hall of Fame/Museum/Library What we used to call "trailers" date from the 1920s; if you pull up to the Foundation in one today, it's an RV. If you left one to come here, it's Manufactured Housing (or, as we used to say, a Mobile Home, although not very M). You'll see the full range here, along with tributes to giants of the industry and extensive archives on this American tradition. *Library*

■ 800 378-8694 • 801 Benham Ave., Elkhart, IN 46516

🚗 Take the SR 19 exit off I-80/90 and go south into the city. The foundation is on 19 in downtown.

🕐 Mon.–Fri. 9 A.M.–4 P.M. Other hours and groups by appointment. No fee.

FAIRMOUNT

Fairmount Historical Museum/James Dean Exhibit James Dean is Fairmount's leading local industry. If you're here at the "wrong" time, like the last week of September, when they have a sort of James Dean festival, you may run into crowds. The museum is full of stuff you'd expect, like motorcycles and bongo drums, but also, in case you doubted he was really a Hoosier, pictures of Jimmy playing basketball. Lots of other local lore too.

■ 765 948-4555 • 203 E. Washington St., Fairmount, IN 46928

🚗 Fairmount is about an hour northeast of Indianapolis. Exit from I-69 onto Route 26W. The museum is 1 block east of the intersection of Washington and Main.

🕐 Mar.–Nov.: Mon.–Sat. 10 A.M.–5 P.M., Sun. noon–5 P.M. Rest of year by appointment. Donation.

FOUNTAIN CITY

Levi Coffin House State Historic Site   Newport, as it was called then, was a stronghold of antislavery Southerners when Levi and Catharine Coffin moved here in 1826. The Coffins soon became the center of a movement to help fugitive slaves, and Newport the "Grand Central Station of the Underground Railroad," with Levi as the Railroad's "president." Some 2,000 slaves may have come through here, including the model for Eliza of *Uncle Tom's Cabin*. Here you can see rooms and passageways used to hide runaways, and the entire house restored to period conditions. *Tours*

■ 765 847-2432 • Fountain City, IN 47341

🚗 Fountain City is in east-central Indiana, near the Ohio line. Take Exit 151 from I-70 at Richmond onto US 27 and go 6 miles north.

🕐 June–Aug.: Tues.–Sat. 1 P.M.–4 P.M. Sept.–Oct.: Sat. 1 P.M.–4 P.M. Call for other times. Fee.

GENEVA

Limberlost State Historic Site   The Limberlost was a swamp then, but now we know it was a wetland. Gene Stratton Porter lived here from 1895 to 1913, and she wrote *Girl of the Limberlost* and other books, painted, and studied the life of the forested region. In 1913 it was drained. Limberlost Cabin, filled with memorabilia, can be seen as a shrine to early environmentalism. If you want to see where the Porters went next, visit the Gene Stratton Porter State Historic Site on Sylvan Lake near Rome City (north-northwest of Fort Wayne); call 219 854-3790 for information.

■ 219 368-7428 • 200 E. 6th St., Geneva, IN 46740

🚗 Geneva is in northeastern Indiana, a half-hour south of Fort Wayne on US 27.

🕐 Mid-Mar.–mid-Dec.: Tues.–Sat. 9 A.M.–5 P.M., Sun. 1 P.M.–5 P.M. Fee.

GREENTOWN

Greentown Glass Museum   Greentown is noted for the glassware it produced early in the century, especially in "chocolate" and "golden agate" colors, developed by the chemist Jacob Rosenthal. A variety of this distinctive product is exhibited here. *Tours*

■ 765 628-6206 • 112 N. Meridian St., Greentown, IN 46936

🚗 Greentown is in north-central Indiana, just east of Kokomo, on US 35 and SR 213. The museum is next to City Hall, just north of the stoplight.

🕐 Mar.–Oct.: Tues.–Fri. 10 A.M.–4 P.M., Sat.–Sun. 1 P.M.–4 P.M.; call for other hours. No fee.

HUNTINGTON

Dan Quayle Center and Museum   Indiana has produced five vice presidents, including J. Danforth Quayle, and this museum is devoted to all of them, but especially to Dan. You'll see exhibits on his life from birth to office, including the law school diploma the dog chewed. *Gift Shop, Screenings*

■ 219 356-6356 • http://www.huntington.in.us/quayle/q.htm • 815 Warren St., Huntington, IN 46750

🚙 Huntington is in northeastern Indiana, half an hour southwest of Fort Wayne. Take I-69 to Exit 102 and follow US 24. Enter Huntington on Jefferson St. and turn left on Tipton; the museum is at Tipton and Warren.

🕐 Tues.–Sat. 10 A.M.–4 P.M., Sun. 1 P.M.–4 P.M. No fee.

INDIANAPOLIS

Indiana Medical History Museum   Built in 1896, this is the former pathology laboratory of the Central Indiana Hospital for the Insane. Then, it was a leading-edge facility. Today, it houses more than 15,000 artifacts of the advance of medical science. You'll get a good idea of how medicine was practiced, researched, and taught, in laboratories, library, photography room, mortuary, and amphitheater. *Tours, Programs*

■ 317 635-7329 • Old Pathology Building, 3045 West Vermont St., Indianapolis, IN 46222

🚙 From downtown, take Washington St. (US 40) west to Tibbs Ave. Turn right (north) on Tibbs, then right (east) on Vermont.

🕐 Wed.–Sat. 10 A.M.–4 P.M. Other hours or days by appointment. Fee.

JEFFERSONVILLE

While you're in the area, see also: Louisville, KY

Howard Steamboat Museum   Of all the riverboats in the great days on the Mississippi, Ohio, and tributaries, half were built by the Howard Shipyards. Here in the imposing 1894 Howard mansion you'll find artifacts and memorabilia including intricate models, tools, and parts. The house, built by Howard craftsmen, reflects the elegance of riverboat travel. *Tours*

■ 812 283-3728 • 1101 East Market St., Jeffersonville, IN 47130

🚙 Jeffersonville is across the Ohio River from Louisville, Kentucky. From I-65N, take Exit #0 onto Court Ave. (east), and turn right on Spring St., then left on Market; southbound, exit directly onto Market and reverse direction as convenient.

🕐 Tues.–Sat. 10 A.M.–3 P.M., Sun. 1 P.M.–3 P.M. Fee.

KOKOMO

While you're in the area, see also: Greentown

Elwood Haynes Museum   Elwood Haynes (1857–1925) was one of America's great inventors. Having made advances in metallurgy and petroleum chemistry, he set about inventing a "horseless carriage," and in 1894, outside Kokomo, made the first successful run of a commercially viable automobile. *Tours, Screenings*
- 765 456-7500 • 1915 S. Webster St., Kokomo, IN 46902
- Kokomo is in north-central Indiana, an hour north of Indianapolis on US 31. Coming into town from the south, branch left onto Washington St. (US 35/SR 22), then turn left on the Boulevard. The museum is at the corner of Boulevard and Webster.
- Tues.–Sat. 1 P.M.–4 P.M., Sun. 1 P.M.–5 P.M. No fee.

MADISON

Dr. William D. Hutchings Office and Hospital   This museum is in a Greek Revival house, where Dr. Hutchings practiced medicine from 1880 until his death in 1903; during that period it was, in effect, the town's hospital, and it remains essentially as he left it, equipment and furnishings on view.
- 812 265-2967 • 120 W. 3rd St., Madison, IN 47250
- Madison is in extreme southeastern Indiana, on the Ohio River and US 421. The museum is 3 blocks west of Jefferson (421) and 1 block north of Main St.
- Apr.–Oct.: Mon.–Sat. 10 A.M.–4:30 P.M., Sun. 1 P.M.–4:30 P.M. Fee.

MITCHELL

Virgil I. Grissom Memorial   "Gus" Grissom, born in Mitchell, was one of the original seven astronauts, the second to go into space. In 1967 he died in a launch-pad fire at Cape Kennedy. Spring Mill State Park was one of his favorite places, and the memorial contains a variety of mementos, including his 1965 Gemini space-craft "Molly Brown" and space suit.
- 812 849-4129 • Spring Mill State Park, Mitchell, IN 47446
- Mitchell is in south-central Indiana, about 2 hours south-southwest of Indianapolis via Route 37. Spring Mill State Park is 3 miles east of town on Hwy 60.
- Mon.–Sun. 8:30 A.M.–4 P.M. Fee.

MUNCIE

Academy of Model Aeronautics/National Model Aviation Museum
Headquarters for a worldwide organization of model plane buffs, the AMA has a

museum here exhibiting planes, engines, radio equipment, and the plans, kits, etc., that go into the pastime. There's space for all related activities. *Programs, Library*

⬛ 765 287-1256 • 5151 E. Memorial Dr., Muncie, IN 47302

🚗 Muncie is an hour northeast of Indianapolis. Take the US 35 loop around the east side, and exit onto Memorial Dr., southeast of downtown.

🕑 Mon.–Fri. 8 A.M.–5 P.M., Sat.–Sun. 10 A.M.–4 P.M. Fee.

Ball Corporation Museum The Ball brothers, who gave their name to the local state university and endowed much else here, made their fortune producing fruit jars. The manufacture has moved elsewhere, but a display on the history of container technology remains.

⬛ 765 747-6100 • 345 S. High St., Muncie, IN 47302

🚗 Take the SR 32/Main St. exit off US 35 and proceed into the center of Muncie, turning left on High St. The museum is at the Ball Corporation headquarters.

🕑 Call for hours and other information.

NASHVILLE

John Dillinger Historical Wax Museum Bad guys in wax! Good guys in wax! The wooden gun! And if your taste for culture heroes is whetted, drive north a piece (five miles) on SR 135 to Bean Blossom, to Bill Monroe's Museum and Bluegrass Hall of Fame Campground; call 812 988-6422 for information.

⬛ 812 988-1933 • 90 W. Washington St., Nashville, IN 47448

🚗 Nashville is an hour south of Indianapolis via I-65, exiting west on SR 46 near Columbus. The museum is just west of the junction with SR 135, in Nashville.

🕑 May–Oct.: Mon.–Sun. 10 A.M.–5 P.M. Call for off-season hours. Fee.

PERU

Circus City Festival Museum Peru is famous as the former winter home to Hagenback-Wallace, Clyde Beatty, Emmett Kelly, and other members of the American circus pantheon. Today a youth circus performs here in July. Then, or at quieter times, you may visit the museum and see uniforms, costumes, trapezes, and other paraphernalia of the shows, along with miniatures, lithographs, photographs, and much other circusana. The nearby Miami County Historical Museum (51 N. Broadway; 317 473-9183) has memorabilia of a quite different entertainment figure, ultrasophisticate composer Cole Porter, including his 1955 Cadillac.

⬛ 765 472-3918 • Circus City Center, 154 N. Broadway, Peru, IN 46970

🚗 Peru is in north-central Indiana, 1.5 hours north of Indianapolis, near the junction of US 24 and US 31. The museum is on Broadway, which is Business Route 31, at the corner of 7th St.

🕑 Apr.–Sept.: Mon.–Fri. 9 A.M.–5 P.M. Rest of year: Mon.–Fri. 9 A.M.–4 P.M. Open till showtime on performance dates. Donation.

SOUTH BEND

Studebaker National Museum   Among the last carmakers to survive Big Three domination of the industry, the Studebakers produced cars until 1963. Their business was based on a wagon and carriage empire, begun in the 1850s. Here you will see just about every kind of conveyance Studebaker made, and there is a science center for kids. *Gift Shop, Hands-on*

■ 219 235-9714 • 525 S. Main St., South Bend, IN 46601

🚗 Business US 31 runs through downtown, with Main St. paralleling (1 block west) Michigan.

🕐 Mon.–Sat. 9 A.M.–5 P.M., Sun. noon–5 P.M. Fee.

TERRE HAUTE

Eugene V. Debs Home   Are we still allowed to cheer for American socialist leaders? All right: "Our engineer is E. V. Debs. . . ." This is his place; he built it in 1890 and lived in it until he died in 1926. You'll see a fine house, with murals on his eventful life and memorabilia from his campaigns. Outside, a memorial wall honors pioneer labor leaders.

■ 812 232-2163 • 451 N. 8th St., Terre Haute, IN 47808

🚗 Terre Haute is in west-central Indiana, 2 hours west-southwest of Indianapolis. Take the 3rd St. (Hwy 41) exit off I-70. Turn right (east) on Wabash Ave., then left (north) on 9th St. Turn left again on Sycamore and left on 8th to park behind the Debs home.

🕐 Wed.–Sun. 1 P.M.–4:30 P.M., or by appointment. No fee.

WAKARUSA

Bird's Eye View Museum of Miniatures   DeVon Rose has been creating this museum since 1967 in his basement, and he will show you around personally. It started with his sons' electric trains. Today it includes Wakarusa itself, and more of Indiana is on the drawing board; right now, Rose is working on nearby Goshen's bag factory.

■ 219 862-2367 • 325 S. Elkhart St., Wakarusa, IN 46573

🚗 Wakarusa is in northern Indiana, half an hour southeast of South Bend, on SR 19, between Elkhart and Nappanee. The museum is 3 blocks south of the center of town.

🕐 Mon.–Fri. 8 A.M.–5 P.M., Sat. 8 A.M.–noon. Fee.

IOWA

Maybe you think the story of Iowa is all corn, with a shucking bee or two to keep the farmers happy. Take a look at these museums, though. You have actors, composers, race drivers, hot air balloonists, Wild West stars, real and imaginary ballplayers, bandleaders, and labor leaders. What farm?

What's Big: And we haven't even talked about events, like Davenport's Bix Memorial Festival—see, you have to be hip, like Iowans, to know about these. Besides, Des Moines has a major Art Center. And at West Branch, there's the Herbert Hoover National Historic Site.

CEDAR FALLS

Ice House Museum   It looks like a cross between a roundhouse and a barn, and it contains vehicles, farm tools, historical displays, and re-created workshops. The most important reason to come here, though, is to learn about the ice business. You'll see the tools used, other artifacts of the trade, and displays illustrating the process of keeping things cool—before technology changed everything.
- 319 266-5149 • First and Clay Sts., Cedar Falls, IA 50613
- Cedar Falls is in east-central Iowa, just west of Waterloo. The museum is at the intersection of US 218 and SR 57.
- May–Oct.: Wed., Sat.–Sun. 2 P.M.–4:30 P.M. No fee.

CEDAR RAPIDS

National Czech and Slovak Museum and Library   Czechs, Slovaks, and Moravians are among the peoples who settled this part of the Midwest in the late 19th century. In this 1995 building, whose row of pitched roofs echoes a historic

Czech townscape, you'll find America's largest collection of ethnic costumes from these homelands, along with decorated eggs and artworks in glass, porcelain, wood, and other mediums. There is a restored immigrant home, and festivals throughout the year. *Tours, Gift Shop, Programs, Library*

🏛 319 362-8500 • 30 16th Ave. SW, Cedar Rapids, IA 52404

🚗 Take I-380N from I-80 into Cedar Rapids, and take Exit 18, turning right on Wilson Ave., then left on J St. SW, then right on 16th Ave. SW. The museum is on the Cedar River, in the Czech Village neighborhood, southeast of downtown.

🕐 Tues.–Sat. 9:30 A.M.–4 P.M. Mid-May to Christmas: Sun. 1 P.M.–4 P.M. also. Fee.

CHARLES CITY

Floyd County Historical Society Museum   They say the word *tractor* was coined here, and Charles City calls itself The Birthplace of the Farm Tractor. You'll see some fine early-20th-century examples from the local Hart-Parr company. There's also the Cretors Popcorn Wagon, which may be selling out front for your enjoyment. You'll find information on suffragist Carrie Chapman Catt, whose house is south of town. And among the museum's other displays is the fully re-created turn-of-the-century drugstore of the intriguingly named John G. Legel.

🏛 515 228-1099 • 500 Gilbert St. (Hwys 18 and 218), Charles City, IA 50616

🚗 Charles City is in northeastern Iowa, an hour north-northwest of Waterloo.

🕐 May–Labor Day: Tues.–Fri. 9 A.M.–4:30 P.M., Sat.–Sun. 1 P.M.–4 P.M. Rest of year: closed weekends. Fee.

CHESTER

Hayden Prairie   This is a real Living Museum—240 acres of the way Iowa, and the eastern Great Plains, used to be. A National Natural Landmark, the preserve is the largest blacksoil prairie left in the state. Late May and the end of summer are especially good times to see wildflowers. Call Iowa's Bureau of Preserves and Ecological Services at 515 281-3891 for more information.

🏛 515 281-5145 • Chester, IA 52134

🚗 Chester is in northeastern Iowa, on the Minnesota border due north of Waterloo. Take US 63 to Davis Corners, turn west on SR 9, and go 4 miles. Turn north on County V26 for 4.5 miles; the Prairie is west of the road.

🕐 Not a closed area. No fee.

CLARINDA

Nodaway Valley Historical Museum   Clarinda isn't big, but it has at least two claims to fame. It was here, in 1901, that teacher Jessie Field launched what became the 4-H movement; you'll see the Goldenrod School, where it began. On a completely different note, bandleader Glenn Miller (*see also* the Fort Morgan, Colorado, museum) was born here in 1904, and you'll see his home and memorabilia.

Tours

📍 712 542-3073 • 1600 S. 16th St., Clarinda, IA 51632

🚗 Clarinda is in southwestern Iowa, 50 miles southeast of Council Bluffs. The museum is just south of the intersection of US 71 and SR 2.

🕐 May–Sept.: Tues.–Sun. 1 P.M.–5 P.M. Rest of year: 2 P.M.–4 P.M. Fee.

CLEAR LAKE

Surf Ballroom   This is where They played The Day the Music Died—*They* being Buddy Holly, Richie Valens, and the Big Bopper (*see also* the Museum of the Gulf Coast, Port Arthur, Texas). The day was February 3, 1959, and on the first weekend in February each year, Clear Lake hosts a big memorial. But at other times, you can tour the old ballroom (which earlier had hosted Big Bands), and get the ambience, helped along by all the memorabilia on the walls.

📍 515 357-6151 • 460 North Shore Dr., Clear Lake, IA 50428

🚗 Clear Lake is in north-central Iowa, just west of Mason City and the I-35/US 18 junction.

🕐 Mon.–Fri. 9 A.M.–5 P.M. Call to confirm and regarding weekends. No fee.

COUNCIL BLUFFS

While you're in the area, see also: Omaha, NE

Squirrel Cage Jail (Pottawattomie County Jail)   "Squirrel Cage" or "Lazy Susan" or whatever you call it (*see also* Crawfordsville, Indiana's Old Jail Museum), it was built in 1885 and features a cellblock that rotated so that guards could see *everything*. Close by, at 605 3rd St. (call 712 322-2406) is the elegant, lavish mansion of Grenville M. Dodge, the man who built the Union Pacific Railroad west from here. We think these two sites make a nice paired visit: Depending on your cast of mind you can regard them as a case of "There but for the grace . . ." or as a parable about the distribution of income.

📍 712 323-2509 • 226 Pearl St., Council Bluffs, IA 51503

🚗 Take Exit 3 off I-80 and go north into downtown. The jail is next to the courthouse.

🕐 Apr.–Sept.: Sat.–Sun. 1 P.M.–5 P.M. Call for appointment at other hours. Fee.

DES MOINES

While you're in the area, see: Indianola, Knoxville, Newton, Van Meter, Winterset

DYERSVILLE

National Farm Toy Museum Isn't it logical that a town in the middle of the Corn Belt should be the Farm Toy Capital of the World? You'd assume that the four manufacturers in Dyersville wouldn't be able to put an inaccurate design past knowledgeable locals. This museum has over 30,000 items on two floors, with dioramas of entire farms and even the machinery the Ertl Company once used to make the little gems. If you're in Dyersville during the season, you'll probably also want to visit what has rapidly become one of the best-known sites in the entire Midwest, the ballfield setting of *Field of Dreams*; call 319 875-8404 for information. *Gift Shop*

🏠 319 875-2727 • 1110 16th Ave. SE, Dyersville, IA 52040

🚜 Dyersville is in east-central Iowa, a half-hour west of Dubuque. Take Exit 294 from US 20 onto SR 136N and turn right on 15th Ave., following signs.

🕐 Mon.–Sun. 8 A.M.–7 P.M. Fee.

ELK HORN

Danish Immigrant Museum Completed in 1994, this museum is now the core of a national cultural center in what is described as America's largest Danish rural community. Nearby are the Danish Windmill (you'll pass it on 173) and the 1908 Bedstemor's (Grandmother's) House. In the museum itself you'll see a Wall of Honor listing many of the roughly 360,000 Danish immigrants to North America. There's also Victor Borge's first piano and a range of artifacts and exhibits on Danish-American life.

🏠 800 759-9192 • 2212 Washington St., Elk Horn, IA 51531

🚜 Elk Horn is in southwestern Iowa, an hour northeast of Council Bluffs. Take Exit 54 off I-80 and proceed north on SR 173, then left on Washington St.

🕐 Mid-May–mid-Sept.: Mon.–Fri. 9 A.M.–6 P.M., Sat. 10 A.M.–6 P.M., Sun. noon–6 P.M. Rest of year: closings at 5 P.M. Fee.

INDIANOLA

National Balloon Museum Indianola has been the scene, since 1970, of the national hot air balloon championships. This new museum, which looks like two huge balloon baskets inverted on the land, has displays on two centuries of ballooning—its technology, personalities, and historic events. Call 515 961-8415 for information on the National Balloon Classic (early August). *Gift Shop*

🏠 515 961-3714 • 1601 N. Jefferson (Hwy 65-69N), Indianola, IA 50125

🚜 Indianola is a half-hour south of Des Moines. The museum is just north of town.

🕐 Mon.–Fri. 9 A.M.–noon and 1 P.M.–4 P.M., Sat. 10 A.M.–4 P.M., Sun. 1 P.M.–4 P.M. No fee.

KEOKUK

Keokuk River Museum/*George M. Verity* Active on the Mississippi and Ohio rivers from 1927 to 1960, the George M. Verity is one of only two remaining of 2,000-odd steam towboats (for the other, *see* Marietta, Ohio). Get a sense of the great river days.

🏠 319 524-4765 • Johnson St., Victory Park, Keokuk, IA 52632

🚗 Keokuk is in extreme southeastern Iowa, on US 136 and 61. The museum is on the river, off Main St. (US 136).

🕐 Apr.–Oct.: Mon.–Sun. 9 A.M.–5 P.M. Fee.

KNOXVILLE

National Sprint Car Hall of Fame and Museum If you grew up getting covered with red dust at the County Fairgrounds; if names like Agajanian, and Bettenhausen, and Leader Card bring a smile; then this facility, opened in 1992, is for you. Here you'll see a salute to the greats, along with cars driven by such luminaries as A. J. Foyt and Johnny Rutherford, Jan Opperman's leather helmet, and other memorabilia of the midget circuit. If you're lucky, someone will be practicing outside. *Gift Shop*

🏠 800 874-4488 • Knoxville Raceway, One Sprint Capital Place, Knoxville, IA 50138

🚗 Knoxville is in south-central Iowa, a half-hour southeast of Des Moines. Take SR 14S from I-80 to the Raceway.

🕐 Mon.–Fri. 10 A.M.–6 P.M., Sat. 10 A.M.–5 P.M., Sun. noon–5 P.M. Fee.

LUCAS

John Lewis Mining and Labor Museum They produce coal in this part of Iowa, and in 1880 they also produced John L. Lewis, who went into the mines at 16 and eventually became one of America's most powerful labor leaders. The museum has a library and theater and displays on the industry and the workers who make it, as well as on John L. himself. *Library*

🏠 515 766-6831 • 102 Division St., Lucas, IA 50151

🚗 Lucas is in south-central Iowa, an hour south of Des Moines, at the US 65/US 34 junction.

🕐 Mid-Apr.–mid-Oct.: Tues.–Sat. 9 A.M.–3 P.M. Group tours by appointment. Fee.

MASON CITY

Van Horn's Antique Truck Museum and Circus Room Display Here's a fine collection of the trucks that worked America's roads early in the century.

They'll give you the sense that the roadscape of the day was filled with what looked like motorized prairie schooners. The manufacturers' names range from the familiar to the completely forgotten, a lesson in the development of a major industry. There's a full-scale model circus too, and gas pumps and paraphernalia, signs, and other arcana. *Gift Shop, Food*

🏠 515 423-0550 • 15272 North St. (US 65), Mason City, IA 50401

🚗 Exit from I-35 at mile 197. Go 8 miles east on County Rd. B20 and left (north) 1 mile on US 65. The museum is 2 miles north of downtown.

🕐 Late May–late Sept.: Mon.–Sat. 9 A.M.–4 P.M., Sun. 11 A.M.–5 P.M. Fee.

MISSOURI VALLEY

Steamship *Bertrand* Display The *Bertrand* was one of dozens of workaday supply boats headed to the Montana goldfields when, in April 1864, she hit a snag and sank in shallow water. Salvage operations stalled, and the river shifted; it was not until 1968 that the vessel was found again, under a nearby field. Today you'll see the goods she was carrying—foods, clothing, tools, and thousands of items forming a coherent record of what frontier consumers would demand.

🏠 712 642-4121 • De Soto National Wildlife Refuge Visitors Center, Missouri Valley, IA 51555

🚗 The De Soto NWR lies along the Missouri River a half-hour north of Omaha, Nebraska. Take I-29N from Omaha–Council Bluffs and turn west on US 30 for 7 miles.

🕐 Visitors Center: Jan.–Dec.: Mon.–Sun. 9 A.M.–4:30 P.M. Excavation site: Mid-Apr.–Sept.: Mon.–Sun. 6 A.M.–10 P.M. Vehicle fee for NWR.

MOUNT PLEASANT

Midwest Old Threshers Heritage Museum and Museum of Repertoire Americana This dual museum seems to sum up Iowa: They're farmers—but *artistic* farmers. The Threshers Museum shows a large collection of steam-powered engines and other machines that brought in the prairies' bounty, as well as displays on farm women, electricity, and other matters. The Repertoire Museum has all kinds of stage props and fittings (dozens of curtains!), tent show relics, and the like. Work hard—but party hard, too. *Gift Shop, Programs*

🏠 319 385-8937 • 1887 Threshers Rd., Mt. Pleasant, IA 52641

🚗 Mt. Pleasant is in southeastern Iowa, at the US 34/US 218 junction, a half-hour northwest of Burlington. The museum is southwest of the intersection, at McMillan Park.

🕐 Threshers: Memorial Day–Labor Day: Mon.–Sun. 9 A.M.–4:30 P.M. Apr.–May and Sept.–Oct.: weekdays only. Fee. Repertoire: by appointment.

NEWTON

Jasper County Historical Society Museum/Maytag Exhibit   This general history museum is special for its exhibit on Maytag, the company that made Newton the Washing Machine Capital of the World. It isn't all washers, as Maytag (and other local companies) have through the years made such items as lawnmowers, other appliances, and aircraft parts.

🔲 515 792-9118 • 1700 S. 15th Ave. West, Newton, IA 50208

🚗 Newton is a half-hour east of Des Moines. From I-80, take Exit 164N (SR 14). Turn right on S. 12th Ave. West and right again on S. 15th.

🕐 May–Oct.: Mon.–Sun. 1 P.M.–5 P.M. Fee. Group tours by appointment.

OKOBOJI

Higgins Foundation/National Bank Note Museum and Library   From the Civil War until the New Deal, the National Bank system was a key component of the American fiscal infrastructure. In Iowa alone 496 national banks issued their own notes. This museum, in a most unlikely setting, details the history of the banks. If you've never seen a ten-dollar bill with your hometown's name on it, you may find one here. *Library*

🔲 712 332-5859 • 1507 Sanborn Ave., Okoboji, IA 51355

🚗 Okoboji is in northwestern Iowa, near the Minnesota line, in the Iowa Great Lakes area. The museum is just off US 71 in the direction of the regional airport.

🕐 Mid-June–Labor Day: Tues.–Sun. 11 A.M.–5:30 P.M.; call to confirm and for off-season hours. No fee.

PELLA

Pella Historical Village Museum   Practically the whole city of Pella has turned itself into a monument to its Dutch founders, who arrived in 1847; the Christmas season and Tulip Time, in May, are especially lively. It's all kind of "big" to our way of thinking, but we include it because there's one wonderful piece of discontinuity: the boyhood home of Wyatt Earp. Try taking in Pella's Old World ambience and thinking about the O.K. Corral at the same time! If you want to stick with Earp, pay a visit to his birthplace over in Monmouth, Illinois. *Tours, Gift Shop, Food, Programs*

🔲 515 628-2409 • 507 Franklin St., Pella, IA 50219

🚗 Pella is in south-central Iowa, about an hour east-southeast of Des Moines on SR 163. The museum is central, 1 block east of the square.

🕐 Apr.–Oct., Dec.: Mon.–Sat. 9 A.M.–5 P.M.; to 6 P.M. June–Aug. Rest of year: closed Sat. Fee.

PRINCETON

Buffalo Bill Cody Homestead   America's premier Wild West showman (*see also* the Buffalo Bill Museums in Golden, Colorado, and Cody, Wyoming) spent part of his boyhood in this 1847 house, or more precisely in, on, and along the nearby river, before his family moved to Kansas. Fittingly, there are live buffalo and a stagecoach on the grounds. In Le Claire, south of Princeton, the Buffalo Bill Museum (201 N. River Rd.; call 319 289-5580) offers displays on Bill's life, as well as on river travel and other Iowa topics.

■ 319 225-2981 • 28050 230th Ave., at Bluff Rd., Princeton, IA 52768

🚗 Princeton is in east-central Iowa, a half-hour northeast of the Quad Cities via US 67. The homestead is actually closer (2 miles south) to McCausland, along 230 above the Wapsipinicon River.

🕐 Apr.–Oct.: Mon.–Sun. 9 A.M.–5 P.M. Fee.

QUASQUETON

Cedar Rock/The Walter Residence   Lowell Walter had Frank Lloyd Wright build him a dream house here in the Wapsipinicon Valley. Completed in 1950, Cedar Rock is one of Wright's last houses, an example of his "Usonian" principles. In 1981, Walter left it to the people of Iowa. There's also a visitors center with displays on the architect.

■ 319 934-3572 • 2615 Quasqueton Diag. Blvd., Quasqueton, IA 52326

🚗 Quasqueton is in east-central Iowa, about 25 miles east of Waterloo. For Cedar Rock, turn off US 20 onto SR 282S, then go northwest 2 miles from Quasqueton on W35.

🕐 May–Oct.: Tues.–Sun. and holidays 11 A.M.–5 P.M. No fee. Group tours by appointment.

SPILLVILLE

Bily Clock Museum/Antonín Dvořák Exhibit   Spillville (originally Spielville) was well known as a Czech town when Antonín Dvořák came here in the summer of 1893 to get away from New York City and touch up his "New World Symphony." Later, the building he lived in became home to the spectacular carved wooden clocks of the Bily brothers, Frank and Joseph, who died in the 1960s. Today you can see the clocks downstairs and displays on Dvořák upstairs; a walk around town will give you a sense of the peacefulness the composer relished.

■ 319 562-3569 • Main St., Spillville, IA 52168

🚗 Spillville is in northeastern Iowa, a half-hour southwest of Decorah. From US 52, take SR 325W into town.

🕐 May–Oct.: Mon.–Sun. 8:30 A.M.–5 P.M. Rest of year: reduced hours; call for appointment in Nov.–Feb. Fee.

VAN METER

Bob Feller Hometown Exhibit How about a rapid stop in Rapid Robert's hometown? The museum, completed in 1995, details the career of the man who began terrifying American League hitters in 1936, at the age of 17. He shows up here himself occasionally.

- 515 996-2806 • 310 Mill St., Van Meter, IA 50261
- Van Meter is about 12 miles west of Des Moines. Take Exit 113 off I-80 and go 1 mile south into town; the museum is just across the tracks.
- Mon.–Sat. 10 A.M.–5 P.M., Sun. noon–4 P.M. Fee.

WINTERSET

Birthplace of John Wayne Here's the Duke's place, fixed up to look like 1907, when Marion Morrison was born. There's all kinds of memorabilia, even the *True Grit* eyepatch. The Gipper came to visit, and you can too. More movie punch: Winterset is the seat of Madison County, and you should see these bridges. *Tours, Gift Shop*

- 515 462-1044 • 216 S. 2nd St., Winterset, IA 50273
- Winterset is 25 miles southwest of Des Moines. Exit west from I-35 onto SR 92.
- Mon.–Sun. 10 A.M.–5 P.M. Fee.

KANSAS

What is it about Kansas? A lot of its museums have to do with going away: Martin and Osa Johnson left Chanute for Africa and the South Seas. Amelia Earhart left Atchison for who knows where. Walter Chrysler left Ellis for Detroit. The thing is, when we non-Kansans get out here, we tend to like it; the open space is refreshing, and if you know where to look, there's lots of interest.

What's Big: The aircraft industry, especially in Wichita. In museum terms, the Combat Air Museum in Topeka is. Hutchinson's Kansas Cosmosphere and Space Center, on a related theme, is also big. Topeka, Wichita, and Lawrence have the range of history, art, science, and natural science museums you'd expect in the capital, largest city, and main university town.

ABILENE

Museum of Independent Telephony Independents are those phone companies that were never gathered into Ma Bell's aprons. They've been around since the 19th century and have covered half the country. One particularly successful one, United Telephone, now Sprint, began here in 1898. The museum displays equipment, re-created work environments, varieties of glass insulators, popular music with a telephone theme (you can listen by phone, of course), manuals, early pay phones, and miniature phones. Across the street is the Eisenhower Center, presidential library, home, and all; on Buckeye a block away is the Greyhound Hall of Fame (913 263-3000), if you feel like going to the dogs. *Tours*

■ 913 263-2681 • 412 S. Campbell St., Abilene, KS 67410

🚙 Abilene is 90 miles west of Topeka via I-70. Exit south onto K-15, which becomes Buckeye Ave. Turn left at 3rd St. and right onto Campbell.

🕑 Apr.–Oct.: Mon.–Sat. 10 A.M.–8 P.M., Sun. 1 P.M.–5 P.M. Fee.

ATCHISON

Amelia Earhart Birthplace   The aviator was born in 1897, in a Victorian house overlooking the Missouri. If her mystery intrigues you, perhaps you'll find a clue in the memorabilia here. Other sites around town have Earhartana also, including the Evah C. Cray Historical Home Museum (805 N. 5th St.; 913 367-3046). There's a memorial forest at the airport, three miles west. And there's more at 200 S. 10th St., where the County Historical Museum shares space with the Atchison Rail Museum (this is also the birthplace of the Santa Fe Railroad).

🖐 913 367-4217 • 223 N. Terrace, Atchison, KS 66002

🚗 Atchison is 40 miles northwest of Kansas City. Entering from the south via US 73, turn right toward the river. The Earhart birthplace is at the corner of N. Terrace and Santa Fe.

🕑 Apr.–Oct.: Mon.–Fri. 9 A.M.–4 P.M., Sat.–Sun. 1 P.M.–4 P.M. Rest of year by appointment. Fee.

CHANUTE

Martin and Osa Johnson Safari Museum   Like Amelia Earhart, the Johnsons left Kansas to roam the world. From 1917 to 1936, they traveled central Africa, Borneo, and the South Seas, and it was through them that the word *safari* gained currency. There are thousands of photographs, movies, pieces of equipment, field journals, letters, and ethnic artifacts here. There's also a large collection of West African masks, an art gallery, and a library on explorers and natural history. *Gift Shop, Library*

🖐 316 431-2730 • 111 N. Lincoln Ave., Chanute, KS 66720

🚗 Chanute is in southeastern Kansas, on US 169. Exit onto Kansas Route 39, and go 2 miles east. Take the Cherry St. exit east to Santa Fe and turn right onto the overpass. The museum is on the right, in the old Santa Fe depot.

🕑 Mon.–Sat. 10 A.M.–5 P.M., Sun. 1 P.M.–5 P.M. Fee.

COFFEYVILLE

Dalton Defenders Museum   October 5, 1892, is the big moment in Coffeyville memory—the day the Dalton Gang rode in to hit two banks, got slowed down by street repairs, and were outgunned by locals. This museum, and various other sites in town, recall the great day. As if the bad guys and good guys weren't enough, locals Walter (Big Train) Johnson and Wendell Willkie are also remembered.

🖐 316 251-5944 • 113 E. 8th St., Coffeyville, KS 67337

🚗 Coffeyville is in southeastern Kansas, near the Oklahoma border, on US 166/169. Exit onto 8th St. west and cross tracks to corner of Patterson Ave.

🕑 Mon.–Sun. 9 A.M.–5 P.M. (to 7 P.M. June–Aug.). Fee.

ELLIS

Walter P. Chrysler Boyhood Home and Museum   The auto giant grew up here and worked in local railroad shops before embarking on a career that took him from trains to cars and from Kansas to New York's Chrysler Building. Behind the period home is a museum with one of his first (1924) autos and other mementos of one local boy who made good. Head into Hays, just east, for Wheels and Spokes (913 628-6477), Jerry Jueneman's collection of historic muscle cars.

■ 913 726-3636 • 102 W. 10th St., Ellis, KS 67637

🚗 In west-central Kansas, 15 minutes west of Hays, Ellis is off I-70 at Exit 145. Turn south and go 10 blocks (on Washington St.) to stop lights, then turn west on 10th.

🕐 May–Sept.: Mon.–Sat. 9 A.M.–5 P.M., Sun. 1 P.M.–5 P.M. Rest of year: Mon.–Sun. 1 P.M.–5 P.M. Fee.

FLORENCE

Harvey House Museum   As the Santa Fe Railroad moved west through Kansas, Fred Harvey opened his first restaurant in Topeka, then created his first restaurant-hotel here in 1878. Harvey revolutionized eating while traveling, and must be seen as the progenitor of today's fast-food industry, although his establishments had better food and a civilized ambience. This "Harvey House" went out of business in 1900; part of it is now a memorial to the "Harvey Girls" who served the food and to the world they worked in.

■ 316 878-4296 • 204 W. 3rd St., Florence, KS 66851

🚗 Florence is in east-central Kansas, 40 miles northeast of Wichita, on US 50. Exit onto 5th St. and go east to Marion, then turn south to the corner of 3rd.

🕐 By appointment. No fee.

GOESSEL

Mennonite Heritage Museum   In 1874 a community of German-speaking Mennonites who had been living in southern Russia arrived in this part of Kansas, enticed by Santa Fe Railroad agents and seeking the freedom to live according to their religion. They brought with them a new kind of wheat, Turkey Red. The rest is Great Plains history, and you'll examine it at the eight-building complex here, which includes the Turkey Red Wheat Palace (with its wheaten Liberty Bell), the spartan Immigrant House, and other homes and common structures. *Gift Shop*

■ 316 367-8200 • 200 N. Poplar St., Goessel, KS 67053

🚗 Goessel is in east-central Kansas, 40 miles north of Wichita and 11 miles north of the N. Newton exit off I-135, on KS 15. Follow signs to Poplar and Centennial.

🕐 May–Sept.: Tues.–Fri. 10 A.M.–5 P.M., Sat.–Sun. 1 P.M.–5 P.M. Rest of year: reduced hours; closed Jan.–Feb. Fee.

GOODLAND

High Plains Museum   This general history museum has dioramas and other displays on the settlement of the High Plains. What's special, though, is the replica of the first patented helicopter in America, which "flew" here (into the water tower, according to some witnesses) in 1910. The inventors, two railroad machinists, left town, and Kansas aviation history resumed elsewhere. There's also a rope-driven car, built in 1902 and more trustworthy than the 'copter.

📱 913 899-4595 • 1717 Cherry St., Goodland, KS 67735

🚗 Goodland is in northwestern Kansas, near the Colorado border and off I-70. Take Exit 17 and proceed north on KS 27. Turn right on 17th St. to Cherry.

🕐 Mon.–Sat. 9 A.M.–5 P.M., Sun. 1 P.M.–4 P.M. No fee.

GREENSBURG

Big Well and Celestial Museum   Stop here and drop in at the World's Largest Hand-dug Well! It's 109 feet deep and 32 feet in diameter, and was created by railroad builders in the 1880s. There are 105 steps to the bottom. Is there a collection at this museum? Yes, a collection of objects found in the well—take a look and see what once made a splash. The Celestial Museum displays a half-ton Pallasite meteorite, which must have made quite an impact in its day. *Gift Shop*

📱 316 723-2261 • 51 S. Sycamore St., Greensburg, KS 67054

🚗 Greensburg is in south-central Kansas, 2 hours west of Wichita on US 54. Turn south on Sycamore St. (1 block west of Main St.) and go 3 blocks.

🕐 Memorial Day–Labor Day: 8 A.M.–8 P.M. Rest of year: 9 A.M.–5 P.M. Fee.

LA CROSSE

Kansas Barbed Wire Museum   Some called it the Devil's Rope. Since the 1860s it has kept Plains cattle from wandering; today it is also used to control prisoners, enemy soldiers, urban youth, you name it. They have over 700 varieties here (some more beautiful than others), along with wire tools and some oddities like a crow's nest made from wire strands (strange birds!). There's a

Barbed Wire Hall of Fame, and you can buy the stuff at the store. And if you were wondering what they attached all that wire to out here on the High Plains, mosey down the block to the Post Rock Museum (913 222-2719). *Gift Shop, Library*

🏠 913 222-9900 • Grass Park, 120 W. 1st St., La Crosse, KS 67548

🚗 La Crosse is in west-central Kansas. Exit from I-70 at Hays and go 26 miles south on US 183, which is Main St. in town. Turn right and go 1 block west on 1st St.

🕐 Apr.–Oct.: Mon.–Sat. 10 A.M.–4:30 P.M., Sun. 1 P.M.–4:30 P.M. Rest of year: call for hours. Donation.

LAWRENCE

Ryther Printing Museum   This one-room museum has a collection of the kinds of machines and paraphernalia now being made to disappear by computers. If you had anything to do with printing more than, let's say, five years ago, you'll know what a slug cutter makes and what a typesetter sets.

🏠 913 864-4341 • Printing Services, University of Kansas, Campus West, 2425 W. 15th St., Lawrence, KS 66044

🚗 Lawrence is 45 minutes west of Kansas City. From I-70, take the Lawrence West Exit (Exit 202) and go south on what becomes Iowa St. Turn west on 15th to Crestline Dr.

🕐 Mon.–Fri. 8 A.M.–5 P.M. No fee. Ask at Printing Services to be admitted.

LUCAS

Garden of Eden and Cabin Home   This is S. P. Dinsmoor's version of Eden and what went wrong, built between 1907 and 1929. Cain kills Abel, but there are also soldiers and Indians out to kill each other. The Goddess of Liberty is spearing the Trusts, but there's also Labor Crucified. Dinsmoor used over 113 tons of concrete, and the result is one of America's oddest landscapes, complete with post-rock limestone "log" cabin and Dinsmoor himself, visible in his mausoleum. *Tours, Gift Shop*

🏠 913 525-6395 • 2nd and Kansas, Lucas, KS 67648

🚗 Lucas is in north-central Kansas, an hour west of Salina. From I-70, exit at mile marker 206 (Hwy 232), go north 16 miles, and follow signs.

🕐 May–Sept.: Mon.–Sun. 10 A.M.–5 P.M. Rest of year: Mon.–Sun. 1 P.M.–4 P.M. Fee.

MARYSVILLE

Original Pony Express Home Station No. 1 Museum   One hundred miles west of the starting point (*see* the Patee House Museum, Saint Joseph, Missouri), this was the Pony Express's first "home" station, where one rider turned the mail over to the next. There are also displays on the building's earlier use as Kansas' first post office, and on regional history, geology, and farming.

■ 913 562-3825 • 106 S. 8th St., Marysville, KS 66508

🚗 Marysville is in northeastern Kansas, 50 miles north of Manhattan, at the junction of US 36 and US 77. The museum is 1 block south of US 36.

🕐 May–Nov.: Mon.–Sun. 9 A.M.–5 P.M. Fee.

MEADE

Dalton Gang Hideout Eva Dalton and her husband, John Whipple, built this home and lived in it from 1887 to 1892. They were upstanding citizens, but something about Eva's brothers didn't sit right, and as the reputation of the Dalton Gang (*see also* Coffeyville) grew, the Whipples abandoned the house. New owners found strange characters hanging around—and then the 95-foot-long tunnel was discovered. *Gift Shop*

■ 800 354-2743 • 502 S. Pearlette St., Meade, KS 67864

🚗 Meade is in southwestern Kansas, 40 miles northeast of Liberal via US 54, on Hwy 23. The hideout is 4 blocks south of 54.

🕐 Memorial Day–Labor Day: Mon.–Sat. 9 A.M.–6 P.M., Sun. 1 P.M.–6 P.M. Rest of year: Mon.–Sat. 9 A.M.–5 P.M., Sun. 1 P.M.–5 P.M. Fee.

MEDICINE LODGE

Carry A. Nation Home America's second most famous axwoman started her campaign here after enduring an alcoholic first husband; unlike Lizzie Borden (*see* Fall River, Massachusetts), Carry took out after inanimate targets—the social institutions that were rendering a lot of her contemporaries inanimate, or at least insensate. Visit the simple house from which Prohibition emerged singing and swinging.

■ 316 886-3553 • 211 W. Fowler Ave., Medicine Lodge, KS 67104

🚗 Medicine Lodge is in south-central Kansas, about 90 minutes southwest of Wichita, at the junction of US Hwys 281 and 160. The home is on W. Fowler at Oak St. and 160.

🕐 Wed.–Sat. noon–5 P.M., Sun. 1 P.M.–5 P.M. Fee.

NORTON

Gallery of Also-Rans Kansas itself, of course, has Wendell Willkie and Bob Dole. They're among the once-famous who adorn the walls of this presidential losers' exhibit. Some, like Grover Cleveland or George Bush, are still famous because they were also-wons. But the roster is limited to "major party" candidates; don't look for E. V. Debs (*see* Terre Haute, Indiana) here.

▪ 913 877-3341 • First State Bank, 105 W. Main St., Norton, KS 67654

🚗 Norton is in northwestern Kansas, at the junction of US 36 and US 283.

🕐 Open when the bank is; call to confirm. No fee.

SEDAN

Emmett Kelly Historical Museum Are you down at the mouth? Emmett Kelly created laughter out of the feeling. Why not pay a call on his hometown, where you'll find his and other clowns' memorabilia, along with seashell, antique print, and other collections?

▪ 316 725-3470 • 202–204 E. Main St. (Hwy 166-99), Sedan, KS 67361

🚗 Sedan is in southeastern Kansas, 40 miles west of Coffeyville, on US 166 and KS 99.

🕐 Mid-Apr.–mid-Oct.: Mon.–Fri. 10 A.M.–noon and 1 P.M.–5 P.M., Sat. 10 A.M.–5 P.M., Sun. 1 P.M.–5 P.M. Rest of year and other hours by appointment. No fee.

WELLINGTON

Chisholm Trail Museum Wellington was one of the towns that prospered during the brief (post–Civil War) heyday of the Chisholm Trail, then went on to other pursuits. This museum is full of artifacts of the agricultural and stock-raising past— 40 rooms and three floors' worth. Informants report being "overwhelmed" by it all.

▪ 316 326-3820 • 502 N. Washington, Wellington, KS 67152

🚗 Wellington is in south-central Kansas, an hour south of Wichita. Take I-35S and turn west on US 160, then south on US 81. It's across from the courthouse.

🕐 June–Aug.: Mon.–Sun. 1 P.M.–4 P.M. Rest of year: weekends or by appointment. No fee.

WEST MINERAL

Big Brutus Big Brutus stands 15 stories high and weighs 11 million pounds. His arms are 150 feet long, and he moves at 0.22 mph. What is he? One of the world's largest electric shovels, used 24 hours a day from 1962 to 1974 to strip the overburden off the coalfields here. Climb him, sit in his operator's seat, and consider how small you are. You can even stay here in your RV, if you don't think he'll give you strange dreams. *Tours, Gift Shop*

▪ 316 827-6177 • West Mineral, KS 66782

🚗 West Mineral is in Kansas' southeast corner. From US 69 go west on KS 102 (south of Pittsburg). Continue 6 miles past junction with KS 7, then turn a half-mile south.

🕐 Mon.–Sun.: hours vary with season. Fee.

WICHITA

The biggest city in Kansas has been famous for cows and cowpokes and more recently for airplanes, and you can check this history out at the Old Cow Town Museum, with its restorations and re-creations of pioneer homes and work-places, as well as regional phenomena like an all-wood grain elevator (call 316 264-0671 for information), or at the Kansas Aviation Museum (316 683-9242). There's also the Indian Center Museum (316 262-5221) for Plains Culture and the Wichita Art Museum (316 268-4921) for High Culture. But if you're looking for lit-tle stuff, we're going to send you out of town—distances here are greater, but people drive them more easily—so we say *see also*: Florence, Goessel, Halstead, Wellington.

KENTUCKY

Once upon a time, in the 18th century, the West was a place of legends, prominent among them a land of promise called Kentucky. When settlers had moved onto its limestone soil and prospered, they said good things about their home, things like "Heaven is a Kentucky of a place." While the museums we've chosen also reveal other Kentucky realities, like the hard life of coal miners, a striking proportion have to do with food, drink, and horses, surely signs of the Good Life (or, if you're a pessimist, that the Good Life has here been enshrined, no longer being possible).

What's Big: Louisville's Kentucky Derby Museum (at Churchill Downs, of course) and Louisville Slugger Museum; the International Museum of the Horse, in Lexington's Kentucky Horse Park; the Shaker Village at Pleasant Hill.

BARDSTOWN

Oscar Getz Museum of Whiskey History   Whiskey history, you say? Why, y-e-e-s-s. Here are documents on George Washington's activities during the Whiskey Rebellion. How about a copy of Abe Lincoln's license to keep a tavern? There's a display on Kentucky's own hatchetwoman, Carry Nation (*see also* the Carry A. Nation Home in Medicine Lodge, Kansas). There's an 1854 Booz (that's E. G. Booz, his name taken in vain ever since) bottle. Some moonshine stills and all sorts of equipment and vessels, legal and otherwise. If you find yourself getting dizzy, you can always step into the Bardstown Historical Museum, in the same building.

🏛 502 348-2999 • Spalding Hall, 114 N. 5th St., Bardstown, KY 40004

🚗 Bardstown is 50 miles west-southwest of Lexington. From the Bluegrass Pkwy, enter Bardstown on US 31E, turn right onto US 62E, and then left on 5th St.

🕐 May–Oct.: Mon.–Sat. 9 A.M.–5 P.M., Sun. 1 P.M.–5 P.M. Rest of year: Tues.–Sat. 10 A.M.–4 P.M., Sun 1 P.M.–4 P.M. No fee.

BENHAM

Kentucky Coal Mining Museum   Benham is a former company town, and the museum, founded in 1994, occupies the former company store. There are displays on all aspects of mining and miners' lives. By the time you get here, Loretta Lynn, "the Coal Miner's Daughter," should have her memorabilia on the third floor, and the Portal 31 Walking Tour, in nearby Lynch, should be ready to give you a first-hand look at the mines. *Tours, Gift Shop*

🏠 606 848-1530 • http://www.uky.edu/~rsilver/CommunityService/ky-coal.htm • Main St., Benham, KY 40807

🚐 Benham is in extreme southeastern Kentucky, on Hwy 160 (Main St.).

🕐 Mon.–Sat. 10 A.M.–5 P.M., Sun. 1 P.M.–4 P.M. Fee. Call for off-hours visits and group tours.

BEREA

Berea College Appalachian Museum   Berea College, where Appalachian students work in return for their education, is famous as an arts and crafts center. This museum depicts the life, work, and culture of the mountain people. You'll see textiles and clothing as well as the tools used in various trades and jobs, and there are changing photographic and arts exhibits.

🏠 606 986-9341 x 6078 • http://www.berea.edu/GalleryV/ • 103 Jackson St., Berea, KY 40403

🚐 Berea is in east-central Kentucky, 30 miles south of Lexington. Take Exit 76 off I-75. Go 2 miles east on Hwy 21 and follow signs.

🕐 Feb.–Dec.: Mon.–Sat. 9 A.M.–6 P.M., Sun. 1 P.M.–6 P.M. Fee.

BOWLING GREEN

National Corvette Museum   The Corvette seems to have been invented with an eye to its nostalgia potential. In this high-tech, architecturally bodacious museum, you get a selection of some 50 Vettes, from 1953 into the future, along with assorted memorabilia. Call 502 745-8419 to see about touring the plant, next door. *Tours, Gift Shop, Programs, Library*

🏠 800 538-3883 • 350 Corvette Dr., Bowling Green, KY 42101

🚐 Bowling Green is in southwestern Kentucky. Take Exit 28 off I-65 and follow signs.

🕐 Mon.–Sun. 9 A.M.–7 P.M. Fee.

CLERMONT

Jim Beam American Outpost   If you didn't find out enough about whiskey in nearby Bardstown, here you can tour the whole process, from limestone to bottle.

There's a cooperage museum and exhibits on ingredients, barreling, etc., and on the Beam family (see T. Jeremiah's tasting parlor). Out back they have what they claim is America's oldest still. *Tours, Gift Shop*

🏠 502 543-9877 • Jim Beam Distillery, Hwy 245, Clermont, KY 40110

🚗 Clermont is 22 miles south of Louisville via I-65. Take Exit 112 and go east on Hwy 245.

🕐 Mon.–Sat. 9 A.M.–4:30 P.M., Sun. 1 P.M.–4 P.M. No fee.

CORBIN

Colonel Harland Sanders Cafe and Museum "Eat Where It All Began!"™ This is where the Colonel developed his pressure-fried chicken recipe in 1940. In 1990, on the centennial of his birth, it reopened as a cafe/restaurant. You'll see the kitchen, model motel room, office, signs, equipment, bust of the Colonel, and other memorabilia. The juke box plays Gene Autry's "Kentucky Babe"; enjoy your meal! *See also* Louisville's Colonel Harland Sanders Museum. *Food*

🏠 606 528-2163 • Junction of US 25E and 25W, Corbin, KY 40701

🚗 Corbin is in southeastern Kentucky, about 80 miles south of Lexington on I-75. Take Exit 29 and go south on 25E for 1 mile, then right on 25W for 0.5 miles.

🕐 Mon.–Sun. 7 A.M.–11 P.M. A working restaurant; no fee to enter.

DANVILLE

McDowell House and Apothecary Shop Imagine this: On Christmas morning, 1809, Dr. Ephraim McDowell in this building removed a sizable ovarian tumor (the first time such a thing had been done) from a patient who, having no anesthetic, sang hymns during the operation. His house and shop illustrate the life and work of a frontier doctor. *Tours*

🏠 606 236-2804 • 125 S. 2nd St., Danville, KY 40422

🚗 Danville is in central Kentucky, 45 minutes southwest of Lexington. The McDowell House is downtown, on Constitution Square, among many historic buildings.

🕐 Mar.–Oct.: Mon.–Sat. 10 A.M.–noon and 1 P.M.–4 P.M., Sun. 2 P.M.–4 P.M. Closed Mon. rest of year. Fee.

ELIZABETHTOWN

Schmidt Coca-Cola Memorabilia Museum This museum is in the process of expansion, after which the number of items on display will jump from 3,000 to 90,000! You'll see advertising signs and objects of all sorts—bottles, trays, Coke machines, the Coca-Cola Santa, calendars, ashtrays, playing cards, thermometers, delivery trucks, and a soda fountain from the 1893 Chicago World's Fair. You may also tour the current assembly line. *Tours*

■ 502 737-4000 • Coca-Cola Bottling Company of Elizabethtown, 1201 N. Dixie Hwy, Elizabethtown, KY 42702

🚌 Elizabethtown is an hour southwest of Louisville. Take I-65 to Elizabethtown Exit and go right on Route 1005 (Ring Rd.). Follow this until it crosses 31W; turn left at light and again following first light.

🕐 Mon.–Fri. 9 A.M.–4 P.M. Fee for museum; plant and production area no fee.

FORT MITCHELL

American Museum of Brewing History and Arts   This claims to be the largest collection of beer-related material anywhere. There are thousands and thousands of promotional items along with brewery artifacts and bottles, cans, and glasses. *Tours, Food*

■ 606 341-2802 • Oldenberg Brewery, I-75 and Buttermilk Pike, Fort Mitchell, KY 41017

🚌 Fort Mitchell is in extreme northern Kentucky, just south of Cincinnati, Ohio, and southwest of Covington. Take I-75 Exit 186 onto Buttermilk Pike, to the Drawbridge Estate.

🕐 Mon.–Sun. 10 A.M.–5 P.M. Fee. Tours of brewery on the hour.

Vent Haven Museum   William Shakespeare Berger (1878–1972) created this monument to, and resource for, the world of ventriloquists. If you're serious about this form of showmanship, you'll find over 500 dummies here, but also all kinds of props, costumes, and memorabilia of the great "vents." *See also* the Magic and Movie Hall of Fame in Las Vegas, Nevada. *Library*

■ 606 341-0461 • http://www.fred.net/karina/vent/museum.html • 33 W. Maple Ave., Fort Mitchell, KY 41011

🚌 Ask for directions when you call for an appointment.

🕐 May–Oct.: Mon.–Fri., by appointment only. Fee.

HENDERSON

John James Audubon Museum and Nature Center   The great painter of birds lived in this area for nine years, during which he did much important work. This museum displays a complete collection of his prints and publications, along with other oils and family papers and artifacts. The adjoining nature center offers kids a variety of hands-on and other programs. *Gift Shop, Hands-on, Programs*

■ 502 827-1893 • John James Audubon State Park, Henderson, KY 42420

🚌 Henderson is in northwestern Kentucky, a half-hour west of Owensboro. The State Park is on US 41 just north of Henderson and across the Ohio River from Evansville, Indiana.

🕐 Mon.–Sun. 10 A.M.–5 P.M. Fee.

HOPKINSVILLE

Pennyroyal Area Museum   The Pennyroyal region is known chiefly for its tobacco. The 1907 Black Patch, or Night Rider, "War"; the split loyalties of the Civil War; and the suffering of the Cherokee on the Trail of Tears are among the museum's foci. Of more recent note is the hometown psychic Edgar Cayce; his memorabilia, and that of another area notable, Jefferson Davis, is shown. *Tours, Gift Shop, Programs*

🏛 502 887-4270 • 217 E. 9th St., Hopkinsville, KY 42241

🚐 Hopkinsville is in southwestern Kentucky, at the junction of US 68 and US 41, which together follow 9th St. in downtown. The museum is in the former post office building.

🕓 Mon.–Fri. 8:30 A.M.–4:30 P.M., Sat. 10 A.M.–3 P.M. Fee.

LEXINGTON

American Saddle Horse Museum   The Kentucky Horse Park is a big facility; the International Museum of the Horse gets most of the attention here. The American Saddle Horse Museum salutes Kentucky's only native breed, not as well known as the thoroughbreds. Here you'll see George Ford Morris paintings, find out how you'd look on various saddlebreds in the "Right Horse for You," and learn the history and lore of the breed. If you're wondering, Mr. Ed was a saddler. *See also* the American Saddlebred Horse Museum in Mexico, Missouri. *Gift Shop*

🏛 606 259-2746 • http://www.wmwoods.edu/asb/asbmusm.htm • 4093 Iron Works Pike, on the grounds of the Kentucky Horse Park, Lexington, KY 40511

🚐 Fifteen minutes north of central Lexington, at Exit 120 (Iron Works Pike) off I-75.

🕓 Memorial Day–Labor Day: Mon.–Sun. 9 A.M.–6 P.M. Rest of year: 9 A.M.–5 P.M. Fee.

Headley-Whitney Museum   This is for decorative arts fans. You'll find porcelains and furniture, textiles and sculpture, along with a Shell Grotto. Founder George W. Headley's designs in metals and jewels—jewelry, cigarette boxes, other bibelots (tchotchkes, if you like) are central to the collection. *Tours, Gift Shop, Library*

🏛 606 255-6653 • 4435 Old Frankfort Pike, Lexington, KY 40510

🚐 It's 6.5 miles northwest of central Lexington; the Old Frankfort Pike is Hwy 1681.

🕓 Tues.–Fri. 10 A.M.–5 P.M., Sat.–Sun. noon–5 P.M. Fee.

LOUISVILLE

Colonel Harland Sanders Museum   After his 1940 fried-chicken breakthrough (*see* Corbin), the Colonel grew his empire, which came to be based in Louisville, into the KFC we all know. Come here to follow the story.

🏛 502 456-8353 • 1441 Gardiner Lane, at KFC Intl. Headquarters, Louisville, KY 40213

🚙 Take Exit 15 off I-264 and go 0.75 mile west on Newburg Rd. to Gardiner Lane.

🕐 Mon.–Thurs. 8:30 A.M.–4:30 P.M.; call for other hours. No fee.

Museum of the American Printing House for the Blind   The APH, established in 1858, is the largest company in the world making products for the blind. Here you can tour the plant and learn how braille books and talking books are produced. The museum has exhibits on Louis Braille and Helen Keller and a collection of artifacts relating to education of the blind. Books date from 1786, and there are mechanical braille writers, a tactile globe, and computer games. *Tours, Gift Shop, Food, Hands-on*

■ 800 223-1839 • http://www.aph.org • 1839 Frankfort Ave., Louisville, KY 40206

🚙 Frankfort Ave. runs east from downtown Louisville. Take 64E and exit at Story Ave. Go left at first light (Spring), left at next light (Mellwood), pass under highway, and turn right on Frankfort.

🕐 Museum: Mon.–Fri. 8:30 A.M.–4:30 P.M. No fee. Tours: 10 A.M. and 2 P.M. No fee.

MURRAY

National Scouting Museum   Originally in North Brunswick, New Jersey, this museum moved in the 1980s into a building here with many high-tech displays expounding on Scout values and history. There's a 50-piece collection of Norman Rockwell scouting paintings, artifacts and illustrations of Lord Baden-Powell and other founders, Scout uniforms since 1910, and other memorabilia indoors. Outdoors, your kids may want to participate in the challenge courses of Gateway Park (reservation required). *Gift Shop, Hands-on, Programs*

■ 800 303-3047 • 1 Murray St., Murray, KY 42071

🚙 Murray is in far western Kentucky, west of the Land Between the Lakes, on US 641 and Hwy 94. The museum is on the campus of Murray State University, at 16th St. and Calloway.

🕐 Mar.–Nov.: Tues.–Sat. 9 A.M.–4:30 P.M., Sun. 12:30 P.M.–4:30 P.M. Fee.

OWENSBORO

International Bluegrass Music Museum   This is bluegrass music country, even if it isn't the Bluegrass region itself; Bill Monroe was born not far from here, in little Rosine. The Victorian home of the IBMM is filled with instruments, costumes, posters, recording equipment, archives—a complete history of the music that developed from early-18th-century Appalachian roots into a pop mainstay. The museum hosts musical and other events. *Gift Shop, Programs*

■ 502 926-7891 • RiverPark Center, 207 E. 2nd St., Owensboro, KY 42303

🚙 Owensboro is in western Kentucky, just southeast of Evansville, Indiana. RiverPark Center is downtown, on the Ohio River; follow signs.

🕐 Memorial Day–Labor Day: Mon.–Sat. 10 A.M.–5 P.M. Call to confirm hours. Fee.

PADUCAH

Museum of the American Quilters Society   If there's a renaissance in quilting going on, the MAQS must be at the heart of it. This elegant museum, opened in 1991, shows quilts old and new, pictorial, geometrical, abstract, or whimsical, from a permanent collection and loans. Its classrooms host workshops and other programs, and its library and bookstore have become a resource to the growing army of quilters. *Gift Shop, Programs, Library*

■ 502 442-8856 • 215 Jefferson St., Paducah, KY 42002

🚙 Paducah is in far western Kentucky, on I-24. Take Exit 4 (I-24 Loop/East) and go 5 miles into downtown; the museum is at the corner of 3rd St. and Jefferson.

🕐 Tues.–Sat. 10 A.M.–5 P.M. Also Sun. 1 P.M.–5 P.M. in Apr.–Oct. Fee.

LOUISIANA

Some say traveling to Louisiana is like visiting another country. Bayous, Spanish moss, Sazeracs, the Big Easy, Jambalaya, jazz, Mardi Gras, Cajun fiddlers, Creole belles, Huey Long, riverboats, pirates, vampires, voodoo, folk art, 'gators, gumbo, gambling, rednecks, and royalty. Well, just as you can't count on the Mississippi to hold on at the levee, the Louisiana cup fizzeth over.

What's Big: In Thibodaux, southwest of New Orleans, The Wetlands Acadian Cultural Center; in New Orleans, Preservation Hall, of course; in Baton Rouge, the Louisiana State Museum of Art; and in Lafayette, the Museum at the University of Southwestern Louisiana for its fabulous annual Festival International de la Louisiane.

AVERY ISLAND

McIlhenny Co. McIlhenny means Tabasco Sauce. And Edmund McIlhenny and his descendants have cultivated the wicked-hot variety of capsicum pepper that makes the sauce so distinctive since just after the Civil War. Breathe deep the aroma; then, after a video about those lean post-war years that inspired its creation, watch it being made right before your eyes. *Tours, Gift Shop*

🏠 800 634-9599/318 365-8173 • Avery Island, LA 70513

🚗 From Lafayette, take US 90S, exit at Hwy 14 (near New Iberia), and turn left to Hwy 329. Turn right, staying on about 6 miles to Avery Island and follow signs.

🕐 Mon.–Fri. 9 A.M.–4 P.M., Sat. 9 A.M.–noon. No fee. Note: Motorcycles not allowed on site.

BATON ROUGE

While you're in the area, see also: Carville, Plaquemine

Center for Political and Governmental History Louisiana has a very juicy political history and no trip would be complete without a look at the controversial reign of the populist Kingfish himself, Governor Huey P. Long. An 1849 crenelated cast-iron and brick fortresslike structure, the Old State Capitol is now home to an interactive video clip and sound-bite library of Louisiana's political orators, oral histories, and old newsreels. To see where he was assassinated in 1935, you must go north a few blocks to the current state capitol building—a 34-story extravagantly marbled Art Deco tower from 1932, replete with WPA murals and a panoramic view of the city. *Hands-on*

■ 504 342-0500 • Old State Capitol, 150 North Blvd., Baton Rouge, LA 70801

🚗 At River Rd.

🕐 Mon.–Sat. 10 A.M.–4 P.M., Sun. noon–4 P.M. Fee.

CARVILLE

John R. Trautman Carville Museum   It was at Carville in 1941 that sulfone drugs were first tested on Hansen's Disease (leprosy), and for the first time in history hope—and a cure—was available. The exhibits here touch on the history of an illness that caused society to treat its victims as worse than pariahs, as well as the early, basically ineffective treatment methods like the palm-derivative Chaulmoogra oil, and the remarkable people who sought the cure and to help the victims. *Tours*

■ 504 642-4755 • Gillis W. Long Hansen's Disease Center, 5445 Point Clair Rd., Carville, LA 70721

🚗 About 20 miles southeast of Baton Rouge. Taking I-10, exit onto Hwy 73 for about 6 miles, turning right at the Mississippi River levee onto Hwy 75. It's about 1.5 miles after 75 becomes Hwy 141.

🕐 Mon.–Fri. 8 A.M.–4:30 P.M. Tours: Mon.–Fri. 10 A.M., 1 P.M. No fee.

EUNICE

The Eunice Museum   Eunice is rich with the Acadian culture that dates back to 1894, as well as Native American settlements for centuries before. Visit this old train depot for pix and artifacts on local history. Highlights include a tape chronicling the rousing and bewitching Cajun country zydeco music for which the area is so well known. *Tours*

■ 318 457-6540 • 220 South C. C. Duson Dr., Eunice, LA 70535

🚗 About 40 miles northwest of Lafayette. Take Hwy 13N from I-10 into town.

🕐 Tues.–Sat. 8 A.M.–noon, 1 P.M.–5 P.M. No fee.

GIBSLAND

Bonnie and Clyde Festival   Well, it's sort of a once-a-year museum (except for some paperwork and other odds and ends they have in the historical museum over in neighboring Mount Lebanon), but the festival really brings them out of the woodwork here in northwestern Louisiana. Folks like to commemorate those psychopath killers Clyde Barrow and Bonnie Parker, who were not quite as romantic as Arthur Penn's 1967 movie depicted, yet still seem to have captured some kind of renegade imagination. The event's always in May on the weekend closest to the 23rd, which is when they met their fate back in 1934 right here in quiet Gibsland. What's claimed to be their bullet-riddled death car is out for all to see, and everyone dresses up in period costume and has a good old time.

🏛 City Hall: 318 843-6141 • Gibsland, LA 71028

🚗 About 45 miles east of Shreveport. Take I-20 to Hwy 154S. The marker's a few miles south of town.

JENNINGS

W. H. Tupper General Merchandise Museum & Louisiana Telephone Pioneer Museum   When W. H. Tupper closed up shop in 1949 he left behind his entire inventory, which was then put in storage until his grandson Joe Tupper, Jr., donated it to the town of Jennings. So the new set-up is just like an old mercantile, and the merchandise—clothing, patent medicine, and auto, often with tags intact, and all in original packaging—provides a picture of the needs and wants of rural Louisiana in the first half of the 20th century. Mr. Tupper used to trade goods for pine-needle baskets with the local Coushatta Indians, and those along with the Tupper Chips he used as payment during the Depression and the early wind-up toys—Charlie McCarthy and Popeye amongst them—are of particular interest, as are the old phones that date back to the beginning of Bell. *Gift Shop*

🏛 318 821-5532 • 311 N. Main St., Jennings, LA 70546

🚗 Thirty-five miles west of Lafayette, take I-10 Exit 64 into historic downtown.

🕐 Mon.–Sat. 10 A.M.–6 P.M. Fee.

LAWTELL

Matt's Museum   Well, Edzin Matt's a unique kind of guy, and if you're up for a romp out to the swamp, and you have a special interest in the Civil War, outlaws, or Indians, this spot's for you. There's an 1800s schoolhouse on the site, loads of historic guns and Indian relics, slavery items, documents back to the 1700s . . . and 50 years of milling stones. *Tours, Library*

🏛 318 543-7223 • McClelland St. and Hwy 190, Lawtell, LA 70550

🚗 Twenty-five miles northwest of Lafayette, take US 190 west of Opelousas 6 miles into Lawtell, following the signs. If you pass the logs you've gone too far.

🕐 Open "when he's there," or call for appointment. Donation.

MARTHAVILLE

Louisiana Country Music Museum From early gospel and string band music to the country sounds of today, the roots are folk traditions in the area and they are all—from bluegrass to Cajun, pop, and swing—celebrated here. Exhibits and artifacts include everything from Roy Acuff's yo-yo to his, and other stars', musical instruments, clothing, photos, and personal interviews. In April every year this is the site of the Louisiana Fiddlers' Championships. *Tours, Programs, Library*

■ 318 472-6255 • Rebel State Commemorative Area, Hwy 1221, Marthaville, LA 71450

🚗 West-central Louisiana, about 70 miles south of Shreveport off I-49.

🕐 Mon.–Sun. 9 A.M.–5 P.M. Fee.

MONROE

Emy-Lou Biedenharn Foundation In this case it seems it's the Bible that goes better with Coca-Cola. In 1913 Joseph A. Biedenharn, inspired pharmacist and Coke's first bottler, moved his family here from Vicksburg, Mississippi. There's a batch of cola memorabilia, as well as daughter Emy-Lou's extensive Bible collection, featuring some of the earliest (1560s) brought to America by English settlers and a 1663 translation into Algonquin. *Tours, Programs, Publications*

■ 800 362-0983/318 387-5281 • 2006 Riverside Dr., Monroe, LA 71201

🚗 I-20 Exit 116-B (Civic Center), to Louisville Ave., turn right, then left on N. 3rd St., then left again on Forsythe Ave., and left onto Riverside.

🕐 Tours of historic home and gardens on the hour: Tues.–Fri. 10 A.M.–3 P.M., Sat.–Sun. 2 P.M.–4 P.M. No fee.

NEW ORLEANS

New Orleans' charms include its old cemeteries, strewn throughout the town. The Historic New Orleans Collection (504 523-4662) is the place for a grand look at local history and culture; the associated Williams Research Center (504 598-7171) has even more, along with a music section that features Louis Armstrong's record collection. And the wonderful resource that is Tulane University should not be overlooked. We refer to the Jazz Archive in the Old Mint listing below, but the Southeastern Architectural Archive and the Tulane University Art/Newcomb Collection (504 865-5327) are also well worth a browse.

Germaine Cazenave Wells Mardi Gras Museum Germaine Cazenave Wells, daughter of the charming but ersatz "Count" Arnaud of restaurant fame, was Queen of the Mardi Gras for an impressive reign that covered 22 balls over a 30-year period. The exotic flavor of Carnival is seen through the fabulous masks, the elaborate Krewe invitations and party favors, and most of all in the Queen of the Royal Repast costumes that had her attired as vintage Champagne and her court of maids dressed as Creole Gumbo, Sizzling Steaks, and other celebrated local dishes.

■ 504 523-5433 • Arnaud's Restaurant, 813 Bienville St., New Orleans, LA 70112

🚗 French Quarter. It's on the 2nd floor of the restaurant.

🕓 Sat. 6 P.M.–10 P.M.; Sun.–Fri. 11:30 A.M.–2:30 P.M., 6 P.M.–10 P.M. No fee.

New Orleans Historic Voodoo Museum

How's your ju-ju? The spirit of the great voodoo queen Marie Laveau presides over the essential New Orleans trip into the lore and practice of this fine art. Surely a bit of custom mix gris-gris herbs and oils, guaranteed to find you love, money, success, or any other desire, is irresistible. And you'll be welcomed into the incense-dank occult room, introduced to the top-hatted skull of Baron Samedi—lord of the cemeteries—in the altar room, and pay a visit to Zombi, a 12-foot Burmese python imbued with spirits all his own. *Tours, Gift Shop, Programs, Library*

■ 504 523-7685 • http://www.voodoomuseum.com • 724 Dumaine St., New Orleans, LA 70116

🚗 French Quarter.

🕓 Mon.–Sun. 10 A.M.–dusk. Fee.

New Orleans Pharmacy Museum

In case you didn't have a personal voodoo priestess, you could always stop in the local pharmacy and have them whip up a potion for, say, Fast Luck (cinnamon, bergamot, and verbena) or just a drop of wa wa water. Or perhaps a leech was what the doctor ordered. This was the place for your antidote, be it a patent medicine or a gris-gris potion, or to satisfy a thirst for a fruit phosphate. And it's in the same beautifully appointed townhouse where Louis J. Dufilho, first licensed pharmacist in the United States, had his practice in the 1820s. *Tours*

■ 504 565-8027 • 514 Chartres St., New Orleans, LA 70130

🚗 French Quarter.

🕓 Tues.–Sun. 10 A.M.–5 P.M. Fee.

Old U.S. Mint: New Orleans Jazz Collection and Carnival Exhibit

Fat Tuesday Mardi Gras parades go back to 1857, and the pre-Lenten celebration goes back even further. The history and traditions of the Krewes, or (formerly) secret Carnival societies, and their costumes are nicely presented here, but short of attending the event itself, you might get a better sense of it all with a visit to Mardi Gras World (233 Newton St.), where you can tour through the artists' and sculptors' workshops. The turn-of-the-century birth of jazz in New Orleans' red-light Storyville neighborhood was about various European forms like quadrilles and parade music blending with African and West Indian beats, then mixing it up with field songs and gospel music. The music made lots of happy feet, and the story of how it spread and changed over time is explored here with a vibrant pix and artifacts collection. Go to the William Ransom Hogan Jazz Archive at Tulane University's Howard-Tilton Memorial Library for its reels and reels of oral histories and rare photographs.

🏠 504 568-6968 • http://www.state.la.us/crt/lsmnet3.htm • 400 Esplanade Ave., New Orleans, LA 70116

🚙 French Quarter.

🕐 Tues.–Sun. 9 A.M.–5 P.M. Fee.

OIL CITY

Caddo–Pine Island Oil and Historical Society Museum From isolated swamp and Native American hunting grounds to overnight boomtown, the Caddo–Pine Island oil field whisked this part of the state out of slumber in the early 1900s and left behind a wealth of memorabilia as tribute to the first Ark-La-Tex wildcat town's delirious heyday. Oil industry photos and artifacts and a small collection of Caddo Indian and Kansas City Southern RR items (the museum is currently housed in the Oil City depot) are joined by a full-size standard rig and a working pumping jack, and the boom-era bank and post office from neighboring Trees City. The new quarters will have greatly expanded exhibits on all aspects of this area's development, including riverboat life and the characters and personalities that traveled through—and how. *Tours, Programs, Publications, Library*

🏠 318 995-6845 • 200 S. Land Ave., Oil City, LA 71061

🚙 About 20 miles north of Shreveport off Hwy 1.

🕐 Mon.–Fri. 9 A.M.–noon, 1 P.M.–5 P.M. Sat. by appointment. Fee.

OPELOUSAS

Jim Bowie Museum Born in Kentucky, Bowie came to Louisiana with his family when he was just a boy, and grew up right here. An early career as a sugar planter led to a stint in the state legislature. Then he got wounded in a duel in the eastern Louisiana town of Vidalia. Things just weren't interesting enough for him here though, so when frontier Texas opportunities beckoned, he was on his way. Despite his marriage to the daughter of the territory's Mexican governor, he joined up with other notable revolutionaries like Davy Crockett, and met his end at the Alamo in 1836. His life and times are commemorated here, as is the invention of the famous bowie knife—patented in the name of his brother.

🏠 318 948-6263 • 941 E. Vine St., Opelousas, LA 70570

🚙 About 20 miles north of Lafayette, off US 190.

🕐 Mon.–Sun. 8 A.M.–4 P.M. Donation.

PLAQUEMINE

Gary J. Hebert Memorial Lockhouse   Bayou Plaquemine (PLACK-uh-minn) was used as a navigable artery to the Mississippi for centuries before it was noted in the journal of a French settler. For a period after the Civil War a levee was constructed across it to prevent flooding. Then in 1895 construction began on the lock to control water levels that way. Made of glazed ceramic brick to reflect light, helpful since there were no lighthouses on the mighty Mississipp', the now-decommissioned Dutch-influenced structure is unique to this area. Photo displays, a working model, and a film documentary are featured.

📷 800 233-3560/504 687-7158 • 57730 Main St., Plaquemine, LA 70764

🚗 Thirteen miles southwest of Baton Rouge off Hwy 1. In the downtown historic district.

🕐 Tues.–Sun. 10 A.M.–4 P.M. Group tours by appointment. No fee.

SHREVEPORT

While you're in the area, see: Oil City

SULPHUR

Brimstone Museum   All sulphur—aka brimstone—may do for you, you think, is conjure up the odor of rotten eggs. But *au contraire*. Here at the Brimstone Museum you'll learn all about the revolutionary melting process that Herman Frasch invented in 1894 to pump sulphur from the ground, thus creating a domestic source and satisfying the huge industrial need this country had for it through the 1920s. The Frasch process is explained and there's a one-ton brick of brimstone for you to appreciate as well as period mining photos and other memorabilia.

📷 318 527-7142 • Frasch Park, 800 Picard Rd., Sulphur, LA 70663

🚗 Just west of Lake Charles, off I-10.

🕐 Mon.–Fri. 9:30 A.M.–5 P.M. Donation.

MAINE

Maine now draws much of its income from visitors and second-home owners, and "Vacationland" has a wide range of small museums and galleries that reflect their importance in its economy. But the state remains essentially a conservative, hard-working society, based on the dual foundation of sea and forest—as suggested by many of the other institutions we list.

What's Big: Two fine-arts museums, the Portland Museum of Art and Rockland's Farnsworth—the latter especially attuned to the Maine scene, displaying work of native and adopted children (Louise Nevelson, the Wyeths).

BATH

Maine Maritime Museum   Increasingly well known, the museum occupies buildings on the site of the 19th-century Percy & Small shipyard. Watch vessels new and old being worked on in the Apprenticeshop, alma mater of shipwrights—and of staff at other museums. There is also much marine art, along with tools, accoutrements, and memorabilia of the nautical life, ship models, small boats, a lobstering display, and more. *Gift Shop, Programs*

📮 207 443-1316 • 263 Washington St., Bath, ME 04530

🚗 About 1.6 miles south of the Route 1 exit in downtown ("Historic") Bath, beyond the Bath Iron Works complex. Mooring on the Kennebec River for visitors' boats.

🕐 Mon.–Sun. 9:30 A.M.–5 P.M. Shipyard tours Apr. 15–Oct. Fee.

BRUNSWICK

Peary-MacMillan Arctic Museum   Robert Peary and Donald MacMillan, two Bowdoin men, were key actors in exploring the North Pole and environs. Here two rooms are devoted to Peary, who did or didn't become the first man to reach the Pole in 1909. The slightly later career of his assistant, MacMillan, is the third room's focus. Expedition gear and logs, Inuit art and artifacts, fur clothing, stuffed animals, and other items establish a little piece of the Arctic way down south in Maine. Next door is the Bowdoin Museum of Art. *Gift Shop, Publications*

🏠 207 725-3416 • Hubbard Hall, Bowdoin College, Brunswick, ME 04011

🚗 Bowdoin is at the corner of Maine St. and the Bath Rd. (Route 24), in central Brunswick.

🕐 Tues.–Sat. 10 A.M.–5 P.M., Sun. 2 P.M.–5 P.M. Closed national holidays. Donation.

BUCKSPORT

Northeast Historic Film   Northeast Historic Film bills itself as an archive of northern New England film and video, with the "largest collection of home movies in North America," as well as peep show machines, flip cards, and other theater equipment and memorabilia—an opportunity to "go to the movies" as one would have in the 1940s. *Gift Shop, Hands-on, Publications, Screenings*

🏠 207 469-0924 • http://www.acadia.net/oldfilm/ • 379 Main St., Bucksport, ME 04416

🚗 In the 1916 Alamo Theatre, 0.5 mile from coastal Route 1.

🕐 Mon.–Fri. 9 A.M.–4 P.M. June–Labor Day: Sat. also. Fee for screenings only.

CARIBOU

Nylander Museum   Olof Nylander, a self-taught scientist and collector born in Sweden, amassed a huge number of fossils, shells, marine organisms, and other specimens from both the region and the world. Rocks and minerals, Indian artifacts, butterflies, and an herb garden are also part of the museum's displays. *Hands-on, Library*

🏠 207 493-4209 • 393 Main St., Caribou, ME 04736

🚗 Caribou is in extreme northern Maine, on Route 1. The museum is just south of the middle of town, on Route 161.

🕐 Mar.–Dec: Wed.–Sun. Hours vary; call ahead. Donation.

FARMINGTON

Nordica Homestead Museum   Lily Norton, born here in 1858, became Lillian Nordica (the Lily of the North), turn-of-the-century opera star. Here are not only traditional household items but, among other memorabilia, a large collection of ornate stage gowns and accessories, as well as all of Madame Nordica's scores.

🏠 207 778-2042 • Holley Rd., Farmington, ME 04938

🚗 Farmington is northwest of Augusta. The homestead is off Route 4, about 2 miles north.

🕐 June–Labor Day: Tues.–Sat. 10 A.M.–noon and 1 P.M.–5 P.M., Sun. 1 P.M.–5 P.M. By appointment until Oct. 15. Fee.

ISLAND FALLS

John E. and Walter D. Webb Museum of Vintage Fashion   Frances Webb Stratton's decades of collecting 1840s–1950s men's, women's, and children's clothing and accessories led in 1983 to the creation of this museum, in a family house. Fourteen rooms are filled with hats, dresses, bridal fashions, infants' togs, and more—largely displayed on mannequins in domestic settings. There's also a tea room and antique dolls. *Publications*

▪ 207 862-3797 (Hampden, weekends) • Island Falls, ME 04747

🚗 It's in the far north, on Route 2 in the village of Island Falls, off Exit 59 on I-95, about 20 miles from Houlton and the Canadian border.

🕐 June–Oct.: Mon.–Thurs. 10 A.M.–4 P.M. Weekends by appointment. Donation.

KENNEBUNKPORT

Seashore Trolley Museum   Trolleys and interurban cars from around the world, some in the process of restoration, some you can ride through local countryside. If street railways ever make a comeback, you and your kids will have seen it here first. *Gift Shop, Food*

▪ 207 967-2712 • http://www.biddeford.com/trolley • Log Cabin Rd., Kennebunkport, ME 04046

🚗 About 3.5 miles north of Kennebunkport on North St., which becomes Log Cabin Rd.

🕐 May–mid-Oct.: Mon.–Sun. Reduced schedule to mid-Nov. Hours vary. Fee.

KINGFIELD

Stanley Museum   The Stanley twins, Francis and Freelan, were the inventors of the Stanley Steamer, one of the best-known early automobiles. But they and other family members also did a little of everything. Sister Chansonetta's photographs and some of the hundreds of Stanley-made violins are also here, in tribute to an outstanding collective example of Yankee inventiveness. *Gift Shop, Publications*

▪ 207 265-2729 • School St., Kingfield, ME 04947

🚗 In the heart of Kingfield, north of Augusta, just off Route 27.

🕐 Year-round except Apr. and Nov.: Tues.–Sun. 1–4 P.M. and by appointment. Fee.

OWLS HEAD

Owls Head Transportation Museum   Operational pre-1930 aircraft are probably the main draw, but the museum has Clara Bow's Rolls-Royce, a Stanley Steamer, and all manner of (chiefly early-20th-century) cycles, carriages, automobiles, and engines. There are air and other shows in the spring and summer. This is one museum you can even fly to, via regular service from Boston! *Gift Shop, Library, Screenings*

📷 207 594-4418 • http://www.midcoast.com/~ohtm/ • Route 73, Owls Head, ME 04854
🚗 Take Route 73 2 miles south of Rockland to the Knox County Airport.
🕐 Apr.–Oct.: Mon.–Sun. 10 A.M.–5 P.M. Nov.–Mar.: weekdays 10 A.M.–4 P.M., weekends 10 A.M.–3 P.M. Fee.

PATTEN

Lumberman's Museum   In nine buildings, the Lumberman's Museum details the history and life of northern Maine's pine and spruce logging industry, for which Shin Pond Road has been "the life-line." Machinery and equipment from the early 19th century to the present are on display, and there is an 1820-style logging camp built without a single nail. *Gift Shop*

📷 207 528-2650 • Shin Pond Rd., Patten, ME 04765
🚗 Patten is in far northern Maine. Take Exit 58 or 59 off I-95. The museum is on Shin Pond Rd. (Route 159), just west of Patten.
🕐 July–Aug.: Tues.–Sun. 10 A.M.–4 P.M. Mid-May–June and Sept.–Columbus Day: Fri.–Sun. 10 A.M.–4 P.M. Other days by appointment. Fee.

PEMAQUID POINT (BRISTOL)

Pemaquid Point Lighthouse and Fisherman's Museum   This spectacularly sited museum focuses on the technology of Maine's long fishing history; the development of nets, traps, harpoons, and other tools of the trade is illustrated. There are a Fresnel lens and other lighthouse equipment, models, and depictions of the life of those who have worked this part of the sea. Nearby are the 17th-century Fort William Henry, other archaeological sites, and an art gallery.

📷 207 677-2494 • Pemaquid Point, Bristol (New Harbor), ME 04554
🚗 Take Route 130S from Damariscotta to Lighthouse Park.
🕐 Memorial Day–Columbus Day: Mon.–Sat. 10:30 A.M.–5 P.M., Sun. 1 P.M.–5 P.M. Donation.

RANGELEY

Wilhelm Reich Museum   Freud's outrageous disciple, who died in prison in 1957 after conviction for promoting his sexual energy–accumulating "orgone box," is buried here at his research center. See for yourself his visionary inventions and the atmosphere he worked in, hidden away in the forests of this most unlikely state. *Hands-on, Library*

📷 207 864-3443 • Orgonon, Dodge Pond Rd., Rangeley, ME 04970

🚗 In western Maine's Rangeley Lakes region. Take Route 4/16 about 4 miles west of the town of Rangeley.

🕐 July–Aug.: Tues.–Sun. 1 P.M.–5 P.M. Sept.: Sun. 1 P.M.–5 P.M. Fee.

ROCKLAND

Shore Village Museum (The Lighthouse Museum)   Lighthouse, Coast Guard, and Civil War displays vie for attention here. The bells, lenses, and other artifacts may comprise the largest lighthouse collection in the country. There are also ship models, scrimshaw, weapons, life-saving gear, old postcards, and any number of other delights to occupy a rainy day. *Gift Shop, Hands-on*

🏠 207 594-0311 • 104 Limerock St., Rockland, ME 04841

🚗 It's in the Grand Army of the Republic Hall, east of Route 1 and just north of Main St.

🕐 June 1–Oct. 15: Mon.–Sun. 10 A.M.–4 P.M. Rest of year by appointment. Donation.

SABBATHDAY LAKE (NEW GLOUCESTER)

Shaker Museum   This is the last active Shaker community in the United States, clustered since 1782 on a hill above little Sabbathday Lake. It's a contemplative place; you can wander quietly around some of the buildings and look over the herb fields, but take one of the tours to learn about the Shakers, their singular lives, their many household and labor-saving innovations, and their thorough sense of design. Just north is Poland Spring, where a look at the scattered remains of one of Maine's biggest and best-known resort hotels may bring on more contemplation. Poland Spring's bottling plant isn't open to visitors, but its Maine State Building, brought back from the 1893 Chicago World's Fair, may be (207 998-4142). *Tours, Gift Shop, Publications*

🏠 207 926-4597 • 707 Shaker Rd. (Route 26), Sabbathday Lake (New Gloucester), ME 04260

🚗 On Route 26 just south of Poland Spring. Take 26N from Exit 11 on the Maine Turnpike.

🕐 Memorial Day–Columbus Day: Mon.–Sat. 10 A.M.–4 P.M. Fee.

SEBAGO (DOUGLAS HILL)

Jones Museum of Glass and Ceramics   Thousands of glass and earthenware, stoneware, and porcelain pieces from around the world and through history draw cognoscenti to this rural spot. Colorful Victorian art glass, a glass violin, oil lamps, and other exhibits are augmented by lectures, a large reference library, and collectibles for sale. *Gift Shop, Library*

🏠 207 787-3370 • Douglas Mt., Sebago (Douglas Hill), ME 04024

🚐 Off Route 107 in Douglas Hill, just south of Sebago and west of Sebago Lake, about 30 miles northwest of Portland.

🕐 May–mid-Nov.: Mon.–Sat. 10 A.M.–5 P.M., Sun. 1 P.M.–5 P.M. Rest of year by appointment. Fee.

SOUTHWEST HARBOR

Wendell Gilley Museum   Woodcarver Wendell Gilley (1904–83) left hundreds of finely detailed bird models. The museum also exhibits the work of other wildlife artists and offers carving demonstrations, workshops, and natural history programs. *Gift Shop, Programs*

📱 207 244-7555 • Main St. and Herrick Rd., Southwest Harbor, ME 04679

🚐 Southwest Harbor is on Mt. Desert Island, just outside Acadia National Park. The museum is on Main St. (Route 102), just north of the harbor.

🕐 June–Oct.: Tues.–Sun. 10 A.M.–4 P.M. May and Nov.–Dec.: Fri.–Sun. 10 A.M.–4 P.M. Jan.–Apr.: by appointment. Fee.

THORNDIKE

Bryant's Museum (Bryant's Stoves and Music, Inc.)   The Bryants, Bea and Joe, founded Bryant Stove Works to preserve the artistry and artisanship of cast-iron stoves and heaters. Some of the 18th- and 19th-century examples are unimaginably ornate. There are also stove tiles, toy stoves, antique cars, music boxes, a doll circus, and other curiosities. Stove aficionados know about Bryant's.

📱 207 568-3665 • Main St., Thorndike, ME 04986

🚐 Thorndike is in south-central Maine. Take Exit 35 (Waterville) from I-95 and follow Route 139 for 30 miles, through Unity. The museum is at the 139/220 junction.

🕐 Mon.–Sat. 8 A.M.–5 P.M. Stove showrooms free; fee for antiquities display.

WISCASSET

Musical Wonder House   This old captain's house contains hidden treasure— music boxes of all sorts. Player pianos, machines that combine music with dancing dolls, and a variety of other devices, some unique, many ornate, all in working order, are here. Outside, High St. and Wiscasset reward the walker with views of magnificent early-19th-century houses. *Tours*

📱 800 336-3725 • 18 High St., Wiscasset, ME 04578

🚐 High St. runs above the green, just off coastal Route 1, in the center of Wiscasset.

🕐 Memorial Day–mid-Oct.: Mon.–Sun. 10 A.M.–5 P.M. Fee.

MARYLAND

Maryland has a lot of flavors: Chesapeake Bay (crabs!) and Atlantic Ocean (board-walk!) coasts, Civil War ghosts, early American industry, wide-open rural space. A chunk of it serves as a Beltway suburb and exurb, and another chunk is enlivened by the wonderful mix that is Baltimore—land of John Waters, Camden Yards, water taxis, and some of our favorite little museums.

What's Big: The Baltimore Museum of Art and the spectacular Cone Collection of very early Matisses; the Ellicott City B & O Railroad Station Museum, the National Capital Trolley Museum in Wheaton, and the Chesapeake Beach Railway Museum; the Chesapeake Bay Maritime Museum and, in Annapolis, the U.S. Naval Academy Museum; and the NASA-Godard Space Flight Visitors Center in Greenbelt. Up north there's the perennial favorite, the Havre de Grace Decoy Museum, and you surely won't want to miss the further paean to our feathered friends—the little Poultry Hall of Fame in the big U.S.D.A. National Library down in Beltsville.

ANNAPOLIS

Banneker-Douglass Museum   This museum, housed in a striking Victorian Gothic structure that was once the Mount Moriah African Methodist Episcopal Church, commemorates the lives of two black Marylanders: Benjamin Banneker (1731–1806) and Frederick Douglass (1818–1895). Banneker, a free African American, was a noted astronomer and land surveyor who assisted in the planning of the District of Columbia. Douglass, born a slave in Maryland, ran away to New York and became a leader of the abolitionist movement in the North during the 1840s. Dipping into a rich repository of African-American material culture, changing exhibits explore different facets of Maryland's heritage. *Tours, Library*

■ 410 974-3893 • 84 Franklin St., Annapolis, MD 21401
🚍 Just off Church Circle.
🕓 Tues.–Fri. 10 A.M.–3 P.M., Sat. noon–4 P.M. No fee.

BALTIMORE

The entire group of Baltimore City Life museums is worth exploring, especially the Center for Urban Archaeology and the Peale Museum. Unfortunately, they're currently closed. We're keeping our fingers crossed for a timely reopening. *While you're in the area, see also*: Linthicum.

American Visionary Art Museum A truly wondrous place, a place of no limits, a place with a wide open sense of possibility. But first, a definition might be useful. Unlike folk art, which is most commonly defined as a tradition passed on between generations or within a cultural community, visionary art is self-taught and arises from an "innate personal vision." So what this museum sets out to do is to be a showplace that revels in the spirit of the individual. And it succeeds wildly, whether the medium is found metal bits, smashed-up tomato crates, aluminum foil, or household paint, and you're apt to find bronco-decorated art cars and whirligigs side-by-side with a full-size foil-clad flying machine. *Gift Shop, Food, Programs, Publications, Library, Screenings*

🖥 410 244-1900 • http://www.doubleclickd.com/avam.home.html • 800 Key Hwy, Baltimore, MD 21230

🚗 Inner Harbor area. From I-95N take Exit 55 (Key Hwy), left at light, go under overpass, and turn left onto Key Hwy. Museum is 1.5 miles on left, at Covington St. Water taxi.

🕐 June–Aug.: Tues.–Thur. and Sun. 10 A.M.–8 P.M., Fri.–Sat. 10 A.M.–10 P.M. Sept.–May: Wed.–Thur. and Sun. 10 A.M.–6 P.M., Fri.–Sat. 10 A.M.–8 P.M. Fee.

Babe Ruth Birthplace and Baseball Center The "Sultan of Swat" was born on the second floor of this former row house, but George Herman Ruth, son of Baltimore, made New York the host of the nation's greatest baseball team before World War II. Yankee Stadium, they said, was "the house that Ruth built." The museum—ironically moments away from the Orioles' home stadium, Camden Yards—has a deluxe collection of all things Ruth, from his boyhood bat, to early personal notes and memorabilia, to photos and artifacts that detail his rise to baseball legend. Also on hand, all kinds of stuff on the Baltimore Orioles and the Colts, and a featured exhibit on the Negro Leagues. Be sure to watch the film documentary on the life of the Babe. *Gift Shop*

🖥 410 727-1539 • 216 Emory St., Baltimore, MD 21230

🚗 Off the 600 block of Pratt St., near the northwest edge of Oriole Park at Camden Yards. Light rail: Pratt and Howard.

🕐 Apr.–Oct.: Mon.–Sun. 10 A.M.–5 P.M. Nov.–Mar.: Mon.–Sun. 10 A.M.–4 P.M. Fee.

Baltimore Museum of Industry Located on the city's Inner Harbor, this collection of manufacturing memorabilia is most fun to get to if you travel by water taxi. Once inside this converted late-19th-century cannery, you will marvel at the exhibits of working machinery (print shop, machine shop, oyster cannery) that formed the core of the Industrial Revolution, and the displays of ephemera on industries that got their start in Baltimore—like Noxema, Martin-Marietta (out at Martin State Airport you'll find more on this company's history—and their actual aircraft—at the Glenn L. Martin Aviation Museum [410 682-6122]), and Head skis. The museum also features the 1906 steam tug, the S.S. *Baltimore*, which once plied the waters of Baltimore harbor. *Tours, Gift Shop, Hands-on, Library*

■ 410 727-4808 • http://www.charm.net/bmi • 1415 Key Hwy, Baltimore, MD 21230

🚗 Inner Harbor area. From I-95N take Exit 55 (Key Hwy), turn left at light, go under overpass, and turn left onto Key Hwy. Museum is immediately on your right. Water taxi.

🕐 Memorial Day–Labor Day: Tues.–Fri. and Sun. noon–5 P.M., Wed. also 7 P.M.–9 P.M., Sat. 10 A.M.–5 P.M. Rest of year: Thurs., Fri., Sun. noon–5 P.M. Fee.

Baltimore Public Works Museum   Located inside the 1912 Eastern Ave. Pumping Station at Pier 7, the museum provides a rare look at urban infrastructure in its infancy as it traces local public works history back to 1730 when Baltimore Town was first surveyed. Municipal services including the provision of water and waste disposal as well as the building of roads and bridges are covered in a lively manner with old photos, a full-size replica of a city street, and original turn-of-the-century equipment including some of the actual wooden water pipes that were used back when. *Tours, Gift Shop, Publications, Library*

■ 410 396-5565 • 751 Eastern Ave., Baltimore, MD 21202

🚗 Inner Harbor area. I-83S, continuing as it turns into President St. It's on the right as you cross Eastern Ave., near the corner of E. Falls Ave. at Pier 7. Water taxi.

🕐 Tues.–Sun. 10 A.M.–5 P.M. Tours of the works by appointment. Fee.

Dr. Samuel D. Harris National Museum of Dentistry   Hey, who said going to the dentist can't be fun? Vintage TV ads; amazing dental feats (don't miss the video of a geriatric Jack LaLanne–type gripping a water ski towline with his choppers); toothbrushes like Dr. Funk's pre-1945 Lingual brush, or a 1920s Kleen-Rite celluloid model with replaceable head; the real truth about our first president's dentures; and a feature on practitioners who dabbled outside of dentistry, like the inventor of—of all things—cotton candy, are all part of a surprising and comprehensive look at a field that goes back to at least 4000 B.C. *Tours, Library*

■ 410 706-0600 • 31 S. Greene St., Baltimore, MD 21201

🚗 Downtown, on the University of Maryland campus. From I-95, take I-395 and exit onto Martin Luther King, Jr., Blvd. At 4th light, turn right onto Baltimore St. Turn left at 2nd light onto Paca St. and enter Baltimore Grand Garage on right. Light rail: Pratt and Howard.

🕐 Wed.–Sat. 10 A.M.–4 P.M., Sun. 1 P.M.–4 P.M. Fee.

Eubie Blake National Museum   The great pianist and composer Eubie Blake is celebrated here with musical memorabilia and personal artifacts that track his contribution to ragtime at the dawn of the jazz age, and onward through the latter part of the 20th century when he received renewed recognition as a veritable national treasure. Period costumes from his Broadway shows are also on hand, set amidst a collection of music and films on the Harlem Renaissance.

🏠 410 371-4155 • 34 Market Pl., Baltimore, MD 21202

🚗 Downtown, in the Brokerage Building. I-83S to Lombard St., turn right, then right again onto Market Pl. Metro: Shot Tower.

🕐 Mon.–Fri. noon–4:30 P.M. Donation.

H. L. Mencken House Mencken, the cranky Baltimore journalist of the 1920s, lambasted the mores of the middle class ("the boobsgeoisie"). He cracked that straitlaced Americans are haunted by the fear that "somewhere someone may be happy." Here is his house, as middle class as the folks he ridiculed in his writing, fully restored and replete with his prized gardens and Tonk baby grand piano. In the parlor there's an audiovisual presentation that documents the life of the "Sage of Baltimore." The museum's unfortunately closed at present; call for details.

🏠 410 396-3523 • 1524 Hollins St., Baltimore, MD 21223

🚗 West on Lombard St. from downtown, it's off Union Square. Metro: Shot Tower.

Lacrosse Hall of Fame Museum This is America's oldest team sport, with its roots in Native American religion. Learn about the 350-year-old history of the game by studying the 50-foot timeline. The museum features a rich collection of vintage equipment and uniforms, trophies, rare historic photos, and modern photomurals of men's and women's teams at play. A videotape captures exciting moments from recent championship games. *Gift Shop*

🏠 410 235-6882 • http://lacrosse.org • 113 West University Pkwy, Baltimore, MD 21210

🚗 Take I-95 north or south to I-395, Downtown Baltimore. Merge right onto Conway St., turning left at 2nd light onto Charles St., and go about 3 miles, turning left onto University Pkwy. It's the first building on left after field.

🕐 June–Feb.: Mon.–Fri. 9 A.M.–5 P.M. Rest of year also open Sat. 10 A.M.–3 P.M. Fee.

Mount Vernon Museum of Incandescent Lighting Here's another dentist who dabbled outside his field. The story goes Dr. Hugh Francis Hicks has collected lightbulbs since his mama discovered they could soothe his tears as a child. He's now got over 60,000 of them and rarely breaks a one. Put together, they provide a seamless history of one of man's most significant inventions. From the largest—a 50,000 watt wonder built to celebrate the 50th anniversary of Edison's 1878 patent—to a pinprick-size bulb used to inspect missile parts, and from Edison and his competitors' earliest, to the eccentric (like a cockpit bulb from the *Enola Gay* juxtaposed with a headlight bulb from Heinrich Himmler's staff car), Dr. Hicks can fill you in about each and every one.

🏠 410 752-8586 • 717 Washington Pl., Baltimore, MD 21201

🚗 About 10 blocks north of the Inner Harbor area, near the corner of Madison and Charles Sts. on the north side of the Washington Monument. Bus: #3.

🕐 By appointment only. Donation.

FORT GEORGE MEADE

National Cryptologic Museum The route to this museum is almost as intriguing as the museum itself. But what better way to get in the mood for revelations of the clandestine and the inscrutable. A lot of the items here have been classified until very recently, adding to the intrigue. Coding devices displayed span over 400 years and feature crude but clever items from the Civil War; the electrifying moments during World War II when the American "Bombe" deciphered the keys on the German "Enigma" cipher machine; the coldest of the Cold War with displays of James Bond–like bugs, including one hidden in a Great Seal of the United States presented to Averell Harriman by Soviet schoolchildren in 1946 (it hung in the ambassador's office until it was discovered in the '60s); and the latest computer technology. *Tours, Gift Shop*

📞 301 688-5848/5849 • http://www.nsa.gov:8080/ • Ft. George G. Meade, MD 20755

🚌 Beltway area. Just east of the intersection of Route 295 (B-W Pkwy) and Route 32, follow signs at the Shell gas station, turning north off of Route 32 onto Colony 7 Road. It's next to the National Security Agency headquarters.

🕐 Mon.–Fri. 9 A.M.–3 P.M., Sat. 10 A.M.–2 P.M., and by appointment. No Fee.

FREDERICK

National Museum of Civil War Medicine This new museum, near the Civil War battlefields at Gettysburg and Antietam, documents the medical side of the battles between the Blue and the Gray. Civil War doctors made advances in the use of anesthesia (see the anesthesia inhaler invented by a Confederate surgeon) and they attempted reconstructive surgery on patients shattered by war. The museum is housed in a building that was used to embalm soldiers killed during the 1862 Battle of Antietam. *Tours, Gift Shop, Programs, Library*

📞 301 695-1864 • http://www.CivilWarMed.org • 48 E. Patrick St., Frederick, MD 21705

🚌 West-central Maryland. I-70W to Exit 56 (Patrick St.); go about 2 miles to the Historic Downtown Section. They're on the left, 1.5 blocks past Carroll St.

🕐 Apr.–Oct.: Mon.–Sat. 10 A.M.–5 P.M., Sun. 11 A.M.–5 P.M. Until 4 P.M. rest of year. Donation.

GLEN ECHO

Clara Barton National Historic Site Known as the "Angel of the Battlefield" for her work with wounded soldiers during the Civil War, Clara Barton went on to become the first president of the American Red Cross in 1881. In addition to her crusade for the humane treatment of wounded soldiers, Barton spoke out in defense of voting rights for the freed slaves and for the rights of women. The three-story building, first used for Red Cross storage, became both her home and the first permanent headquarters of the organization in 1897. Tour guides re-create her fascinating life as they take you through the house. *Tours, Gift Shop, Library*

🖼 301 492-6245 • 5801 Oxford Rd., Glen Echo, MD 20812

🚗 Beltway area. Take I-495S Exit 40 onto Cabin John Pkwy. After it merges into Clara Barton Pkwy, exit at Glen Echo onto MacArthur Blvd., then left on Oxford Rd.

🕐 Mon.–Sun. 10 A.M.–5 P.M. Tours hourly on the half hour. No fee.

LINTHICUM

Historical Electronics Museum Technological development and electronics have gone hand in hand, especially in the last 50 years or so. Again we have electro-mechanical code cipher machines like the Enigma, and other exotic items like one of the 1969 lunar TV cameras. And while hands-on displays offer an original Edison cylinder phonograph for your listening pleasure, and telegraph machines to test your Morse Code skills, the more dramatic displays may be more large scale—like the SCR-584, the first automatic tracking and gunfire control radar. That one's set up outdoors, and you can climb right into it. *Tours, Hands-on, Library*

🖼 410 765-3803 • 1735 W. Nursery Rd., Linthicum, MD 21090

🚗 From Baltimore, take 295S (B-W Pkwy) to first exit on right, turning left onto W. Nursery Rd. It's just before Elkridge Landing Rd., on the left.

🕐 Mon.–Fri. 9 A.M.–3 P.M., Sat. 10 A.M.–2 P.M. No fee.

NEW CARROLLTON

Museum of Menstruation (MUM) Who would argue that Harry Finley is an unusual man? After all, he comes from a family known for creating "monuments to women." For instance his grandfather founded the Miss America contest. So perhaps it's only natural he would become interested in this most personal aspect of female biology, the field of feminine hygiene. So here in his very own home you may take a tour of the products (and their packaging), their history and advertising, and the myths and lore about our favorite aunt from Red Bank.

🖼 301 459-4450 • http://www.mum.org • 5905 Mentana St., New Carrollton, MD 20784

🚗 Beltway area. Call for directions. Washington, DC Metro: Orange/New Carrollton.

🕐 Weekends, by appointment only. No fee.

OCEAN CITY

Ocean City Life-Saving Station Museum Last used by the Coast Guard in 1962, the red-roofed Victorian structure built in 1891 displays lifesaving equipment used to rescue the crews of ill-fated ships that ran into trouble off the Del-Mar-Va coast. See artifacts from the *Jacob Jones*, a ship torpedoed off the coast of Ocean City by a German submarine during World War II, and china from the *Andrea Doria*, which sank in 1956. On a (much) lighter note, the museum also features some really itchy beach fashions from the early 1900s; a nostalgic selection of beach-going toys, shades, and boardwalk memorabilia; a Mermaid Room (over 50 examples); and a "Sands from Around the World" exhibit. *Gift Shop*

■ 410 289-4991 • Boardwalk at the Inlet, Ocean City, MD 21842

🚗 Eastern shore. US 50 into Ocean City, then right on Philadelphia Ave. to the south end of the boardwalk.

🕐 June–Sept.: Mon.–Sun. 11 A.M.–10 P.M. May and Oct.: Closes 4 P.M. Nov.–Apr.: Sat.–Sun. noon–4 P.M., and by appointment. Fee.

SILVER SPRING

George Meany Memorial Archives   This Bronx plumber went on to lead the largest labor federation in the noncommunist world. Under Meany's leadership, the AFL-CIO represented about a quarter of America's work force. Those were the glory days of a union movement that has been in sharp decline since Meany's death in 1980. The archives bearing Meany's name contain written records documenting the evolution of the AFL-CIO. In addition to records chiefly of interest to scholars, the museum also features a wide assortment of labor-action related buttons, banners, caps, bumper stickers, photos, signs, and other ephemera.

■ 301 431-5451 • 10000 New Hampshire Ave., Silver Spring, MD 20903

🚗 Beltway area. On the campus of George Meany Center for Labor Studies. One block north of US 495, Exit 28A, and west of the intersection of New Hampshire Ave. and Powder Mill Rd. Washington, DC Metro: Red/Silver Spring.

🕐 Mon.–Fri. 9:30 A.M.–4 P.M. No fee.

Massachusetts

So much History, and so little time! Not to mention the Culture. The Commonwealth probably isn't embarrassed by its riches; they may be New Englanders, but we swear we've heard them brag. To make the most of a visit, you should really do some reading first. Then accept that you'll come up against things you didn't anticipate, because there's still a lot happening in Massachusetts.

What's Big: Boston's Freedom Trail, Faneuil Hall, Museum of Fine Arts, Isabella Stewart Gardner Museum, New England Aquarium, etc., etc., etc.; in Cambridge, Harvard's museums and libraries; the historical complexes and accompanying theme sites at Plymouth, Salem, Lexington-Concord, and Quincy; the re-creation complex at Sturbridge Village; the Basketball Hall of Fame in Springfield, and the museums on that city's Quadrangle; and, way out west, the new Massachusetts Museum of Contemporary Art, in North Adams.

BOSTON

The Athens of America and Hub of the Universe has a plethora of "big" museums and sites—the stops along the Freedom Trail, the U.S.S. *Constitution*, the Boston Museum of Fine Arts, the Isabella Stewart Gardner Museum, and others. Here we're going to list a few places you may have overlooked. And since this is a relatively small central city in a large metropolitan area, don't forget that the visitor's "Boston" includes many adjacent municipalities. *While you're in the area, see also*: Brookline, Cambridge, Dedham, Lincoln, Waltham, Watertown, Weston.

Boston Athenaeum   Is the Athenaeum a museum? Let's put it this way: If 19th-century Boston was the "Athens of America," you're on the Acropolis here. This is a museum of the mind. Established in 1807, it's the country's premier private library. In addition to the tradition- and atmosphere-rich reading rooms, there are portraits by Stuart, Sargent, and others on the walls. Most of the original art collection moved to the Museum of Fine Arts in the 1870s.

■ 617 227-0270 • 10½ Beacon St., Boston, MA 02108

🚗 It's on Beacon Hill, just down the street from the State House.

🕐 First two floors: Mon.–Fri. 9 A.M.–5:30 P.M., Sat. 9 A.M.–4 P.M. Tours of Athenaeum Tues. and Thurs. at 3 P.M.; call 24 hrs. ahead for appointment. No fee.

Computer Museum   This museum gets less "little" all the time, but we include it especially for your kids. There's a huge walk-through computer with a giant mouse and other parts, robots, a virtual reality gallery, and all sorts of interactive displays. But there is also, for serious students of cybernetics, "the most comprehensive" collection available of computers past, present, and future. For students of more earthbound cyberconnections, the Museum of Dirt now has a local physical space to go with its exalted website (by appointment only, 617 574-4800). *Tours, Gift Shop, Hands-on, Programs, Publications*

■ 617 423-6758 • http://www.tcm.org • 300 Congress St., Boston, MA 02210

🚗 It's a short walk across the Congress St. Bridge from South Station. Take Exit 23 (southbound) from I-93 and go left on Congress. Or take the Downtown/Chinatown exit (northbound) and go right on Kneeland, left on Atlantic, and right on Congress. From I-90, take the South Station exit and go 3 lights, then right on Congress.

🕐 Winter: Tues.–Sun. 10 A.M.–5 P.M. Summer: Mon.–Sun. 10 A.M.–6 P.M. Fee.

BROOKLINE

Frederick Law Olmsted National Historic Site   America's famous park builder set up shop here in 1883, establishing the world's first true landscape architecture practice, carried on by his sons and other disciples. The house and office complex are surrounded by Fairstead, the small estate laid out according to Olmsted's principles. Not far away, in Brookline and in Boston's Back Bay, Jamaica Plain, and Dorchester sections, is Olmsted's Emerald Necklace, one of the most famous of his urban oases. Another noted 19th-century figure, Mary Baker Eddy, the founder of Christian Science, is remembered at the Longyear Museum (617 277-8943), a short walk from the Olmsted site. *Tours, Gift Shop, Publications*

■ 617 566-1689 • 99 Warren St., Brookline, MA 02146

🚗 About a quarter-mile south of Boylston St. (Route 9), in the heart of Brookline. Bus: #60. Subway: Green Line, Riverside branch/Brookline Hills.

🕐 Fri.–Sun. 10 A.M.–4:30 P.M. Groups other days by appointment. Fee.

CAMBRIDGE

Mount Auburn Cemetery   In the 19th century, "rural" cemeteries were regarded not only as fitting memorials to the deceased, but as places of public resort. Eventually, the concept gave birth to our urban public parks. Mount Auburn, established in 1831, was the pioneer. Today you can see the graves of notables from Margaret Fuller to Buckminster Fuller, from Henry Wadsworth Longfellow to Bernard Malamud, as well as a historic landscape, a magnificent collection of statuary, and hundreds of species, most identified, of trees and shrubs. *Tours, Programs*

🏠 617 547-7105 • 580 Mount Auburn St., Cambridge, MA 02138

🚗 It's about 1.5 miles west of Harvard Square, just west of Mount Auburn Hospital and Fresh Pond Pkwy. Buses from Harvard Square stop at the cemetery.

🕐 Mon.–Sun. 8 A.M.–5 P.M. Open to 7 P.M. during daylight savings time. No fee.

DALTON

Crane Museum   This is about paper, high-quality paper. Your wedding announcement, your thank-you notes, your tracing paper, your stock certificates, even your cash may have come from Dalton. Crane has been making paper, especially the top-of-the-line all-rag stuff, since the beginning of the 19th century. You'll see a model depiction of the original vat house, and displays on the history of American papermaking. It's all found in a building of great beauty and serenity.

🏠 413 684-2600 • Housatonic St., Dalton, MA 01226

🚗 Dalton is in western Massachusetts, 5 miles east of Pittsfield. Crane & Company is on SR 8/9. The museum is in the Old Stone Mill, behind company offices.

🕐 June–mid-Oct.: Mon.–Fri. 2 P.M.–5 P.M. No fee.

DEDHAM

Museum of Bad Art   If you ever dreamed that your very own paintings might end up on the walls of a museum, this is the museum that proves that dreams can come true! Of course, we aren't necessarily talking about *good* dreams. . . . We understand the full meaning of the term *provenance* when we think about MOBA's prizes, because some of them came straight off the streets of nearby Jamaica Plain, and we used to live along those streets. (Fortunately, we weren't attempting to paint in those days.) But look, the world is full of artists, and, on garbage nights especially, the streets are full of art. All it took was a few geniuses like MOBA's founders to make the necessary connections. They rotate the really "good" stuff in this basement display. The documentation is awesome. *Gift Shop, Publications*

🏠 781 325-8224 • http:www//glyphs.com/moba • Dedham Community Theater, 580 High St., Dedham, MA 02026

🚗 Dedham is just outside Boston's southwestern city limits. High St. runs east from US 1 through downtown. MOBA is in the Community Theater's basement.

🕐 Open during theater hours: Mon.–Fri. 6:30 P.M.–10:30 or 11 P.M. Weekends: 1:30 P.M.–10:30 or 11 P.M. No fee for museum.

FALL RIVER

Fall River Historical Society   In a mill owner's mansion, this general history museum depicts Fall River's textile and maritime history. You've probably come for the Lizzie Borden exhibit, which includes some of the actual evidence, along with other memorabilia. If you want more, why not take a tour (on the half hour, 11 A.M.–3 P.M., seven days a week) at the nearby Lizzie Borden Bed and Breakfast Museum, in the very house where the crime occurred. Call them (508 675-7333) for further information, or if you'd like to spend the night!

🏛 508 679-1071 • 451 Rock St., Fall River, MA 02720

🚗 From I-195E, take the exit after Battleship Cove. Turn right, and right again on 3rd, which becomes Rock St. north of Bedford.

🕐 Mar.–Nov.: Tues.–Fri. 9 A.M.–4 P.M. Sat. and Sun. 1 P.M.–5 P.M. in summer. Fee.

Marine Museum at Fall River   Many visitors come here for the *Titanic* model and memorabilia (*see also* the *Titanic* Museum in Springfield), but this museum chiefly recalls the heyday (into the 1930s) of the coastal steamships of the Old Fall River Line, and has some 150 other models of ships of all sorts.

🏛 508 674-3533 • 70 Water St., Fall River, MA 02721

🚗 It's just south of Battleship Cove and the I-195 bridge, on the waterfront.

🕐 May–Oct.: Mon.–Fri. 9 A.M.–5 P.M.; Sat.–Sun. noon–5 P.M. Nov.–Apr.: Tues.–Fri. 9 A.M.– 5 P.M.; Sat.–Sun. noon–5 P.M. Fee.

FISKDALE

Saint Anne Shrine   In a quiet pastoral setting a short distance from Sturbridge Village's bustle, this Assumptionist center, which includes an active church, is known for its collection of Russian icons, some from the 17th century. Exhibits and accompanying materials reveal the fine points of an art rarely seen in America. On the grounds is a collection of religious statuary. *Gift Shop, Programs*

🏛 508 347-7461/Group Programs: 347-7338 • 16 Church St., Fiskdale, MA 01518

🚗 The shrine is off Route 20, 1 mile west of Sturbridge Village (take Exit 9 from Mass Pike or Sturbridge Village exit from I-84).

🕐 Mon.–Fri. 10 A.M.–4 P.M., Sat.–Sun. 10 A.M.–6 P.M. Donation.

HARVARD

Fruitlands Museums   Fruitlands is a complex of four museums. The 1843 farmhouse was home to the Con-Sociate Family, led by transcendentalist Bronson Alcott and others. There is also a Shaker museum, with Mother Ann Lee's chair; the Picture Gallery, featuring Hudson River School and other 19th-century paintings and folk art; and the Indian Museum, with many items relating to the spiritual life of Native Americans, as well as basketry and King Philip's war club. *Tours, Gift Shop, Food, Programs, Library*

■ 978 456-3924 • http://www.USA1.comFruitland • 102 Prospect Hill Rd., Harvard, MA 01451

🚗 Harvard is 30 miles west of Boston. Exit from Route 495 to Route 2, and proceed west to Exit 38A. Go right from exit and right on Old Shirley Rd. for 2 miles.

🕐 Museums open mid-May–mid-Oct.: Tues.–Sun. and Mon. holidays 10 A.M.–5 P.M. Fee. Grounds open daily year-round, 10 A.M.–5 P.M.

LEOMINSTER

National Plastics Center and Museum   Leominster was once the comb capital and in 1900 began to use a then-new material, celluloid, in its major product. The NPC&M, opened by the John Wesley Hyatt Society in 1992, focuses on developing methods for educating children and adults on the plastic industry, uses of plastic, recycling, and related matters. *Tours, Gift Shop, Programs*

■ 508 537-9529 • http://www.Polymers.com/npcm/ • 210 Lancaster St., Leominster, MA 01453

🚗 Leominster is in north-central Massachusetts, north of Worcester. Take Exit 7 off I-190, and go 2 miles west on Route 117.

🕐 Wed.–Sat. 11 A.M.–4 P.M. Closed major holidays. Fee.

LINCOLN

DeCordova Museum and Sculpture Park   Hidden in this affluent suburb is a fine art museum, focusing on 20th-century New England and American painters, with a sculpture garden and 35-acre park. On weekends, you can drive down nearby Baker Bridge Rd. and see the home of Bauhaus architect Walter Gropius (617 227-3956). At the end of Baker Bridge Rd. is Walden Pond, on the Concord town line. *Programs*

■ 781 259-8355 • http://www.decordova.org • 51 Sandy Pond Rd., Lincoln, MA 01773

🚗 Lincoln is a suburb just outside Boston's Route 128. Take Exit 28 off I-95/128 and follow Trapelo Rd. west to Sandy Pond Rd.

🕐 Tues.–Fri. 10 A.M.–5 P.M., Sat.–Sun. noon–5 P.M. Fee. Park open daily 8 A.M.–10 P.M. No fee.

LOWELL

American Textile History Museum   Lowell more or less *is* American textiles. It was created in the 1820s as a model industrial center, and its history since then, including its recent metamorphosis into a combination high-tech manufacturer/historical park, tells a story that echoes all over this country. This museum, moved from nearby North Andover in 1997, has a huge collection of machinery and products, tools and equipment, and artifacts of the millworkers' culture. *Tours, Gift Shop, Food, Programs*

🔲 978 441-0400 • 491 Dutton St., Lowell, MA 01854

🚗 Lowell is 25 miles northwest of Boston. From I-495, take the Lowell Connector (Exit 35C) and follow to Exit 5N (Thorndike St.). The museum is on the left just after the 4th traffic light on Thorndike.

🕐 Tues.–Fri. 9 A.M.–5 P.M., Sat.–Sun. 10 A.M.–4 P.M. Fee. Call to reserve for tours.

Boott Cotton Mills Museum   Boott Mills was a key factor in Lowell's industrial heyday. Renovated in the 1980s, the complex now houses the Tsongas Industrial History Center, the New England Folklife Center, and displays including the huge (and noisy!) Weave Room, with 88 power looms. Rangers and audiovisual exhibits help detail labor, industrial, and ethnic history; one even played the dulcimer for friends of ours. *Tours, Gift Shop, Programs*

🔲 978 970-5000 • 400 Foot of John St., Lowell National Historical Park, Lowell, MA 01852

🚗 Take I-495 or Route 3 to Lowell Connector to Exit 5N. Go right on Thorndike St., then right on Dutton to LNHP Visitors Center for free parking. John St. runs from Merrimack St. to the river, a short walk away.

🕐 Mon.–Sun. 9:30 A.M.–5 P.M. Fee.

New England Quilt Museum   Like MAQS (*see* Paducah, Kentucky), this is a center for quilters, with a library, workshops and other programs, research undertakings, and changing and visiting as well as permanent exhibits. An idea of the range of interests represented among members and exhibitors is suggested by the 1997 schedule, which includes shows on landscape quilts, mourning and healing quilts, quilts of the Depression, and the work of leading contemporaries. *Gift Shop, Programs, Library*

🔲 978 452-4207 • 18 Shattuck St., Lowell, MA 01852

🚗 Shattuck St. is across from the visitors center (*see* Boott Cotton Mills directions).

🕐 May–Dec.: Tues.–Sat. 10 A.M.–4 P.M., Sun. noon–4 P.M. Jan.–Apr.: no Sun. hours. Fee.

NORTHAMPTON

Words and Pictures Museum of Fine Sequential Art   Comic books? The term seems hardly adequate to describe the genre this museum is all about. Through permanent and rotating gallery exhibits, "themed environments" (like futuristic fantasy or paleolithic story), interactive and computer displays, and other means, the story of comic art from the beginning—but chiefly in recent decades—is told. *Gift Shop, Hands-on*

📱 413 586-8545 • 140 Main St., Northampton, MA 01060
🚗 Take Exit 18 off I-91. Go left on Route 5 1 mile to first traffic light, then left onto Main St.
🕐 Tues.–Sun. noon–5 P.M. Extended hours Fri., Sat., summer, holidays. Fee.

NORTH EASTON

Shovel Museum/Arnold B. Tofias Archives   Oliver Ames founded the O. Ames Shovel Company in North Easton in 1803, and the town became the center of the American industry. The company is gone, but the Ames Estate became Stonehill College, and the college has perhaps the largest shovel collection in the world. Archivist Louise Kenneally points out that the collection is mainly records and correspondence, but there are some 800 of the humble tools. It's tempting to say: you dig?

📱 508 565-1396 • Stonehill College, 320 Washington St., North Easton, MA 02357
🚗 North Easton is about 20 miles south of Boston and 5 miles west of Brockton. Follow signs for Stonehill College and look for Donahue Hall.
🕐 By appointment only. Sept.–May: Mon.–Fri. 8:30 A.M.–4:30 P.M. No fee.

ONSET

Porter Thermometer Museum (Dick Porter—Thermometer Man)
At last count, Dick Porter had 2,579 thermometers and related items in his collection. But there will be more by the time you arrive; Guinness and Ripley's both list him as number one. He has thermometers, he has a batch of degrees, and he isn't shy. If you can't get here, maybe you'd like to book one of his lectures.

📱 508 295-5504 • Onset, MA 02558
🚗 Onset is in southeastern Massachusetts, just east of the I-495/I-195 junction, on the way to Cape Cod's Bourne Bridge. Call for directions and reservations.
🕐 Open "365 days a year, 24 hours a day"; call ahead. No fee.

ORLEANS

French Cable Station Museum   From 1890 through 1959, except when the World War II German occupation closed things down at the other end, this small building received the news from France—news like that of Lindbergh's 1927 landing—via cable lying on the Atlantic's floor. Now it is both a monument to those who manned it and a reminder of the complex technology of those pre-satellite days. *Publications*

📱 508 240-1735 • Route 28 at Cove Rd., Orleans, MA 02653

🚗 Orleans is at the "elbow" of Cape Cod. Take Exit 12 from the Mid Cape Hwy (Route 6) and follow 6A into town. Cross Main St. and turn right on Cove Rd.

🕐 July–Aug.: Tues.–Sat. 2 P.M.–4 P.M., or by appointment. Fee.

PETERSHAM

Fisher Museum of Forestry   Harvard Forest comprises 3,000 acres, on which Harvard and other researchers study ecological and botanical issues, and through which there are self-teaching trails. The Fisher Museum is noted for its dioramas—vivid representations of the historical development of New England forests, from first settlement to today. *Programs*

📱 978 724-3302 • http://www.fas.harvard.edu/peabody/museum_fisher.html • at the Harvard Forest, Petersham, MA 01366

🚗 Harvard Forest is 70 miles west of Boston on Route 2, then 3 miles south on Route 32. From I-91, exit at Greenfield and take Route 2 25 miles east to the Route 32 junction.

🕐 Jan.–Dec.: Mon.–Fri. 9 A.M.–5 P.M. May–Oct.: also Sat.–Sun. noon–4 P.M. Fee. Groups by appointment.

ROCKPORT

Paper House   Looking for a museum of newspapering? How about a museum *of newspaper*—newspaper and glue? Beginning in 1922, Elis Stenman built this whole house of folded and pasted newspapers. Even the fireplace. All right, he covered some parts with newspaper. There's a grandfather clock made from the dailies in 48 state capitals. Stenman's grandniece still feels an obligation to show the world his wonderful whim.

📱 978 546-2629 • Pigeon Hill St., Pigeon Cove, Rockport, MA 01966

🚗 Rockport is on Cape Ann, northeast of Boston. Take Route 127N through town to Pigeon Cove, and follow Curtis St. to Pigeon Hill St.

🕐 Apr.–mid-Oct.: Mon.–Sun. 10 A.M.–5 P.M. Fee.

SANDWICH

Sandwich Glass Museum   Sandwich was a glass center in the mid-19th century, noted especially for its engraving technique and use of delicately shaded colors. The museum shows engraved, blown, cut, and pressed glass in a wide variety of forms and designs. There are also a diorama of the old plant and displays of furniture, paintings, books, and local historical artifacts. *Gift Shop, Programs*

📱 508 888-0251 • 129 Main St., Sandwich, MA 02563

🚐 Sandwich is on the north shore of the "shoulder" of Cape Cod. The museum is at the corner of Tupper Rd. and Route 130, across from Town Hall.

🕐 Apr.–Oct.: Mon.–Sun. 9:30 A.M.–4:30 P.M. Rest of year except Jan.: Wed.–Sun. 9:30 A.M.–4 P.M. Fee.

Thornton W. Burgess Museum   Located in the 1756 Eldred House, this is a nature center, with fine mounted collections, rocks, minerals, fossils, and a wild-flower garden. But you probably came to see the home of the inventor of Peter Rabbit, and it tells his story through manuscripts, illustrations from his books, and other memorabilia.

🏠 508 888-4668 • 4 Water St. (Route 130), Sandwich, MA 02563

🚐 See directions for Sandwich Glass Museum. The Burgess Museum is on Route 130.

🕐 Mon.–Sat. 10 A.M.–4 P.M., Sun. 1 P.M.–4 P.M. Fee.

SPRINGFIELD

While you're in the area, see also: Northampton

Indian Motocycle Museum and Hall of Fame   No, it's not *Motorcycle*. That's the generic; this is the home of the Indian Motocycle, the first American motorcycle, built in Springfield from 1901 to the 1950s. The museum is now also home to a large collection of Columbia bicycles, toy motorcycles, and other rolling objects, along with photos and other memorabilia of the Two-Wheeled World.

🏠 413 737-2624 • 33 Hendee St., Springfield, MA 01139

🚐 Take I-291 to the St. James Ave. exit. Go right on Page Blvd., then right on Hendee St.

🕐 Mon.–Sun. 10 A.M.–5 P.M. Fee.

Springfield Armory National Historic Site   George Washington commissioned an arsenal here in 1777, and it was central to American military history until the 1960s. The "Organ" of Civil War–era muskets (subject of a noted Longfellow poem) is the great attention-getter, but the development of weapons—and general industrial technology—is shown in many other displays, which include machinery like the first practical mass-production wood lathe as well as a variety of experimental arms. *Tours, Gift Shop, Programs, Publications*

🏠 413 734-8115 • http://nps.gov • One Armory Square, Springfield, MA 01105

🚐 Armory Square is in the center of Springfield, between State and Pearl Sts. Take Exit 4/5 off I-91 and proceed east on State St., following signs.

🕐 Tues.–Sun. 10 A.M.–5 P.M. No fee.

Titanic Museum   If you're fascinated by the story of the *Titanic*, this small museum created by Ed Kamuda, founder of the *Titanic* Historical Society, is the place for you. There are items from the ship, letters mailed from her, memorabilia of survivors, material on her sister ships and the White Star and Cunard lines, and all sorts of oddities. You may want to join the society or visit the *Titanic* model and other artifacts at Fall River's Marine Museum. *See also* the Cottage Grove, Oregon, Museum. *Gift Shop, Publications*

🏛 413 543-4770 • 208 Main St., Springfield (Indian Orchard), MA 01151

🚗 Indian Orchard, now part of Springfield, is 7 miles from downtown. Take Exit 7 off the Mass Pike, go south 1 mile on Route 21, cross bridge and turn right on Main St. The museum is across from Grand Theater. From I-91, take I-291E/Route 20 (Exit 5A), and turn left on Berkshire Ave., left on Oak St., and right on Main.

🕐 Mon.–Fri. 10 A.M.–4 P.M., Sat. 10 A.M.–3 P.M. Donation.

WALTHAM

Charles River Museum of Industry   For an understanding of the range of technologies that have made this area an industrial powerhouse for 200 years, this is a good stop. From the first Industrial Revolution to the high-tech "Massachusetts Miracle," the devices and systems here, which include many working machines, have played central roles. *Tours*

🏛 781 893-5410 • 154 Moody St., Waltham, MA 02154

🚗 Waltham is just west of Boston. Exit from I-95/Route 128 and take Route 20E into the center, then turn right on Moody St.

🕐 Thurs., Sat. 10 A.M.–5 P.M. or by appointment. Fee.

WATERTOWN

Blindiana/Tactual Museum/Museum on the History of Blindness
This is America's most famous institution for the blind. The Blindiana Museum displays artifacts and materials on the education of the blind from ancient to modern times. In the Tactual Museum the message is "*Do* touch!" The Samuel P. Hayes Research Library is open for reference use. *Tours, Hands-on, Library*

🏛 617 924-3434 • Howe Bldg., Perkins School for the Blind, 175 N. Beacon St., Watertown, MA 02172

🚗 Watertown is immediately west of Boston. North Beacon St. is the extension of Boston's Beacon St. From the west, exit at Waltham from I-95/Route 128 onto Route 20E, which becomes Beacon St.

🕐 Mon.–Fri. 8:30 A.M.–5 P.M. No fee. Call to confirm; museum being redesigned. For information on tours of school, call 617 923-8874.

WESTON

Cardinal Spellman Philatelic Museum   Four million stamps! Francis Cardinal Spellman started it in 1963, but there are other collections, including those of Dwight D. Eisenhower, Jascha Heifetz, and Douglas MacArthur. The philatelic library has 40,000 volumes, and there are photographic and research laboratories. *Gift Shop, Programs, Publications, Library*

- 781 894-6735 • Regis College, 235 Wellesley St., Weston, MA 02193
- Weston is a suburb of Boston. From Route 128, take the Route 30W exit, go about 1 mile west, and turn right at traffic light onto Wellesley St. The museum is on the left.
- Tues.–Thurs. 9 A.M.–4 P.M., Sun. 1 P.M.–5 P.M. No fee.

WILLIAMSTOWN

While you're in the area, see also: Bennington, VT

Sterling and Francine Clark Art Institute   Our friends tell us that the Clark, already well known, is getting less "little" all the time; still, it's in a small town that you might not have visited otherwise. This is Renoir Central, and there are lots of other Impressionists, as well as 19th-century American classics. The grounds are great for picnicking. Vermont's Bennington Museum is a half-hour north. *Tours, Gift Shop, Publications, Library*

- 413 458-9545 • 225 South St., Williamstown, MA 01267
- Williamstown is in Massachusetts' northwest corner. The Clark Institute is just south of the intersection of Routes 2 and 7; look for signs.
- Tues.–Sun. 10 A.M.–5 P.M. July–Aug.: Mons. also. No fee.

WORCESTER

While you're in the area, see also: Fiskdale, Leominster

American Sanitary Plumbing Museum   Worcester is a hardware town, and in 1979 Charles Manoog decided that his specialty, plumbing technology, needed its own historical showplace. Hence this tribute to the necessary and usually overlooked. They tell us that most of their visitors are in the profession, but you can remedy that if you're simply interested in learning about something real and universal. They welcome donations of old fixtures, tools, manuals, etc., by the way.

- 508 754-9453 • 39 Piedmont St., Worcester, MA 01610
- It's off I-290 in central Worcester; call for directions.
- Jan.–June, Sept.–Dec.: Tues., Thurs. 10 A.M.–2 P.M. No fee.

Higgins Armory Museum   John Woodman Higgins had a thing about suits of armor, and here you can benefit from his passion. It has an Art Deco exterior, but inside, the museum is all ancient, medieval, and Renaissance—swords, pikes, helmets, breastplates, the trappings of falconry, the ritual of the tourney, and more. Here's a place to learn about heraldry and its cousin genealogy too. Lots for kids to do. *Tours, Gift Shop, Hands-on, Programs, Screenings*

🏠 508 853-6015 • 100 Barber Ave., Worcester, MA 01606

🚗 Take Exit 1 off I-190 in Worcester and follow Route 12N. Pass the Greendale Mall on right and turn right on Barber Ave. The museum is a tall steel and glass structure with flags on top.

🕐 Tues.–Sat. 10 A.M.–4 P.M., Sun. noon–4 P.M. Fee.

MICHIGAN

In the end, Michigan may be seen as the ultimate boom state. Many of the museums listed here have to do with three economic explosions: In the Upper Peninsula, iron and copper, mined and shipped from the 1840s, created wild towns, some of which, now that things have quieted, retain monuments to their heyday. In the northern Lower Peninsula, the lumber boom that came after the Civil War has left similar traces. And in the southeast, the auto industry, now fighting decline, created vast wealth in the 20th century, making possible estates and activities now memorialized in a variety of museums.

What's Big: See our comments on Detroit and its museums. Elsewhere, there are such possibilities as the cluster of university-related museums in Ann Arbor, Henry Ford's museum and Greenfield Village in Dearborn, the Gerald R. Ford Museum in Grand Rapids, Mackinac Island, and the Soo Locks.

ACME

Music House   Devices that entertained in 19th-century parlors (that is, when the entertainment wasn't live) could be wonderfully ornate and imposing. The Amaryllis, a Belgian theater dance organ, is itself the size of a two-car garage. It's just one of the many machines you'll be introduced to here. Nickelodeons, organs, a Grand Reproducing Piano, late Stone Age radios and televisions, phonographs, juke boxes—now, this is entertainment! *Tours, Gift Shop, Food*

🏠 616 938-9300 • Harmony Village, 7377 US 31N, Acme, MI 49610

🚗 Acme is in the northwestern Lower Peninsula, just east of Traverse City. The museum is 1.5 miles north on US 31, just north of the junction with SR 72.

🕐 May–Oct.: Mon.–Sat. 10 A.M.–4 P.M., Sun. noon–4 P.M. Mid-Nov.–Dec.: Fri.–Sat. 10 A.M.–4 P.M., Sun. noon–4 P.M. Fee.

ANN ARBOR

Kelsey Museum of Archaeology   Of the University of Michigan's several major museums, we'll send you to this one, which reflects much work in the lands of the ancient Egyptians, Greeks, and Romans. You'll see artifacts of all sorts— even objects like cosmetic applicators and a 2,000-year-old piece of bread. And if you like mummies, here they have not only humans, but birds, cats, dogs, and even a grain mummy; ask about it.

🏛 734 763-3559 • http://www.umich.edu~kelseydb/ • 434 S. State St., Ann Arbor, MI 48109

🚗 From I-94 take State St. exit. Go approximately 2 miles north into the city center. The museum is on the left, 2 buildings past the Michigan Union.

🕐 Mon.–Fri. 9 A.M.–4 P.M., Sat.–Sun. 1 P.M.–4 P.M. No fee.

BARAGA (ASKEL)

Hanka Homestead Ulkomuseo (Living Outdoor Museum)   If you don't know much about the Finns except that their saunas once made them suspect among "moral" Americans, you owe yourself a visit to this farm the Hankas established in the North Woods in 1896. Now it looks as it did in the 1920s, its buildings and tools made by the family, its blacksmith shop ready for work, its kitchen ready for visitors, its lawns and orchard patrolled by one relaxed Jersey cow. This is truly pastoral.

🏛 906 353-7116 • Baraga (Askel), MI 49908

🚗 Baraga is in the northwestern Upper Peninsula, just west of L'Anse. The homestead is actually in Askel, 10 miles northwest. Take US 41N from Baraga and turn left on Arnhiem Rd. for 7 miles, following signs.

🕐 Memorial Day–second week of Oct.: Tues., Thurs., Sat.–Sun. and holidays noon–4 P.M. Rest of year by appointment. Fee.

BLOOMFIELD HILLS

Cranbrook Art Museum   The widely known Cranbrook Educational Community is a 315-acre center for the arts, with gardens, outdoor sculpture, schools, concert programs, an Institute of Science, and the original 1908 arts-and-crafts manor home of George and Ellen Booth. Here you're going to see works of all kinds by the recently famous and the soon to be famous. And you can spend the rest of the day seeing Eliel Saarinen's house and wandering the grounds. *Tours, Gift Shop, Programs*

🏛 248 645-3312 (recorded information) • http://www.cranbrook.edu/museum.htm • 1221 N. Woodward Ave., Bloomfield Hills, MI 48303

🚗 Bloomfield Hills is a northwestern suburb of Detroit; Cranbrook is about 20 miles from downtown on Woodward Ave. (SR 1). Or you can exit from I-696 onto Woodward and proceed north for about 8 miles.

🕐 Wed.–Sat. 10 A.M.–5 P.M. (to 9 P.M. Thurs.), Sun. noon–5 P.M. Fee.

DETROIT

Detroit, the great engine of American industrial prosperity for so long, has taken some hits recently, and has lost a lot of its residents to the 'burbs; the fact that most of the little museums we found in the area are outside the city testifies to this. However, there is life in the Motor City yet. For instance, something Big and New is the recently reopened Museum of African-American History (313 494-5800), which has been getting much press. Other related sites include the Tuskegee Airmen's Museum (call the Detroit Historical Society at 313 833-1805), for a look at the legendary World War II fighter pilots; the Motown Museum (313 875-2264), where you'll follow the history of the black pop music explosion of the 1960s and beyond; and the International Afro-American Sports Hall of Fame (313 838-8056). We don't promise you that these museums are "little," but they represent variations on a theme. Other local sites for different interests include the Dossin Great Lakes Museum (also run by the D.H.S.) and the Pewabic Pottery (313 822-0954), which will excite you if you liked our listings for Parsippany, New Jersey, and East Aurora, New York. Nearby, of course, is Bigsville itself—Henry Ford's Greenfield Village and museum in Dearborn—with Buckminster Fuller's Dymaxion House and all sorts of other American icons. *While you're in the area, see also*: Ann Arbor, Bloomfield Hills, Farmington Hills, Novi, Plymouth.

FARMINGTON HILLS

Marvin's Marvelous Mechanical Museum   Marvin Yagoda says he gets thousands of visitors a week, but we decided we wouldn't let that stop you. Bring all your spare change. Every kind of boardwalk and sideshow machine (leaving aside all the magic-show posters, etc.) you've ever thought of is crammed in here somewhere; there are "over 1,000 electrical outlets, all used." You'd probably better decide not to be a *student* of gameology while you're here; be a little too serious and the Bimbo Box might jump up and get you.

📱 248 626-5020 • 31005 Orchard Lake Rd., Farmington Hills, MI 48334

🚗 It's in a northwestern Detroit suburb. Take the Orchard Lake Rd. exit north from I-696. The museum is just south of 14 Mile Rd., on the left, in a shopping mall; look for the tell-tale backwards clock.

🕐 Mon.–Thurs. 10 A.M.–10 P.M., Fri.–Sat. 10 A.M.–11 P.M., Sun. 11 A.M.–9 P.M. No fee, but bring change.

FLINT

Labor Museum and Learning Center of Michigan   Flint is the scene of one of the most famous American labor struggles, the 1937 sitdown at the Fisher Body plant. This museum tells this and other stories using videos, interactive displays, and a variety of other materials. Not far away, at 1221 E. Kearsley St., you can see some of the cars built by Flint workers, at the Alfred P. Sloan Museum, named for the longtime chairman of General Motors, of which Flint claims to be the birthplace; call 810 760-1169 for information. *Hands-on, Screenings*

■ 810 341-1206 • 711 N. Saginaw St., Flint, MI 48503

🚗 Flint is 50 miles northwest of Detroit. Saginaw St. is downtown, just west of the junction of I-69 and I-475; the museum is in the Job Center–Walter Reuther Building.

🕐 Tues.–Fri. 10 A.M.–5 P.M. Fee.

GAYLORD

Call of the Wild   C'est touristique, but you kids (unless you scare easily) will love the 150-odd American animals you'll see here, realistically mounted and in some cases with r-r-real sound piped in. There's a display on the trapper's life, and even a Poetry Nook, where you can relax with some doggerel (or should it be bearrerel?). You can eat health and nonhealth foods and even buy your boots and outdoor gear—a one-stop natural experience. And if you'd like to stay off the highway for a little longer, why not check out the Bottle Cap Museum (call 517 732-1931), ten minutes east in Sparr? *Gift Shop, Food*

■ 517 732-4336 • 850 S. Wisconsin Ave., Gaylord, MI 49735

🚗 Gaylord is in the north-central Lower Peninsula, an hour south of the Straits of Mackinac. From I-75, take Exit 282 and go east on SR 32. Turn right at the first light, on Wisconsin Ave., and go 6 blocks.

🕐 Mid-June–Labor Day: Mon.–Sun. 8:30 A.M.–9 P.M. Rest of year: 9:30 A.M.–6 P.M. Fee.

HANOVER

Lee Conklin Antique Organ Museum   The 1911 Hanover High School is now home to Lee Conklin's collection of reed organs, melodeons, and music machines once carried by circuit-riding ministers. There are also some nonmusical items like a foot-powered press and a dog-powered(!) butter churn. *Tours, Gift Shop*

■ 517 563-2311 • 105 Fairview St., Hanover, MI 49241

🚗 Hanover is in south-central Michigan, about 10 miles southwest of Jackson. Fairview St. is at the east end of Main St.

🕐 Apr.–Oct.: first and third Suns. 1 P.M.–5 P.M. Fee.

HOLLAND

Holland Museum (formerly the Netherlands Museum) Since the 1840s, Holland has been one of America's best-known Dutch towns; today it has a spring Tulip Time, wooden shoe factories, and other reminders of this heritage. The museum not only has exhibits on many things Dutch, it even has displays on previous displays on things Dutch—items from the 1939 New York World's Fair; is this what they mean by Double Dutch? *Gift Shop*

■ 616 392-9084 • 31 W. 10th St., Holland, MI 49423

🚗 Holland is a half-hour southwest of Grand Rapids. Follow the I-96 Business Route (8th St.) into the city; turn left on Central, then right on 10th to the corner of River.

🕐 Mon., Wed.–Sat. 10 A.M.–5 P.M. (to 8 P.M. Thurs.), Sun. 2 P.M.–5 P.M. Fee.

IRON MOUNTAIN

Cornish Pumping Engine and Mining Museum The Menominee Range is one of the richest American iron sources, but there were serious problems with groundwater here. The answer was the Cornish Pumping Engine, said to be the largest steam engine ever built in North America. The museum displays artifacts from the region's hardrock history, and also, surprisingly, an exhibit on the military gliders built nearby for use in World War II.

■ 906 774-1086 • Kent St., Iron Mountain, MI 49801

🚗 Iron Mountain is in the Upper Peninsula, on the Wisconsin line and the Menominee River. The museum is central, 2 blocks west of US 2 (Stephenson St.).

🕐 May–mid-Oct.: Mon.–Sat. 9 A.M.–5 P.M., Sun. noon–4 P.M. Fee.

ISHPEMING

U.S. National Ski Hall of Fame and Ski Museum How odd that the National Ski Hall of Fame should be in a state as flat as Michigan, you say. Yes, but Ishpeming is a ski *jumping* center. So here it is—displays on the honorees, Olympic medals, and everything you'd expect. There's also a 10th Mountain Division display, a diorama on the Birkebeiners, a replica of a 4,000-year-old ski and pole found in a Swedish bog, and much else.

■ 906 485-6323 • Ishpeming, MI 49849

🚗 Ishpeming is in the Upper Peninsula, just west of Marquette. The museum is on US 41 at the corner of 3rd St.

🕐 Mon.–Sun. 10 A.M.–5 P.M. (to 8 P.M. in summer). Fee.

LANSING

Michigan Museum of Surveying   We know that George Washington got his start as a surveyor, don't we? But we don't know much else about surveying, do we? So we had better get ourselves over to this museum, hadn't we? It's got the instruments, artifacts, and archives that tell the story, as well as a video library. And the director says it is *not* crowded. Everyone else has probably gone to the R. E. Olds Transportation Museum, which is next door. Library

🔲 517 484-6605 • 220 S. Museum Dr., Lansing, MI 48933

🚐 Lansing has a downtown Museum District, a few blocks east of the Capitol. Museum Dr. extends south from Michigan Ave. between Grand Ave. (W) and Cedar St. (E).

🕐 Mon.–Fri. 8 A.M.–noon and 1 P.M.–5 P.M., or by appointment. No fee.

MARSHALL

American Museum of Magic   Marshall is noted for its Victorian buildings. Who knows what lurks behind those grand façades? We can tell you that this one conceals entire hatfuls, or is it sleevefuls, or trunkfuls, of magical stuff. Of course, magicians aren't happy if you reveal their secrets, so we won't. But expect to see all kinds of publicity and memorabilia as well.

🔲 616 781-7666 (recording) • 107 E. Michigan Ave., Marshall, MI 49068

🚐 Marshall is in the south-central Lower Peninsula, 10 miles southeast of Battle Creek. Michigan Ave. is Business Route 94.

🕐 Mar.–Labor Day: Sat. 11:30 A.M.–5 P.M., Sun. 12:30 P.M.–4 P.M. Fee.

MIDLAND

Herbert H. Dow Historical Museum   Local brine soils gave Herbert H. Dow his start (extracting bromine) in 1890, and his business has given Midland its Midland Center for the Arts, the Dow Gardens, and other sites. The museum celebrates the founder's brains, application, inventiveness, business sense, and philanthropies, with reconstructions of his workshop and office, his wife's kitchen, and the original manufacturing plant. Call 517 636-8659 if you'd like to tour the Dow Chemical Company, known for hundreds of products from pharmaceuticals to napalm.

🔲 517 832-5319 • 3100 Cook Rd., Midland, MI 48640

🚐 Midland is in the middle of the Lower Peninsula, a half-hour northwest of Saginaw. Cook Rd. runs west from W. Main St., which is accessible from SR 20.

🕐 Wed.–Sat. 10 A.M.–4 P.M., Sun. 1 P.M.–5 P.M. Tours by appointment. Fee.

MONROE

Monroe County Historical Museum   The city of Monroe was the longtime home of George Armstrong Custer and his kin. If you're a Custer buff, you'll want to see the memorabilia here, and the museum will also provide you with a guide to the Custer-related sites in Monroe. If the War of 1812 is your thing, you'll want to drop over to 1403 E. Elm, to see the River Raisin Battlefield Visitor Center (administered with the Museum), which, oddly, memorializes one of the other most notable American military disasters. *Library*

🏠 734 243-7137 • 126 S. Monroe St., Monroe, MI 48161

🚗 Monroe is a half-hour north of Toledo, Ohio. Take Exit 14 off I-75. Go west on E. Elm Ave., then left on Monroe St. The museum is 3 blocks south.

🕐 May–Sept.: Mon.–Sun. 10 A.M.–5 P.M. Rest of year: Wed.–Sun. Tours by appointment. Fee in June–Aug. only.

MUSKEGON

Muskegon Museum of Art   Here you'll find some Old Masters, some French Impressionists, and a wide range of artworks including much in glass. But the key to the museum is the American collection, which includes John Steuart Curry's *Tornado over Kansas*, Hopper's *New York Restaurant*, and other items you didn't realize were in Michigan. *Tours, Gift Shop, Programs*

🏠 616 722-2600 • 296 W. Webster Ave., Muskegon, MI 49440

🚗 Muskegon is in the west-central Lower Peninsula, a half-hour northwest of Grand Rapids. The museum is downtown, on South Business 31 between 2nd and 3rd Sts.

🕐 Tues.–Fri. 10 A.M.–5 P.M., Sat.–Sun. noon–5 P.M. No fee.

NEGAUNEE

Michigan Iron Industry Museum   In the heart of the Marquette Iron Range, this museum employs displays, interactive exhibits, and walking trails to tell the story of the industry and its people. Among the machinery you'll see is the 1868 "Yankee" mine locomotive. *Hands-on*

🏠 906 475-7857 • 73 Forge Rd., Negaunee, MI 49866

🚗 Negaunee is in the center of the Upper Peninsula, 8 miles west of Marquette. Exit from US 41 onto County Rd. 492E; go left onto Forge Rd.

🕐 May–Oct.: Mon.–Sun. 9:30 A.M.–4:30 P.M. No fee.

NOVI

Motorsports Hall of Fame of America   If you can race it on land, on water, or in the air, this place knows about it. There are NASCAR vehicles, jet cars, the fastest open-cockpit powerboat, dragsters, and the Novi Special Indy car. There are also slot racing and other games if you just can't control the itch to speed. *Gift Shop, Hands-on*

🏠 800 250-RACE [7223] • http://www.mshf.com • Novi, MI 48376

🚗 Novi is a northwestern Detroit suburb, just west of the I-275/I-696 junction, on I-96. Take Exit 162 (Novi Rd.) south to the Novi Expo Center water tower.

🕐 Mon.–Sun. 10 A.M.–5 P.M. Fee. Simulations and games extra.

PETOSKEY

Little Traverse Regional Historical Museum   This museum is notable for displays on two local writers. The historian Bruce Catton was a native. Ernest Hemingway was not, but he spent youthful summers here and later lived in or near Petoskey; much of the background to his man-in-nature stories is drawn from his experiences in these surroundings.

🏠 616 347-2620 • 1 Waterfront Park, Petoskey, MI 49770

🚗 Petoskey is in the northwestern Lower Peninsula, 30 miles south of the Straits of Mackinac, on US 31. The museum is central, in the old railroad station.

🕐 May–Labor Day: Mon.–Sat. 10 A.M.–4 P.M. Sept.–Oct.: closed Mon. Fee.

PLYMOUTH

Plymouth Historical Museum   This is a general historical museum made particularly interesting because among its varied exhibits it displays two local manufactures. One is a 1916 touring car called the Alter, something you won't see anywhere else. The other is something you may have seen anywhere—the Daisy air rifle, made here from 1886 to 1954, and about as close to innocent as any gun can get. The museum has lots of Daisys and other models. *Tours*

🏠 734 455-8940 • 155 S. Main St., Plymouth, MI 48170

🚗 Plymouth is a western suburb of Detroit, about 20 miles from downtown and just west of I-275. The museum is downtown, at the corner of Main and Church Sts.

🕐 Wed.–Thurs. and Sat. 1 P.M.–4 P.M., Sun. 2 P.M.–5 P.M. Fee.

ROSCOMMON

Civilian Conservation Corps Museum/Higgins Lake Nursery   Over 100,000 Michiganders worked in the CCC ("Roosevelt's Tree Army"), and some donated equipment and memorabilia to establish this museum. You'll get a sense of what CCC life was like—if you don't already have it from camping in Michigan, which is done largely on CCC-created sites. Also here is the former Higgins Lake Nursery, whence, from 1903 to 1962, millions of evergreen seedlings went forth to replenish our forests.

🏠 517 821-6125 • North Higgins Lake State Park, 11252 N. Higgins Lake Dr., Roscommon, MI 48653

🚗 Roscommon is in the north-central Lower Peninsula, 15 minutes south of Grayling. From US 27 take Military Rd. exit; Higgins Lake Nursery and museum are 1 mile on left. From I-75 take Exit 244; nursery and museum are within 5 miles on right.

🕐 Mid-June–early Sept.: Mon.–Sun. 9 A.M.–5 P.M. Vehicle fee for park.

SAINT JAMES

Beaver Island Historical Society/Mormon Print Shop Museum and Marine Museum   This is fishing and resort country, and in these two museums you'll find exhibits on Indians, on lake trades, on the Irish who settled here after the mid-1850s, and on Feodor Protar (who died in 1925), an Estonian immigrant who became a local healer. But at the print shop you'll encounter the "kingdom" of the breakaway Mormon leader Jesse Strang, who arrived here in 1847 and ran a theocracy until two of his followers killed him in 1856. It's jarring history to have occurred in such a place. *Gift Shop*

🏠 616 448-2254 • Main and Forest Sts., Saint James, MI 49782

🚗 Beaver Island is 2 hours off the northwestern Lower Peninsula via ferry from Charlevoix.

🕐 Mid-June–Labor Day: Mon.–Sat. 11 A.M.–5 P.M., Sun. noon–3 P.M. Reduced hours in May, early June, and Sept., or by appointment. Fee.

MINNESOTA

Minnesota has gotten to be pretty funny recently. Garrison Keillor has had a lot to do with it, and the Coen Brothers; now we're all aware that the place is rife with odd-talking Lutherans. Actually, to judge from some of the museums we're recommending, Minnesotans have been acting unusual for some time. Sinclair Lewis strafed Sauk Centre, and the town has practically been renamed for him. Judy Garland used to claim she came from Grand Rapids, *Michigan*, but her Minnesota hometown loves her anyway. See, it isn't all just mining and farming, although there are some great places to explore those straightforward lifestyles.

What's Big: Lots in the Twin Cities, from the Walker Art Center through Fort Snelling. The Planes of Fame Air Museum in nearby Eden Prairie. Duluth's Depot and Lake Superior Transportation Museum. Ironworld USA, in Chisholm. And for something Bigger than Big—and perhaps readable as a museum to Bigness—how about the Mall of America in Bloomington?

ALEXANDRIA

Runestone Museum   Is the 200-pound stone Olaf Ohman dug from under a tree on his farm in nearby Kensington in 1898 really a message left by a 1362 Viking expedition? Experts can't agree; so why not come here and see it for yourself? *Tours, Gift Shop, Programs*

📷 320 763-3160 • 206 Broadway, Alexandria, MN 56308

🚗 Alexandria is in west-central Minnesota, 125 miles northwest of the Twin Cities. From I-94, take the SR 29/Broadway exit north for 5 miles.

🕐 Apr.–Sept.: Mon.–Sat. 9 A.M.–5 P.M., Sun. noon–5 P.M. Rest of year: Mon.–Fri. 9 A.M.–5 P.M., Sat. noon–5 P.M. Fee.

AUSTIN

First Century Museum (the Hormel Museum)   We're not sure what the nickname "Spamtown USA" means for the high school football team, but for the rest of the world, it names the product that put Austin on the map. The Hormel company began operations (as George Hormel's butcher business) in 1891. In 1991 they created a centennial exhibit, which proved so popular it's become a museum. See George and Gracie advertising Spam, which first appeared in 1937. Learn all about Hormel achievements, which include Hormel lard and Hormel chili con carne. Get here in July and join in the "hog jog" and all the fun of Spam Jam. *Gift Shop*

🏛 800 444-5713 • Oak Park Mall, Austin, MN 55912

🚗 Austin is in southeastern Minnesota. The museum is in the northwest corner of Oak Park Mall, in the northeast quadrant of the intersection of I-90 with 14th St. NW.

🕐 Mon.–Fri. 10 A.M.–9 P.M., Sat. 10 A.M.–5 P.M., Sun. 11 A.M.–5 P.M. No fee.

CHISHOLM

Minnesota Museum of Mining   Here you are in the Mesabi Range (*see also* Eveleth and Hibbing), one of the most famous mining areas in the world. You won't have missed Ironworld USA, the huge theme-park-but-also-serious-historical-center just south on US 169. But you also shouldn't miss the MMM, which is in town and has mining, rail, and road vehicles; a 1916 White, the first intercity bus; drills galore; an elaborate diorama on steam trains at work in the iron range; and other artifacts of the industry. If you're a serious student of regional history and newspapers, call or write ahead to the Iron Range Research Center (PO Box 392; 218 254-3321), which has an extensive archive of the journals that have recorded Mesabi history since the 1890s.

🏛 218 254-5543 • Memorial Park, Main St., Chisholm, MN 55719

🚗 Chisholm is in northeastern Minnesota, just north of Hibbing and 15 minutes west of Virginia and Eveleth, on US 169 and SR 73. Follow 73 into town.

🕐 Memorial Day–Labor Day: Mon.–Sun. 9 A.M.–6 P.M. Call for off-season tours. Fee.

ELY

International Wolf Center   In the category of museums to things we hope *don't* belong to the past, here's an institution devoted to *Canis lupus*, who lives hereabouts and may even someday come back to your neighborhood, if you're lucky.

There is artwork, as well as films and other presentations, and of course there are the beasts themselves. *Programs*

🔲 800 359-9653 • 1396 Hwy 169, Ely, MN 55731

🚗 Ely is in northeastern Minnesota, about 60 miles northeast of Hibbing, on SR 169 and 1. The center is on the east side of town.

🕐 May–late Sept.: Mon.–Sun. 8 A.M.–8 P.M. Fee.

EVELETH

United States Hockey Hall of Fame   This is a long way from the sport's urban centers, but it's hockey country, and the Hall of Fame has displays on the evolution of skates and other equipment and on noted players. There's an original 1950s Zamboni, for those who have always savored the moments between periods. The chief focus is on the 1960 Olympics and on the 1980 games, when the United States won its famous victory over the Evil Empire.

🔲 800 443-7825 • 801 Hat Trick Ave., Eveleth, MN 55734

🚗 Eveleth is in northeastern Minnesota, just south of Virginia and 15 minutes east of Hibbing and Chisholm. Take the Hall of Fame exit off US 53 onto Hat Trick Ave.

🕐 Mon.–Sat. 9 A.M.–5 P.M., Sun. 11 A.M.–5 P.M. Fee.

GRAND RAPIDS

Judy Garland Historical Center in the Central School Heritage and Arts Center   Frances Gumm, later to become Judy Garland, apparently liked her birthplace even less than Sinclair Lewis liked Sauk Centre. But that was then, of course, and now the third floor of this local history complex presents the entertainer's life—her career began here as an infant in her parents' vaudeville house—in varied memorabilia, and the town even has a Judy Garland Festival, in late June.

🔲 218 326-6431 • Hwys 2 and 169, Grand Rapids, MN 55744

🚗 Grand Rapids is in north-central Minnesota, 30 miles southwest of Hibbing, on US 2 and US 169. The Central School is at the junction of the highways.

🕐 Memorial Day–Labor Day: Mon.–Sat. 9:30 A.M.–5 P.M., Sun. 11 A.M.–4 P.M. Rest of year closed Sun. Fee.

HIBBING

Greyhound Bus Origin Center   If you've spent time on the 'Hound, you'll be interested to see this tribute to the business Carl Wickman began with a 1914 Hupmobile, carrying miners from Hibbing to nearby Alice. There are models you won't see on the road anywhere north of Mexico, leading to the 1956 Scenicruiser. There's the first Bookmobile. There are audiovisual representations of company history, from "Hibbing to Everywhere."

🔲 218 263-5814 • Hibbing Memorial Buildings, 23rd St and 5th Ave. East, Hibbing, MN 55746

🚗 Hibbing is in northeastern Minnesota, just south of Chisholm and 15 minutes west of Virginia and Eveleth. Exit from US 169 directly onto 23rd St. headed west.

🕐 Mid-May–mid-Sept.: Mon.–Sat. 9 A.M.–5 P.M. Rest of year: call for appointment (218 262-3895 or 262-4166). Fee.

HINCKLEY

Hinckley Fire Museum Fire buffs: Here's a town (one of six) that was destroyed by a huge forest fire on September 1, 1894. The Saint Paul and Duluth depot now houses a museum telling the story in dioramas, artifacts, and other displays; it'll also give you a sense of the high days of railroading. Nearby is the gravel pit townspeople huddled in to escape the firestorm.

🔲 320 384-7338 • 106 Old Hwy 61, Hinckley, MN 55037

🚗 Hinckley is in east-central Minnesota, an hour north of the Twin Cities via I-35. The museum is 6 blocks west of I-35, on Old Hwy 61.

🕐 May–mid-Oct.: Mon.–Sun. 10 A.M.–5 P.M. Fee.

INTERNATIONAL FALLS

Grand Mound Interpretive Center International Falls prides itself on being "The Icebox of America"; in the winter this area is, to be technical, colder than hell. Nevertheless, Grand Mound is 136 feet by 98 feet, and 25 feet high, and reveals that people have been living here for over 5,000 years! The center illustrates this amazing history. *Programs*

🔲 218 285-3332 • http://www.mnhs.org • 6749 Hwy 11, International Falls, MN 56649

🚗 International Falls is in north-central Minnesota, on the Rainy River and the Ontario border. Grand Mound is 17 miles west, along the river, on SR 11.

🕐 May–Labor Day: Mon.–Sat. 10 A.M.–5 P.M., Sun. noon–5 P.M. Sept.–Oct.: Sat. 10 A.M.–5 P.M., Sun. noon–4 P.M. Fee.

Koochiching County Historical Museum/Bronko Nagurski Museum
They had a gold rush here in 1893, and logging (and paper) is central to the economy. The museum details this history, but may be most surprising because it also details the life of local man Bronko Nagurski. Who? Well, if you know that football existed before television, you may know that some people think he was the greatest player ever—and he returned here, to the lakes and woods, after his career, something it's hard to imagine any of today's stars doing.

🔲 218 283-4316 • Smokey Bear Park, 6th Ave. and 2nd St., International Falls, MN 56649

180 . . . Minnesota

🚐 The museum is in Smokey Bear Park, in the center of the city.
🕐 Mid-May–mid-Sept.: Mon.–Sat. 11 A.M.–5 P.M., Sun. and holidays 1 P.M.–5 P.M. Fee.

LE SUEUR

Le Sueur Museum   It's been nagging you all these years: Where *is* the Valley of the Jolly Green Giant? Search no more, ho ho ho. This museum has a little of every-thing about local history, but lots about the Green Giant company, which has been canning those peas and other goodies here for 75 years.
🏠 612 665-2050 • 709 N. 2nd St., Le Sueur, MN 56058
🚐 Le Sueur is in south-central Minnesota, 50 miles southwest of the Twin Cities via US 169. The museum is off Main St., behind the creamery.
🕐 Memorial Day–Labor Day: Mon.–Sun. 1 P.M.–4:30 P.M. and by appointment. No fee.

LITTLE FALLS

Charles A. Lindbergh House   He was one of the most famous, unusual, and controversial Americans. By the time he landed in Paris in 1927, the family had moved away from this house, and it was virtually stripped by the celebrity-mad. Later it was refurbished, and it now offers exhibits on Lindy, his father (the antiwar congressman), and the rest of the family—as well as the chance to gauge the atmosphere such a man grew up in.
🏠 612 632-3154 • Lindbergh Dr., Little Falls, MN 56345
🚐 Little Falls is 90 miles northwest of the Twin Cities on US 10. Take SR 27W for 0.5 mile, then turn south on Lindbergh Dr.
🕐 May–Labor Day: Mon.–Sat. 10 A.M.–5 P.M., Sun. noon–5 P.M. Reduced hours Sept.–Oct. Fee.

MINNEAPOLIS–SAINT PAUL

While you're in the area, see also: Shoreview

American Swedish Institute   The 33-room mansion of Swan Turnblad and family became home to the ASI in 1929. You may find the house itself boggling. Everything Swedish is here, in murals on emigration, glass, porcelain, *kakelugnar* (tile stoves), metalwork, clothing, books and papers, changing art exhibits, a coffee shop, and on and on. *Gift Shop, Food, Programs, Library*
🏠 612 871-4907 • 2600 Park Ave., Minneapolis, MN 55407

🚗 The Institute is 5 minutes south of downtown, at the corner of 26th St. and Park Ave. Take the 11th St. exit off I-94 and go south on Portland, then left on 28th and left again on Park. From I-35W, take the Lake/31st exit and go east on Lake, then left on Park.

🕑 Tues.–Sat. noon–4 P.M. (Wed. to 8 P.M.), Sun. 1 P.M.–5 P.M. Fee.

Museum of Questionable Medical Devices   Depending of course on your ability to pay, the inventions displayed in this museum could make you younger, better endowed, supple of limb, clear of complexion, cancerless . . . sound familiar? It must be that *these* devices were just a little cruder than the ones still out there. Test yourself on a phrenology machine—who knows what lurks in your mind? Hands-on

📱 612 379-4046 • 219 Main St. SE, Minneapolis, MN 55414

🚗 In the St. Anthony Main section, north of the river. Take Exit 18 (University Ave.) off I-35W. The museum is 2 blocks from the north end of the new Hennepin Ave. Bridge.

🕑 Tues.–Thurs. 5 P.M.–9 P.M., Fri. 5 P.M.–10 P.M., Sat. 11 A.M.–10 P.M., Sun. noon–5 P.M. Donation.

The Bakken: A Library and Museum of Electricity in Life   Earl Bakken, inventor of the first wearable cardiac pacemaker, founded this institution in 1976. The Bakken is a high-concept museum and archive on electricity's promise and uses, since the fourth century B.C., in the health sciences. You'll see electric fish and eels here, and learn about their powers. There are also the progenitors of numerous familiar devices, a garden of medicinal herbs, and an extensive library of research documents. *Programs*

📱 612 927-6508 • http://www.bakkenmuseum.org • 3537 Zenith Ave. South, Minneapolis, MN 55416

🚗 The Bakken is about 4 miles southwest of downtown, in West Winds, a 1928 mansion on the southwest shore of Lake Calhoun. It is 1 block west of the Lake Calhoun Pkwy, at 36th and Zenith.

🕑 Mon.–Sat. 10 A.M.–5 P.M. Fee.

MOORHEAD

While you're in the area, see also: Fargo, ND

Heritage *Hjemkomst* Interpretive Center   The Hjemkomst (Homecoming) was Robert Asp's dream. He began building the 76-foot Viking ship replica in 1972, hoping to sail it to his ancestral Norway. Asp died in 1980, but in 1982 four of his children and nine others sailed the vessel 6,000 miles, from Duluth to the Norwegian port of Bergen. The center and neighboring Clay County Museum present a wide range of historical exhibits, but you'll want to see the ship most of all. *Gift Shop*

📱 218 233-5604 • http://www.atpfargo.com/hjem • 202 1st Ave. North, Moorhead, MN 56560

🚗 Moorhead is in east-central Minnesota, across the Red River from Fargo, North Dakota. Take Exit 1A off I-94 and go north on US 75 for 2.5 miles and turn left on 1st Ave. North. The center is on the right, and looks like a large tent.

🕐 Mon.–Sat. 9 A.M.–5 P.M. (to 9 P.M. Thurs.), Sun. noon–5 P.M. Fee.

NORTHFIELD

Northfield Historical Museum   Jesse James and the gang came here to hit the bank in this building on September 7, 1876. Instead, the townspeople hit them—only Jesse (*see also* the James museums in Kearney, Saint Joseph, and Stanton, Missouri) and brother Frank escaped. This general history museum has a special exhibit on the raid, and Northfield re-enacts it every year. *Tours*

🏛 507 645-9268 • Scriver Bldg., 408 Division St., Northfield, MN 55057

🚗 Northfield is in southeastern Minnesota, 35 miles south of the Twin Cities. Exit off I-35 onto SR 19 and go 7 miles east. The museum is just north of 5th St.

🕐 Tues.–Sat. 10 A.M.–4 P.M., Sun. 1 P.M.–4 P.M. Other times by appointment. Fee.

PIPESTONE

Pipestone County Historical Museum   Most visitors to Pipestone head straight for the National Monument (just northwest), with its ancient quarries and cultural center displays. You should not overlook coming into town, where this museum has displays on the famous calumet stone of the Dakota and on native quillwork and beadwork, pioneer life, the artist George Catlin, the Civil War, and other matters. The neighborhood is filled with handsome buildings of Sioux quartzite. *Hands-on, Programs, Library*

🏛 507 825-2563 • http://www.pipestone.mn.us/museum/homepa~1.htm • 113 S. Hiawatha Ave., Pipestone, MN 56164

🚗 Pipestone is in the southwestern corner of Minnesota, at the junction of US 75 with SR 23 and SR 30. It's in the Old City Hall, near the corner of Hiawatha and Main.

🕐 Mon.–Sun. 10 A.M.–5 P.M. Extended hours during Hiawatha Pageant (midsummer). Fee.

SAUK CENTRE

Sinclair Lewis Boyhood Home   He said terrible things about "Gopher Prairie," and now his townspeople love him for it—of course, he *is* a major source of income. His home provided setting and material for much of his writing, and you'll see memorabilia of his father's medical career and the boy's carriage-house loft retreat, where the writing began. *Tours, Gift Shop*

🏛 320 352-5201 • 812 Sinclair Lewis Ave., Sauk Centre, MN 56378

🚗 Sauk Centre is in central Minnesota, 90 miles northwest of the Twin Cities, on I-94. Take Exit 127 (the Sinclair Lewis Interpretive Center is at the exit) onto US 71N (Main St.), and turn left on Sinclair Lewis Ave.

🕐 Memorial Day–Labor Day: Mon.–Sat. 9:30 A.M.–5 P.M., Sun. 10:30 A.M.–5 P.M. Rest of year by appointment. Fee.

SHOREVIEW

American Museum of Asmat Art/Bishop Sowada Gallery   The Asmat are a rain forest people of Irian Jaya, in Indonesia. Since the 1950s the Crosiers, a religious order, have been bringing Asmat art and artifacts to America. This museum, opened in 1995, displays woodcarvings, drums, a 17-foot "soulship," ancestor skulls, war shields, and other ceremonial objects. Much of the Crosiers' collection is in the Crosier Asmat Museum, in Hastings, Nebraska (call 402 463-3188).

📞 612 486-7456 • 3510 Vivian Ave., Shoreview, MN 55126

🚗 Shoreview is a northern suburb of Saint Paul, on I-694. Exit onto Lexington Ave. and go south to City Rd. East, east to Vivian Ave., then south.

🕐 Mon.–Thurs. 8:30 A.M.–4 P.M., Fri. 8:30 A.M.–noon. No fee.

WINONA

Polish Cultural Institute/Polish Museum   Founded in 1976, the Polish Cultural Institute seeks to preserve the history and traditions of Poles who came to this part of America, particularly the Kashubians who settled in Winona, but also Silesians who found minework nearby. The institute presents cultural and commemorative events and maintains a large archive of documents and newspapers from the immigration period. *Gift Shop, Programs, Library*

📞 507 454-3431 • 102 Liberty St., Winona, MN 55987

🚗 Winona is in extreme southeastern Minnesota, on the Mississippi River, about 100 miles southeast of the Twin Cities. From I-90, exit onto SR 43N, following it into the city. The museum is at the corner of 2nd St. and Liberty.

🕐 May–Nov.: Mon.–Fri. 10 A.M.–3 P.M. Call for weekend hours. Donation.

MISSISSIPPI

Mississippi is the kind of place you wander around in pursuit of a theme. Antebellum and Civil War sites are the most obvious items on many travelers' itinerary. The music and culture of the Delta, in the northwest, is another organizing principle. The life of the Gulf Coast could be a third. The museums we've come up with here, though, mostly fall out of these categories. To be sure, some could be bases for theme traveling—see Clarksdale regarding the Delta, or Biloxi regarding the Gulf Coast. But taken as a whole they could best be said to represent individualism: the passions of a number of imaginative souls with very different interests.

What's Big: The entire community of Natchez; if you can see only one site, try Longwood, the magnificent unfinished octagonal house. On the way north to Vicksburg (more antebellum and war sites), stop off at Port Gibson and Grand Gulf. In the northeast, it isn't so much the Civil War that will put you in a crowd, we think, as Elvis. See Holly Springs for our Elvis choice, but remember Tupelo too.

BELZONI

Catfish Capitol Museum   Catfish farming began in earnest in the mid-1960s in a depressed part of the Delta, and now the name Belzoni is known far and wide. Here, in a redeveloped depot, you'll see displays on the breeding and raising of catfish as well as a sizable collection of fish and fish-farming art, including the 40-foot King Cat. Except during the World Catfish Festival in April, fellow museumgoers won't school around you in large numbers.

📫 800 408-4838 • http://www.capital2.com/catfish.htm • 111 Magnolia St., Belzoni, MS 39038

🚗 Belzoni is about 80 miles north of Jackson. From US 49W, turn east into Belzoni and proceed approximately 0.5 mile on Jackson St. Turn right onto Magnolia.

🕐 Mon.–Fri. 9 A.M.–5 P.M. No fee.

Ethel Wright Mohamed Stitchery Museum ("Mama's Dream World")
This is the home of "the Grandma Moses of Stitchery," whose daughter Carol Ivy
will show visitors a house full of her late mother's work (more is in the Smithsonian). In the elaborate pieces you'll see the history of this family and their Delta
community. *Tours, Gift Shop*
- 601 247-1433 • 307 Central St., Belzoni, MS 39038
- See Catfish Capitol directions. Continue 3 blocks farther east along Jackson and turn
left on Central. The museum is on the left after Bowles St.
- By appointment. Fee.

BILOXI

While you're in the area, see also: D'Iberville

Mardi Gras Museum   Biloxi has been around as long (since 1699) as American forms of Mardi Gras, but the city didn't develop its own parades and attendant
highjinks until the 20th century. Nevertheless, the tradition is well established
now, and you don't have to go to New Orleans to see displays of costumes and
memorabilia, pictures of the Krewes, and all that wild and crazy stuff. And the
Lewis Hine photo collection is just one good reason to stop at the Maritime and
Seafood Industry Museum (601 435-6320), where the displays harken back to the
days when Biloxi was the "Seafood Capital of the World."
- 601 435-6245 • Magnolia Hotel, 1st floor, 119 Rue Magnolia, Biloxi, MS 39530
- The hotel is 1 block from US 90 on the Rue Magnolia walking mall; look for signs.
- Mon.–Fri. 9 A.M.–4 P.M., Sat. 11 A.M.–4 P.M. No fee.

BOVINA

Earl's Art Gallery   Earl Simmons is a painter, but he makes art out of almost
anything, and you'll find much of it in and around his little home here. This is an
intimate look into the life and work of the kind of artist big-city galleries don't
always find out about.
- 601 636-5264 • Natchez Trace Pkwy, Bovina, MS 39180
- Bovina is just east of Vicksburg. Take Bovina exit off I-20; follow main road, take left at
stop sign, and cross the tracks. Stay to the left and look for Earl's sign.
- Call for hours. Fee.

CLARKSDALE

Delta Blues Museum   This is Blues Country, and the museum is engaged in
preserving what was once an elusive heritage, giving the lives and art of itinerant

musicians a home to which visitors come from all over the world. If it isn't overrun it's because Americans still don't know about blues; your fellow visitor is apt to be German or Japanese. You'll find recordings, videos, and all sorts of memorabilia of the greats, local and slightly less local. They'll put you onto other Clarksdale sites and events. *Gift Shop, Programs, Library*

- 601 627-6820 • http://www.clarksdale.com/blusmuseu.htm • Carnegie Public Library, 114 Delta Ave., Clarksdale, MS 38614
- Clarksdale is an hour south of Memphis, Tennessee, via US Hwy 61, which becomes State St. in town. The library and museum are at the corner of 1st and Delta, 2 blocks east of the Sunflower River and near the Historic District.
- Mon.–Thur. 9 A.M.–5:30 P.M., Fri. 9 A.M.–5 P.M., Sat. 10 A.M.–5 P.M. No fee.

D'IBERVILLE

Warren L. Fuller Breweriana Collection   Warren Fuller says he gets "very few" visitors each week, so you're sure to get his attention. What do you say to more than 20,000 cans and bottles, arranged by country and brand name? Trays, tap knobs, openers, advertising posters, glasses, mugs, and steins, all by the light of beer signs? Does it get any better than this?

- 601 392-2150 • 3298 Bay Shore Dr., D'Iberville, MS 39532
- D'Iberville is just north across the bay from Biloxi. From I-10, take Exit 46. Go south on I-110 to Exit 2. Turn right, then immediately left on 5th, and left again on Boney. When you reach Bay Shore Dr., turn left and look for black mailbox #3298 on left.
- Call ahead for appointment. No fee.

GREENWOOD

Prayer Museum   This is William Hony's home, and the anthropologist has amassed religious items from around the world. There are prayer beads, a Tibetan human bone rattle, a Buddhist prayer wheel, an early New York Bible with a hand-written account of a cholera epidemic, bells, prayer flags and rugs, and other items he's happy to show you and explain. It's a personal seminar on world religion, length depending on your degree of interest. And Greenwood's Cottonlandia Museum (601 453-0925) offers a somewhat more objective, yet complete, overview of the history and culture of this region.

- 601 453-7306 • 611 W. Market St., Greenwood, MS 38930
- Greenwood is in the central Delta, 100 miles north of Jackson, 20 miles west of I-55, on US 82 and US 49E. The museum is 3 blocks west of the courthouse, where Market St. dead-ends.
- Call for appointment. Donations.

HOLLY SPRINGS

Graceland Too   Paul MacLeod and son Elvis Aaron are about as serious about the King as you can be, and if you want to avoid the crowds at Graceland One, come here and see their collection, which runs from bizarre (death certificate of a woman who expired watching *Jailhouse Rock*) to everyday. There's also a huge archive.

■ 601 252-7954 • http://ocasr.teclink.net/~elvisgto • 200 E. Gholson Ave., Holly Springs, MS 38635-3012

🚗 Holly Springs is in north-central Mississippi, 50 miles northwest of Tupelo and 30 miles southeast of Memphis, Tennessee, on I-78.

🕐 Call for directions and appointment. Fee.

LUCEDALE

Palestinian Gardens   With one yard equaling one mile, the Holy Land at the time of Christ covers 20 acres down here in the Mississippi woods. Jericho, the Dead Sea, Jacob's Well, Mount Hermon, Bethlehem—if you've ever had trouble learning biblical geography, or visualizing the Bible story, this is the place for you.

■ 601 947-8422 • 201 Palestine Gardens Rd., Lucedale, MS 39452

🚗 Lucedale is in extreme southeastern Mississippi, 35 miles north of Pascagoula. From Lucedale take Hwy 198 to US 98, and go 0.75 mile west. Turn right onto Bexley Rd. at Carolyn's grocery. Go 3.5 miles to stop, turn right, and go for 1.5 miles to gardens.

🕐 Mon.–Sat. 8 A.M.–6 P.M., Sun. 1 P.M.–6 P.M. Fee. Tours by appointment.

MERIDIAN

Jimmie Rodgers Museum   He lived only from 1897 to 1933, when tuberculosis cut him down, but Jimmie Rodgers is known variously as "the Singing Brakeman" (he worked hereabouts on the railroad), "the Blue Yodeler," and "the Father of Country Music." This memorial has musical and railroading memorabilia. They hold a festival here in the week that includes his death date (May 26). Meridian was also home to Hartley Peavey, the amplifier king. The Peavey Museum (601 486-1460) has historic equipment Rodgers himself might have used, family memorabilia, and the Peavey Walk of Wisdom. *Gift Shop*

■ 800 748-9970 • Highland Park, 1725 Jimmie Rodgers Dr., Meridian, MS 39304

🚗 Meridian is in east-central Mississippi. For the museum, take Exit 153 off I-20 onto 22nd Ave. north, turn left on 8th St., and follow signs.

🕐 Mon.–Sat. 10 A.M.–4 P.M., Sun. 1 P.M.–5 P.M. Fee.

MISSISSIPPI STATE

Templeton Music Museum and Archives   In an early-20th-century faculty house, this museum holds the collection of MSU alumnus and local businessman Charles Templeton. There are more than 15,000 records and 22,000 pieces of turn-of-the-century sheet music, but you're most likely to find yourself admiring handsome old machinery or marveling at the song of the hundred-year-old French "finches." Nearby there are other MSU museums, and if you head back west on US 12 you can stop at Starkville's C. C. Clark Memorial Coca-Cola Museum (601 323-4150 or 4317).

■ 601 325-8301 • http://msinfo.ur.msstate.edu/temple.ton • Mississippi State University, 46 Blackjack Rd., Mississippi State, MS 39762

🚗 Mississippi State adjoins Starkville on the east. From US 12 in Starkville, turn right onto Spring St. Continue past College of Veterinary Medicine. At fork (Shell station), stay left and you will be on Blackjack Rd.

🕐 Mon.–Fri. 9 A.M.–5 P.M. No fee.

PETAL

International Checker Hall of Fame   Charles Walker, an insurance millionaire, established this facility on part of his estate in 1979. No, it's not about taxicabs, it's about Mind Sports, in particular the game Walker used to play while waiting for his date to get ready. You'll find yourself on a giant checkerboard here, and you'll see pictures of the greats as well as other memorabilia. *Tours, Gift Shop, Hands-on, Programs*

■ 601 582-7090 • 220 Lynn Ray Rd., Petal, MS 39465

🚗 Petal, in southeastern Mississippi, adjoins Hattiesburg's east side. The ICHF is off Hwy 42; call for specific directions.

🕐 By appointment Mon.–Fri. 9 A.M.–5 P.M. No fee.

PINEY WOODS

Laurence C. Jones Museum   It's the picture this museum gives of life and work at Piney Woods School that makes this stop worthwhile. Laurence Jones began the school in 1909, and after his death in 1975 his home was turned into a memorial. Piney Woods is about primarily poor black kids and their education, which was once chiefly vocational but now sends almost all of them to college. *Gift Shop*

■ 601 845-2214 x232 • Old Community House, Piney Woods Country Life School, Hwy 49S, Piney Woods, MS 39148

🚗 The school and museum are 22 miles southeast of Jackson off Hwy 49S.

🕐 Tues.–Fri. 8 A.M.–5 P.M., Sat. 9 A.M.–5 P.M. No fee.

RULEVILLE

American Costume Museum   Luster Bayless left Ruleville in 1959 for Hollywood, found success as a costume designer, and in 1985 bought a hometown department store to create this museum. Fan of the Duke? Bayless worked closely with him, and there's lots of John Wayne stuff here. Also Marilyn, Redford and Newman, Cagney, and others. Starstruck or clothesstruck, you'll like it.

📱 601 756-2344 • Hollywood Outpost, 104 N. Ruby St., Ruleville, MS 38771

🚗 Ruleville is in the central Delta, a half-hour south of Clarksdale, on US 49W.

🕐 Tues.–Sat. 9:30 A.M.–5 P.M. Call to confirm. Fee.

VALLEY PARK

Valley Park Shortline Railroad/Agriculture/Historic Museum (C. B. "Buddie" Newman Museum)   Buddie Newman is not your usual curator. He spent 40 years in the Mississippi legislature, 12 as Speaker of the House. In the early 1980s, when the Illinois Central abandoned its local line, Newman bought it and some rolling stock, and now he devotes his efforts to preserving the railroad era. Not that it's all rail: He has the furniture from his former (Speaker's) office, for instance, and World War II artifacts from the Philippines, along with cotton farming and blacksmithing implements and more. He says that "only a few" people come to see him; why not you?

📱 601 636-0345 • Valley Park, MS 39177

🚗 Valley Park is on US 61, 21 miles north of Vicksburg. The museum is on abandoned Illinois Central land, next to the Valley Park post office and along Hwy 61.

🕐 Call for appointment. No fee.

VAUGHAN

Casey Jones Museum   The whole story is a curiosity: A white engineer, John Luther (Casey) Jones, wrecks the *Cannon Ball* one night in 1900 in Vaughan, Mississippi. There were many—and many worse—crashes those days; but a black maintenance man, Wallace Saunders, is Casey's friend, and the ballad he writes about this one becomes one of the most familiar of all American songs. Here, in a former railway station, you can see artifacts, memorabilia, and portraits detailing the story, as well as much on Southern railroading in general.

📍 601 673-9864 • Casey Jones Museum State Park, Vaughan, MS 39179

🚗 Vaughan is 35 miles north of Jackson via I-55. Follow signs off Exit 133E.

🕐 Mon.–Fri. 8 A.M.–4 P.M. (Wed. to noon only), Sat. 8 A.M.–noon. Fee.

VICKSBURG

While you're in the area, see also: **Bovina, Valley Park**

Corner Drug Store   Waiting for a prescription to be filled is no problem in Joe Gerache's drugstore. The place has the latest pharmaceuticals, but it also has herbs from the Bible, antique medical instruments and bottles, all sorts of forgotten medicines, and medical memorabilia. We think it's the Civil War artifacts, though, that'll really perk you up: How about guns and swords hanging among the remedies? There are bullets and shells galore, even a cannon. In the medical line, there's also a moonshiner's still.

📍 601 636-2756 • 1123 Washington St., Vicksburg, MS 39180

🚗 Take the Clay St. exit off I-20 into downtown Vicksburg. Turn right on Walnut. Go 1 block, turn left, and go 1 block. It is on your right.

🕐 Mon.–Sat. 8 A.M.–6 P.M., Sun. 9 A.M.–11 A.M. No fee.

Missouri

Here's a state, one of few, with two bona fide metropolitan areas—Saint Louis and Kansas City. Furthermore, both rose to importance as gateways to the West. The difference is time, about half a century: The eastern city grew the minute the Louisiana Purchase was concluded, the western not until the era of the overland trails. You can see this even in their museums; those in Saint Louis speak of an economy and culture that peaked in the late 19th century, those in Kansas City suggest instead the 1920s and 1930s.

What's Big: Much in the two cities, but we'd like to point out Kansas City's Arabia Steamboat Museum and Hallmark Visitors Center in particular. Purina Farms, in Gray Summit; the George Washington Carver National Monument, in Diamond; and the Mark Twain Home and Museum, in Hannibal, are also among places we thought were probably a little too traveled. And we are *not* sending you to Branson!

DES PERES

American Kennel Club Museum of the Dog (formerly the Dog Museum) Here's our best friend, seen through the eyes of painters, sculptors, and other artists, but also in instructional videos. *Gift Shop*
🔲 314 821-DOGS [3647] • 1721 S. Mason, Des Peres, MO 63131
🚗 The museum is in the Jarville House, in Queeny Park, Des Peres, about 20 minutes from downtown Saint Louis and 2 miles south of I-64.
🕐 Tues.–Sat. 9 A.M.–5 P.M., Sun. noon–5 P.M. Fee.

FORT LEONARD WOOD

U.S. Army Engineer Museum This is a museum of military engineering (which is not to be confused with the work of the Army Corps of Engineers). It details army history from the 19th century to the present. Bridges, mines, various ordnance up to and including an atom bomb, surveying equipment, weapons, and a computer firing range can be seen in a complex of several World War II–era buildings at this outpost in the Ozark foothills.

- 573 596-0780 • http://www.wood.army.mil/museum/t_ency.htm • Fort Leonard Wood, MO 65473
- Fort Leonard Wood is in south-central Missouri, 120 miles southwest of Saint Louis and just south of I-44. From the Main Gate follow Missouri Ave., go left on North Dakota and right on Nebraska, then left on South Dakota.
- Mon.–Sat. 10 A.M.–4 P.M. No fee.

FULTON

Winston Churchill Memorial and Library in the United States   Westminster was an obscure Midwestern college in 1946 when Churchill delivered his "Iron Curtain" speech in the gym. Next, to commemorate the occasion and Anglo-American unity, the 1677 Church of Saint Mary the Virgin, Aldermanbury, designed by Christopher Wren and demolished during the London blitz, was brought here and reconstructed. Then, in 1989, part of the "fallen" Berlin Wall was brought here to symbolize the end of the Iron Curtain. You will see much Churchill memorabilia, including some of his paintings. *Tours*

- 573 592-1369 • http://www.westminster-mo.edu • Westminster College, 501 Westminster Ave., Fulton, MO 65251
- Westminster is 20 miles east of Columbia. Exit south from I-70 at Kingdom City, onto US 54, then take County Rd. F east into town.
- Mon.–Sun. 10 A.M.–4:30 P.M. Fee.

HAZELWOOD

Museum of Western Jesuit Missions   In a noted Federal-style building, this museum details the history of Jesuit activities in the Louisiana Purchase and the West. Saint Stanislaus Seminary educated missionary "Black Robes"—the best known being P. J. De Smet—for 150 years, until 1971. Here you'll see both antique church items (chalices, monstrances, carvings of the Madonna) and tools, other artifacts, and books on the West.

- 314 837-3525 • Rock Bldg., Saint Stanislaus Seminary, 700 Howdershell Rd., Hazelwood, MO 63042
- Hazelwood is a northern Saint Louis suburb. Take the McDonnell Blvd. exit from I-270, head north, and stay right on Howdershell Rd.
- Sun. 1 P.M.–4 P.M. Group tours by appointment other days. No fee.

INDEPENDENCE

Leila's Hair Museum   Hair art: In the 19th century it was widely practiced. One kept mementos in the form of brooches. Lovers exchanged hair "jewelry." Especially luxuriant tresses might end up woven into wreaths. This is said to be the only place in America where you can see this vanished medium (but *see* Saint Louis' Museum of Cosmetology Arts and Sciences also).

- 816 252-HAIR [4247] • 815 W. 23rd St., Independence, MO 64055
- On the east side of Kansas City. Take I-435 Exit 61 and go east on SR 78 (23rd St.)
- Tues.–Sat. 8:30 A.M.–4:30 P.M. Fee.

National Frontier Trails Center   On the site of a mill and watering spot where travelers on the Santa Fe, Oregon, and California trails stopped before heading out onto the Great Plains, this center tells the story of the westward pioneers through such artifacts as covered wagons and trail diaries and relics, along with film and other historical displays. *Library*

- 816 325-7575 • 318 W. Pacific St., Independence, MO 64050
- I-70 to Noland Rd. (County Rd. V), exit north to downtown, then left on Pacific.
- Apr.–Oct.: Mon–Sat. 9 A.M.–4:30 P.M., Sun. 12:30 P.M.–4:30 P.M. Nov.–Mar.: Mon.–Fri 10 A.M.–4 P.M., weekends 12:30 P.M.–4 P.M. Fee.

KANSAS CITY

While you're in the area, see also: Independence, Kearney

Black Archives of Mid-America   Kansas City has long been the black capital of the Midwest, so this is a logical place to look into African-American regional history. The 18th and Vine district was a hotbed of jazz in the 1920s and 1930s, and this is one area of focus (ask about the long-planned International Jazz Museum); but all areas of black life in Missouri, Oklahoma, and Kansas are within the archives' bailiwick.

- 816 483-1300 • 2033 Vine St., Kansas City, MO 64108
- A short walk from the Negro Leagues Baseball Museum (see following entry).
- Mon.–Fri. 9 A.M.–4:30 P.M. Fee. Weekend group tours by appointment.

Negro Leagues Baseball Museum   Until Jackie Robinson broke the Major Leagues' color barrier in 1947, there was another whole world of American baseball, one most whites were completely unaware of. It was the world of Satchel Paige and Josh Gibson and other titans—the Negro Leagues. Here you'll see uniforms, photographs, video, timelines, and other displays that lay out a long and proud history. *Gift Shop*

- 816 221-1920 • 1601 E. 18th St., Kansas City, MO 64108

🚙 The museum is in the 18th and Vine Historical District, just southeast of downtown. Exit south from I-70 on the Paseo, and turn east (left) on 18th St.

🕐 Tues.–Sat. 10 A.M.–4:30 P.M., Sun. noon–4:30 P.M. Fee.

Thomas Hart Benton Home and Studio State Historic Site   Many think of Benton as *the* Midwestern painter. He lived here a long time (1939–75), working in the adjoining carriage house (he died there, while painting). You'll see some of his works, and you'll also get a sense of the environment in which much significant American art was produced. *Tours*

■ 816 931-5722 • 3616 Belleview Ave., Kansas City, MO 64111

🚙 South of downtown, near the Kansas line and just southwest of Penn Valley Park.

🕐 Mid-Apr.–Oct.: Mon.–Sat. 10 A.M.–4 P.M., Sun. noon–5 P.M. Rest of year: same except Sun. 11 A.M.–4 P.M. Fee.

Toy and Miniature Museum of Kansas City   In a refurbished 1911 mansion are many houses—dollhouses, along with all sorts of toys, precisely crafted modern miniatures, and toy environments (like farm settings).

■ 816 333-2055 • 5235 Oak St., Kansas City, MO 64112

🚙 The museum is 5 miles south of downtown and just south of Ward Pkwy, in the University of Missouri–Kansas City neighborhood.

🕐 Wed.–Sat. 10 A.M.–4 P.M., Sun. 1 P.M.–4 P.M. Fee.

KEARNEY

Jesse James Farm and Museum   One of America's favorite badmen is an industry in this part of Missouri. Born and raised on this farm, he became a Confederate guerrilla at 16; as soon as that Cause was Lost, he became a bank robber. Having toured the farm and seen Jesse's guns, coffin, and birth bed, as well as the Pinkerton Bomb, you'll want to take it on the lam back down I-35 into Liberty, to the Jesse James Bank Museum, and see the site of America's pioneer daylight bank job (call 816 781-4458 for hours). *See also* James Museums in Saint Joseph and Stanton, and the Northfield, Minnesota, museum. *Tours, Gift Shop*

■ 816 628-6065 • 21216 Jesse James Farm Rd., Kearney, MO 64060

🚙 Kearney is 15 minutes northeast of Kansas City via I-35. Take Exit 26 and go east on SR 92, following signs onto Jesse James Farm Rd.

🕐 June–Sept.: Mon.–Sun. 9 A.M.–4 P.M. Open daily, reduced hours, rest of year. Fee.

KIRKSVILLE

Still National Osteopathic Museum   Kirksville is where Andrew Taylor Still (1827–1917) developed his new and controversial methods of manipulation of body parts and systems from 1875, and where in 1892 he founded the first osteo-pathic school (Kirksville College). This memorial to his life and work displays a dis-sected human nervous system along with medical instruments and other memorabilia, including much on women in osteopathy. *Gift Shop*

■ 800 626-5266 x2359 • 800 W. Jefferson St., Kirksville, MO 63501

🚗 Kirksville is in north-central Missouri, 2 hours north of Columbia via US 63. The museum is on the campus of Kirksville College.

🕐 June–Oct.: Mon.–Fri. 10 A.M.–4 P.M., Sat. noon–4 P.M. Rest of year weekdays only. No fee.

MANSFIELD

Laura Ingalls Wilder–Rose Wilder Lane Home and Museum Readers (and viewers) of the *Little House* series will want to see this house on Rocky Ridge Farm, where all of the books were written; it's also where Rose Wilder Lane grew up. Manuscripts and Ingalls and Wilder family artifacts are in the adjacent museum. Those who are really serious about following "Little House" history should know that it involves some traveling. Laura Ingalls was born in Pepin, Wis-consin, in the "Little House in the Big Woods"; the Pepin Historical Museum (call 715 442-3161) shows summer visitors some early memorabilia. Walnut Grove, Min-nesota, on Plum Creek, was home in 1874–79 (for the Wilder Museum in Walnut Grove call 800 761-1009). Finally, there is De Smet, South Dakota, home in 1879–94, where Laura taught school and met Almanzo Wilder; call 605 854-3383 for information on sites there. *Gift Shop*

■ 417 924-3626 • 3068 Hwy A, Mansfield, MO 65704

🚗 Mansfield is in south-central Missouri, 35 miles east of Springfield on US 60. Take Busi-ness 60S to the town square, and continue 1.5 miles east on Hwy A.

🕐 Mar. 15–Oct. 15: Mon.–Sat. 9 A.M.–5 P.M., Sun. 12:30 P.M.–5:30 P.M. Rest of year: hours slightly reduced. Fee.

MEXICO

American Saddlebred Horse Museum This has been horseracing country since the mid-19th century, and the Saddlebred Horse Museum displays paintings and memorabilia of famed horses (like Rex McDonald) and trainers (like Tom Bass); it bills itself as the oldest such museum in the country. *See also* the American Saddle Horse Museum in Lexington, Kentucky.

■ 573 581-3910 • 501 S. Muldrow, Mexico, MO 65265

🚗 Mexico is in east-central Missouri, on US 54, 20 miles north of I-70 and an hour north-east of Columbia. In town, turn left off 54 onto the Boulevard, then right on Muldrow.

🕐 Tues.–Sat. 1 P.M.–4 P.M., Sun. 2 P.M.–5 P.M. Fee.

NEW MADRID

New Madrid Historical Museum   The local T-shirts say "It's Our Fault!" and boy, did it let go in December of 1811, at about 8.6 on the Richter Scale, changing the course of the Mississippi. You may be aware that it's going to happen again—someday—but why not visit now? The museum has exhibits on this history, on local Civil War activity, on prehistory, and other matters.

■ 573 748-5944 • 1 Main St., New Madrid, MO 63869

🚗 New Madrid is in extreme southeastern Missouri's Bootheel region, on the Mississippi River and just off I-55. The museum is downtown, at the corner of Main and Water.

🕓 Mon.–Fri. 9 A.M.–4 P.M., Sat. 10 A.M.–4 P.M., Sun. 1 P.M.–4 P.M. In summer, to 5 P.M. Fee.

POPLAR BLUFF

Margaret Harwell Art Museum   Here's a fine-arts museum that puts on changing exhibits also involving folk arts, period clothing, photography, and other expressions of the area, in the Ozark foothills. *Tours*

■ 573 686-8002 • http://www.ims-1.com/nonprof/mham/ • 421 N. Main St., Poplar Bluff, MO 63901

🚗 Poplar Bluff is in southeastern Missouri, 50 miles west-northwest of New Madrid, at the junction of US 60 and US 67.

🕓 Wed.–Sun. 1 P.M.–4 P.M. No fee.

SAINT JOSEPH

While you're in the area, see also: Atchison, KS

Albrecht-Kemper Museum of Art   This is an important regional fine-arts museum, much less visited than its collection merits. You'll see Thomas Hart Benton's version of Custer's Last Stand, and works by Fitzhugh Lane, Bierstadt, Cassatt, William Merritt Chase, Thiebaud, Grooms, and other major figures from the 18th century on. *Gift Shop, Programs*

■ 816 233-7003 • 2818 Frederick Blvd., Saint Joseph, MO 64506

🚗 Saint Joseph is an hour north of Kansas City on I-29. Exit onto Frederick Ave.; the museum is about 2 miles west.

🕓 Tues.–Sat. 10 A.M.–4 P.M., Sun. 1 P.M.–4 P.M. Fee except on Sun.

Glore Psychiatric Museum   Will we ever understand the workings of the mind? If you think we're a long way off now, you should see some of the approaches taken in the past. How about a "tranquilizer chair" (six months strapped in place)? This museum displays devices and methods to restrain, shock, disorient, and reintegrate—whatever seemed promising. There are also artworks and artifacts (some quite bizarre) of patients of the past.

■ 816 387-2300 • Saint Joseph State Hospital, 3400 Frederick Ave., Saint Joseph, MO 64506

🚗 It's 10 minutes northeast of downtown. From I-29/US 71, exit west on Frederick Blvd., which becomes Frederick Ave.; the hospital is on the south side.

🕐 Mon.–Fri 8:30 A.M.–4 P.M., weekends and holidays 1 P.M.–5 P.M. Donation.

Patee House Museum/Jesse James House Museum   The brief (1860–61) and romantic Pony Express experiment was run (businesswise) from an office in the Patee House, an Italianate 1850s hotel, where today you'll see artifacts of the service and the period. On the grounds is the house Jesse James lived in as "Mr. Howard," and in which Robert Ford shot him (but see the entry for Stanton!) in 1882; the building has been restored (except for an important bullet hole) and contains Jamesana. Down the street is the Pony Express National Monument, the stables from which the daring young riders departed.

■ 816 232-8206 • 12th and Penn Sts., Saint Joseph, MO 64503

🚗 Penn St. runs east from downtown Saint Joseph. The Pony Express National Monument is closer to the center, at 914 Penn, the Patee and James Houses 3 blocks away.

🕐 Patee House: Apr.–Oct.: Mon.–Sat. 10 A.M.–5 P.M., Sun. 1 P.M.–5 P.M. Weekends only Feb.–Mar. and Nov. James House hours slightly different; call to confirm. Fee.

SAINT LOUIS

While you're in the area, see also: Des Peres, Hazelwood. *In Illinois, see*: Edwardsville

Bowling Hall of Fame and Museum   From the Pharaohs to Earl Anthony—and beyond! Bronze busts, portraits, shirts, trophies, pinsetters, videos, antique and modern lanes, balls, pins, computerized records, hands-on (ball-on?) displays. They don't say, but you probably should bring your shoes. *Gift Shop, Hands-on*

■ 314 231-6340 • 111 Stadium Plaza, Saint Louis, MO 63102

🚗 It's downtown, near the I-64/I-70 junction, across from Busch Memorial Stadium.

🕐 Mon.–Sat. 9 A.M.–5 P.M., Sun. noon–5 P.M. Fee.

Mercantile Money Museum   Here's lucre in many forms, including numismatists' delights as well as the Almighty Dollar. Benjamin Franklin speaks from beyond the grave (audiovisually), and another shady character discusses the art (and pitfalls) of counterfeiting.

■ 314 421-1819 • Mercantile Tower, 7th St. and Washington Ave., Saint Louis, MO 63101

🚗 The Mercantile Tower is downtown, 8 blocks north of Busch Stadium and just west of Laclede's Landing; there is a light rail station 2 blocks west on Washington.

🕐 Mon.–Sun. 9 A.M.–4 P.M. No fee.

Museum of Cosmetology Arts and Sciences   *Cosmetology* is the professional term for practices carried on for millennia, most recently in parlors, or at stylists'. We're talking hair, for the most part, and this museum has, among other things, a fully re-created 1920s salon, a Cosmetology Hall of Fame, a library of hairstyles, a permanent wave machine, a Magic Fingers massager, steamers, irons, dryers, ornaments, and hair art. Come here and learn about Madame C. J. Walker and other giants of the industry. *See also* Leila's Hair Museum in Independence.   *Library*

■ 314 652-4333 • 3510 Olive St., Saint Louis, MO 63103

🚌 The museum is in the Grand Center Cultural Arts District, in the former Godefroy Cosmetics factory, near the corner of Olive St. and Grand Ave., west of downtown and 3 blocks from the Fox Theatre.

🕑 The museum is in a process of expansion. Call for information.

National Video Game and Coin-Op Museum   If you can put down your computer games for a minute, here's an educational experience: Come and learn about the dinosaurs—Pinballosaurus and the others—who, back in the mists of time, lurched around the bars and arcades of what is now North America.

■ 314 621-2900 • 801 N. 2nd St., at Laclede's Landing, Saint Louis, MO 63102

🚌 Laclede's Landing is the restoration district on the riverfront, just north of the Jefferson National Expansion Memorial. The museum is on 2nd St. north of Washington Ave.

🕑 Mar.–Sept.: Mon.–Sat. 10 A.M.–10 P.M., Sun. noon–8 P.M. Reduced hours rest of year. No fee, but bring change.

Scott Joplin House State Historic Site   This is the only surviving space occupied (1900–1903) by the great ragtime composer. It has been restored to illustrate the kind of surroundings a successful black artist of the period would have lived in; the rest of the building is a museum with exhibits on Joplin and on the Saint Louis of that period. If you're headed west in Missouri and want more ragtime, check out the Sedalia Ragtime Archives (call 816 826-7100 for information).   *Tours*

■ 314 533-1003 • 2658 Delmar Blvd., Saint Louis, MO 63103

🚌 The Scott Joplin House is in north-central Saint Louis, near the corner of Delmar and Jefferson Ave. Exit north off US 40/I-64 onto Jefferson, then turn left at Delmar.

🕑 Mon.–Sat. 10 A.M.–4 P.M., Sun. noon–6 P.M. (5 P.M. winter). Fee.

STANTON

Jesse James Wax Museum   After visiting the Jesse James House in Saint Joseph you probably think you know the end of the story, right? Oh, no, no, no, no, no—not according to these folks! They say it was all a ruse back in 1882: A lookalike got plugged. Jesse lived on until—are you ready?—19-ought-51! There are wax figures and all sorts of other artifacts here to prove the case; you be the jury. And listen, now that you're in the mood: You're only about an hour from Wright City, where you could drop in at the Elvis Is Alive Cafe and Museum (call 314 745-3154). Is this Show Me, or what?

■ 573 927-5233 • Stanton, MO 63079

🚗 Stanton is on I-44, about 50 miles southwest of Saint Louis. The museum is at Exit 230.

🕑 June–Aug.: Mon.–Sun. 8 A.M.–6 P.M. Hours slightly reduced rest of year. Fee.

MONTANA

Big Sky, big open spaces. A state whose Native American heritage goes from the extremes of the Battle of Little Bighorn to the surrender of Chief Joseph. A state whose fossil record boasts the first T-rex in the United States—and the state fossil is a duck-billed dinosaur. Where wild and woolly was marked by the building of the Northern Pacific Railroad, and the brief flare of the era of the cattle kings in the eastern part of the state was snuffed by the devastating weather that plagues those parts. Where the copper kings made the western half of the state. Where grain elevators are the skyscrapers on the horizon . . . and the remains of subterranean Minuteman silos are our memory of the Cold War. And where fly-fishing and bronc-riding compete for the two favorite sports.

What's Big: The mineral trove in Montana wasn't just copper, of course. Butte's World Museum of Mining and Hell Roarin' Gulch is on the site of the old Orphan Girl silver and zinc mine, and the good news is that local residents thought to preserve associated enterprises—the IWW ("Wobblies") Union Hall and the Quong Fong Laundry, for example—and brought them intact to the mine, helping to provide a real feel for the times with no re-creations in sight. Up in the northeast, Fort Peck Dam, one of the world's largest earth-filled dams, dramatically does its job. The Little Bighorn Battlefield National Monument lies just southeast of Billings. And for scenic spectacular, we must send you to Glacier National Park in the way northwest. Finally, we'd be remiss if we didn't mention the giant steer reported to be parked in front of the O'Fallon Historical Museum, way east in Baker.

BILLINGS

While you're in the area, see also: Worden

Moss Mansion   Designed by Henry Janeway Hardenbergh and built in 1903, a depth of detail evinces the frontier version of turn-of-the-century wealth. Eclectic as all get out, with styles from Louis XVI to an Art Nouveau sitting room, from minimalist modern to a Moorish-styled entryway, it all somehow has a western twang. Banker Preston B. Moss, and then descendants of his family, lived here until 1984, and stained-glass windows, hand-wrought furnishings and effects, Persian rugs, and rich polished woods are all pristine. *Tours, Gift Shop*

🏠 406 256-5100 • http://www.blgs.com/moss • 914 Division St., Billings, MT 59101

🚗 Downtown. From I-90 Exit 450 (Billings/27th St.) turn left onto 3rd Ave. and go about 7 blocks to the end.

🕐 June 1–Labor Day: Mon.–Sat. 10 A.M.–4 P.M., Sun. 1 P.M.–3 P.M. Rest of year: Mon.–Sun. 1 P.M.–3 P.M. Guided tours on the hour. Fee.

Oscar's Dreamland   Three hundred Rare Gas Tractors—No Duplicates . . . World's Largest Revolving Clock . . . Airplanes and Motors . . . Tallest Air Motor Windmill . . . Wooden Oil Well Rig . . . Ancient Hand Tool Display. Might give you the idea that Oscar O. Cooke collected everything, but then we'd be forgetting to mention the old buildings he relocated here too—like the First Schoolhouse in Yellowstone County . . . Fire Station (including Houdini Collection) . . . Church with Oldest Steeple in Billings . . . Old-Time Jail and Padded Cell . . . *Tours, Food*

🏠 Museum: 406 656-0966/Owner: 406 245-4598 • 3100 Harrow Dr., Billings, MT 59102

🚗 I-90E: Exit 437, and go east on S. Frontage Rd. to Shiloh Rd. overpass, then south 1 mile. I-90W: Exit 446, and go west 3.5 miles on S. Frontage Rd., turning left at the Market Basket store, then south 1 mile.

🕐 May–Sept.: Mon.–Sun. 9 A.M.–6 P.M. Fee.

BOZEMAN

While you're in the area, see also: Livingston

American Computer Museum   The Babylonians did it. The Egyptians did it. For over 4,000 years people have sought ways to speed up their calculations. And here is a timeline of the myriad devices used from ancient times to the techiest of the present, from a simple slide rule to the bloated megaton mainframes of the 1950s to the minuscule microchip appliances of today. *Tours, Hands-on*

🏠 406 587-7545 • http://www.compustory.com • 234 E. Babcock St., Bozeman, MT 59715

🚗 Downtown.

🕐 June–Aug.: Mon.–Sun. 10 A.M.–4 P.M. Sept.–May: Tues.–Wed., Fri.–Sat. noon–4 P.M. Fee.

BROADUS

Mac's Museum   Tucked amidst the stuffed stuff ("everything from a mouse to a moose"), here is one man's collection of starfish and seashells, slews of nicely mounted arrowheads and other Indian artifacts, and a selection of rocks and minerals. You might want to poke around the pioneer corner too, highlighted with oral histories and video interviews, a photo collection, school memorabilia, a working still, and the Espy family's ornately carved 19th-century pump organ. *Library*

🔲 406 436-2977 • Powder River Taxidermy, 708 S. Park Ave., Broadus, MT 59317

🚌 Broadus is in southeastern Montana. I-90 Exit 510, onto US 212E 100 miles. It's 1 block north of the traffic light, on the town square.

🕐 Memorial Day–Sept.: Mon.–Sat. 9 A.M.–5 P.M. Donation.

CHINOOK

Blaine County Museum In 1887 Chief Joseph and the Nez Perce were forced to surrender to the U.S. Army at a site near here that was within 40 miles of the Canadian border—and freedom. The battle and related events are addressed in a multimedia exhibit and tours to the battleground site in Bear's Paw State Historic Park. In Havre (HAV-ver), the H. Earl Clack Memorial Museum has a good display of artifacts salvaged from the nearby Plains Indian *pishgun*, or bison jump, site. *Tours*

🔲 406 357-2590 • 501 Indiana St., Chinook, MT 59523

🚌 About 20 miles east of Havre in north-central Montana, off US 2.

🕐 May–Sept.: Tues.–Sat. 8 A.M.–5 P.M., Sun. 2 P.M.–4 P.M. Oct.–Apr.: Mon.–Fri. 1 P.M.–5 P.M. Donation.

CIRCLE

Montana Sheepherders Hall of Fame Circle is named for the cattle brand used by Major Seth Mabrey, a pioneer Texas-to-Montana driver. While cattle was king in eastern Montana only for the brief period from the early 1880s until the devastating winter of 1886–87, cattle ranchers and sheep growers still have their mark on the area, and you'll find tributes to both along with modern and historic brands, like the "Round-topped T." Locally found T-rex fossils here too.

🔲 406 485-2414 • McCone County Museum, 801 1st Ave. South, Circle, MT 59215

🚌 In northeastern Montana. Take US 2 to Wolf Point, then 50 miles south on Hwy 13 to Hwy 200 into town.

🕐 Mon.–Fri. 9 A.M.–5 P.M. Fee.

HELENA

Montana Historical Society Museum Once known as Last Chance Gulch, Montana's state capital is the home of a good collection of Western artifacts. From unique musical instruments like a guitar zither, to frontier-era surveyor's transits, fly-fishing equipment, fossils, mining and ranching history, Native American col-

lections, and the late-19th- and early-20th-century Northern Pacific Railroad and Yellowstone Park photos of F. Jay Haynes, as well as the seemingly ubiquitous artwork of Charles M. Russell. *Tours, Gift Shop, Programs, Publications, Library*
🏠 406 444-2694 • 225 N. Roberts, Helena, MT 59620
🚗 Across from the state capitol, at 6th Ave.
🕐 Memorial Day–Labor Day: Mon.–Fri. 8 A.M.–6 P.M., Sat.–Sun. 9 A.M.–5 P.M. Rest of year: Mon.–Fri. 8 A.M.–5 P.M., Sat. 9 A.M.–5 P.M. No fee.

LIVINGSTON

International Fly Fishing Center If your woolly-bugger tying skills are wanting, you might want to stop here. Housed in the historic Lincoln School, the museum moved not too long ago from West Yellowstone to Calamity Jane territory (and east of Norman McLean's turf) here in Livingston. Exotic and fragile-looking flies, antique rods, reels, and creels, and multimedia exhibits where you might pick up a tip or two about plumbing that perfect fishing hole. *Programs*
🏠 406 222-9369 • 215 E. Lewis St., Livingston, MT 59047
🚗 About 20 miles east of Bozeman. From I-90 Exit 333 (US 89) travel north 1.5 miles, then turn left onto B St. It's 1.5 blocks down on the right.
🕐 May 30–Sept. 15: Mon.–Sun. 10 A.M.–6 P.M. Fee.

MILES CITY

Range Riders Museum and Huffman Pictures Bronco alert! When the Northern Pacific roared in here in 1881, this little white settlement in the eastern plains began to boom. Cattle was herded here from all over and a wild and exciting time was had by all. Miles City folks were quick to figure out they'd better find some way to hold on to what they had, so in 1938, starting with a one-room log cabin, they began the museum. Now in eight buildings, each room has a neatly organized specialty that chronicles the era in one way or another. They've got a Telegraph Insulator Collection, a wealth of women's hats, original cattle brands, guns, broad axes, Indian history, a replica of the L.O. Ranch, and tons of great photos.
🏠 406 232-4483/586-0170 • W. Main St., Miles City, MT 59301
🚗 120 miles east of Billings. I-94 Exit 138, go 1 mile west on US 10/I-94 Business Loop, across the Tongue River Bridge.
🕐 Apr.–Oct.: Mon.–Sun. 8 A.M.–8 P.M. Other times by appointment. Fee.

MISSOULA

Smokejumper and Aerial Fire Depot It seems every year we learn of more devastating fires in our wilderness areas. The nation's largest training base for smokejumpers is in Missoula and offers tours by experienced Forest Service jumpers who have firsthand accounts of this perilous and exhausting career at the ready. Historical photos and artifacts at the visitors center are complemented by a visit to the nearby CCC-built Ninemile Remount Depot Visitors Center (406 626-5201). Ninemile was active from 1930 to 1953 and tells the story of the days firefighting and backcountry work were handled by packing in over land. *Tours*

🏛 406 329-4934 • US 93/Alt. I-90, AFD Box 6, Missoula, MT 59802

🚗 From Missoula, take W. Broadway (US 93/Alt. I-90) 7 miles west. It's about 0.5 mile past the Johnson Bell Airport.

🕐 Memorial Day–Labor Day: Mon.–Sun. 8:30 A.M.–5 P.M. Donation.

PHILIPSBURG

Ghost Town Hall of Fame   In the historic Courtney Hotel, a swell collection of pictures shows Montana's now-abandoned mining towns at their peak. We're told at least 20 of these sites can be found within 40 miles of Philipsburg. Before you go, stop and take a look at the museum's sapphire and mineral displays.

🏛 406 859-3020 • Granite County Museum and Cultural Center, Hwy 1, Box 502, Philipsburg, MT 59858

🚗 Fifty miles west of Butte, on Hwy 1. It's behind the Club Bar, 1 block off Broadway.

🕐 May–mid-Dec.: Mon.–Sun. 10 A.M.–4 P.M. Fee.

POLSON

Montana Fiddlers Hall of Fame   Now Gil and Joanne Mangels are "stuff" experts. So after you've tapped your toes a bit in the fiddle section (fiddling all-stars pix and memorabilia; fiddle-making tools and instruments, spoons and bones), jig on over to the tractor seat collection (a surprising range of patterns and colors), or sheep-powered 1898 treadmill, or the coin-operated "Violano" violin-piano, or perhaps the motorized toboggan. . . . It's all kind of a breathtaking jumble of Americana, so give yourself some time. *Tours, Hands-on*

🏛 406 883-6804 • Miracle of America Museum, 58176 US 93, Polson, MT 59860

🚗 About 60 miles due north of Missoula, on US 93, 2 miles south of town.

🕐 April–Sept.: Mon.–Sun. 8 A.M.–5 P.M. Rest of year by chance or appointment. Fee.

SHELBY

Marias Museum of History and Art   Shelby's a railroad cum oil town cum grain center that had a particularly big moment in 1923, a year after oil was discovered and everyone was thinking big, though the population count then was only pushing 500. Expecting a crowd for the upcoming Jack Dempsey–Tommy Gibbons World Heavyweight fight, the town decided a 40,000-capacity arena was just the thing to have on hand. It wasn't . . . but 15 rounds later Dempsey won anyway. Fight pix and artifacts, oil industry ephemera, and local history.

🏠 406 434-2551 • 206 12th Ave. North, Shelby, MT 59474

🚗 In north-central Montana, just east of I-15. Exit US 2S onto 12th Ave., then continue to the corner of 1st St.

🕐 June–Aug.: Mon.–Fri. 1 P.M.–5 P.M., 7 P.M.–9 P.M.; Sat. 1 P.M.–4 P.M. Sept.–May: Tues. noon–4 P.M. Other times by appointment. No fee.

VIRGINIA CITY

Thompson-Hickman Memorial Museum   Not to be confused with Virginia City, Nevada, though the profile is quite similar: outlaws, reprobates, and gold. The mission of the museum is to preserve and display state and local history. These are some of their favorite things: 1. the club foot of the eponymous Club Foot George, an outlaw hanged in 1864; 2. a piece of "dried or petrified" birthday cake made for a child of an early family (we don't know if *Great Expectations* had been written yet); and 3. a petrified cat (not dried). By the way, there's a nice old gas station across the street.

🏠 406 843-5386 • 215 E. Wallace St., Virginia City, MT 59755

🚗 About 75 miles southeast of Butte and 75 miles southwest of Bozeman. Take US 287S to Ennis, then take State Hwy 287W 15 miles into town.

🕐 May 15–Sept.: 10 A.M.–5 P.M. Fee.

WOLF POINT

Louis Toav's John Deere Collection   Okay, so Louis Toav has a few Model T Fords and Lincoln Continentals, but his true love, his passion, is John Deere tractors. He's got more than 500 of them on his farm, every one that they made from 1923 to 1953, each one painted with the same standard green or yellow paint. Over 80 himself, he's still collecting, and he fixes up and restores every one that he finds. *See also* Deere & Co. in Moline, Illinois.

🏠 406 392-5224 • Box 2045, Wolf Point, MT 59201

🚗 In northeast Montana, off US 2. Call for directions.

🕐 By appointment only. No fee.

WORDEN

Huntley Project Museum of Irrigated Agriculture   Stop by the third week in August for the annual Threshing Bee, or any other time for this exhibit devoted to the history of homesteading. All kinds of farm machinery's on hand, with an especially large selection for harvesting sugar beets. They're glad to demo the smaller equipment and chat about homestead home-style and school days.

■ 406 967-2881 • 2561 S. 22nd Rd., Worden, MT 59088

🚗 Twenty miles northeast of Billings. Take US 212, 3 miles east of Huntley.

🕐 June–Aug.: Mon.–Sun. 9 A.M.–4 P.M. No fee.

NEBRASKA

The Great American Desert is really a lot more fun than it sounds. Sure there are lots of wide open spaces, with tall grasses, short grasses, and everything in between. But the rich prairie lands are steeped in history, and many a traveler on the Oregon Trail decided to stop right here and settle in. You had Buffalo Bill and Wild Bill, Wright Morris, Willa Cather, Mari Sandoz, and Mark Twain traveling through; the Sioux, the Pawnee, and the Cheyenne always thought it was swell—at least until some of the rest of these other folks started showing up; the Mormons came by, and so did the Pony Express, French trappers and traders, missionaries, and bird-watchers. Why, even jackalope like it here. It's been nuclear-central for the Strategic Air Command, and James Michener set one of his epics here. It's a rich history and a warm people here on the lone prairie.

What's Big: Omaha: Joslyn Art Museum, Strategic Air Command Museum, Western Heritage Museum; Lincoln: University of Nebraska State Museum (largest elephant skeleton in the world), Museum of Nebraska History; North Platte: Buffalo Bill State Historical Park, Lincoln County Historical Museum; Crawford: Fort Robinson; and Kearney: Museum of Nebraska Art.

ALLIANCE

Carhenge   Just sitting out there on this lonely stretch of US 385 is Nebraska's answer to Cadillac Ranch. Given that we live in a car culture, we thought it fitting to list James Reinders' Stonehenge-like construction of a variety pack of vehicles from Caddies to pick-ups, all painted over in a soothing shade of gray.
- Chamber of Commerce: 308 762-1520 • US 385, Alliance, NE 69301
- In west-central Nebraska, just north of town and the junction with SR 2.
- Mon.–Sun. daylight hours. No fee.

AURORA

Plainsman Museum   While the main gist of this museum is regional history told through murals and mosaics, we especially like it for its special exhibit on Harold Edgerton, the local inventor of what he called a "double-piddler stop machine," better known as a strobe light (we'll help you out here—his experiments involved two streams of water). Other exhibits include iron toys and dolls, and an 1859 log cabin plus a sod house replica. *Publications, Library*
- 402 694-6531 • 210 16th St., Aurora, NE 68818
- About 20 miles east of Grand Island. Take I-80 to SR 14, go north 3 miles.
- Apr.–Oct.: Mon.–Sat. 9 A.M.–5 P.M., Sun. 1 P.M.–5 P.M. Nov.–Mar: Mon.–Sun. 1 P.M.–5 P.M. Fee.

BANCROFT

John G. Neihardt Center   John Neihardt, "Poet Laureate in Perpetuity" of Nebraska, left an invaluable selection of literature in *Black Elk Speaks* and *The Cycle of the West* that preserves for us a way of life, and a way of living, that may otherwise not have been recorded. The Sacred Hoop Prayer Garden here was designed by Neihardt and is a living interpretation of Oglala Lakota Black Elk's vision of the universe. *Tours, Publications, Library*
- 402 648-3388 • Elm and Washington, Bancroft, NE 68004
- About 70 miles northwest of Omaha. Take I-29N through Iowa, getting off onto Route 175W, which becomes Nebraska SR 51, and then it's about 15 miles into Bancroft.
- Mon.–Sat. 9 A.M.–5 P.M., Sun. 1:30 P.M.–5 P.M. No fee.

BOYS TOWN

Boys Town Hall of History   Boys Town—from Spencer Tracy's silver screen version of Father Flanagan to Newt Gingrich's big idea to send off the poor kids of America—this is a place that makes us think maybe things were really simpler back when. There's a shrine to the man who believed "there's no such thing as a bad boy" and a pictorial Hall of History dating to its founding in 1917. *Tours, Library*
- 402 498-1185 • 14057 Flanagan Blvd., Boys Town, NE 68010
- It's 15 miles west of Omaha; take Exit 6 off I-680.
- Mon.–Sun. 9 A.M.–4:30 P.M. Tour and summer hours vary. Donation.

CHADRON

Museum of the Fur Trade   Traders, trappers, and Native Americans. Here's a place you can get a really solid feel for the mix of cultures and events that shaped the West—and influenced the direction of things to come from the 1700s through the 1900s. The commerce of the American fur trade with its mix of European and Scandinavian players is represented by pelts from sea otter to beaver and buffalo, weaponry, textiles, and costumes, as well as the minutiae of day-to-day life on the Great Plains, like checkerboards and whiskey bottles. *Tours, Programs, Publications, Library, Screenings*

🔲 308 432-3843 • E. Hwy 20, Chadron, NE 69337

🚗 In northwestern Nebraska, it's 3 miles east of Chadron on US 20.

🕐 Memorial Day–Labor Day: Mon.–Sun. 8 A.M.–5 P.M. Rest of year by appointment. Fee.

COZAD

Robert Henri Museum and Historical Walkway A whiff of mystery—and notoriety—surrounds the town of Cozad on the 100th Meridian. And, of course it redounds to this museum here in the old Hendee Hotel, once the boyhood home of Robert Henri, founder of the famous "Ash Can" school of modern painting and son of the gambling man who founded the town itself. While mostly this is a home furnished in period (late 1800s), there's a bit of family memorabilia, an Henri painting and a few of those of his students and contemporaries, sketches, and a video documentary, as well as a nearby original Pony Express station. Check out the Museum of Nebraska Art in Kearney for more of Henri's work, as well as that of George Catlin and Thomas Hart Benton. *Gift Shop*

🔲 308 784-4154 • 218 E. 8th St., Cozad, NE 69130

🚗 In south-central Nebraska. Take I-80 Exit 222; then it's 1 mile into town.

🕐 May–Sept.: Mon.–Sat. 9 A.M.–5 P.M., Sun. 1 P.M.–5 P.M. By appointment at other times. Fee.

DANNEBROG

National Liars Hall of Fame Back in 1986 Roger "Captain Nebraska" Welsch got together with his pals Eric Nielsen and Bruce Davis, as they were wont to do, and cooked up this memorial to tall-tale tellers and truth-stretchers everywhere. It's a small exhibit, appropriate to this small, cozy one-tavern town ("Have you lived in Dannebrog all your life?" "No, not yet"). The portrait of Richard Nixon has found a most appropriate home along with the stuffed jackalope and bottle of dehydrated water. Don't forget to send in your entry for the annual Pinocchio award.

🔲 308 226-2493 • Eric's Tavern, 115 Mill St., Dannebrog, NE 68831

🚗 It's 24 miles northwest of Grand Island. Take US 281N to SR 58W into town.

🕐 Mon.–Sat. 4 P.M.–1 A.M. No fee, but have a beer.

ELM CREEK

Chevyland U.S.A. All Chevies, all the time . . . over 100 of them, vintage 1914 on up, and they're all running. Also featured are lots of original literature and spanking new hubcaps. Pick out one you like and drive it home—they're all for sale, from Corvette to Corvair, Nomad to Bel Air.

🚪 308 856-4208 • Elm Creek, NE 68836

🚗 About 15 miles west of Kearney, take I-80 Exit 257, then go 1 mile east of the Skelly station on the gravel road.

🕐 May 1–Labor Day: Mon.–Sun. 8 A.M.–5 P.M.; by appointment rest of year. Fee.

HASTINGS

See: *American Museum of Asmat Art, Shoreview, Minnesota.*

HOLDREDGE

Phelps County Historical Museum From the outside this extensive prairie-life museum looks like a warehouse, but don't be deterred. Take your time and go to the areas that capture your interest—perhaps the array of 30 or so sod-buster plows; or the orphan train collection; or the Buffalo Bill Wild West Show stuff; or pharmaceuticals, medical, and dental equipment; or newspapers dating from 1884. But be sure not to miss the exhibit on the local WWII German POW camp that left its mark on nearby Atlanta, NE. *Tours, Publications, Library*

🚪 308 995-5015 • North Hwy 183, Holdredge, NE 68949

🚗 See Elm Creek. Take I-80 Exit 257 onto US 183S for about 15 miles. It's 1 mile north of town.

🕐 Mon.–Sat. 10 A.M.–5 P.M., Sun. 1 P.M.–5 P.M. Donation.

LINCOLN

National Museum of Roller Skating Did you know the first patented roller skate (1819) was an in-line model? Designed by M. Petitbled in Paris, France, the three wheels came in wood, metal, or ivory; it looks like a Dr. Scholl's on wheels. These folks are expert, and the collection is an absolute joy . . . and revelation. Hottest TV event in 1949? Roller Derby. Latest new/old sport? Roller Basketball (begun in the 1920s, it's back). Rolling stilts? Skates for Fido? They've got 'em—and everything else, from a nostalgic collection of skate keys to the stories of the roller rink's Golden Age and the first recorded attempts to get a man on wheels in 1735. *Tours, Gift Shop, Publications, Library*

■ 402 483-7551 • http://www.usacrs.com/museum.htm • 4730 South St., Lincoln, NE 68506
�car Near downtown. I-80 to Exit 403S (27th St.), go south on 27th St. to South St., turn left, then left again onto 48th St. It's on the northwest corner.
🕐 Mon.–Fri. 9 A.M.–5 P.M. Hours may extend in summer. No fee.

MINDEN

Harold Warp Pioneer Village On your way down during March and early April, make a point of stopping along the Platte at sunrise or sunset to see the magnificent sandhill cranes. You might get so distracted at the more mundane wonders in the Pioneer Village that you'd forget to look up. Now get ready for Harold Warp's story of America—the story of progress. Brought up right here in the Great Plains, from turn-of-the-century farm roots to his invention of Flex-O-Glass—an early-20th-century plastic that brought better living to the chicken coop—he developed a sense of what drives America early on. And he's saved it all (and we mean *all*) for you: washing machines, bicycles, flying machines, snowmobiles, automobiles, and farm machinery. Oh, yes, and a steam-powered carousel, music machines, hat pins, outboard motors, and . . . all dating as far back as 1830. *Gift Shop, Food, Hands-on, Programs*
■ 800 445-4447/308 832-1181 • http://www.web-guides.com-pionvill.htm • US 6/34 and Hwy 10, Minden, NE 68959
�car About 15 miles south of Kearney. I-80 to Exit 279; take Hwy 10S to US 6/34.
🕐 Mon.–Sun. 8 A.M.–dusk. Fee.

OMAHA

Omaha hospitality is legend, and we have especially fond memories of late-night cattle-town coffee shops. And waitresses with big, big hair. The designated national golfer, President Gerald Ford, was born here, and his birth site (the actual home took a stumble and burned down in 1971) has an exhibit that of course includes his clubs (402 444-5955). The General Crook House Museum (402 455-9990) is also here. This is a good stop to learn about the 1870s Indian Wars commander who, while a committed American military man of that era, was also influential in the eventual granting of Constitutional rights to Indians. And don't miss the Union Pacific Railroad section (still housed in a 1930 former station) of the giant Western Heritage Museum (402 271-3530) for the truly DeMille-scope saga of the first (1869's the date) transcontinental railroad. *While you're in the area, see also*: Boys Town. *In Iowa, see*: Missouri Valley.

Great Plains Black Museum Bertha Calloways' mission has been to support and preserve all aspects of the black experience on the Great Plains, from the contributions of the range cowboys to those who ran the Underground Railroad to the long railroad history of the Pullman porters to civil-rights activists. For the men and women athletes, musicians, farmers, soldiers, scientists, philanthropists, and politicians—she has kept witness, and collected an invaluable trove of photos and artifacts. *Tours, Programs, Publications, Library*

🏛 402 345-2212 • 2213 Lake St., Omaha, NE 68110

🚗 Just north of downtown. From I-480/US 75, exit east onto Lake St. It's at 16th and Lake.

🕐 Mon.–Fri. 10 A.M.–2 P.M.; other times by appointment. Fee.

University of Nebraska Medical Center Library   A wide assortment of arcane and unusual medical instruments is yours for the viewing, but you'll have to make an appointment for special access to some of it.

🏛 402 559-6221 • University of Nebraska, 600 S. 42nd St., Omaha, NE 68198

🚗 Midtown. From Dodge St. (US 6), turn south onto S. 42nd St.; it's on the left. The displays are on the 6th, 7th, and 8th floors of Wittson Hall.

🕐 Mon.–Thurs. 7:30 A.M.–midnight, Fri. 7:30 A.M.–9 P.M., Sat. 9 A.M.–5 P.M., Sun. 7 P.M.–midnight. Hours vary in summer. By appointment for research collection. No fee.

ROYAL

Ashfall Fossil Beds State Park   The Mount Vesuvius of fossil beds. Frozen in time ten million years ago by volcanic fallout, remarkably intact skeletons of three-toed horses, complete herds of rhinoceros, saber-toothed deer, camels, and birds may be observed as the paleontologists' excavation exposes them.

🏛 402 893-2000 • 6 miles north of US 20, Royal, NE 68773

🚗 In northeastern Nebraska. Take Hwy 13N to US 20, head west to Hwy 59, then north again, following the signs.

🕐 May 1–Sept. 30 only. Memorial Day–Labor Day: Mon.–Sat. 9 A.M.–5 P.M., Sun. 11 A.M.–5 P.M. Other times: Wed.–Sat. 10 A.M.–4 P.M., Sun. 1 P.M.–4 P.M. Fee.

Nevada

First off, you have to understand that there are at least two Nevadas. Vegas-style Nevada, of course, and all the rest. Wild and whomping in its own way (think Comstock Lode, Virginia City, Pony Express), historic Nevada also has its austere side. Startling areas of stark scenic beauty. The desert alive, just minutes from the Vegas glare. Whether you're traveling the much-tauted US 50, "The Loneliest Road in America," or the recently dubbed "Extraterrestrial Highway" (that's Highway 375 for you mapgazers), there are indeed extremes of all kinds to wonder at in this most sparsely settled of American states.

What's Big: High rollers and hot desert—and big open spaces between, where you'll find cultural oases like Reno's Wilbur D. May Museum and Arboretum and Carson City's Nevada State Railroad Museum, the Nevada State Museum, and the Stewart Indian Museum. And don't forget the Cowboy Poetry Festival, held every January in Elko.

BOULDER CITY

Boulder City/Hoover Dam Museum   When you've had enough of the glitz and glare of Vegas, come here to the Nevada equivalent of a dry town—there's no gambling allowed in Boulder City. But given that you're in sight of Hoover Dam, a genuine "American Engineering Wonder of the World," you won't miss the ubiquitous slots at all. The town was built to house the 4,000 workers brought in to build the dam in the '30s, and with striking plotos and exhibits the museum covers the experimental nature of this planned community, as well as the early tent-city living conditions, and the dam construction itself. *Gift Shop, Programs*

702 294-1988 • 444 Hotel Plaza, Boulder City, NV 89005

Twenty-three miles southeast of Las Vegas on US 93/95.

Mon.–Sun. 10 A.M.–4 P.M. Donation.

CALIENTE

Caliente Railroad Boxcar Museum Let Maryellen Sadovich explain it all for you. Nevada history is revealed à la Michener, from the day the dinosaurs ruled the earth right up through the hot scorch of the Atomic Age. A past president of the Nevada Historical Society, she knows her stuff, and will take you through her personal boxcar museum (soon to expand into an adjacent caboose) with pertinent documents, maps, and photos taped to the walls, there to jog her memory as much as anything. She's as apt to weave together the connection between local petroglyphs and Mayan hieroglyphs as to tell you about Einstein's famous alert letter to FDR, and the local effects of the atomic testing that followed.

702 726-3199 • Hwy 93, Caliente Railroad Depot, Caliente, NV 89008

In southeastern Nevada, about 165 miles northeast of Las Vegas, right in town.

By appointment and "when they're there." Donation.

EUREKA

Eureka Sentinel Museum One of the liveliest towns on US 50, the old Pony Express route, silver-rich Eureka's boom began in 1869 when smelters that could separate the silver from its lead ore were finally developed. The *Sentinel's* presses started up soon thereafter, bringing all the news that fits to the then heavily polluted "Pittsburgh of the West." Eureka history, including 1879's famed Charcoal War, and all the original late-1800s presses and clip files are on display. Step over to the other side of the street and take a look at the Eureka Theatre and Opera House's grand hand-painted stage curtain from the '20s silent film days.

702 237-5010 • US 50, PO Box 82, Eureka, NV 89316

In central Nevada, on US 50, about 90 miles west of Ely.

Apr.–Oct.: Mon.–Sat. 10 A.M.–4 P.M. Sun. 10 A.M.–3 P.M. Donation.

GENOA

Genoa Courthouse Museum John A. "Snowshoe" Thompson may have been the guy who carried the mail over the Sierras between Genoa (Jen-NO-ah) and Sacramento, but the display on his career is rivaled by the museum's Buckaroo Room, which features snowshoes fitted for a horse. Otherwise somewhat standard pioneer home 'n' ranch stuff is highlighted with a Washoe Indian artifact exhibit, and the story of the original Ferris wheel, which—introduced at the 1893 World's Columbian Exposition in Chicago—was designed and built by native son George Ferris, an engineer inspired by waterwheels he saw in his youth. *Gift Shop*

702 782-4325/2555 • Main and 5th St., Genoa, NV 89411

🚐 About 12 miles south of Carson City. Take Genoa Lane from Hwy 395, and turn right at the 4-way stop sign.

🕐 May 1–Oct. 15: Mon.–Sun. 10 A.M.–4:30 P.M. Donation.

LAS VEGAS

Claes Oldenberg has kindly provided Las Vegas with a Flashlight should there be a sudden power shortage. In case of emergency, the 38-foot steel sculpture may be found on the UNLV campus. Las Vegas has found another unique way to bring culture to the harried slot-pursuing populace—the Valley Bank of Nevada has a growing collection of Western art, with a strong representation of Taos Founders artists. And finally, the real art. After you've seen the Mirage's volcano explode just one too many times, drive, drive away, out to the Red Rocks. You won't regret it. *While you're in the area, see also*: Boulder City, Overton, Searchlight.

King Tut's Tomb and Museum   Didn't catch the traveling Tut show a number of years ago? No immediate plans to cruise the Nile? No matter, the Luxor has redefined Pyramid Power, and using the Power of the Green has re-created—they say precisely—the tomb of the boy king Tut, just as Howard Carter and the good Lord Carnarvon found it back in 1922. *See also* the Gold Pyramid House in Wadsworth, Illinois.

🏛 702 262-4822 • Luxor Las Vegas, 3900 Las Vegas Blvd. South, Las Vegas, NV 89119

🚐 Right on The Strip.

🕐 Mon.–Thurs. and Sun. 9 A.M.–11 P.M., Fri.–Sat. 9 A.M.–11:30 P.M. Fee.

Liberace Museum   Those of us "of a certain age" may well recall Mr. Showmanship's stint on the tube—the candelabra, the costumes, the capes, the glitter, the Grand(s). The music—well, that's something else. But nothing exemplifies Vegas excess better than Liberace's flamboyantly feathered and mirror-ladened collection (Elvis has nothing on the Lib sartorially, anyway), maybe even more so because of the sedate presentation. We especially like his red, white, and blue hotpants suit and the Austrian-rhinestone encrusted '34 Mercedes. *Gift Shop*

🏛 800 626-2625/702 798-5595 • 1775 E. Tropicana Rd., Las Vegas, NV 89119

🚐 Just off The Strip.

🕐 Mon.–Sat. 10 A.M.–5 P.M., Sun. 1 P.M.–5 P.M. Fee.

Magic and Movie Hall of Fame   And you thought just Liberace did it all with mirrors. Valentine Vox actually does a lot of it with ventriloquism too. And it's this longtime performer's extensive collection of dummies and ventriloquist props from biblical times to the present that was the starter for this museum that covers the greats of the smoky arts (*see also* the Vent Haven Museum in Fort Mitchell, Kentucky—the ultimate spot for voice-throwers and their stuff). Houdini memorabilia including the infamous Water Torture Cell, antique automatons, and clockwork toys are also on hand. The magicians among you will need to conjure up your best tricks to gain access to David Copperfield's private collection (International Museum of the Conjuring Arts)—its location is top secret. *Gift Shop*

■ 702 737-1343 • O'Shea's Casino, 3555 Las Vegas Blvd. South, Las Vegas, NV 89109

🚌 Right on The Strip, next to the Flamingo.

🕐 Tues.–Sat. 10 A.M.–6 P.M. Fee.

OVERTON

Lost City Museum   Back in the 1920s, no one expected to find Pueblo Indian sites west of the Colorado River, though ruins in nearby salt caves had been noted by explorer Jedidiah Smith a century earlier. The 20th-century "rediscovery" got archaeologists working overtime, as they uncovered evidence of occupation going back to the 10,000-year-old Desert Culture and continuing through the Pueblos and a reoccupation by the Paiutes about 1,000 years ago. Hunters and farmers, miners and traders (salt and turquoise), the Anasazi people's homes and ceramic and stone artifacts are displayed in this nice old adobe structure, along with some items of the Mormon settlers who arrived on the scene in 1865.

■ 702 397-2193 • 721 S. Moapa Valley Blvd., Overton, NV 89040

🚌 In southeast Nevada, about 48 miles northeast of Las Vegas. Take I-15, Exit 93 (Logandale/Overton), turn right onto Hwy 169 (Moapa Valley Blvd.), for 13 miles.

🕐 Mon.–Sun. 8:30 A.M.–4:30 P.M. Fee.

RACHEL

Little A'Le'Inn/Area 51 Research Center   You know, people see things out here. Stuff they, well, can't quite explain. Stuff the Air Force, it seems, won't come clean about. Lights in the sky, odd-shaped objects floating by, an extraterrestrial being or two. Stop down at the Inn's cafe and swill back a potent "Beam Me Up, Scotty" and enjoy the encounter pix on display. For more serious study, you can pick up an *Area 51 Viewer's Guide* at the nearby research center. *Food, Publications*

■ Little A'Le'Inn: 702 729-2515 • Hwy 375, Rachel, NV 89001

🚌 In south-central Nevada, about 130 miles north of Las Vegas. Take US 93N to Hwy 375W.

🕐 Mon.–Sun. 8 A.M.–10 P.M. No fee.

RENO

We don't see how you'd miss it should you find yourself outdoors, but just in case, watch for the sun glinting off the giant geodesic ball atop the National

Bowling Stadium. It's the kegling equivalent of Minnesota's Mall of America. *While you're in the area, see also*: Genoa, Virginia City. *In Northern California, see*: Donner Summit, Truckee.

Liberty Belle Antique Slot Machine Collection   Did Charlie Fey, "the Thomas Edison of slots," picture those busloads of little old ladies in tennis shoes planting roots in front of his one-armed bandits? The record doesn't show, but when he dreamed up the 4–11–44 in 1895, he was embarking on a 50-year career devoted to slots, machines that are still the most popular ones in use today. Draw poker slots, the double-life of a Liberty Bell G-U-M vendor, Silver Dollar slots, all the work of this Bavarian mastermind, and on display along with early dice machines, roulette games, and a beautiful turn-of-the-century rosewood bar. *Food*

🔲 702 825-1776 • Liberty Belle Saloon & Restaurant, 4250 S. Virginia St., Reno, NV 89502

🚗 I-80, Exit 13 onto S. Virginia (US 395 business route).

🕐 Mon.–Sat. 11 A.M.–2:30 P.M., 5 P.M.–10 P.M.; Sun. 5 P.M.–10 P.M. No fee.

SEARCHLIGHT

Searchlight Historical Museum   Another amazing disappearing gold and silver mining town that managed to keep it together despite a population dip to 50 by 1927. Now virtually booming at pop.: 800, the biggest controversy is over how the town got its name. And the fondest memory is about the silent-film personalities and other characters—like Clara Bow, Rex Bell, Scott Joplin, and Edith Head—who had ties to the town's heyday early in this century.

🔲 702 455-7955/297-1682 • Searchlight Community Center, 200 Michael Wendel Way, Searchlight, NV 89046

🚗 Fifty-five miles south of Las Vegas, on US 95 and Route 164.

🕐 Mon.–Fri. 9 A.M.–5 P.M., Sat. 9 A.M.–1 P.M. Donation.

TONOPAH

Central Nevada Museum   In case you were traveling from Tehachapi to Tonopah, we thought you might like to stop here. And as might be fitting, the outside ain't much, but there's plenty of parking for truckers. Silver is what made Tonopah's fortune, in 1900. And it was a good thing for the state too, since the Comstock had run dry. Displays on Tonopah "Queen of the Silver Camps," nearby Goldfield, "The Greatest Gold Camp on Earth," and other area boomtowns like Bullfrog and Rhyolite, are joined by a variety pack of boomtown-era items, like original outhouses, a Chinese tank house, a bootlegger's still, and mining equipment. A 1913 Tonopah movie and slide programs are available on request. In the ruins of Rhyolite, about 85 miles south near Beatty, you'll still find a house built almost entirely of bottles and an impressive railroad depot. *Tours, Library*

🔲 702 482-9676 • Logan Field Rd., Tonopah, NV 89049

🚗 About 20 miles west of Las Vegas, just south of where US 95 meets US 6.

🕐 Apr.–Sept.: Mon.–Sun. 9 A.M.–5 P.M. Oct.–Mar.: Tues.–Sat. 11 A.M.–5 P.M. No fee.

VIRGINIA CITY

Fourth Ward School Museum Virginia City 101: The Comstock Lode is discovered in 1859, and with a roaring boom the town is on its way. "One of the richest strikes in history" (both gold and silver) did, like most all of the rest, dry up, and the city's fortunes were not helped by the fire that swept through in 1875, destroying most of the wooden town. While rebuilt almost immediately (this time in brick), the town's moment had more than passed by 1880. But what a time! Samuel Clemens, using his pen name for the first time, reporting for the *Territorial Enterprise* along with Bret Harte, started pulling our legs back then, and the tradition resumed when Lucius Beebe revived the paper in the 1950s with a tale of a camel race, only to have it become a real-life annual event. Its first-year participants featured ostriches and director John Huston (on hand at that time for the locally filmed movie *The Misfits*). Pix and history up to the touristy present. *Gift Shop*

🔲 702 847-0975 • 537 S. C St., Virginia City, NV 89440

🚗 About 25 miles southeast of Reno. Take US 395S to Hwy 341, then east into town to the corner of C St.

🕐 May 15–Oct. 15: Mon.–Sun. 10 A.M.–5 P.M. Donation.

Julia C. Bullette Red Light Museum Miss Julia was Virginia City's most famous prostitute, and you will learn about madam here along with an impressive assortment of equipment for the trade, like antiquated condoms and other contraceptives, sexual ephemera of all manner including pornographic postcards, quack medical cure-alls, and a variety of opium paraphernalia.

🔲 702 847-9394 • 5 C St., Virginia City, NV 89440

🚗 See above. It's at the corner of Union St.

🕐 Mon.–Sun. 11 A.M.–5 P.M. Fee.

Virginia City Radio Museum Cowboy movie star Hoot Gibson's Victor 9-54 Radiola-Electrola, a radio that cost him $1,365 back in 1929, is one of the favorites of the slew of vintage wireless and radio apparatus on display here in ham-fan (WA7YBS) Henry Rogers' well-documented and homey collection. Rare vacuum tubes, from the early audion to the nuvistor, are also a hit—and if you don't know why, this is a great spot to find out. Also on hand: a working vintage amateur radio station and a wonderful selection of photos of the popular radio stars of yesteryear. For a look at vintage 1880s entertainment— from the days when the likes of Edwin

Booth, Lotta Crabtree, and David Belasco were as likely to find themselves performing here as in San Francisco—stroll over to Piper's Opera House (702 847-0433).

■ 702 847-9047 • 109 S. F St., Virginia City, NV 89440

🚗 See above. It's at the corner of Taylor.

🕐 April–October: Mon.–Sun. 11 A.M.–5 P.M. Nov.–Mar: Sat.–Sun., hours vary. Fee.

WINNEMUCCA

Buckaroo Hall of Fame and Heritage Museum   Here's where those old bronc-riding cowhands who had a way with a rope finally get their due. To make it here, selected buckaroos must have led a "worthy life" out on the range, and the displays and artifacts—diaries, clothing, tools, photos, and illustrations—make it clear that getting out there every day a-riding and a-roping was no easy task.

■ 702 623-2225 • Winnemucca Convention Center, 50 W. Winnemucca Blvd., Winnemucca, NV 89445

🚗 North-central Nevada, at I-80 and US 95.

🕐 Mon.–Fri. 8 A.M.–4 P.M., and during special events. No fee.

NEW HAMPSHIRE

Living Free or Dying, these days, seems to mean either residing in what is essentially a lower-tax part of the Boston metropolitan area, in the south, or in smaller cities and towns similar to those in neighboring Maine and Vermont—some with economies based on tourism and outdoor recreation, some on logging and related manufacturing, some squeezing by on light industries and retail trade. The museums we've found are, logically, a mixed bunch.

What's Big: Strawbery Banke, a re-created neighborhood in Portsmouth where the houses include that of John Paul Jones; otherwise, outdoor sites like Mount Washington and Hampton Beach, and shopping, but not museums.

ALLENSTOWN

Museum of Family Camping   Part of a complex that includes museums to the New Deal's Civilian Conservation Corps (CCC) and to snowmobiling, this one aims to illustrate just how rugged camping could be in the old days—from the 19th century through the 1940s. There are some nifty trailers, but you'll be glad you're not out there with this equipment. The Family Camping Hall of Fame is here, honoring such rough-and-ready types as Teddy Roosevelt. *Gift Shop, Screenings*

■ 603 485-9874 • http://www.channel1.users/Brosius/museum.htm • Bear Brook State Park, Allenstown, NH 03275

In Bear Brook State Park off Route 28, about 12 miles north of Manchester.
Memorial Day–Columbus Day: Mon.–Sun. 10 A.M.–4 P.M. Fee to enter park.

BETHLEHEM

Crossroads of America   It's an old boarding house, but inside is a whole country in ³⁄₁₆ scale. Model train buffs, this is for you. You'll see model cars, trucks, ships, planes, animated toys, antique outboard motors, and more.

603 869-3919 • 6 Trudeau Rd., Bethlehem, NH 03574

In northern New Hampshire, take Exit 40 off I-93 and proceed east through the center of Bethlehem. Crossroads is 2.5 miles east of the village, on Route 302.

June–Foliage Season: Tues.–Sun. 9 A.M.–6 P.M. Fee.

CORNISH

Saint-Gaudens National Historic Site   Augustus Saint-Gaudens (1848–1907) moved into this former inn in 1885 and did much of his later sculpting here; by the early 1900s an artists' colony had grown around him. Many of his smaller works are here, along with casts of some of his monumental larger pieces found in Washington and elsewhere. The gardens, the stables, and the view are special.

603 675-2175 • Cornish, NH 03745

Off Route 12A north of Claremont, overlooking the Connecticut River.

Memorial Day–Oct. 31: Mon.–Sun. 8:30 A.M.–4:30 P.M. Fee.

ENFIELD

Museum at Lower Shaker Village   Active from 1793 to 1923, this community includes Ammi Young's 1837 Great Stone Dwelling, the largest of Shaker buildings, along with a dozen other structures and noted gardens. Crafts demonstrations and workshops are a feature. *Hands-on, Programs*

603 632-4346 • Route 4A, Enfield, NH 03748

Take Exit 17 off I-89 and proceed east on Route 4, then on 4A along Mascoma Lake.

June–Oct. 15: Mon.–Sat. 10 A.M.–5 P.M., Sun. noon–5 P.M. Oct. 16–May: Sat. 10 A.M.–4 P.M., Sun. noon–4 P.M. Fee.

FRANCONIA

New England Ski Museum   Videos, artworks, outmoded gear, and a wide variety of other artifacts detail the history of downhill skiing in New England and the world. *Gift Shop*

603 823-7177 • Franconia Notch, Franconia, NH 03580

🚐 On the Franconia Notch Pkwy section of I-93, just north of the Old Man of the Mountain, next to the Cannon Mountain Tramway.
🕓 Memorial Day–mid-Oct. and Dec.–Mar.: Tues.–Thurs. noon–5 P.M. No fee.

LACONIA

Carpenter Museum of Antique Outboard Motors Outboard engines are a special passion. Enthusiasts will here find a collection ranging from the early 1900s. There are also related items, like advertisements and engine manuals.
🏠 603 524-7611 • Laconia, NH 03246
🚐 The museum is on Route 3, south of Laconia. Call for directions.
🕓 By appointment. Donation.

MANCHESTER

While you're in the area, see also: Allenstown

Lawrence L. Lee Scouting Museum and Max I. Silber Library The history of the Boy Scouts is detailed in displays of Scout paraphernalia, including the collection of Lord Baden-Powell himself. Pennants, badges, kerchiefs, and all the other necessaries are here, along with magazines, postage stamps, books, and other celebrations of Scouting. You can camp while visiting. *Gift Shop, Hands-on, Library*
🏠 603 669-8919 • Camp Carpenter, Bodwell Rd., Manchester, NH 03109
🚐 Take I-93 to Exit 5, on the southeast side of Manchester, and follow signs.
🕓 July–Aug.: Mon.–Sun. 10 A.M.–4 P.M. Sept.–June: Sat. only. No fee.

PORTSMOUTH

The big attraction in this little city is Strawbery Banke, a restoration complex displaying buildings and artifacts from the 18th century on, like John Paul Jones' house; call 603 433-1100 for information. Students of American art may want to call the Isles of Shoals Steamship Company (800 441-4620) to see if there's a boat going to Appledore, where Celia Thaxter's Garden was a subject for several noted painters. But we suggest something quite different:

Red Hook Brewery Before the Prohibitionists had their little fling, Portsmouth was the Ale Capital of the United States. In 1981 Seattle-based Red Hook opened a brewery here, and at the adjoining Cataqua Public House you'll find a display on the glory days and on Frank Jones, the Ale Man. Yes, Portsmouth has had a history since the Revolution. *Tours, Gift Shop, Food*

🏠 603 430-8600 • http://www.homepage.redhook.com • 35 Corporate Dr., Portsmouth, NH 03801

🚗 Red Hook is in the Pease International Tradeport, at the corner of Corporate Dr. and International Blvd. Follow signs off I-95 or the Spaulding Tpke (Route 4/16).

🕐 The display at the Cataqua Public House may be viewed when the pub is open: Mon.–Sat. 11:30 A.M.–11 P.M., Sun. noon–8 P.M. No fee, but your kids may be carded. Call the brewery for tour information. Fee.

WOLFEBORO

Wright Museum of American Enterprise   The museum celebrates American life during World War II. There are a tank and other military items; but the focus is on the Home Front, with re-creations of domestic ambience, costumes, and other artifacts from that Age of Nostalgia. *Gift Shop, Screenings*

🏠 603 569-1212 • 77 Center St., Wolfeboro, NH 03894

🚗 In downtown Wolfeboro, on the southeast shore of Lake Winnipesaukee, near the junction of Routes 109 and 28.

🕐 Memorial Day–mid-Oct.: Mon.–Sun. 10 A.M.–4 P.M. Weekend hours rest of year. Fee.

Ｎew Jersey

One of the hoariest cliches about New Jersey is that what everyone knows about it is the Turnpike—and nothing else. In fact, the road is the *least* typical part of the state. But it does do one very important thing: It roughly marks the division between two very different places. To the south and east is coastal plain, at least until recently characterized chiefly by orchards, pine woods, and open space. To the north and west is a densely populated industrial and suburban zone. The museums we've listed reflect this difference. One batch, along the Jersey Shore from north of Atlantic City to down near Cape May, have mostly to do with leisure and nature. The other group, from Trenton north, are diverse historical, industrial, arts, and conceptual sites—what you'd expect to find in an area where so much has gone on for so long.

What's Big: In addition to state, Newark, and Princeton University museums, there are such sites as Wheaton Village, in Millville, a major glass industry complex; the Edison National Historic Site in West Orange; and Morristown's Morris Museum. There are also entire towns, like Cape May (Victorian resort architecture) and Batsto (Pine Barrens history), as well as numerous historic homes.

ATLANTIC CITY

While you're in the area, see also: Margate City, Oceanville, Tuckerton

Atlantic City Historical Museum   A lot of people think of A.C. only as Las Vegas East, a clump of air-conditioned casinos a bus ride from Megalopolis. As a remedy, we suggest a catechism, something like: "Boardwalk. Under the Boardwalk. Monopoly. Club Harlem. Salt Water Taffy. Mr. Peanut. Miss America. The Diving Horse. Take Your Tongue for a Sleighride. Next Week, Steel Pier." Or words to that effect. At any rate, this museum will give you perspective. You'll see posters and photographs and videos and artifacts of more than a century of fun. You'll see examples of sand art, an ancient form. You'll see ancient bathing suits. You'll see the most ancient of picture postcards. Across the pier you can stop in at the Atlantic City Art Center too.

🏠 609 347-5839 • http://www.nj.com/acmuseum • Garden Pier, New Jersey Ave. and the Boardwalk, Atlantic City, NJ 08404

🚗 Entering Atlantic City from either the Atlantic City Expwy or US 30 (Absecon Blvd., then Virginia Ave.), turn left on Pacific, then right on New Jersey.

🕐 Mon.–Sun. 10 A.M.–4 P.M. No fee.

Kentucky Avenue Museum Behind the façade of Boardwalk and casino, A.C. has long been a black entertainment center. Some of this history may be seen at the Atlantic City Historical Museum. But you may also want to drop by here. Kentucky (the "Strip") and Arctic were the key streets, the Club Harlem was the key venue, and the heyday was the 1930s and afterward.

🏠 609 348-8906 • 42 N. Kentucky Ave., Atlantic City, NJ 08401

🚗 The museum is just south of City Hall, between Atlantic and Arctic Aves.

🕐 Sat.–Sun. 10 A.M.–6 P.M. Donation. Call to confirm hours.

FAR HILLS

Golf House/USGA Museum and Library The most widely played of all sports, from Scotland to the Moon (Alan Shepard's 1971 club is on display), is celebrated in this appropriately affluent setting. You'll see artworks, medals and trophies, early paraphernalia, and high-tech expositions of the game's history and fine points. Iron Byron, the USGA robot, may be out driving balls on the test range. *Library*

🏠 908 234-2300 • Liberty Corner Rd., Far Hills, NJ 07931

🚗 Far Hills is in north-central New Jersey, a half-hour west of Newark. From I-287, take Exit 18 onto US 202N, then turn right on County Rd. 512.

🕐 Mon.–Fri. 9 A.M.–5 P.M., Sat.–Sun. 10 A.M.–4 P.M. No fee.

FORT MONMOUTH

United States Army Communications-Electronics Museum A World War I base that grew into one of the army's most important technological centers, Fort Monmouth displays its history in this facility, everything from carrier pigeons to the use of satellites. Radar, walkie-talkies, night vision devices, spy cameras, and many other innovations are part of the story. While you're here, and if a slightly different form of communications interests you, inquire about the U.S. Army Chaplain Museum (call 908 532-5809 for information). *Tours*

🏠 732 532-2440 • Kaplan Hall, Building 275, Fort Monmouth, NJ 07703

🚙 At the north end of the Jersey Shore. From the Garden State Pkwy, take Exit 105 east to Eatontown, turn north on SR 35, and enter the Fort on the Ave. of Memories, following signs.

🕐 Mon.–Fri. 1200–1600 hours. No fee.

FRANKLIN

Franklin Mineral Museum This is about as close to New York City as you'll find a mining museum. The hills here were mined for iron in Revolutionary times, and for zinc until the 1950s. The museum displays thousands of samples of minerals, many of them fluorescent, along with other items found in digging: fossils, Indian artifacts, and more. A mine replica gives an idea of the zinc mines, and you may dig in the Buckwheat Dump, using what you learned in the museum (and its UV lights) to identify your finds. Even closer to the city is the nearby Sterling Hill Mine and Museum, in Ogdensburg. There you may visit an actual mine; they don't encourage you to bring small children, and do suggest sweaters and good shoes (call 201 209-7212 for information). *Tours, Gift Shop*

💼 973 827-3481 • Evans St., Franklin, NJ 07416

🚙 Franklin is 35 miles northwest of Newark. From SR 23, follow blue signs; the museum is on Evans between Main and Buckwheat.

🕐 Apr.–Nov.: Mon.–Sat. 10 A.M.–4 P.M., Sun 12:30 P.M.–4:30 P.M. By appointment in Mar. Fee.

HALEDON

American Labor Museum/Botto House National Landmark The home of immigrant silkworkers, the Botto House became a haven for workers and union leaders during the great 1913 Paterson strike; its second-floor balcony was a much-used speakers' platform. Today you'll see displays on the history of that event, on American labor in general, and on immigrant life. *Tours, Gift Shop, Programs*

💼 973 595-7953 • 83 Norwood St., Haledon, NJ 07508

🚙 Haledon is a suburb immediately northwest of Paterson, in northeastern New Jersey. From US 80W, take the Union Blvd. (Totowa/Paterson) exit, and turn right on Union, left on W. Broadway, hard right on Barbour St., and left on Mason Ave.; the Botto House is at the corner of Mason and Norwood.

🕐 Wed.–Sat. 1 P.M.–4 P.M., Sun. by appointment. Fee.

LYNDHURST

Trash Museum/Hackensack Meadowlands Development Commission Environment Center This is the real answer to "Whatever happened to . . . ?" At the Trash Museum, you can walk through the stuff you so cavalierly tossed out. We mean through, not over: They've built a Garbage Tunnel for you. There are artworks made from trash, but the main focus is on the problem we're creating for ourselves and nature. The natural/unnatural history of the Meadowlands is detailed. *Tours, Gift Shop, Hands-on, Programs*

📱 201 460-8300 • 2 DeKorte Park Plaza, Lyndhurst, NJ 07071

🚗 Lyndhurst is 5 miles north of Newark. From the NJ Tpke, take Exit 16W. Follow Route 3W to Route 17S (Lyndhurst exit); from the ramp, go left on Polito Ave. to end. Go left on Valley Brook Ave. for 1.5 miles, to end. Cross tracks, keeping to left. The center is the first building on the left after the tracks.

🕐 Mon.–Fri. 9 A.M.–5 P.M., Sat. 10 A.M.–3 P.M. Fee.

MARGATE CITY

Lucy the Margate Elephant   We've included six-story, 90-ton Lucy because she is a logical follow-up to the Atlantic City Historical Museum, and an emblem of an entire period of Americana. And if you'd like more elephants, and have a little spare time, how about a drive to Mister Ed's? *See* Orrtanna, Pennsylvania. *Tours*

📱 609 823-6473 • 9200 Atlantic Ave., Margate City, NJ 08402

🚗 Margate City is "downbeach" from Atlantic City, just beyond Ventnor City. Follow Atlantic Ave. and you can't miss Lucy.

🕐 Mid-June–Labor Day: Mon.–Sun. 10 A.M.–8 P.M. Apr.–June and Sept.–Oct.: weekends, 10 A.M.–4:30 P.M. Fee.

MENLO PARK (EDISON)

Thomas A. Edison Memorial Tower and Museum   Edison's laboratory in West Orange, where he worked from 1887 to 1931, is now within the Edison National Historic Site. He wasn't called the "Wizard of Menlo Park" for nothing, however. This tower and museum mark the spot where he made his first (1876–86) breakthroughs. A 13-foot, 3-ton incandescent bulb celebrates the original, and there are also huge sound-reproducing devices, and a number of other early inventions, along with Edison memorabilia. In a sense all this, created in 1937, is a museum to the way we remembered our geniuses back then. If you haven't had enough on bulbs, though, see our listing on the Mount Vernon Museum of Incandescent Lighting in Baltimore, Maryland. *Tours*

📱 732 549-3299 • 37 Christie St., Menlo Park (Edison), NJ 08820

🚗 Menlo Park is part of Edison, about 15 miles southwest of Newark. Take Exit 131 off the Garden State Pkwy onto Route 27S. Turn right on Christie St.

🕐 Memorial Day–Labor Day: Tues.–Fri. 12:30 P.M.–4 P.M., Sat.–Sun. 12:30 P.M.–4:30 P.M. Rest of year: same except closed on Tues. No fee.

MONTCLAIR

Montclair Art Museum   Here's a good example of the fine-arts museum that isn't "big" because it's near so many that are. Montclair has American Impressionists, 18th-century portraiture, Hopper, Shahn, Bearden, Motherwell, Lawrence, Hartley, Bellows, Marin, and a highly regarded collection of Native American arts and crafts. And you can take it all in without feeling crowded. *Tours, Gift Shop, Programs, Library*

🏠 973 746-5555 • 3 South Mountain Ave., Montclair, NJ 07042

🚗 Montclair is 10 miles north of Newark and 12 miles northwest of downtown New York City. Take Exit 148 off the Garden State Pkwy, head north on Bloomfield Ave. through downtown, and turn left on Mountain Ave.

🕐 Tues.–Wed. and Fri.–Sat. 11 A.M.–5 P.M., Thurs. and Sun. 1 P.M.–5 P.M. In summer, Wed.–Sun. noon–5 P.M. Fee.

MORRISTOWN

Macculloch Hall Historical Museum   This Federal-style mansion is now a decorative-arts museum, with American and European materials from the 18th and 19th centuries and fine gardens. But there's also something special: a collection of works by Thomas Nast, the father of political cartooning, who lived nearby.

🏠 973 538-2404 • 45 Macculloch Ave., Morristown, NJ 07960

🚗 Morristown is 15 miles northwest of Newark, on I-287. The museum is in the Morristown Historic District, downtown. Call for directions.

🕐 Apr.–Dec.: Thurs. and Sun. 2 P.M.–4:30 P.M. Groups also by appointment Mon.–Fri. Fee.

NESHANIC

Doyle's Unami Farms/Corn Maze   Here's one that's strictly for fun—or, if you're inclined, reflection. The Doyles have been running this farm for five generations. Since the 1920s Richard, now the elder, has been collecting arrowheads and other artifacts (the Unami, a branch of New Jersey's Lenni Lenape, or Delaware, left many signs of their years here) and natural objects; informal educational programs based on his interests have gradually expanded. In 1996 younger Doyles created a huge walk-through-or-get-lost-in corn maze, hoping to attract enough visitors to offset a decline in farm income. Give them a call: You city dwellers and your kids might enjoy an educational outing—and you could regard Unami Farms as a sort of museum to family farming. *Tours, Food*

🏠 908 367-3187 • 771 Mill Lane, Neshanic, NJ 08553

🚗 Neshanic is in west-central New Jersey, 5 miles east of Flemington. Take US 202W from Somerville. Exit south on Pleasant Run Rd. (at the Texaco station); turn left on Amwell Rd. (County Rd. 514), left again on Old Amwell Rd., and left on Mill Lane.

🕐 Call for information on events and fees in summer and fall.

NEWARK

While you're in the area, see also: Lyndhurst, Menlo Park (Edison), Montclair, Morristown, Teterboro

Institute of Jazz Studies   The Institute of Jazz Studies is at the heart of scholarship on American music, and this is a stop especially for those of you who would like to do a little archival work. There are some thematic displays, but there's much, much more here you can lose yourself in if you care to dig, which jazz people tend to do. *Library*

📷 973 648-5595 • Rutgers University-Newark, 185 University Ave., Newark, NJ 07102

🚗 The Rutgers-Newark campus is in central Newark, just south of Central Ave. Ask for directions when you call to arrange a visit.

🕐 Mon.–Fri. 9 A.M.–5 P.M. No fee, but call ahead to use archives.

OCEANVILLE

Noyes Museum of Art   The Noyes is a fine- and folk-arts museum, part of whose charm is its seashore setting. Here are paintings, sculpture, and crafts by regional artists. Appropriately, one of the highlights is a major collection of waterfowl decoys, and another is a 112-room purple martin "palace."

📷 609 652-8848 • http://www.users.aol.com/noyesnews • Lily Lake Rd., Oceanville, NJ 08231

🚗 Oceanville is on the south Jersey shore, 15 minutes north of Atlantic City. The museum is just off US 9, adjacent to the Edwin B. Forsythe National Wildlife Refuge.

🕐 Wed.–Sun. 11 A.M.–4 P.M. Fee.

PARSIPPANY

Craftsman Farms/Gustav Stickley Museum   Craftsman Farms became headquarters for the operations of design giant Gustav Stickley (1858–1942) just before World War I. You may tour his home here, and there are changing exhibits on such aspects of his work as the development of Mission furniture and Arts and Crafts metalwork. *See* East Aurora in Upstate New York, and Detroit, Michigan, for more related sites. *Tours*

📷 973 540-1165 • 2352 Route 10W (at Manor Lane), Parsippany, NJ 07054

🚗 Parsippany is in north-central New Jersey, 5 minutes north of Morristown on I-287. Take Exit 35 onto Route 10W and look for signs.

🕐 Tours: Thurs. and Sun. 2 P.M.–5 P.M. Fee.

PATERSON

Paterson Museum/Rogers Mill This is a good place to begin an examination of Paterson's fascinating industrial story, which dates from 1790 and Alexander Hamilton. There are extensive exhibits on the silk industry, along with much on the archaeology and geology of the region. The most surprising item may be J. P. Holland's pioneer submarine. For a rounded look at Paterson's industry, why not go from here to Lambert Castle, in the Garrett Mountain Reservation, where you'll find art and historical displays and a noted spoon collection in the 1890s home of one of the silk barons (call 201 881-2761), and then take another short jaunt to the Botto House (*see* Haledon).

📱 973 881-3874 • 2 Market St., Paterson, NJ 07501

🚗 In the Great Falls Historic District, downtown. Take Exit 57 off I-80 and follow signs.

🕐 Tues.–Fri. 10 A.M.–4 P.M., Sat.–Sun. 12:30 P.M.–4:30 P.M. Fee.

RAHWAY

Herman Abrams, Archaeologist of Himself Wondering if you could, or should, start your own museum? If you need encouragement, why not visit Herman Abrams, who wants to show you his collection of *everything* from the past 60 years. This means not just his old baseball glove, but six decades' worth of Cracker Jack toys, and the wishbone from every turkey he has consumed. There is no history more local than the history you'll see at Herman Abrams'. This would be a good visit to pair with one to Lyndhurst, half an hour northeast.

📱 732 388-1381 • 1546 Lambert St., Rahway, NJ 07065

🚗 Rahway is in north-central New Jersey, just southwest of Linden and 10 miles southwest of Newark, on SR 27 and US 1 and 9.

🕐 "I'm home all day; I'm retired." Mr. Abrams invites you to walk up, but we advise calling for directions and an appointment. No fee.

SOMERVILLE

United States Bicycling Hall of Fame From early heroes like Major Taylor (one of his cycles is here), through the high days of the six-day racers and others in the 1920s and '30s, to modern stars like Greg LeMond, this growing facility salutes the greats of one of America's "secret" sports. Why Somerville? For one thing, it's home to the end-of-May Tour of Somerville, the oldest continuously run U.S. race. Displays include jerseys, bikes, plaques, murals, ribbons, cups, posters, and more. A related attraction, out West, is the Mountain Bike Hall of Fame, in Crested Butte, Colorado; call 970 349-7382 if you're headed that way.

■ 800 BICYCLE [242-9253] • 166 W. Main St., Somerville, NJ 08876

🚙 Somerville is in north-central New Jersey, on I-287 and US 22, 202, and 206. From 22, exit onto Bridge St. into town. Turn right on Main St. for 2 blocks; the Hall of Fame is next to the telephone building.

🕐 Mon.–Fri. 11 A.M.–noon and 1 P.M.–3 P.M. No fee, but call ahead at 908 722-3620.

TENAFLY

African Art Museum of the S.M.A. Fathers   For 15 years, in this quiet suburban setting, the Society of African Missions has offered a display of eye-catching African arts and crafts, including statues, textiles, ritual objects, bead-work, and, especially, masks that transfix the viewer.

■ 201 567-0450 • The Mission, 23 Bliss Ave., Tenafly, NJ 07670

🚙 Tenafly is in extreme northeastern New Jersey, on the Palisades Interstate Pkwy, 10 minutes north of the George Washington Bridge. Call for precise directions.

🕐 Mon.–Fri. 9 A.M.–5 P.M. Weekends also, but no staff is available. No fee.

TETERBORO

Aviation Hall of Fame and Museum of New Jersey   Teterboro is part of the earlier aviation history of the nation's largest metropolis. Today only private planes use the airport, and the old control tower has become one of the two parts of this museum. There's an airliner to walk around, engines and other equipment, displays on New Jersey's older airports and on noted airborne and space-exploring New Jerseyans, films, Arthur Godfrey's private collection, and the opportunity to watch and hear air traffic controllers at work. *Tours*

■ 201 288-6344 • Teterboro Airport, Teterboro, NJ 07608

🚙 Teterboro Airport is in northeastern New Jersey, just south of Hackensack and north of the Meadowlands Sports Complex. Take Exit 18 off I-95/the NJ Tpke, and go west on US 46 to Fred Wehran Dr. Or approach from the south via SR 17, following signs.

🕐 Tues.–Sun. 10 A.M.–4 P.M. Fee.

TUCKERTON

Barnegat Bay Decoy and Baymen's Museum   Tuckerton was the third designated U.S. port of entry, in 1791, and the town looks for a return to importance through tourism; a projected Tuckerton Seaport should bring crowds. But until then, you can visit this museum, in a replica of a hunting shanty, and find a trove of artifacts of the hunting, fishing, oystering, clamming, eeling, boatbuilding life of Barnegat Bay—decoys and waterfowl carvings, baskets, knots, nets, bird calls, sailmaking tools, fyke nets, sneakboxes, garveys—the names alone should bring you here. *Gift Shop, Programs*

■ 609 296-8868 • 137 W. Main St. (US 9), Tuckerton, NJ 08087

🚗 Tuckerton is about 10 miles north of Atlantic City and just off the Garden State Pkwy. The museum is on Main St. (US 9).

🕐 Wed.–Sun. 10 A.M.–4:30 P.M. Fee.

WEST TRENTON

New Jersey State Police Museum and Learning Center The New Jersey State Police were created in 1921 and placed under the leadership of Col. Norman Schwarzkopf—no, his father. Here they'll show you such specialties as confiscated guns, a squad car you can sit in, and a crime scene to investigate. But you'll probably most want to see what they have on the Crime of the Century: the Lindbergh Kidnapping.

■ 609 882-2000 x6402 • River Rd. (Route 175), West Trenton, NJ 08628

🚗 The museum is at the State Police Headquarters on River Rd. betwen I-95 and W. Upper Ferry Rd. Take Exit 1 south off I-95.

🕐 Mon.–Sat. 10 A.M.–4 P.M. No fee.

WILDWOOD

George F. Boyer Museum and National Marbles Hall of Fame Wildwood is slightly less well known than Cape May or Atlantic City, but it's one of the Jersey Shore's premier resorts. That makes you think beach, boardwalk, bands, etc.; but if you know, you also think marbles. The national championship has been held here since 1922, and this museum salutes the great shooters. If you remember your time on the floor, this is the place for you. *Gift Shop, Library*

■ 609 523-0277 • 3907 Pacific Ave., Holly Beach Mall, Wildwood, NJ 08260

🚗 Wildwood is in extreme southern New Jersey, just northeast of Cape May. Take Exit 4 off the Garden State Pkwy and proceed into town on SR 47, which becomes Rio Grande Ave. Turn left on Pacific to the corner of Spencer.

🕐 May–Sept.: Mon.–Fri. 9:30 A.M.–2:30 P.M., Sat.–Sun. 10:30 A.M.–2:30 P.M. Rest of year: Thurs.–Sun. 10:30 A.M.–2:30 P.M. Donation.

NEW MEXICO

At minimum New Mexico is a remarkable confluence of three primary cultures: Native American, Spanish, and Anglo. But the feel of it is as much informed by the remarkable light and terrain, as well as the mix of other cultures, religions, and ways of life the area seems to attract so readily. Land of Enchantment, Land of Contrasts, Land of the Best Chiles, you bet.

What's Big: The aforementioned chiles, red and green of course, hot air balloons, archaeology, space-age history, Carlsbad Caverns, and in Albuquerque there's the Albuquerque Museum, the Indian Pueblo Cultural Center, and the New Mexico Museum of Natural History to be reckoned with; in Grants, the New Mexico Mining Museum; in Santa Fe, the absolutely not-to-be-missed Museum of International Folk Art, the Museum of Fine Arts, and the Wheelwright Museum of the American Indian; and in Taos, the Millicent Rogers Museum.

ABIQUIU

You may be able to tour the nearby Dar al-Islam Mosque (505 685-4515), particularly interesting because of its adobe arches, unknown in traditional Southwestern adobe structures. A few miles north of the O'Keeffe house you'll hit the Ghost Ranch Living Museum, with local animals and their habitats; you might also stop at the Florence Hawley Ellis Museum of Anthropology.

Georgia O'Keeffe House   Georgia O'Keeffe lived and worked at her Abiquiu home from 1949 up until her death in 1986, and its setting amongst the cottonwoods will be familiar to those who know her art. The adobe house—parts of it dating back to the early 18th century—has been maintained exactly as she left it, redolent with her aesthetic and full of the Southwestern icons and images she was so fond of. You can also visit the new Georgia O'Keeffe Museum in Santa Fe. *Tours*

505 685-4539 • PO Box 40, Abiquiu, NM 87510

🚙 About 50 miles northwest of Santa Fe, off US 84.

🕐 Tours Tues., Thurs., Fri. by appointment only. Minimum donation required.

ALBUQUERQUE

Albuquerque can look like any urban sprawl, with strip shopping centers at every turn. But what it's also got, just like the rest of the state, is big sky, mountains (Sandias) to the east, volcanos, desert, and mesas to the west. And Route 66 (Central Ave.)—and some remnants of the early days—still running through it. Downtown almost missed the preservation boat, but what it lost in its old train station is challenged by the knockout restoration of the KiMo Theater—a Pueblo Deco extravaganza. And when you're on UNM's campus don't miss the Maxwell Museum of Anthropology (505 277-4404). Also, take some time to explore the old part of the library and other fine examples of John Gaw Meem's Pueblo Revival architecture. The Ernie Pyle Memorial Branch Library at 900 Girard SE (505 256-2065) is the late WWII correspondent's former home and is filled with memorabilia. *While you're in the area, see also*: Sandia Park.

American International Rattlesnake Museum   Former bio teacher Bob Myers makes snakes fun, even for the squeamish. With separate labels for kids and adults, and a wide selection of specimens—all captive-bred—from around the world placed in natural habitats, he reveals the ways rattlers and other "less desirable" (read: scorpions and their toxic friends) animals have influenced American history, native culture, and science and medicine. *Gift Shop, Hands-on*

📱 505 242-6569 • 202 San Felipe NW, Albuquerque, NM 87104

🚙 In Albuquerque's Old Town, at the southeast corner of the main plaza.

🕐 Mon.–Sun. 10 A.M.–6 P.M. Fee.

Food Museum (aka Potato Museum)   In a state that's screaming for a chile museum, the closest we've found is this transplanted (first from Brussels, then D.C.) former Potato Museum. Meredith and Tom Hughes, however, always envisioned a museum dedicated to all kinds of caloric fuel, and while they are still featured, potatoes were just the beginning. They now have small but pithy monthlong exhibits, like the recent "Pomme d'Amour: The Tomato," that present a particular foodstuff (and recently they did cover peppers, or "Captivating Capsicums") in a global historic and cultural context. *Food, Programs*

📱 505 898-0909 • http://www.foodmuseum.com/~hughes/first.htm • Wild Oats Supermarket, San Mateo Blvd. NE and Academy Blvd. NE, Albuquerque, NM 87109

🚙 Northeast Heights, in the shopping center on the northeast corner of San Mateo Blvd. NE and Academy Blvd. NE.

🕐 Mon.–Sun. 8 A.M.–10 P.M. No fee.

Meteorite Museum   It shouldn't be any surprise that a state renowned for its sightings of items extraterrestrial (*see* Roswell) should also have a museum for meteorites. As research has revealed, however, this seemingly mundane (albeit four to six billion years old) detritus from outer space may itself hold secrets to life, and certainly solar system history. With meteorites from Mars, the moon, and the second largest stone meteorite in the world (weighing in at over one ton, it dented Kansas in 1948), this is the place to come for fascinating and beautiful rocks that are literally from out of this world.

■ 505 277-1644 • http://www.tem.unm.edu/meteor.htm • Institute of Meteoritics, Northrop Hall, University of New Mexico, Albuquerque, NM 87131

🚙 On the UNM campus, about 2 blocks north of Central Ave. on Yale NE.

🕐 Mon.–Fri. 9 A.M.–noon, 1 P.M.–4 P.M. No fee.

National Atomic Museum   This is where old bombs and other air force, navy, Marine, and army thermonuclear weapons and their carriers go on retirement, and the exhibits include actual Cold War veterans like a B-29 "Superfortress" similar to the *Enola Gay*, as well as replicas of the bomb casings for the infamous first-of-the-atom-bombs Fat Man and Little Boy and models of nuclear-powered submarines and ships. The story of the Atomic Age is presented from the earliest days of the Manhattan Project through peacetime applications, particularly in medicine. Check out our listing in Los Alamos for other aspects critical to New Mexico's role in nuclear history. *Gift Shop, Screenings*

■ 505 284-3243 • http://www.sandia.gov/AtomMus/AtomMus.htm • Wyoming Blvd. SE, Kirtland Air Force Base, Albuquerque, NM 87117

🚙 Enter Kirtland AFB at either the Wyoming or Gibson Gate and get a pass. It's about 1 mile inside, on Wyoming SE between Gibson Blvd. and Central Ave.

🕐 Mon.–Sun. 9 A.M.–5 P.M. No fee.

CAPITAN

Smokey Bear State Historical Park   Found clinging to a tree after surviving a devastating Lincoln Forest blaze in 1950, baby Smokey became a live—not to mention endearing and effective—version of the cartoon national fire prevention symbol created in 1944. He led a good life, hanging out at D.C.'s National Zoo until 1976. But he's buried here, beside this log cabin museum dedicated to him and the story of forest fire fighting and prevention. If four-legged creatures are your theme, consider the Museum of the Horse in nearby Ruidoso. *Gift Shop*

■ 505 354-2748 • Visitors Center, US 380, Capitan, NM 88316

🚙 About 70 miles west of Roswell, stay on US 380 into town.

🕐 Mon.–Sun. 9 A.M.–5 P.M. Fee.

FORT SUMNER

Billy the Kid Museum   Call him William H. Bonney, Henry Antrim, or Henry McCarty; while his background may be vague—he may or may not have been born in Manhattan, down by the Brooklyn Bridge—Billy the Kid most definitely met his end here in Fort Sumner. While it was at the Lincoln County Courthouse about 120 miles to the southwest that he made his getaway, Pat Garrett traced him here. His grave is at the site of the old fort, though as with other outlaw legends, there seems to be some dispute as to whether he's in it or not. What's not in dispute is the authenticity of the variety of Billy finds—amongst the hodgepodge of other local history items—the Sweet family has collected since the 1950s: Billy's rifles, a door he danced through on his last night on earth, and a set of his fancy spurs from when he was out cutting the rug the more traditional way. *Gift Shop*

🏠 505 355-2380 • 1601 E. Sumner, Fort Sumner, NM 88119

🚗 East-central, at the junction of US 60 and US 84, about 85 miles north of Roswell.

🕐 May 15–Oct. 1: Mon.–Sun. 8:30 A.M.–5 P.M. Rest of year: Mon.–Sat. 8:30 A.M.–5 P.M., Sun. 11 A.M.–5 P.M. Closed first 2 weeks of Jan. Fee.

GALLUP

The little Gallup Historical Museum covers the coal-mining roots of the town, but the building it's in—the former Rex Hotel—is perhaps more interesting for its history as a former bar and brothel. While we're on buildings, a stop is in order for the El Rancho, a restored 1937 hotel and motel to the stars. Celebrity photos adorn the grand two-story Western-rustic lobby. About 40 miles south are the new Navajo museum in Ramah (505 783-4677) and the Zuni Pueblo museum, the A:shiwi A:wan Museum and Heritage Center (505 782-4403).

Navajo Code Talkers Room   During WWII the Marines cleverly recruited rural Navajos to develop an impenetrable code to stymie the Japanese—the complex syntax and intricate tonal qualities of their unwritten language were a natural for the task. An initial corps of 29 grew to 400 by the end of the war. These men, considered so valuable each had been assigned a personal bodyguard, were credited with enabling the Marines to take Iwo Jima. The remaining vets get together here monthly, and there's a small photo, document, and uniform display covering the Navajo role and the cryptographic history. *See also* the U.S. Army Signal Corps Museum in Fort Gordon, Georgia, and the National Cryptologic Museum in Fort George Meade, Maryland.

🏠 505 722-2228 • 103 W. Historic Route 66, Gallup, NM 87305

🚗 Downtown Gallup in the Gallup-McKinley County Chamber of Commerce.

🕐 Mon.–Fri. 9 A.M.–5 P.M., but best to call ahead. No fee.

LAS VEGAS

City of Las Vegas Museum and Rough Riders Memorial Collection

Las Vegas, a key stop along the Santa Fe Trail and a spot known in the 1880s as "one of the roughest towns on the frontier," became, with the help of the railroad, New Mexico's primary mercantile center by the turn of the century. Teddy Roosevelt had recruited heavily in the West for his "Rough Riders" unit for the 1898 Spanish-American War, and a large contingent of his fighters came from New Mexico. The veterans' annual reunions in Las Vegas were rousing affairs, and the museum documents these and other local events as well as the war itself, with an extensive photo collection, artifacts, and memorabilia. By the way, Las Vegas managed to save its old train station (and many of its other historic buildings), which you can visit, peeking in at the old Harvey House Castaneda Hotel across the way. The bar downstairs is still open at times.

🏠 505 425-8726 • 725 N. Grand Ave., Las Vegas, NM 87701

🚙 Take the I-25 University exit. Turn downtown at the end of the ramp; it's on the right.

🕐 Mon.–Fri. 9 A.M.–noon, 1 P.M.–4 P.M., and by appointment. Donation.

LOS ALAMOS

Los Alamos Historical Museum

In 1943, when Gen. Leslie Groves gave the order to clear out the area for the Manhattan Project, the relocatees included Pueblo Indians, a few ranchers, and the students at the exclusive Los Alamos Ranch School. The school's guest house is now a fitting home for this collection that describes a most unusual local history. Geologically explosive, archaeologically impressive, the area that became the temporary home of some of the greatest scientific minds of our time was encased in secrecy from 1943 until 1957. The town known simply as Box 1663 (for the Santa Fe mailing address) and the lab as Project Y, life in the military-run "Secret City" was difficult for the young (average age 24) civilian scientists and their families. Eras Cenozoic to Atomic are highlighted here, punctuated with the fascinating day-to-day life on the Manhattan Project exhibit, and pix like that of "an admiral about to cut a slice of cake in the shape of a mushroom cloud." The more techno Bradbury Science Museum is nearby. It's a must-stop if you're hot on the Atomic trail, as is the city's walking tour. If archaeology is more up your alley, it's Bandelier for you. *Gift Shop, Programs, Library*

🏠 505 662-6272 • http://www.losalamos.com/lahistory • 1921 Juniper St., Los Alamos, NM 87544

🚙 About 35 miles northwest of Santa Fe. Take I-25 to US 84N, then turn west onto Hwy 502. It's off Central Ave. and 20th St., next to the Fuller Lodge Visitor Center.

🕐 Summer: Mon.–Sat. 9:30 A.M.–4:30 P.M., Sun. 11 A.M.–5 P.M. Winter: Mon.–Sat. 10 A.M.–4 P.M., Sun. 1 P.M.–4 P.M. No fee.

NAGEEZI

Chaco Culture National Historical Park   It's a rugged drive out to Chaco, but the exquisitely masoned Anasazi ruins you'll encounter at the end of the trail will more than compensate. The visitors center does a fine job of introducing you to the history and culture of the Pueblo occupation here, which predominately ranged from 900 to 1150 A.D., as well as the more recent (and current) Navajo presence. Give yourself plenty of time to walk some of the eight self-guided trails to appreciate the vast multi-storied ruins set among the stark sandstone mesas. *Tours, Gift Shop, Programs, Publications, Camping*

🏠 505 786-7014/988-6716 • PO Box 220, Nageezi, NM 87037

🚙 Northwestern New Mexico. I-40W to Thoreau (Exit 53), following signs from Hwy 371 to Hwy 9, then Hwy 57 into the park. Call for northern access instructions from Hwy 44. Both routes are dirt for the last 20–26 miles.

🕐 Memorial Day–Labor Day: 8 A.M.–6 P.M. Rest of year: 8 A.M.–5 P.M. Fee. Note: Facilities are extremely limited. Call ahead, especially if you plan to camp.

NAMBE

Liquid Paper Museum   Ex-Monkee Michael Nesmith's mom, Bette Graham, invented that vital fluid, Liquid Paper, in Dallas. While it was first catching on, she relocated manufacturing operations from the small trailer behind her Texas home to Nambe, just north of Santa Fe. So here's where it all happened in the '60s, with all the original equipment still in place. *Tours*

🏠 505 455-3848 • Gihon Foundation, Nambe, NM 87501

🚙 Near Santa Fe. Call for directions.

🕐 By appointment only. No fee.

ORGAN

Space Murals Museum   Sort of the people's version of Alamogordo's high-gloss Space Center, this museum, a vision of former New Jerseyite Lou Gariano, features murals of the space program painted on a 1.2-million-gallon water tank that's surrounded by a Space Shuttle–shaped pond. They've also got a nose and tailpiece from a V-2 rocket; a pair of boots hand-labeled "These boots walked on the moon," with dirt on the soles to show for it; a ⅛ scale model of the Challenger; and slews of space photos, craft parts, and now-declassified memorabilia, all of which has been donated by astronauts and space fans in response to Lou's requests, or built by the Gariano family themselves. The White Sands Missile Range Museum and Missile Park is just a few miles away. *Gift Shop*

🏠 505 382-0977 • 15450 Hwy 70E, Organ, NM 88052

🚐 It's 12 miles east of Las Cruces, across from NASA's White Sands Test Facility turnoff.
🕐 Mon.–Sat. 9 A.M.–6 P.M., Sun. 10 A.M.–6 P.M. No fee.

PORTALES

Bill Dalley's Windmill Collection   Former Peanut Capital Portales may be in a dry county—to look at its flat, barren plains, it's easy to imagine no water here either—but it has in fact a good source of shallow ground water, and the very knowledgeable Mr. Dalley has been busy collecting the windmills used to pump it up. His fascinating field of mills (or, more accurately, "multi-vaned wind pumps"), about 75 of them, include some of the oldest wooden models, more "modern" (starting from 1883) steel ones, and some remarkable homemade devices using oil drums and car parts. Evocatively named models like the Go Devil, the Battle-Ax, and Wonder Model B are joined by the Ant-Killer. Which, it turns out—like other power mills used for tasks like shelling corn or cutting wood—was designed to do just that. About seven miles northeast of town, you'll encounter signs of much older civilization—Clovis and Folsom Paleoindian cultures from 11,300–8,500 B.C. to be exact—at the Black Water Draw Museum (505 562-2202) and its nearby dig site. Another 12 miles north gets you to Clovis and other rock (like Buddy Holly) history at the Norman Petty Recording Studio (tours by appointment: 505 356-6422).
📱 505 356-6263 • 1506 S. Kilgore, Portales, NM 88130
🚐 In eastern New Mexico. Take US 70 into town, then south on Kilgore.
🕐 By appointment only. No fee.

QUEMADO

The Lightning Field   In this land of military installations, outer space sightings, and oversize space detectors (the Very Large Array radio telescope installation is in Magdalena, 77 miles east of Quemado, just down the road a piece in New Mexico terms), a grid of 400 stainless steel rods—set in a horizontal plane at a height averaging 20 feet and 7.5 inches (diameter: two inches), and spaced precisely 220 feet apart—pointed toward the sky might be brushed off as having some top-secret, or scientific, purpose. But you'd be wrong. Earthwork artist Walter De Maria created this piece out in the middle of nothing else in 1977, and it's been attracting people who like to see what happens during a New Mexico thunderstorm ever since. For dessert, you can visit nearby Pie Town.
📱 505 898-3335 • http://www.diacenter.org • Information: The Lightning Field, PO Box 2993, Corrales, NM 87048
🚐 Quemado is in western New Mexico. Call for directions.
🕐 By appointment only. Access is limited to the months of May through October. Fee. Note: site visit requires overnight stay; accommodations included in fee.

ROSWELL

Roswell is not just UFOs, you know. It's got Billy (the Kid, that is) too, not that you could miss him just about anywhere you go in this stretch of southeastern New Mexico. Look quick, Lincoln County's just to the west, Fort Sumner's to the north. And don't forget Carlsbad and its caverns, too (to the south). *While you're in the area, see also*: Capitan.

International UFO Museum and Research Center   Roswell, quietly sitting in farm and ranch lands in southeastern New Mexico, usually gets its excitement from annual events like the Great Milk Carton Boat Race in nearby Dexter. And since rocket scientist Dr. Robert H. Goddard, working in the '30s and early '40s, did the testing here that eventually got us into the space race, who would have thought that there could be such brouhaha about a bit of saucer-shaped metal seen flashing across the sky on a fateful day in 1947? As you all recall from UFO 101, we're talking about the "Roswell Incident." You know—object crashes, Air Force cover-up, three little aliens hidden away, weather balloon story released to press. Unless you've been out of the country the last few years, you know at least as much about it, probably more, than we do. There are two museums in town that will gladly fill in any blanks. This first is the one with the mysterious metal sample, a trove of Air Force documents released through the Freedom of Information Act, and displays on how to distinguish a possible UFO photo from a hoax and how to properly report any peculiar encounters. *Gift Shop, Publications, Screenings*

🔲 505 625-9495 • http://www.lookingglass.net/commercial/ufo/ufo.html • 400–402 N. Main St., Roswell, NM 88202

🚌 In southeastern New Mexico. Take I-25S to US 380E into US 70E and downtown Roswell.

🕐 Mon.–Sun. 1 P.M.–5 P.M. No fee.

UFO Enigma Museum   And this is the one that's right next to the old P-3 Hangar, where the wreckage and the aliens were allegedly taken and "prepared for shipment" (submit your hypotheses as to where). It has the Blue Room with its detailed crash site re-creation (Ed Wood would be proud), a display on UFOs and the movies (this museum began life as a video store specializing in UFO flicks), and oodles of supporting saucer pix and documents from around the world. By the way, there's a nice planetarium and little exhibit on Goddard and early rocket technology in the Roswell Museum and Art Center. And Bitter Lake National Wildlife Refuge is just a few miles away if you'd like to see some exquisite high-flying objects of the avian variety. *Gift Shop, Publications, Screenings*

🔲 505 347-2275 • http://members.gnn.com/ufoenigma/index.htm • 6108 S. Main St., Roswell, NM 88202

🚌 See above. Then it's 4 miles south near the old Roswell Army Air Field Base gate.

🕐 Mon.–Sat. 9:30 A.M.–5 P.M., Sun. noon–5 P.M. Fee.

SANDIA PARK

Tinkertown Museum The path to Tinkertown screams Tourist Trap, but hey, you were going to the Crest anyway. Besides, what we have here is quite swell. The result of Ross Ward's youthful fascination with the mechanical shows that accompanied the traveling carnivals he grew up with in the Midwest, it's a marvel of 35 years' worth of intricate wood carving, with a completely animated miniature three-ring circus and a finely detailed Western village. The museum walls are a marvel too—they're built with glass bottles . . . over 40,000 of them. *Gift Shop*

● 505 281-5233 • http://www.tinkertown.com/museum • 121 Sandia Crest Rd., Sandia Park, NM 87047

🚗 From I-40 Exit 175, just east of Albuquerque, take Hwy 14N to Hwy 536W (the Sandia Crest National Scenic Byway) and follow the signs.

🕐 Apr.–Oct.: Mon.–Sun. 9 A.M.–6 P.M. Fee.

SANTA FE

Santa Fe's restrictive adobe-style only building codes may leave you feeling more than a bit like a *turista* in a theme park. A bit north of town is the also well-touristed but still compelling Santuario de Chimayó, a pilgrimage for the faithful and those not so. Healing mud is available for all. If you're still in a shrine frame of mind, out by Santa Fe's airport you'll find the exuberant Tibetan Buddhist Temple, where you'll be alerted to View Appearance as Delusion. *While you're in the area, see also*: Abiquiu, Las Vegas, Los Alamos.

Bataan Memorial Military Museum and Library The 200th Coast Artillery Regiment, many of its men New Mexicans tied to the regiment's prior life as a state cavalry unit, was sent to the Philippines in 1942 and returned with less than half the soldiers they began with. This museum is dedicated to all such veterans and its exhibits touch on the state's role from the Civil War through Desert Storm. Director Harrison Taylor gladly supplements the display labels with tales about such things as the French field rations from the Gulf War—complete with foie gras—looked upon jealously by Americans stuck with suspect MREs; or the World War I convertible horse-drawn transport vehicle with detachable metal glides for winter travel. Also includes a striking wall display of 2,000 shoulder patches from most branches of the armed forces. If you're up early, join a small group of the surviving "Battling Bastards of Bataan" vets here for their morning coffee. *Library*

● 505 474-1670 • 1050 Old Pecos Trail, Santa Fe, NM 87505

🚗 From the plaza, go out Old Santa Fe Trail about 1 mile. It's on the right just before the Cordova Rd. intersection.

🕐 Tues.–Sat. 7:30 A.M.–4:30 P.M. Donation.

Indian Arts Research Center Traditional Southwest Indian arts and arti-facts spanning the 450-year period from Spanish contact to the present are beau-tifully presented on the grounds of a formerly private historic adobe estate. Exquisitely detailed Hopi and Zuni kachinas, 19th- and 20th-century Navajo and Pueblo weavings, and pottery from virtually every stylistic and technical tradition from the 1600s to modern times; basketry, jewelry, paintings, and a significant selection of ethnographic items, featuring musical instruments. *Tours*

🏠 505 982-3584 • School of American Research, 660 Garcia St., Santa Fe, NM 87504

🚕 From the plaza, take the first right off Canyon Rd. onto Garcia St., proceed 0.5 mile, entering at the second gate on the right (marked "IARC").

🕐 Scheduled tour by reservation only: Fri. 2 P.M. Other times by appointment. Fee.

TAOS

Harwood Foundation A gem of a collection in a historic adobe that is the second oldest museum in the state features 20th-century American art and the work of the infamous Taos Society of Artists (Ernest Blumenschein, Victor Hig-gins), modernists like Marsden Hartley and Andrew Dasburg, and a special collec-tion of work by contemporary artist Agnes Martin. Nineteenth-century Taos artists and artisans are well presented too, most dynamically with painted wood Santos and complex tinwork. Rustic hand-carved New Mexican and Spanish Colonial fur-niture complements the exhibits, and an extensive photo collection completes the picture. *Tours, Gift Shop, Library*

🏠 505 758-9826 • 238 Ledoux St., Taos, NM 87571

🚕 In town, near the plaza. From Hwy 64, turn in on Camino de la Placita, proceed 1 block to Ledoux and turn left to the end.

🕐 Tues.–Sat. 10 A.M.–5 P.M.; open Sun. in summer. Tours by appointment only. Fee.

TRUTH OR CONSEQUENCES

Geronimo Springs Museum Could it be only in America that we'd name a town after a popular '40s and '50s quiz show? Nope, no frontier roots in the name, though the cowboys used to like to poke around the soothing mineral springs next door. Don't miss the Ralph Edwards Room (Ralph began the show on radio; you may recall Bob Barker as a later TV emcee) with tapes aplenty of the old show, and the scoop on how T or C came to call itself Hot Springs no more. Other displays of interest: the New Mexico Old Time Fiddlers Hall of Fame; a "weird but tasteful" coprolite collection; and a Hispanic Heritage Room. Nearby stops include Calla-han's Auto Museum (with lots of early auto advertising stuff, like maps, packaging, and road signs; 505 894-6900); ghost towns like Chloride and Hillsboro; and the early 1900s Elephant Butte Dam. And you're just 90 miles from Silver City's Western New Mexico Museum and its unparalleled collection of Mimbres pottery. *Gift Shop*

📍 505 894-6600 • 211 Main St., Truth or Consequences, NM 87901

🚗 In southern New Mexico. I-25 Exit 79N, following Main St. into downtown.

🕐 Mon.–Sat. 9 A.M.–5 P.M. Fee.

NEW YORK

We're dividing this state into three sections—New York City, Upstate, and Long Island. Here's a special tip: We're New Yorkers, and we're aware just how provincial we can be. It has often been noted that some City people don't know much more about either Upstate or the Island than a few beaches they escape to from time to time, and the fact that state government goes on somewhere Up There. But we imagine that visitors to the City—by some accounts the most visited place in the world—unless they are coming from elsewhere in New York, know even less about the hinterlands. We hope here to suggest not only that in New York City you can find almost anything imaginable, but that it would be worth your while to consider what's at the other (outer) end of those notorious Bridges and Tunnels. Let the Gothamites continue in their heedless provincialism! Fire up your rented car, or check out the Long Island Rail Road, Metro-North, or PATH trains, and head for the hills!

NEW YORK CITY

THE BRONX

The Bronx is a disparate place, its large parks and institutions like Yankee Stadium and the Zoo—excuse us, the International Wildlife Conservation Park—coexisting with residential neighborhoods unknown to anyone but the residents. Its long and varied history will someday be captured in museums big and little. For the moment, we're sending you off to the northwest, to Riverdale.

Judaica Museum There are big Jewish institutions in Manhattan, but since you've come to this quiet corner of the city, one of many to which Downtown's immigrants eventually moved, why not take in a collection of hundreds of pieces of Judaica? In addition to devotional objects from the European tradition, the museum has changing exhibits depicting life in the New World. As befits its setting, this is a place of long memory. *Programs*

📱 718 548-1006 • Hebrew Home for the Aged, 5961 Palisade Ave., Bronx, NY 10471

🚗 It's in northern Riverdale, just south of W. 261st St. Heading north on the Henry Hudson Pkwy, Exit 253rd St./Riverdale Ave., go to 261st and turn left (west). Subway: 1, 9/231st St., then transfer to bus: BX7 or BX10/Riverdale Ave. and W. 261st St.

🕐 Mon.–Thurs. 1 P.M.–4:30 P.M., Sun. 1 P.M.–5 P.M. No fee.

Wave Hill   Its full title is the Wave Hill Center for Environmental Studies. If you think New York City's physical setting isn't spectacular, wait till you get here. And the site has been masterfully elaborated by landscape designers and architects (the current chief horticulturist, Marco Polo Stufano, enjoys near-legend status). There is a range of horticultural, environmental, and cultural programs, tours, and exhibits. And for lovers of historical ambience, the Manor, Wave Hill's main building, has been home to people with names like Thackeray, Teddy Roosevelt, Mark Twain, and Toscanini. *Tours, Programs*

📱 718 549-3200 • 675 W. 252nd St. (entrance 249th and Independence), Bronx, NY 10471

🚗 By car, take the Henry Hudson Pkwy (Route 9) to 246th St. exit and continue to 252nd St., crossing back (left) over the Pkwy. Turn left, then right on 249th, and look for signs. Subway: 1, 9/231st St. or A/207th St., then transfer to bus: BX7/252nd St. and walk west.

🕐 Tues.–Sun. 10:30 A.M.–4:30 P.M. Fee. Call for tour and event information.

BROOKLYN

Here's a storied land with two million residents, some neighborhoods that are well known even to those who don't know they're part of Brooklyn, other neighborhoods no one seems to know about despite their pungent character, lots of fine domestic architecture, and people—native and from everywhere else—full of ideas. So what are we doing? We're limiting ourselves to describing two places we think are *echt* Brooklyn. We're not telling you about the Harbor Defense Museum, or the New York Transit Museum, or the Kurdish Library, or Weeksville, not to mention the big places. Just these two:

Coney Island Museum and Sideshows-by-the-Seashore   "You'd have to be insane to run a business here," says Dick Zigun. He says it, not us (actually, he's talking about the hard weather that shortens the Coney Island season). This is "the national center of Americano-Bizarro," per another account. We know the *Americano* part is true: Coney Island is known far and wide, even in Muskogee, Oklahoma, where once we were offered a "coney" (hot dog). *Bizarro* you'll judge for yourself. In a second-story loft, formerly a Child's restaurant and later a topless joint, looking out at the Cyclone and the Wonderwheel, you'll find an original Steeple-chase horse, "bumping" cars, Boardwalk chairs, funhouse mirrors, and all manner of Coney Island memorabilia and tchotchkes. Around the corner, the Sideshows people are still doing unspeakable things with swords, nails, chains, flame, and other cosmetic devices. *Gift Shop, Food, Programs*

📷 718 372-5159 • 1208 Surf Ave. (Museum) and 3006 W. 12th St. (Sideshows), Brooklyn, NY 11224

🚗 At the corner of Surf and W. 12th, in the heart of Coney Island's amusement zone. Take Exit 7S from the Belt Pkwy; follow Ocean Pkwy and turn right at Surf Ave. Subway: B, D, F, N/Stillwell Ave.

🕐 Museum: May–Sept.: Wed.–Sun. noon–sundown. Rest of year: Sat.–Sun. only. Call for Sideshows hours. Separate fees for the two establishments.

Green-Wood Cemetery   You're calling this a *museum*? You're calling this *little*? Yeah—you gotta problem with that? The displays include Currier and Ives (the men, not the prints); Tiffany (the man, not the glass); Tiffany (the other man, not the store); Squibb and Pfizer (the men, not the pharmaceutical items); Richard Upjohn (the man *and* the architecture); Lola Montez (she's here; the fame must be hovering about); and Boss Tweed (he's here; ditto the scandal). There are also thousands and thousands of others, from the noble obscure to yesterday's mobsters. It's their monuments you'll see, of course, and great landscaping and views. From its opening in 1840, this was *the* place to come for New Yorkers, until Central Park was built. Today access is limited, which hardly seems necessary since the city's people have forgotten about Green-Wood. Bring good shoes. Bring your camera and sketchpad. Bring birding glasses. *Tours*

📷 718 768-7300 • 5th Ave. and 25th St., Brooklyn, NY 11232

🚗 It's in the Sunset Park neighborhood, just southwest of Prospect Park. By car, avoid the Gowanus and Prospect Expwys, which are always under construction, or something; from the Brooklyn-Battery Tunnel, go straight ahead to 5th Ave. and turn right. Subway: M, N, R/25th St. and walk (uphill, 5 minutes).

🕐 Call for information on tours, etc.

MANHATTAN

Manhattan is, of course, the extreme of all of New York City's boroughs—a place of sublime sophistication and architectural grandeur, at the same time suffering from a decaying infrastructure and cost-of-living pressure. But no matter how you slice the apple, it's a place with a bite that's distinctly its own, and at the turn of every corner there's something to see we're sure you'd never find in Iowa.

We should note that our selection here is truly idiosyncratic. The museums in this town have already filled a book or two, and there are another few being built as we speak. The NYC Police Academy Museum, NYC Fire Museum, Abigail Adams Smith Museum, the Nicholas Roerich Museum, and the American Numismatic Society are perennial "small" museum favorites, for good reason. A bit bigger, but still far from the Met, are Asia Society, Bard Graduate Center for Studies in the Decorative Arts, Studio Museum in Harlem, Cooper-Hewitt, Schomberg Center, Pierpont Morgan Library, the Frick, El Museo del Barrio, Museum of the City of New York, and the Cloisters. While we're talking local museums, say good-bye to the building on 42nd St.—now in the throes of Goofy-Goes-Gotham—that housed one of the last remnants of the old Times Square, the flea circus and "amusement center" known as Hubert's Museum.

Eldridge Street Synagogue   In 1887, Eastern European Jewish immigrants built this gloriously intimate Moorish-Gothic synagogue that has evocatively been called "a majestic collage of psychedelic polychromy and ruinous decay." The decay is in arrest, but like many, you may find a visit there now—before restoration is complete—a most meaningful sojourn with the spirits of a century past. You're within blocks of the Lower East Side Tenement Museum (212 431-0233) and the Museum of the Chinese in the Americas (212 619-4785), both not to be missed. *Tours, Gift Shop, Library, Programs*

🏠 212 219-0888 • 12 Eldridge St., NY, NY 10002

🚗 Between Grand and Canal Sts., 1 block west of Allen St. Subway: B, D/Grand St.; F/East Broadway.

🕐 Tours only: Sun. 11 A.M.–4 P.M., on the hour; Tues.–Thurs. by appointment. Donation.

First National Church of the Exquisite Panic   Robert Delford Brown has been a presence in the New York art scene since the early '60s. While that scene has gone through many a permutation since then, Brown has kept a lively and watchful eye out for those who might take it all just a little too seriously. We're big fans of the church (also known as Funkup! or the Great Building Crack-up), which features a Chapel of Pharblongence (pull out your Rosten), and is devoted to laughter, art, and the road to Nevada. While the church is moving to Houston, we expect the exterior embellishments to remain on this historic Richard Morris Hunt building with Paul Rudolph interior touches. But, who knows!

🏠 713 523-4093 • http://funkup.com • 251 W. 13th St., NY, NY 10014

🚗 West Village, just east of Greenwich Ave. Subway: A, C, E, 1, 2, 3/14th St.

🕐 Outside exhibits: 24-hour access. Events: Check website or call Mon.–Fri. 10 A.M.–5 P.M. No fee.

***Forbes* Magazine Galleries**   From the moment you step into the *Normandie*-bedecked Deco foyer of the museum and hear the delightful seagoing tune playing in the background, you're hooked. The late Malcolm Forbes may have been famous for his Fabergé eggs and motorcycles (oh, and money), but we give him highest marks for his (and his curators' and exhibition designers') accomplishments with this wonderfully laid-out space filled with his personal collections of toy boats, toy soldiers, Monopoly game history, and political memorabilia. Look for the painting of a blue ship son Tim Forbes made as a child.

🏠 212 206-5548 • 62 5th Ave., NY, NY 10011

🚌 Greenwich Village, at 12th St. Subway: 1, 2, 3, 4, 5, 6, F, N, R/14th St./Union Square.
🕐 Tues.–Sat. 10 A.M.–4 P.M. No fee.

Glove Museum   Curator Jay Ruckel, a glove cutter by trade, found the inspiration to begin this museum from a close encounter with an exquisite pair of embroidered gloves from the 1600s. His appreciation for all aspects of the fine craft of glovemaking is apparent in his careful selection and display of an array of antique tools—including a mooning knife just like the one William Shakespeare's dad would have used—as well as elegant stretchers, delicate button hooks, two centuries of wonderfully detailed ladies' gloves and the various travel bags designed to hold them, metal gauntlets (the perfect complement to a suit of armor), and even the rubber molds used to make astronauts' gloves. If you're lucky, he'll have a few minutes to share the surprising wealth of glove lore he's accumulated as well.
🏢 212 594-2223 • LaCrasia Gloves, 304 5th Ave., Manhattan, NY 10001
🚌 Midtown, between 31st and 32nd Sts. Subway: 6/33rd St.; N, R/28th St.
🕐 By appointment only. No fee.

Joe Franklin's Office   While *The Joe Franklin Show* is only on radio these days, the man himself—a veritable show-biz icon—lives on, and boy does he have the stuff to show for it. On sheer quantity alone—100,000 celebrity pix (particularly of movie people known for a comedy edge, like Georgie Jessel and W. C. Fields) and 20,000 lobby cards in pristine condition—you stand to be impressed, but the esoterica takes it over the top. The uncatalogued collection going back to the late 1800s is apt to turn up anything from Dixie cup ice cream tops from the '30s with movie stars' pictures on them to RKO Palace programs featuring the "Golden Age of the Irresistibles" or trinkets from the epics of Cecil B. DeMille.
🏢 212 956-1693 • 300 W. 43rd St., NY, NY 10036
🚌 Midtown, near 8th Ave. Subway: A, C, E/42nd St.
🕐 By appointment only. No fee.

Maidenform Museum   A seemingly simple garment, yet to properly fit, the design details warrant the consideration of an engineer (Patent No. 1,648,464 issued in 1927 proves it!). From the finest of gossamer silks and the simple lines of the '20s and '30s, to the World War II models in sturdier gingham (one of the ways women—and clever company buyers—did their bit for the conservation needs of the war effort) and the B-52 form of the '50s, the history of the brassiere and the company that began life as Enid Frocks is traced delightfully with a special look at the "I Dreamed I . . ." ads that put the company on the map for generations.
🏢 212 684-6641 • NY, NY 10016
🚌 Midtown. Call for current information.
🕐 By appointment only. No fee.

Museum at the Fashion Institute of Technology   Clever and insightful interpretations and fearless exploration of both high and low fashion are the hallmarks of the changing exhibits culled from the museum's extensive 20th-century costume and textile collections. One of the largest such repositories in the world, this is the place to come to see the creative process melded exquisitely with craft, to see for yourself how fashion constantly reinvents itself, or just for plain old sartorial inspiration. *Tours, Library*

■ 212 217-5800 • 7th Ave. at 27th St., NY, NY 10001

🚌 Midtown South, near Madison Square Garden. Subway: A, C, E/34th St.; C, E/23rd St.

🕐 Tues.–Fri. noon–8 P.M., Sat. 10 A.M.–5 P.M. Group tours by appointment. No fee.

Museum of American Financial History

Housed in a most appropriate location—the early-20th-century Standard Oil Building in the heart of the financial district—these items from the annals of American financial history dating back to the mid-1800s were selected to balance the stereotype that equates Wall Street with avarice. It certainly fosters an appreciation for the contribution the world of money makes to New York City. Artifacts and memorabilia on hand include early ticker-tape machines, John D. Rockefeller's strong box, Bernard Baruch's conference chair, and a selection of finely engraved stock and bond certificates, including one signed by George Washington. *Gift Shop, Library*

■ 212 908-4519 • http://netresource.com/math • 24 Broadway, NY, NY 10004

🚌 Lower Manhattan, opposite Bowling Green Park. Subway: 4, 5/Bowling Green; 1, 9/Rector St.; N, R/Whitehall St./South Ferry; M/Broad St.

🕐 Mon.–Fri. 11:30 A.M.–2:30 P.M. and weekends by appointment. No fee.

Museum of Postal History

Next time you're in the beautiful old McKim, Mead, and White main post office, perhaps mailing your taxes at the last minute, take a few more minutes and stroll from one end of the lobby to the other and see some of the tucked-away postal history items, like a huge collection of foreign postal badges and a number of decommissioned postal boxes from around the world. Don't miss the display cases that do a nice job of covering air mail history with photos and telegrams, as well as the selection of letter carrier chapeaux. Or come back and take a tour with curator Joe Cohen, a font of information on all things postal. *Tours, Library*

■ 212 330-3291 • James A. Farley Bldg., 421 8th Ave., NY, NY 10199

🚌 Midtown, between 31st and 33rd Sts. Subway: A, C, E/34th St.

🕐 Lobby exhibits: 24-hour access (but limited at Christmas). Tours: Wed. 10 A.M.–3 P.M., by appointment only. No fee.

Rose Museum at Carnegie Hall

The Rose Museum is a gem tucked into a gem of a music hall. Saved from the wrecking ball in the 1960s, its centennial in 1986 inspired this archives and memorabilia collection. Spanning the hall's use not only for all kinds of music and dance performances, but for political and religious events as well, are evocative items like Arturo Toscanini's baton, a souvenir book from the Beatles' 1964 Carnegie Hall debut, original plan drawings and the silver trowel used by Mr. Louis Carnegie at the cornerstone ceremony, and Benny

Goodman's clarinet. Just a few blocks away is the Museum of the American Piano (212 246-4646; open only to groups, by reservation only) with a wonderful collection of historic pianos and related tools and memorabilia. *Gift Shop*

🔲 212 247-7800 • 154 W. 57th St., NY, NY 10019

🚌 Midtown, off 7th Ave. Subway: N, R/57th St.; B, D, E/7th Ave.

🕐 Mon.–Sun. (closed Wed.) 11 A.M.–4:30 P.M., and during concert hours. No fee.

Skyscraper Museum   Currently in temporary space amongst the highrise-lined canyons of Lower Manhattan, the core exhibit of this museum-in-the-works "The Architecture of Business/The Business of Buildings" celebrates the historical development of the skyscraper right in its birthplace. A symbol and metaphor for the exponential wealth of New York's captains of industry, these achievements of architectural inspiration and engineering skills have, of course, shaped much more than the skyline, standing as a tribute to the social, political, and economic forces that continue to shape the city today.

🔲 212 968-1961 • http://www.skyscraper.org • 44 Wall St., NY, NY 10005

🚌 Lower Manhattan. Subway: 2, 3, 4, 5/Wall St.

🕐 Tues.–Sat. noon–6 P.M. No fee. Call to confirm location.

Tamiment Institute Library/Wagner Labor Archives   The Tamiment Collection is a unique repository for materials about modern radical movements, but more so from the '20s, '30s, and '40s, and so covers critical periods in labor history and in the evolution of socialist, communist, progressive, and new-left activism in the United States and elsewhere in the world. Exhibits tap into an overwhelming archive and may feature items like subscription blanks to the *Black Panther*, the little red songbook of the I.W.W., a copy of anarchist Emma Goldman's *Mother Earth* journal, a "Repeal Taft-Hartley" necktie, and items associated with the Scottsboro case and Southern Negro suffrage. *Programs, Library*

🔲 212 998-2630/2640 • New York University, Bobst Library, 10th Floor, 70 Washington Square South, NY, NY 10012

🚌 Greenwich Village, off La Guardia Pl. Subway: A, B, C, D, E, F/W. 4th St.

🕐 Spring/Fall terms: Mon., Thurs. 10 A.M.–9 P.M.; Tues., Wed., Fri. 10 A.M.–5:45 P.M.; Sat. 10 A.M.–5 P.M. Hours vary rest of year. Request pass at main entrance. No fee.

QUEENS

Queens is the most diverse county in the United States. Some *neighborhoods* in Queens have more national groups than the United Nations. The borough is just beginning to wake up to the potential this represents, and down the road this could be Little Museum Heaven. Now we're going to send you to see the museum of a one-man U.N. But first, a few remarks on museum-going in Queens. At the moment, there are two "complexes" of museums here. One, in and around Flushing Meadows–Corona Park, where the 1939 and 1964 World's Fairs were held, has such big attractions as the interactive-wonderland New York Hall of Science and the Queens Museum of Art (with its thousands-of-buildings diorama of the *entire* city). Out this way there are two places that should be listed as Coming Attractions: One is the Museum of the World's Fairs projected for the near future in the park. At the moment, there is a display of World's Fairana at the QMA (call 718 592-9700 for information), and that's a place to keep up with any developments on the new museum. Over at Queens College's Rosenthal Library (63-50 Kissena Blvd., also in Flushing) is the Louis Armstrong Archives. Director Michael Cogswell tells us that the conversion of Armstrong's home in nearby Corona into a full-scale museum should be completed in 1998. In the meantime, there are things to see at the library; call 718 997-3670 for information. This one is exciting because the great musician was also a great collector, and his house will obviously be filled with good stuff.

Now, about the other Queens museum complex, and about that one-man United Nations:

Isamu Noguchi Garden Museum   Isamu Noguchi (1904–88) was Japanese in the America of his mother, and American in the Japan of his father; the result was an international man. Fittingly, he became an artist in many media. Here, in his former workshop and its adjoining buildings, once an ink plant, you'll see examples of his stage decor, paper lampshades, metal sculpture, photographs of gardens and public settings he created around the world, and examples of much else. But as with the traditional Japanese garden, the real story here is stone. If the things that can be done, and expressed, with stone interest you, pay a call; there's everything from granite expressing the spirit of massiveness and solidity to vivid marble to the coarse gravel used to fine effect in the garden. The industrial setting is highly appropriate. Across Vernon Blvd. is the Socrates Sculpture Park (call 718 956-1819), an outdoor collection (and setting) just beginning to acquire a name. Not far away is the American Museum of the Moving Image, in part of the former Kauffmann Astoria Studios, where you can examine movie history (718 784-0077). And a short drive south, as for Noguchi, it's also in Long Island City, is the P.S. 1 Contemporary Art Center, the largest contemporary and alternative art museum in the United States not based on a permanent collection (call 718 784-2084 for information). *Tours, Gift Shop*

■ 718 721-1932 • 32–37 Vernon Blvd., Long Island City, Queens, NY 11106

🚙 Vernon Blvd. runs along the East River between Long Island City and Astoria, across from Roosevelt Island. The museum entrance is at the corner of 33rd Rd. and Vernon. Call for driving directions and for shuttle bus information. Subway: N/Broadway, then walk west on Broadway and south on Vernon (about 15 minutes).

🕐 Apr.–Nov.: Wed., Sat.–Sun. 11 A.M.–6 P.M. Fee.

STATEN ISLAND

Some Staten Islanders are continually saying they'd like to break away from the rest of the City. That's mostly about taxes and the cost of services; but when you come out here you feel as though you *have* broken away. The island, developed largely since the Verrazano Bridge opened in 1964, has always been the "other" among the City's boroughs. It's now a weird soup of fast suburban development mixed with historic small towns. These two sites are both quite "other."

Garibaldi and Meucci Museum of the Order Sons of Italy in America
Great cities are often havens to revolutionaries and exiles from elsewhere, and New York is no exception. The Italian republican lived here in the early 1850s, waiting for the opportunity to get back to his nation-building work at home. Antonio Meucci, his friend whose house this was, had another claim to fame as well: He invented a forerunner of the modern telephone, for which he never, his supporters will tell you, received sufficient credit. You'll find memorabilia here of both careers and of the time in exile.

🏠 718 442-1608 • 420 Tompkins Ave., Staten Island, NY 10305

🚗 It's in the Rosebank neighborhood, along New York Bay north of the Verrazano Bridge and south of the Ferry terminal. From the Verrazano, exit onto Hyland Blvd. (right at 2nd light). Go left on Tompkins (the 1st light on Hyland) to corner of Chestnut.

🕑 Tues.–Sun. 1 P.M.–5 P.M. Call to confirm winter hours. Donation.

Jacques Marchais Museum of Tibetan Art   In the middle of the island, on the east side of its central hill, is this evocation of a Tibetan mountainside temple, with gardens and walkways, where Jacques Marchais and his successors created (from the 1940s) one of the most surprising spots in New York City. Religious statuary, paintings, metalwork, wall hangings, and other art objects are presented here in understated charm, a small tribute to the peoples of the Himalayas. There is a range of lectures, concerts, and other programs; call ahead for information.
Gift Shop, Programs

🏠 718 987-3500 • 338 Lighthouse Ave., Staten Island, NY 10306

🚗 From I-278, exit south on Richmond Ave. and go 5 miles south. Take a right on Lighthouse Ave. and go up the hill; the museum is around the first bend, on the right.

🕑 Apr.–Nov.: Wed.–Sun. 1 P.M.–5 P.M., or by appointment. Fee.

UPSTATE NEW YORK

Upstate is everything north of the New York City line, and includes some wildly disparate areas—Westchester County and near suburbs; the Hudson and Mohawk valleys; the North Country, Thousand Islands, and Adirondacks; the Southern Tier, along the Pennsylvania border; the Finger Lakes, in the center; and the lakeshore areas around Buffalo and farther west. There are old and wealthy cities out here, and there is rich farmland, and there is deep wilderness. The museums we've looked at are also wildly disparate, and there are a lot of them. Because life is short and art long, we're going to quickly name some categories, and some museums that fall into them that we haven't included. In **Aviation:** the Old Rhinebeck Aerodrome and Geneseo's National Warplane Museum. (*See* Elmira for one we did include.) Among the **Natives:** the Iroquois Indian Museum at Howes Cave (Cobbleskill); William Pryor Letchworth Museum at Letchworth State Park (Castile); National Shrine of Blessed Kateri Tekakwitha at Fonda; the Turtle (Native American Center for the Living Arts) in Niagara Falls; Seneca-Iroquois National Museum in Salamanca. For **Shakers:** the Shaker Museum in Old Chatham; Mount Lebanon Shaker Village in New Lebanon. For **Sports fans:** the National Soccer Hall of Fame in Oneonta; International Boxing Hall of Fame in Canastota; National Museum of Racing in Saratoga Springs; Harness Racing Hall of Fame and Museum in Goshen. On the **Military front:** the Watervliet Arsenal; West Point Museum. **Historic Homes and Sites:** the Harriet Tubman House in Auburn; John Brown Farm in Lake Placid; National Women's Hall of Fame in Seneca Falls; Susan B. Anthony House in Rochester; Slabsides, the John Burroughs home in West Park. And as for **Arts and Culture:** Among the sites it pained us most to leave out are the Everson Museum in Syracuse, the Strong Museum and the Eastman House (International Photography Center) in Rochester, and above all, Frederic Church's Olana in Hudson. **We love it but it's too big:** the Adirondack Museum in Blue Mountain Lake.

BALLSTON SPA

National Bottle Museum   The study of bottles combines an examination of manufacturing history (glassmaking was a key 18th- and 19th-century industry in this part of the country), an appreciation of the artistry involved before machinery standardized containers, and, we think, curiosity about social history. There are thousands of artifacts here, along with videos and knowledgeable docents. This is a membership organization, and meetings, auctions, and other programs are part of its appeal. *Programs, Library*

- 518 885-7589 • 76 Milton Ave., Ballston Spa, NY 12020
- Ballston Spa is 15 minutes southwest of Saratoga Springs and a half-hour north of Albany via I-87. Take Exit 12 and go west, then north on NY 50 (Milton Ave.).
- June–Sept.: Mon.–Sun. 10 A.M.–4 P.M. Rest of year: weekdays only. Fee.

BOLTON LANDING

Marcella Sembrich Opera Museum   Marcella Sembrich, born in Poland in 1858, was the most unusual of musicians—not only a great diva but also a virtuoso violinist and pianist, and the founder of the vocal departments at the Juilliard School and Curtis Institute. This museum, in her lakeside summer teaching studio, is filled with memorabilia of Sembrich, her colleagues, and the world of opera. *Programs*

📱 518 644-9839 • Lake Shore Dr., Bolton Landing, NY 12814

🚗 Bolton Landing is 60 miles north of Albany, on Lake George. From I-87 (the Northway), take Exit 22 or 24 to NY 9N. The museum is just south of the town center.

🕐 Mid-June–mid-Sept.: Mon.–Sun. 10 A.M.–12:30 P.M. and 2 P.M.–5:30 P.M. Donation.

BREWSTER

Southeast Museum Wonderful eclecticism is the key here in Brewster (which used to be called Southeast). The development of one of New York's far suburbs is detailed through displays on the Harlem Line railroad. There are artifacts of early circuses, which once wintered in the area. The beginnings of the condensed-milk empire of local Gail Borden are another focus. And there are minerals and other reminders of Southeast's mining days.

📱 914 279-7500 • 67 Main St., Brewster, NY 10509

🚗 Brewster is an hour north-northeast of New York City, near the junction of I-84 with I-684. The museum is in the center of town, in the old Town Hall building.

🕐 Apr.–late Dec.: Tues.–Thurs. noon–4 P.M., Sat.–Sun. 2 P.M.–4 P.M. No fee.

BUFFALO

While you're in the area, see: East Aurora, Eden, North Tonawanda, Orchard Park

CLAYTON

Antique Boat Museum Everything from birchbark canoes to the 48-foot (!) runabout *Pardon Me*, from boatbuilding tools to the earliest gas outboard to racing speedboats to presidential craft to King Gustav V's sloop. This must be freshwater Boat Heaven. *Gift Shop, Programs, Publications*

📱 315 686-4104 • 750 Mary St., Clayton, NY 13624

🚗 Clayton is in the Thousand Islands region, on the St. Lawrence River. Take Exit 47 off I-81 and follow NY 12N into Clayton, where it becomes James St. Turn left at Mary St. to the waterfront.

🕐 May 15–Oct. 15: Mon.–Sun. 9 A.M.–4 P.M. Fee.

CORNING

Rockwell Museum Corning is a glass-producing center, and this museum has the largest displays of Frederic Carder's Steuben glass and sculpture. There is also a large toy collection. But what the Rockwell really stands out for is its Western art holdings; if you want to stay East and see West, this is the place. You'll see Remington, Bierstadt, Russell, Sharp, Taos artists, Navajo weavings, Colt firearms, Southwestern ceramics and baskets, and much more.

📞 607 937-5386 • 111 Cedar St., Corning, NY 14830

🚗 Corning is in the Southern Tier, a half-hour west of Elmira. The museum is at the corner of Cedar St. and Denison Pkwy (NY 352) in downtown's Market St. Historic District. From NY 17 take Exit 46 and go south 0.5 mile.

🕐 June–Oct.: Mon.–Sat. 9 A.M.–5 P.M., Sun. noon–5 P.M. Rest of year: weekdays opens 10 A.M. Fee.

CROGHAN

American Maple Museum   Major funding for the museum is from pancake breakfasts—how could you pass *this* up? There's a maple industry Hall of Fame, and re-creations of the sugarbush, sugar house, evaporator room, and all the other special environments of the maple trade. Croghan is a quiet little village, but this is "the geographic center of the North American Maple Region." *See also* the New England Maple Museum in Pittsford, Vermont. *Gift Shop*

📞 315 346-1107 • Main St. (Route 812), Croghan, NY 13327

🚗 Croghan is in the North Country, about 25 miles east-southeast of Watertown, on NY 812, which is Main St. The museum is central, in a former school building.

🕐 July–Labor Day: Mon.–Sat. 11 A.M.–4 P.M. May–June and Sept.–Oct.: Fri.–Sat. and Mon. 11 A.M.–4 P.M. Fee.

DEANSBORO

Musical Museum   A hobby that grew into a family undertaking, this is a wonderland of mechanical music, and one where you yourself can play a lot of the old instruments (they *are* wary of young kids getting their hands on them, though). So if you've been wondering just what are the sounds of a nickelodeon, melodeon, harmonium, pandemonium . . . here are 17 rooms of them! *Hands-on*

📞 315 841-8774 • Route 12B, Deansboro, NY 13328

🚗 Deansboro is a half-hour southwest of Utica. From the Thruway (I-90), exit south on I-790/SR 12, then branch right on 12B through Clinton to Deansboro.

🕐 Apr.–Dec.: Mon.–Sun. 10 A.M.–4 P.M. Fee.

EAST AURORA

Elbert Hubbard Roycroft Museum   East Aurora is the town where the intellectual/entrepreneur Elbert Hubbard (1856–1915) established the Roycroft Press and soon became the leader of the American wing of the Arts and Crafts movement (*see also* Detroit, Michigan, and Parsippany, New Jersey), attracting designers, architects, and others to his "campus." This museum displays the coherent aesthetic that flourished early in the century.

🏠 716 652-4735 • ScheideMantel House, 363 Oakwood Ave., East Aurora, NY 14052

🚗 East Aurora is a southeastern suburb of Buffalo, and is just northeast of Orchard Park. Oakwood Ave. parallels Main St. (NY 20A) on the south. The museum is near the corner of Oakwood and Center.

🕐 June–Oct. 15: Wed., Sat.–Sun. 2 P.M.–4 P.M. Other times by appointment. Donation.

EDEN

Original American Kazoo Company Factory and Museum   If you were in the Kazoo Band in college, you already know what this is about. They make 'em all here—even the gold-plated Executive Kazoo—and have since World War I, on the same equipment. You'll see antiques like the liquor bottle kazoos that celebrated the 21st Amendment, and you can catch a glimpse of new kazoos rolling (or buzzing?) off the line. *Gift Shop*

🏠 716 992-3960 • 8703 S. Main St., Eden, NY 14057

🚗 Eden is a half-hour south of Buffalo. From the Thruway (I-90), take Exit 57A and go east on Evans Center Rd.. There's a huge metal kazoo on the museum's roof.

🕐 Mon.–Sat. 10 A.M.–5 P.M., Sun. noon–5 P.M. No fee.

ELMIRA

While you're in the area, see also: Corning

National Soaring Museum   Military gliders have been built hereabouts, and the museum has the "largest collection of sailplanes in the world." This includes fabric from a 1903 Wright Brothers model, 66 actual craft, and 120-odd models showing the evolution of this kind of vehicle (did you know the space shuttle is a glider?). Try your hand in a flight simulator, see videos and other action displays, and perhaps take a ride, weather permitting. *Gift Shop, Hands-on, Programs*

🏠 607 734-3128 • Harris Hill, 51 Soaring Hill Dr., Elmira, NY 14903

🚗 Elmira is in the Southern Tier, an hour west of Binghamton via NY 17. Take Exit 51 and follow signs to County Route 64, then up Harris Hill Rd.

🕐 Mon.–Sun. 10 A.M.–5 P.M. Fee.

HAMMONDSPORT

Wine Museum of Greyton H. Taylor   Wine was made in this building beginning in the late 19th century. Production has moved into newer buildings nearby, but you can see the old equipment, along with tools and other memorabilia of the region's best-known industry. Abe Lincoln's glass from Ford's Theatre is part of the glassware collection. Don't drink and fly, but you may want to drop in at the Glenn H. Curtiss Museum in Hammondsport (call 607 569-2160 for information) to see displays on the aviation pioneer. *Tours, Gift Shop, Food*

🏠 607 868-4814 • Bully Hill Vineyards, 8843 Greyton H. Taylor Memorial Dr., Hammondsport, NY 14840

🚗 Hammondsport is in the western Finger Lakes region, at the foot of Keuka Lake. From NY 17, exit onto NY 54N at Bath. Go left on 54A through Hammondsport village, then go left on County Route 76, following signs to Bully Hill.

🕐 Mid-May–Nov.: Mon.–Sat. 9 A.M.–5 P.M., Sun. noon–4:30 P.M. Donation.

HASTINGS-ON-HUDSON

Newington Cropsey Foundation Gallery of Art and Cultural Studies Center/Ever Rest   This new museum displaying the work of Hudson River School landscapist Jasper Francis Cropsey (1823–1900) has attracted architecture fans for its Palladian exterior and partially Gothic interior. Ever Rest, Cropsey's cottage, is next door (call 914 478-1372 for information). A visit to both is a step from the modern world into something either past or future, we're not sure which.

🏠 914 478-7990 • Hastings-on-Hudson, NY 10706

🚗 Hastings is a half-hour north of Manhattan via I-87, US 9 (Broadway), or Metro-North train from Grand Central Station. Call for directions.

🕐 Tours by appointment. No fee.

ILION

Remington Firearms Museum and Country Store   Eliphalet Remington built a rifle here in 1816, and the rest is history. This is a combination factory tour/factory store/museum opportunity. What the museum shows is the evolution of high-quality firearms over two centuries, but also the involvement of Remington in making cash registers, knives, bicycles, typewriters, etc. There's also much sporting art. But the guns are the main thing. *Tours, Gift Shop*

🏠 315 894-9961 • Catherine St. off Route 5S, Ilion, NY 13357

🚗 Ilion is 12 miles southeast of Utica. Take Exit 30 off the NY State Thruway (I-90) and follow Route 5S into town.

🕐 Mon.–Fri. 8 A.M.–5 P.M., Sat. 10 A.M.–5 P.M., Sun. noon–5 P.M. Factory tours: Mon.–Fri. 9 A.M.–noon and 12:30 P.M.–2 P.M. No fee.

LEROY

Jell-O Museum (LeRoy House)   If we tell you that Jell-O was 100 years old in 1997, will you finally believe that America has a history? All that jiggling started here, and at LeRoy House they celebrated with special exhibits that soon jelled (sorry!). If this doesn't take you back, nothing will.

🏠 716 768-7433 • 23 Main St., LeRoy, NY 14482

🚗 LeRoy is in western New York, a half-hour southwest of Rochester. Take Exit 47 off the Thruway (I-90) and go south on SR 19 into town.

🕐 Tues.–Fri., Sun. 2 P.M.–4 P.M. Tours by appointment. No fee.

LIVERPOOL

Salt Museum Salt built Syracuse: Lake Onondaga's brine, reduced in the works here, became "white gold." At this museum, built from parts of old salt ware-houses, you'll see exhibits on an industry that flourished into the 20th century but is now largely forgotten. *Gift Shop*

🏠 315 453-6715 • Onondaga Lake Park, Onondaga Lake Pkwy, Liverpool, NY 13088

🚗 Liverpool is on the northwest side of Syracuse. The park is off Route 370 (the Onondaga Lake Pkwy); look for signs.

🕐 May–Sept.: Tues.–Sun. and Monday holidays, noon–5 P.M. Fee.

MOUNTAINVILLE

Storm King Art Center Storm King (named for the mountain) is 400 acres of breathtaking scenery enhanced by over 120 works of sculpture by such as Calder, Noguchi, and Nevelson. There are also changing exhibits, concerts, and other pro-grams. What a place for a picnic! *Tours, Programs*

🏠 914 534-3190 • Old Pleasant Hill Rd., Mountainville, NY 10953

🚗 Mountainville is in the Hudson Valley, just west of West Point and south of Newburgh. From the Thruway (I-87), exit west on NY 17 at Harriman, then turn north on NY 32 past Central Valley toward Cornwall, and look for signs.

🕐 Apr.–mid-Nov.: Mon.–Sun. 11 A.M.–5:30 P.M. Tours at 2 P.M. Fee.

NORTH CHILI

Victorian Doll Museum and Chili Doll Hospital Among doll museums this one—which has over 1,000 dolls, along with dollhouses, a miniature circus, other toys, an action puppet theater, and more—is special in displaying the parts and apparatus of doll repairing (the actual work in the Doll Hospital, like the actual work in most human hospitals, is not seen). *Gift Shop*

🏠 716 247-0130 • 4332 Buffalo Rd. (Route 33), North Chili, NY 14514

🚗 North Chili is 20 minutes west of Rochester. From I-490W, take Exit 7B onto NY 33W. The museum is on the right at 4.5 miles, just past Roberts Wesleyan College.

🕐 Nov.–Dec.: Tues.–Sat. 10 A.M.–4:30 P.M., Sun. 1 P.M.–4 P.M. Rest of year closed Sun. Also closed month of Jan. Fee.

NORTH TONAWANDA

Herschell Carrousel Factory Museum   This carousel museum is not just for lovers of the painted horses and atmosphere but for those who would like to understand the work and lives of the people who made it all happen. You and your kids can ride, of course, in 1916 style. *Gift Shop, Programs*

📱 716 693-1885 • 180 Thompson St., North Tonawanda, NY 14120

🚗 North Tonawanda is just north of Buffalo. From I-290, take Exit 1 and go north on Delaware St. (384) through Tonawanda into North Tonawanda, to Thompson St.

🕐 July–Aug.: Mon.–Sun. 1 P.M.–5 P.M. Apr.–June, Sept.–Dec.: Wed.–Sun. 1 P.M.–5 P.M. Fee.

ORCHARD PARK

Burgwardt Bicycle Museum   This facility boasts over 300 bicycles from the 19th century on. There are bicycles that float and bicycles that shook your bones. Bicycles World War II paratroopers carried as they jumped. Kids' wheels. And, of course, bicycles built for two. Lots of other bike-related paraphernalia too.

📱 716 662-3853 • 3943 N. Buffalo Rd., Orchard Park, NY 14127

🚗 Orchard Park is a half-hour south of Buffalo. The museum is on Route 240/277, north of the center of town.

🕐 Apr.–Dec.: Mon.–Fri. 11 A.M.–5 P.M., Sun. 1:30 P.M.–5 P.M. Rest of year: closed Tues.–Thurs. Fee.

PALMYRA

Alling Coverlet Museum   Palmyra is chiefly known as the home of Joseph Smith and the birthplace of the Mormon church; the Hill Cumorah, its sacred site, is four miles south via Route 21. Back in town, this little museum has the largest handwoven coverlet collection in the United States and also shows quilts, rugs, and the kind of equipment all are made on. There's a lot of history worked into these pieces. *Gift Shop*

📱 315 597-6737 • 122 William St., Palmyra, NY 14522

🚗 Palmyra is 22 miles southeast of Rochester, at the intersection of Routes 21 and 31. The museum is 1 block east of the intersection and just north of Main St. (Route 31).

🕐 June–Sept.: Mon.–Sun. 1 P.M.–4 P.M. Other times by appointment. No fee.

PAUL SMITHS

White Pine Camp   The Adirondack Museum, an hour south of here in Blue Mountain Lake, is a tremendous resource. But if you're in this part of the Adirondacks, or if you'd like to see something a little different, this was Calvin Coolidge's Summer White House in 1926. It has been a refuge to other notables, and now it is being developed into a museum *of* the summer camp. On 35 acres there are at least 18 buildings open to view, along with paths and gardens. Historical displays focus on the architecture and social history of the "Great Camps" for which this region is famous. *Tours, Gift Shop, Food*

📱 518 327-3030 • White Pine Rd., Paul Smiths, NY 12970

🚗 Paul Smiths is in the northern part of Adirondack Park, about 10 miles northwest of Saranac Lake via Route 86. White Pine Rd. is on the right, half a mile before the junction of 86 with Route 30. White Pine Camp is 2 miles into the woods.

🕐 Late May–mid-Oct.: Mon.–Sun. 10 A.M.–5 P.M. Rest of year: guided tour daily at 1:30 P.M., or by appointment. Fee.

PURCHASE

Neuberger Museum of Art   This noted campus museum is based on the 20th-century American art collection of Roy Neuberger, whose interests range from Social Realism to Abstract Expressionism and in various other directions. There are also more recent European and Mexican acquisitions. And across Anderson Hill Rd. is Pepsico world headquarters, home to the Donald M. Kendall Sculpture Gardens (world-class outdoor sculpture, and fine landscaping too; call 914 253-2900 for information).

📱 914 251-6100 • State University of New York at Purchase, 735 Anderson Hill Rd., Purchase, NY 10577

🚗 Purchase is about an hour north-northeast of Manhattan. From the Hutchinson River Pkwy, take Exit 28. Go north on Lincoln Ave. and right on Anderson Hill to SUNY.

🕐 Tues.–Fri. 10 A.M.–4 P.M., Sat.–Sun. 1 P.M.–5 P.M. Fee.

WHITEHALL

Skenesborough Museum/Whitehall Urban Cultural Park Visitor Center   This little town in the most-fought-over area in America calls itself "the

Birthplace of the U.S. Navy," because Benedict Arnold built a fleet here in 1776 to fight for Lake Champlain. There's a diorama of that shipyard in the museum. But get this assortment of other displays: 19th-century fire equipment hanging from rafters, boat models, high-button shoes, antique dolls, Buel spoons (pioneering fishing lures), railroad and canal memorabilia, farming artifacts, and so on. Sound like you could get lost in here?

🔲 518 499-1155 • Skenesborough Dr., Whitehall, NY 12887

🚗 Whitehall is in northeastern New York, at the head (south end) of Lake Champlain. From I-87 take Exit 20 (Glens Falls) and follow Route 149E to Ft. Ann, then US 4 into Whitehall. Go left on Skenesborough Dr. just before the Champlain Canal.

🕐 Mid-June–Labor Day: Mon.–Sat. 10 A.M.–4 P.M., Sun. noon–4 P.M. Sept.–Oct.: Sat. 10 A.M.–3 P.M., Sun. noon–3 P.M. Other times by appointment. Fee.

· ·

LONG ISLAND

When we say Long Island, we mean Nassau and Suffolk counties, the land beyond Brooklyn and Queens. We have a feeling that this is a big (2.7-million-inhabitant) Unknown to people from outside New York City—and to many in the City too. So here is an assortment of museums, some having to do with early history (whaling, fishing, farming), some having to do with recent developments (abstract expressionism, guitars). For travelers, the Long Island Expressway (or L.I.E.) is I-495, and the Long Island Rail Road goes almost everywhere; the North and South Forks are at the East End; and most of the older, richer towns are along the North Shore, while the big beaches are along the South.

What's Big: In this category we place two institutions: the Museums at Stony Brook, a complex especially known for its carriage museum; and Old Bethpage Village Restoration, a 19th-century reconstruction complete with costumed guides.

BRIDGEHAMPTON

Bridgehampton Historical Museum   This is a good place to get a grip on the history of the Hamptons, as it maintains collections of such working artifacts as farm machinery, engines, and a wheelwright's tools but also mounts exhibits on such nonworking artifacts as resort clothing. There's a story here. *Tours*

🔲 516 537-1088 • Main St. at Corwith Ave., Bridgehampton, NY 11932

🚗 Bridgehampton is on the South Fork, between Southampton and East Hampton. Main St. is the Montauk Hwy (Route 27).

🕐 June–Labor Day: Thurs.–Sat. noon–4 P.M. Donation.

COLD SPRING HARBOR

Cold Spring Harbor Whaling Museum   A whaleboat, tools of the trade, hundreds of pieces of scrimshaw, paintings, models, and other displays detail the whaling history of this town, but for modern tastes there's also a focus on our cousins the whales.

🏠 516 367-3418 • Main St. (Route 25A), Cold Spring Harbor, NY 11724

🚗 Cold Spring Harbor is on the North Shore, just west of Huntington.

🕐 Memorial Day–Labor Day: Mon.–Sun. 11 A.M.–5 P.M. Rest of year: closed Mon. Fee.

EAST HAMPTON

Home, Sweet Home Museum   East Hampton didn't become a famous exurban artists' center until the post–World War II period, but long ago local boy John Howard Payne (1791–1852) had occasional success in a career that included acting and playwriting (as well as diplomacy). He is best known for the verse that gives this museum its name. You'll see fine period furniture and ceramics as well as an early-19th-century windmill and an herb garden. *Tours*

🏠 516 324-0713 • 14 James Lane, East Hampton, NY 11937

🚗 East Hampton is on the South Fork, beyond Southampton and Bridgehampton. The museum is on the green, facing Route 27.

🕐 Mon.–Sat. 10 A.M.–4 P.M., Sun. 2 P.M.–4 P.M. Fee.

Pollock-Krasner House and Study Center   This *is* the artists' East Hampton. The works of contemporary painters and others, including associates of Jackson Pollock and Lee Krasner, are shown in changing exhibitions, and you get to see the house. It's all run by SUNY Stony Brook. For more Hamptons art, there's also the Parrish Museum in Southampton (call 516 283-2118 for information).

🏠 516 324-4929 • 830 Fireplace Rd., East Hampton, NY 11937

🕐 By appointment only; call for directions.

HUNTINGTON STATION (WEST HILLS)

Walt Whitman Birthplace State Historic Site   Is this the suburban Long Island of today? Or is it the Paumanok of the poet's imagination? You could start your investigations at his first home, where they have a collection of books and manuscripts along with other artifacts and period furnishings. There's a Calder sculpture of Walt, too, and Himself's voice, preserved on wax cylinder. A good place to loaf and invite your soul. In Huntington Village there's also the Heckscher Museum, an esteemed fine-arts showplace, in Heckscher Park (call 516 351-3250 for information). *Tours, Gift Shop, Programs, Library*

🏠 516 427-5240 • 246 Old Walt Whitman Rd., Huntington Station (West Hills), NY 11746

🚗 Huntington Station is near the North Shore and just east of Cold Spring Harbor. From the Long Island Expwy, take Exit 49N onto Route 110N and follow signs.

🕐 Wed.–Fri. 1 P.M.–4 P.M., Sat.–Sun. 10 A.M.–4 P.M. No fee.

LOCUST VALLEY

John P. Humes Japanese Stroll Garden For a break from urban museum-going, we're suggesting a visit to a garden even garden people don't know about. Diplomat John P. Humes retired here and turned part of his estate into the classic garden in which one walks in tranquillity and reflectiveness before sitting down to tea. For a stroll in Japanese culture, we recommend this. Call about tea.

🏠 516 676-4486 • 347 Oyster Bay Rd., Locust Valley, NY 11560

🚗 Take the Long Island Expwy to Exit 39N. Go north and turn right on 25A for 3 miles. Turn left on Wolver Hollow Rd. to end, then right on Chicken Valley Rd. At 1.8 miles, turn right on Dogwood Lane and look for entrance on right.

🕐 Call for hours and fees.

NEW HYDE PARK

American Guitar Museum Everything from lutes and lutemakers' tools to high technology is featured in this salute to the ubiquitous instrument, of which there are also striking examples. It's not just a museum; they do repairs and service metropolitan-area guitarists in other ways. If you're one, you'll feel right at home. *Gift Shop*

🏠 516 488-5000 • 1810 New Hyde Park Rd., New Hyde Park, NY 11040

🚗 It's just over the line from Queens, and just west of Garden City. From the Long Island Expwy, exit south on New Hyde Park Rd., through North New Hyde Park.

🕐 Tues.–Fri. 10 A.M.–6 P.M. (Thurs. to 10 P.M.), Sat. 9 A.M.–5 P.M., Sun. and Mon. group tours by arrangement. No fee.

UPTON

Brookhaven National Laboratory (BNL) Science Museum Like Cold Spring Harbor, Brookhaven has been the scene of revolutionary developments in science—in nuclear energy production in particular. This museum's in the first reactor! There are all sorts of hands-on (how about a skeletal handshake?) displays, along with artifacts (if that's the right term) of research history. *Tours, Hands-on*

🏠 516 282-4049 • William Floyd Pkwy, Upton, NY 11973

🚗 Brookhaven is in eastern Long Island. Take Exit 68 north off the Long Island Expwy onto William Floyd Pkwy (SR 46).

🕐 Call for information. No fee.

NORTH CAROLINA

It was hard to find a certain type of "off-the-beaten-path" museum for North Carolina. Many of its institutions are rooted in its rich history, and with good reason. It's a contrast of coast, piedmont, and mountain life. It's the Venus's-Flytrap Capital of the World, the source of one of the first gold strikes in the United States, where Pepsi-Cola got invented, where the first airplane took off, the home of Thomas Wolfe, where the first lunch-counter sit-in took place. Scarred greatly by the Civil War, the former "Rip Van Winkle" state is booming these days as the big T of tourism (Appalachian Mountain crafts, the Wilmington movie-making mecca, the exquisite beaches of the Outer Banks, the drive down the incomparable Blue Ridge Parkway) replaces the holy trio of textiles, tobacco, and furniture-making.

What's Big: In the mountains, the Museum of the Cherokee Indian in Cherokee and the Biltmore Estate in Asheville. The mid-state Piedmont section has the Duke Homestead State Historic Site in Durham, which will tell you all about a really big North Carolina theme, tobacco history. In Greensboro, stop at the Mattye Reed African Heritage Center. And in Winston-Salem is the Reynolda House Museum of American Art (besides the fine art collection, you may be interested to discover the bowling alley in this former tobacco-money home); the Museum of Early Southern Decorative Arts; and, at Wake Forest University, the Museum of Anthropology. On the southern coast, stop at Wilmington and see the extensive Mary Cassatt collection at St. John's Museum of Art and Michael Jordan's shoes at the Cape Fear Museum.

ASHEVILLE

Just a few miles east off the Blue Ridge Parkway is the town of Black Mountain, with its roots as a spiritual center (for the Cherokees, and now for more religious retreats than you could shake a snake at) and as a hotbed for artists and intellectuals from the '30s through the '50s at Black Mountain College. We send you there now because it's just plumb pretty, and for Pepper's Sandwich Shop, all decked out with a museum's worth of Dr. Pepper memorabilia. *While you're in the area, see also*: Lake Junaluska.

Thomas Wolfe Memorial   This 28-room white frame house from 1883 is Wolfe's boyhood home, and it's been restored to look like the boardinghouse it was when he was growing up in the 1920s. The story goes that his mother was so eager to please her boarders that young Tom was left to use whatever room happened to be vacant. You'll see how he preserved the atmosphere of the place in his writing. While you're here, don't miss Riverside Cemetery (704 258-8480), where you'll find Wolfe (and a replica of the angel from *Look Homeward . . .*), O. Henry (Wm. Porter), and a full complement of war heroes. *Tours, Gift Shop*
- 704 253-8304 • 48 Spruce St., Asheville, NC 28802
- Downtown.
- Apr.–Oct.: Mon.–Sat. 9 A.M.–5 P.M., Sun. 1 P.M.–5 P.M. Nov.–Mar.: Tues.–Sat. 10 A.M.–4 P.M., Sun. 1 P.M.–4 P.M. Fee.

AURORA

Aurora Fossil Museum   *Jaws*, up close and personal, but not all that scary because these shark teeth are millions of years old. Prehistoric shark teeth are among the favorite attractions at a museum that explains the geological and paleontological origins of the Coastal Plain. One room provides a view of ocean life 5 and 15 million years ago. Get your picture taken in the model of a giant shark's jaw.
- 919 322-4238 • 400 Main St., Aurora, NC 27806
- About 35 miles east of Greenville, right off Route 33, off Pamlico Sound near the coast.
- June–Aug.: Tues.–Fri. 9 A.M.–4:30 P.M., Sat. 9 A.M.–2 P.M. Sept.–May: Mon.–Fri. 9 A.M.–4:30 P.M., and by appointment. Hours may vary. No fee.

BAILEY

Country Doctor Museum   Before HMOs, before Dr. Kildare and Marcus Welby, M.D., there was the country doctor, a noble figure who made house calls in the dead of night. This museum lovingly re-creates the 19th-century offices of two of them, complete with all the tools of the trade plus their trusty 1912 Model T.
- 919 235-4165 • Vance St., Bailey, NC 27807
- About 25 miles east of Raleigh. Take US 64 to US 264 into town.
- Tues.–Sat. 10 A.M.–4 P.M., Sun. 2 P.M.–5 P.M. Fee.

BELHAVEN

Belhaven Memorial Museum   By the time of her death in 1962 (at the age of 92), farm wife and sometimes bear-hunter (she liked to wrangle with a rattlesnake every so often as well, we understand) Eva Blount Way had collected just about everything: 30,000 buttons, a pin from a cousin's hip, eyeglasses sized for a chicken, a dress from a 700-pound woman, an eight-legged pig, petrified walrus tusks, and, oh, the usual range of stuff in jars, like a 10-pound tumor, and a bunch of human hair. What drove the spirited Ms. Way? It's not certain, but, the way these things go, after a while Tar Heel folk knew they could find a home for whatever no longer fit in theirs. So she happily took it all in, wrote up its story (it's the story that makes this work), and saved it all for us.

🏠 919 943-3055/942-2242 • Main St., Belhaven, NC 27810

🚙 About 35 miles east of Greenville on Route 99, off Pamlico Sound near the coast.

🕐 Thurs.–Tues. 1 P.M.–5 P.M. Other times by appointment. No fee.

CHARLOTTE

While you're in the area, see: Kannapolis, Stanfield, Waxhaw

FAYETTEVILLE

John F. Kennedy Special Warfare Museum   Remember the Green Berets? They were Special Forces units that used guerrilla tactics against enemy troops in Vietnam. This museum tells their story and the story of special operations beginning in the 18th century. One odd fact about the Green Berets: they wore their legendary headgear without official authorization for almost ten years. The 82nd Airborne Division War Memorial Museum is just 1.5 miles to the west. *Gift Shop*

🏠 910 432-1533 • Bldg. D-2502, Fort Bragg, Fayetteville, NC 28307

🚙 Fort Bragg is just west of town. Follow signs to Ardennes St. and Reilly Rd.

🕐 Tues.–Sun. 11:30 A.M.–4:00 P.M. No fee.

FUQUAY-VARINA

Marvin and Mary Johnson's Gourd Museum   Marvin Johnson, a former high school math teacher, has spent a lifetime turning an ugly hard-rinded vegetable into art and oddities. Behind his ranch-style home 20 miles from Raleigh is a veritable gourd-fest that features more than 200 varieties of this unlikely art object. Ask Mr. Johnson to show you the intricately patterned and carved gourds that have been made into everything from "simple" painted penguins to model cars, a steam train, cartoon characters, musical instruments, and even a Madonna.

■ 919 639-2894 • PO Box 666, Fuquay-Varina, NC 27526

🚗 About 12 miles south of Raleigh, at US 401 and Hwy 55, opposite Kennebec Airport.

🕑 Mon.–Sun. dawn to dusk. No fee.

GREENSBORO

While you're in the area, see: High Point, Randleman, Winston-Salem

HIGH POINT

While you're in the area, see also: Winston-Salem

Furniture Discovery Center and the Furniture Hall of Fame　Located in the Furniture Capital of the World (125 furniture plants in the area), this museum of furniture manufacturing gives visitors a "hands on" introduction to the process of making furniture. Visitors can handle an air-powered nail gun to get the experience of assembling a frame for a loveseat or pick up a spray gun to apply the finish on a Queen Anne Highboy. Or design your own sofa or chair with a computer. Adjacent to the Discovery Center, located in a renovated warehouse, is the Angela Peterson Doll and Miniature Musuem, which houses a collection of 1,600 dolls, miniatures, and artifacts. *Tours, Gift Shop, Hands-on*

■ 910 887-3876 • http://www2.hpe.com/discovery • 101 W. Green Dr., High Point, NC 27260

🚗 From I-85 exit onto US 311W (Main St.). It's at the southeast corner of Main and Green.

🕑 Mon.–Sat. 10 A.M.–5 P.M., Sun. 1 P.M.–5 P.M. Closed Mon. from Nov.–Mar. Fee.

KANNAPOLIS

Fieldcrest Cannon Textile Exhibition　If you peek into Grandma's linen closet, you'll probably find a handful of towels with the Cannon label. Here's where it all began: a company town founded in the late 19th century, whose name (ka-NA-polis, Greek for "City of Looms") pays homage to the area's historic textile industry. The exhibition features the world's largest towel, an antique loom, and cotton fabric from a 1,700-year-old Egyptian tomb, and tells you everything you've ever wanted to know about sheet-making, short and otherwise.

■ 704 938-3200 • Cannon Village Visitors Center, 200 West Ave., Kannapolis, NC 28081

🚗 Northeast of Charlotte, take Kannapolis Exit 58 or 63 off I-85 and follow signs.

🕑 Mon.–Sat. 9 A.M.–5 P.M., Sun. 1 P.M.–6 P.M. No fee.

KILL DEVIL HILLS

Wright Brothers National Memorial On December 17, 1903, Wilbur Wright—lying astride the 40-foot, 605-pound Flyer—made aviation history, after a few false starts, by keeping his primitive craft aloft for 59 seconds before it hit the sand at Kill Devil Hills. Now the beach is the site of a memorial that marks the distance of the four flights made by the brothers Wright on that first hallmark day back in 1903. Check out the full-scale reproduction of their original flying machine. Naturally, there is a 3,000-foot paved airstrip for visitors who want to fly to the memorial.

■ 919 441-7430 • US 158 Bypass, Kill Devil Hills, NC 27948

🚗 In the Outer Banks, just south of Kitty Hawk off the US 158 bypass, at Milepost 8.

🕐 Mon.–Sun. 9 A.M.–5 P.M. Fee.

LAKE JUNALUSKA

World Methodist Museum Methodism, under the leadership of John Wesley, began in England during the early 18th century as a dissenting force against the dominant Anglican Church. This museum tells that story. Among the artifacts you will find are John Wesley's "traveling pulpit," a lock of his hair, and some surprising items from the annals of religious history like the horse vertebra painted to look like a preacher—it was once used in saloons for target practice. *Tours, Library*

■ 704 456-9432 • 30 Lakeshore Dr., Lake Junaluska, NC 28745

🚗 About 25 miles west of Asheville, I-40 Exit Maggie Valley/Lake Junaluska and follow signs to the Methodist Assembly grounds.

🕐 Summer: Mon.–Fri. 9 A.M.–5 P.M., Sat. 9 A.M.–noon, 1 P.M.–5 P.M. Winter: Mon.–Fri. 9 A.M.–5 P.M. Donation.

NEW BERN

New Bern Civil War Museum Civil War buffs will be delighted with the large collection of Union and Confederate weaponry displayed here. You'll find a LeMat pistol, Colt revolving rifles, and rare carbines. Uniforms and camp furniture are also on display. The museum is located in the Colonial and Federalist period capital of North Carolina. Take the self-guided tour of this historic town, stopping at the New Bern Firemen's Museum (919 636-4087). *Tours, Gift Shop*

■ 919 633-2818 • http://www.collectorsnet.com/museums/nbmus.htm • 301 Metcalf St., New Bern, NC 28560

🚗 Take US 70E; it's off Pamlico Sound near the coast. At the corner of Pollock St. and Metcalf, and down the block from Tryon Palace.

🕐 Apr. 1–Sept. 30: Tues.–Sun. 10 A.M.–4 P.M. Fee.

RALEIGH/DURHAM

While you're in the area, see: Bailey, Fuquay-Varina, Smithfield

RANDLEMAN

Richard Petty Museum   He won hundreds of stock car races but lost his bid to be elected North Carolina secretary of state in 1996. Unlike stock car racing, victory in politics does not always go to the quick. Still, Petty is a Tar Heel legend whose accomplishments are heralded in displays of cars, trophies, and racing suits. Further tribute is offered in a 25-minute film that describes the life of the legend.

📞 910 495-1143 • 311 Branson Mill Rd., Randleman, NC 27317

🚗 Ten miles south of Greensboro, take the US 220 Level Cross exit, then follow signs east on Branson Mill Rd. 1 mile.

🕐 Mon.–Sat. 9 A.M.–5 P.M. Fee.

SMITHFIELD

Ava Gardner Museum   Ava Gardner was a rural Tar Heel girl, blessed with a beautiful face, who got into the movie business after her brother-in-law sent photographs of her to MGM. Several years later she signed a seven-year movie contract, married Mickey Rooney, quickly divorced him, and then married band leader Artie Shaw. She married once more (to Frank Sinatra) and starred in a host of classic films including *One Touch of Venus*, *The Sun Also Rises*, *Seven Days in May*, and *The Night of the Iguana*. This museum captures it all with film clips, costumes, and posters. While in Smithfield, visit the Howell Theatre, which has been delivering movie magic since 1935. *Tours, Gift Shop*

📞 919 934-5830/0887 • 205 S. 3rd St., Smithfield, NC 27577

🚗 Southeast of Raleigh, take US 70 (Business) into town, turning right onto 2nd St., then left on Johnson St. to 3rd St.

🕐 Mon.–Sun. 1 P.M.–5 P.M. Fee.

STANFIELD

Reed Gold Mine State Historic Site   Think of the nation's first gold rush and you might think of California in 1849, but gold fever hit North Carolina decades earlier when John Reed discovered the valuable element on his farm east of Charlotte back in 1799. The site of Reed's farm—the first documented gold strike in the U.S.—now features exhibits of mining equipment and the popular underground tour through 400 feet of tunnels 50 feet underground. Don't miss the steam hoist, which was used to haul miners and ore up and down the shafts. *See also* Dahlonega, Georgia's Dahlonega Courthouse Gold Museum. *Tours, Hands-on*

🚹 704 786-8337 • 9621 Reed Mine Rd., Stanfield, NC 28163

🚐 Northeast of Charlotte, take Route 24/27 (Albemarle Rd.) east, crossing US 601, and continuing on about 2 miles and over the Rocky River bridge, taking the left (Reed Mine Rd.) immediately after the bridge. It's a very curvy 2 miles down, on the right.

🕐 Apr.–Oct.: Mon.–Sat. 9 A.M.–5 P.M., Sun. 1 P.M.–5 P.M. Nov.–Mar.: Tues.–Sat. 10 A.M.–4 P.M., Sun. 1 P.M.–4 P.M. No fee, except for panning.

WAXHAW

Museum of the Alphabet   The origin of the world's languages is explored in a museum affiliated with an organization that translates and ships Bibles all over the world. You won't be saying "it's Greek to me" after examining exhibits on the Cyrillic, Roman, Aramaic, and Hebrew alphabets. East Asian and Native American languages, as well as the many oral traditions that are still unwritten, are also featured here. The exhibits' biblical interpretations aside, the analysis of how written languages are developed is covered quite nicely. *Tours, Gift Shop, Library*

🚹 704 843-6066 • JAARS Center, Davis Rd., Waxhaw, NC 28173

🚐 Just south of Charlotte at the intersection of Hwys 16 and 75.

🕐 Mon.–Sat. 9 A.M.–noon, 1 P.M.–3:30 P.M. Donation.

WINSTON-SALEM

While you're in the area, see also: High Point

R. J. Reynolds Tobacco   Forget about cancer and heart disease. This is the place to learn how cigarettes (up to 275 million daily) are made. A visit to R. J. Reynolds' 1.5-million-square-foot plant includes a tour of the spankingly sterile high-tech manufacturing floor as well as historical exhibits on tobacco growing, harvesting, and auctioneering. The tobacco industry's side of the story, and maybe the only place it's available these days since Philip-Morris chickened out and no longer welcomes visitors. *Tours, Gift Shop*

🚹 910 741-5718 • Whitaker Park Manufacturing Center, Reynolds Blvd. at N. Cherry St., Winston-Salem, NC 27102

🚐 Just north of downtown, take US 52/Hwy 8N to Akron Dr. exit, turning west onto Reynolds Blvd. and follow signs.

🕐 Memorial Day–Labor Day: Mon.–Fri. 8 A.M.–8 P.M. Rest of year closes 6 P.M. By tour only. No fee.

NORTH DAKOTA

The middle of a continent can be a hard place, and North Dakota is sure enough the middle of this one. People came here to shelter in the occasional river valley and eke out a farmer's life, or to hunt the buffalo. Later they came because railroads promoted the fertility of the prairie, and because there was so much land. While not proposing to deny that there are joys in the open spaces, we say Hats Off to everyone who made it here, and we imagine most of the museums in North Dakota will make you feel the same way.

What's Big: Unless you include the International Peace Garden, shared with Manitoba—and even there you aren't going to run into crowds—not a thing.

BELCOURT

Turtle Mountain Heritage Center This area became home to the Pembina Chippewa (Ojibwa), originally from the Great Lakes region, in the 19th century. In their fur trading, the band established relationships especially with the Métis, people of mixed French and native blood. The Heritage Center displays Chippewa and Métis arts and crafts, and there are dioramas and other displays and archives on local history. When you're here, you should also visit the Anishinaubag Intercultural Center, just north of Belcourt, where you'll see native habitations of several kinds (ask for directions at the Heritage Center). *Gift Shop*

🏛 701 477-6451 • Belcourt, ND 58316

🚗 Belcourt is in extreme northern North Dakota, just southeast of the International Peace Garden and the Manitoba line, on SR 5.

🕐 Memorial Day–Labor Day: Mon.–Fri. 8 A.M.–4:30 P.M., Sat.–Sun. 1 P.M.–5 P.M. No fee.

DICKINSON

Dakota Dinosaur Museum   A new (1994) presence on Dickinson's Museum Drive, this museum features ten full-scale dinosaur reconstructions, along with a wealth of bones, eggs, teeth, and other reptilian remains. There's a popular fluorescent rock display, along with fossils, minerals, and seashells. They love dinosaurs out here—on Father's Day weekend (Dinosaur Days), they even have a Dinosaur Hollering Contest! *Tours, Gift Shop, Hands-on, Programs*

■ 701 225-DINO [3466] • http://www.ctctel.com/dino • Museum Center at Dickinson, 200 Museum Dr., Dickinson, ND 58601

🚙 Dickinson is in southwestern North Dakota. Take I-94 to Exit 61, go south on Route 22, and turn left at first light (Museum Dr.) for the Museum Center at Dickinson.

🕐 June–Aug.: Mon.–Sun. 9 A.M.–6 P.M. Rest of year: Tues.–Sat. 9 A.M.–5 P.M., Sun. noon–5 P.M. Fee.

FARGO

While you're in the area, see also: Moorhead, MN

Roger Maris Museum   He was born in Hibbing, Minnesota, but Roger Maris grew up in Fargo, where he was a star high school footballer and played American Legion baseball. In 1983, when he was dying, Jim McLaughlin and others decided that the man who hit "61 in '61" needed his own "Hall of Fame," and here it is—his uniforms, bats, home run balls, gold glove award, earlier memorabilia, along with video replays of the end of his 1961 season. You can see it all by just coming to the mall. If you want to see Roger's grave, go to Holy Cross Cemetery, at 32nd Ave. North and University Dr., east of Fargo's Hector Airport.

■ 701 282-2222 • West Acres Shopping Center, Fargo, ND 58107

🚙 West Acres is at I-29 (take Exit 64) and 13th Ave. South in Fargo. If you're on I-94, take the I-29 exit. The museum is in a hallway at the mall, across from Sears, on the east side.

🕐 Jan.–Oct.: Mon.–Fri. 10 A.M.–9 P.M., Sat. 10 A.M.–7 P.M., Sun. noon–6 P.M. Nov.–Dec.: also till 9 P.M. Sat. No fee.

HATTON

Hatton-Eielson Museum   Carl Ben Eielson (1897–1929) is largely forgotten now, except perhaps in Alaska, where he flew the first airmail route (*see also* the Alaska Aviation Heritage Museum, Anchorage). After growing up in this house, he barnstormed the region, moved to Alaska in the early 1920s, and later pioneered transpolar flight, in both the Arctic and Antarctic, before crashing in the Bering

Strait. Here you'll see memorabilia of his youth, but also parts from the wreckage of his plane, returned from Russia in the 1990s.

🏠 701 543-3726 • 405 8th St., Hatton, ND 58240

🚗 Hatton is in eastern North Dakota, north-northwest of Fargo. From I-29, take Exit 111 onto Route 200W, through Mayville and Portland, then turn north on Route 18.

🕐 Mid-May–mid-Sept.: Sun. 1 P.M.–4:30 P.M. Other hours by appointment. Fee.

JAMESTOWN

National Buffalo Museum Here's the place to learn all about the American bison—and how we almost eradicated it. There are pictures, artifacts, and artwork inside, and a small herd of the animals outside. You also won't be able to avoid seeing "the World's Largest Buffalo" at the adjacent Frontier Village. Jamestown is also supposed to be building a museum to native Louis L'Amour. We think they should have one for native Peggy Lee also, but we haven't heard any rumors. *Gift Shop*

🏠 800 22-BISON [222-4766] • Jamestown, ND 58402

🚗 Jamestown is in southeastern North Dakota, on I-94. Take Exit 258N (Route 281) and turn right on 17th St. SW, following signs.

🕐 Summer: Mon.–Sun. 9 A.M.–8 P.M. Rest of year: Mon.–Sat. 10 A.M.–5 P.M., Sun. noon–5 P.M. Fee.

MAKOTI

Makoti Threshers Museum Out here in the wide open spaces, the Makoti Threshing Association maintains what it says is "the largest collection of stationary engines under one roof in the world." If you want to see the steam and gas engines that bring in the sheaves, come here. They put on a big Threshing Show each year in early October.

🏠 701 726-5594 • http://minot.ndak/cnatc/makoti.htm • Makoti, ND 58756

🚗 Makoti is in northwestern North Dakota, about 2 hours northwest of Bismarck. Take US 83 to ND 23 and go 24 miles west, then 1 mile south on Ward County Route 9.

🕐 Call 701 726-5643 for appointment, or stop by Makoti Cafe to arrange. Fee.

NEW TOWN

Three Affiliated Tribes Museum When Lewis and Clark came here in 1804, the Mandan and Hidatsa had been living along the Missouri River for some time, farming. They were later joined by the Arikara, a more southerly people. The museum details the history and displays the crafts of the three peoples. The nearby Four Bears Casino draws the crowds, but we think you're more serious than that.

🏠 701 627-4477 • North Dakota Hwy 23, Fort Berthold Indian Reservation, New Town, ND 58763

🚗 New Town is in northwestern North Dakota. See directions to Makoti. From Makoti, stay on Hwy 23 to New Town; museum is 4 miles west of town.

🕐 Mon.–Sun. 10 A.M.–6 P.M. In winter, may be closed due to severe weather. Fee.

RUGBY

Geographical Center Pioneer Village and Museum   You came here so you could stand smack in the center of the North American continent (there's a cairn marking the spot). To your surprise, you find a village/museum complex with a little bit of everything—old railroad depot, telephone switchboards, schoolhouse, hobo jungle, jail, etc. etc.—even a life-size replica of Clifford Thompson, a local who stood 8 ft. 7 in. tall! It takes at least an hour and a half to tour all this. *Tours, Gift Shop*

🏠 701 776-6414 • Rugby, ND 58368

🚗 Rugby is in north-central North Dakota, at the junction of US 2 and North Dakota Hwy 3. The museum is just east of the junction.

🕐 May–Sept.: Mon.–Sat. 8 A.M.–7 P.M., Sun. 1 P.M.–7 P.M. Fee.

STRASBURG

Ludwig and Christina Welk Homestead/Lawrence Welk Birthplace The bandleader was born and grew up here, practicing the accordion in the barn loft. The Welks were among the "Volga Germans," a people of whom many, having lived in central Russia for generations, came to the Great Plains in the late 19th century, bringing with them their agricultural techniques and their culture. Here you have not only the unlikely home of a television fixture, but a look at the life of a group important in Western history. *See also* the Lawrence Welk Museum in Escondido, California.

🏠 701 336-7519 • Strasburg, ND 58573

🚗 Strasburg is in southern North Dakota, an hour southeast of Bismarck. Take US 83N from Strasburg for 0.7 mile, then follow signs west (2 miles) and north to Homestead.

🕐 Mid-May–mid-Sept.: Mon.–Sun. 10 A.M.–6 P.M. Off-season: call for appointment. Fee.

OHIO

The first "Western" state to be heavily settled, Ohio thus has a relatively long history. It also has a lakefront, clay and silica, proximity to coalfields, and a number of other industrial necessaries. It is no surprise that it is as filled with museums to industry, invention, and economic history as any state in the Union. There are also, of course, all sorts of other showplaces, as the following selections will reveal.

What's Big: The Toledo Museum of Art; Dayton's U.S. Air Force Museum; Canton's Pro Football Hall of Fame; Akron's Inventure Place (National Inventors' Hall of Fame); major art and other museums in the three Cs—Columbus, Cincinnati, and Cleveland; and speaking of Cleveland, how about that Rock and Roll Hall of Fame?

AKRON

While you're in the area, see also: Kent

Goodyear World of Rubber   Akron's wealth was built on rubber (pardon the image), and here's a record of the empire Charles Goodyear began. There's Goodyear memorabilia and a re-creation of his workshop, as well as a depiction of later manufacturing processes and their chief end-product: tires. But it's not all auto industry: There's also a rubber-tree "forest" and an exhibit on another important Ohio rubber product, the blimp.

🏠 216 796-7117 • 1144 E. Market St., Akron, OH 44308
🚗 Exit off I-76 on the east side of Akron, onto SR 18, which is Market St. in the city.
🕐 Mon.–Fri. 8:30 A.M.–4:30 P.M. No fee.

BAINBRIDGE

Dr. John Harris Dental Museum   You may not have heard of Bainbridge, but certainly we all can relate to this: This little town is the "Cradle of Dental Education" in America. From John Harris' 1820s home office, now the museum, the first trained dentists spread out across the country. What you'll see includes antique instruments, tooth powder boxes, the world's largest display of Japanese wooden teeth, brushes, picks, and other artifacts, in addition to exhibits on the advances in dentistry through the 19th and early 20th centuries.

📱 614 634-2228 • Route 50, Bainbridge, OH 45612

🚗 Bainbridge is in south-central Ohio, about 20 miles southwest of Chillicothe and 65 miles east of Cincinnati on US 50.

🕐 Mid-June–August. Call for hours. Donation.

BARNESVILLE

Barbara Barbe Doll Museum   No, it's not "Barbie," although there is a collection of them here, among 3,500 dolls of all sorts. There are the Dionne Quintuplets, handmade by Barbara Barbe (1925–89), and there are the tin-headed Shirley Temples, Kewpies, Schoenhuts, and other types known to aficionados. It's a personal place, housed in a small onetime female seminary building.

📱 614 425-2301 • 211 N. Chestnut St., Barnesville, OH 43713

🚗 Barnesville is 25 miles west of Wheeling, West Virginia. From I-70, take Route 800 6 miles south into Barnesville. The museum is on the left at the 1st traffic light.

🕐 May–Sept.: Wed.–Sun. 1 P.M.–4 P.M., or by appointment. Fee.

BELLEVUE

Post Mark Collectors Club Museum   The Post Mark Collectors Club is a growing organization of those devoted not so much to stamps as to the ways stamps are canceled, and the ways letters were marked before stamps existed. The PMCC museum here keeps growing with new members and marks. It's in the old Lyme, Ohio, post office. Hobbyists as well as the historically minded will enjoy this stop. *Tours, Gift Shop*

📱 419 483-4949 • Historic Lyme Village, Bellevue, OH 44811

🚗 Bellevue is in northern Ohio, 50 miles west of Cleveland. Historic Lyme Village is 2 miles east of town on Route 113. From I-80/90, exit for Milan and take 113W.

🕐 Village: June–Aug.: Tues.–Sun. 1 P.M.–5 P.M. Call for other hours and specifics on PMCC Museum. Fee.

CAMBRIDGE

Degenhart Paperweight and Glass Museum   Cambridge is in the heart of Glass Country, which embraces eastern Ohio, western Pennsylvania, and northern

West Virginia. Elizabeth Degenhart, owner of Crystal Art Glass, left her collection to found this museum in 1978; in it you'll find those enchanting collectibles, paper-weights, along with pattern glass, glassware, and novelties. There are exhibits on techniques, and a research library. If you're a glass aficionado, Cambridge has several other sites you shouldn't miss. In town is the Cambridge Glass Museum (812 Jefferson Ave.; 614 432-3045), featuring the well-known local glass, ceramics, and marbles. At the US 40 exit off I-77 is the Museum of Cambridge Glass (614 432-4245), with a research library. And in town you can also see glass being made at Boyd's Crystal Art Glass (1203 Morton Ave.; 614 439-2077). One of the Cambridge Boyds, by the way, became the cowboy star Hopalong Cassidy (*see also* the American Heritage Center in Laramie, Wyoming); you'll find his memorabilia at the downtown Artisan Center (call 800 933-5480). In addition to a Glass Show in June, the city holds a Hopalong Cassidy Festival in May. *Gift Shop, Library*

🏠 614 432-2626 • Highland Hill Rd., junction of I-77 and US 22, Cambridge, OH 43725

🚗 Cambridge is in east-central Ohio. For the Degenhart Museum, exit from I-70 onto I-77N, then again onto US 22 toward the city.

🕐 Mar.–Dec.: Mon.–Sat. 9 A.M.–5 P.M., Sun. 1 P.M.–5 P.M. Jan.–Feb.: Mon.–Fri. only. Fee.

CENTERVILLE

International Women's Air and Space Museum   An 1806 house might seem an odd place for such a museum, but it's the house of Asahel Wright, the great-uncle of Wilbur, Orville, and Katharine. You haven't heard about Katharine, but she was an important supporter of her brothers. Some of the other women celebrated here are better known—women like Amelia Earhart, the sound barrier–busting Jacquelines (Cochran and Auriol), and Sally Ride.

🏠 513 433-6766 • 26 N. Main St., Centerville, OH 45459

🚗 Centerville is a southeastern suburb of Dayton. The museum is at the northeast corner of SR 48 and 725.

🕐 Sat. 10 A.M.–4 P.M. Special tours by request. No fee. The museum is developing; call regarding research library and other facilities.

CINCINNATI

While you're in the area, see also: Fort Mitchell, KY

Stowe House   Harriet Beecher Stowe lived here (it was actually the Beechers' house) in 1833–50, the period during which she heard the tales of slavery and escapes that led to *Uncle Tom's Cabin*. Today the house is a memorial to her and her family's efforts against slavery, and a museum of black life in the Cincinnati area. You may also want to visit the Rankin House, an hour southeast of Cincinnati in the little Ohio River town of Ripley, where the Rankin family hid and sent on their way to freedom hundreds of slaves, including the original of "Eliza" (call 513 392-1627 for information).

🏠 513 632-5120 • 2950 Gilbert Ave., Cincinnati, OH 45221

🚗 The Stowe House is 15 minutes northeast of downtown. Seventh Ave. becomes Gilbert Ave. as it approaches I-71; it is also SR 3.

🕐 Tues.–Thurs. 10 A.M.–4 P.M. Donation.

CIRCLEVILLE

Ted Lewis Museum   "Is Everybody Happy?" If you remember who asked, you may want to stop in at this little shrine to the bandleader (1890–1971) and see his famous top hat, his clarinet, and other memorabilia.

🏠 614 477-3630 • 133 W. Main St., Circleville, OH 43113

🚗 Circleville is in south-central Ohio, an hour south of Columbus on US 22 just off US 23.

🕐 Call for hours and other information.

CLEVELAND

Cleveland Police Historical Society, Inc., and Museum   Many policing innovations occurred in Cleveland, and here you'll see displays on the first traffic light, first call box, first use of ballistics in investigation, and first camera recording of a bank holdup. For crime fans, there's material on the 1935 Kingsbury Run Murders. For TV fans, there's material on Eliot Ness' post-Chicago career. Confiscated weapons, motorcycles, a jail cell, and narcotics paraphernalia fill the corners. *Tours*

🏠 216 623-5055 • Justice Center, 1300 Ontario St., Cleveland, OH 44113

🚗 It's downtown, at the corner of Ontario and St. Clair. The museum is in Police Headquarters, on the Justice Center's first floor.

🕐 Mon–Fri. 10 A.M.–4 P.M. No fee. Tours by reservation only.

Dittrick Museum of Medical History   In the heart of an educational/ medical complex, this museum has been collecting materials since 1894, and now has some 75,000 medical, dental, and pharmaceutical items, many displayed in period offices and a pharmacy. The evolution of the microscope is featured, along with such devices as surgical instruments and X-ray tubes. Down the road, at 8911 Euclid Ave., is the much bigger and splashier Health Museum of Cleveland (call 216 231-5010 for information), with Juno the Transparent Talking Woman. *Tours*

🏠 216 368-3648 • http://www.cwru.edu/cwru/chsl/museum.htm • Allen Memorial Medical Library, 11000 Euclid Ave. (University Circle—Case Western Reserve University), Cleveland, OH 44106

🚗 University Circle is 5 miles east of downtown. If on I-90, take Martin Luther King, Jr., Dr. south 3 miles, then left on Euclid. The museum is at the corner of Euclid and Adelbert, on the 3rd floor of the Library.

🕐 Mon.–Fri. 10 A.M.–5 P.M. No fee. Groups by appointment; fee for tours.

COLUMBUS

While you're in the area, see also: Plain City, Westerville

Thurber House   The ghost got in. The bed fell. Walter Mitty lived in glory. The Battle of the Sexes raged. Assorted dogs, men, and women carried on in their inimitable ways. With all this history, how could you stay away from James Thurber's home? Now there's also a Thurber Center, with various programs, next door at 91 Jefferson. There's a fine bookshop. And if all this isn't enough, and in tribute to Thurber's struggles with failing vision, you may want to nip over to the Ohio State campus and check out the eyeglasses of the great at the Optometry Museum; call 614 292-2788 for information. *Tours, Gift Shop, Programs, Library*

📞 614 464-1032 • 77 Jefferson Ave., Columbus, OH 43215

🚗 It's on the east side of Columbus, just west of the I-71/E. Broad St. (US 62) intersection.

🕐 Mon.–Sun. 10 A.M.–4 P.M. No fee.

DAYTON

While you're in the area, see also: Centerville, Vandalia

Paul Laurence Dunbar State Memorial   The son of former slaves, Paul Laurence Dunbar (1872–1906) was working as an elevator operator in Dayton when his dialect poems suddenly shot him to fame in 1896; for the rest of his brief life he was perhaps the most prominent African-American poet. In his house you'll see personal belongings and memorabilia of his career.

📞 937 224-7061 • 219 N. Paul Laurence Dunbar St., Dayton, OH 45407

🚗 The Dunbar House is west of downtown, off W. 3rd St. (SR 4).

🕐 Memorial Day–Labor Day: Wed.–Sat. 9:30 A.M.–4:45 P.M., Sun. noon–4:45 P.M. Reduced hours rest of year. Fee.

DELPHOS

Museum of Postal History   This is the Delphos post office. On the ground floor, if you ignore a few computers, you could have stepped back into 1933. But knock on Gary Levitt's "Postmaster" door, and step downstairs, and you'll really go back. There's a turn-of-the-century postal buggy, ancient uniforms and all sorts of gear, an inspector's room with displays on mail fraud, a stamp room, a collection of collection boxes, and much other postal incunabula.

🏠 419 695-2811 • 131 N. Main St., Delphos, OH 45833

🚗 Delphos is in northwestern Ohio, a half-hour northwest of Lima. Take US 30W from I-75 to 5th St. Delphos exit. Go south into city and left on Main St.

🕐 Mon., Wed., Fri. 1:30 P.M.–3:30 P.M. Call for other hours. No fee.

DENNISON

Dennison Railroad Depot Museum Dennison was a rail hub in the late 19th century, and this museum has rolling stock and artifacts and memorabilia of all sorts. But we suspect the reason many of you will want to visit is that in the 1940s this was Dreamsville—they estimate that 1.5 million GIs were solaced by volunteers at the Dennison canteen. Perhaps you were one of them; come back and they say they'll do it again. *Gift Shop, Food, Programs*

🏠 614 922-6776 • 400 Center St., Dennison, OH 44621

🚗 Dennison is an hour south of Canton, at the junction of US 250, US 36, and Ohio 800. Take the Dennison exit off 250, go south on 2nd St., and turn left on Center.

🕐 Tues.–Sat. 10 A.M.–5 P.M., Sun. 11 A.M.–5 P.M. Fee.

DOVER

Warther Museum Ernest "Mooney" Warther was one of those people who makes his particular kind of art—here, intricate carvings of trains, buildings, a "tree of pliers," etc.—from almost anything. Some is ivory, some ebony. You'll also see Frieda Warther's collection of over 70,000 buttons. *Tours, Gift Shop*

🏠 216 343-7513 • 331 Karl Ave., Dover, OH 44622

🚗 Dover is in east-central Ohio, a half-hour south of Canton on I-77. Take Exit 83; the museum is just east, on the way into town.

🕐 Mon.–Sun. 9 A.M.–5 P.M. Fee.

EAST LIVERPOOL

Museum of Ceramics There was clay and there was coal, and for a long time East Liverpool was Crockery City. Populated largely by immigrants from Stafford-shire, England, it peaked from 1870 to 1910, turning out the famous Lotus Ware and other varieties. Then the industry collapsed. Today, in the 1909 post office building, you'll see this history preserved. There are life-size dioramas of workspaces and machinery, along with artifacts and illustrations of East Liverpool's heyday.

🏠 216 386-6001 • 400 E. 5th St., East Liverpool, OH 43920

🚗 East Liverpool is in northeastern Ohio, on the Pennsylvania line, on the Ohio River. US 30 and Ohio Routes 7 and 11 enter the city. The museum is at the corner of Broadway.

🕐 Mar.–Nov.: Wed.–Sat. 9:30 A.M.–5 P.M., Sun. and holidays noon–5 P.M. Fee.

GRANVILLE

Granville Life-Style Museum (H. D. Robinson House)   What is it? It's the home of Hubert and Oese Robinson, and it's filled with family possessions going back to the early 19th century. When Oese died, in 1981, she stipulated that everything be kept as it was. If you're with a group, you may see a program like "Victorian Undergarments" ("appropriate for all ages . . . men and women") and learn to flirt with a paper fan. *Tours, Programs*

🏠 614 587-0373 • 121 S. Main St., Granville, OH 43023

🚗 Granville is in central Ohio, 35 miles east of Columbus. Exit from I-70 onto Ohio 37N to Ohio 661; this becomes S. Main St.

🕐 Mid-Apr.–mid-Oct.: Sun. 1 P.M.–4:30 P.M. Group tours by appointment, mid-Mar. through mid-Dec. Fee.

GREENVILLE

Garst Museum (Darke County Historical Society Museum)   This may be the ultimate example of eclecticism in a county historical museum. Here's some of what you'll see: Howard Chandler Christy's original painting *The Treaty of Green Ville*; a model of the Stutz Bearcat, which was designed by a local; the world's largest collection of Annie Oakley memorabilia; a representation of the Lohmann Telescope shop; a display honoring the greats of horse shoe pitching (Greenville is the "World Horse Shoe Pitching Capital"); Ed Schilling's Choo-Choo the Clown costume; the Iddings' Special "93" sprint car driven by Al Unser and others; and an exhibit on Harness Racing Hall of Famer Gene Riegle. Oh, and Lowell Thomas' (*see also* the Lowell Thomas Museum in Victor, Colorado) childhood home, which is next door. *Gift Shop*

🏠 937 548-5250 • 205 N. Broadway, Greenville, OH 45331

🚗 Greenville is 2 hours west of Columbus at the junction of US 36 and US 127.

🕐 Feb.–Dec.: Tues.–Sat 11 A.M.–5 P.M., Sun. 1 P.M.–5 P.M. Donation.

KENT

Kenneth W. Berger Hearing Aid Museum and Archives   This museum, named for its founder, who died in 1994, holds the world's largest collection of hearing devices, along with technical materials, advertising, and patents relating to them. From horns, trumpets, and mechanical resonators the collection moves through electronic and transistorized devices.

🏠 330 672-2672 • Music and Speech Building, Kent State University, Kent, OH 44242

🚍 Kent is just northeast of Akron. The Music and Speech Building is on Route 59 (Main St.).

🕐 Mon.–Fri. 8 A.M.–5 P.M. No fee.

KENTON

Dougherty House–Victorian Wedding Museum   Courtship and marriage in 19th-century America is the theme of this museum. Here you'll find costumes, furnishings, and other artifacts of romance gone by, with exhibits explaining customs we now think quaint (imagine if roles were reversed!). There are also toys, books, and games for children—logically. A block over, at 223 N. Main St., the Sullivan-Johnson Museum has displays including a sizable collection of Kentontoys, the cast-iron toys that made the city famous from 1893 to 1952.

🏠 419 673-7147 (Hardin County Historical Museums Inc.) • 215 N. Detroit St., Kenton, OH 43226

🚍 Kenton is in northwestern Ohio, about midway between Columbus and Toledo, on US 68 (which becomes Detroit St.) and US 31 (which becomes Main St.) The Dougherty House is in the 2nd block north of the courthouse.

🕐 Apr.–Dec.: Thurs.–Sun. 1 P.M.–4 P.M. Weekend hours Jan.–Mar. Group tours by appointment. Donation.

MARIETTA

Campus Martius: The Museum of the Northwest Territory/Ohio River Museum   Marietta is the oldest Ohio settlement, the gateway to the Northwest Territory and the settlement of the Midwest. Campus Martius was a fortification begun in 1788 to protect the move westward. Today, Rufus Putnam's home, Ohio's oldest, survives within the museum grounds. There are displays detailing the history of westward expansion, and on the subsequent move from the farms and from Appalachia into Ohio's cities. The adjacent Ohio River Museum tells the story of steamboats (and other craft) on the Ohio River, the main artery of westward expansion before the railroads. The 1918 W. P. *Snyder* is among the craft on view, along with a large collection of artifacts and displays on all aspects of river travel.

🏠 800 860-0145 • 601 2nd St., Marietta, OH 45750

🚍 Marietta is in southeastern Ohio, on the Muskingum and Ohio Rivers. Take Exit 1 off I-77 onto Route 7S, following signs for "Valley Gem Sternwheeler, Museums." The museum is at the corner of 2nd and Washington.

🕐 May–Sept.: Mon.–Sat. 9:30 A.M.–5 P.M., Sun. noon–5 P.M. Rest of year: closed Mon.–Tues. Fee.

MARION

Wyandot Popcorn Museum   Wow! Dozens of antique popping machines and peanut roasters! Clowns (it's a circus theme)!! A Popcorn Festival right after Labor Day!!! You may want to visit this museum before *or* after you drop in at the home of Warren Gamaliel Harding, which is also in town. *Gift Shop*

■ 614 387-HALL [4255] • Heritage Hall, 169 E. Church St., Marion, OH 43302

🚗 Marion is 45 miles north of Columbus on US 23. Exit onto SR 95W into the city; this is Church St., and Heritage Hall is the home of the Marion County Historical Society.

🕐 May–Oct.: Wed.–Sun. 1 P.M.–4 P.M. Rest of year: Sat.–Sun. only. Groups by appointment at other times. No fee.

NEWARK

National Heisey Glass Museum   The A. H. Heisey Company made fine glass in Newark from 1896 to 1957. The museum, in the 1831 King House, has eight rooms full of this highly collectible product, with patterns, molds, tools, experimental pieces, and other artifacts of the business. If the museum particularly inspires you, the Heisey Collectors of America headquarters are next door. *Gift Shop*

■ 614 345-2932 • W. Church St. and 6th St., Newark, OH 43055

🚗 See directions for following entry. Continue north on SR 79 into Newark, cross Main St., and turn right on Church St.

🕐 Mon.–Sun. 1 P.M.–4 P.M. Fee.

Ohio Indian Art Museum/Moundbuilders State Memorial   The people of the Hopewell culture (100 B.C.–A.D. 500) left the Newark area with the most extensive earthworks in the United States, spread over four square miles. In the immediate vicinity are the Moundbuilders, Wright, and Octagon sites, collectively the Newark Earthworks. This museum, the first devoted to the art of prehistoric Americans, shows items taken from the earthworks, including necklaces, bracelets, beads, ear ornaments, and items whose use is unclear. Also nearby is the noted Dawes Arboretum, which gives an idea of what the area's forest was like before white settlement (call 800 443-2937 for information). *Gift Shop*

■ 800 600-7174 • 99 Cooper Ave., Newark, OH 43055

🚗 Newark is 45 minutes east of Columbus. From I-70 exit onto SR 79N toward Newark; the memorial is across from Rockwell International's Newark facility.

🕐 Museum: Memorial Day–Labor Day: Wed.–Sat. 9:30 A.M.–5 P.M., Sun. noon–5 P.M. Reduced hours Sept.–Oct. Grounds: Jan.–Dec.: Mon.–Sun. daylight hours. Fee.

NORTH CANTON

Hoover Historical Center   The Hoovers lived here after the Civil War, and the museum details their life and displays equipment from their tannery. But then they bought the patent for an Electric Suction Sweeper. The rest is history, and you'll see it—rooms full of the new model Hoovers as they have appeared through the years, presented as a history of the American home. *See also* the Vacuum Cleaner Museum in Portland, Oregon, and while you're there, check out the Gabe Self-Cleaning House in Newberg, Oregon. *Gift Shop, Programs, Library*

🏠 330 499-0287 • 2225 Easton St. NW, North Canton, OH 44720

🚗 The museum is 15 minutes north of downtown Canton, near the intersection of SR 43 with Easton St. Take Exit 111 off I-77 and follow Portage St. east, following signs to Walsh University.

🕐 Tues.–Sun. 1 P.M.–5 P.M. No fee.

NORWICH

National Road/Zane Grey Museum   The National Road, which by 1840 extended from Maryland to Illinois, was the main land artery of western migration before the railroads came. Among early settlers were the family of the noted Western writer Zane Grey, who grew up in nearby Zanesville. This museum celebrates the road, with displays of vehicles and other artifacts, and Grey, with his trophies, manuscripts, and memorabilia (*see also* the Zane Grey Museum in Lackawaxen, Pennsylvania). It also celebrates Zanesville's importance as an early-20th-century art pottery center, with decorative vessels and tiles.

🏠 800 752-2602 • 8850 East Pike (US Route 40), Norwich, OH 43767

🚗 Norwich is in east-central Ohio, halfway between Cambridge and Zanesville. Exit from I-70 onto US 40 and follow signs.

🕐 May–Sept.: Mon.–Sat. 9:30 A.M.–5 P.M., Sun. noon–5 P.M. Rest of year: closed Mon.–Tues. Fee.

PLAIN CITY

Select Sires Bull Hall of Fame   The Hall of Fame, honoring at least 17 (the count as of August 1996) stud bulls with portraits and plaques, is only one part of the Select Sires complex, where you may tour the facilities, including the Production Center, and meet some of the workers themselves. This is said to be the world's largest artificial insemination operation. *Tours*

🏠 614 873-4683 • http://www.selectsires.com • 11740 US 42N, Plain City, OH 43064

🚗 Plain City is just northwest of Columbus. Take I-270 to US 33 and exit onto US 42N. Select Sires is at 1.7 miles on the right.

🕐 Mon.–Sun. 8:30 A.M.–4 P.M. No fee. Groups call to schedule tour.

SANDUSKY

Merry-Go-Round Museum   In the old post office building, this is an elegant setting for a fully restored carousel. There is also a re-created Dentzel shop (based on the 1867 original in Philadelphia), in which you can see the artistry and labor that went into the classic merry-go-rounds. *Tours, Gift Shop*

▪ 419 626-6111 • http://www.acess.digex.net/~rburgess • W. Washington (SR 6) and Jackson Sts., Sandusky, OH 44870

🚗 Sandusky is on Lake Erie, an hour west of Cleveland. Washington St. is SR 6; the museum is on the square, just west of the intersection with Columbus Ave. (SR 4).

🕐 Memorial Day–Labor Day: Mon., Wed.–Sat. 11 A.M.–5 P.M.; Sun. noon–5 P.M. Rest of year: closed Mon. Fee.

VANDALIA

Trapshooting Hall of Fame and Museum   This is the American Trapshooting Association's national headquarters, site of their annual tournament. The Hall of Fame has photographs and plaques of trapshooting greats, but the museum also houses displays of traps, targets, cartons, shells, guns (including celebrity items), pins, trophies, posters, and other artifacts of the sport. There's also a research library. *Programs, Library*

▪ 513 898-1945 • 601 W. National Rd., Vandalia, OH 45377

🚗 Vandalia is 15 minutes north of Dayton via I-75, and just north of the I-75/I-70 interchange. Exit from I-75 onto US 40W (National Rd.) and follow signs.

🕐 Mon.–Fri. 9 A.M.–4 P.M. Fee.

VERMILION

Inland Seas Maritime Museum (formerly the Great Lakes Museum)
This is the museum of the Great Lakes Historical Society, and it contains the Clarence S. Metcalf Library, a major source of research materials on the Lakes. There are also the pilothouse of the laker *Canopus*, a full-size replica of the Vermilion lighthouse, timbers from Commodore Perry's *Niagara*, and many models, engines, paintings, and other artifacts. *Gift Shop, Publications, Library*

▪ 800 893-1485 • 480 Main St., Vermilion, OH 44089

🚗 Vermilion is in north-central Ohio, on Lake Erie, an hour west of Cleveland. The museum is on the waterfront.

🕐 Mon.–Sun. 10 A.M.–5 P.M. Fee.

WAPAKONETA

Neil Armstrong Air and Space Museum   Neil Armstrong was the first Buckeye (and also the first human) on the moon, but hardly the first to defy gravity. This high-tech museum—which, nestled into rolling ground, looks a bit like the famous photo of earthrise from the moon—tells the story of Ohioans like the Wright Brothers, as well as the Armstrong story. You'll see the Gemini VIII craft, a spacesuit, a gallery of moon rocks, the airframe from the pioneer airship *Toledo*, a 1913 Wright seaplane, and much more. Kids especially will enjoy getting disoriented in the Infinity Room. *Gift Shop, Programs, Publications*

🏠 419 738-8811 • I-75 and Bellefontaine Rd., Wapakoneta, OH 45895

🚗 Wapakoneta is in northwestern Ohio, a half-hour south of Lima via I-75. The museum is at Exit 111 off I-75, outside town.

🕐 Mon.–Sat. 9:30 A.M.–5 P.M., Sun. and holidays noon–5 P.M. Fee.

WESTERVILLE

Motorcycle Heritage Museum   The AMA (that's the American Motorcyclist Association) is behind this celebration of cycles. Members have loaned many of the classic models in the continually changing displays. This place is about design, technology, competition, and experiment, but also about lifestyle and the image bikers have acquired. *Tours, Gift Shop*

🏠 614 891-2425 • 33 Collegeview Rd., Westerville, OH 43081

🚗 Westerville is just northeast of Columbus. From I-270 take the Cleveland Ave. North exit, go 1.5 miles and turn right on W. Main St., then right on Collegeview.

🕐 Mon.–Fri. 8:30 A.M.–5 P.M., Sat. 10 A.M.–4 P.M., Sun. noon–4 P.M. Donation.

WILBERFORCE

National Afro-American Museum and Cultural Center   Wilberforce is a name long prominent in abolitionism and black education. This new museum, on Wilberforce University's old campus, is a growing research center on African-American history and culture. Its main exhibit depicts the life of American blacks on the eve of the Civil Rights revolution of the 1950s and 1960s; both historic events and everyday life are detailed through artifacts and materials on lifestyles, arts, education, and history. *Tours, Library*

🏠 937 376-4944 • 1350 Brush Row Rd., Wilberforce, OH 45384

🚗 Wilberforce is in southwestern Ohio, a half-hour east of Dayton and just northeast of Xenia. Take US 42 into town and turn left (north) on Brush Row Rd.

🕐 Tues.–Sat. 9 A.M.–5 P.M., Sun. 1 P.M.–5 P.M. Fee.

YOUNGSTOWN

Youngstown Historical Center of Industry and Labor Have you been wondering where the Rust Belt is? The Mahoning Valley, with Youngstown its chief city, is at the buckle. This was Iron and Steel Country. When the industry had collapsed, in the early 1980s, this center was created to tell the story. In a striking Michael Graves building, you'll see who the workers were, where they came from, how they worked and lived, and some of the items they produced. Come here and see what it was like when the business of America was making things. *Programs, Library*

⬛ 330 743-5934 • 151 W. Wood St., Youngstown, OH 44501

🚗 Take I-680 into the city and exit for Market St. north. Go left on Wood St.

🕐 Wed.–Sat. 9:30 A.M.–5 P.M., Sun. and most holidays noon–5 P.M. Fee.

OKLAHOMA

▼▼▼▼▼▼▼▼▼▼▼▼▼▼▼▼▼▼▼▼▼▼▼▼▼▼▼▼▼▼▼▼▼▼▼▼▼▼▼

In Oklahoma you find everything and everyone seems to have even less than the normal six degrees of separation from Will Rogers. But it seems fitting, since, to paraphrase Mr. Rogers, it's hard to find anything about this state not to like, or certainly not to pique your interest. And its museums cover most all of its rich heritage—though notably missing a dedicated spot for native Woody Guthrie . . . and we still don't have word on a real twister museum either.

What's Big: As a respite from the ubiquitous Heckle & Jekyll oil pumps, and the *Okie from Muskogee* tune rambling around your brain, we offer you Muskogee's Five Civilized Tribes Museum; Tulsa's Gilcrease Institute and the Fenster Museum of Jewish Art; the Lynn Riggs Memorial in Claremore, celebrating the author of *Oklahoma!*'s original story (yes, they have a surrey); Oklahoma City with at least four different Halls of Fame (cowboys, photography, softball, and gymnastics); and in Tahlequah, the Cherokee National Museum.

ANADARKO

National Hall of Fame for Famous American Indians   Set in an outdoor garden, bronze sculptures of a select group of Indians (and people of Indian descent) who made contributions to both native society and to the American "way of life" are displayed and interpreted in a self-guided tour. The tour publication offers an in-depth background and history of each inductee as well as his or her tribe, and so provides a cultural panorama as well as a deeper appreciation of impressive individuals like Nez Perce leader Chief Joseph; Seminole chief Alice Brown Davis; Kiowa artist T. C. Cannon; Shawnee statesman Tecumseh; and the humorist formerly known as "The Cherokee Kid," Will Rogers. *Gift Shop*

📷 405 247-5555 • US 62E, Anadarko, OK 73005

🚗 About 65 miles southwest of Oklahoma City, take I-44S, then west on Hwy 9.

🕐 Mon.–Sat. 9 A.M.–5 P.M., Sun. 1 P.M.–5 P.M. No fee.

ARDMORE/MARIETTA LANDING

Mom-Pop's Grocery Store   Say you've been to the Gene Autry Museum a few miles north of Ardmore, and you'd still like to toodle around a bit. Well, we can send you in a search for Mom-Pop's Grocery Store, which it seems everyone has seen, but no one has been to—at least not anyone who lives nearby. Word is they have a copious baseball cap collection, some of them even autographed. If you strike out, you can visit the Tucker Tower Nature Center in Lake Murray State Park. Besides housing a meteorite that, in best 4-H style, is "one of the largest of its kind," it's an opportunity to see WPA dollars and labor put to work for leisure pursuit in this never-occupied medieval-fortress-style governor's retreat. *Food*

🏠 405 223-7765 • Hwy 77S, Lake Murray, Ardmore/Marietta Landing, OK
🚙 In south-central Oklahoma, take I-35S exiting onto US 77S. It's off the lake, between Ardmore and Marietta.
🕐 Store hours. No fee.

BARTLESVILLE

Bartlesville Museum in the Price Tower/Shin'enKan   Frank Lloyd Wright's only skyscraper—copper and glass-clad and based on a diamond module of 30- and 60-degree triangles—is the striking home of an art museum that features permanent exhibits on the eclectic architectural history of Bartlesville, "The City That Oil Built," including architect Bruce Goff's fantastical Shin'enKan or "Home of the Faraway Heart," with its feather-coated ceiling and walls of coal, tile, and glass. Unfortunately the actual Goff site burned down in late 1996, but this is the place to come to see some of the salvaged decorative elements, photos from as-it-was, and an in-depth video. *Tours*

🏠 Museum: 918 336-4949/Tours: 918 661-7471 • 510 Dewey Ave., Bartlesville, OK 74006
🚙 Forty miles north of Tulsa. Take US 75N to US 60, turning east to Dewey Ave., then north 2 blocks.
🕐 Museum: Tues.–Sat. 10 A.M.–3 P.M., Sun. 12:30 P.M.–3 P.M. Building Tours: Thurs. 1 P.M.–3 P.M. and by appointment. Donation.

CHICKASHA

Muscle Car Ranch   No sedate collection of muscle cars here. You're as apt to find a front end of a "Plum Crazy" purple 1970 Dodge Super B converted into a street light or a '69 Camaro Z-28 frame jutting nose first from a fish pond as you are to find all kinds of auto-related original porcelain and neon advertising signs. Seventy acres and seven barns full of the stuff, and a "car corral" showing off the best and most pristine of the classic cars and motorcycles Curtis Hart has been collecting these last 35 years. The local Grady County Museum (405 224-6480) also has transportation memorabilia, but with more of a railroad flavor and featuring Harvey House items.

🏛 405 222-4910 • http://www.okdirect.com/musclecarranch • 3609 S. 16th St., Chickasha, OK 73018

🚗 Thirty miles southwest of Oklahoma City. Take the second Chickasha exit off I-44 onto US 81S, proceed to the 3rd light and turn west onto Country Club Rd., then go 1 mile to 16th St. and turn south for 0.5 mile.

🕐 Mon.–Sat. 8 A.M.–8 P.M. No fee.

CLAREMORE

J. M. Davis Arms and Historical Museum   Woody Allen would have had a huge selection of "gubs" to choose from if he'd come here before his failed heist in *Take the Money and Run*. Over 20,000 of them in fact, all from Mr. Davis' personal collection and reflecting his goal to have one of everything. He's also got a great collection of World War I posters (and beer steins, musical instruments, and music boxes). A 500-year-old Chinese hand-cannon and the world's smallest manufactured gun get featured space along with a "Gallery of Outlaw Guns," and an exhibit on Samuel Colt's unique revolver design that took the Old West by storm—and whose manufacture led the way in America's industrial revolution. *Gift Shop*

🏛 918 341-5707 • http://www.state.ok.us/~jmdavis/ • 333 N. Lynn Riggs Blvd., Claremore, OK 74017

🚗 About 20 miles northeast of Tulsa, right on old Route 66.

🕐 Mon.–Sat. 8:30 A.M.–5 P.M., Sun. 1 P.M.–5 P.M. No fee.

CLINTON

Oklahoma Route 66 Museum   In case you somehow missed it, Route 66 "The Mother Road" has been rediscovered, luring as many or more overseas visitors as natives in their desire to look for America via its byways and off-road attractions. The first segments were officially designated in 1926, and the route grew to eventually extend from Chicago all the way to Santa Monica. And while you'll find a number of small and less formal repositories along the route, here in Oklahoma—the state with the most old-road miles (396 to be exact) intact—is the slickest and most complete tribute to the celebrated "auto river of the American West." For a true taste of the road-as-she-was, toot on over about 20 miles east to Hydro and cruise the stretch off Exit 89 just north of I-40, being sure to stop at octagenarian Lucille Hamons' 1941 souvenir stand and former gas station. *Tours, Gift Shop*

🏛 405 323-7866 • 2229 Gary Blvd., Clinton, OK 73601

🚗 About 75 miles due west of Oklahoma City, take I-40 Exit 65.

🕐 Memorial Day–Labor Day: Mon.–Sat. 9 A.M.–7 P.M., Sun. 1 P.M.–6 P.M. Rest of year: Tues.–Sat. 9 A.M.–5 P.M., Sun. 1 P.M.–5 P.M. Closed first week of Jan. Fee.

COYLE

Gerald Johnson Free Museum   Gerald Johnson's collection of "everything that ever was" does indeed cover as eclectic an assortment of cultural detritus as ever was. A sampling: Pancho Villa's doctor's utensils, a spot of the original wallpaper from Oklahoma's first capitol in Guthrie, a camel saddle from Casablanca, and a group of Pueblo Indian artifacts. A craftsman and ex-wrangler in his own right, Mr. Johnson grew up in this area, then ranched in New Mexico for years. What you see here is really his life, and boy, is it impressive. Now here's the deal. Mr. Johnson has just donated his entire collection to the Washington Irving Museum (405 624-9130) in Stillwater, a place he feels is copacetic in attitude. In his words, he expects the joint enterprise to be a great success because it "will have the facts that pertain to the Oklahoma history and not the movie picture of the people that played the life of the cowboy. We actually lived the life of the cowboy." A good chunk of the Indian relics are going there first, along with some of the cowboy stuff. The rest of the collection remains packed in its current home, an 1891 former saloon, for as long as Mr. Johnson wants to keep it going.

🏠 405 466-2440 • 216 E. Main St., Coyle, OK 73027

🚗 About 40 miles north of Oklahoma City. From I-35N, exit at Guthrie onto Hwy 33E for about 12 miles.

🕐 Mon.–Wed., Fri. by appointment. No fee.

DEWEY

Tom Mix Museum   He's not stuffed like Trigger, but silent western film star Mix's horse Tony—and his many ornate saddles and his unique leather stage shoes—is here in life-size replica along with oodles of early film and radio memorabilia from the career of Mix himself. *Gift Shop, Screenings*

🏠 918 534-1555 • 721 N. Delaware, Dewey, OK 74029

🚗 About 50 miles due north of Tulsa, on US 75.

🕐 Tues.–Sat. 10 A.M.–4:30 P.M., Sun. 1 P.M.–4:30 P.M. Closed Jan. Fee.

ENID

Mr. and Mrs. Dan Midgley Museum   Libbie and Dan Midgley liked rocks, so over the years, collect they did. They did so well as wheat and hay farmers in fact, that they were able to have their house especially constructed of the over 30 unusual types of rocks they'd gathered up through World War II. As you might have suspected, they'd gathered a few other things in their travels as well: Libbie and Dan's wedding cigars and toothpicks, an original hand-painted stage curtain, a large gypsum selenite crystal, one of the first electric toasters, a stuffed 1,800-pound buffalo, and a 7,000-pound petrified tree stump. *Gift Shop*

■ 405 234-7265 • 1001 Sequoyah Dr., Enid, OK 73703

🚗 Enid is in north-central Oklahoma at US 64 and US 81. It's at the corner of Owen K. Garriott and Van Buren Sts.

🕐 Apr.–Oct.: Tues.–Fri. 10 A.M.–5 P.M., Sat.–Sun. 2 P.M.–5 P.M. Nov.–Mar.: Wed.–Sat. 1 P.M.–5 P.M. No fee.

ERICK

100th Meridian Museum   Its largest collection is the historic photos that tell the story of of an early-20th-century railroad town, its population never growing larger than 1,700, and that was over 50 years ago. Named for its proximity to the western state line, the museum's housed in a bank building that's as old as Oklahoma's statehood—1907. The small town had its own kind of big days, as evidenced in the pictures, and farmers and ranchers, bankers and shopkeepers all played a part, as did the first autos in town and the local stretch of Route 66 and its steady pace of transcontinental traffic, the dustbowl days, Saturday at the local movie theater, and Friday night football games.

■ 405 526-3221 • 114 N. Main St., Erick, OK 73645

🚗 Western Oklahoma, right off I-40, 7 miles before the Texas border.

🕐 By appointment only. No fee.

FOYIL

Totem Pole Park   Foyil's been on the map since Cherokee homeboy Andy Payne won the 1928 "Bunion Derby" marathon across the United States. While most of that was run on the Route 66 stretch from L.A. to Chicago, and went right through Foyil, you'll need to head east a bit for this next attraction. The recently restored site of Ed Galloway's 1937–62 folk art creation includes a 70-foot concrete totem covered with birds, fish, and other mythical symbols of American Native tribes. Working out of an 11-sided single story building on site, he also built fiddles and the 12-foot arrowhead and assorted outdoor tables, chairs, and gateposts you'll find there today, all fashioned from carved and painted concrete.

■ Hwy 28A, Foyil, OK 74031

🚗 About 35 miles northeast of Tulsa, a few miles north of the Will Rogers Memorial. Take old Route 66 into Foyil, then turn east for 4 miles on Hwy 28A.

🕐 Dawn to dusk. No fee.

GAGE

Jim Powers Junk Art Museum   Jim Powers invites you to see some of his unusual art, all of which was made possible by "a Lincoln welder, a Victor cutting torch, and a lot of Junk discarded by the People of this area." But he does want you to know that not all people like his "type of art and you can feel free to call it the way you see it . . . you won't make anyone mad." We think it's worth a gamble. Some of his favorites are a balance beam that lets you move over 1,000 pounds with your little finger, the Baby Elephant, the Baby Camel, a space ship, and the Famous Jimmy Bird.

■ 405 923-7935 • Hwys 15 and 46, PO Box 145, Gage, OK 73843

🚙 Just inside the Panhandle, off US 283 at the junction of Hwys 15 and 46S on the south side of the baseball field.

🕑 By appointment only. No fee.

GENE AUTRY

Gene Autry Oklahoma Museum   Dedicated to "the Singing Cowboys of the 'B' Westerns," it's an especial tribute to 1937–42 "number one film cowpoke," Gene Autry. From the day in 1941 when 35,000 people showed up for the official town name-change from Berwyn to Gene Autry (pop.: 97 today), the loyalty and interest in these parts has not let up. The old schoolhouse is now the home of singing cowboy *and* cowgirl memorabilia, featuring all sorts of stuff from Autry's Melody Ranch and his radio show. While they haven't been able to lure Gene yet (90 in '97), the museum's late September annual Film and Music Festival is the place to be for a hit parade of Western stars of yesteryear. *Gift Shop, Programs*

■ 405 389-5335/294-3155 • PO Box 67, Gene Autry, OK 73436

🚙 In south-central Oklahoma, take I-35 Exit 40 (Springer) onto Hwy 53E for 7 miles.

🕑 Sat. 10 A.M.–4 P.M., Sun. 1 P.M.–4 P.M., and by appointment. No fee.

GOODWELL

No Man's Land Historical Museum   Oklahoma's panhandle was literally no man's land for the period prior to 1890 when it became part of the Oklahoma Territory. While no state or other territory had a claim on it then, its unfortunate location at the heart of the 1930s Dust Bowl tragedy certainly put it on the map decades later. This museum covers that history and a bit more of geology, paleontology, pioneer and American Indian artifacts, and includes the Duckett alabaster carvings collection. *Tours, Library*

■ 405 349-2670 • Panhandle State University, 207 W. Sewell St., Goodwell, OK 73939

🚙 Off US 54 in the heart of the Panhandle.

🕑 Tues.–Sat. 9 A.M.–noon, 1 P.M.–5 P.M. No fee.

GUTHRIE

National Lighter Museum   Ted and Pat Ballard have been collecting what they enjoy calling "Mechanical Pyrotechnic Apparatus" for decades, and now they certainly have more than anyone else (20,000 at last count), spanning more time (3,000 years) than anyone else. But what they also have is a contagious enthusiasm for their subject, which includes anything and everything that has to do with fire-making, from perpetual lighters from the 1700s to the stalwart Zippo. They're especially taken with the 20th-century use of lighters as "pocket billboard" corporate giveaways and have a healthy selection of these along with a remarkably varied range of devices, often clever in construct and in craftsmanship.

📠 405 282-3025 • 107 S. 2nd St., Guthrie, OK 73044

🚗 Off I-35 30 miles north of Oklahoma City, it's downtown next to, yes, the fire station.

🕐 Mon.–Sun. 10 A.M.–6 P.M. No fee.

HOMINY

Marland Station Wall of Memories   Hominy has gained some modern-day fame as a "City of Murals," with many local buildings now painted by Black-foot artist Cha' Tullis. But at least one wall, the one adjacent to the 1925 triangular Marland filling station, harkens to a different—though not without its Native American connection—heritage. The display of historic oil industry signs—Skelly, The Texas Co. (now Texaco), Cities Service (went Citgo), Gulf, Fire Chief, and Sunray-DX among them—and '20s and '30s road map collection reflect an era when a gas station was all about service. And an industry that in these parts owes its existence to the Osage Tribal Council's fateful 1896 decision to lease its reservation for petroleum and gas rights, leading to one of the greatest oil discoveries in U.S. history.

📠 918 885-4939 • Hominy Heritage Association, E. Main and S. Wood, Hominy, OK 74035

🚗 At junction of Hwys 99 and 20, about 35 miles northwest of Tulsa.

🕐 Outdoor signs have 24-hr. access. Call for other collection hours. No fee.

LAWTON

Percussive Arts Society Museum   No drum solo jokes, please. The Percussive Arts Society has put together a most impressive collection of historic instruments from around the world: an 11-foot wind chime, an aged Royal Air Force rope-tension drum, a 1941 Deluxe "Neo Classic" concert Grand Vibraphone, a New Guinea lizard-skin-headed Kundu, and a Balinese Joget Bun Bung. Its library is no slouch either—its archives range from vintage drum manufacturer catalogs to a Xylophone Marimba Collection with over 2,000 78s and 50 Edison wax cylinder recordings and the machine to play them on. *Gift Shop, Hands-on, Library*

📷 405 353-1455 • http://www.pas.org • 701 NW Ferris Ave., Lawton, OK 73502

🚗 In southwestern Oklahoma, take I-44 Exit 39B (2nd St.) onto Business Route 281S to NW Ferris, then turn right.

🕐 Mon.–Sat. 10 A.M.–3 P.M. Fee.

OKLAHOMA CITY

While you're in the area, see also: Coyle, Guthrie

Lee Way Motor Freight Museum   Begun by former employee Frank Swindle as sort of a memorial after the Lee Way Motor Freight Co. closed down in 1984, the collection has grown to include such items from the annals of motor freight history as a 1912 and a 1932 International (Lee Way's original vehicle-of-choice); slews of photos, driver awards, and trophies; Lee Way signs and promo materials; and a growing assortment of the same from other trucking and motor freight companies.

📷 405 682-8858/Appointment: 405 685-7968 • 2640 SW 59th St., Oklahoma City, OK 73119

🚗 Near the airport, take I-44 Exit 116A onto SW 59th St.

🕐 Tues.–Sat. 10 A.M.–2 P.M., and by appointment. No fee.

PAWNEE

Pawnee Bill Museum   Showman first and last, Gordon "Pawnee Bill" Lillie, Wild West show entrepreneur and sometime partner of Buffalo Bill Cody, left his mark on the West not just for his wild and wily reputation but for his prescient move to save the dying buffalo population at the turn of the century. Now you can visit the ranch where the former buffalo hunter and trapper and his wife—sharp-shooter and showstopper May Willie—spent their later years, and where indeed, the buffalo still roam.

📷 918 762-2513 • US 64, PO Box 493, Pawnee, OK 74058

🚗 Between Enid and Tulsa, east of I-35 on US 64.

🕐 Tues.–Sat. 10 A.M.–5 P.M., Sun.–Mon. 1 P.M.–4 P.M. No fee.

SHATTUCK

Shattuck Windmill Museum and Park   The brightly colored wind machines stand like giant children's playthings strewn about a backyard, but are in reality a testament to the earliest settlers and their sod-busting days as homesteaders here in the arid High Plains. Windmills were invented in New York in 1854 by Daniel Halladay, and the collection here—Althouse-Wheeler Giant, Elgin Hummer, Duplex vaneless, open-geared Dempster, and Challenge O.K. mills among them—dates almost as far back and includes some of the earliest wooden-wheeled models as well as early steel windmills. *Programs*

📷 405 938-2818/5146 • Hwy 15 and US 283, Shattuck, OK 73858

🚙 Just inside the Panhandle, at the junction of Hwy 15 and US 283.

🕐 Mon.–Sun. Daylight to dusk. No fee.

STILLWATER

National Wrestling Hall of Fame and Museum   The Oldest Sport has no connection to the Oldest Profession as far as we know, but the razzle-dazzle associated with it in the TV era gives one pause. Nevertheless, the sport considered here is one with a most respectable pedigree, and its American champions old and new, collegiate, Olympic, and otherwise famous—from George Washington to Stormin' Norm Schwarzkopf—are given their due. For the scoop on Norm Sr. check out the New Jersey State Police Museum (West Trenton). *Gift Shop, Library*

📷 405 377-5243 • 405 W. Hall of Fame Ave., Stillwater, OK 74075

🚙 About midway between Oklahoma City and Tulsa, it's 17 miles east of I-35 off Hwy 51, on the northeast corner of the Oklahoma State University campus.

🕐 Mon.–Fri. 9 A.M.–4 P.M., other times by appointment. Donation.

Sheerar Museum   Oklahoma is known for many things, but we'd bet you didn't know that it's also the home of the very first parking meter. Brainchild of Oklahoma City newpaper editor Carl Magee in 1935, it's no surprise it was more popularly known as a snitching post. The Sheerar is dedicated to state and local history, a rich heritage indeed, its survival as a Boomer settlement credited to "shrewd horse trading, prairie chicken, and champagne." It's also known for the Sheerar Button Collection, featuring over 3,500 of them dating from the 1740s to the 1930s. *Tours, Programs*

📷 405 377-0359 • 7th and Duncan Sts., Stillwater, OK 74076

🚙 See above. From Hwy 51 (it becomes 6th St.), turn right on Duncan to 7th St.

🕐 Tues.–Fri. 11 A.M.–4 P.M., Sat.–Sun. 1 P.M.–4 P.M. Tours by appointment. No fee.

TULSA

While you're in the area, see: Claremore, Hominy

OREGON

This is the paradise at the end of the Trail, and you can see from the museums we've listed below that all kinds of people have found it. But another "trail" appears to be feeding Oregon too—the trail from California to the rest of the world: There's a high proportion of truly idiosyncratic stuff here, some of it suspiciously close to major north-south highways. Oh well. It's an expansive state, and there are still vastnesses to lose yourself in.

What's Big: How about physically big? Two of the largest items in aircraft history are in Oregon, and oddly—*and* appropriately—they're made of wood. Howard Hughes' "Spruce Goose," the largest plane ever to fly, is at McMinnville's Evergreen AirVenture Museum; try going there and *not* seeing it. And Tillamook's Naval Air Station Museum incorporates Hangar B, built for World War II blimps; it's made of Douglas fir and encloses over seven acres—the "largest clear span wood structure in the world"! As for museums, we thought the Warm Springs Tribal Museum and Ashland's Pacific Northwest Museum of Natural History both looked intriguing but a bit heavily traveled for our purposes. And perhaps we don't need to point out, but we will, that the city of Portland has lots more than we've mentioned.

BROWNSVILLE

Living Rock Studios   Howard and Faye Taylor have here created a "memorial and monument" of agate, petrified wood, flagstone, concrete, and other materials. Most unusual are the seven large "living rock" pictures Howard created using thin-cut stone that is backlit; these depict the Flight into Egypt, Golgotha, and other biblical scenes. There are also sculptures (many of Oregon wildlife) carved from 100 different kinds of wood, and all sorts of stone—a complete geology of the country, Howard says. A petrified tree holds stairs to an upper level. *Tours, Gift Shop*

◼ 541 466-5814 • 911 W. Bishop Way, Brownsville, OR 97327

🚗 Brownsville is in east-central Oregon, 45 minutes north of Eugene. Take I-5 to Exit 216 and go 3 miles east on SR 228, to the city limits. The museum is easy to spot.

🕐 Tues.–Sat. 10 A.M.–5 P.M. Other times by appointment; call ahead to confirm. Fee.

COTTAGE GROVE

Cottage Grove Museum   This part of the Willamette Valley's promised land saw gold mining late in the 19th century, and the museum has an impressive ore stamp mill and collection of tools from the Bohemia District. But there are other reasons to stop by. This is the only octagonal public building (once it was a Catholic church) in the Pacific Northwest. There's an assortment of pioneer artifacts and memorabilia. And for *Titanic* enthusiasts (*see also* the *Titanic* Museum in Springfield, Massachusetts) there's a small exhibit based on belongings of a local resident who survived.

📷 541 942-3963 • H St. and Birch Ave., Cottage Grove, OR 97424

🚗 Cottage Grove is 20 miles south of Eugene via I-5.

🕐 Mid-June–Labor Day: Wed.–Sun. 1 P.M.–4 P.M. Rest of year: weekends only. No fee.

FLORENCE

Fly Fishing Museum   Put a master fine-arts framer and mounter together with master fly tyers and you get a special kind of art. Collect these miniatures and you get this museum, which displays the work of the late William Cushner. He didn't fish, but Cushner was consumed, as many have been, by the beauty and mystique of flies. Here they are combined with photographs and other artworks on the theme.

📷 541 997-6102 • 280 Nopal St., Florence, OR 97439

🚗 Florence is midway up Oregon's coast and 50 miles west of Eugene, on US 101 (the Pacific Coast Hwy). The museum is in the Old Town section east of 101.

🕐 Mid-May–Sept.: Mon.–Sun. 10 A.M.–5 P.M. Other times by appointment. Fee.

HOOD RIVER

Luhr Jensen Fishing Tackle Museum   The Luhr Jensen Company got its start in the Depression—what better time to go fishing?—and has expanded over the years, creating an empire by catering to the needs of sportsfishermen. A visit here will show you antique tackle and lures as well as tools formerly used to make lures; as for the modern stuff, you can take a factory tour. Hood River is also a mecca for windsurfers; ask these folks for information about tours of surfboard plants as well as the carousel museum almost next door. The Hood River County

Historical Museum (541 386-6772) is particularly strong in materials on the local fruit industry. *Tours*

📞 541 386-3811 • 400 Portway Ave., Hood River, OR 97031

🚗 Hood River is 63 miles east of Portland via I-84. Take Exit 63 and turn left over the freeway. Turn left onto Riverview St. and see Luhr Jensen Building on right.

🕐 Mon.–Fri. 9 A.M.–5 P.M., Sat. 9 A.M.–1 P.M. No fee. Groups should call ahead.

JOHN DAY

Kam Wah Chung and Company Museum Among the 19th-century gold rushers who came to California and then to areas like eastern Oregon, many were from the southern provinces of China. In the late 1870s, in fact, most of the non-native residents of this area were Chinese. This building, originally an 1860s trading post and later housing businesses (including herbal medicine) and immigrants, was central to the life of the Chinese community until World War II. *Tours*

📞 541 575-0028 (City Hall) • 450 E. Main, John Day, OR 97845

🚗 The city of John Day is in east-central Oregon, at the junction of US 395 and US 26.

🕐 May–Oct.: Mon.–Thurs. 9 A.M.–noon and 1 P.M.–5 P.M., Sat.–Sun. 1 P.M.–5 P.M. Fee.

MONMOUTH

Paul Jensen Arctic Museum Paul "Angyalik" Jensen died in 1995, but his museum remains one of few in the Lower 48 (*see also* the Peary-MacMillan Arctic Museum in Brunswick, Maine) at which you can get an impression of life and nature in the far north. Here you'll see polar bears, musk oxen, arctic wolves, and other magnificent animals; tools, clothing, and artwork of the region's people; and video and other representations of the arctic environment. *Tours, Hands-on, Programs*

📞 503 838-8468 • Western Oregon State College, 590 W. Church St., Monmouth, OR 97361

🚗 Monmouth is in northwestern Oregon, a half-hour west of Salem, on SR 99W. Take Main or Jackson St. west from 99W to Stadium Dr. Turn right and go to Church St.

🕐 Tues.–Sat. 10 A.M.–4 P.M. No Fee. Tours by appointment.

NEWBERG

Gabe Self-Cleaning House/Business Building Authority Frances Gabe wants you to know that this is *not* a museum. What it is, is the house she's spent decades developing into a place where women (or anyone, we assume) will be freed forever from the tyranny of housework. If that's been your fantasy, call her and arrange for a visit to see the inventions she's filled the "SCH" with (a few teasers: self-dusting books! a sprinkler system that doesn't wait around for a fire!). *Tours*

■ 503 538-4946 • Newberg, OR 97132

🚗 Newberg is 20 miles south of Portland. Call for directions.

🕐 By appointment only. Fee.

PENDLETON

Pendleton Round-up Hall of Fame   Pendleton's Round-up, in September, is one of America's biggest rodeos, and dates back to 1910. So there's a lot of "Wild West" history here. The centerpiece is Warpaint, a bucking bronc who has you under his (fortunately, post-taxidermist) hoof. Feast yourself on all sorts of gear, Indian artifacts, and pictorial tributes to the sport's greats.

■ 800 524-2984 (outside OR)/800 824-1603 (in OR)/541 276-2553 • 1205 SW Court Ave., Round-up Grounds, Pendleton, OR 97801

🚗 Pendleton is in northeastern Oregon, on I-84. The Hall of Fame is under the south grandstand of Round-up Stadium; use Exit 207 off highway.

🕐 Memorial Day–Sept.: Mon.–Sun. 10 A.M.–4 P.M., or by appointment. Donation.

PORT ORFORD

Prehistoric Gardens   This is a roadside attraction more than a museum, a good place to stop with your kids and stroll through a rain-forest valley where you'll come face to face with life-size dinosaurs and their contemporaries, looming among lush ferns and mosses. This is E. V. Nelson's passion, assembled pains-takingly since 1953. *Gift Shop*

■ 541 332-4463 • 36848 Hwy 101S, Port Orford, OR 97465

🚗 Prehistoric Gardens is on the Pacific Coast Hwy (US 101) about midway between Port Orford (north) and Gold Beach (south), in Oregon's southwestern corner.

🕐 Mon.–Sun. 8 A.M.–dusk. Fee.

PORTLAND

While the Cowboys Then and Now Museum has moved to Union, there's still plenty to consider in Portland. Like the apron exhibit at Powell's City of Books, or Kidd's Toy Town, or the windows at Van Calvin's Manikin Restoration Shop. And look for the Toaster Museum (currently on the Web), scheduled to pop up here from their old place in Seattle. *While you're in the area, see also*: Newberg, Saint Benedict. *In Washington, see*: Castle Rock, Stevenson.

American Advertising Museum   Opened in 1986, this museum celebrates the industry with displays of print, audio, and video advertising. Ads you'll see run from 18th-century trade notices through neon signs through claymation and celebrity endorsements. One of the most unusual items is the original Philip Morris bellhop's uniform. *Tours, Gift Shop, Library*
- 503 226-0000 • 50 SW 2nd Ave., at Ankeny St., Portland, OR 97204
- From I-5N take Exit 300B (City Center/Oregon City). Take next exit (Morrison Bridge/ City Center), cross bridge, then turn right onto 2nd Ave. From I-5S, take Exit 1A (City Center/Naito Ave.) and continue through 3 lights, turning right on 2nd. MAX: Skidmore Fountain.
- Wed.–Sun. 11 A.M.–5 P.M. Fee.

24-Hour Church of Elvis   Elvis acolytes on the West Coast have a friend in Stephanie Pierce, self-styled "celebrity spokesmodel/minister" who will welcome you to her realm of Elvisana and will arrange a wedding for you just as enthusiastically, legal and not. *Gift Shop*
- 503 226-3671 • http://www.churchofelvis.com • 720 SW Ankeny St., Portland, OR 97205
- Downtown between Broadway and Park, it's upstairs above the Thai restaurant. MAX: Pioneer Place.
- Fri–Mon. 9 A.M.–5 P.M., 8 P.M.–midnight; Tues.–Thurs. hours may vary. No fee.

UFO Museum   Does Lex Loeb know UFOs, or does he know UFOs? This place has everything you could ask for about space aliens and their machines, and Lex will explain it all. A Psychological Museum may join the UFOs soon, and Lex will explain *that* too. Look, where else can you see a streetwalker alien? Where but here is the Elvis Abduction Chamber? This is truly a "refuge from reality." (Well, almost. Major flooding in 1997 temporarily shut their doors, so call for current location.) *Tours, Gift Shop*
- 503 227-2975 • Portland, OR 97205
- The UFO Museum plans to stay in downtown Portland.
- Thurs.–Sun. 1 P.M.–6 P.M., Thurs.–Sat. 9 P.M.–midnight. Call to confirm. Fee.

Vacuum Cleaner Museum   They plan to redesign it, but for the moment the Stark's museum is a wonderfully cluttered room full of obsolete machinery. "Vacuum cleaners" have gone through various phases since the 19th century. There are pump types (think of pulling the air *out* of your bicycle tires), friction types, bellows types, and now there are entire houses with built-in intakes (you won't see one of *those* here). The dinosaurs are hiding out at Stark's. For the official history, *see* North Canton, Ohio, for the Hoover Historical Center.
- 503 232-4101 • http://www.starks.com • Stark's Vacuum Cleaner Sales and Service, 107 NE Grand Ave., Portland, OR 97232
- From downtown, cross the Burnside St. bridge (headed east) and turn left on Grand.
- Mon.–Fri. 8 A.M.–6 P.M. (to 8 P.M. Mon. and Fri.), Sat. 9 A.M.–6 P.M. No fee.

REDMOND

While you're in the area, see also: Sisters

Petersen Rock Gardens   Rasmus Petersen, a Danish immigrant farmer, began these gardens in the 1930s, and before he died in 1952 had covered several acres with castles, ponds, and bridges, using rocks he found in this part of Oregon. Part of the attraction is his artistry, and part is the rock samples themselves; many of the more unusual are in the museum, along with a fluorescent display. Watch out for the peacocks. *Gift Shop*

■ 541 382-5574 • 7930 SW 77th St., Redmond, OR 97756

🚐 Redmond is in west-central Oregon, on US 97. The gardens are about 7 miles south of Redmond (on the way to Bend) and 2.5 miles west of 97; look for signs.

🕐 Garden: open daily in summer 9 A.M.–9 P.M., winter 9 A.M.–dusk. Museum: open to 6 P.M. summer, 4:30 P.M. winter. Donation.

SAINT BENEDICT

Mount Angel Abbey Museum   This museum is known to some as "the Hairball Museum." Why? Its large-animal collection includes what is said to be the world's largest example, weighing some 2 pounds, from the stomach of a swine. What's going on here? Well, it helps to know that monasteries have a long history of maintaining museums. Mount Angel's happens to have a fine animal collection, but most of its displays have to do with monastic history and religious matters. Despite the hairball, this is actually a contemplative kind of place.

■ 503 845-3030 • One Abbey Lane, Saint Benedict, OR 97373

🚐 Saint Benedict is a half-hour south of Portland via I-5. Exit east at Woodburn to Hwy 214 to Mount Angel, then take Church St. east to the abbey and seminary.

🕐 Mon.–Sun. 10 A.M.–11:30 A.M., 1 P.M.–5 P.M. No fee.

SEASIDE

Seaside Museum and Historical Society   Seaside is where Lewis and Clark reached the Pacific in 1806. Since the late 19th century it has been a major ocean resort, reached from Portland before modern highways by the "Daddy Train," which reunited city men with their families on summer weekends. This had been home to the Clatsop, now completely gone. The virtue of this museum is that it tells the story of both peoples, through artifacts, pictorial displays, and restored buildings. *Gift Shop*

■ 503 738-7065 • 570 Necanicum Dr., Seaside, OR 97138

🚗 Seaside is 80 miles northwest of Portland, on US 101. From 101 (Roosevelt Ave.), turn west on 1st Ave. and north on Necanicum.

🕐 Mon.–Sun. 10:30 A.M.–4:30 P.M. No fee.

SISTERS

World Famous Fantastic Museum   Like its sibling in Yakima, Washington, this museum displays a bewildering assortment of celebrity, everyday, trivial, and peculiar items. Like Al Capone's vest and shotgun. Or over one million buttons. A huge collection of business cards. Barnum and Bailey's "Olaf the Giant" (a nine-foot mummy, according to some accounts). And so on. And so on. And so on. If your kids don't cotton to this kind of museum, there's pizza, bumper boats, and miniature golf too.

📱 541 549-4253 (Chamber of Commerce) • 222 W. Hood St., Sisters, OR 97759

🚗 From Redmond, it's 20 minutes west on Hwy 26.

🕐 Mon.–Sat. 9 A.M.–5 P.M., Sun. noon–5 P.M. Fee.

UNION

Cowboys Then and Now Museum   Once based in Portland, this collection has found a new home out in ranch country at the well-curated Union County Museum. Some of the exhibits here are about beef, not surprisingly, but it's mainly about the men (and some women) who took care of the beef on the hoof. You'll see everything from everyday apparatus (including a full chuckwagon) to that great downsizer of the profession, barbed wire, to round-up memorabilia (*see* Pendleton) to cowboy movie stuff—did someone say from the sublime to the ridiculous? Not us! It's laid out along a timeline, and there's a holographic cowpuncher. *Tours, Gift Shop, Hands-on, Library*

📱 800 848-9969/541 562-6003 • Union County Museum, 333 S. Main St., Union, OR 97883

🚗 Union is in northeastern Oregon. Just south of LaGrande, take I-84 Exit 265 onto Route 203S. It's about 12 miles to the center of town.

🕐 Mother's Day–Halloween: Mon.–Sat. 10 A.M.–4:30 P.M., Sun. 1 P.M.–4 P.M. Tours at other times by appointment. Fee.

PENNSYLVANIA

Pennsylvania has a museum problem. It's a problem more states should have. Put simply, it's that there's so much here it makes your head spin. Consider: This was one of the founding states, and has always been one of the most populous. Philadelphia was not only Pennsylvania's but the United States' first big city. Major events of the Revolutionary period and of the Civil War occurred here. All sorts of religious and national groups, along with certain remarkable individuals, settled here. There are rich farmlands and forests. And as if this weren't enough, Pennsylvania sits on top of vast deposits of hard coal (in the east), soft coal and iron ore (in the west), and even oil (northwest), so that when it was already rich in history and economy, it became, in the mid-19th century, critical to American industrial and transportation development.

Naturally, there are *lots* of museums. We've found it difficult to winnow them. In addition to some of the "big" museums, we're going to briefly mention sites in three key categories—coal, railroads, and oil.

Coal: The eastern hard coal country—the Anthracite Belt—is where the museum action is in this category. Three places you could explore in a day—they're in a line about 50 miles long, northeast to southwest—are Scranton's Anthracite Heritage Museum; the reconstructed miners' village of Eckley; and the Museum of Anthracite Mining in Ashland.

Railroads: The most significant railroad town in Pennsylvania is Altoona, where the Alleghenies were crossed and the Pennsylvania Railroad had its shops. The Railroaders Memorial Museum there could be the center of a trip that also takes in the nearby Allegheny Portage Railroad (remnants of a failed rail-and-canal scheme of the 1820s–30s) and Horseshoe Curve (where, in the 1850s, an effective all-rail conquest of the mountains occurred). Back east in Scranton, the new Steamtown National Historic Site has amassed a large collection of steam locomotives. In the Pennsylvania Dutch Country, just east of Lancaster, are the Railroad Museum of Pennsylvania (in Ronks) and National Toy Train Museum (in Strasburg). And if trolleys are your special passion, there's the Pennsylvania Trolley Museum in Washington, in the far southwest.

Oil: In the northwestern oil field, we've listed the Otto Cupler Company in Pleasantville. The big attraction in those parts is the Drake Well Museum in Titusville—

the site of the *first* oil well. A visit there might be combined with one to Historic Pithole City in Pleasantville (and to the Cupler museum).

What Else Is Big: See the Philadelphia and Pittsburgh entries for museums in those cities. Other sites we considered include the Johnstown Flood Museum, Brandywine Museum in Chadds Ford, Little League Museum in Williamsport, Cornwall Iron Furnace, Ephrata Cloister, and others. Some entire towns, like Gettysburg and Hershey, don't need a boost from us.

ALLENTOWN

The two museums we list here are actually in communities close to Allentown. They are both operated by the Lehigh County Historical Society (610 435-4664, PO Box 1548, Allentown, PA 18105).

Lock Ridge Furnace Museum   Anthracite coal and iron ore came together in the 1860s to make Alburtis a booming company town, a key to the Lehigh Valley's prosperity. At Lock Ridge you'll see the remains, partially restored, of an iron furnace complex that closed in 1921, and you'll also tour office, housing, and church, all part of the company complex. *Tours*

🏛 610 435-4664 • 525 Franklin St., Alburtis, PA 18011

🚗 Alburtis is just southwest of Allentown. From I-78/US 22, take PA 100S to Spring Creek Rd. and turn right. Cross the tracks and fork left on Church St. At the white church, fork right, then follow large brown signs.

🕐 May–Sept.: Sat.–Sun. 1 P.M.–4 P.M. No fee.

Saylor Cement Museum   At about the same time the anthracite-powered furnaces were at their peak, the Lehigh Valley was producing 75 percent of America's cement. David O. Saylor, a local, held the first U.S. patent for Portland cement. This museum is dominated by the spectacular Schoefer vertical kilns. As at Alburtis, you'll tour various buildings and learn about the lives and work of those who made this industry hum. *Tours*

🏛 610 435-4664 • 245 N. 2nd St., Coplay, PA 18037

🚗 Coplay is just north of Allentown. From US 22 take PA 145N to Lehigh St. Turn right, then left on Front St. into Coplay, where it becomes 2nd St.

🕐 May–Sept.: Sat.–Sun. 1 P.M.–4 P.M. No fee.

BEAVER FALLS

Air Heritage Museum and Aircraft Restoration Facility   This is an air museum at which you can get close to the work of restoration. Air Heritage focuses on World War II craft; you'll see a P-39, a P-40, and a B-25, among others. Memorabilia from both world wars, Korea, Vietnam, and aviation history in general is on display. *Gift Shop*

🏠 412 843-2820 • Beaver County Airport, Beaver Falls, PA 15010

🚗 Beaver Falls is 25 miles northwest of Pittsburgh. The airport is north of the city. From PA Route 60, take the Chippewa Route 51 exit west. Look for Taco Bell on right, then turn left at used car lot and look for signs to airport.

🕐 Mon.–Sat. 10 A.M.–6 P.M., Sun. noon–6 P.M. Donation.

BETHLEHEM

Kemerer Museum of Decorative Arts Annie Kemerer founded this museum in 1954 with her collection of furnishings and needlework, and it has grown into a well-respected showplace for 250 years of furniture, folk art, fine paintings, and other decorative items. Cast-iron toys, maps, glass and china, and clocks are among items in the permanent collection. Changing exhibits take on such themes as a century of American children's sleds. *Tours, Gift Shop*

🏠 610 868-6868 • 427 N. New St., Bethlehem, PA 18018

🚗 Bethlehem is in east-central Pennsylvania, just east of Allentown and west of Easton, in the Lehigh Valley. From US 22, take 378S to Center City exit. Go right at stop sign, and right again; proceed straight, then right onto New St.

🕐 Tues.–Sun. noon–5 P.M. Groups by appointment. Fee.

BIGLERVILLE

National Apple Museum This is apple country (names like Mott's and Musselmans come from the vicinity). It's appropriate that since 1990 this museum has been explicating the history of an industry developed by Scots-Irish and German farmers using stock from Russia and elsewhere. Find out about the old varieties and early methods of tending, picking, sorting, and processing. There's even a local Apple Core Band and National Apple Museum Dance Band—talk about going to "the Apple"! *Tours, Gift Shop, Library*

🏠 717 677-4556 • 154 W. Hanover St. (Route 394), Biglerville, PA 17307

🚗 Biglerville is in south-central Pennsylvania, 7 miles north of Gettysburg. The museum is just west of town, at the junction of Routes 234 and 394.

🕐 Apr.–Oct.: Sat. 10 A.M.–5 P.M., Sun. noon–5 P.M.; tours other times by appointment. Fee.

BOOTHWYN

Real World Computer Museum The Delaware Valley was the first Silicon Valley—home to ENIAC and Sperry Univac—and here they have displays from early calculating devices through computer-generated art and music. You can guide yourself through the history of computing or get them to take you around. *Tours, Gift Shop, Programs*

■ 610 494-9000 • http://www.uscphl.com/museum • Naamans Creek Center, 7 Creek Pkwy, Boothwyn, PA 19061

🚗 Boothwyn is in extreme southeastern Pennsylvania, on the Delaware border. From I-95S take Exit 3A (West Chester) and go 3 miles on US 322 (Conchester Rd.) to Naamans Creek Center; turn right.

🕐 Mon–Fri 9 A.M.–5 P.M., or by appointment. No fee.

COLUMBIA

Watch and Clock Museum of the National Association of Watch and Clock Collectors If you want to "know time," this is a good place to start. They have 10,000 items, everything from ancient water clocks and sand glasses through 19th-century monumental clocks to a working model of the first atomic clock. The museum of a large national organization, this is a place for serious researchers and horologists—but also for serious gawking. *Publications, Library*

■ 717 684-8261 • http://www.nawcc.org/nawcc/ • 514 Poplar St., Columbia, PA 17512

🚗 Columbia is in south-central Pennsylvania, 10 miles west of Lancaster. The museum is just off (south of) US 30; follow signs to Poplar and 5th.

🕐 Tues.–Sat. 9 A.M.–4 P.M. Also Sun. noon–4 P.M. in May–Sept. Fee.

CUSTER CITY

Penn-Brad Oil Museum Nowadays we think of Texas, Louisiana, or Alaska; but Pennsylvania was where the American oil industry started. Here, marked by a 72-foot wooden drilling rig, is a museum to the heyday of the 1870s–80s, when the Bradford area became "the first billion-dollar oil field." You'll see all sorts of antique equipment and early devices, as well as artifacts of oil country home life and a large collection of postcards and other visual materials. Industry veterans are on hand to talk oil talk. *Tours, Gift Shop*

■ 814 362-1955 • Route 219, Custer City, PA 16725

🚗 Custer City is in north-central Pennsylvania, 25 miles southeast of Jamestown, New York, and 3 miles south of Bradford, on US 219.

🕐 Memorial Day–Labor Day: Mon.–Sat. 10 A.M.–4 P.M., Sun. noon–5 P.M. Fee.

DOYLESTOWN

Fonthill Museum Doylestown has a remarkable cluster of museums, of which Fonthill is probably the least known. It is the castlelike home of Henry Chapman

Mercer (1856–1930), archaeologist, designer, ceramics innovator, writer, and anti-quarian. Built in 1908–10 of concrete, Fonthill is startling from without and amazing within, a monument to the Arts and Crafts period crammed with tiles, prints, and other decor. Next door is the Moravian Tile Works, where you'll see (and may buy) tiles made in Mercer's styles. In the center of town, at 84 S. Pine St., is the much more heavily visited Mercer Museum, where his huge collection of antique tools—anything you can imagine, and some stuff you can't, like a "vampire killing kit"—is spectacularly displayed (call 215 345-0210 for information). As if the "Mercer Mile" weren't enough, Doylestown is also home to the new (1988) but already well-known James A. Michener Art Museum (138 S. Pine St.; 215 340-9800), whose exhibits include works of a wide range of regional and nationally known artists and the furniture of Bucks County's George Nakashima. *Tours, Gift Shop, Programs*

■ 215 348-9461 • http://www.libertynet.org/~bchs • E. Court St. and Route 313 (Swamp Rd.), Doylestown, PA 18901

🚗 Doylestown is 25 miles north of Philadelphia. From the Pennsylvania Tpke, take Exit 27 and follow Route 611N into town. Turn right on E. Court St.

🕐 Mon.–Sat. 10 A.M.–5 P.M., Sun. noon–5 P.M. Guided tours only (last at 4 P.M.); reservations advised. Fee.

EASTON

Canal Museum   Here you're at the junction of the Lehigh and the Delaware, an appropriate place to learn about the history of America's canals, which flourished just before the railroads came, and made areas like the Lehigh Valley boom. Displays detail life on the barges as well as the development of a national canal system. In the summer you can ride on a canal boat. And it's an easygoing visit for you and your kids before or after a tour of Binney & Smith's Crayola Hall of Fame and factory, downtown's big attraction (at Two Rivers Landing, Centre Square; call 610 515-8000 or access http://www.crayola.com for information). *Tours*

■ 610 250-6700 • Hugh Moore Park, 200 S. Delaware Dr., Easton, PA 18044

🚗 Easton is 15 minutes east of Bethlehem and Allentown. Take Exit 22 off I-78 and go north into South Easton, where Hugh Moore Park is on PA 611 (S. Delaware Dr.).

🕐 Mon.–Sat. 10 A.M.–4 P.M., Sun. 1 P.M.–5 P.M. Fee. Call for information on boat rides.

ERDENHEIM

Business Card Museum   Ken Erdman has something like 400,000 items in his collection, and it sounds like a concept gone wild: There are cards made of everything from paper to leather to chocolate, cards in shapes you wouldn't have thought of, flashy cards, weird cards, celebrity cards. . . . But what this museum really constitutes, Erdman says, is heaven for graphic designers. Don't worry; you can come here and be serious too. *Gift Shop*

📍 215 836-0555 • 402 Bethlehem Pike (Route 309), Erdenheim, PA 19038

🚗 Erdenheim is just north of Philadelphia. From the Pennsylvania Tpke, take Route 309S from the Fort Washington interchange. Go about 3 miles and see the museum, a former school building with white columns, on the left side.

🕐 Call for appointment, preferably Mon.–Fri. 9 A.M.–5 P.M. No fee.

EXTON

Thomas Newcomen Library and Museum in Steam Technology and Industrial History/James R. Muldowney Printing Museum   The Newcomen Society, most of whose activities are devoted to celebrating "entrepreneurial ingenuity," the "American free enterprise system," and "corporate entities and other organizations" that represent the success of that system, here maintains a library devoted to steam technology's history. Included is a display of over 50 steam engines, from early-18th-century models of the Cornish inventor Newcomen (whose pioneer device may be said to have set off the Industrial Revolution, making the American system possible) through later American machines. Call ahead and arrange also to see James Muldowney's print shop/museum, where the Society's publications are produced, and where Mr. Muldowney will show thousands of etchings, demonstrate techniques, and answer questions on printing. *Tours, Publications, Library*

📍 610 363-6600 • http://www.libertynet.org/~newcomen • 412 Newcomen Rd., Exton, PA 19341

🚗 Exton is 20 miles west of Philadelphia via the Pennsylvania Tpke. Exit at Downington and take PA 100S, then exit east on Ship Rd. and go left on Newcomen.

🕐 Mon.–Fri. 10 A.M.–3 P.M. Weekends and evenings by appointment. No fee.

HARMONY

Harmony Museum   Harmony was the first home (1804–14) of George Rapp's Harmony Society, German pietists and communalists who settled here and flourished for ten years before moving to what is now New Harmony, Indiana (to follow their story there, visit the New Harmony Athenaeum; call 812 682-4488 for information). In 1824 the Society returned to Pennsylvania, establishing Old Economy at Ambridge, half an hour south of here. This original Harmony became a Mennonite town. The museum has displays on the Harmonists' background and American beginnings.

📍 412 452-7341 • on the Diamond, Harmony, PA 16037

🚗 Harmony is about 25 miles north of Pittsburgh via I-79, exiting west onto PA 68. Follow signs; the museum is in the town center.

🕐 June–Sept.: Tues.–Sun. 1 P.M.–4 P.M. Rest of year by appointment. Fee.

KENNETT SQUARE

Mushroom Museum at Phillips Place Visitors to the Brandywine's famous museums and gardens (in Pennsylvania and Delaware) are often reminded, when the wind is right, that they are in mushroom-growing country. This place details the history of mushrooms and gives you an idea of what their culture is like, through film, dioramas, other media, and, of course, fungi. *Gift Shop*

■ 610 388-6082 • 909 E. Baltimore Pike (US 1), Kennett Square, PA 19348

🚗 Kennett Square is in extreme southeastern Pennsylvania, 25 miles west-southwest of Philadelphia. Phillips Place is on US 1 just west of Longwood Gardens.

🕐 Mon.–Sun. 10 A.M.–6 P.M. Fee.

KUTZTOWN

Cut and Thrust Edged Weapons Museum/Co-op Gallery In this unlikely place (no, Kutztown doesn't get its name from "cut") you'll find a former bank filled with striking displays of swords, poles, battle axes, maces, shields, daggers, crossbows, helmets, and suits of armor. Ron and Lisa Howell, the proprietors, are engaged in trade, but during the summer you don't have to be a buyer or dealer to see all this steel, silver, and gold. *Gift Shop*

■ 610 683-5683 • 211–213 W. Main St., Kutztown, PA 19530

🚗 Kutztown is in east-central Pennsylvania, 20 miles west of Allentown via US 222.

🕐 Summer: Thurs.–Fri. and Sun. noon–5 P.M., Sat. 9 A.M.–5 P.M. Fee. Rest of year: dealers and collectors only. Call to confirm hours.

LACKAWAXEN

Zane Grey Museum The trail of renowned Western writer Zane Grey takes you to some unlikely places. Would you believe *Riders of the Purple Sage* was written in Lackawaxen? Or that the author had previously been a dentist, and you can see his instruments here? There's also his Morris chair, his drawings, his baseball shoes, photos of his prize fishing catches, and his former office and study. If you think it takes spurs and a ten-gallon hat to write Westerns, ride on over this way, pardner. *See also* the National Road/Zane Grey Museum in Norwich, Ohio.

■ 717 685-4871 • Scenic Dr., Lackawaxen, PA 18435

🚗 Lackawaxen is in extreme northeastern Pennsylvania, along the Upper Delaware River and the New York border, 35 miles east of Scranton. From I-84 at Port Jervis, New York, take NY 97N along the river to the Delaware Aqueduct/Roebling Bridge, cross to Pennsylvania, and follow signs.

🕐 Memorial Day–Sept.: Mon.–Sun. 10 A.M.–4:30 P.M. Reduced hours Apr.–May and Oct.–Nov. No fee.

LANCASTER

While you're in the area, see also: Columbia, Lititz

Lancaster Newspapers Newseum Here's a museum you don't even go into: Along Queen St., where the Lancaster Newspapers are produced, is a half-block-long window display of printing machinery, front pages, and other items detailing Lancaster's 200-year, 27-paper journalistic history, from stories of the post-Revolutionary era through the flexographic press that turns out today's dailies.

📞 717 291-8600 • http://www.lancnews.com • 28 S. Queen St., Lancaster, PA 17603

🚗 Lancaster is 60 miles west of Philadelphia. The Newseum is in the center city, 1 block south of Penn Square, along Queen St.

🕐 Open at all hours, but night is suggested. No fee, but dress according to weather.

LITITZ

Candy Americana Museum What did they do before chocolate was discovered? That's a good question, but not the one that's answered here. What did they do *after* chocolate was discovered? That's what this museum is about. There are artifacts of all aspects of the candy business, but the focus is on brown gold. Pots up to 200 years old, used to make candies and drinking chocolate, will excite you if you've somehow missed the scent from the adjoining factory. Don't worry—there's a candy store.

📞 717 626-3249 • Wilbur Chocolate Company Bldg., 46 N. Broad St., Lititz, PA 17543

🚗 Lititz is in southeastern Pennsylvania, 15 minutes north of Lancaster. Broad St. is Route 501; the museum is just north of the tracks and the Route 772 intersection.

🕐 Mon.–Sat 10 A.M.–5 P.M. No fee.

MERION

Barnes Foundation Here it is, possibly the most famous "little museum" in the world. They keep it little by limiting admissions, and their treasures are shown in intimate settings. There's nothing little about the collection, though—180

Renoirs? Sixty Matisses? When they lend this material out, attendance records are broken at the *big* museums. Albert Barnes, whose fortune was based on an anti-septic, had interests that were anything but lifeless, as the explosion of beauty here attests.

📍 610 667-0290 • 300 N. Latch's Lane, Merion, PA 19066

🚗 Merion is a suburb on Philadelphia's west side. Exit from the Schuylkill Expwy (I-76) onto US 1 (City Line Ave.) headed southwest, and turn right on Old Lancaster, then left on Latch's. Train: R5 from center city to Merion Station. Bus: #44.

🕐 Sept.–June: Thurs. 12:30 P.M.–5 P.M., Fri.–Sun. 9:30 A.M.–5 P.M. Admissions limited and on first-come, first-served basis; no children under 12 or unaccompanied under 15. Fee. Call to confirm hours and fees.

MIDDLETOWN

Three Mile Island Visitors Center   Videos, computer games, fiber optics, replicas of nuclear defueling tools, and other displays explain how at Three Mile Island "we make electricity safely and reliably" and how the plant "operates in harmony with the environment."

📍 717 948-8829 • Route 441S, Middletown, PA 17057

🚗 Middletown is 15 minutes southeast of Harrisburg. Three Mile Island is about 3 miles south of town along the Susquehanna River. Follow 441S, pass the plant, and look for the visitors center, another 0.75 mile on the left.

🕐 Thurs.–Sat. noon–4:30 P.M. Sun. also in June–Aug. No fee.

MIFFLINBURG

Mifflinburg Buggy Museum   We forget now that the American automobile industry was built on the foundation of the American carriage industry. If we remembered, the name of William Heiss, who built buggies here for 50 years, into the 1920s, would be heard along with names like Chevrolet and Ford. This museum preserves Heiss' home and the workshop, tools, and other appurtenances of a business that was once very big in this part of Pennsylvania. *Tours, Gift Shop*

📍 800 45-VISIT [458-4748] • 523 Green St., Mifflinburg, PA 17844

🚗 Mifflinburg is in central Pennsylvania, 15 minutes west of Lewisburg on Route 45. The museum is 2 blocks south of 45 (Chestnut St.), between 5th and 6th streets.

🕐 Thurs.–Sun. afternoons in summer, or by appointment; call for specifics. Fee.

NAZARETH

Martin Guitar Company   This modern plant is in the hands of the sixth generation of Martins—the original arrived from Germany in the 1830s, already a master of the craft. A tour here will show you the entire process of creating the instrument; the attached museum exhibits vintage guitars and other items relating to company history. *Tours, Gift Shop*

🏠 610 759-2837 • 510 Sycamore St., Nazareth, PA 18064

🚗 Nazareth is in east-central Pennsylvania, in the Lehigh Valley, north of Bethlehem and Allentown and northwest of Easton. The factory and museum are on the north side of town: take Broad St. north and turn right on Beil Ave. to Sycamore.

🕐 Mon.–Fri. 9 A.M.–5 P.M. Factory tours at 1:15 P.M. No fee.

NORTHUMBERLAND

Joseph Priestley House In England, Joseph Priestley (1733–1804) was a prominent Unitarian minister, a pioneer in the study of electricity and optics, and the first to isolate oxygen and to describe photosynthesis. Persecuted for his support of the American and French Revolutions, the "founder of modern chemistry" came to Pennsylvania in 1794 and continued his experiments, identifying carbon monoxide as well as writing on religion. Here are the home and relics of a man who even in old age remained in the scientific vanguard.

🏠 717 473-9474 • 472 Priestley Ave., Northumberland, PA 17857

🚗 Northumberland is in east-central Pennsylvania, about 45 miles north of Harrisburg. From I-80, exit on PA 54 to Danville, then proceed west (south) on US 11. In Northumberland, the Priestley House is 1 block south of 11.

🕐 Tues.–Sat. 9 A.M.–5 P.M., Sun. noon–5 P.M. Fee.

ORRTANNA

Mister Ed's Elephant Museum This is "the world's only gift/candy shop and elephant museum." Ed Gotwalt, who used to be a peanut dealer (no kidding) caught the pachyderm bug in the late 1960s, and now he has over 5,000 elephants—in every medium you can think of except flesh and blood. There's elephant clothing, elephant furniture, even elephant hair dryers. After this, if you feel like a little drive, you should pay a call on Lucy. *See* Margate City, New Jersey. *Gift Shop, Food*

🏠 717 352-3792 • 6019 Chambersburg Rd., Orrtanna, PA 17353

🚗 Orrtanna is in south-central Pennsylvania, 12 miles west of Gettysburg on US 30. Look for the white fiberglass, ear-flapping, talking Miss Ellie, who is over 9 feet tall.

🕐 Mon.–Sun. 10 A.M.–5 P.M. No fee.

PHILADELPHIA

Plan to spend a week. Or a month. Possibilities here get as "big" as the Philadelphia Museum of Art or the Franklin Institute. Among places we considered but didn't include are the Atwater Kent Museum (history of Philadelphia, in the original Franklin Institute building and named for a radio pioneer—enough to make you go out of curiosity); the Balch Institute for Ethnic Studies; and the Edgar Allan Poe National Historic Site. But don't miss former American Bandstand dancer Ron Caldera's Marilyn Museum. Yes, *that* Marilyn. (Call between 1 P.M. and 6 P.M. 215 755-5989, it's by appointment only.) *While you're in the area, see also*: Boothwyn, Erdenheim, Merion, Pottstown.

American Swedish Historical Museum   New Sweden was created in the Delaware Valley in 1638, and this, appropriately, is the oldest Swedish museum in the United States. Festivals and events occur through the year; call for information. If you're just dropping by, you'll see historical murals, Orrefors glass, a 1,000-year-old Viking sword, a re-created farmhouse (*stuga*) interior, artworks and artifacts of such noted Swedish-Americans as Carl Milles, John Ericsson, and Carl Larsson, and rooms devoted to Swedes who influenced America, among them Jenny Lind and Emanuel Swedenborg. *Gift Shop, Programs, Library*

📧 215 389-1776 • http://www.libertynet.org/~ashm • 1900 Pattison Ave., Philadelphia, PA 19145

🚗 It's in South Philadelphia's F. D. Roosevelt Park, just west of Broad St. (PA 611) and Veterans Stadium, near the corner of 20th and Pattison. Bus: #17.

🕐 Tues.–Fri. 10 A.M.–4 P.M., Sat.–Sun. noon–4 P.M. Fee.

Center for the History of Foot Care and Foot Wear (The Shoe Museum)   You think your feet could tell stories? Wait till you see this place! They've got everything from the tiny slippers once worn by Chinese women whose feet had been bound from birth to celebrity shoes of today. *Tours*

📧 215 625-5243 • Pennsylvania College of Podiatric Medicine, 8th and Race Sts., 6th floor, Philadelphia, PA 19107

🚗 It's a half-mile northeast of City Hall, and just southwest of Franklin Square, an easy walk from Independence National Historic Park. Subway: Broad St./Chinatown.

🕐 Wed., Fri. 9 A.M.–5 P.M., by appointment only. No fee.

Fabric Workshop and Museum   The Fabric Workshop has a growing reputation for its artist-in-residence program and the apprenticeships connected with it. What you'll see on exhibit here is representative of the forefronts of fabric art—installations, costumes, print multiples, works on paper, sculpture. The names are big, the students are talented, and the museum shop sells many items they produce. *Tours, Gift Shop, Programs, Publications*

📧 800 713-1315 • 1315 Cherry St., 5th floor, Philadelphia, PA 19107

🚗 It's just north and a block east of City Hall, near the corner of Cherry and 13th. Subway: Broad St./City Hall or Race-Vine.

🕐 Mon.–Fri 9 A.M.–6 P.M., Sat. noon–4 P.M. No fee.

Historic Bartram's Garden   In this now-industrial landscape sits the first American botanical garden, on the 1728 estate of the "father of American horticulture." If you're talking plant science, it doesn't get more "historic" than this. Linnaeus himself called Bartram the greatest botanist in the world. Here is the *Franklinia altamaha*, which he saved from extinction and named for his friend Ben Franklin. Here is the survivor of the first ginkgoes brought to this country, in the 1790s. There are 44 acres, with Bartram's house, outbuildings, arboretum, and surprising views of the city. *Tours, Gift Shop*

🏠 215 729-5281 • 54th St. and Lindbergh Blvd., Philadelphia, PA 19143

🚗 It's in southwest Philadelphia, on the Schuylkill River, across from downtown. From I-95S, take Exit 12 (Bartram Ave.) and turn right onto Island Ave., then right on Lindbergh Blvd. and go 3 miles to 54th St. Or take the #36 westbound trolley from City Hall.

🕐 Grounds open dawn to dusk year-round. No fee. Tours: May–Oct.: Wed.–Sun. noon–4 P.M. Rest of year: Wed.–Fri., same hours. Fee.

Mario Lanza Museum   Two blocks from his birthplace, this museum celebrates the meteoric career and brief life of the tenor, born in the year Caruso died and seen by Koussevitzky and others as a worthy successor, but who became a movie star so quickly there was little time left for opera. You'll see all sorts of personal items and memorabilia, and there are videos of his films. *Tours, Gift Shop, Screenings*

🏠 215 468-3623 • Mario Lanza Institute, at the Settlement Music School, 416 Queen St., 3rd floor, Philadelphia, PA 19147

🚗 It's in the heart of South Philadelphia. From I-95, take the Center City exit, follow signs to Historical Area, and go south on 6th St. past Independence Hall, then turn left on Christian St. for 1 block to Settlement Music School (on left). Bus: #57, 63.

🕐 Mon.–Sat. 10 A.M.–3:30 P.M. Closed Sat. in July–Aug. No fee.

Mummers Museum (New Year's Shooters and Mummers Museum)
O Dem Golden Slippers! If you've been around Philadelphia on New Year's Day, you know what this is about. Serious—and we do mean serious—silliness: America's largest parade of men in feathers and spangles. It's been going on for a long, long time. Here you'll see costumes and memorabilia, but even better, they'll teach you to strut to the famous string-band music. *Tours, Gift Shop, Library*

🏠 215 336-3050 • 1100 S. 2nd, at Washington Ave., Philadelphia, PA 19147

🚗 It's about 1.5 miles southeast of City Hall. Second St. parallels I-95; Washington Ave. crosses Broad St. Bus: #57.

🕐 Tues.–Sat. 9:30 A.M.–5 P.M., Sun. noon–5 P.M. Fee. Call to reserve guided tour.

Museum of Nursing History   The Pennsylvania Hospital is the nation's oldest (1751), and a fitting place for this tribute to the people who do the hardest jobs in health care. The focus of the permanent exhibits is on nursing artifacts—

uniforms, badges, obsolete nursing apparatus, and the like—but the archives have been growing since 1974 with diaries and other memorabilia of nurses all over the country, and some of this material is always available in changing displays. Also in the building is the hospital's famed surgical amphitheater. *Tours, Library*

🏠 215 951-1430 • Old Pine Building, Pennsylvania Hospital, 8th and Pine Sts., Philadelphia, PA 19141

🚗 It's a half-mile southeast of City Hall, near Society Hill, on the 3rd floor of the Pine Building, which is just south of Pennsylvania Hospital's main buildings. Bus: #40, 47, 90.

🕐 Mon.–Fri. 9 A.M.–5 P.M. No fee.

Mütter Museum, College of Physicians of Philadelphia

History of science, or cutting edge of taste? Among medical museums, this one may attract more thrill-seekers than others. It's where you come to see a tumor from Grover Cleveland's jaw, for instance, or parts from other prominent bodies. There is a skull collection, and an astonishing assortment of swallowed objects. It's also serious, though; you'll see all sorts of outmoded instruments, and you'll learn that advances in technique and technology have dealt with the problems that led some of the "contributions" to this museum.

🏠 215 563-3737 • 19 S. 22nd St., Philadelphia, PA 19103

🚗 It's 8 blocks west of City Hall and 1 block south of Market St., at the corner of 22nd and Ludlow. Trolley: 22nd St. Bus: #7, 12.

🕐 Tues.–Fri. 10 A.M.–4 P.M. Fee.

Rosenbach Museum and Library

This quiet museum and library preserves the legacy of the Rosenbach brothers, world-famous rare book, manuscript, and fine and decorative arts dealers. Imagine finding, in the same place, the manuscript of *Ulysses*, Marianne Moore's archives, Tenniel's original *Alice in Wonderland* drawings, the oldest (1482) printed Hebrew Pentateuch, huge amounts of Maurice Sendak's work, letters of Washington and Lincoln, thousands of oil portrait miniatures, Chippendale and Hepplewhite furniture . . . (pant, pant). *Tours, Gift Shop, Library*

🏠 215 732-1600 • 2010 DeLancey Pl., Philadelphia, PA 19103

🚗 It's about a half-mile southwest of City Hall, and just southwest of Rittenhouse Square. From Broad St. southbound, go right on Spruce, left on 21st, and immediately left on DeLancey. Bus: #17, 90.

🕐 By tour only, Tues.–Sun. 11 A.M.–4 P.M. (last tour 2:45 P.M.). Fee. Research library by appointment, Mon.–Fri 9 A.M.–5 P.M.

Wanamaker Museum

The former Wanamaker's store, with its famous eagle, organ, and interior court, is a sight you should see. Up on the eighth floor they've preserved the founder's office (having pioneered "department" stores, he died in

1922). Wanamaker was paternalistic, moralistic, and various other things charac-
teristic of many of the 19th century's merchant and industrial giants; this little
shrine will give you the picture.

📞 215 241-9000 • Lord & Taylor, 8th floor, 1330 Market St., Philadelphia, PA 19107

🚗 It's just east of City Hall. Subway: Broad St./City Hall; Market-Frankford/13th-Market.
Bus: #12, 17, 33, 48, 76. Trolley: 10, 11, 13, 34, 36.

🕐 Call to confirm hours. Fee.

PITTSBURGH

There's lots in the "big" category in Pittsburgh, much of it funded by big old
Pittsburgh money. The Carnegie, located (all but one unit) at the University of
Pittsburgh, is the premier complex of art, natural history, and science museums.
Farther east, in Point Breeze, is the Frick Art & Historical Center. And in the
North Side is the Carnegie's newest unit, the Andy Warhol Museum, which calls
itself the "largest single artist museum in the world." We think too many of you
are already headed for the Warhol for us to list it here—perhaps, you might say,
we were 15 minutes too late.While you're in the area, see also: Beaver Falls.

James L. Kelso Bible Lands Museum   Archaeological work in the Holy Land
has created the collections at this museum, where you'll see the kinds of pottery on
which a chronology of ancient Palestine is based, along with artifacts from Qumran,
Tell Beit Mirsim, and other sites. Cuneiform seals, coins, part of the Dead Sea Scrolls'
wrapping, ancient brick, and tools and utensils like a potter's wheel and comb are
among the finds contributing to an understanding of the biblical era. Not far away, if
you'd like to continue on the theme, is Carnegie-Mellon University's Rodef Shalom
Biblical Botanical Garden (4905 5th Ave.; call 412 621-6566 for information and
directions), where plants and setting illustrate religious history. *Tours, Programs*

📞 412 362-5610 • Long Administration Building, Pittsburgh Theological Seminary, 616 N.
Highland Ave., Pittsburgh, PA 15206

🚗 The seminary is in Pittsburgh's East End, about 5 miles from downtown and just south
of Highland Park and the Zoo.

🕐 Sept.–May: Wed. 9 A.M.–2 P.M. Other times, and tour guides, by appointment. No fee.

Mattress Factory   They did make mattresses here once, but now they make
installation art. If you think *museum* suggests the past, they'll adjust your attitude
at the Mattress Factory. Everything and anything, including yourself, may be part of
the work. The Andy Warhol Museum is ten minutes away.

📞 412 231-3169 • http://www.mattress.org/MFhome.html • 500 Sampsonia St., Pittsburgh, PA 15212

🚗 It's on the North Side, in the Mexican War Streets neighborhood. Take Federal St. north from Allegheny Center. Go left on Jacksonia to corner of Monterey. Park in lot on Jacksonia and walk around corner (down Monterey) into Sampsonia.

🕐 Tues.–Sat. 10 A.M.–5 P.M., Sun. 1 P.M.–5 P.M. No fee.

Stephen C. Foster Memorial For all the rustic aura of his compositions, Stephen Foster came from Lawrenceville, now part of Pittsburgh, and his native city remembers him with an archive and collection of artifacts relating to his and other American music. This is quite a contrast to the museum in White Springs, Florida, and the two together say something about the concept of "folk" music. *Tours, Library*

📞 412 624-4100 • University of Pittsburgh, Forbes Ave., Pittsburgh, PA 15260

🚗 The university is in the East End's cultural complex. The memorial is at the Cathedral of Learning, which is impossible to miss.

🕐 Mon.–Fri. 9 A.M.–4 P.M. Fee.

PLEASANTVILLE

Otto Cupler Torpedo Company's Nitroglycerin Museum Watching Civil War shelling gave the founder of this company the idea for the "torpedo," which blasts holes for oil drilling. The process was so successful, and so easy to imitate, that the period 1866–83 became known hereabouts as the Nitroglycerin or Torpedo Wars, as legitimate "shooters" and "moonshiners" fought for business. They don't use nitro in wells anymore, but the Otto Cupler people will show you the gear and artifacts, and, weather permitting, treat you to a blast or two. *Tours*

📞 814 827-2921 • 46730 Enterprise Rd., Pleasantville (East Titusville), PA 16341

🚗 Pleasantville is in northwestern Pennsylvania's oil field, 10 miles northeast of Oil City and just east of Titusville. Take Route 27E from Titusville to East Titusville and go left on Enterprise Rd. for 1 mile to Quonset hut on left.

🕐 By appointment only. Fee. Special effects tour subject to appropriate weather.

POTTSTOWN

Streitwieser Foundation Trumpet Museum Pottstown started with iron-making, and Pennsylvania is noted for its brass players (think the Bach Choir; think the Dorsey Brothers). What more suitable location for a trumpet museum? Horns are usually beautiful, always impressive objects, and here the acoustics are well thought of. The collection goes back thousands of years. How's your embouchure?

📞 610 327-1351 • 880 Vaughan Rd., Pottstown, PA 19464

🚗 Pottstown is 30 miles northwest of Philadelphia, on US 422. The museum is south of town. Exit from 422 onto PA 724 headed east, then turn south onto Vaughan Rd.

🕐 By appointment: Tues.–Fri. 10 A.M.–5 P.M., Sun. 1 P.M.–5 P.M. Fee.

TOWANDA

French Azilum   The story of fugitive French aristocrats, fleeing the Revolution or the uprising in Haiti, has given various American localities romantic myths. Here there actually were exiles, settled in the wilderness through the intervention of prominent Pennsylvanians. Marie Antoinette didn't make it, but the 84-foot-long Grande Maison (only traces remain) may have been built for her; Talleyrand and Louis-Philippe did visit. The houses were of log, which seems incongruous, but the wine cellar has been discovered, so life couldn't have been too harsh. You can tour the settlement and see its traces, along with reconstructions of buildings and gardens of the period. *Tours, Gift Shop*

■ 717 265-3376 • Towanda, PA 18848

🚗 Towanda is in northeastern Pennsylvania, about 45 miles northwest of Scranton. Take US 6N to Wyalusing, cross the Susquehanna (west), and proceed about 10 miles north on PA 187.

🕐 June–Aug.: Wed.–Sun. 11 A.M.–4:30 P.M. May and Sept.–mid-Oct.: weekends only. Fee.

UNIVERSITY PARK

Frost Entomological Museum   Penn State is highly successful at football, but nowhere near as successful as insects are at living; drop by the Frost museum to see some real winners. There are up to half a million of them here. Most have seen their day, but among those still buzzing you may see—and perhaps handle—giant cockroaches, gypsy moths, tarantulas, and related arthropods. There's also a functioning "bee tree." *Tours, Hands-on, Library*

■ 814 863-2865 • http://www.ento.psu.edu • Pennsylvania State University, Headhouse Three, Curtin Rd., University Park, PA 16802

🚗 University Park is part of State College, smack in the center of Pennsylvania. Exit from US 322 onto Park Ave. west, and turn into the campus on Shortlidge Rd. (left). Get a parking permit and map at the kiosk in front of Eisenhower Auditorium, in the 2nd block on the left.

🕐 Mon.–Fri. 9 A.M.–noon and 1:30 P.M.–4:30 P.M. No fee. Guided tours by appointment.

WHITE MILLS

Dorflinger Glass Museum   In the 19th century, Christian Dorflinger lead crystal was the top of the line in cut glass. Here's a display of dazzling glass along with artifacts of the works, seen in Dorflinger's home, the whole within a 600-acre wildlife sanctuary. In the summer there are also music and art festivals in this restful setting.

■ 717 253-1185 • http://www.ibcco.com/dorflinger • Dorflinger-Suydam Wildlife Sanctuary, Long Ridge Rd., White Mills, PA 18473

🚙 White Mills is in northeastern Pennsylvania, 25 miles east-northeast of Scranton. From US 6, turn east at the yellow blinker in White Mills and go uphill, through an intersection (stop sign) to the Dorflinger-Suydam Wildlife Sanctuary.

🕐 Mid-May–late Oct.: Wed.–Sat. 10 A.M.–4 P.M., Sun. 1 P.M.–4 P.M. Fee.

YORK

Harley-Davidson Motorcycle Plant and Museum (Rodney C. Gott Museum) Harleys are assembled here, although Milwaukee, Wisconsin, is headquarters. This is primarily a plant tour—you'll see new hogs that have never known black leather!—but the museum, with cycles from 1903 on, and related displays, provides background. Note that the plant is closed to tours when model changeover is going on (roughly, in July), but you can still see the museum. *Tours*

■ 800 673-2429 xHD • 1425 Eden Rd. (junction with US 30), York, PA 17402

🚙 US 30 and I-83 cross just north of York. From I-83 take Exit 9 and follow US 30E to Eden Rd., which runs north after about 0.7 mile.

🕐 Mon.–Fri. 10 A.M.–2 P.M. No fee. Kids under 12 not allowed on plant tour.

Weightlifting Hall of Fame Strongmanism doesn't have anything to do with Papa Doc or Marshal Tito. Like powerlifting, Olympic lifting, and bodybuilding, it has to do with weights. Here the York Barbell Company and the U.S. Weightlifting Federation laud the "Mighty Men of Old," as well as more recent standouts, male and female. Barbells, belts, photographs, competition data, and memorabilia of powermen and powerwomen are here. There's even a life bust of the "French Angel," the acromegalic wrestler Maurice Tillet. *Gift Shop*

■ 717 767-6481 • 3300 Board Rd., York, PA 17402

🚙 From I-83, take Exit 11. Board Rd. parallels the highway on the east side; the Hall of Fame is just north of the exit, in the York Barbell Company complex.

🕐 Mon.–Sat. 10 A.M.–4 P.M. No fee.

RHODE ISLAND

The formal title, "Rhode Island and Providence Plantations" (*plantation* was a form of colonial government), hints at the story. One part of Rhody—the islands and lower Narragansett Bay, basically—has been a playground, even with the naval presence. The Providence area, though—the top of the bay, the Blackstone Valley, and environs—started as a religious haven but long ago turned into an industrial and business hub. Most of what you'll find in the smallest state reflects this dichotomy.

What's Big: Newport. Consider visiting off-season, if possible.

BRISTOL

Haffenreffer Museum of Anthropology This is Brown University's anthropological museum. Its site is historically crucial: The Wampanoag lived here, and the death of Metacomet (King Philip) in a nearby ambush in 1676 ended the most serious of native wars against the settlers. The museum details not only North American traditional cultures but those of South and Middle America, Africa, Asia, and Oceania as well. *Gift Shop, Programs, Publications*

■ 401 253-8388 • 300 Tower St., Mount Hope Grant, Bristol, RI 02809

🚗 Take I-195 east from Providence to Exit 2, and go south on Route 136 for 7.5 miles. Watch for signs; the museum is 1.4 miles to the left on Tower St.

🕐 Sept.–May: Sat.–Sun. 11 A.M.–5 P.M. June–Aug.: Tues.–Sun. 11 A.M.–5 P.M. Other hours by appointment. Fee.

Herreshoff Marine Museum/America's Cup Hall of Fame Herreshoff is one of the big names in American yachting. The company built powerboats as well as sailing vessels including America's Cup defenders before closing in the 1940s. Now you may see examples, models and memorabilia, and displays on the famed races. *Gift Shop, Programs*

■ 401 253-5000 • 7 Burnside St., Bristol, RI 02809

🚐 It's just south of downtown Bristol, 1.4 miles north of the Mount Hope Bridge. Burnside St. runs east, away from the bay, off Route 114.

🕐 May–Oct.: Mon.–Fri. 1 P.M.–4 P.M., Sat.–Sun. 11 A.M.–4 P.M. Fee.

NEWPORT

International Tennis Hall of Fame and Museum   The Newport Casino is where American tennis really got going with the 1881 U.S. Championships, which developed into the U.S. Open. The grass courts still host professional tournaments.

■ 401 849-3990 • http://www.tennisfame.com • at the Newport Casino, 194 Bellevue Ave., Newport, RI 02840

🚐 Bellevue Ave. runs south from the center of Newport.

🕐 Mon.–Sun. 9:30 A.M.–5 P.M. During tournaments in July and Sept., ticketholders only. Fee.

Museum of Yachting   The Hall of Fame for Single-handed Sailors is of special interest, but the museum also has an America's Cup Gallery and a wide variety of small craft, many restored here. Regattas and other programs are an important part of the institution's life. *Gift Shop, Programs*

■ 401 847-1018 • Fort Adams State Park, Ocean Drive, Newport, RI 02840

🚐 Fort Adams is southwest of downtown Newport, across the harbor. Take Thames or Bellevue Ave. south from the center and follow signs.

🕐 Mid-May–Oct.: Mon.–Sun. 10 A.M.–5 P.M. Winter: by appointment. Fee.

Rhode Island Fisherman and Whale Museum   Here's one (actually, two) for the kids. The museum aims to increase feeling for the life of the sea via hands-on exhibits (Pet a shark! Find out how difficult knots are to tie!) and educational programs. Out at the aquarium, kids explore the surf; at summer's end, they release sharks and other "displays" back to the ocean. *Hands-on, Programs*

■ 401 849-1340 • 18 Market Square (Seamen's Church Institute), Newport, RI 02840

🚐 Market Square is in the heart of downtown Newport. The Newport Aquarium is at Easton's Beach, on Route 138 east of town.

🕐 Mon., Thurs.–Sun. 10 A.M.–5 P.M. Fee. Aquarium open in summer: Mon.–Sun. 10 A.M.–5 P.M.

Touro Synagogue   You may visit the Touro only with a guide, and it is not always open; but we think you should not miss it. Built in 1763 for a Sephardic congregation, it is America's oldest active Jewish house of worship. Peter Harrison's design is justly famed. Nearby is the 17th-century Jewish cemetery.

■ 401 849-7385 or 847-4794 • 85 Touro St., Newport, RI 02840

🚐 Touro St. is just east of Newport's center. The synagogue is near the intersection with the north end of Bellevue Ave.

🕐 Open via tour only. Not open Sat. or on Jewish holidays. Hours vary; call for appointment. No fee.

PAWTUCKET

Slater Mill Historic Site   This is one of the most important American technological sites, where in 1793 Samuel Slater opened one of the country's first true factories on the Blackstone River. Today the historic complex specializes in group tours for students, but don't let that keep you older travelers from seeing the huge waterwheel, spinning machines, processing demonstrations, etc. *Tours, Programs*

■ 401 725-8638 • Roosevelt Ave., Pawtucket, RI 02862

🚗 It's just north of Providence. Take Exit 27 or 28 from I-95 and follow signs for Slater Mill.

🕐 June–Labor Day: Tues.–Sat. 10 A.M.–5 P.M., Sun. 1 P.M.–5 P.M. Mar.–May and Labor Day–Dec.: weekend hours. Fee.

PROVIDENCE

While you're in the area, see also: Bristol, Pawtucket

American Diner Museum   The big news in Providence is the 12-museum Heritage Harbor complex planned for the year 2000 in the old South Street Power Station. The first phase of construction has a temporarily abridged version of the Diner Museum opening at the complex. Housed next door to what else but a vintage diner, its displays are designed to "restore people's memories" and document the distinctive structures, from native Rhode Islander Walter Scott's first night-lunch wagon in 1872 through the 20th century. We can smell the coffee now. *Gift Shop, Food, Library*

■ 401 331-8575 x102 (Rhode Island Historical Society) • 360 Eddy St., Providence, RI 02901

🚗 I-95 Exit 20, onto I-95E to Exit 2 (Wickenden St.). At end of ramp turn right, going over the Point St. Bridge to the traffic light (Eddy St.). Turn right on Eddy and proceed 0.1 mile; it's on the right.

🕐 Mon.–Sat. 11 A.M.–4 P.M. No fee.

Culinary Archives and Museum at Johnson and Wales University   It calls itself "the Smithsonian of the Food Service Industry," and if you're a gastronome, you'll seek it out. The tools of the trade range back 5,000 years, but there's also plenty of modern equipment, along with the memorabilia of presidential chefs, a 16th-century Turkish culinary costume, more cookbooks than you can imagine, and thousands of other cooking, entertainment, and hospitality items. *Tours*

■ 401 598-2805 • 315 Harborside Blvd., Providence, RI 02905

🚗 Take I-95 to Thurbers Ave. (Exit 18) in Providence. Go east and turn right on Allens Ave., then left on Northup, downhill and into first parking lot. The museum is in a warehouse with an Art Deco–style arch.

🕐 Mon.–Fri. 9 A.M.–5 P.M., Sat. 10 A.M.–5 P.M. Closed major holidays. Fee.

SOUTH CAROLINA

Here's a state that, like Virginia and Massachusetts, has "big" history, and "big" sites, in profusion. The South Carolina visitor, unless headed for the beach, is probably going to get a heavy dose of life before the Civil War. Only recently, with the development of the I-85 corridor (Spartanburg, Greenville) has a Second Front opened; someday there will be lots of little museums there. In the meantime, we've identified a scattering of places around the state that are *not* Fort Sumter.

What's Big: Charleston, the whole nine yards; nearby gardens and plantations, like Drayton Hall, Boone Hall, and Middleton Place.

AIKEN

Aiken Thoroughbred Racing Hall of Fame and Museum   Aiken has been one of the nation's richest playgrounds. Here in C. Oliver Iselin's former carriage house you'll get a real sense of the life of the horsey set. Portraits, trophies, silks, sculpture, and a polo room contribute to the shrine.

🏠 803 642-7758 • Hopeland Gardens, Whiskey Rd. and Dupree Pl., Aiken, SC 29802
🚗 Aiken is in west-central South Carolina. Hopeland Gardens is off Whiskey Rd., which is Route 19, just south of the town center.
🕐 Oct. 15–May 15: Tues.–Sun. 2 P.M.–5 P.M., or by appointment. Donation.

CHARLESTON

Macaulay Museum of Dental History   Here we offer something entirely out of keeping with Charleston's houses and gardens—unless, we're tempted to say, all that beauty makes your teeth hurt. At the Macaulay you'll see things that will make you *very* glad for the advance of science. We're sure the same could be said for Charleston's new Medical Leech Museum (call 803 577-9143 if you dare).

■ 803 792-2288 • Medical University of South Carolina, 171 Ashley Ave., Charleston, SC 29403

🚗 Ashley Ave. runs roughly north-south, west of the center of downtown Charleston. The Medical University is north of Calhoun St.

🕐 Mon.–Fri. 9 A.M.–5 P.M. No fee.

COLUMBIA

South Carolina Criminal Justice Hall of Fame   A memorial to South Carolina lawmen killed in the line of duty, this is also of interest to cops and robbers buffs because it holds memorabilia of "G-man" Melvin Purvis, Dillinger's nemesis. You can learn a lot about the pursuit of moonshiners too.

■ 803 737-8600 • 5400 Broad River Rd., Columbia, SC 29210

🚗 Broad River Rd. is Route 176; the Hall of Fame is 10 miles northwest of downtown, next to the Criminal Justice Academy.

🕐 Mon.–Fri. 8:30 A.M.–5 P.M., Sat. 10 A.M.–5 P.M., Sun. 1 P.M.–4 P.M. No fee.

DARLINGTON

NMPA Stock Car Hall of Fame/Joe Weatherly Museum   The best time to be here, obviously, is nowhere near a race day. The museum has cars from Johnny Mantz's 1950 Plymouth, the first Southern 500 winner, to Bill Elliott's 1985 Ford. There are displays on each of the Hall of Fame members, and other arcana such as illegal items removed from competitors' machines. *Gift Shop, Screenings*

■ 803 395-8821 • Darlington Raceway, 1301 Harry Byrd Hwy, Darlington, SC 29532

🚗 Darlington is in northeastern South Carolina, near Florence. Exit from I-95 onto US 52N, then SC 151/34W, following signs.

🕐 Mon.–Sun. 8:30 A.M.–5 P.M. Fee.

GEORGETOWN

Rice Museum   Georgetown, at the mouth of the Pee Dee River behind the Grand Strand, was once the rice exporting capital of the world. This museum tells the story of Low Country rice culture in artifacts, dioramas, paintings, photographs, and a model rice mill.

■ 803 546-7423 • Front and Screven Sts., Georgetown, SC 29440

🚗 Georgetown is in coastal northeastern South Carolina, at the junction of Routes 17 and 701. The museum is in the Old Market Building.

🕐 Mon.–Sat. 9:30 A.M.–4:30 P.M. Fee.

GREENVILLE

Bob Jones University Art Gallery and Museum   The Baroque Era is especially well represented in this collection, which has works by Rubens, Cranach, van Dyck, Rembrandt, Titian, Botticelli, and others. There are Russian icons, Renaissance furniture, vestments, and the Bowen Bible Lands Collection, which includes items from Egypt, Syria, and Israel, some 4,000 years old. *Tours*

■ 864 242-5100 x 1050 • 1700 Wade Hampton Blvd., Greenville, SC 29614

🚍 Wade Hampton Blvd. is Route 29; the university is on Greenville's northeast side. Ask at the Welcome Center for directions to the gallery.

🕐 Tues.–Sun. 2 P.M.–5 P.M. Closed some holidays. No fee. Dress modestly.

LAURENS

World's Only Ku Klux Klan Museum   Want to do a little fieldwork for us? The question is, does John Howard intend to exalt the Klan, of which he is a (former?) member, or is he just trying to tell its story—a cautionary tale, as it were? There have been rallies against Howard's operation, which started in 1996 with the Redneck Shop, selling Klan and Confederate souvenirs; you may have to pass pickets to find out. *Gift Shop*

■ 864 984-7484 • Laurens, SC 29360

🚍 Laurens is about 60 miles northwest of Columbia via I-26, then I-385. Take Exit 9 off 385 and proceed south into town via US 221. The Redneck Shop and museum are in the old Echo Theater building, just off the central square.

🕐 Call them for hours and terms of admission.

PARRIS ISLAND

Parris Island Museum   The Parris Island Museum is chiefly about the Marine Corps, and you'll find uniforms, weaponry, and other artifacts. But this is also an area that saw both French and Spanish attempts at settlement in the 16th century, and there are exhibits dealing with that part of history too.

■ 803 525-2951 • Marine Corps Recruit Depot, Parris Island, SC 29905

🚍 Parris Island is in extreme southern South Carolina. Take Exit 8 off I-95 and follow Route 21S, following signs. The museum is in Building 111.

🕐 Mon.–Sun. 10 A.M.–4:30 P.M. No fee.

ROCK HILL

Museum of York County   MYCO plans soon to relocate in downtown Rock Hill, where there's a thriving arts community. Out here on Mount Gallant Rd., the big attraction is the collection of over 200 African mammals, mounted in dioramas. There's also a collection of the work of illustrator Vernon Grant, changing exhibits of regional art, and lots of natural history and science for the kids. The Catawbas, York County's original inhabitants, are well represented. Downtown, check out the Center for the Arts at 121 E. Main St.; there was a stimulating show of outsider art when we were there (call 803 328-2787 for information). *Gift Shop, Hands-on, Programs*

● 803 329-2121 • http://web.cetlink.net/~myco.mycohome • 4621 Mt. Gallant Rd., Rock Hill, SC 29732

🚗 Rock Hill is 15 minutes south of Charlotte, North Carolina. From I-77, take Exit 82A. At the 2nd stoplight, turn right on Mount Gallant, and go 6 miles.

🕐 Mon.–Sat. 10 A.M.–5 P.M., Sun. 1 P.M.–5 P.M. Fee.

SAINT HELENA ISLAND

York W. Bailey Museum Penn Center was founded in 1862, once Union forces had taken control of the island, to educate freed slaves. The museum recounts the history of African-American Sea Islanders. Gullah, their language, is a focus of tape collections and research here.

● 803 838-2235 • Penn Center Historic District, Martin Luther King Dr., Saint Helena Island, SC 29920

🚗 It's in extreme southern South Carolina. Take Exit 8 off I-95 and follow Route 21S.

🕐 Tues.–Fri. 11 A.M.–4 P.M. Donation.

SPARTANBURG

George E. Case Collection of Antique Keyboards Members of the Case Brothers Piano Company family have placed their collection of early keyboards on permanent loan here. You will see pieces from the late 17th through the 19th century—reed organs, harpsichords, fortepianos, and others—affording an idea of the instruments the great composers wrote for.

● 864 503-5611 • Library, University of South Carolina at Spartanburg, 800 University Way, Spartanburg, SC 29303

🚗 Spartanburg is in northwestern South Carolina. The university is north of the city, at the I-85/I-585 junction; from I-85, take Exit 73B south or 74 north.

🕐 Library hours or by appointment; call for information. No fee.

Sᴏᴜᴛʜ Dᴀᴋᴏᴛᴀ

One of the things you'll notice in South Dakota is that what we list as "little" is often quite big—in size. It's a state with big, open stretches, so maybe that affects how people collect. We don't know. But we do know this is also a place that bears some of the greatest sweeps of America's history as well. Think about it: Mount Rushmore, North by Northwest; Pine Ridge, Sioux, Gold!, Custer!, Wild Bill; Deadwood Gulch; Wall Drug; trappers, traders, miners. Is there more? Sure. The big Mo River, giant Mammoth Site, a heritage that goes way back before the first European ever showed up, and the Black Hills, where the scenery wins hands down over the "attractions" and Lakota Sioux still consider the ground to be sacred.

What's Big: On the west end, visit Badlands National Park, located partly on the Pine Ridge Indian Reservation, and stop to pay your respects at the site of Wounded Knee; in Lead (that's leed, as in lode, not lead, get it?) tour the Homestake mine (in action since 1876) and visit the Black Hills Mining Museum; around Custer, the Crazy Horse Memorial beckons, as do the National Museum of Woodcarving and the Rushmore-Borglum Story in nearby Keystone. On the east end, in Mitchell, the big thing is the Soukup and Thomas International Balloon and Airship Museum.

CHAMBERLAIN

Akta Lakota Museum and Cultural Center   Donations from friends and alumni of Saint Joseph's Indian School form the core of this collection that strives to capture and preserve the Lakota Sioux way of life for generations to come. Using the displays as a way of carrying on the storytelling traditions of the Lakota, weaponry, ceremonial dress, tools, and antique and contemporary art are laid out in dioramas to help the visitor "hear" the historic experience. Rare and significant Native art and artifacts include a medicine necklace that belonged to Sitting Bull, quilled and beaded ceremonial horse masks, and a spectacular painted buffalo robe. Visiting artists frequently offer demonstrations. *Tours, Gift Shop, Programs*

■ 605 734-3455 • Saint Joseph's Indian School, Chamberlain, SD 57326

🚍 South-central South Dakota. I-90, Exit 263, then north 2 miles through downtown.

🕐 May–Sept.: Mon.–Sat. 8 A.M.–6 P.M., Sun. 1 P.M.–5 P.M. Oct.–Apr.: Mon.–Fri. 8 A.M.–4:30 P.M. Tours by appointment. No fee.

Old West Museum   The Olsons—Gene, Alice, and Greg—clearly have a great time with their six buildings' worth of frontier-era finds. What's here? A whole range of horse-drawn vehicles like a Spanish-American War ambulance; a 13-notched Remington and a Colt revolving rifle; a bunch of coin-operated animated and music machines, like the piano with a racetrack on top and eight horses running to its musical accompaniment; dolls of all sorts—including a rare bedroom doll, complete with cigarette; quack medical equipment like the infamous Wagensteen suction machine; and an indispensable thundermug . . . You get the idea.

■ 605 734-6157 • Hwy 16, Chamberlain, SD 57325

🚍 See above. I-90, Exit 260 (Oacama), then go east on Hwy 16 back toward Chamberlain.

🕐 Apr.–Oct.: Sun.–Mon. Hours vary. Fee.

DEADWOOD

Adams Memorial Museum   Born in the gold rush of 1876, Deadwood Gulch was an instant magnet for gamblers and gunfighters—Wild Bill Hickok, Calamity Jane (aka Martha Canary), Doc Holliday, and Wyatt Earp among them. This is the place to come for more on them (this tourist town is full of the stuff), but also for mining history and a fine mineral collection—highlighted with Potato Creek Johnny's record-setting gold nugget, vintage clothing, the first locomotive in the Black Hills, and the mysterious Thoen Stone. But it's off to Old Style Saloon #10 on Main St., if it's the actual site of Wild Bill's Dead Man's Hand you're after or Chinatown tours (we liked it better when it was called The Chinese Opium Tunnel Museum; 605 578-3561) to experience one aspect of the Chinese contribution to life in the gulch. *Gift Shop, Library*

■ 605 578-1714 • 54 Sherman, Deadwood, SD 57732

🚍 Forty-four miles northwest of Rapid City. I-90 Exit 30, onto US 14A going west.

🕐 May–Sept.: Mon.–Sat. 9 A.M.–6 P.M., Sun. noon–5 P.M. Oct.–Apr.: Mon.–Sat. 10 A.M.–4 P.M. Donation.

HURON

Cheryl Ladd Room   You know Huron is former veep Hubert Humphrey's hometown too. But there was a time—and we guess there still is, that Cheryl Jean

Stoppelmoor had a much greater hold on the public's attention. And they do have a soft spot for her here, from the days when she was just serving up the daily special. So all you *Charlie's Angels* fans can now stop by for some eggs *and* a Cheryl Ladd fix of photos, posters, and memorabilia. *Food*

■ 605 352-9238 • The Barn Restaurant, Hwy 37, Huron, SD 57350
🚗 I-90 to Hwy 37 (at Mitchell) north, about 55 miles. It's just before town, on the left.
🕐 Mon.–Sun. 9 A.M.–9 P.M. No fee.

LAKE NORDEN

South Dakota Amateur Baseball Hall of Fame   This is hometown baseball, when the game was fun. Ninety-five amateur players are honored here amongst a collection of pix and homemade equipment dating back to the turn of the century. *Programs*

■ 605 785-3553 • 519 Main Ave., Lake Norden, SD 57248
🚗 About 80 minutes north of Sioux Falls. I-29 to Exit 150, take SR 28W about 20 miles.
🕐 Mid-May–mid Oct.: Mon.–Sun. 9 A.M.–7 P.M. Donation.

LEMMON

Petrified Wood Park and Museum   Rampant petrified wood and plant and animal life—from immense logs to prehistoric grasses—along with unusual globular formations, caught the attention of early-20th-century amateur geologist Ole S. Quammen. Lucky for us. And lucky for the men, artists really, he hired in a privately run WPA-type project to turn the remarkable material into this wondrous park with its castles, pyramids, local history museum, and Chamber of Commerce building (originally an Independent Oil station) all built with it.

■ 605 374-5716 • 500 Main Ave., Lemmon, SD 57638
🚗 In the west on the North Dakota border, at the junction of Hwy 73 and US 12.
🕐 Memorial Day–Labor Day: Mon.–Sun. 10 A.M.–6 P.M. No fee.

MITCHELL

Corn Palace   Known officially as the "World's Only Corn Palace," once you've seen it you'll have no doubt there's nothing else like it. Its first incarnation, in 1892, was as the venue for Mitchell's first Corn Belt Exposition. While it's been rebuilt twice since, the exterior has always been decorated with murals and contrasting patterns using various grasses, corn, and grains nailed right onto the Moorish-themed surface, replete with minarets, turrets, and kiosks. While the outside decorations are replaced each year, the public space inside has permanent works by the late Yanktonai Sioux artist Oscar Howe. The Oscar Howe Art Center at 119 W. 3rd St. features his wonderful 1940 WPA dome mural. *Tours, Gift Shop*

🏛 800 257-CORN [2676]/605 996-7311 • 604 N. Main St., Mitchell, SD 57301

🚗 I-90 Exit 330 or 332. Follow signs for 1 mile.

🕐 Memorial Day–Labor Day: Mon.–Sun. 8 A.M.–10 P.M. Rest of year: Mon.–Fri. 8 A.M.–5 P.M. No fee.

MURDO

Pioneer Auto Show   Okay. It's B-I-G. But America just has so much stuff and someone has to keep track of it. In this case it was the watchful eye of A. J. "Dick" Geisler, who started the collecting, and his sons, John and Dave, who have kept it up. While the exhibits change now and again, there's always a slew of great old cars and motorcycles, jukeboxes, rocks and minerals, a "Ladies Style Show," bygone toys and games, a special Tom Mix–Packard room . . . and a swell assortment of cream separators (and other farm equipment). Oh yes, they have Elvis' motorcycle and an original Tucker car too. *Gift Shop, Food*

🏛 605 669-2691 • I-90 and US 83, Murdo, SD 57559

🚗 In south central South Dakota, it's at I-90 Exit 192.

🕐 June–Aug.: Mon.–Sun. 7 A.M.–10 P.M.; Apr.–May, Sept.–Oct.: Mon.–Sun. 8 A.M.–6 P.M. Fee.

RAPID CITY

While you're in the area, see: **Deadwood, Spearfish, Sturgis**

SIOUX FALLS

Sioux Empire Medical Museum   This is a swell medical history collection, and as the curators say, "iron lung, bleeders, surgery—it's all very special." Exhibits are historically accurate re-creations of hospital areas, with mannequins wearing period uniforms, altogether providing a great feel for medical progress. While you're in this neck of the woods, you might want to take a look at the early-20th-century murals by Norwegian-born artist Ole Runing in the Old Courthouse Museum.

🏛 605 333-6397 • Sioux Valley Hospital, 1100 S. Euclid Ave., Sioux Falls, SD 57117

🚗 I-29 to 12th St. exit, then east to Grange, and south to the hospital. The museum is in the East Patient Building.

🕐 Mon.–Fri. 10 A.M.–4 P.M. Donation.

SPEARFISH

National Fish Culture Hall of Fame and Museum   How to move fish faster and farther? Get a fish car, of course. Actually a real highlight of hatchery history is the successful development of rail transport of young shad and striped bass to spawning grounds as far away as California. Tour the beautiful grounds and visit one of the largest known collections of fish-culture artifacts and antique equipment, housed in the original 1899 hatchery building. *Tours*

- 605 642-7730/5668 • http://www.fws.gov/~r6dcbth/dcbooth.html • 423 Hatchery Circle, Spearfish, SD 57783
- Forty-six miles northwest of Rapid City. I-90, Exit 12, following Jackson Blvd. to Canyon St., turn left to the hatchery.
- Mid-May–mid-Sept.: Mon.–Sun. 10 A.M.–8 P.M., tours and museum. Fee. No fee for grounds, which are open year round.

SAINT FRANCIS

Buechel Memorial Lakota Museum   Father Eugene Buechel, in the 35 years he spent living and working as a missionary among the Sioux, made a rare contribution—and showed a rare compassion—by first learning the Lakota language, then painstakingly evolving a writing system and grammar for it. His work and other ethnographic collections here emphasize the reservation period of the Pine Ridge and Rosebud Sioux. Extensive photo library available on request. *Tours, Gift Shop, Publications, Library*

- 605 747-2361 • Saint Francis Indian Mission, 350 S. Oak St., Saint Francis, SD 57572
- South-central. I-90 to Murdo, Exit 192 onto US 83S for 40 miles to US 18E for about 2 miles, then south on road toward Rosebud/Saint Francis.
- Memorial Day–Labor Day: Mon.–Sun. 9 A.M.–6 P.M. Appointment only rest of year. Donation.

STURGIS

National Motorcycle Museum and Hall of Fame   Grown up around Sturgis' biker rally—held annually in August since 1938—this museum honors the sport's best. Featured: Dot Robinson, "First Lady of Motorcycling," and founder J. C. "Pappy" Hoel; and, among over 100 bikes on display, the "Mona Lisa of Motorcycles," a 1907 Harley in—as the owners are proud to say—original, unrestored, and running condition. *Gift Shop*

- 605 347-4875 • 2438 S. Junction Ave., Sturgis, SD 57785
- Twenty-eight miles northwest of Rapid City, take I-90 Exit 32.
- Memorial Day–Labor Day: Mon.–Sun. 9 A.M.–8 P.M. Closes 6 P.M. rest of year. Fee.

VERMILLION

Shrine to Music Museum The exquisite artistry of the instruments here would be compelling enough, but when you consider the further transformation when in the hands of the right musician, well. . . . The makers' craft is celebrated with over 6,000 instruments from virtually all cultures and historical periods, and you'll delight to such rare and remarkable gems as a hand-painted Persian drum, Italian stringed instruments from the Renaissance, a magnificent arched harp, and a crocodile-shaped zither. *Tours, Gift Shop, Programs, Publications, Library*

■ 605 677-5306 • University of South Dakota, 414 E. Clark St., Vermillion, SD 57069

🚗 Fifty-six miles south of Sioux Falls. I-29 Exit 26 onto SR 50W into town on the business route. It's on campus, at the corner of Clark and Yale Sts.

🕐 Mon.–Fri. 9 A.M.–4:30 P.M., Sat. 10 A.M.–4:30 P.M., Sun. 2 P.M.–4:30 P.M. Donation.

TENNESSEE

Davy Crockett was born on a mountaintop here. The Chattanooga Choo-Choo chugged through here. The TVA *and* atomic energy, harnessing water and nuclear energy, found some of their first homes here. Appalachian crafts, scenic wonders. Blues, bluegrass, and bourbon have all found a home here. It ain't just country.

What's Big: Chattanooga: Rock City, the National Medal of Honor Museum of Military History, and of course the Chattanooga Choo-Choo; Lynchburg: the Jack Daniel's distillery; Nashville: Ryman Auditorium; the Museum of Appalachia in Norris; and the Lost Sea in Sweetwater. And the giant guitar, which is all that's left of Bristol's Grand Guitar Music Museum.

ADAMSVILLE

Buford Pusser Home and Museum While national memory may have faded a bit, the town of Adamsville has immortalized Buford "Walking Tall" Pusser, local sheriff and defender of the law. Some say zealot, and in the '60s and early '70s, you could rest assured that no gambler, moonshiner, or scofflaw would be missed by Mr. Pusser's big stick. Video and lots of Buford true-crime stuff. Note! They've got yet more Pusser memorabilia over at Carbo's Smoky Mountain Police Museum in Pigeon Forge. *Gift Shop*
- 🏠 901 632-4080 • 342 Pusser St., Adamsville, TN 38310
- 🚗 Southwest Tennessee. Take I-40 Exit 108 onto Hwy 22, and head south to US 64.
- 🕐 May–Oct.: Mon.–Sat. 9 A.M.–5 P.M., Sun. noon–6 P.M.; Nov.–Apr.: Wed.–Sat. 10 A.M.–4 P.M., Sun. 1 P.M.–5 P.M. Fee.

CHATTANOOGA

While you're in the area, see also: Dayton. *In Georgia, see*: Dalton, Summerville

International Towing and Recovery Hall of Fame and Museum

Once you had the cars, could the wreckers be far behind? This collection, based on a Chattanooga-born industry, dates back to 1916 and includes, among a wonderful assortment of beautifully restored vintage tow trucks, a selection built on Ford Model A and Model T chassis. Pix of towing luminaries from around the world, a historical photo gallery of wreckers-in-action, and a group of toy tow trucks are also on display. *Tours, Gift Shop, Food*

🔲 423 267-3132 • 401 Broad St., Chattanooga, TN 37402

🚗 Downtown via Hwy 27N. Take 4th St. exit (1C) to 4th and Broad Sts.

🕐 Mon.–Fri. 10 A.M.–4:30 P.M., Sat.–Sun. 11 A.M.–5 P.M. Longer hours in summer. Fee.

National Knife Museum
Ceremonial knives, commemorative knives, turquoise-handled knives, knives used for cutting open oysters, and knives used in the Bronze Age. Knives, swords, sabers, anything that cuts, from all countries, and from just about any time—the rare and pedestrian side-by-side.

🔲 423 892-5007 • 7201 Shallowford Rd., Chattanooga, TN 37421

🚗 I-75, Exit 5.

🕐 Mon.–Fri. 9 A.M.–4 P.M., Sat. 10 A.M.–4 P.M. Fee.

CROSSVILLE

Homesteads Tower Museum
The "Showplace of the New Deal," Crossville is believed to have the last intact homesteading unit of 100 rural settlements founded by FDR's administration in the late '30s and early '40s. Photos and documents of the program and the era, as well as floor plans, house details, and day-to-day items from the homes are displayed in the octagonal sandstone tower that had been the Cumberland Homesteads Project administrative offices.

🔲 615 456-9663 • US 127S and SR 68, Crossville, TN 38555

🚗 About 60 miles west of Knoxville. Take I-40 Exit 317 onto US 127S for 4 miles to SR 68.

🕐 Apr.–Nov.: Mon.–Sat. 10 A.M.–5 P.M., Sun. noon–5 P.M. Donation. Fee for observatory.

DAYTON

Scopes Museum/Rhea County Courthouse
Now *this* could more fairly be known as the Trial of the Century. And walking into this majestic 1891 courthouse, you feel the gravity of the confrontation between those two titans of oratory, William Jennings Bryan and Clarence Darrow. The 1925 trial, challenging the legal right for evolution to be taught in the public schools in the state of Tennessee, is documented in a small museum two floors below the still-used courtroom.

🔲 423 775-7801 • 1475 Market St., Dayton, TN 37321

🚗 Thirty-five miles northeast of Chattanooga, on US 27.

🕐 Mon.–Thurs. 8 A.M.–4 P.M., Fri. 8 A.M.–5:30 P.M. No fee.

GRAND JUNCTION

National Bird Dog Museum and Field Trial Hall of Fame As their brochure says: "Yesterday . . . Today . . . Tomorrow in the world of bird dogs." Bird-dogging in North America goes back 300 years, and if ever you wanted to visit a place that extols the friendship of a man and his dog, this is it. The hunting, shooting, and field-trial traditions that involve over 40 breeds of sporting dogs are celebrated through photos, paintings, and sport memorabilia. *Programs, Library*

■ 901 764-2058/878-1168 • 505 W. Hwy 57, Grand Junction, TN 38039

🚗 Fifty miles east of Memphis, on Hwy 57, 0.75 mile east of SR 18.

🕐 Tues.–Fri. 10 A.M.–2 P.M., Sat. 10 A.M.–4 P.M., Sun. 1 P.M.–4 P.M. Donation.

HENDERSONVILLE

House of Cash Johnny Cash's Georgian-style mansion is a fine house of collectibles from his long country-music career. Just as he seems to be able to dip into a well and regularly renew his career, his eclectic assortment of antique stuff and music-biz mementos—including guitars, photos, and many awards—are refreshing in their own right. He's even handwritten some of the display cards.

■ 615 824-5110 • 700 Johnny Cash Pkwy, Hendersonville, TN 37077

🚗 Eighteen miles north of Nashville, off US 31E.

🕐 Apr.–Oct.: Mon.–Sat. 9 A.M.–4:30 P.M. Fee.

JOHNSON CITY

Museum of Ancient Brick While a couple of the bricks here go back to the Neolithic, and some may be larger, or more finely crafted, the curator's "pride and joy" is a sun-dried mud brick from the Ziggurat at Ur, a site many archeologists believe was the Tower of Babel. What makes it especially remarkable is that it bears the impression of its maker's fingers from 4,500 years ago. The company's round 16-sided building itself is a modern brickwork marvel. Just down the pike from Davy Crockett's birthplace.

■ 423 282-4661 • General Shale Products Corp., 3211 N. Roan St., Johnson City, TN 37601

🚗 In northeast Tennessee, take I-81 to US 23E to Roan St. North, staying to the left at the fork. It's a round brick building on the left, without signs.

🕐 Mon.–Fri. 8 A.M.–5 P.M. No fee.

KNOXVILLE

While you're in the area, see: Norris, Oak Ridge, Pigeon Forge, Vonore

MEMPHIS

National Civil Rights Museum   The museum is housed in the restored Lorraine Hotel, a place indelibly etched in our memories as the site where Martin Luther King, Jr., was assassinated in 1968. It traces the landmark moments in the struggle for civil rights in this country, using interpretive exhibits to aid the visitor in experiencing the era and its events: on boarding a restored bus, the tension is palpable as the driver's voice raises, and repeats, seemingly endlessly, his order to move to the back. *Tours, Gift Shop*

■ 901 521-9699 • 450 Mulberry St., Memphis, TN 38103

🚗 I-40 Exit 1A, south of Beale St. to Mulberry between Vance and Calhoun.

🕐 June–Aug.: Mon., Wed.–Sat 10 A.M.–6 P.M.; Sun. 1 P.M.–6 P.M. Sept.–May: Mon., Wed.–Sat 10 A.M.–5 P.M.; Sun. 1 P.M.–5 P.M. Tours by appointment. Fee.

National Ornamental Metal Museum   At this spectacular spot overlooking the Mississippi is an equally spectacular museum dedicated to the fine art—and craft—of metalsmithing. Changing exhibitions frequently focus on 20th-century artisans from all points on the globe, some of whom can be seen in action at the on-site smithy. Objects like exquisite mixed-metal openwork gates, avant-garde tea sets, and historic filigree work using precious metals are just a taste of what you'll find here. *Tours, Gift Shop, Programs, Library*

■ 901 774-6380 • 374 Metal Museum Dr., Memphis, TN 38106

🚗 Exit 12C off I-55 at the bridge, just south of downtown.

🕐 Tues.–Sat. 10 A.M.–5 P.M., Sun. noon–5 P.M. Fee.

Pink Palace Museum   Recently reopened in the pink marble mansion of Clarence Saunders, self-serve shopping's original genius. The founder of Piggly-Wiggly, the very first supermarket chain, he gained and lost three separate fortunes from his marketing concepts from the '30s into the '50s, including Keedoozle (say: key does all) and Foodelectric, two sort of retail-goes-Automat systems that used keys instead of nickels. Now that the Pink Palace has been gussied up they assure us that their evergreen Polar Bear and Shrunken Head displays will be there still, along with the Piggly-Wiggly grocery store replica, and the Memphis history exhibits that focus on its music, especially W. C. Handy and Elvis, and on King Cotton. *Gift Shop, Food, Hands-on, Programs, Library*

■ 901 320-6320 • http://www.memphismuseums.org • 3050 Central Ave., Memphis, TN 38111

🚗 From I-240 Exit 29 take Lamar Ave. to Central—it's between E. Parkway and Highland.

🕐 Memorial Day–Labor Day: Mon.–Wed. 9 A.M.–4 P.M., Thurs. 9 A.M.–8 P.M., Fri.–Sat. 9 A.M.–9 P.M., Sun. noon–5 P.M. Rest of year: Mon.–Wed. 9 A.M.–5 P.M., Thurs.–Sat. 9 A.M.–9 P.M., Sun. noon–5 P.M. Fee.

Sincerely Elvis   Sure you'll go on the Graceland tour, but in case you're dazed and dazzled by the frou-frou of his career and lifestyle, we thought we should remind you to stop at this small museum on the far side of the complex, which will tell you about Mr. Presley's *private* side. Yeah, you may have to cough up a few more bucks to get in (same goes for the Auto Museum and the Elvis Airplanes tour), but hey, they've got a photo of the King with President Richard M. Nixon (we're sure he was a big fan), and more importantly, they have the TV that Elvis famously shot out *and* his favorite loungewear and his jammies—now that's stuff you don't see every day. *Tours, Gift Shop, Food, Screenings*

📷 800 238-2000/901 332-3322 • http://www.Elvis-Presley.com • Graceland, 3734 Elvis Presley Blvd., Memphis, TN 38116

🚗 From I-240 take I-55 then get off at Exit 5B onto US 51S (Elvis Presley Blvd.).

🕐 Summer: Mon.–Sun. 8 A.M.–6 P.M. Closed Tues. in winter. Fee.

MILLERSVILLE (GOODLETSVILLE)

Museum of Beverage Containers and Advertising   Collectors everywhere can empathize with Tom Bates, who began by casually retrieving beer cans from the trash on the way home from school, then next thing you know, Dad pitches in and is picking up soda cans. Grown out of the family den years ago, the 36,000 cans-to-date—and over 9,000 soda bottles and myriad other advertising paraphernalia, neon and otherwise—are now computer-inventoried and impressively organized floor to ceiling, by brand and collection-type. From political collectibles (remember Goldwater—the soft drink—and Johnson Juice?) to long-lost brand names like Derry's Delaware Punch or Dix Drinks, it's a tribute to graphic design and the beverage business and, given that over 80 percent of the cans here are no longer produced, a rare archive indeed. By the way, you're just down the road from Twitty City and Oscar Mayer's "wiener wonderland." Visit the Beer Can House in Houston to commune with a kindred spirit. *Gift Shop*

📷 615 859-5236 • 1055 Ridgecrest Dr., Millersville (Goodletsville), TN 37072

🚗 Fifteen minutes north of Nashville. Take I-65 Exit 98 going toward Millersville for 1.3 miles, then turn left on Cartwright Circle North, then right onto Ridgecrest.

🕐 Mon.–Sat. 9 A.M.–5 P.M., Sun. 1 P.M.–5 P.M. Fee.

NASHVILLE

While you're in the area, see also: Hendersonville, Millersville (Goodletsville)

Hank Williams, Jr., Family Tradition Museum   Alas, the man who wrote "Your Cheatin' Heart," "I'm So Lonesome I Could Cry," and "Hey, Good

Lookin'" didn't get out of this world alive, but he did leave behind his '52 pink Cadillac, his son Hank Williams, Jr., suits by famed dresser-to-the-CW-stars Nudie, a collection of his favorite hand-painted ties, and his rare Martin guitars. And the remarkable body of unsurpassed tunes and lyrics in a way-too-short career. This one covers the whole Hank family; scoot down to Georgiana, Alabama, for Hank Sr.'s Boyhood Home—the museum there is dedicated to his career alone. But while you're here, and have that lump in your throat and twang in your ears, don't forget Nashville's Jim Reeves Museum, covering his baseball and music careers. *Screenings*

🔲 615 242-8313 • 1524 Demonbreun St., Nashville, TN 37202

🚙 One block south of I-40 Exit 209B on Music Row.

🕐 Mon.–Sun. 8 A.M.–6 P.M. Fee.

Museum of Tobacco Art and History   Whatever your feelings are on tobacco, the range, variety, and sheer craftsmanship of the art and antiques on display in this museum will be a revelation. Objects like a 1760s Staffordshire puzzle pipe, Native American peace pipes, hand-blown English glass pipes circa 1800, Chinese snuff bottles carved from carnelian and agate, French 19th-century meerschaums, playful American pottery tobacco jars, tobacco tins, advertising posters, and cigar-store Indians, testify to the social and economic contribution made by tobacco from pre-Columbian times to the present. *Tours, Gift Shop, Publications, Library*

🔲 615 271-2349 • U.S. Tobacco Building, 800 Harrison St., Nashville, TN 37203

🚙 Downtown. From I-265 take 8th Ave. North to the corner of Harrison St.

🕐 Mon.–Sat. 9 A.M.–4 P.M. No fee.

NORRIS

Lenoir Museum   Will G. Lenoir and his wife, Helen Hudson, collected what interested them from the rural life of early settlers in east Tennessee, then donated it to the state. You'll find a ten-tune playing barrel organ, with 140 wooden pipes and hand-carved figures that move to the music; the usual assortment of household utensils and farm implements; Confederate scrip; Indian relics; and a mousetrap collection bar none. Sunday afternoons find a varied group of local bluegrass and country musicians gathered to play—a living museum of mountain music. *Programs*

🔲 423 494-9688 • Hwy 441N, Norris, TN 37828

🚙 About 30 miles northwest of Knoxville. Take I-75N, at Exit 122 go east on Hwy 61 about 1.5 miles, then left on US 441 (Norris Fwy) for about 3 miles. It's on the right.

🕐 Apr. 15–Nov. 15: Wed.–Sun. 9 A.M.–5 P.M. Nov. 16–Apr. 14: Sat. 9 A.M.–5 P.M., Sun. 1 P.M.–5 P.M. No fee.

OAK RIDGE

American Museum of Science and Energy Opened in 1949 at the same time as the gates to the previously secret city of Oak Ridge, the exhibits use interactive techniques, but like the nearby Graphite Reactor (423 574-4160), have a real '50s feel—immediately evoking that duck-and-cover instinct. Newer exhibits may have more modern razzle-dazzle, but always the focus on sharing the wonder and reality of how energy works is paramount, hugely effective, and *fun*. *Hands-on*

■ 423 576-3200 • 300 S. Tulane Ave., Oak Ridge, TN 37830

🚗 About 30 miles northwest of Knoxville. Take I-40 to SR 162N, then continue north on SR 62; turn right on Tulane.

🕐 June–Aug.: Mon.–Sun. 9 A.M.–6 P.M.; closes at 5 P.M. rest of year. No fee.

PIGEON FORGE

Carbo's Smoky Mountain Police Museum Well, no, we don't want you to think of Tennessee as a "police" state, but they do have great respect for the law (besides Buford Pusser's place, you should also know about the Memphis Police Museum, over on the other side of the state). But while you're here, speaking of Mr. Pusser, you can view his famed "death" Corvette, and oodles of law enforcement items, domestic and international. A trove of badges, billy clubs, uniforms, and all kinds of confiscated stuff.

■ 423 453-1358 • 3311 Parkway, Pigeon Forge, TN 37868

🚗 Just east of Knoxville, take I-40 Exit 407 onto US 441. It's right near Dollywood.

🕐 Apr.: Fri.–Sun. 10 A.M.–5 P.M.; May–Oct. Mon.–Sun. 10 A.M.–5 P.M. Fee.

TRENTON

Trenton Teapot Museum In early May each year, Trenton celebrates this world-renowned collection of over 500 porcelain *veilleuse-théières* (nightlight teapots) from the late 18th and early 19th centuries with a two-week festival. Functioning like the food warmers that actually were their precursors, the delicate, transluscent teapots—created in all manner of whimsical and figurative forms, then set atop a candle hidden in a base—are shown off by lighting each one. During the rest of the year, while not lit, they are still delightful to look at. *Tours, Publications*

■ 901 855-2013 • 309 S. College St., Trenton, TN 38382

🚗 In northwestern Tennessee. I-40 to Jackson, then north on US 45W, which becomes College St. It's at the corner of 3rd St., in the City Hall building.

🕐 Mon.–Fri. 8 A.M.–5 P.M. No fee. Call ahead for group lecture/tour.

VONORE

Sequoyah Birthplace Museum   The Cherokees were the first Native American tribe to have a written language, for which they are indebted to the determined scholarship of Sequoyah, a soldier and statesman who made his mark throughout the course of Anglo-Native relations. His story, and a riveting exploration of Cherokee myths and legends, history and culture, are what's in store at this Native-run museum.

- 423 884-6246 • Hwy 360, Vonore, TN 37885
- About 30 miles southwest of Knoxville. US 129 to US 411, then 1 mile east on Hwy 360.
- Mon.–Sat. 9 A.M.–5 P.M., Sun. noon–5 P.M. Fee.

WAVERLY

World o' Tools Museum   World o' Tools is Mr. Hunter Pilkinton's personal wonderland of the over 25,000 tools he's been collecting since the early '50s. He loves tools and has made a real study of them—he will tell you all about them and their manufacturing history. While the anvil and wrench collections get an especially strong response, his large reference library and its exhibits of tool-themed objects and oddities capture their share of attention. By the way, you're just down the road a piece from the Coal Miner's Daughter Loretta Lynn's Hurricane Mills ranch and museum, replete with Butcher Holler home replica. *See* the Kentucky Coal Mining Museum in Benham, Kentucky, for more on Lynn. *Tours, Library*

- 615 296-3218 • 2431 Hwy 13S, Waverly, TN 37185
- About 60 miles west of Nashville. Take I-40, Exit 143, and it's about 16 miles north on Hwy 13. Look for "Pilkinton" on the mailbox.
- Call ahead for appointment. Donation.

TEXAS

A look at little museums in Texas is like capturing the essence of the American individualist along with a healthy shake of the elements that have made the America we know today. Texas museums are as diverse as the land is big. Along with the inevitable showplaces exploring those wild and woolly frontier days, you'll find all kinds of museums showcasing the high points and high jinks and other key moments in Texas history, from political scandal to creation theory, from the birth of big oil to the birth of Dr. Pepper, from the events at the Texas Book Depository to a collection housing Lee Harvey Oswald's can opener.

What's Big: W-e-l-l. What kind of a danged question is that for Texas? Nevertheless, we'll attempt some random notes on the topic. In the Dallas–Fort Worth area there's the National Museum of Communications (in Irving) and the Cattleman's Museum (in Fort Worth); in Austin there's the National Wildflower Research Center and in Fredericksburg, the Admiral Nimitz Museum; in Hereford there's the National Cowgirl Hall of Fame; in El Paso, the Bullfight Museum; and in Beaumont, the Texas Energy Museum.

ALBANY

Old Jail Art Center   Fine arts in the county jail, a restored 1878 jail, that is. And the art on the walls is some of the best in, um, captivity. In this little mid-Texas town (pop.: 1,987) you'll get an intimate look at modern works from the likes of Henry Moore, Pablo Picasso, and Louise Nevelson along with Chinese art dating back to the Han and Ming dynasties. *Library*

🏠 915 762-2269 • Texas St. (Route 6), Albany, TX 76430

🚗 North central Texas. Take I-20 to US 283, then north 25 miles.

🕐 Tues.–Sat. 10 A.M.–5 P.M., Sun. 2 P.M.–5 P.M. No fee.

ARLINGTON

Smith's Sewing Machine Museum   You may know Arlington as the home of the Texas Rangers, baseball team that is, but it's also proud to be known as the site of the world's largest sewing machine. Based on an 1864 model and built to commemorate the 150-year anniversary of Elias Howe, Jr.'s invention, it stands 10 feet high and 16 feet long. It's now on permanent display outside the museum. But don't stop there—Frank Smith has a display of sewing patterns and antique buttons along with a serious collection of over 145 standard-size machines dating from 1853 up to 1950. *Hands-on*

🏠 817 275-0971 • 804 W. Abram St., Arlington, TX 76103

🚗 Arlington is midway between Dallas and Fort Worth, just off of I-20.

🕐 Mon.–Sat. 9 A.M.–5 P.M. Fee.

BEAUMONT

While you're in the area, see also: Nederland, Port Arthur. *In Louisiana, see*: Sulphur

Babe Didrikson Zaharias Museum   Beaumont's Mildred "Babe" Didrickson Zaharias is considered one of the world's all-time best athletes, in a career spanning a gold-netting 1932 L.A. Olympics through a golfing blitz that lasted into the '50s. Basketball, javelin, hurdles, baseball, golf—you name it, she played it, and she excelled at it all. This museum/memorial is designed with the Olympic rings in mind. Her husband George, a pro wrestler, had a hand in starting it, and you can test your own prowess out at the 18-hole putting green right next door.

🏠 409 833-4622/880-3749 • 1750 I-10E, Beaumont, TX 77701

🚗 In southeastern Texas take I-10, Exit 854 (Martin Luther King Pkwy/Magnolia).

🕐 Mon.–Sun. 9 A.M.–5 P.M. No fee.

Eye of the World Museum   Here at the J & J Steakhouse, besides a good meal, you'll find the work of the late John Gavrelos, a visionary artist whose medium was tomato crates. Not that that's what you think of when you see his sculptures. Rendered from splintered crates, the surfaces then refinished, intricate constructions like *Betsy Ross & the First American Flag*, *Aristotle's Big Mistake*, *Ancient Persian Palace of Xerxes*, and *Pyramid of Egypt* enthrall and astound. *Food*

🏠 409 898-0801 • J & J Steakhouse, 6685 Eastex Fwy, Beaumont, TX 77708

🚗 From I-10, take the Lufkin exit for 69/96N, exiting at Sour Lake/Hwy 105, staying on the service road loop back under the overpass. J & J is on the right.

🕐 Open steakhouse hours, Mon.–Sat. 7 A.M.–10 P.M. No fee.

CANTON

Brewer's Bell Museum   Virginia Belle Brewer was given a Tiffin crystal bell in the fall of 1940. Over half a century later, her collection has grown to 4,000 bells, bells of all types, shapes, sounds, and provenances. A particularly warm and personal collection, and Ms. Brewer can tell you a story about every one of them.

🔲 903 567-4632 • Route 7, Box 314, Canton, TX 75103

🚗 Call ahead for directions.

🕑 By appointment only. No fee.

CORPUS CHRISTI

International Kite Museum   Kites through history, with some surprising uses: as weapons, experimental devices, and as works of art.

🔲 512 883-7456 • 3200 Surfside, Corpus Christi, TX 78403

🚗 Take I-37S into US 181S, then across the Harbor Bridge to the first exit (Burleson St.); follow the USS *Lexington*/Aquarium signs. It's in the Best Western Sandy Shores Resort.

🕑 Mon.–Fri. 9 A.M.–5 P.M., Sat.–Sun. 10 A.M.–5 P.M. Fee.

CORSICANA

Lefty Frizzell Country Music Museum (Pioneer Village)   Let the kids check out the standard pioneer village (genuine mid-1800s structures relocated here and restored) while you find the Lefty stuff tucked inside. The local boy who made it big is further celebrated with a life-size statue, embellished with the handprints of that Okie from Muskogee, Merle Haggard, and other country stars.

🔲 903 654-4846 • Pioneer Village, 912 W. Park Ave., Corsicana, TX 75110

🚗 About 60 miles southeast of Dallas. Take I-45S to Hwy 31 (Corsicana exit), turning right to 15th St., then right again to Park Ave. Turning left onto Park, it's 3 blocks down.

🕑 Mon.–Sat. 9 A.M.–5 P.M., Sun. 1 P.M.–5 P.M. Fee.

CROWELL

Gafford Family Museum   Years ago Mrs. Bettie B. Gafford traded her cowboy boots for a china cabinet and now she has 13 showcases and a house full of stuff that other people felt was important, but just couldn't see hanging onto themselves. Like a corn husking machine, or the more notorious stuff, like Lee Harvey Oswald's can opener and other Oswald detritus from a stay his mom made at the Gafford residence.

🔲 940 655-3395 • Box 609, Crowell, TX 79227

🚗 Crowell (say "kroll") is at the junction of Route 6 and I-70.
🕐 Visitors must call for appointment (and directions). Closed in winter. No fee.

DALLAS

While you're in the area, see also: Arlington, Denton, Fort Worth, Plano

Celebrity Shoe Museum   For no fee at all, while you're looking for a respite from your shopping adventure in what's claimed to be America's largest shoe store for men, stop at their espresso bar or take a gander at their celebrity shoe museum. It's a small collection and dispersed around, but take a close look and you'll find Marilyn Monroe's suede pumps, Don Adams' *Get Smart* shoe phone, JFK's wing tips, Cher's shoes, Vincent Price's *Ten Commandments* footgear, and even Gerry Ford's golf shoes. And soon they'll be at other Larry's branches too (throughout Texas and Colorado). It's not Toronto's incredible Bata Shoe Museum, but it's a nice taste. *See also* Philadelphia's Center for the History of Foot Care and Foot Wear.
🖼 972 731-4961 • Larry's Shoes, 15340 Dallas N. Pkwy, Dallas, TX 75248
🚗 In North Dallas in the Prestonwood Court East Shopping Center.
🕐 Mon.–Sat. 10 A.M.–9 P.M., Sun. noon–6 P.M. No fee.

The Conspiracy Museum   The inspiration and obsession of "assassinologist" R. B. Cutler, a Harvard-educated architect who, for an entry fee ($7 when we visited) will take you on a personal tour of exhibits tracing the American history of assassinations back to the age of Andrew Jackson, but will focus your attention on his very specific JFK conspiracy theories. And to complement the story while you're in the neighborhood, you can go to the nearby Texas Book Depository and check out The Sixth Floor museum, which features photos and artifacts on Kennedy's life and legacy—or take the macabre re-creation tour that follows the route of that ill-fated motorcade. To further develop your own conspiracy theories, you may also want to look under El Paso, for the Billie Sol Estes Museum. *Tours*
🖼 214 741-3040 • 110 S. Market St., Dallas, TX 75202
🚗 Three blocks from Dealy Plaza, it's across the street from the Kennedy Memorial in the Katy Building at the corner of Market and Commerce Sts.
🕐 Mon.–Sun. 10 A.M.–6 P.M. Museum tours: Fri., Sat., Sun., same hours. Fee.

Mary Kay Museum   Get ready to Think Pink. Whether you see the museum as the maraschino cherry to top off the plant tour, or you just stop in for the exhibits, the Mary Kay Museum: Dreams Come True is worth a stop. This paean to the cosmetics queen is an Art Deco showcase and fashion show of MK career apparel since 1963, including gowns worn by Mary Kay herself, among other memorabilia. If you're lucky, your tour may include Ms. Kay's private office. *Tours*
🖼 972 687-6300/5720 (tours) • Mary Kay International, 8787 Stemmons Fwy, Dallas, TX 75247

🚍 Regal Row exit off Stemmons Fwy.

🕐 Mon.–Fri. 9 A.M.–5 P.M. No fee. Tours by appointment only.

Olde Fan Museum   Who would have thought there could be so many non-freon-type cooling devices? At the moment, the Fan Man's collection goes back to 1860, and ranges back up to 1960. Dedicated to mechanical fans, from Spring-load types to steam-powered to ac and dc, he's got fans of all powers and purposes (except those accordion paper ones your fourth-grade teacher tried to ban). He's also got a felicitous assortment of other historic small household appliances: radios, phonographs, waffle irons, mixers, juicers, electric razors, and hair driers among them.

🏠 214 826-7700 • 1907 Abrams Rd., Dallas, TX 75214

🚍 Near downtown in Lakewood Shopping Center. Take the I-30 Munger St. exit, turning north on Munger to the 2nd light (Columbia Ave.), turn right and proceed 1.5 miles (Columbia becomes Abrams). It's on the left.

🕐 Mon.–Fri. 9 A.M.–6 P.M., Sat. 10 A.M.–4 P.M. No fee.

DENTON

World's Only Pecan Art Museum   Inspired by the contours of the humble pecan (that's pah-CAHN), B. W. Crawford ("the Pecan Picasso") reveals the major figures of our time, as well as his family and neighbors, through his remarkable painted likenesses. The ultimate miniature. Picture Ronald Reagan—or Dolly Parton—on a pecan. While you're there you are invited to watch the Crawfords' Pecan Cracking Machine tackle up to 75 pounds of nuts per hour.

🏠 940 321-3461 • 138 Chaparral Estates, Denton, TX 76208

🚍 About 40 miles north of Dallas–Ft. Worth, in Shady Shores, near Denton. From I-35E take Exit 461, turn right onto Shady Shores Rd. to first left, then go about 2 blocks, turning right onto Chaparral.

🕐 Phone first, but generally open 10 A.M.–4 P.M. Donation.

DUBLIN

Dr. Pepper Bottling   This is the grandaddy of Dr. Pepper bottling operations. From the drink's beginnings in a Waco drugstore in 1885, this first plant opened six years later with the original recipe and good old-fashioned cane sugar. Well, over 100 years later the recipe's the same, the equipment's the same, and unlike all the other Dr. P bottlers, they've stuck with real sugar too. Mmm, mmm. While you can go down on Route 6 about 75 miles to Waco for the slick Dr. Pepper Museum in a 1906 plant (restored soda fountain, fancy audio-visual displays), you might just want to get yourself a cold one right here in Dublin first. You don't get to see a factory operation like this much anymore, and loads of memorabilia dating back to the founding are at hand as well. *Tours*

■ 254 445-3466 • 221 S. Patrick, Dublin, TX 76446

🚗 Take Hwy 67 or 377 southwest from Dallas-Fort Worth about 100 miles, right into town.

🕐 Mon.–Fri. 8 A.M.–noon, 1 P.M.–5 P.M.; Sat. 10 A.M.–noon, 1 P.M.–3 P.M. Bottling happens only on Tues. 9 A.M.–11:30 A.M., 1 P.M.–3:30 P.M. No fee.

EL PASO

Billie Sol Estes Museum   Tucked into daughter Pam Padget's antiques shop in downtown Granbury you'll find an exhibit devoted to Billie Sol Estes, a headline name some of you may remember as synonymous with political scandal back in 1961. And you may also recall that his was the first-ever televised trial and the last until recently—the judge at the time said something about the excessive publicity affecting the fairness of it all. Sound familiar? For you conspiracists out there, he's still with us—in fact, does book signings (*Billie Sol, King of Texas Wheeler-Dealers* is the title of the bio) once a month at the museum—and still has yet to speak out on the various deaths and cover-ups that surrounded the JFK/RFK-requested FBI investigation of his various enterprises, and his connections to then–vice president LBJ. *See also* The Conspiracy Museum in Dallas.

■ 800 351-6024 (Visitors Bureau) • El Paso, TX 79901

🚗 The museum's Granbury location is now closed. It is scheduled to re-open in El Paso sometime in 1998.

🕐 Call for information.

U.S. Border Patrol Museum   "Border patrol" these days conjures up grim images of impoverished aliens risking their lives to make it into the United States undetected. Of course the history is broader than that, and covers our coastal borders as well as Canada and Mexico. Photos and equipment displays cover the low-tech days of the Old West through modern cyber-technology used in current operations. *Library*

■ 915 759-6060 • 4315 Transmountain Rd., El Paso, TX 79924

🚗 On the north side of Loop 375 (Transmountain Rd.) about half a mile west of the Patriot Fwy interchange.

🕐 Tues.–Sun. 9 A.M.–5 P.M. No fee.

FORT WORTH

While you're in the area, see also: Arlington, Dallas, Denton, Plano

American Airlines C. R. Smith Museum   It's big and glitzy but it's the only airlines museum included, and it's kind of interesting to trace commercial aviation not just through the small planes that first made it possible, but through the service industry that grew from it. Did you know that American provided compact typewriters for inflight work sessions during the '30s? *Tours, Gift Shop, Hands-on, Screenings*

🏠 817 967-1560 • 4601 Hwy 360 at FAA Rd., Fort Worth, TX 76155

🚙 Just south of Dallas–Ft. Worth International Airport, take the FAA Rd. exit from either Hwy 183 or Hwy 360, turn right at stop sign; it's on the right.

🕙 Wed.–Sat. 10 A.M.–6 P.M., Sun. noon–5 P.M., Tues. 10 A.M.–7 P.M. No fee.

FREDERICKSBURG

Bauer Toy Museum   Don and Betty Bauer love toys and that's made clear in the very neat and clever displays showing off their wonderful collection of historic (1870–1960) toys—especially the old painted metal ones. All kinds of airplanes, fire trucks, riding toys, and toy tools and a fine selection of small trinket toys including Cracker Jack and premium giveaways.

🏠 830 997-9394 • 233 E. Main St., Fredericksburg, TX 78624

🚙 About 60 miles northwest of San Antonio, downtown.

🕙 Wed.–Mon. 10 A.M.–5 P.M. Hours may vary in winter. Donation.

Gish's Old West Museum   Old West stuff, but not the usual. Relics and attire from 1870 to 1920, all of it used, each item with its story. Let Joe Gish tell you about his long interest in frontier history and how his collection started from props he accumulated in his commercial art career—until he finally had to build a separate house for it all.

🏠 210 997-2794 • 502 N. Milam St., Fredericksburg, TX 78624

🚙 Downtown, heading west on Main St. from Pioneer Plaza, turn right on N. Milam.

🕙 "Open when here" or call for appointment. No fee.

GLEN ROSE

Creation Evidences Museum   Here's what's here: items that claim to support a "scientific basis for the creation of the world versus the standard evolutionary theory." Confused? Just picture a universe where humans walked with the dinosaurs. The evidence: They've got the fossil footprints . . . and a human finger in Cretaceous stone. *Gift Shop, Publications*

🏠 254 897-3200 • FM 205 at Paluxy Bridge, Glen Rose, TX 76043

🚙 From Dallas, take US 67S about 60 miles, then turn north on FM 205 4 miles west of town.

🕙 Tues.–Sat. 10 A.M.–4 P.M. Fee.

GREENVILLE

American Cotton Museum   Here in Greenville, where "Cotton Was King," you'll learn all about the history and impact of the cotton industry in these parts, and throughout the United States. Ain't just cotton, though—don't leave without checking out the Coca-Cola and local-boy Monty Stratton exhibits or taking a stroll in their wildflower meadow.

■ 903 450-4502/454-1990 • 600 I-30E, Greenville, TX 75403-0347

🚙 About 25 miles northeast of Dallas, take I-30E just past where it crosses US 69.

🕑 Tues.–Fri. 9 A.M.–5 P.M., Sat. 9 A.M.–5 P.M. Fee.

HOUSTON

This is a city with museum *personality*. What else would you expect from the town that's home to the Annual Art Car Weekend and Ball (Fruitmobile! Grass Car!), as well as the recently relocated First National Church of the Exquisite Panic (713 523-4093, and *see* our listing in Manhattan, New York).

American Funeral Service Museum   A collection of coffins that the vampire Lestat would be proud of is just a small part of this museum that seeks to enlighten the public about one of our most important cultural rituals, at the same time preserving related artifacts from the 19th and 20th centuries. Changing exhibits like Fantasy Coffins from Ghana (in shapes that reflect the lives of the dearly deceased—like cars and exotic amphibious creatures) and permanent displays like the Funerals of the Famous Gallery and a full-size replica of King Tut's sarcophagus are all sure to give you fresh thoughts for the afterlife—and perhaps a new appreciation of a most respectable service.

■ 713 876-3063 • 415 Barren Springs Dr., Houston, TX 77090

🚙 In Houston take I-45N, taking the Airtex exit west to Ella Blvd., then turn right to Barren Springs Dr. Museum is on the right.

🕑 Tues.–Sat. 10 A.M.–4 P.M., Sun. noon–4 P.M. Fee.

Beer Can House   You'll really want to call ahead so you can be sure to catch Mary Milkovisch at home. She put up with her late husband John's home-improvement projects for many years, and now she and her sons are in charge of keeping it up. The first thing you might notice is the marbles-and-metals-embedded concrete lawn. It seems John just "got sick of mowing the grass." Then again, it might be the thick beer can tab fringe that hangs from the awnings that catches your eye, or the split and flattened cans that upholster the sides of the house (indeed, Mr. Milkovisch was an upholsterer by trade), or the various decorations that cover most every surface of the property in one man's inspired ode to aluminum.

■ 713 862-3238 • 222 Malone St., Houston, TX 77007

🚐 It's in the West End section close to Memorial Park, near downtown.
🕐 By appointment or "by chance." Fee for commercial tours only.

The Orange Show   Everything oranges, it's sort of a Watts Towers of citrus, brought to you by Jeff McKissack, the Simon Rodia of Houston. McKissack, a post-man by trade, was a man who viewed oranges as the staff of life and then died within a year of completing this tribute in 1979. A personal vision that is a creative inspiration for those who visit, this tableau of folk art, mechanical whirligigs, mazes, and mosaics, is preserved for your viewing pleasure. Here's the place to come for the word on folk art environments throughout the area, and beyond. *Tours*
📞 713 926-6368 • 2401 Munger St., Houston, TX 77023
🚐 I-45N to the Tellepsen exit, turn left, then left again and go under the underpass. Take the next immediate left and go 3 blocks to Munger and turn right. From I-45S, take the Telephone Rd. exit, then proceed 2 blocks to Munger and turn right.
🕐 Memorial Day–Labor Day: Wed.–Fri. 9 A.M.–1 P.M., Sat.–Sun. noon–5 P.M. Closed mid-Dec.–mid-Mar. Rest of year: Sat.–Sun. noon–5 P.M. Group tours by appointment. Fee.

MARFA

Chinati Foundation/La Fundación Chinati   This is sculptor Donald Judd's site for displaying his and others' work in a space in which it belongs: "Some-where . . . a strict measure must exist for the art of this time and place." His view was that an alternative was needed to traditional museums, with their temporary exhibitions and inability to consistently provide appropriate space for modern work. So he developed Chinati in various former military buildings and ware-houses as well as outdoor sites in and around the flat open range of Marfa, moun-tains looming in the distance. Here's where you'll find pieces by Dan Flavin, John Chamberlain, Claes Oldenburg, and Carl Andre appearing as each artist intended. And the apparent austerity of the settings—and the sense that you are with the work alone—truly brings one closer to appreciating that intent.
📞 915 729-4362 • One Cavalry Row, Marfa, TX 79843
🚐 Two hundred miles southeast of El Paso, take I-10 to Van Horn, then US 90 to Marfa. Chinati is just off of US 67 after you've come into Marfa.
🕐 Thurs.–Sat. noon–5 P.M. and by appointment. No fee.

El Paisano Hotel   This 1928 Spanish Colonial hotel—listed on the National Register of Historic Places—was used as operations central for George Stevens' filming of *Giant* in 1955. Clippings and pictures from the shooting are on display and every year in May there's a reunion festival.
📞 915 729-3145 • 207 N. Highland, Marfa, TX 79843
🚐 In the far southwest, take I-10 to Route 17 60 miles south into town.
🕐 Hotel lobby hours. No fee.

MCLEAN

Devil's Rope Museum and Route 66 Museum Well, this is a two-for-one. Two separate museums, both in the same spot—an old bra factory. But this entire town and the roadways in the vicinity are the real Route 66 "museum." Stop at the exhibit for inspiration, pick up some maps and hot tips, and hit the road. As for Devil's Rope, this Panhandle spot claims to have the largest collection of barbed wire artifacts in the world (a visit to the Kansas Barbed Wire Museum in La Crosse, Kansas, may be in order if you want to be certain you've seen it all. . . .) and also features historical displays from the XIT, JA, Frying-Pan, and other local big ranches. *Gift Shop*

■ 806 779-2225 • Old Route 66 at Kingsley St., McLean, TX 79057-0290
🚐 Sixty miles east of Amarillo. I-40 Exit 141–142 eastbound, Exit 143–142 westbound.
🕐 May 1–Oct. 31: Tues.–Sat. 10 A.M.–4 P.M., Sun. 1 P.M.–4 P.M. Nov. 1–Apr. 30: Fri.–Sat. 10 A.M.–4 P.M., Sun. 1 P.M.–4 P.M. Donation.

NEDERLAND

Windmill Museum/Tex Ritter Museum Welcome to Nederland (that's Nee-der-land), City of Programmed Progress, and home to country star Tex Ritter. This museum's built in a motor-operated windmill as a tribute to the area's Dutch heritage. But watch for a French museum to be built next door to note the Acadian wave that occurred soon after the Dutch settled in. Ritter mementos are displayed along with cultural history artifacts. *Gift Shop*

■ 409 723-1545 • Tex Ritter Park, 1515 Boston, Nederland, TX 77627
🚐 About 15 miles southeast of Beaumont off US 96.
🕐 Mar.–Aug.: Tues.–Sun. 1 P.M.–5 P.M. Sept.–Feb.: Thurs.–Sun. 1 P.M.–5 P.M. No fee.

PHARR

Old Clock Museum Antique clocks, over 2,000 of them. Some date back as far as 1690; many are exquisite and quite unusual. *Library*

■ 956 787-1923 • 929 E. Preston St., Pharr, TX 78577
🚐 Pharr is about 50 miles west of Brownsville in southern Texas. From the junction of US 281 and old Hwy 83, proceed on 83 past the schoolhouse, turn right, then left onto Preston.
🕐 Usually Mon.–Sun. 10:30 A.M.–noon, 2:30 P.M.–4 P.M., but call ahead. No fee.

Smitty's Juke Box Museum See one of the last of the 1942 Wurlitzer "950" jukeboxes here in Pharr. Their oldest item is a 1929 Electramuse, as well as early RCA and Edison victrolas and an archaic pinball machine. Leo "Smitty" Schmitt, Sr., no longer runs his jukebox service route, but he and his sons have found a way to keep the juke-joint spirit alive. Bob Wills sounds just like he was meant to coming out of that restored "Bubbler."

📱 956 787-0131 • 116 W. State, Pharr, TX 78577

🚙 See above. Smitty's is at US 281 and old Hwy 83, "directly behind Dunkin Donuts."

🕐 Mon.–Fri. 9 A.M.–5:30 P.M. No fee. Bring quarters and nickels for the jukeboxes, though.

PLANO

Cockroach Hall of Fame   Michael Bohdan's exterminating service on the north side of Dallas is no ordinary Pest Shop. Mr. Bohdan offers us roach tableaux, featuring roaches in costume as "Ross Peroach" and "Liberoachi." But the display that gets the most attention is his live Madagascar "hissing roaches." *Gift Shop*

📱 972 519-0355 • 2231-B W. 15th St., Plano, TX 75075

🚙 It's just north of Dallas. Take US 75N, Exit 29, then 1.5 miles west to 15th St. and Custer.

🕐 Mon.–Fri. 12:15 P.M.–5 P.M., Sat. noon–3 P.M. No fee.

JCPenney Historical Museum and Archives   James Cash Penney, a Missouri native, made his retail start with the Golden Rule stores in Wyoming in 1902. But now corporate headquarters along with the company collections—historic store photos and advertisements, early catalogs and merchandise, fashion photos and business records—have found a home in Texas. Imagine the frontier developing without mail order. . . . *Tours, Library*

📱 Museum: 214 431-7928/Tours: 214 431-TOUR [8687] • 6501 Legacy Dr., Plano, TX 75024

🚙 Dallas North Tollway north to Legacy Dr. exit. Turn left onto Legacy, then right onto Communications Pkwy, then left onto Headquarters Dr.

🕐 Mon.–Fri. 8 A.M.–5 P.M. No fee. Tours by appointment only: Tues.–Thurs. 10 A.M.–2 P.M.

PORT ARTHUR

Museum of the Gulf Coast   As their brochure says, this one covers it all—from the Jurassic to Janis Joplin, the Buccaneers to the Big Bopper (known to his mom as J. P. "Jape" Richardson). Janis stuff, from religious artwork from her Port Arthur childhood to stage attire and memorabilia, stands as a shrine of its own. But you'll want to make time for displays on other local legends (Jimmy Johnson, Robert Rauschenberg, George Jones) and nice early history and decorative arts (particularly the Snell glass collection) exhibits as well. *See also* Clear Lake, Iowa, for more on Mr. Richardson from his last gig at the Surf Ballroom. *Gift Shop*

📱 409 982-7000 • http://www.pa.lamar.edu/museum/gulf.html • 700 Procter St., Port Arthur, TX 77640

In southeastern Texas. Downtown, at the corner of Beaumont Ave. and 4th St.

Mon.–Sat. 9 A.M.–5 P.M., Sun. 1 P.M.–5 P.M. Fee. Group tours by appointment.

SAN ANTONIO

Barney Smith's Toilet Seat Art Museum Former master plumber Barney Smith had to sell his Winnebago to make room in his garage for his toilet seat art display (411 of 'em at last count). Neatly covering the walls from floor to ceiling, you can appreciate the sweep of Mr. Smith's *oeuvre*, from the early days of simply decorating the discarded seats with little antlers and a few turkey feathers to full-scale tableaux inspired by his travels, like a recent trip to the Dead Sea, or even one to his dentist. The carefully constructed pieces often use applied bits of oil paintings (his own) and dip into his inventory of finds like Boy Scout badges, false teeth, sea corals, perhaps a portion of a bowling bowl, and, more often than not, motel keys—another collecting passion of the eclectic Mr. Smith. *See also* American Sanitary Plumbing Museum in Worcester, Massachusetts.

210 824-7791 • 239 Abiso, San Antonio, TX 78209

On the north side of town, in the Alamo Heights section. It's 2 blocks off Broadway, inside the I-410 Loop. Go around to the rear of the house, the collection's in his garage and the entrance is on Arbutus St.

He's retired and it's open "whenever he's around." He keeps the garage door open, and you can just stop in. No fee.

Buckhorn Hall of Horns, Texas History, Fins, Feathers and Boar's Nest Known for its eclectic displays of fauna-of-all-nations and Texas historical artifacts, you'll find something for everyone at this modern-day brewery site that also features the late-19th-century home and memorabilia of Texas-native short-story writer, O. Henry. And you can even quaff back a cold one (local Lone Star hops or fountain root beer), gratis, at the historic 1881 Buckhorn Bar, used as a key setting in *Lonesome* Dove. *Gift Shop*

210 270-9465 • Lone Star Brewery, 600 Lone Star Blvd., San Antonio, TX 78204

About 1.5 miles south of downtown, off Saint Mary's St., near the junction I-10/I-37.

Mon.–Sun. 9:30 A.M.–5 P.M. Fee. Call to confirm location—a move to downtown is planned.

Church of Anti-Oppression Folk Art This is a walk or drive-by, as the "museum" is the artwork you'll find decorating the outside of this residence. Displays change at the whim of the artist inhabitants, but please do not knock.

no phone • 622 Ave. East, San Antonio, TX 78200

Just north of the Alamo.

Daylight hours. No fee. Exterior only—do not request access.

Hangar 9/Edward H. White II Memorial Museum   Dedicated to Edward H. White II, San Antonio native and first American to walk in space (and ultimately, die on the launch pad), this is the only remaining World War I hangar in the United States. It features displays, photos, and memorabilia dealing with historic flight medicine and the development of manned space flight, and you can check out an original Jenny as well as a Rotational Simulator used to prepare astronauts for space travel. *Gift Shop*

■ 210 536-2203 • 8008 Inner Circle Dr., Brooks AFB, San Antonio, TX 78235
🚐 Ten-minute drive southeast of downtown, off Hwy 37.
🕐 Mon.–Fri. 8 A.M.–4 P.M. Sat. by appointment. No fee.

Hertzberg Circus Collection and Museum   Twenty thousand items of circus stuff, from King Charles II through P. T. Barnum, from rare posters to Emmet Kelly, Sr.'s shoes. Features Tom Thumb's personal coach, sideshow personalities, a complete miniature circus, costumes, and lots of lore. *Gift Shop, Publications, Library*

■ 210 207-7819 • 210 W. Market St., San Antonio, TX 78205
🚐 Near the Alamo, between Presa and Dolorosa.
🕐 Summer: Mon.–Sat. 10 A.M.–5 P.M., Sun. 1 P.M.–5 P.M. Rest of year: closed Sun. Fee.

Magic Lantern Castle Museum   Housed in a refurbished former San Antonio nightclub with a castle theme, this lovingly restored pseudo-feudal structure contrasts with and somehow complements the serious collection within. Concentration on magic lanterns from the 1700s through the 20th century and their history throughout the world; glass slides, prints, books, accessories, and related paraphernalia; worldwide scientific instruments for optical projection. *Programs, Library*

■ 210 805-0011 • 1419 Austin Hwy, San Antonio, TX 78209
🚐 Ten-minute drive northeast of downtown, right near the airport.
🕐 By appointment only. No fee.

SHINER

Edwin Wolters Memorial Museum   Here in Shiner, the "Cleanest Little City in Texas," is the 1900 home of Wolters, founder of the museum. A seemingly "typical" mix of local history, industry, Indian artifacts, archaeology, costumes, botany, dolls, and period furniture is jazzed up with a freak egg collection and an impressive group of salt and pepper shakers.

■ 512 594-3774 • 306 S. Ave. I, Shiner, TX 77984
🚐 Midway between San Antonio and Houston, exit onto TX 95S from I-10. In Shiner, go 6–7 blocks south of the Yoakum Moulton Hwy (TX 90-A).
🕐 Mon.–Fri. 8 A.M.–5 P.M., every 2nd and 4th Sun. 2 P.M.–5 P.M. Donation.

TURKEY

Bob Wills Museum   Bob Wills is still the king (of Western Swing, that is), and this museum in the small town of Turkey (pop.: 516) happily helps keep that thought alive. See his fiddles, band pictures and awards, clothes, boots, clippings. You'll want to come back for their annual Bob Wills Day, featuring many of the former Texas Playboys, always on the last Saturday in April.

📱 806 423-1253 • 6th and Lyles, Turkey, TX 79261

🚗 In the Panhandle to the east of Amarillo and Lubbock. Take I-27 to TX 86E about 50 miles into Turkey. It's in the old school building.

🕐 Mon.–Fri. 8 A.M.–11 A.M., 1 P.M.–5 P.M., and by appointment.

Hotel Turkey   Founded in 1927, this hotel is kind of a museum itself. It's completely furnished and decorated with 1920s-era stuff and even the food's prepared with period appliances. Special events feature cowboy poetry readings. And, yes, Bob Wills sang here.

📱 800 657-7110 • 3rd and Alexander, Turkey, TX 79261

🚗 See above. Take TX 86E into Turkey.

🕐 Hotel lobby hours. No fee.

WACO

Loud Cry Museum   Amo Bishop Roden, a Branch Davidian herself, is the self-appointed curator of the museum she erected on the site of the deadly 1993 confrontation with Federal agents; she provides maps of the compound with possible tunnels and "escape routes" that she says might have been taken by the sect leader, David Koresh, and chronicles the group's history. Note: A fire in early '97 destroyed the museum so you will need to call or write for an update.

📱 254 863-5264 • Route 7, Box 741 B, Waco, TX 76705

🚗 Ten miles outside Waco, in Mount Carmel near the village of Elk.

🕐 By appointment. Donation.

UTAH

Stunning natural features dwarf human endeavor here, except along the Wasatch Front, where the Mormons built Deseret, only to see miners and other outsiders turn it into Utah. Many of the state's museums focus on things that come out of the earth, others on the tiny figures that beetle across its surface from time to time.

What's Big: in Salt Lake City, the major sites relating to Mormon history; Ogden's Hill Aerospace Museum and Union Station.

DELTA

Great Basin Museum   This regional museum has displays and archives on the settlement and history of this agricultural edge of the Great Basin. What sets it apart are its exhibits on the nearby Topaz relocation camp, one of the isolated sites to which Japanese Americans were sent during World War II.
- 801 864-3362 • 328 W. 100 North, Delta, UT 84624
- Delta is 100 miles south-southwest of Salt Lake City; the museum is 1 block north of US 6/50, the through highway.
- Mon.–Sat. 10 A.M.–4 P.M., holidays 1 P.M.–4 P.M. Call to confirm winter hours. No fee.

EUREKA

Tintic Mining Museum   Eureka means "I found it!" and in 1869 they found it here—gold, silver, lead, and copper. The mines worked into the 1950s. The museum shows tools, mineral samples, other artifacts of the boom days, photographs, period rooms, and dioramas, and has a large archive of Eureka newspapers for researchers. Library
- 801 433-6842 • 241 West Main, Eureka, UT 84628

🚗 Eureka is in central Utah, about 50 miles south-southwest of Salt Lake City, on US 6/50. The museum is central, in the old City Hall and railroad depot.

🕐 Open by request, Mon.–Sun. 10 A.M.–4 P.M. No fee.

GRANTSVILLE

Donner-Reed Pioneer Museum   In harsh country, this small museum commemorates the famous Donner Party, which crossed the Great Salt Lake Desert in 1846 before becoming disastrously stranded in the Sierra Nevada. Here you'll see items abandoned by westbound pioneers as the going got tougher. *See also* the Emigrant Trail Museum in Truckee, Northern California.

■ 801 884-3348 • 90 N. Cooley, Grantsville, UT 84029

🚗 Grantsville is about 20 miles southwest of Salt Lake City, on Route 138.

🕐 Call for appointment and directions. Donation.

GREEN RIVER

John Wesley Powell River History Museum   The Green and Colorado Rivers were among the last parts of North America to be explored by whites, and it was not until John Wesley Powell ran the rivers in small boats beginning in 1869 that parts of them were known at all. This museum salutes his daring, and the exploits of others, in a River Runners' Hall of Fame, and displays replicas and models of craft used in the voyages. It also details the geology, geography, and history of the Colorado Plateau and its rivers. *See also* the museums in Page, Arizona, and Green River, Wyoming. *Gift Shop, Screenings*

■ 801 564-3427 • 885 E. Main St., Green River, UT 84525

🚗 Green River is in east-central Utah. East Main is the I-70 business route in the city.

🕐 Summer: Mon.–Sun. 8 A.M.–8 P.M. Winter: Mon.–Sun. 9 A.M.–5 P.M. Donation.

LEHI

John Hutching's Museum of Natural History   It started with a family operation, and now is noted for diversity. It isn't all natural history; although there are tropical seashells, minerals, fossils, birds and eggs, there's also pioneer history—weapons and the like.

■ 801 768-7180 • 685 N. Center St., Lehi, UT 84043

🚗 Lehi is on I-15 between Salt Lake City and Provo. The museum is central.

🕐 Mon.–Sat. 9:30 A.M.–5 P.M. Fee.

MOAB

Hole N' The Rock   If you've been visiting Arches National Park, you might want to come down here to see what a man and a woman can do to the same kind of rock. This is a 5,000-square-foot home carved into a sandstone cliff. You don't often see rooms like these. Albert and Gladys Christensen are gone now (actually, they're interred, if that's the word, within the rock), but the paintings, the lapidary room, the rock bathtub, the studio with donkey are all still here, and Franklin D. Roosevelt still looks down from above. *Tours, Gift Shop*

■ 801 686-2250 • 11037 S. Hwy 191, Moab, UT 84532

🚗 It's 15 miles south of Moab, in southeastern Utah. You will not be able to miss it.

🕐 Summer: Mon.–Sun. 9 A.M.–6 P.M. Rest of year: Mon.–Sun. 9 A.M.–5 P.M. Fee.

MONUMENT VALLEY

Goulding's Museum   Monument Valley is backdrop country, and at Goulding's you'll find memorabilia of movies made in the area. There's local history also, and then there's personal history—exhibits on Harry and Mike Goulding, who started the trading post in the 1920s—the ultimate museum material. *Gift Shop, Food*

■ 801 727-3231 • Monument Valley, UT 84536

🚗 Goulding's is near the Arizona border, in extreme southeastern Utah. Take US 163 to the Monument Valley turnoff, then 2 miles west to Goulding's Lodge.

🕐 Apr.–Dec.: Mon.–Sun. 11 A.M.–8 P.M. By appointment rest of year. Donation.

PROVO

Earth Science Museum at Brigham Young University   Is this the real Jurassic Park? They have skulls, skin impressions, eggs, bones—all from creatures that were actually lumbering around Utah a while back. You can watch personnel at work, touch fossils, and, when you're done with dinosaurs, visit other campus museums. *Tours, Gift Shop*

■ 801 378-3680 • 1683 N. Canyon Rd., Provo, UT 84602

🚗 North of Provo, exit from I-15 onto Route 265, which becomes University Pkwy. Go left at N. Canyon Rd. The museum is immediately west of the football stadium.

🕐 Mon. 9 A.M.–9 P.M., Tues.–Fri. 9 A.M.–5 P.M., Sat. noon–4 P.M. Donation.

SALT LAKE CITY

While you're in the area, see: Grantsville, Lehi

$\bigvee$ERMONT

Part of the state is New York exurb, part is distant mountain republic—and then there's the Northeast Kingdom. Vermonters fought to keep off their neighbors' mitts, and then ran their own show for some years before becoming a state in 1790. Throw in the landscape, and it's easy at times to think you've crossed an ocean instead of a state line. But Vermont is very New England in having sent its people and ideas across America, and in its museums you'll encounter some of them.

What's Big: The Shelburne Museum, outside Burlington, is the best-known in Vermont. Financial stress has recently forced it to shed parts of its collections. Let's hope it doesn't become "little."

BENNINGTON

Bennington Museum   This fine regional museum has Vermont-made glass and ceramics, furniture, early American painting and sculpture, and Battle of Bennington artifacts. It's the large collection of Grandma Moses works and memorabilia that draws many visitors, though; even her schoolhouse, moved from Eagle Bridge, New York, is here. *Tours, Gift Shop, Programs, Library*

📍 802 447-1571 • West Main St., Bennington, VT 05201

🚗 Bennington is in Vermont's southwest corner, on Routes 7 and 9. The museum is 1 mile west of the town's main intersection (West Main St. is Route 9).

🕐 Nov.–May: Mon.–Sun. 9 A.M.–5 P.M. June–Oct.: Mon.–Sun. 9 A.M.–6 P.M. Fee.

BURLINGTON

While you're in the area, see also: Shelburne

Williams Hall Art Museum of Kitsch Art (WHAMKA)   WHAMKA, founded by Prof. Ed Owre, has Last Suppers, space aliens, little boys fishing, the guts of various music boxes playing unavoidable pop tunes that occasionally come into sync, Elvis, Sno Cones, hula hoops. . . . A lot of the art is hot-glued to the walls—"We're at the forefront of display technology"—and it's all covered with dust from a nearby woodshop. A closet may soon become a western annex, as the collection grows. Two minutes out the back door is UVM's Robert Hull Fleming Museum, where, if you really want, there's plenty of good stuff. WHAMKA, according to "goad and scourge" Prof. Frank Owen, is the kind of museum one never gets to because one had to do something else. But you can change that.

🛍 802 656-2014 (UVM Art Dept.) • Williams Hall, University of Vermont, Burlington, VT 05405

🚐 It's in the first-floor hallway of the Art Dept. building, on Colchester Ave.

🕐 The building's open 7 A.M.–11 P.M. weekdays, 9 A.M.–9 P.M. weekends. For other hours, "call Security." No fee.

GLOVER

Bread and Puppet Museum   New York's radical Bread and Puppet Theater established this museum in 1974, making use of a large old dairy barn. Here you will find yourself among hundreds of surreal figures, especially the enigmatic heads that have bobbed above so many parades, festivals, and demonstrations. It's a sort of cloth-and-plaster Easter Island, hidden in the Northeast Kingdom.

🛍 802 525-3031 • Route 122, Glover, VT 05839

🚐 The Bread and Puppet Farm is in far northern Vermont, on Route 122 about 1 mile east of the junction with Route 16, south of the center of Glover. Take Exit 24 (Wheelock) off I-91 and proceed west toward Glover.

🕐 May–Oct.: Mon.–Sun. 10 A.M.–5 P.M. Rest of year by appointment. Donation.

HUNTINGTON

Birds of Vermont Museum   Bob Spear began carving birds as a teenager, in the 1930s. This museum's collection is now some 350 carvings and over 200 species strong. There are special presentations on bird song, nests and eggs, and endangered species, as well as woodcarving workshops. *Hands-on*

🛍 802 434-2167 • 900 Sherman Hollow Rd., Huntington, VT 05462

🚐 Huntington is a half-hour southeast of Burlington. Take Exit 11 (Richmond) off I-89, turn right in Richmond Village, toward Huntington, and follow signs.

🕐 May–Oct.: Mon.–Sun. 10 A.M.–4 P.M. Rest of year by appointment. Fee.

MANCHESTER VILLAGE

American Museum of Fly Fishing   Flies—the kind constructed from floss, feathers, and so on—are in focus here. The museum details the history of the sport ("as old as civilization") in this country, where Manchester claims to be its birthplace. Celebrity rods and gear, including that of our fishing presidents, are a key attraction. *Gift Shop, Publications*

- 802 362-3300 • Seminary Ave. and Route 7A, Manchester Village, VT 05254
- Manchester is in Vermont's southwest corner. Route 7A parallels (to the west) Route 7. The museum is on Manchester's southwest edge.
- May–Oct.: Mon.–Sun. 10 A.M.–4 P.M. Nov.–Apr.: Mon.–Fri. 10 A.M.–4 P.M. Fee.

PITTSFORD

New England Maple Museum Here is the story of maple sugaring since before Europeans arrived in America, detailed by artifacts and in visual presentations. There are sap sleds, tanks, buckets, over 150 feet of murals, and more. Comparison tastings and demonstrations of bucket and candy making are part of the fun. *See also* the American Maple Museum in Croghan, in upstate New York. *Gift Shop, Programs*

- 802 483-9414 • Route 7, Pittsford, VT 05763
- It's on Route 7, 10 minutes north of Rutland.
- Memorial Day–Oct.: Mon.–Sun. 8:30 A.M.–5:30 P.M. Mar.–Memorial Day and Nov.–Christmas Mon.–Sun., 10 A.M.–4 P.M. Fee.

PROCTOR

Vermont Marble Exhibit The Hall of Presidents (the head men, in bas-relief) is a big draw, but the museum also offers the opportunity to watch sculptors and other artisans at work, and displays of industry machinery. There is marble to buy too—only the size of your pocketbook (or recreational vehicle) limits you. *Gift Shop, Food*

- 802 459-2300 • 62 Main St., Proctor, VT 05765
- Proctor is just northwest of Rutland, in south-central Vermont. Main St. here is Route 3.
- May–Oct.: Mon.–Sun. 9 A.M.–5:30 P.M. Nov.–Apr.: Mon.–Sat. 9 A.M.–4 P.M. Fee.

SAINT JOHNSBURY

Fairbanks Museum and Planetarium This red sandstone, barrel-vaulted, and delightfully ornamented Victorian building would be interesting no matter what it housed. But inside you'll find all kinds of wonders, especially appealing to children. There are stuffed birds and mammals, "bug art" (yes, made from insects), historical tableaux, thousands of antique dolls, political memorabilia, Civil War stuff, Polynesian items, minerals, shells, rocks, tools, toys, and, and, and . . . and planetarium shows! *Gift Shop, Programs*

📞 802 748-2372 • http://www.fairbanksmuseum.org • 83 Main St., Saint Johnsbury, VT 05819

🚗 Saint Johnsbury is on the south edge of Vermont's Northeast Kingdom. Take Exit 21 off I-91 and proceed 1.5 miles east to the center of town.

🕐 July–Aug.: Mon.–Sat. 10 A.M.–6 P.M., Sun. 1 P.M.–5 P.M. Rest of year: Mon.–Sat. 10 A.M.–4 P.M., Sun. 1 P.M.–5 P.M. Fee.

SHELBURNE

National Museum of the Morgan Horse   The Morgan horse is one of Vermont's well-known contributions to American life. Here is a celebration of its role in history, in paintings, glass and sculpture, training carts, and other artifacts. If you'd like even more on Morgans, there's also the University of Vermont's Morgan Horse Farm, half an hour south in Middlebury (call 802 388-2011).

📞 802 985-8665 • 3 Bostwick Rd., Shelburne, VT 05482

🚗 Shelburne is 15 minutes south of Burlington, on Route 7. The Morgan horse museum is on the southern edge of the Shelburne Museum's complex; look for signs.

🕐 Mon.–Fri. 9 A.M.–4 P.M. Mid-May–Oct.: weekends, also, 10 A.M.–2 P.M. Fee.

WINDSOR

American Precision Museum   Machine tools, Windsor guns, typewriters, sewing machines, and other precision items are the focus here in the former armory where Robbins and Lawrence were the first (in the 1840s) to produce interchangeable parts on a practical level. There are scale models and other displays detailing the history of precision, unique devices like the "Etheric Force Main Stator," and examples of the work of machinist (and artist) Maxfield Parrish.

📞 802 674-5781 • http://ourworld.compuserve.com/homepages/Precision_Museum • 196 S. Main St., Windsor, VT 05089

🚗 Windsor is in southeastern Vermont, just south of the I-91/I-89 junction. Exit from I-91 into downtown, where Main St. is Route 5.

🕐 Memorial Day–Nov. 1: Mon.–Fri. 9 A.M.–5 P.M., weekends, holidays 10 A.M.–4 P.M. Fee.

WOODSTOCK

Vermont Raptor Center   The Northeast's only living museum devoted to rehabilitating birds of prey displays 24 species of hawk, eagle, owl, and falcon. You'll see them and learn how they are cared for. There are also reptiles and tarantulas, and at times wolves and other visitors. *Gift Shop, Hands-on, Programs, Publications*

■ 802 457-2779 • Woodstock, VT 05091

🚗 Woodstock is in south-central Vermont, just west of where I-91 and I-89 meet at White River Junction. The VINS (Vermont Institute of Natural Science and Raptor Center) is 1.5 miles southwest of Woodstock's green, on Church Hill Rd.

🕐 May–Oct.: Mon.–Sun. 10 A.M.–4 P.M. Nov.–Apr.: Mon.–Sat. 10 A.M.–4 P.M. Fee.

VIRGINIA

It will seem like most everything in Virginia is housed in a 1700s–1800s Colonial building. Locals are *very* attached to their past here. And for a while, of course, after the devastation of the Civil War, that seemed like all Virginians had. But the fact is there really is quite a bit of diversity—you just have to take a look inside these venerable old buildings.

What's Big: The scenic beauty of the Skyline Drive, of course; after that we've got the spanking new state-of-the-art Newseum in Arlington; McCormick's Farm in Steeles Tavern; Walton's Mountain Museum, for you diehard nostalgia buffs, in Schuyler; the Museum of the Confederacy in Richmond; the Museum of Valor in Spotsylvania; and Frank Lloyd Wright's Pop-Leighey House in Mount Vernon.

ALEXANDRIA

Adams Center for the History of Otolaryngology—Head and Neck Surgery Good-bye, tonsils. Hello, nasal douche. The ear, nose, and throat (and neck and head) people have been probing around for centuries, and here on display you'll find the most remarkable-looking medical equipment, surgical instruments, illustrations, and historical ephemera. A set of tonsil screws is one of their most unusual items; the 1880 beehive ear trumpet is one of our favorites. *Programs, Library*

🔹 703 519-1568/836-4444 • http://www.entnet.org • AAO-HNS Foundation, 1 Prince St., Alexandria, VA 22314

🚗 D.C. metro area. In Old Town, near Union St. intersection. Metro: King St.

🕐 Mon.–Fri. 9 A.M.–5 P.M. Library and storage collections are by appointment only. No fee.

George Washington Masonic Memorial The masons know how to build a monument and this one, modeled after Alexandria, Egypt's ancient lighthouse, is no exception. Dedicated to Lodge No. 22's 1st Worshipful Master (aka President

Washington), it's got exotic mason stuff from around the world plus the requisite humdinger of an Ark of the Covenant and a bunch of founding father memorabilia—but you'll have to go to the new dental museum in Baltimore to see his not-so-wooden teeth. *Library*

🏛 703 683-2007 • 101 Callahan Dr., Alexandria, VA 22301

🚗 D.C. metro area. 1 mile from the Telegraph Rd. I-95 (Beltway) exit. It's at the west end of King St. Metro: King St.

🕐 Mon.–Sun. 9 A.M.–5 P.M. No fee.

ARLINGTON

U.S. Patent and Trademark Museum One thousand ninety-three patents owned by one person? Yep. Thomas Edison (read about them in Menlo Park, New Jersey). Now that's American ingenuity at its peak. But America's been fertile ground for inventors of all stripes, and one of the highlights here is the old Patent Office exhibit, which from 1840 to 1893 also housed 250,000 patent models, and was a major tourist attraction of its day. Nowadays, only a few models are on display (*see* Fort Smith, Arkansas, for more). But there's always a lively feature on how particular contraptions have changed—like how the wooden-spoked Velocipede became today's lightweight bicycle. *Tours, Gift Shop*

🏛 703 305-8341 • http://www.uspto.gov • 2121 Crystal Dr., Arlington, VA 22202

🚗 D.C. metro area. From D.C. cross the 14th St. Bridge, exiting left to Crystal City (Route 1). Turn left at 23rd St., then left at Crystal Dr. Follow museum sign and turn right. It's in Crystal Park Two. Metro: Crystal City.

🕐 Mon.–Fri. 8:30 A.M.–4:30 P.M., tours and other times by appointment. No fee.

CHINCOTEAGUE

Oyster Museum We've heard this called a pearl of an oyster museum, and its size and presentation may well have you thinking the same. Oysters and oystering from the 1600s to the present.

🏛 757 336-6117 • Maddox Blvd., Chincoteague, VA 23336

🚗 On the Del-Mar-Va peninsula, take Hwy 175 into town, then left onto Main St. for 0.5 mile, then turn east onto Maddox Blvd. for 1.5 miles.

🕐 Memorial Day–Labor Day: Mon.–Sun. 10 A.M.–5 P.M. Hours vary rest of year. Closed Dec.–Feb. Fee.

DUMFRIES

Weems-Botts Museum Another kind of invention, this time involving the early 1800s biographer to the founding fathers, the Reverend Mason Locke Weems.

Seems our first president wasn't so beloved later in his career, and the good Parson Weems thought a bit of spin was in order. So whipping in a tall tale of chopped cherry trees to his best-selling *Life of Washington* seemed just the thing to win over a hero-hungry public. Wonder what Honest George made of it? This is where Weems lived, it's very old, and they have a nice assortment of Colonial finds that were unearthed right on the property. *Hands-on*

- 703 221-3346 • 300 Duke St., Dumfries, VA 22026
- About 25 miles south of D.C. I-95 Exit 51, then take a left onto Duke, it's on the left just past Cameron St.
- Tues.–Sun. Hours vary. Donation.

MOUNT SOLON

National Jousting Hall of Fame   Iroquois lacrosse players may quibble, but in Virginia they consider jousting the "oldest continually held sporting event in America." Begun here in 1821, lances were poised not to kill, but to snare small rings hanging on a limp string. Our horseback heroes' contest was at that time, the story goes, over the hand of a maiden. Historic pix, great limestone formations for castlelike atmosphere, and jousting events every third Saturday in June and August. *Programs*

- 540 350-2510 • Natural Chimneys Park, Route 1, Box 286, Mount Solon, VA 22843
- In western Virginia, about 12 miles north of Staunton off I-81 on Hwy 607.
- Open all park hours. Mar.–Sept.: Mon.–Fri. 9 A.M.–5 P.M., Sat.–Sun. 9 A.M.–7 P.M. Oct.–Feb.: Sun., Mon., Wed., Thurs. 10 A.M.–5 P.M., Fri.–Sat. 9 A.M.–7 P.M. Fee.

NEW MARKET

Bedrooms of America   Yes it does look just like a tourist trap, despite the building's 1765 pedigree. But you're here for the 11 bedrooms they promise, which are indeed decorated with authentic period furniture from William and Mary (circa 1650) through Art Deco (circa 1930), and should satisfy your requirements for American Furniture 101. *Gift Shop*

- 540 740-3512 • 9386 Congress St., New Market, VA 22844
- In northwestern Virginia take I-81 Exit 264, to Congress and Old Cross Rd.
- Memorial Day–Labor Day: Mon.–Sun. 9 A.M.–8 P.M. Closes 5 P.M. rest of year. Fee.

PAEONIAN SPRINGS

American Work Horse Museum   How could you not like and, surely, respect these big guys? Pictures and artifacts tell the on-the-job story of these equine Teamsters, used to haul all kinds of farm and military equipment before the combustion engine downsized most of them out to an early retirement. *Library*

🏠 540 231-4152 • Route 662, PO Box 88, Paeonian Springs, VA 22129

🚗 In northern Virginia on Route 662, 4 miles west of Leesburg.

🕐 By appointment only. Donation.

PETERSBURG

U.S. Slo-Pitch Softball Association Hall of Fame Museum Two million people play under Slo-Pitch rules, and now that this version of softball has been introduced in Russia, who knows how far it will go. Meanwhile though, it's fun right here, checking out the team jerseys with names that rival bowling's best, like Elite Coating of Gordon, Georgia, and the descriptive displays that will tell you things like how the softball evolved from a twine-wrapped boxing glove in 1887 to the still hand-stitched, but now poly-core, ball of today. *Gift Shop*

🏠 804 733-1005 • 3935 S. Crater Rd., Petersburg, VA 23803

🚗 Petersburg is 25 miles south of Richmond. From I-95S take the Rives Rd. exit, go 0.5 mile and turn left onto Route 301 (S. Crater Rd.).

🕐 Mon.–Fri. 9 A.M.–4 P.M., Sat. 10 A.M.–4 P.M., Sun. noon–4 P.M. Fee.

RICHMOND

Black History Museum In the historic Jackson Ward district, the 1832 home of this museum has also been the home to a roster of firsts for blacks. The collections and archives reflect that with changing exhibits that might feature African-American inventors or traditional art, and permanent displays on people and events you won't find much on elsewhere like the World War II Tuskegee airmen, Bojangles, and business and entertainment history of the area. *See also* Detroit, Michigan. *Tours, Gift Shop, Programs, Library*

🏠 804 780-9093 • 00 Clay St., Richmond, VA 23219

🚗 I-95 Exit 76A (Chamberlayne Ave.). Turn left at the light, then left again onto Leigh St. Turn right onto Saint James St.—it's at the end of the block.

🕐 Tues.–Sat. 11 A.M.–4 P.M. Appointment necessary for tours. Fee.

Edgar Allan Poe Museum Seems like Poe hung his hat in a lot of different towns, but he does have long-standing family roots here in Richmond. The museum is in the oldest building in Richmond (circa 1737), and no, he did not live here, but they did bring over an entire staircase, furnishings, and personal effects from his nearby home and office. Besides the somber and mood-setting 1880s James Carling illustrations for "The Raven," we are most fascinated by the re-creation of his childhood bedroom, looking for clues to his dark and brooding imagery. *Tours, Gift Shop, Programs, Publications, Library*

🏛 804 648-5523 • 1914–1916 E. Main St., Richmond, VA 23223

🚗 Shockoe Bottom district, at the corner of E. Main and 20th St.

🕐 Mar.–Oct.: Tues.–Sat. 10 A.M.–4 P.M., Sun.–Mon. noon–4 P.M. Nov.–Feb.: Sun.–Fri. noon–4 P.M., Sat. 10 A.M.–4 P.M. Tours begin on the hour. Fee.

Money Museum   A husk of corn . . . a large flat stone with a hole in the center . . . shell beads on a string . . . a compressed brick of tea . . . What do these have in common? Like the Katanga "wife-buying cross" showcased here, they've all been used as money at one time or another. Currency old (back to 30 centuries ago) and new, from the "Far East to the New World," is joined with exhibits on the tools of the trade and dramatic show-and-tells like an uncut sheet of $100,000 gold certificates.

🏛 804 697-8108 • Federal Reserve Bank of Richmond, 701 E. Byrd St., Richmond, VA 23219

🚗 From I-95 from the north, exit onto 3rd St. and proceed to Byrd St., then turn left.

🕐 Mon.–Fri. 9:30 A.M.–3:30 P.M. No fee.

VIRGINIA BEACH

Old Coast Guard Station Museum   This museum really brings the war back home, with exhibits detailing the U-boat activity and enemy mining of the Chesapeake Bay during World War II. Also on deck are stirring pix and artifacts that tell the story of shipwrecks, hurricanes, and lifesaving efforts dating back to 1878. *Gift Shop, Publications*

🏛 757 422-1587 • 24th St. and Atlantic Ave., Virginia Beach, VA 23458

🚗 Route 44 (Norfolk/Virginia Beach Expwy) into town, which becomes 21st St. Follow 21st down to Atlantic Ave., then turn left to 24th St.

🕐 Memorial Day–Sept. 30: Mon.–Sat. 10 A.M.–5 P.M., Sun. noon–5 P.M. Closed Mon. rest of year. Fee.

WAVERLY

First Peanut Museum in U.S.A.   The peanut novice may be surprised to learn that peanuts don't grow on trees, but since around 1842, when Dr. Matthew Harris grew the first commercial crop in the United States here in Sussex County, the mighty peanut has proliferated. Here's a wonderfully cozy museum dedicated to a favorite nut, with pictures and equipment from its farming and factories, and wood-carved folk art by the late Miles B. Carpenter and other local artists. Another

unusual site feature: outhouses from one of FDR's lesser-known WPA projects.
Tours, Programs, Library

🏠 804 834-3327/2151 • Miles B. Carpenter Museum Complex, 201 Hunter St., Waverly, VA 23890

🚙 Forty-five miles southeast of Richmond, on US 460, near Route 40.

🕐 Mon., Thurs.–Sun. 2 P.M.–5 P.M. Donation.

WINCHESTER

Patsy Cline at the Kurtz Cultural Center A tragic year for this country, 1963 started off badly when Patsy's plane went down in Tennessee that March. You can "Celebrate Patsy" with a walking tour in her hometown and follow up with a visit to the small exhibit in this local and Civil War history museum that features her mink, personal effects and letters, gold records, and her own postage stamp. Unfortunately Patsy's mom, who lives nearby, isn't quite ready to give up her trove of Cline outfits and other stuff, but we hope she'll change her mind when the hoped-for Patsy-dedicated museum eventually gets built. The "Singing Girl of the Shenandoah Valley," whose warm country voice just wraps itself around you, is due for star treatment. *Tours, Gift Shop*

🏠 540 722-6367 • 2 N. Cameron St., Winchester, VA 22601

🚙 Northern Virginia, 60 miles west of Washington, D.C. From I-81N take Exit 313; from I-81S, take Exit 315. It's in the Old Town section, at the corner of Boscawen St.

🕐 Mon.–Sat. 10 A.M.–5 P.M., Sun. noon–5 P.M. No fee. Self-guided walking tour.

WASHINGTON

What do you think of when you think Washington? Oh-so-liveable Seattle? Starbucks? Microsoft? Boeing? Mount Saint Helens? Mount Rainier? Apples? Cranberries? *Twin Peaks*? Columbia Gorge? Grand Coulee Dam? Don Brown's Rosary Collection? Turns out Washington is one of those states where the littlest tidbit of info is inspiration enough to make you want to seek it out. Especially when it comes to descriptions of natural beauty. We think you'll be lured all over this state—where things most mundane seem fresh, the arcane seems right at home, and absolutely everyone's hopped up on java.

What's Big: Any of the spots we've mentioned above, along with the Lewis and Clark Interpretive Center in Ilwaco; in Seattle, the Museum of Flight and the forthcoming Experience Music Project; and in Tacoma, Lakewold's (Medieval Knot) Gardens.

BELLINGHAM

Roeder Home   Built in 1908 in Bracketed Gothic (sort of heading to Craftsman-style), the Roeder Home exemplifies what big bucks can do in providing all the modern conveniences. The fantastic attention to detail that Victor Roeder, bank founder and scion of local pioneering families, insisted on extended to the installation of a built-in vacuum system—vents installed throughout the house allow you to attach a hose at each location and suck away. Interesting—and the period wall murals are nice too. *Tours, Programs*

🏠 360 733-6897 • 2600 Sunset Dr., Bellingham, WA 98225

🚐 About 85 miles north of Seattle. Take I-5 to Sunset Dr. Exit 255. Go west on Sunset, turning right at the end onto W. Illinois, then left onto Cornwall, then right onto Broadway going up 1 block to Sunset again. It's on the right.

🕐 Mon.–Thurs. 9 A.M.–4 P.M. and by appointment. Closed Dec. No fee.

BICKLETON

Whoop-n-Holler Museum Local history, old cars, and a lot of the personal touch from Ada Ruth and Lawrence Whitmore. Savers nonpareil, for everything they've got—from display cases of miniature rock furniture to an electric lunch pail—they can tell you a story, and that's half the fun. Back in town don't miss the still-in-action 1882 Bluebird Inn with its 1903 Brunswick pool table.

🔲 509 896-2344 • 1 Whitmore Rd., Bickleton, WA 99322

🚢 South-central. From Goldendale go east to Bickleton, then south 12 miles on East Rd., turning west onto Whitmore.

🕐 Apr.–Sept.: Mon.–Sun. 10 A.M.–4 P.M. Fee.

CASTLE ROCK

Castle Rock Exhibit Hall When Mount Saint Helens blew on May 18, 1980, lives and terrain were changed throughout the area. Castle Rock provides oral histories from eyewitnesses as well as dramatic photos and a small re-creation of the blast zone. Another side of people's lives here is told through the story of loggers like Hap Johnson, who won 23 world championships and is a member of a rare breed of competitive woodsfolk whose specialties include speed climbing, tree topping, axe throwing, log rolling, and Jack & Jill bucking. There's more on Mount Saint Helens in this area, but you must just go see it. *Hands-on, Programs*

🔲 360 274-6603 • 147 Front St., Castle Rock, WA 98611

🚢 In southwestern Washington, take I-5 Exit 49, going 0.5 mile southwest into downtown Castle Rock. You'll be on Huntington Ave.; turn right onto Front.

🕐 May–Sept.: Mon.–Sun. 9 A.M.–6 P.M. Oct.–Apr.: Wed.–Sat. 10 A.M.–2 P.M. Donation.

CLE ELUM

Cle Elum Historical Telephone Museum Cle Elum's telephone history is a history of lasts—last in this country to give up their operator-assisted manual switchboard system and switch to direct-dial phones (1966), last to get Touchtone, and one of the last to get auto dialing (1991). But here are the switchboards in all their developing complexity, and the rich stories of the operators that served this mining town—all of whom were required to speak at least two languages due to the many nationalities of the local mine and railroad workers. *Gift Shop*

🔲 509 674-5702 • 221 E. 1st St., Cle Elum, WA 98922

🚢 In central Washington, off I-90 Exit 84. It's downtown, at E. 1st and Wright Ave.

🕐 Memorial Day–Labor Day: Tues.–Fri. 9 A.M.–4 P.M.; Sat., Sun., Mon. noon–4 P.M. Fee.

CONCRETE

Camp Seven Museum   Concrete, once known as Cement City, has known both the logging and the cement industries, and a selection of artifacts—like timber branding irons—and historical pix from both are here at Camp Seven. Also on hand, from Herb Larsen's personal collection, is an unusual assortment of items from the old homestead—like washing machines, refrigerators, and some very special typewriters, including an old Remington with the key pad set underneath the chassis.

■ 360 853-8304 • 117 Railroad Ave., Concrete, WA 98237

🚗 About 80 miles northeast of Seattle, take I-5 to Hwy 20E 23 miles into town. From Main St. turn right onto Thompson St., then right again onto Railroad Ave.

🕐 May–Aug.: Mon.–Sun. usually noon–4 P.M. Sept.–Apr.: By appointment only. Fee.

ELECTRIC CITY

Gehrke Windmill Garden   Phantasmogorical windmills in the shadow of the Grand Coulee Dam make a wondrous contrast to the concrete technological wonder that is the Coulee. Constructed of found material—from Jell-O molds to hubcaps and chandeliers—by the late Emil Gehrke (an ironworker and millwright by trade) and painted by Vera Gehrke, his wife, this field of over 100 windmills and whirligigs spins playfully along.

■ Hwy 155/North Dam Rest Area, Electric City, WA 99123

🚗 In central Washington, 1 mile southwest of Grand Coulee Dam. It's in the North Dam rest area as you're coming into Grand Coulee on Hwy 155.

🕐 Year-round, daylight hours. No fee.

FORKS

Hoh Rain Forest Visitors Center   The visitors center provides a fine orientation to the flora and fauna of the Hoh Rain Forest, distinctive because it is one of only a very few temperate rain forests to be found in the world—you'd have to go to New Zealand or Chile to see the others. Distinctive also because it is a virtual wonderland of soft mossy greenery, almost delicate in appearance, and certainly magical as light filters through the boughs of the giant Sitka spruce and western hemlock. It's not an insult when we tell you to take a hike. For tales (and exhibits) about the local timber industry, stop at the Forks Timber Museum (360 374-9663).

■ 360 374-6925 • 18195 Upper Hoh Rd., Forks, WA 98331

🚗 On the Olympic Peninsula, take US 101 to 12 miles south of Forks, then turn off onto the Upper Hoh Rd. It's 18 miles to the visitors center.

🕐 July–Aug.: Mon.–Sun. 9 A.M.–6:30 P.M. Sept.–June: Mon.–Sun. 9 A.M.–4 P.M. No fee.

FRIDAY HARBOR/SAN JUAN ISLAND

Pig War Museum   Once upon a time, when the Brits still laid claim to portions of the New World—specifically the San Juan Islands, which, despite the British claim in 1792, were declared as American soil in 1841—there was an altercation over a pig. Well, it was a big pig—a prize black boar to be precise, owned by the British manager of the Hudson's Bay Co. farm—and it seems the beast kept wandering into the potato patch of a neighboring American miner who got fed up and shot him. So to avoid a big war, Kaiser Wilhelm I was called in to arbitrate, and 13 years after the war of 1859 he declared the San Juans for the United States once and for all. Ms. Emilia Bave has singlehandedly preserved this moment in history. Don't miss it.

▪ 360 378-6495/378-4830 • 620 Guard St., Friday Harbor, San Juan Island, WA 98250

🚗 Take the ferry to Friday Harbor. It's at the corner of Guard and Tucker.

🕑 Memorial Day–Labor Day: Wed.–Sat. 1 P.M.–4 P.M. Rest of year by appointment. Fee.

GOLDENDALE

Maryhill Museum of Art   *The Cast*: Sam Hill—Quaker, stock-market million-aire, and Harvard-educated man-of-the-world; Queen Marie of Romania; Loie Fuller, a Folies-Bergère dancer with connections; and Alma Spreckels, sugar mil-lionairess. *The Scenario*: 1907. Hill envisions Maryhill as his family's home and the cornerstone of a Quaker farm community. While he completes his nearby Stone-henge replica—built as a tribute to the World War I dead—he never finishes Mary-hill. He does, however, heed the advice of Ms. Fuller that he turn it into an art museum. Good fortune, and a little pull all around, brings him 52 Rodin originals and Queen Marie herself for a dedication, even though it's still just a concrete shell. Everyone dies, except Ms. Spreckels, who gets the doors open in 1940. *The Present*: A wow of a museum featuring the Rodins; a "glittering grouping" of Queen Marie's Romanian ball gowns, jewels, and other royal art and effects; fantastically attired miniature French fashion mannequins conceived by the designers and credited with the rebirth of post–World War II Paris couture; and acclaimed chess set and Native American collections. *Tours, Gift Shop, Food, Programs*

▪ 509 773-3733 • 35 Maryhill Museum Dr., Goldendale, WA 98620

🚗 South-central, south of Yakima. Take I-90 to I-82, then south on US 97 at Toppenish, about 50 miles.

🕑 Mar. 15–Nov. 15: Mon.–Sun. 9 A.M.–5 P.M. Fee.

GRAYLAND

Furford Cranberry Museum   Julius Furford's automated picker changed the way of cranberry picking here in the heart of Washington bog country back in 1956.

Now you can stop by and see the old and new methods and machines and learn all about this labor-intensive Thanksgiving-indispensable crop. *Food*

📷 360 267-3303 • 2395 State Route 105, Grayland, WA 98547

🚗 On the coast, 60 miles west of Olympia. Follow Hwy 105S through Grayland. It's on the right side, behind the Furford manufacturing facility.

🕐 Mar.–Nov.: Hours vary, call ahead. No fee.

LONG BEACH

Marsh's Free Museum   A veritable "stuff" emporium. The most well known inhabitant is "Jake" the Alligator Man, but he's in fine company in this sideshow of a museum on the Long Beach strip. The still family-run (founded by tavern-owner Wellington Marsh, Sr., when he started swapping beers for mementos in 1935) enterprise has a skedillion seashells, a fine corset collection, nickel peep shows like a dime Kiss Tester (Ice Cold! to Hot Stuff!!), and lots more. *Gift Shop, Food*

📷 360 642-2188 • 409 S. Pacific Ave., Long Beach, WA 98631

🚗 On the southwest coast, take US 101S into Seaview, then 1 mile north on Pacific Hwy 103 (S. Pacific Ave.) to S. 5th.

🕐 Summer: Mon.–Sun. 9 A.M.–9 P.M. Winter: Mon.–Fri. 9 A.M.–6 P.M., Sat.–Sun. 9 A.M.–7 P.M. No fee.

World Kite Museum and Hall of Fame   Kite-flying conditions are great here in Long Beach–28 miles of open sand, brisk winds, and uncluttered sky—so no wonder this is the home of a major annual (kite) flying festival in August. There's also a collection of kites from around the world, old and new, giant (as big as 550 square meters) and tiny, from fighter kites to sport kites to night-light kites. Special features on kite history, from Ben Franklin through military defense, and their use in flying photography. *Gift Shop, Hands-on, Programs, Library*

📷 360 642-4020 • 3rd St. NW, Long Beach, WA 98631

🚗 See above. From Pacific Hwy 103 (S. Pacific Ave.) north, turn left onto 3rd St.

🕐 June–Aug.: Mon.–Sun. 11 A.M.–5 P.M. Sept.–Oct.: Fri.–Mon. 11 A.M.–5 P.M. Nov.–May: Sat.–Sun. 11 A.M.–5 P.M. Fee.

NEAH BAY

Makah Cultural and Research Center   The Makah village of Ozette, per-fectly preserved by a mudslide, was re-exposed by tidal erosion in 1970, over 500 years later. This remarkable discovery, painstakingly excavated over an 11-year period, has helped re-create the Makahs' past as whalers and sealers, bas-ketweavers and craftspeople, and warriors. One of the most significant archaeo-logical finds in North America, the workmanship of the artifacts and dugout canoes are complemented with the thoughtful exhibits that include marine-environment dioramas and a feeling for the life of Makah people to the present day. *Gift Shop, Hands-on*

📷 360 645-2711 • Hwy 112, Neah Bay, WA 98357

🚗 On the Olympic Peninsula, from US 101 get on Hwy 112 just west of Port Angeles. Then go west about 60 miles to the end.

🕐 June–Sept. 15: Mon.–Sun. 10 A.M.–5 P.M. Sept. 16–May: Wed.–Sun. 10 A.M.–5 P.M. Fee.

PORT GAMBLE

Of Sea and Shore Museum Starting with a science-fair project run amok, Tom Rice has amassed over 25,000 shells over the last 20 or so years. He can also tell you all about the inner workings of the gumboot chiton and a sea snail's favorite camouflage tricks. Housed in the same 1914 building as the Port Gamble Historic Museum, stop by there for the story of this company town, where the oldest lumbermill in the country is still in operation. *Gift Shop, Programs, Publications*

📷 360 297-2426 • Country Store Building, Rainier Ave., Port Gamble, WA 98364

🚗 Puget Sound area. Take Hwy 16N from Tacoma about 45 miles into Hwy 104.

🕐 May 15–Sept. 15: Tues.–Sun. 11 A.M.–4 P.M. Sept. 16–May 14: Sat.–Sun. 11 A.M.–4 P.M. Other times by appointment. No fee.

PULLMAN

Washington State University has a collection of something for everyone: Nez Perce Music Archive; Drucker Collection of Oriental furniture, textiles, and art; Museum of Anthropology; Maurice T. James Entomological Collection for those with a thing for bugs; and the Mycological Herbarium, for those with a thing for fungus growing in the dark.

Smith Soil Monolith Collection It ain't just dirt. Soil monoliths are actually vertical profiles, up to eight feet in length, painstakingly extracted from the earth to preserve all details of texture, stratigraphy, effects of erosion and weathering, and other information useful to those whose studies of such things inform the rest of us not just about changes on our planet, but, for instance, what makes one area good for agriculture, and another not. We understand the University of Idaho (in Moscow, Idaho; call Dr. Paul McDaniel: 208 885-7012) has an even bigger, more accessible collection. And we're reminded to tell you about one of our favorite websites, the Dirt Museum (http://www.planet.com/dirtweb/dirt.html). *Tours*

📷 509 335-1859 • Johnson Hall 114, Washington State University, Pullman, WA 99164

🚗 Eastern Washington, about 76 miles south of Spokane off US 195.

🕐 Observation window: Mon.–Fri. 8 A.M.–5 P.M. Call Dr. Alan Busacca ahead for tours. No fee.

RICHLAND

Columbia River Exhibition of History, Science, and Technology

When the Department of Energy decided to shut down the visitors center for the Hanford Nuclear Site, the community rallied. Having salvaged hands-on exhibits, like a mock-up "Hot Cell" with a robotic manipulator arm for handling highly radioactive materials, that go back to the days of Hanford's role in the Manhattan Project, they recently reopened with a mission not only to preserve the history and legacy of the nuclear era but to investigate local technology and environment issues into the next century. *Gift Shop, Hands-on, Programs, Publications*

■ 509 943-9000 • 95 Lee Blvd., Richland, WA 99352

🚌 South-central. From I-82 or I-182, take the George Washington Way exit. Turn right onto Lee Blvd., then an almost immediate right again at the Allied Arts Gallery.

🕐 Mon.–Sat. 10 A.M.–5 P.M., Sun. noon–5 P.M. Fee.

SEATTLE

Seattle is a hopping town, so while you've got the buzz, here are a few more places to look into: Center for Wooden Boats, The Royal Brougham Collection at the Kingdome Sports Museum, Smith Tower, and the nearby Bainbridge Island Vineyards and Winery—for their collection of antique wineglasses.

General Petroleum Museum

One of the charms of a good road trip is wandering the old highways and stumbling across an ancient gas station, hopefully with some old signage and a glass pump intact. Jeff and Susan Pedersen think so too, and have made it their mission to collect and display all things, as they say in the trade, "petroleana." Gasoline-sales history is chronicled with pumps of all kinds, neon signs, all the toys, games, and map giveaways, and two (of only five ever made) mechanical Mobil Pegasus horses used for promo around the country. Come to enjoy the atmosphere—replete with an accurate deco gas station replica—but also to absorb a chunk of auto history from this carefully researched and archived collection.

■ 206 323-4789 • 1526 Bellevue Ave. East, Seattle, WA 98122

🚌 Capitol Hill area, at the corner of Bellevue and Pine St. The entrance is at the rear.

🕐 By appointment only. No fee.

Memory Lane Museum at Seattle Goodwill

A trip to Goodwill is often a trip down memory lane. Great for new finds, and great for the feeling of relief that that avocado-colored toaster's not yours anymore. But what you'll find here is some pretty unusual stuff from some pretty unusual attics: *Miss Bardahl*, a world-champion hydroplane, is here; so is a complete mechanic's garage, Fiesta dinnerware, an 11-foot tall Alaskan brown bear, and lots of vintage clothing and accessories.

● 206 329-1000 • Seattle Goodwill, 1400 S. Lane St., Seattle, WA 98144

🚗 I-5, Dearborn St. exit, south of downtown. It's at the corner of Rainier Ave. South and S. Dearborn St.

🕐 Mon.–Fri. 10 A.M.–8 P.M., Sat. 9 A.M.–7 P.M., Sun. 10 A.M.–5 P.M. No fee.

Saint Charles Archery Museum   Lions, and tigers, and bears, oh yes. The archers that you might find in the shop while you're touring the museum are indeed representative—this is a bow-hunting crowd, and the displays, from a recent acquisition of an unusual mounted African lion rug shot by Art Young back in 1925 to the presentation of five arrows made by Ishi, the last Yahi Indian, whose survival at the turn of the century depended on his bow skills, reflect that. Over 200 antique bows and bow-making tools, countless arrowheads, and super high-tech modern flight (distance) shooting equipment. *Library*

● 206 878-7300 • Northwest Archery Co., 19807 1st Ave. South, Seattle, WA 98148

🚗 South of downtown near the airport. I-5 Exit 151 (200th St. South), continue west 2.5 miles to 1st Ave. South, turn right. It's just up the block, on the left.

🕐 Tues.–Fri. 10 A.M.–6 P.M., Sat. 10 A.M.–5 P.M. No fee.

Thorniley Collection of Type   An old hand in the printing trade, curator John DeNure will take you on a very special personal tour of the world of hot metal type. This showcase of American typography and printing ingenuity is a growing repository for the tools of a craft all but lost to desktop computers. Here's the place to see original wooden fonts like Cincinnati Ornamental, Union Pearl, and Antique Pointed; the presses they were used on; and get a whiff of what it really means to have printer's blood in your veins.

● 800 451-2737/206 850-1800 • West Coast Paper Co., 23200 64th Ave. South, Kent, WA 98032

🚗 Just south of Seattle's Kingdome, between I-5 and Route 99, and just to the east of Seattle-Tacoma Airport.

🕐 Wed. 9 A.M.–5 P.M., by appointment only. No fee.

Vintage Telephone Equipment   Run by the Telephone Pioneers of America and staffed with former employees of the old Bell System, you're in expert hands as you tour—and try out—this carefully restored collection of telephone equipment from the old magnetos (crank phones) to switchboards, teletypes, and an entire "central office." Telephone ephemera like a set of Seattle telephone directories dating back to the early days is joined by an overview of what else Western Electric was up to back when. Check out the selection of fans, sewing machines, and cookstoves. *Tours, Hands-on, Library*

● 206 767-3012/789-4761 • 7000 E. Marginal Way South, Seattle, WA 98108

🚐 South Seattle ("Georgetown"), I-5 Exit 163 (Corson Ave./Michigan Ave.), staying on Corson Ave. Just before the 2nd traffic light (and right across from the huge but kaput Hat N Boot gas station), enter the US West building driveway on the left.

🕑 Tues. 8:30 A.M.–2:30 P.M. and by appointment. Donation.

Wing Luke Asian Museum   Devoted to Asian Pacific American culture, history, and art, the exhibits here are renowned for their cross-cultural, community-based approach to a diverse population. The 200-year story of immigration and settlement in Washington state is that of ten major groups including Pacific Islanders, Southeast Asian Hill Tribes, Cambodians, Japanese, Chinese, Vietnamese, Koreans, Laotians, South Asians, and Filipinos. Gorgeous hand-painted kites, masks, and artwork are counterpointed with displays on World War II internment camps for American-born Japanese and all aspects of work and day-to-day life in Seattle's unusual pan-Asian community. *Tours*

🏛 206 623-5124 • 407 7th Ave. South, Seattle, WA 98104

🚐 I-5, Dearborn St. exit south of downtown. At the end of the off-ramp head west (toward the Kingdome), turning right onto 7th Ave. South for 3.5 blocks.

🕑 Tues.–Fri. 11 A.M.–4:30 P.M., Sat.–Sun. noon–4 P.M. Fee.

SPOKANE

Bing Crosby Library   Der Bingle's alma mater, and happy home for career and golfing memorabilia of the consummate crooner, Harry Lillis "Bing" Crosby. For the diehard aficionado, a trip to Kohala Coast, Hawaii, to the Eva Parker Woods Cottage for the story of his trademark feather in his fedora might be in order.

🏛 509 328-4220 x4277 • Gonzaga University, 502 E. Boone Ave., Spokane, WA 99202

🚐 Northeast of downtown, take US 395 (Division St.) north and turn right at Boone.

🕑 Sept.–Apr.: Mon.–Fri. 8:30 A.M.–4:30 P.M., Sat.–Sun. 11:30 A.M.–4:30 P.M. May–Aug.: Mon.–Fri. 9 A.M.–4:30 P.M. Hours vary during semester breaks. No fee.

STEILACOOM

Bair Drug and Hardware Co. Living Museum   A thriving all-around drug and hardware store back in the trolley era, these days you come here for the old (1906) fountain, great fresh blackberry shakes, and old-time atmosphere with pharmaceutical displays, original hardware merchandise, and early post office still intact. It fits right in with the town that's the state's oldest incorporated one, and home to its first library and many other venerable old buildings. *Food*

🏛 253 588-9668 • 1617 Lafayette St., Steilacoom, WA 98388

🚐 About 15 miles south of Tacoma. At Tacoma take I-5 Exit 129, then follow signs to Steilacoom. It's in the historic district. Bair is at Lafayette and Wilkes St.

🕑 Mon.–Sun. 9 A.M.–4 P.M. Fri. also 6 P.M.–9 P.M. No fee.

Steilacoom Tribal Cultural Center and Museum   Steilacoom is the aboriginal homeland of the Steilacoom tribe and was named by them after the abundant Indian Pink plant found on the surrounding bluffs. Housed in a 1903 grey clapboard church, the simple rustic structure with its pulpit view of the Sound seems the perfect setting to this austere collection representing the Steilacoom and other Coast Salish people. Featured: an archaeological dig wall dating back to 1430, prehistory of the Tacoma Basin, and historic and contemporary lifestyles like "Float House" construction. *Tours, Gift Shop, Food, Hands-on, Programs*
- 📞 253 584-6308 • 1515 Lafayette St., Steilacoom, WA 98388
- 🚗 See above. It's in the historic district, at the corner of Pacific St.
- 🕐 Tues.–Sun. 10 A.M.–4 P.M. Fee. Call ahead for tour.

STEVENSON

You're right on top of the Bonneville Dam here, and while things look great from the Washington side, you will want to cross over to the Oregon side and get a good look at the Cascade Locks too.

Don Brown Rosary Collection   While Catholic prayer beads have strictly circumscribed guidelines as to how they are to be worn (*not* as a fashion accessory, please), by whom (Catholic church officials), and how many (each is made of five sets of ten beads plus one special bead between the sets), the sky's the limit when it comes to how they're made—and of what. So that explains the absolutely—some might say, inspired—eclectic assortment that's found its way into Don Brown's hands, and now the museum's, since his death in 1975. Ping-pong balls; glow-in-the-darks (for night driving . . . or the bijou); water chestnuts; ancient amber; hand-carved deer horns; rifle shells; some exquisite, some tiny (one fits in an acorn); all remarkable. When you come to the rosary collection, leave yourself some time to poke around this huge new interpretive center for the cultural and natural history of the Gorge. *Tours, Gift Shop*
- 📞 509 427-8211 • Columbia Gorge Interpretive Center, 990 SW Rock Creek Dr., Stevenson, WA 98648
- 🚗 Just northeast of Portland, Oregon. I-5 Exit 27 onto WA Hwy 14E about 35 miles. Turn left on Rock Creek Dr.
- 🕐 Mon.–Sun. 10 A.M.–5 P.M. Fee.

TOPPENISH

American Hop Museum   The museum begins from the outside, with murals (you'll see them throughout the town also) depicting hop cultural and harvest scenes from 1900 and before. Inside you'll find exhibits that cover (and allow you to taste-test) the beers the Colonialists were drinking, and historic photos, memorabilia, and interpretive displays on the industry. *Food*

🏠 509 865 HOPS [4677] • 22 S. B St., Toppenish, WA 98948

🚗 Just south of Yakima. I-90 Exit 110, south on US 82 about 40 miles to Exit 50 onto US 97S.

🕐 Apr.–Oct.: Mon.–Sun. 11 A.M.–4 P.M. Donation.

WENATCHEE

North Central Washington Museum Housed in historic early-20th-century Federal buildings, including the former Wenatchee Post Office, one of the first things you'll notice are the WPA murals of Peggy Jo Strong, revealing the saga of the U.S. Postal Service. Then there's the early Clovis archaeological exhibit, a display on the first trans-Pacific flight, the 1919 working Liberty Theatre pipe organ, the in-service miniature Great Northern Railway train, and the even more miniature Charbeau-Warren collection of tiny stuff—scenes painted on a pinhead, binky crocheted hats, etc.—and, an entire section devoted to the apple industry with a working antique apple packing line, complete with apple wiper and catapult sorter. There's also the Washington Apple Commission Visitors Center. And the Lake Chelan Historical Society Museum, up about 35 miles on US 97, has a fine collection of applebox labels too. The bonus there is the movie projector and curtain salvaged from Chelan's old Ruby Theater. *Tours, Gift Shop, Hands-on, Programs, Library*

🏠 509 664-3340 • 127 S. Mission St., Wenatchee, WA 98801

🚗 Central Washington, 138 miles east of Seattle. Just south of US 2 and US 97, the museum's 1 block from downtown at Mission and Yakima Sts.

🕐 Mon.–Fri. 10 A.M.–4 P.M., Sat.–Sun. 1 P.M.–4 P.M. Closed weekends in Jan. Fee. Tours by appointment.

YAKIMA

World Famous Fantastic Museum Jim Schmit and his partner, Del Matthews, bought up the 1962 Seattle World's Fair—and a few other things—and are sharing it with you. Their locations here and in Sisters, Oregon, can only be described as the homes of the ultimate detritus of a pop-culture society. Stuffed into a circa 1910 fruit warehouse seems to be all the "stuff" money can buy, and their bent leans heavily on celebrity items—like Liz Taylor's entire dressing room and Elvis' pink caddie, *and* his mom's; antique toys, featuring the world's largest pedal-car collection; and miniature golf and nickel arcade concessions. *Gift Shop*

🏠 509 575-0100 • 15 W. Yakima Ave., Yakima, WA 98902

🚗 South-central Washington, about 142 miles east of Seattle, off I-82 and US 97.

🕐 Mon.–Sat. 10 A.M.–6 P.M., Sun. noon–5 P.M. Fee.

WEST VIRGINIA

There's something about West Virginia that has a timeless quality to it. Perhaps it's the twisty mountain roads that tend to isolate chunks of it. Or the fact that coal mining and glassmaking, industries founded early on, are still vital parts of the economy. Regardless, it's a great state of side roads and scenic wonders, and evocative place names—like Horse Shoe Run and Left Hand—that rival Alabama's.

What's Big: In Wheeling, the Wheeling Suspension Bridge, but also the Oglebay Institute–Mansion Museum and Glass Museum. In Parkersburg there's the Blennerhasset Museum with the Aaron Burr story. All the glass manufacturers (Blenko in Milton, Pilgrim in Ceredo, and Fentor in Williamstown) offer exhibits and tours. And of course there's Harpers Ferry to visit, and, in Greenbank, the National Radio Astronomy Observatory is regularly scouring the universe for extragalactic signals.

BERKELEY SPRINGS

Homeopathy Works At one point Dizzy Gillespie apparently claimed two revelations in his life: "The first was be-bop, and second was homeopathy." Given its age—homeopathy was developed in the 1790s—and historic following, especially in Europe, and the strength of its current resurgence, you might begin to agree this ain't no snake oil. Remedies are created by "potentizing" plants, minerals, and other substances, then dispensing them in microdose quantities—and in seemingly contrarian fashion, the more dilute, the more potent. The result are tiny little pills, the appropriate ones dispensed according to a concept Hippocrates himself introduced—the Law of Similars, or "like curing like." Housed in a restored turn-of-the-century building, you can watch remedy-making in action at the factory and museum of historic pill-making machines. *Gift Shop, Programs*

🔲 304 258-2541 • 124 Fairfax St., Berkeley Springs, WV 25411

🚗 It's 35 miles north of Winchester, Virginia, on US 522, 6 miles south of I-68.

🕑 Mon.–Sun. 10 A.M.–5 P.M. No fee.

Museum of the Berkeley Springs   George and Martha's spa of choice, the still-bubbling circa 1820 Old Roman Bath House is a destination for its restorative mineral springs and its displays on the history of the Bath (Berkeley Springs was earlier known as "Bath") resort hotels, a jazzy collection of old swimsuits, as well as the local history and geology of the springs that once served the Colonial elite—and Indians for miles around long before that—at a pleasantly uniform temperature of 74° F. *Gift Shop, Programs*

■ 304 258-3743/2711 • Berkeley Springs State Park, 121 S. Washington St., Berkeley Springs, WV 25411

🚗 See above. It's on US 522, near the center of town.

🕐 Museum: Memorial Day–mid-Oct.: Mon.–Tues. 9 A.M.–noon, Thurs.–Fri. 2 P.M.–5 P.M., Sat. 10 A.M.–4 P.M., Sun. noon–4 P.M. Donation. (Note: The spa is open year-round.)

CLIFFTOP

Camp Washington-Carver   Not too many prize cows lurking in the hills of West Virginia, but there was still plenty for the kids at this 4-H camp to do. What is really significant about this one, a 1939 WPA project built with CCC assistance as well as prison labor, is that it was the first 4-H camp built for blacks in the United States. And it stayed so from 1942 when it opened, up through the '60s. Which tells you a lot about segregation in this part of the country. So do the photos and video, which cover the building of the rare chestnut log structure, as well as the local version of summer fun. *Programs*

■ 304 438-3005 • HC 35, Box 5, Clifftop, WV 25831

🚗 About 60 miles east of Charleston. Take US 60E to Hwy 41S.

🕐 May–Oct.: Mon.–Fri. 8 A.M.–6 P.M. Nov.–Apr.: Mon.–Fri. 8:30 A.M.–5 P.M., during administration office hours, but note the camp building is not heated in winter. No fee.

GRAFTON

International Mother's Day Shrine   Others may argue they were first to establish a Mother's Day event, but fact is West Virginia Governor Glasscock did sign an official resolution in 1908, which was followed by President Wilson's in 1914. And the story is that if it weren't for the singleminded efforts of Anna Jarvis to credit and preserve the estimable Civil War accomplishments of her mother, Ann Marie Jarvis, Hallmark and FTD wouldn't have quite so much to celebrate today. The shrine commemorates the first few Mother's Day observances, which took place here, with photo and document ephemera. A short trip four miles south to Webster on US 119 takes you to the Anna Jarvis Birthplace Museum (304 265-5549), which digs deeper into family history and will fill you in on the week in 1861 when General George B. McClellan came to stay.

■ 304 265-1589/265-1177 • Main St., Grafton, WV 26354

🚗 About 25 miles south of Morgantown in north-central West Virginia. Take I-79 to US 50E about 18 miles into town. In the former Andrews Methodist Church, it's across from the train station.

🕐 Mothers Day–Labor Day: 9 A.M.–3:30 P.M. And by appointment. Donation.

HUNTINGTON

Museum of Radio and Technology No soap, radio. And a good batch of early televisions, telegraph items, and computers too. From the earliest 1920s Atwater Kent breadboard radio to the colorfully snazzy transistor imports of the '50s and '60s—and all the Bakelite and Deco consoles in between. Especially unusual here is the fully stocked vintage radio repair shop, the world's largest (4½ feet high!) vacuum tube, and a '50s-era radio station for reliving the moment when rock first broke over the airwaves. *Gift Shop, Library*

📱 304 525-8890 • http://www.library.ohiou.edu/MuseumR&T/museum.htm • 1640 Florence Ave., Huntington, WV 25701

🚗 I-64, Exit 6, turning right onto Madison Ave., right again onto 14th St. West, across the tracks to turn right onto Memorial Blvd., then take a quick left onto Harvey Rd., then left again onto Florence. It's in the former Harvey Town Grade School.

🕐 Fri.–Sat. 10 A.M.–4 P.M., Sun. 1 P.M.–4 P.M., and by appointment. Donation.

MOUNDSVILLE

Prabhupada's Palace of Gold All that glitters . . . yikes. Bring your Ray-Bans. Lest you think the saffron-robed Hare Krishnas faded into the woodwork—or floated away—they actually have alighted here in an unlikely spot in the hills of West Virginia. Now you can see how they put their airport collections to use, building a "Taj Mahal of the West" as a memorial to His Divine Grace A. C. Bhaktivedanta Swami Prabhupada, and wowing tourists from hither and yon. It's almost too fabulous to describe, but we're certain that this is a place where Leona Helmsley would feel at home. *Tours, Gift Shop, Food, Publications*

📱 304 843-1600/1812 • New Vrindaban, Rd. 1, NBU #24, Moundsville, WV 26041

🚗 Just south of Wheeling. Take I-470 Exit 2 (Bethlehem) onto Route 88S, turn west onto US 250, continue on for 2 miles to palace signs, then turn left and it's 3 more miles.

🕐 Mon.–Sun. 9 A.M.–9 P.M. Fee.

WEST LIBERTY

Women's History Museum Stop by, or let librarian Jeanne Schramm roll her cleverly converted yellow women's history school bus to you. What she has here is a tightly focused collection of all original documents, photos, artifacts, and posters covering a select group of women who have made their mark, then passed on. Material from the likes of Florence Nightingale, Dorothea Dix, Elizabeth Cady Stanton, Harriet Beecher Stowe, and Susan B. Anthony serves to bring attention to the important roles women have always played in history—and the context they played them in. *Programs*

🏠 304 336-7159 • http://vaxa.wvnet.edu/~WL260033/museum.html • 108 Walnut St., Box 209, West Liberty, WV 26074

🚗 Just north of Wheeling. Take I-70 Oglebay Park exit onto Route 88N going 6 miles past Oglebay Park; signs are posted in West Liberty.

🕐 Sat. 10 A.M.–2 P.M. and by appointment. Fee.

WHEELING

You could venture way up into the northernmost nook of West Virginia and take a tour of the Homer Laughlin Fiesta Ware factory in Newell. Or, appreciate pottery—and other artifacts of the advanced Adena culture—of a far more ancient vintage at the Delf Norona museum in Grave Creek Mound State Park, just to the south in Moundsville. *While you're in the area, see*: Moundsville, West Liberty.

WHITE SULPHUR SPRINGS

Presidents Cottage Museum   The Greenbrier has a remarkable history, dating back over two centuries. Attracting the lame and the wealthy for its mineral springs and spa, and a popular vacation home of some of our early presidents, it traded hands between the Union and the Confederacy a number of times during the Civil War, each using it as a hospital. After the war it became a favored roost of Robert E. Lee, and, expanding when the C & O Railway purchased it in the early 1900s, it then became an internment center for German and Japanese diplomats during World War II, when it was once again used as a hospital, this time by the U.S. Army. Finally peace came to the valley, and the resort was completely restored, its history preserved with photos, documents, paintings, and memorabilia in the period-furnished 1835 cottage.

🏠 304 536-1110 • The Greenbrier Hotel, Route 60W, White Sulphur Springs, WV 24986

🚗 In southeastern West Virginia. From I-64W, Exit 181 (White Sulphur Springs): take a right at end of ramp, proceeding 1.5 miles to entrance on right. I-64E, Exit 175 (White Sulphur Springs): take a left at end of ramp, turning right at stop sign, then proceeding 3.5 miles to entrance on left.

🕐 April–Thanksgiving: Mon.–Sat. 9 A.M.–5 P.M., Sun. 10 A.M.–3 P.M. No fee.

Wisconsin

There are logging museums in Wisconsin, and dairying and other agricultural museums, and mining museums, and tribal museums, and maritime museums. So far, you follow. But why the circus museums? Why the cutting-edge architecture and politics? The answer might be, as our uncle, who came from "older" British stock and grew up west of Milwaukee, once hinted, that all those other people—the Germans, Scandinavians, and so on—brought real fresh air with them when they arrived, and that Wisconsin has remained a land full of energy and ideas.

What's Big: Among the places we considered and decided were a little too "mainstream" are Hayward's National Freshwater Fishing Hall of Fame (see your family in a muskie's mouth!); the EAA Air Adventure Museum in Oshkosh; and Spring Green's combination of Frank Lloyd Wright sites and the bodacious House on the Rock. There's also the Packer Hall of Fame in Green Bay, not to mention the civic and university museums in Madison and Milwaukee.

APPLETON

Outagamie Museum and Houdini Historical Center   This is largely a museum of technology, with material relating to electric power and regional industries. But you may be here because Appleton was the boyhood home of the great Houdini, and there's a collection of his belongings and memorabilia—handcuffs and locks, posters and other publicity—evidences of a career that still causes heads to shake.

- 🔲 920 735-9370 • 330 E. College Ave., Appleton, WI 54911
- 🚗 Appleton is in east-central Wisconsin, just north of Lake Winnebago. From US 10, exit onto SR 125/Business Route 41 east toward Lawrence University.
- 🕑 Tues.–Fri. 10 A.M.–4 P.M., Sat. 10 A.M.–5 P.M., Sun. noon–5 P.M. Fee.

ASHIPPUN

Honey of a Museum   Did you miss out on the birds and bees? Here's the bee part. Seriously: If you don't know how important bees are to us, you'll find out here. You'll see slides as well as active hives, learn the history, economics, and science of beekeeping, and get to taste some of the good stuff.

■ 920 474-4411 • Honey Acres, N1557 Hwy 67, Ashippun, WI 53003

🚗 It's an hour west-northwest of Milwaukee. Take Exit 282 off I-94 and proceed 12 miles north on SR 67. Honey Acres is 2 miles north of Ashippun.

🕐 May 15–Oct.: Mon.–Fri. 9 A.M.–3:30 P.M., Sat.–Sun. noon–4 P.M. Rest of year: weekdays only. No fee.

AUGUSTA

Dells Mill Water-Powered Museum   "Down by the old mill stream" is an image that still has a lot of resonance. Here's the real thing: a five-story mill built in the 1860s, long the economic and social mainstay of a farm region, and still doing occasional milling. You can walk through and see in its intricacy (3,000 feet of belting; 175 pulleys) the operation of that most elegant of concepts—having running water turn wheat into flour. *Gift Shop*

■ 715 286-2714 • E18855 County Rd. V, Augusta, WI 54722

🚗 Dells Mill is in west-central Wisconsin, 20 miles southeast of Eau Claire and 3 miles north of the town of Augusta. Take County Rd. V east from US 12.

🕐 May–Oct.: Mon.–Sun. 10 A.M.–5 P.M. Fee.

BARABOO

Circus World Museum   A visit to Baraboo will remind you that the circus is essentially a rural and small-town phenomenon. It was here in the 1880s that the five Ringling brothers got the show biz bug, and the rest is history. Lots of wagons and all kinds of paraphernalia and memorabilia. In the summer, parades, concerts, etc. Archives for the serious-minded. *Tours, Gift Shop, Food, Programs, Library*

■ 608 356-0800 (recorded information) • 426 Water St. (Hwy 113), Baraboo, WI 53913

🚗 Baraboo is in south-central Wisconsin, an hour northwest of Madison and 15 minutes south of Wisconsin Dells. Exit from I-90/94 onto SR 33W and look for signs.

🕐 Early May–early Sept.: Mon.–Sun. 9 A.M.–6 P.M. (to 9 P.M. late July–Late Aug.). Rest of year: Mon.–Sat. 9 A.M.–5 P.M., Sun. 11 A.M.–5 P.M. Fee.

BAYFIELD

Hokenson Brothers Fishery   Lake Superior's fisheries declined after the opening of the Saint Lawrence Seaway, when an invasion of lampreys combined with overfishing to decimate stocks. This museum shows how one family fished the lake from the 1920s into the 1960s. You'll be shown the Twine Shed, Ice House, Pound Nets, Dock and Herring Shed, and other aspects of the trade, including the 38-foot *Twilite*. In Bayfield itself, stop in at the operational Booth Cooperage (1 Washington Ave.; call 715 779-3400) to see how the barrels that carried the fish were made. *Tours, Gift Shop*

■ 715 779-3397 • Little Sand Bay, Apostle Islands National Lakeshore, Bayfield, WI 54814

🚗 Bayfield, in extreme northern Wisconsin, 60 miles east of Duluth, Minnesota, is headquarters for the Apostle Islands National Lakeshore. Little Sand Bay is 10 miles northwest, off SR 13 and County Rd. K. The fishery is next to the visitors center.

🕐 Memorial Day–Labor Day: Mon.–Sun. 10 A.M.–4 P.M. No fee.

CLEAR LAKE

Clear Lake Historical Museum   In this little town the local museum has feature exhibits on two native sons that form a strange juxtaposition—one on Senator Gaylord Nelson, the founder of Earth Day (you might call him Mr. Clean), and the other on pitcher Burleigh Grimes, who rode his spitball into the Baseball Hall of Fame (you might call him Mr. Not-So-Clean).

■ 715 263-3050 • 450 5th Ave., Clear Lake, WI 54005

🚗 Clear Lake is in northwestern Wisconsin, 50 miles northwest of Eau Claire, on US 63.

🕐 Memorial Day–Labor Day: Mon.–Fri. 11 A.M.–4 P.M., Sat.–Sun. 1:30 P.M.–4:30 P.M. Donation.

COUDERAY

The Hideout   It's just your average hunter's retreat—the huge fireplace, the antlers on the walls, the staircases, the machine-gun ports. *Machine-gun ports?* Well, yes. See, the hunter who got away from it all here was one Al Capone. Stock up on images from all your favorite movies, then come and take the tour.

■ 715 945-2746 • County Rd. CC, Couderay, WI 54835

🚗 Couderay is in the woods of northwest Wisconsin, about an hour west of Phillips, on SR 70. The Hideout is 6 miles north, on County Rd. CC.

🕐 Memorial Day–mid-Sept.: Mon.–Sun. noon–10 P.M. Tours on the hour. Call for other hours and to confirm. Fee.

FORT ATKINSON

Dairy Shrine/Hoard Historical Museum   The Dairy Shrine offers a full introduction—with all kinds of artifacts, dioramas, audiovisual displays, and salutes to breed champions—to the industry most associated with Wisconsin. The Hoard museum has an exhibit on the Black Hawk War and varied other displays including quilts and mounted birds. Just west of town, on SR 106, is the Panther Intaglio Mound, an ancient effigy whose use, probably religious, is debated.

🏠 920 563-7769 • 407 Merchants Ave., Fort Atkinson, WI 53538

🚗 Fort Atkinson is an hour west of Milwaukee. Exit from I-94 south on SR 26 through Jefferson, or take US 12 from northeastern Illinois. Merchants Ave. is US 12.

🕐 June–Aug.: Tues.–Sat. 9:30 A.M.–4:30 P.M., Sun. 1 P.M.–5 P.M. Rest of year: Tues.–Sat. 9:30 A.M.–3:30 P.M., and first Sun. of month. No fee.

LAC DU FLAMBEAU

George W. Brown, Jr., Ojibwe Museum and Cultural Center (formerly Lac du Flambeau Chippewa Museum and Cultural Center)   The Ojibwe (Chippewa) here display aspects of their North Woods culture, in exhibits of artifacts, video presentations, theatrical performances, storytelling, and other activities and illustrations. There's a 24-foot-long canoe more than 250 years old, a seven-foot sturgeon caught locally, birchbark and bead crafts, wild rice and maple sugaring displays, arts and crafts workshops, all within a large wooden building representing the traditional round ("no beginning and no end") tribal structure. Nearby is Waswagoning, a traditional Ojibwe village re-created; call 715 588-3560 for information. *Tours, Programs*

🏠 715 588-3333 • 603 Peace Pipe Rd., Lac du Flambeau, WI 54538

🚗 Lac du Flambeau is in north-central Wisconsin, on the reservation of the same name. The museum is downtown just off SR 47, south of the Indian Bowl.

🕐 May–Oct.: Mon.–Sat. 10 A.M.–4 P.M. Rest of year: Tues.–Thurs. 10 A.M.–2 P.M. Fee.

MADISON

If you're here, we know you'll want to look into the Toilet Tissue Museum (608 251-8098). *While you're in the area, see*: Baraboo, Fort Atkinson, Milton, Mount Horeb, Wisconsin Dells

MILTON

Milton House Museum   The hexagonal Milton House, said to be the first grout (poured concrete) structure in the United States, was built as a stagecoach inn in 1844. But Joseph Goodrich wasn't just entertaining travelers—he was harboring runaway slaves as well, and you'll see his tunnel, "the only segment of the Underground Railroad that was actually underground," and the log cabin the slaves came up in, should they have to flee suddenly. This is history at ground level. *Tours*

📞 608 868-7772 • http://www.inwave.com/Milton/MiltonHouse/ • 18 S. Janesville St., Milton, WI 53563

🚗 Milton is an hour southeast of Madison. From I-90 take Exit 171A, following SR 26N; the museum is just north of the railroad tracks and intersection with SR 59.

🕐 Memorial Day–Labor Day: Mon.–Sun. 10 A.M.–5 P.M. May and Sept: weekends only. Fee.

MILWAUKEE

While you're in the area, see also: Fort Atkinson, Watertown

America's Black Holocaust Museum   This museum expresses the person and the experience of James Cameron, sole survivor of a 1930 lynching in Indiana. Although there was much publicity after its 1988 opening, you won't find crowds here. You will find stark photographs and other items detailing the history of racial violence in America. This is not entertainment.

📞 414 264-2500 • 2233 N. 4th St., Milwaukee, WI 53212

🚗 The museum is at the corner of N. 4th St. and North Ave. Take Exit 73C from I-43 and proceed west on North Ave.

🕐 Mon.–Fri. 9 A.M.–5 P.M. Fee. Call to confirm and for weekend hours.

International Clown Hall of Fame and Research Center   Relocated in 1997 from Delavan, where it was born into a community that had been home to a number of early circuses, the Hall of Fame documents one of the great entertainment traditions. The costumes and props of funny men and women are here among all manner of portraiture and other memorabilia. Keeping clowning alive is the happy aim of this organization. *Programs*

📞 414 319-0848 • Grand Avenue Mall, 275 W. Wisconsin Ave., Milwaukee, WI 53205

🚗 The Grand Ave. Mall is in the center of downtown Milwaukee, at 2nd and Wisconsin.

🕐 Call for hours and fees.

MOUNT HOREB

Mount Horeb Mustard Museum   Pass the ketchup? Not around here. There are at least 1,700 kinds of mustard, though (call for the latest count), and mustard history, mustard advertising, mustard folklore. Barry Levenson is said to have heard a voice saying, "If you collect us they will come"—by the time you leave Mount Horeb you'll be hearing voices too. *Gift Shop, Food*

■ 608 437-3986 • 109 E. Main St., Mount Horeb, WI 53572

🚗 Mt. Horeb is a half-hour west of Madison, on US 18/151.

🕐 Mon.–Sun. 10 A.M.–5 P.M. No fee.

NEENAH

Bergstrom-Mahler Museum   The mid-19th century was the classic age of paperweight design. How appropriate that Neenah, a paper town, has the world's leading collection of these beauties, begun by Evangeline H. Bergstrom, wife of the Bergstrom Paper Company's founder. There are over 2,000 pieces here, along with exhibits on technique and artistry and a schedule of arts programs involving various other mediums. *Tours, Gift Shop, Hands-on, Programs*

■ 920 751-4658 • 165 N. Park Ave., Neenah, WI 54956

🚗 Neenah is in east-central Wisconsin, on the northwest shore of Lake Winnebago. From US 41, take the Main St. exit east into the city, and continue as Main becomes Wisconsin Ave.; then turn left onto North Park Ave.

🕐 Tues.–Fri. 10 A.M.–4:30 P.M., Sat.–Sun. 1 P.M.–4:30 P.M. Donation.

ONEIDA (DE PERE)

Oneida Nation Museum   The Oneida (On∧yote?aka, or People of the Standing Stone) were part of New York's Iroquois Confederacy. In the 1820s, moving ahead of white encroachment, some of them found land that seemed homelike and settled here. Their museum tells the people's history and details the traditional lives of men and women, spiritual and political activities, and arts and crafts. A longhouse adjoins the modern building. *Tours, Gift Shop, Hands-on*

■ 920 869-2768 • W 892 EE Rd., Oneida (De Pere), WI 54155

🚗 De Pere is 7 miles west of Green Bay, in northeastern Wisconsin. The museum is in the middle of the Oneida Reservation, at the junction of County Rds. EE and E.

🕐 Tues.–Fri. 9 A.M.–5 P.M., Sat.–Sun. 10 A.M.–2 P.M. Call to confirm. Fee.

PHILLIPS

Wisconsin Concrete Park   Logging legend, tavern owner, ginseng farmer, and dancehall musician Fred Smith began in 1950 (when he was 65 and suffering from arthritis) to render his world in outdoor sculpture. He worked for 14 years, using wooden frames, cement, and various surface ornamentation. You'll see Paul

Bunyan, Sacajawea, Lincoln, a double wedding, movie heroes, an eight-horse beer wagon, and other marvels—some 3.5 acres of them.

- 715 339-4505 (Price County Forestry and Tourism) • Hwy 13S, Phillips, WI 54555
- Phillips is in north-central Wisconsin, 90 miles northwest of Wausau and 12 miles north of the junction of US 8 and Hwy 13. The park is on the south edge of town.
- Year-round, daily, in daylight hours. No fee; donations appreciated.

PLATTEVILLE

Rollo Jamison Museum/Mining Museum Here's a twofer: The Rollo Jamison Museum is one of those places created by a man who collected *everything*. The 20,000 items and their settings preserve early-20th-century Wisconsin life. The Mining Museum is based on the 1845 mine where Lorenzo Bevans got rich on lead; wear good shoes and a sweater for the descent into the cool earth. There's a mine train ride, if weather permits.

- 608 348-3301 • http://www.uwplatt.edu/Platteville • 405 and 385 E. Main St., Platteville, WI 53818
- Platteville is 60 miles southwest of Madison and 20 miles northeast of Dubuque, Iowa. From US 151, exit north onto Water St. (SR 80/81) and turn right on Main.
- May–Oct.: Mon.–Sun. 9 A.M.–5 P.M. Reduced schedule rest of year. Group tours by appointment. Fee.

PRAIRIE DU CHIEN

Fort Crawford Medical Museum At this important army post, Dr. William Beaumont performed operations on a patient who happened to have a "hole in his stomach"—operations on which medical knowledge of digestion are based. You'll see dioramas on the progress of surgical technique, a completely furnished 1890s pharmacy, a dentist's office of the same period, and the Transparent Twins, who "talk" about the body parts you're looking at.

- 800 545-0634 • 717 S. Beaumont Rd., Prairie du Chien, WI 53821
- Prairie du Chien is in southwestern Wisconsin, on the Mississippi River near the mouth of the Wisconsin River. Entering the city from east or west on US 18 (Wisconsin St.), turn south on Beaumont and go 2 blocks to the museum.
- May–Oct.: Mon.–Sun. 10 A.M.–5 P.M. Fee.

SHELL LAKE

Museum of Woodcarving Joseph Barta (1904–72) carved from childhood. In the last 30 years of his life he focused his energies on creating the Bible in wood. Here you can see a 26-foot Last Supper, Daniel in the Lions' Den, the Crucifixion, Jesus in Prayer, the Serpent and Eve, Doubting Thomas, and other life-size figures including a hanging Judas, as well as over 400 miniatures. The display has become a place of pilgrimage, both for the religious and for wood-carving aficionados.

■ 715 468-7100 • Hwy 63N, Shell Lake, WI 54871

🚗 Shell Lake is in northwestern Wisconsin, 60 miles northwest of Eau Claire, on US 63.

🕐 May–Oct.: Mon.–Sun. 9 A.M.–6 P.M. Fee.

WATERTOWN

Octagon House/America's First Kindergarten   Two different interests may draw you here. Octagon House is a spectacular 1854 example of a building style that was the rage in the mid-19th century. Out back is the 1856 structure, moved from downtown, in which Margarethe Schurz, wife of reformer Carl Schurz, introduced Froebelian methods of teaching children to the United States.

■ 920 261-2796 • 919 Charles St., Watertown, WI 53094

🚗 Watertown is in southeastern Wisconsin, 40 miles west-northwest of Milwaukee, on SR 26 and SR 16. Take Main St. east from downtown and follow signs to Octagon House.

🕐 Memorial Day–Labor Day: Mon.–Sun. 10 A.M.–4 P.M. May, Sept.–Oct.: 10 A.M.–3 P.M. Fee.

WISCONSIN DELLS

H. H. Bennett Studio Foundation Museum   That Wisconsin Dells is today a major tourist center is owed in large part to Henry Hamilton Bennett, the pioneer landscape photographer whose studio you will see here. An innovator in action photography, panoramas, and other genres, Bennett left thousands of glass plates, from which prints are made today. This is for photography buffs, but is also, in a sense, a museum of the Dells.

■ 608 253-2261 • 215 Broadway, Wisconsin Dells, WI 53965

🚗 Wisconsin Dells is in south-central Wisconsin, 40 miles north-northwest of Madison. From I-90/94, take Exit 87 (SR 13, also Broadway) across the river.

🕐 Memorial Day–Labor Day: Mon.–Sun. noon–9 P.M. Sept.–Oct.: Sat.–Sun. noon–5 P.M. Other times by appointment. No fee.

WOODRUFF

Doctor Kate Museum   "The Angel on Snowshoes" is what Dr. Kate Newcomb was called, for her persistence in serving her North Woods patients in the harshest

weather. In the early 1950s, wanting to build a hospital, she had the idea of collecting a million pennies. Television liked it, and the nation (and world) joined in.
We don't know if Dr. Kate is featured down south in Beloit's Angel Museum (call
608 365-4838 for information), but we do know that while you're up here in the
woods, you might like to pay a call on Rhinelander's Logging Museum (call 715
362-2193), half an hour southeast. At Rhinelander they have forestry displays, a re-
creation of the life of CC workers, a Soo Line depot circa 1900, *and* (don't ask us to
explain, and don't let anyone else in on the secret once you've been there), safe in
its cage, the world's one and only remaining *hodag*!

▪ 715 356-6896 • 923 2nd Ave., Woodruff, WI 54568

🚗 Woodruff is in north-central Wisconsin, 20 miles northwest of Rhinelander, on US 51.

🕐 Mid-June–Labor Day: Mon.–Fri. 11 A.M.–4 P.M. Other hours by appointment. Donation.

WYOMING

Now, Nebraska may have adopted the critter, but we must make it perfectly clear that the jackalope is a Wyoming native. You may in fact think you've entered a wildlife museum or two as you travel the state and stop at its diners and cafes. That may be as close to their natural habitat as you get, seeing the rare hybrid jack rabbit–antelope stuffed, or perhaps mounted, along with a more common grizzly, and other fauna. But Wyoming is a magnificently beautiful state, and you're likely to be spending as much time as possible outdoors.

What's Big: Devil's Tower, the Grand Tetons, and of course, Yellowstone.

CHEYENNE

Cheyenne Frontier Days Old West Museum   This is a rodeo town, and this is the museum to tell you all about it. While its displays include Oglala Sioux Indian artifacts, period costumes and carriages, a Union Pacific exhibit, and Western art, the romance of the West is most clearly felt through its Frontier Days rodeo collection, celebrating the century-long story of the cowboys and cowgirls and their bucking broncs. *Tours, Gift Shop, Hands-on, Programs, Library*
- 307 778-7290 • 4501 N. Carey, Cheyenne, WY 82003
- I-25N, exit onto Central Ave. heading east, turn right onto Kennedy, then left onto Carey.
- Memorial Day–Labor Day: Mon.–Fri. 8 A.M.–6 P.M., Sat.–Sun. 10 A.M.–5 P.M. (8 A.M.–8 P.M. for Frontier Days, always the last full week in July). Rest of year: Mon.–Fri. 9 A.M.–5 P.M., Sat.–Sun. 11 A.M.–4 P.M. Hours may be shorter Jan.–April. Fee.

CODY

Buffalo Bill Historical Center   Five-for-one here: Not only the most comprehensive Buffalo Bill Cody—and his Wild West show—collection to be found, but also a spectacular Plains Indian museum, the world's largest American firearms display, a significant group of Western art masterworks, and the Harold McCracken Research Library, which supports each of the four museums with extensive photographic, advertising, and other resource archives. *See also* Golden, Colorado's Buffalo Bill Memorial Museum and Grave and the Buffalo Bill Cody Homestead in Princeton, Iowa. *Tours, Gift Shop, Food, Programs, Publications, Library*

🏛 307 587-4771 • 720 Sheridan Ave., Cody, WY 82414

🚗 About 52 miles from the east entrance of Yellowstone, at the junction of US 14/16/20 with Sheridan Ave.

🕐 June–Sept.: Mon.–Sun. 7 A.M.–8 P.M.; Oct.: Mon.–Sun. 8 A.M.–5 P.M.; Nov.–Apr.: Mon.–Sun. 10 A.M.–2 P.M.; May: Mon.–Sun. 8 A.M.–8 P.M. Fee.

DIAMONDVILLE

Stolen Bell Museum   This a small historical museum, featuring items donated mostly by the local citizens, and you might get a kick at seeing some of it, like the old moonshine still and old-time fire equipment. Ask about the stolen bell. Then skip over to Kemmerer for Missouri native J. C. Penney's home and a look at the "Mother Store," the first in the Golden Rule chain, and the beginning of his empire. *See* Plano, Texas, for the JCPenney Historical Museum and Archives.

🏛 307 877-6676 • 316 Diamondville Ave., Diamondville, WY 83116

🚗 In western Wyoming just south of Kemmerer off US 30. It's in the old firehouse.

🕐 Hours vary. Donation.

EVANSTON

Uinta County Historical Museum   You're in Union Pacific and Mormon Trail country here, in a valley surrounded by the Uinta and Wasateh mountains. The Chinese who came in with the railroad left a legacy that included one of only three Joss Houses, or sacred temples, built in this country back in the 1880s. While it burned in 1922, items rescued from it are on view here and in a nearby replica of the temple. Found here along with Chinese ceremonial items like a many-legged silk dragon are day-to-day items from the Anglo, Chinese, and Native American cultures like Indian spear points and beadwork, and gambling and bootleg whiskey paraphernalia. *Tours, Programs, Screenings*

🏛 307 789-3655 • 36 10th St., Evanston, WY 82930

🚗 Take I-80 to the far southwest corner of the state.

🕐 Memorial Day–Labor Day: Mon.–Fri. 9 A.M.–5 P.M., Sat.–Sun. 10 A.M.–4 P.M. Rest of year: closed weekends. No fee.

GREEN RIVER

Sweetwater County Historical Museum Don't be fooled by this sterile courthouse building—it houses a great collection of historic photos covering such subjects as the native Shoshone and Ute, mountain men in full furry regalia, the coming of the railroad and the coal-mining boom in next-door Rock Springs, the start of John Wesley Powell's Green River expedition in 1869, and the significant strike of trona ore (for soda ash). Also on hand to further reflect the mix of cultures in the area is a collection of Chinese textiles and a selection of Sioux ledger art dating to the early Indian School days. *See also* Page, Arizona's John Wesley Powell Memorial Museum and the John Wesley Powell River History Museum in Green River, Utah. *Tours*

- 🏛 307 872-6435 • 80 W. Flaming Gorge Way, Green River, WY 82935
- 🚗 I-80 to Exit 91, follow signs for US 30/Flaming Gorge Way. Note: They're planning to move into the historic building next door by 2001.
- 🕐 July–Aug.: Mon.–Fri. 9 A.M.–5 P.M., Sat. 1 P.M.–5 P.M. Sept.–June: Closed Sat. No fee.

JACKSON

Jackson Hole Museum and Historical Center Perhaps you were thinking of wrassling a bear? Trappers and mountain men are the focus here and the collection of hand-forged knives will give you an idea of the appropriate tool to have on hand as back-up. Homestead items and other typical pioneer and Plains artifacts are here too, but the Moosehead Ranch pole furniture selection is pretty special, as is a historic exhibit on local skiing. The unheated museum is closed in winter, but you can mosey over to the historical/research center, which has a trade bead and Plains Indian collection and super photo archives. *Tours, Programs, Library*

- 🏛 Museum: 307 733-2414/Historical Center: 733-9605 • Museum: Glenwood at Deloney, Historical Center: Glenwood at Mercill, Jackson, WY 83001
- 🚗 Western Wyoming off US 191. The museum is 1 block west off the town square. The historical center is 2 blocks north of the town square.
- 🕐 Museum: May 24–Sept. 28: Mon.–Sat. 9:30 A.M.–6 P.M., Sun. 10 A.M.–5 P.M. Fee. Historical Center: Year-round: Mon.–Fri. 8 A.M.–5 P.M. No fee.

LARAMIE

American Heritage Center Antoine Predock's futuristic structure contrasts sharply with the more territorial-style native sandstone campus buildings. While the building's got your attention, stop in for a rousing visit to the real and mythic West. Its collections include the saddles of Hollywood legends Hopalong Cassidy (*see also* the Degenhart listing in Cambridge, Ohio) and Tim McCoy, memorabilia of aviation pioneer Roscoe Turner, Western art, and photos, maps, and artifacts on the region's mining past and its performing arts. *Programs, Library*

🏛 307 766-2570 • University of Wyoming, 22nd St. and Willett Dr., Laramie, WY 82071

🚌 In the campus centennial complex.

🕐 June–Aug.: Mon.–Fri. 7:30 A.M.–4:30 P.M., Sat. 11 A.M.–5 P.M. Sept.–May: Mon.–Fri. 8 A.M.–5 P.M., Sat. 11 A.M.–5 P.M., Sun. 10 A.M.–3 P.M. No fee.

Geological Museum   They say there are only five on exhibit in the world, and a complete skeleton of one of these rare *Apatosauruses* (previously known as *Brontosaurus*, for those not up on their dino data) is right here on this lovely campus in Laramie. An *Allosaurus* display keeps it company, as does a goodly selection of rocks, minerals, and fossils dating back two billion years. North American cultural history is nicely covered at the university's Anthropology Museum. *Tours*

🏛 307 766-4218 • University of Wyoming, Laramie, WY 82071

🚌 In the east wing of the S.H. Knight Geology Building on the northwest corner of the campus.

🕐 Mon.–Fri. 8 A.M.–5 P.M. Sat.–Sun. 10 A.M.–3 P.M. No Fee.

RAWLINS

Wyoming Frontier Prison Museum   Rawlins attracted more than its share of lawless riffraff and it must have seemed the perfect place to build a replacement when Laramie's territorial prison was outgrown. Begun in 1888, the harsh and spartan 104-cell penitentiary opened to its "guests" in 1901 and stayed open until 1981. Tours and exhibits provide a grim yet fascinating picture of an era with criminal escapades that included train robbery and poisoning by plum pie. The original gas chamber attracts a particular macabre interest, as might the selection of homemade weapons confiscated from the inmates. The Carbon County Museum nearby will regale you with the grisly true-life tale of 19th-century train bandit "Big Nose" George Parrott. *Tours, Gift Shop*

🏛 307 324-4422 • 500 W. Walnut St., Rawlins, WY 82301

🚌 On I-80, 100 miles west of Laramie. At 5th and Walnut.

🕐 Memorial Day–Labor Day: Tours on the hour Mon.–Sun. 8:30 A.M.–5:30 P.M., and by appointment Fri.–Sat. 9:30 P.M. Rest of year: tours at 8:30 A.M., 10:30 A.M., 1:30 P.M., 3:30 P.M., and by appointment. Fee.

SHERIDAN

Don King's Western Museum   They *are* still making them like they used to. Saddles, chaps, and spurs, but saddles particularly. Don King, a renowned saddle-maker himself, has put together this historic collection ranging from an 1870s silver-trimmed Mexican saddle, to one from a Conestoga wagon, to a 17th-century Japanese saddle found in Okinawa during World War II. Tucked into his family-owned saddlery shop, the display invites appreciation of the craftsmanship and tooling of the leather, as well as the wide variety of styles found not only in the saddles, but in the angora chaps and spurs found here. Fact is, the hand-prepared coils of rope he sells are like a museum display themselves.

■ 307 672-2702/2755 • King's Saddlery, 184 N. Main, Sheridan, WY 82801
🚗 I-90, to the center of town. It's on the left heading north.
🕐 Mon.–Sat. 8 A.M.–5 P.M. No fee.

THERMOPOLIS

Hot Springs County Historical Museum and Cultural Center Yup. Farming and oil-drilling, mining and wildlife photos and stuff, but also the cherry-wood bar where Butch and Sundance and the rest of the Hole-in-the-Wall gang are said to have tossed back a cold one every so often.

■ 307 864-5183 • 700 Broadway, Thermopolis, WY 82443
🚗 About 130 miles west of Casper in central Wyoming. Take US 20/26W to Shoshoni, then US 20N. It's across the river in the center of town.
🕐 Mon.–Sat. 8 A.M.–5 P.M. Fee.

Virtual Museums

As in the book, we've tried to seek out the "smaller" websites, but have indeed provided a few of the mainstream monoliths. We've also taken into consideration, since this is sort of a travel book (armchair or otherwise), that you might be interested in various roadside sites (and publications), so we've included a number of these. They often link to museums as well. Note: Art museum sources abound—for more of these try some of our Big Sources below. And for the biggest searches—by collection, museum name, or what have you—use an established engine like Alta Vista http://www.altavista.digital.com, Infoseek http://www.infoseek.com, Lycos http://www.lycos.com, or Yahoo! http://www.yahoo.com

Big Sources for Museum Data:

- Links to Aboriginal Resources—http://www.io.org/~jgcom/aborl.htm
- Local History Web Resources—http://www.spcc.com/ihsw/lhsresor.htm
- The Natural History Museum of Los Angeles County—http://www.nhm.org
- Nedsite List of Museum Indices—http://www.nedsite.nl/search/museum.htm
- New York Museums, etc.—http://www.webcom.com/~village
- Online Museums/Canada—http://www.chin.gc.ca/Government/PCH/CHIN/
- Online Museums/U.S.—http://www.w3.org/pub/DataSources/bySubject/overview.html
- WebMuseum—http://sunsite.unc.edu/wm/
- World Wide Arts Resources—http://www.concourse.com/wwar/defaultnew.html
- WWW Virtual Library Museums Pages—
  http://www.comlab.ox.ac.uk/archive/other/museums.html

Other Places to Visit:

- Alabama Music Hall of Fame—http://www.alamhof.org
- American Museum of Fire Fighting—http://www.artcom.com/museums/
- Antiques—http://www.ic.mankato.mn.us/antiques/Antiques.html
- Art Crimes—http://www.gatech.edu/desoto/graf/Index.Art_Crimes.html

- ArtDirect—http://artdirect.com
- Arte Maya Tz'utuhil Museum & Gallery—http://www.artemaya.com
- Barbie Dolls—http://deepthought.armory.com/~zenugirl/barbie.html
- Blenko Glass Co. and Museum—http://www.citynet.net/blenko
- Cahokia Mounds State Historic Site—
  http://medicine.wustl.edu/~kellerk/cahokia.html
- Canadian Wildlife & Wilderness Art Museum—http://intranet.ca/cawa/
- Chiat Day Idea Factory—http://www.chiatday.com/factory/
- Coins—http://atheist.tamu.edu/~ratboy/Coins/coins.html
- Columbia Welcome Center/Archives—http://www.webcolumbia.com/ca/caindex
- Dali Virtual Museum of Art—http://www.nol.net/~nil/dali.html
- Detroit Institute for the Arts—http://www.dia.org
- Dia Center for the Arts—http://www.diacenter.org
- Diego Rivera Museo Virtual—http://www.diegorivera.com
- Digital Library Project—http://elib.cs.berkeley.edu/flowers
- EiNet Galaxy Archaeology Directory—http://galaxy.einet.net/galaxy/Social-
- Electronic Prehistoric Shark Museum—
  http://turnpike.net/emporium/C/celestial/epsm.htm
- Encounter with Duchamp—http://www.val.net/~tim/duchamp-aug96.html
- Experience Music Project/"Jimi Hendrix Museum"—http://www.experience.org
- Extraterrestrial Highway—http://www.best.com/~schmitz/ufo.html
- Fermi National Accelerator Laboratory and Lederman Science Center—
  http://www-ed.fnal.gov
- FindArts—http://www.Find-Arts.com
- "First Virtual" Mousepad Museum—http://www.expa.hvu.nl/ajvdhek/mouse.htm
- Folk Art and Craft Exchange—http://www.folkart.com
- Ford's Theatre Museum—http://nps.gov/foth
- Frederic Remington Art Museum—http://www.northnet.org/broncho
- Friends of the Sea Otter—http://infomanage.com/mbk/mbkfos.html
- Furniture Discovery Center and the Furniture Hall of Fame—
  http://www2.hpe.com/discovery
- Gallery Guide On-line—http://www.gallery-guide.com
- Gold Coast Railroad Museum—http://www.elink.net/goldcoast
- Golden Gate Railroad Museum—http://www.io.com/~fano2472/ggrm
- Golden Nugget Museum—http://fly.hiwaay.net/~dddorf/gnm/gnm.cgi
- Gothic Gardening—http://www.arches.uga.edu/~maliced/gothgard/index2.html
- Graphions's Online Type Museum—http://www.slip.net/~graphion/museum.html
- HCS Virtual Computer History Museum—
  http://www.cyberstreet.com/hcs/museum/museum.htm
- Hudson River Museum of Westchester—http://www.hrm.org
- il museo chenoncè—http://abruzzo.abol.it/museo
- Indian Pueblo Cultural Center—
  http://hanksville.phast.umass.edu/defs/independent/PCC/PCC.html

- International Crane Foundation—http://www.baraboo.com/bus/icf/whowhat.htm
- International Interactive Genetic Art—http://robocop.modmath.cs.cmu.edu:8001/
- International Museum of Art—http://www.nettap.com/~iart/
- Jamestown Rediscovery Archaeology Project—http://www.widomaker.com/~apva/
- Judah L. Magnes Museum—http://www.jfed.org/Magnes/Magnes.htm
- Keigwin and Mathews Collection of Rare and Historical Documents—http://www.bluewater.com/bluewater/keigwin_mathews
- Kooks Museum, The—http://www.teleport.com/~dkossy/index.html
- Lords of the Earth—Maya/Aztec/Inca Exchange—http://www.realtime.net/maya/
- Lost Museum of Sciences—http://www.netaxs.com/people/aca3/ATRIUM.HTM
- Material Culture Resources—gopher://gopher.inform.umd.edu:70/11/EdRes/Topic/MatCulture/ReadRoom/NuPub
- Mattye Reed African Heritage Center—http://www.huenet.com/nc/nc.htm
- Maxwell Museum of Anthropology—http://www.unm.edu/~Maxwell/Maxwell/MMhp.html
- Meg's Museum Links—http://www.educ.msu.edu/homepages/ropp/Museums.html
- Mexican Fine Arts Museum (Museo de Bellas Artes Mexicanas)—http://mafcm@artswire.org
- Mingie—Two Centuries of Japanese Folk Art—http://www.star.net/salem/pem/mingei/
- Monticello—The Home of Thomas Jefferson—http://www.monticello.org
- Mount Vernon—http://www.mountvernon.org/
- Museum of Creation and Earth History—http://www.icr.org
- Museum of Dirt—http://www.planet.com/dirtweb/dirt.html
- Museum of Geology, South Dakota School of Mines and Technology—http://www.sdsmt.edu/campus/oharra/museum/museum1.htm
- Museum of Non-Primate Art—http://www.netlink.co.nz/~monpa/
- Museum of Slavery in the Atlantic—http://squash.la.psu.edu/plarson/smuseum/homepage.html
- Museum of the City of San Francisco—http://www.sfmuseum.org
- Museum of Tolerance—http://www.wiesenthal.com
- Museum of Woodworking Tools—http://www.antiquetools.com
- National Postal Museum (U.K.)—http://www.royalmail.co.uk/collect/museum1.htm
- National Postal Museum (U.S.)—http://www.si.edu/postal/intro.htm
- National Radio Astronomy Observatory Visitor's Center—http://www.nrao.edu
- National Softball Hall of Fame and Museum Complex—http://www.softball.org
- Newseum—http://www.freedomforum.org
- Nicholas Roerich Museum—http://www.roerich.org
- Noah Webster House/Museum of West Hartford History—http://www.ctstateu.edu/~noahweb/noahWebster.html
- Ocean Planet—http://seawifs.gsfc.nasa.gov/ocean_planet.html
- Old-Time Radio—http://www.old-time.com
- Online DC-3 Aviation Museum—http://www.centercomp.com/dc3/

- Parrish Museum—http://www.thehamptons.com
- Peavey Museum and Visitors Center—http://www.Peavey.com
- Picasso and Portraiture—http://www.clubinternet.com/picasso/homepage.html
- Postcards—
  http://www.cris.com/~Felixg/POSTCARDS/cards.html
  http://www.xmission.com/grue/postcards/
  http://www-iwi.unisg.ch/~mmarchon/postcard/index.html
  http://postcards.www.media.mit.edu/PO-bin/cardClaim.perl/
  http://postcards.www.media.mit.edu/Postcards/
- Quilts and Textiles/Shelburne Museum—
  http://www.cybermalls.com/cymont/shelmus/text001.html
- Rail Road Museum List—http://www.panix.com/~ni2p/tour/mainidx.html
- Rockhounds—http://www.rahul.net/infodyn/rockhounds/rockhounds.html
- Skeptics Society—http://www.skeptic.com/skeptics-society.html
- Smithsonian Institution—http://www.si.edu
- Society for the Preservation of Natural History Collections—
  http://iscssun.uni.edu/vidal/spnhc
- Stamps—http://www.mbnet.mb.ca/~lampi/stamps.html
- Tech Museum of Innovation—The HyperTech—San Jose, California—
  http://www.thetech.org/hyper
- Technology Museum of Innovation—http://www.the tech.org/thetech.html
- Texas Energy Museum—http://hal.lamar.edu/~wwwmgr/energy/museum.html
- "The Place" by Joseph Squier—http://gertrude.art.uiuc.edu/ludgate/the/place.html
- The Thing—http://www.thing.net/thingnyc
- Tinker Swiss Cottage Museum—http://www.tinkercottage.com
- Toaster Museum—http://www.spiritone.com/~ericn
- Transnational Church of Life on Mars—http://www.meat.com
- United States Brig *Niagara*—http://www.ncinter.net/~niagara
- U.S. Department of the Interior Museum—http://www.ios.doi.gov/isc/isc.html
- U.S. Space and Rocket Center—http://www.spacecamp.com
- Valdez Museum—http://www.alaska.net/~vldzmuse/index.html
- Victoriana (Museum & Historical Society links)—http://www.victoriana.com
- Virtual Garden—http://vg.com
- Weather Vane Home Page—http://www.denninger.com
- Williams Research Center—http://www.hnoc.org
- wNetStation (Visionary Art)—http://www.wnet.org
- Ye Olde Curiosity Shoppe—http://www.seattlesquare.com/curiosity
- Zoology Museum at Tring and Down House (the Home of Charles Darwin)—
  http://www.nhm.ac.uk/tring/tring.html

Roadside Sources:

- Mapquest—http://www.mapquest.com
- *Route 66* magazine—http://www.neonroad.com
- Route 66—
  http://www.cs.kuleuven.ac.be:80/~swa/route66/main.html
  http://www.cs.kuleuven.ac.bez/~swa/route66/main.html
- *Roadside* magazine—http://www1.usa1.com/~roadside/
- Drive-Ins—http://ezinfo.ucs.indiana.edu/~csherayk/drive-ins.html
- *Out West*: The Newspaper That Roams—http://www.outwestnewspaper.com
- Outtahere—http://outtahere.wvs.com
- Roadside Attractions—http://www.brettnews.com
- *Roadside America*—http://www.roadsideamerica.com
- Roadside Commentary—http://www.doremi.co.uk/road/favs.html
- *Road Trip* USA—http://www.moon.com/rt.usa/rdtrip/rdtrip.html
- *Vagabond Monthly*—http://www.globaldialog.com/~tpatmaho
- Wanderlust—http://www.salonmagazine.com/wanderlust

Index by Category

ADVERTISING & COMMERCE

American Advertising Museum, 301
American Bicentennial Museum, 2
American Diner Museum, 323
American Museum of Brewing History and Arts, 131
Black History Museum, 367
Business Card Museum, 308–9
California Route 66 Museum, 42
Canal Museum, 308
Candy Americana Museum, 311
Carpenter Museum of Antique Outboard Motors, 222
Cockroach Hall of Fame, 352
Colonel Harland Sanders Cafe and Museum, 130
Colonel Harland Sanders Museum, 132–33
Corner Drug Store, 190
Curt Teich Postcard Exhibit and Archives, 101
Dells Mill Water-Powered Museum, 386
Dr. Pepper Bottling, 346–47
Emy-Lou Biedenharn Foundation, 138
Feet First, 94
Floyd County Historical Society Museum, 112
General Petroleum Museum, 376
Geographical Center Pioneer Village and Museum, 274
Goulding's Museum, 358
Greyhound Bus Origin Center, 178–79
Harvey House Museum, 122
Higgins Foundation/National Bank Note Museum and Library, 117
International Museum of Surgical Science and Hall of Immortals, 95

JCPenney Historical Museum and Archives, 352
Johnson Victrola Museum, 62–63
Julia C. Bullette Red Light Museum, 218
Kam Wah Chung and Company Museum, 299
Le Sueur Museum, 180
Lunchbox Museum, 6
Maidenform Museum, 248
Marland Station Wall of Memories, 294
Marsh's Free Museum, 374
Marvin's Marvelous Mechanical Museum, 169
Max Nordeen's Wheels Museum, 102
Mercantile Money Museum, 197
Mount Horeb Mustard Museum, 389–90
Muscle Car Ranch, 289–90
Museum of American Financial History, 249
Museum of American Political Life, 60
Museum of Cosmetology Arts and Sciences, 198
Museum of Independent Telephony, 120
Museum of Menstruation (MUM), 153
Museum of Neon Art, 39
Museum of Postal History (Delphos, OH), 279–80
Museum of Postal History (NYC), 249
Museum of Questionable Medical Devices, 181
Museum of the Fur Trade, 208–9
Museum of Tobacco Art and History, 339
National Lighter Museum, 294
North Central Washington Museum, 380
Oklahoma Route 66 Museum, 290–91
Oldest Store Museum, 75
100th Meridian Museum, 292
Patee House Museum/Jesse James House Museum, 197

Paterson Museum/Rogers Mill, 230
Pink Palace Museum, 337
Post Mark Collectors Club Museum, 276
R. J. Reynolds Tobacco, 270
Remington Firearms Museum and Country Store, 257
Roy Rogers–Dale Evans Museum, 43
Schmidt Coca-Cola Memorabilia Museum, 130–31
Sheldon Jackson Museum, 11
Skyscraper Museum, 250
Smallwood Store Museum, 68–69
Steamship *Bertrand* Display, 116
Tamiment Institute Library/Wagner Labor Archives, 250
Thomas Newcomen Library and Museum in Steam, Technology and Industrial History/James R. Muldowney Printing Museum, 309
Valentine Museum, 99
Van Horn's Antique Truck Museum and Circus Room Display, 115–16
Vintage Telephone Equipment, 377–78
W. H. Tupper General Merchandise Museum & Louisiana Telephone Pioneer Museum, 137
Wal-Mart Visitor Center, 22–23
Wanamaker Museum, 316–17
Warren L. Fuller Breweriana Collection, 186
Wolfsonian, The (formerly Collection of Decorative and Propaganda Arts), 72–73
World o' Tools Museum, 341

ANIMALS & BUGS

Aiken Thoroughbred Racing Hall of Fame and Museum, 324
American International Rattlesnake Museum, 234
American Kennel Club Museum of the Dog (formerly the Dog Museum), 191
American Saddlebred Horse Museum, 195
American Saddle Horse Museum, 132
American Work Horse Museum, 366–67
Appaloosa Horse Club Museum, 91
Arizona–Sonora Desert Museum, 20
Ashfall Fossil Beds State Park, 212
Aurora Fossil Museum, 265
Bailey-Mathews Shell Museum, 75
Belhaven Memorial Museum, 266
Birds of Vermont Museum, 360
Buckhorn Hall of Horns, Texas History, Fins, Feathers and Boar's Nest, 353

Call of the Wild, 170
Catfish Capitol Museum, 184
Cockroach Hall of Fame, 352
Cold Spring Harbor Whaling Museum, 262
Dairy Shrine/Hoard Historical Museum, 388
Dakota Dinosaur Museum, 272
Dog Mushing Museum, 9
Earth Science Museum at Brigham Young University, 358
Fairbanks Museum and Planetarium, 361–62
Fred Bear Museum, 71
Frog Fantasies Museum, 23–24
Frost Entomological Museum, 319
Geological Museum, 397
Hoh Rain Forest Visitors Center, 372
Honey of a Museum, 386
International Wolf Center, 177–78
John James Audubon Museum and Nature Center, 131
John May Museum Center, 47
Kelsey Museum of Archaeology, 168
Lucy the Margate Elephant, 227
Ma'Cille's Museum of Miscellanea, 7
Mac's Museum, 201–2
Mr. and Mrs. Dan Midgley Museum, 291–92
Mister Ed's Elephant Museum, 313
Montana Sheepherders Hall of Fame, 202
Mount Angel Abbey Museum, 202
Museum of the Fur Trade, 208–9
Museum of York County, 326–27
National Bird Dog Museum and Field Trial Hall of Fame, 336
National Buffalo Museum, 273
National Fish Culture Hall of Fame and Museum, 332
National Museum of the Morgan Horse, 362
Of Sea and Shore Museum, 375
Paul Jensen Arctic Museum, 299
Pawnee Bill Museum, 295
Pig War Museum, 373
Prehistoric Gardens, 300
Rhode Island Fisherman and Whale Museum, 322
Saint Charles Archery Museum, 377
Select Sires Bull Hall of Fame, 284–85
Sheldon Jackson Museum, 11
Smokey Bear State Historical Park, 235
Thompson-Hickman Memorial Museum, 205
University of Alaska Fairbanks Museum, 9
Vermont Raptor Center, 362–63

ANTHROPOLOGY & ARCHAEOLOGY

Akta Lakota Museum and Cultural Center, 328–29
American Funeral Service Museum, 349
American Museum of Asmat Art/Bishop Sowada Gallery, 183
Amerind Foundation, 14
Anasazi Heritage Center, 49
Appaloosa Horse Club Museum, 91
Bailey House Museum (Maui Historical Society Museum), 87
Banneker-Douglass Museum, 148
Baranov Museum, 10
Bead Museum, 17
Black History Museum, 367
Blaine County Museum, 202
Buechel Memorial Lakota Museum, 332
Caliente Railroad Boxcar Museum, 214
Carrie M. McLain Memorial Museum, 10
Casa Malpais, 19–20
Center for Puppetry Arts, 79
Central Nevada Museum, 217–18
Chaco Culture National Historical Park, 238
Dairy Shrine/Hoard Historical Museum, 388
Desert Caballeros Western Museum, 20
Edwin Wolters Memorial Museum, 354
Eldridge Street Synagogue, 247
Eva Parker Woods Cottage, 85–86
Fort Morgan Museum, 49
Fruitlands Museums, 158–59
General Petroleum Museum, 376
George W. Brown, Jr., Ojibwe Museum and Cultural Center (formerly Lac du Flambeau Chippewa Museum and Cultural Center), 388
Gerald Johnson Free Museum, 291
Geronimo Springs Museum, 242–43
Gila River Cultural Center, 18
Gold Pyramid House, 101
Grand Mound Interpretive Center, 179
Great Plains Black Museum, 211–12
Haffenreffer Museum of Anthropology, 321
Hammond Museum of Bells, 24
Herman Abrams, Archaeologist of Himself, 230
Hopi Cultural Center, 19
Indian Arts Research Center, 242
Indian Temple Mound Museum, 70
Institute for American Indian Studies, 59–60
Jacques Marchais Museum of Tibetan Art, 252
James L. Kelso Bible Lands Museum, 317
Japanese Cultural Center of Hawaii, 88

John G. Neihardt Center, 208
John Wesley Powell Memorial Museum, 16
Judiciary History Center, 88
Kam Wah Chung and Company Museum, 299
Kelsey Museum of Archaeology, 168
King Tut's Tomb and Museum, 215
Koshare Indian Kiva Museum, 50–51
Little Traverse Regional Historical Museum, 174
Los Alamos Historical Museum, 237
Lost City Museum, 216
Mac's Museum, 201–2
Makah Cultural and Research Center, 374–75
Malibu Lagoon Museum and Historic Adamson House, 40
Martin and Osa Johnson Safari Museum, 121
Matt's Museum, 137
Museum of the Alphabet, 270
Museum of Tobacco Art and History, 339
Museum of Western Colorado, 50
Nanticoke Indian Museum, 63
National Hall of Fame for Famous American Indians, 288
National Jewish American Sports Hall of Fame/B'nai B'rith Klutznick National Jewish Museum, 67
Navajo Code Talkers Room, 236
Navajo Tribal Museum, 21
New Orleans Historic Voodoo Museum, 139
No Man's Land Historical Museum, 293
Ohio Indian Art Museum/Moundbuilders State Memorial, 283
Oneida Nation Museum, 390
Paul Jensen Arctic Museum, 299
Peary-MacMillan Arctic Museum, 142–43
Pipestone County Historical Museum, 182
Plainsman Museum, 208
Pratt Museum, 9–10
Prayer Museum, 186
Range Riders Museum and Huffman Pictures, 203
Raven Site Museum/White Mountain Archaeological Center, 18–19
Rockwell Museum, 254–55
Saint Charles Archery Museum, 377
Seaside Museum and Historical Society, 302–3
Sheldon Jackson Museum, 11
Smoki Museum, 18
Sweetwater County Historical Museum, 396
Textile Museum, The, 67
Three Affiliated Tribes Museum, 273–74
Totem Heritage Center, 10

Turtle Mountain Heritage Center, 271
Uinta County Historical Museum, 395
Ute Indian Museum, 52
William Breman Jewish Heritage Museum, 80
Wing Luke Asian Museum, 378
York W. Bailey Museum, 327

ARCHITECTURE & DESIGN
American Diner Museum, 323
American Heritage Center, 396–97
American Swedish Institute, 180–81
Arcosanti, 14
Ave Maria Grotto, 1–2
Baltimore Public Works Museum, 150
Bartlesville Museum in the Price Tower/
    Shin'enKan, 289
Bedrooms of America, 366
Beer Can House, 349
Bird's Eye View Museum of Miniatures, 110
Boulder City/Hoover Dam Museum, 213
Business Card Museum, 308–9
Camp Washington-Carver, 382
Carole and Barry Kaye Museum of Miniatures,
    38–39
Cedar Rock/The Walter Residence, 118
Century House Museum (Sanguinetti House),
    21
Chaco Culture National Historical Park, 238
Cottage Grove Museum, 298
Craftsman Farms/Gustav Stickley Museum,
    229–30
Cranbrook Art Museum, 168–69
Elbert Hubbard Roycroft Museum, 255–56
El Paisano Hotel, 350
Fabric Workshop and Museum, 314
Fonthill Museum, 307–8
Frederick Law Olmsted National Historic Site,
    156
George Washington Masonic Memorial,
    364–65
Georgia O'Keeffe House, 233–34
Ghost Town Hall of Fame, 204
Gila River Cultural Center, 18
Gold Pyramid House, 101
Green-Wood Cemetery, 246
Headley-Whitney Museum, 132
Hill-Stead Museum, 57
Hitchcock Museum (John Tarrant Kenney
    Hitchcock Museum), 59
Hole N' The Rock, 358

Holland Museum (formerly the Netherlands
    Museum), 171
Homesteads Tower Museum, 335
Home, Sweet Home Museum, 262
House of the Temple Library/Museum, 66
Kemerer Museum of Decorative Arts, 306
Lightner Museum, 75
Lotusland, 34–35
Louis H. Sullivan Architectural Ornament
    Collection, 96
Lucy the Margate Elephant, 227
Macculloch Hall Historical Museum, 228
Malibu Lagoon Museum and Historic
    Adamson House, 40
Mattatuck Museum, 60
Mattress Factory, 317–18
Milton House Museum, 388–89
Mr. and Mrs. Dan Midgley Museum, 291–92
Moss Mansion, 200–1
Mount Auburn Cemetery, 156–57
Museum of Ancient Brick, 336
National Building Museum, 66
National Corvette Museum, 129
National Ornamental Metal Museum, 337
Newington Cropsey Foundation Gallery of Art
    and Cultural Studies Center/Ever Rest,
    257
Octagon House/America's First Kindergarten,
    392
Paper House, 162
Petrified Wood Park and Museum, 330
Prabhupada's Palace of Gold, 383
Presidents Cottage Museum, 384
Roeder Home, 370
Rosenbach Museum and Library, 316
Skyscraper Museum, 250
Smitty's Juke Box Museum, 351–52
Southern California Institute of Architecture
    (SCI-Arc), 39
Tabor Opera House, 51
Thomas Wolfe Memorial, 265
Tinkertown Museum, 241
Touro Synagogue, 322
Trianon Museum and Art Gallery, 48
Watts Towers of Simon Rodia, 39
White Pine Camp, 260
Winchester Mystery House, 33–34
Wolfsonian, The (formerly Collection of
    Decorative and Propaganda Arts),
    72–73

ART & CRAFTS

African Art Museum of the S.M.A. Fathers, 231
Akta Lakota Museum and Cultural Center, 328–29
Albrecht-Kemper Museum of Art, 196
Alling Coverlet Museum, 259–60
American Funeral Service Museum, 349
American Kennel Club Museum of the Dog (formerly the Dog Museum), 191
American Museum of Asmat Art/Bishop Sowada Gallery, 183
American Saddle Horse Museum, 132
American Swedish Historical Museum, 314
American Swedish Institute, 180–81
American Visionary Art Museum, 149
Amerind Foundation, 14
A. R. Mitchell Memorial Museum of Western Art, 53
Baranov Museum, 10
Barnegat Bay Decoy and Baymen's Museum, 231–32
Barnes Foundation, 311–12
Barney Smith's Toilet Seat Art Museum, 353
Bead Museum, 17
Beer Can House, 349
Bennington Museum, 359
Berea College Appalachian Museum, 129
Bergstrom-Mahler Museum, 390
Bily Clock Museum/Antonin Dvořák Exhibit, 118
Birds of Vermont Museum, 360
Bob Jones University Art Gallery and Museum, 326
Boston Athenaeum, 155–56
Bread and Puppet Museum, 360
Brewer's Bell Museum, 344
Buffalo Bill Historical Center, 394–95
Carhenge, 207
Carole and Barry Kaye Museum of Miniatures, 38–39
Center for Puppetry Arts, 79
Charles Hosmer Morse Museum of American Art, 77
Chinati Foundation/La Fundación Chinati, 350
Church of Anti-Oppression Folk Art, 353
Cold Spring Harbor Whaling Museum, 262
Cookie Jar Museum, 97
Corn Palace, 330–31
Craftsman Farms/Gustav Stickley Museum, 229–30

Cranbrook Art Museum, 168–69
Curt Teich Postcard Exhibit and Archives, 101
Cut and Thrust Edged Weapons Museum/Co-op Gallery, 310
DeCordova Museum and Sculpture Park, 159
Degenhart Paperweight and Glass Museum, 276–77
Delaware Agricultural Museum and Village, 62
Denver Museum of Miniatures, Dolls and Toys, 48
Desert Caballeros Western Museum, 20
Don Brown Rosary Collection, 379
Dorflinger Glass Museum, 319–20
Earl's Art Gallery, 185
East Martello Museum and Gallery, 71–72
Edgar Allan Poe Museum, 367–68
Elbert Hubbard Roycroft Museum, 255–56
Ethel Wright Mohamed Stitchery Museum ("Mama's Dream World"), 185
Eye of the World Museum, 343
Fabric Workshop and Museum, 314
Fairbanks Museum and Planetarium, 361–62
First National Church of the Exquisite Panic, 247
Fleischer Museum, 19
Fly Fishing Museum, 298
Folger Shakespeare Library, 65
Fonthill Museum, 307–8
Forbes Magazine Galleries, 247–48
Fruitlands Museums, 158–59
Furniture Discovery Center and the Furniture Hall of Fame, 267
Garden of Eden and Cabin Home, 124
Gehrke Windmill Garden, 372
Georgia O'Keeffe House, 233–34
Harwood Foundation of UNM, 242
Headley-Whitney Museum, 132
Henry Miller Memorial Library, 34
H. H. Bennett Studio Foundation Museum, 392
Hill-Stead Museum, 57
Hungarian Folk Art Museum, 74
Indian Arts Research Center, 242
Inland Seas Maritime Museum (formerly the Great Lakes Museum), 285–86
International Bioregional Old Route 66 Visitor Center and Preservation Foundation, 15
Isamu Noguchi Garden Museum, 251
Jacques Marchais Museum of Tibetan Art, 252
Jim Powers Junk Art Museum, 293

John James Audubon Museum and Nature Center, 131

Jones Museum of Glass and Ceramics, 146–47

Kemerer Museum of Decorative Arts, 306

Koshare Indian Kiva Museum, 50–51

Lace Museum, 34

Leila's Hair Museum, 193

Lightner Museum, 75

Lightning Field, The, 239

Living Rock Studios, 297–98

Louis P. Klein Broom and Brush Museum, 93–94

Lunchbox Museum, 6

Macculloch Hall Historical Museum, 228

Magic Lantern Castle Museum, 354

Malibu Lagoon Museum and Historic Adamson House, 40

Margaret Harwell Art Museum, 196

Martin and Osa Johnson Safari Museum, 121

Marvin and Mary Johnson's Gourd Museum, 266–67

Maryhill Museum of Art, 373

Mattatuck Museum, 60

Mattress Factory, 317–18

Merry-Go-Round Museum, 285

Miller Comb Museum, 9

Montana Historical Society Museum, 202–3

Montclair Art Museum, 228

Morikami Museum and Japanese Gardens, 69

Museum at Lower Shaker Village, 221

Museum at the Fashion Institute of Technology, The, 248–49

Museum of Bad Art, 157

Museum of Death, 44–45

Museum of Holography, 95

Museum of Neon Art, 39

Museum of Ordinary People (MOP), 4–5

Museum of the American Numismatic Association, 47

Museum of the American Quilters Society, 134

Museum of the Gulf Coast, 352–53

Museum of Tobacco Art and History, 339

Museum of Woodcarving, 391–92

Museum of York County, 326–27

Muskegon Museum of Art, 173

National Bottle Museum, 253

National Czech and Slovak Museum and Library, 111–12

National Gallery of Caricature and Cartoon Art, 66–67

National Jewish American Sports Hall of Fame/B'nai B'rith Klutznick National Jewish Museum, 67

National Knife Museum, 335

National Ornamental Metal Museum, 337

Navajo Tribal Museum, 21

Neuberger Museum of Art, 260

New England Quilt Museum, 160

Newington Cropsey Foundation Gallery of Art and Cultural Studies Center/Ever Rest, 257

Noyes Museum of Art, 229

Nut Museum, 58–59

Old Clock Museum, 351

Old Jail Art Center, 342

Old Jail Museum, 104–5

Orange Show, The, 350

Paradise Garden, 83

Parker Ranch Visitor Center and Museum, 85

Pasaquan, 80

Peace Museum, 95

Petersen Rock Gardens, 302

Petrified Wood Park and Museum, 330

Phippen Museum of Western Art, 18

Pollock-Krasner House and Study Center, 262

Pratt Museum, 9–10

Remington Firearms Museum and Country Store, 257

Robert C. Williams American Museum of Papermaking, 79

Robert Henri Museum and Historical Walkway, 209

Rockwell Museum, 254–55

Rollo Jamison Museum/Mining Museum, 391

Rosenbach Museum and Library, 316

Saint Anne Shrine, 158

Saint Charles Archery Museum, 377

Saint-Gaudens National Historic Site, 221

Sandwich Glass Museum, 162–63

Shore Village Museum (The Lighthouse Museum), 146

Sloane-Stanley Museum/Kent Furnace, 58

Space Murals Museum, 238–39

Stanley Museum, 144

Stephen Foster State Folk Culture Center, 76

Sterling and Francine Clark Art Institute, 165

Storm King Art Center, 258

Streitwieser Foundation Trumpet Museum, 318

Super Museum, 98

Tattoo Art Museum, 33

Teddy Bear Museum of Naples ("Frannie's"), 73
Textile Museum, The, 67
Thomas Hart Benton Home and Studio State
    Historic Site, 194
Thornton W. Burgess Museum, 163
Tinkertown Museum, 241
Totem Heritage Center, 10
Totem Pole Park, 292
Trenton Teapot Museum, 340
Trianon Museum and Art Gallery, 48
24-Hour Church of Elvis, 301
Valentine Museum, 99
Vermont Marble Exhibit, 361
Warther Museum, 280
Watts Towers of Simon Rodia, 39
Wendell Gilley Museum, 147
Whoop-n-Holler Museum, 371
William S. Hart Museum, 40
Williams Hall Art Museum of Kitsch Art
    (WHAMKA), 359–60
Wisconsin Concrete Park, 390–91
Wolfsonian, The (formerly Collection of
    Decorative and Propaganda Arts), 72–73
Words and Pictures Museum of Fine
    Sequential Art, 160
World o' Tools Museum, 341
World's Only Pecan Art Museum, 346

AVIATION & SPACE
Academy of Model Aeronautics/National
    Model Aviation Museum, 108–9
Air Heritage Museum and Aircraft Restoration
    Facility, 305–6
Alaska Aviation Heritage Museum, 8
Amelia Earhart Birthplace, 121
American Airlines C. R. Smith Museum, 347–48
Aviation Hall of Fame and Museum of New
    Jersey, 231
Big Well and Celestial Museum, 123
Black History Museum, 367
Champlin Fighter Aircraft Museum, 16
Charles A. Lindbergh House, 180
Cornish Pumping Engine and Mining Museum,
    171
Fairbanks Museum and Planetarium, 361–62
Fred E. Weisbrod Aircraft Museum/
    International B-24 Museum, 52
Hangar 9/Edward H. White II Memorial
    Museum, 354
Hatton-Eielson Museum, 272–73

High Plains Museum, 123
International Kite Museum, 344
International UFO Museum and Research
    Center, 240
International Women's Air and Space Museum,
    277
John May Museum Center, 47
Little A'Le'Inn/Area 51 Research Center, 216
Meteorite Museum, 235
Motorsports Hall of Fame of America, 174
Museum of Alaska Transportation and
    Industry, 11–12
Museum of Postal History (NYC), 279–80
National Atomic Museum, 235
National Balloon Museum, 114
National Soaring Museum, 256
Neil Armstrong Air and Space Museum, 286
Oscar's Dreamland, 201
Owls Head Transportation Museum, 144–45
Space Murals Museum, 238–39
UFO Enigma Museum, 240
UFO Museum, 301
Virgil I. Grissom Memorial, 108
Wine Museum of Greyton H. Taylor, 256–57
World Kite Museum and Hall of Fame, 374
Wright Brothers National Memorial, 268

CONCEPTUAL
American Visionary Art Museum, 149
Ave Maria Grotto, 1–2
Barney Smith's Toilet Seat Art Museum, 353
Beer Can House, 349
Business Card Museum, 308–9
Carhenge, 207
Conspiracy Museum, The, 345
Creation Evidences Museum, 348
Doyle's Unami Farms/Corn Maze, 228–29
Eye of the World Museum, 343
First National Church of the Exquisite Panic,
    247
Garden of Eden and Cabin Home, 124
Gehrke Windmill Garden, 372
Herman Abrams, Archaeologist of Himself, 230
International UFO Museum and Research
    Center, 240
Jim Powers Junk Art Museum, 293
L. Ron Hubbard Life Exhibition, 37–38
Lightning Field, The, 239
Little A'Le'Inn/Area 51 Research Center, 216
Lucy the Margate Elephant, 227

Ma'Cille's Museum of Miscellanea, 7
Max Nordeen's Wheels Museum, 102
Mister Ed's Elephant Museum, 313
Museum of Bad Art, 157
Museum of Death, 44–45
Museum of Jurassic Technology, 36
Museum of Ordinary People (MOP), 4–5
Museum of Questionable Medical Devices, 181
National Liars Hall of Fame, 209
Orange Show, The, 350
Palestinian Gardens, 187
Paradise Garden, 83
Pasaquan, 80
Peace Museum, 95
Petersen Rock Gardens, 302
Petrified Wood Park and Museum, 330
Prehistoric Gardens, 300
Space Murals Museum, 238–39
Totem Pole Park, 292
Trash Museum/Hackensack Meadowlands Development Commission Environment Center, 226–27
24-Hour Church of Elvis, 301
UFO Enigma Museum, 240
UFO Museum, 301
Watts Towers of Simon Rodia, 39
Wisconsin Concrete Park, 390–91

FARM & RANCH

Alexander and Baldwin Sugar Museum, 86
American Cotton Museum, 349
American Hop Museum, 379–80
American Saddlebred Horse Museum, 195
American Work Horse Museum, 366–67
Basque Museum and Cultural Center, 90
Berea College Appalachian Museum, 129
Bill Dalley's Windmill Collection, 239
Bridgehampton Historical Museum, 261
Buckaroo Hall of Fame and Heritage Museum, 219
Chisholm Trail Museum, 126
City of Las Vegas Museum and Rough Riders Memorial Collection, 237
Cowboys Then and Now Museum, 303
Dairy Shrine/Hoard Historical Museum, 388
Danish Immigrant Museum, 114
Deere & Co. Administrative Center, 98
Delaware Agricultural Museum and Village, 62
Dells Mill Water-Powered Museum, 386
Devil's Rope Museum and Route 66 Museum, 351
Doyle's Unami Farms/Corn Maze, 228–29
First Peanut Museum in U.S.A., 368–69
Floyd County Historical Society Museum, 112
Furford Cranberry Museum, 373–74
Gafford Family Museum, 344–45
Genoa Courthouse Museum, 214–15
Geographical Center Pioneer Village and Museum, 274
Great Plains Black Museum, 211–12
Hanka Homestead Ulkomuseo (Living Outdoor Museum), 168
Harold Warp Pioneer Village, 211
Hartung's License Plate and Automotive Museum, 97
Henry and Rubye Connerly Museum, 23
Honey of a Museum, 386
Huntley Project Museum of Irrigated Agriculture, 205–6
Ice House Museum, 111
Idaho's World Potato Exposition, 89–90
Jackson Hole Museum and Historical Center, 396
Jasper County Historical Society Museum/ Maytag Exhibit, 117
Jesse James Farm and Museum, 194
Kansas Barbed Wire Museum, 123–24
Kona Historical Society Museum, 85
Lenoir Museum, 339
Louis Toav's John Deere Collection, 205
Ludwig and Christina Welk Homestead/ Lawrence Welk Birthplace, 274
Makoti Threshers Museum, 273
Max Nordeen's Wheels Museum, 102
Mennonite Heritage Museum, 122–23
Midwest Old Threshers Heritage Museum and Museum of Repertoire Americana, 116
Montana Sheepherders Hall of Fame, 202
Morikami Museum and Japanese Gardens, 69
Museum at Lower Shaker Village, 221
Museum of Alaska Transportation and Industry, 11–12
Mushroom Museum at Phillips Place, 310
National Apple Museum, 306
National Farm Toy Museum, 114
New England Maple Museum, 361
Nodaway Valley Historical Museum, 112–13
No Man's Land Historical Museum, 293
North Central Washington Museum, 380

100th Meridian Museum, 292
Oscar's Dreamland, 201
Parker Ranch Visitor Center and Museum, 85
Pennyroyal Area Museum, 132
Phelps County Historical Museum, 210
Pinal County Historical Museum, 14–15
Pink Palace Museum, 337
Rice Museum, 325
R. J. Reynolds Tobacco, 270
Royal Aloha Coffee Mill and Museum, 84–85
Select Sires Bull Hall of Fame, 284–85
Shaker Museum, 146
Shattuck Windmill Museum and Park, 295–96
Stolen Bell Museum, 395
Valley Park Shortline Railroad/Agriculture/
    Historic Museum (C. B. "Buddie" Newman
    Museum), 189

FASHION & BEAUTY
American Costume Museum, 189
American Swedish Historical Museum, 314
American Textile History Museum, 159–60
Bead Museum, 17
Belhaven Memorial Museum, 266
Boott Cotton Mills Museum, 160
Celebrity Shoe Museum, 345
Center for the History of Foot Care and Foot
    Wear (The Shoe Museum), 314
Danbury Scott-Fanton Museum/Charles Ives
    House, 56–57
Don King's Western Museum, 397–98
Dougherty House–Victorian Wedding Museum,
    282
Elizabeth Sage Historic Costume Collection,
    104
Fabric Workshop and Museum, 314
Fieldcrest Cannon Textile Exhibition, 267
Germaine Cazenave Wells Mardi Gras
    Museum, 138–39
Gish's Old West Museum, 348
Glove Museum, 248
Granville Life-Style Museum (H. D. Robinson
    House), 281
Henry and Rubye Connerly Museum, 23
Hungarian Folk Art Museum, 74
JCPenney Historical Museum and Archives,
    352
John E. and Walter D. Webb Museum of
    Vintage Fashion, 144
Lace Museum, 34

Leila's Hair Museum, 193
Lingerie Museum, 38
Maidenform Museum, 248
Margaret Harwell Art Museum, 196
Maryhill Museum of Art, 373
Mary Kay Museum, 345–46
Memory Lane Museum at Seattle Goodwill,
    376–77
Miller Comb Museum, 9
Mummers Museum (New Year's Shooters and
    Mummers Museum), 315
Museum at the Fashion Institute of
    Technology, The, 248–49
Museum of Cosmetology Arts and Sciences,
    198
Museum of the Berkeley Springs, 382
National Czech and Slovak Museum and
    Library, 111–12
Old U.S. Mint: New Orleans Jazz Collection and
    Carnival Exhibit, 139–40
Plymouth Historical Museum, 174
Potts Inn Museum, 26
Skenesborough Museum/Whitehall Urban
    Cultural Park Visitor Center, 260–61
Smith's Sewing Machine Museum, 343
Tattoo Art Museum, 33
Teutopolis Monastery Museum, 100–1
Textile Museum, The, 67
Warther Museum, 280
Windham Textile and History Museum, 60
Wolfsonian, The (formerly Collection of
    Decorative and Propaganda Arts), 72–73

FOOD & DRINK
Alexander and Baldwin Sugar Museum, 86
American Diner Museum, 323
American Hop Museum, 379–80
American Maple Museum, 255
American Museum of Brewing History and
    Arts, 131
Bair Drug and Hardware Co. Living Museum,
    378
Ball Corporation Museum, 109
Banana Museum, 36
Buckhorn Hall of Horns, Texas History, Fins,
    Feathers and Boar's Nest, 353
Burlingame Museum of Pez Memorabilia, 31
Call of the Wild, 170
Candy Americana Museum, 311
Carry A. Nation Home, 125

Catfish Capitol Museum, 184
Colonel Harland Sanders Cafe and Museum, 130
Colonel Harland Sanders Museum, 132–33
Cookie Jar Museum, 97
Corn Palace, 330–31
Cowboys Then and Now Museum, 303
Culinary Archives and Museum at Johnson and
  Wales University, 323
Dairy Shrine/Hoard Historical Museum, 388
Dells Mill Water-Powered Museum, 386
Dr. Pepper Bottling, 346–47
Emigrant Trail Museum, 30
First Century Museum (the Hormel Museum),
  177
First Peanut Museum in U.S.A., 368–69
Food Museum (aka Potato Museum), 234
Furford Cranberry Museum, 373–74
Germaine Cazenave Wells Mardi Gras
  Museum, 138–39
Harvey House Museum, 122
Henry and Rubye Connerly Museum, 23
Honey of a Museum, 386
Idaho's World Potato Exposition, 89–90
Jell-O Museum/Leroy House, 257–58
Jim Beam American Outpost, 129–30
Le Sueur Museum, 180
Marvin and Mary Johnson's Gourd Museum,
  266–67
McDonald's Museum, 95–96
McIlheny Co., 135
Mini Cake Museum, 40–41
Mount Horeb Mustard Museum, 389–90
Museum of Beverage Containers and
  Advertising, 338
Mushroom Museum at Phillips Place, 310
National Apple Museum, 306
New England Maple Museum, 361
North Central Washington Museum, 380
Nut Museum, 58–59
Oldest Store Museum, 75
Orange Show, The, 350
Oscar Getz Museum of Whiskey History, 128
Oyster Museum, 365
Pink Palace Museum, 337
Red Hook Brewery, 222–23
Rice Museum, 325
Royal Aloha Coffee Mill and Museum, 84–85
Salt Museum, 258
Schmidt Coca-Cola Memorabilia Museum,
  130–31

Southeast Museum, 254
Warren L. Fuller Breweriana Collection, 186
W. H. Tupper General Merchandise Museum &
  Louisiana Telephone Pioneer Museum,
  137
Wine Museum of Greyton H. Taylor, 256–57
World's Only Pecan Art Museum, 346
Wyandot Popcorn Museum, 283

FRONTIER

Adams Memorial Museum, 329
Alaska Aviation Heritage Museum, 8
Appaloosa Horse Club Museum, 91
Arcosanti, 14
Bailey House Museum (Maui Historical
  Society Museum), 87
Baranov Museum, 10
Basque Museum and Cultural Center, 90
Beaver Island Historical Society/Mormon Print
  Shop Museum and Marine Museum, 175
Billy the Kid Museum, 236
Black American West Museum and Heritage
  Center, 48
Blaine County Museum, 202
Boise Basin Museum, 91
Buckaroo Hall of Fame and Heritage Museum,
  219
Buckhorn Hall of Horns, Texas History, Fins,
  Feathers and Boar's Nest, 353
Buffalo Bill Historical Center, 394–95
Buffalo Bill Memorial Museum and Grave, 50
Campus Martius: The Museum of the Northwest
  Territory/Ohio River Museum, 282
Carrie M. McLain Memorial Museum, 10
Cheyenne Frontier Days Old West Museum,
  394
Chisholm Trail Museum, 126
City of Las Vegas Museum and Rough Riders
  Memorial Collection, 237
Cle Elum Historical Telephone Museum, 371
Cottage Grove Museum, 298
Cowboys Then and Now Museum, 303
Dalton Gang Hideout, 125
Danish Immigrant Museum, 114
Desert Caballeros Western Museum, 20
Dr. Kate Museum, 392–93
Dog Mushing Museum, 9
Don King's Western Museum, 397–98
Donner Reed Pioneer Museum, 357
Edwin Wolters Memorial Museum, 354

Emigrant Trail Museum, 30
French Azilum, 319
Frontier Relics Museum, 14
Geographical Center Pioneer Village and
    Museum, 274
Gerald Johnson Free Museum, 291
Ghost Town Hall of Fame, 204
Gish's Old West Museum, 348
Great Basin Museum, 356
Hanka Homestead Ulkomuseo (Living Outdoor
    Museum), 168
Harmony Museum, 309–10
Harold Warp Pioneer Village, 211
High Plains Museum, 123
Hot Springs County Historical Museum and
    Cultural Center, 398
Jackson Hole Museum and Historical Center,
    396
Jim Bowie Museum, 140
John Hutching's Museum of Natural History, 357
John Wesley Powell Memorial Museum, 16
John Wesley Powell River History Museum, 357
Kalmar Nyckel Foundation and Shipyard, 64
Kam Wah Chung and Company Museum, 299
Kansas Barbed Wire Museum, 123–24
Klondike Gold Rush National Historical Park,
    11
Laura Ingalls Wilder–Rose Wilder Lane Home
    and Museum, 195
Limberlost State Historic Site, 106
Little Traverse Regional Historical Museum, 174
Ludwig and Christina Welk Homestead/
    Lawrence Welk Birthplace, 274
Mac's Museum, 201–2
Marjorie Kinnan Rawlings State Historic
    Site, 69
McDowell House and Apothecary Shop, 130
Mennonite Heritage Museum, 122–23
Montana Historical Society Museum, 202–3
Montana Sheepherders Hall of Fame, 202
Moss Mansion, 200–1
Museum of the Fur Trade, 208–9
Museum of Western Jesuit Missions, 192
National Buffalo Museum, 273
National Czech and Slovak Museum and
    Library, 111–12
National Frontier Trails Center, 193
National Road/Zane Grey Museum, 284
New Madrid Historical Museum, 196
Northfield Historical Museum, 182

Old West Museum, 329
100th Meridian Museum, 292
Oneida Nation Museum, 390
Original Pony Express Home Station No. 1
    Museum, 124–25
Oscar's Dreamland, 201
Overland Trail Museum, 52–53
Parker Ranch Visitor Center and Museum, 85
Parris Island Museum, 326
Pawnee Bill Museum, 295
Peary-MacMillan Arctic Museum, 142–43
Pella Historical Village Museum, 117
Phelps County Historical Museum, 210
Pinal County Historical Museum, 15
Pioneer Auto Show, 331
Pipestone County Historical Museum, 182
Polish Cultural Institute/Polish Museum, 183
Range Riders Museum and Huffman Pictures,
    203
Robert Henri Museum and Historical Walkway,
    209
Rockwell Museum, 254–55
Runestone Museum, 176
Smallwood Store Museum, 68–69
Steamship *Bertrand* Display, 116
Stolen Bell Museum, 395
Sweetwater County Historical Museum, 396
Teton Flood Museum, 92
Thompson-Hickman Memorial Museum, 205
Tiny Town, 25
Turtle Mountain Heritage Center, 271
Twenty-Mule Team Museum, 41–42
Uinta County Historical Museum, 395
University of Alaska Fairbanks Museum, 9
Western SkiSport Museum, 29
William S. Hart Museum, 40
Winchester Mystery House/Winchester Products
    Museum/Winchester Historic Firearms
    Museum, 33–34
Wyoming Frontier Prison Museum, 397

GARDENS & LANDSCAPE

Arizona–Sonora Desert Museum, 20
Bakken, The: A Library and Museum of
    Electricity in Life, 181
Century House Museum (Sanguinetti House),
    21
Cranbrook Art Museum, 168–69
DeCordova Museum and Sculpture Park, 159
Emy-Lou Biedenharn Foundation, 138

Eva Parker Woods Cottage, 85–86
Frederick Law Olmsted National Historic Site, 156
Green-Wood Cemetery, 246
Hill-Stead Museum, 57
Historic Bartram's Garden, 315
Hoover Historical Center, 284
Isamu Noguchi Garden Museum, 251
James L. Kelso Bible Lands Museum, 317
Jim Beam American Outpost, 129–30
John G. Neihardt Center, 208
John P. Humes Japanese Stroll Garden, 263
Lotusland, 34–35
McDowell House and Apothecary Shop, 130
Morikami Museum and Japanese Gardens, 69
Mount Auburn Cemetery, 156–57
Museum at Lower Shaker Village, 221
New Orleans Pharmacy Museum, 139
Paradise Garden, 83
Petersen Rock Gardens, 302
Prehistoric Gardens, 300
Saint-Gaudens National Historic Site, 221
Storm King Art Center, 258
U.S. Bicycling Hall of Fame, 230–31
Ute Indian Museum, 52
Wave Hill, 245

GEMS & MINERALS

Arizona Mining and Mineral Museum, 16
Bauxite Museum, 22
Bead Museum, 17
Big Well and Celestial Museum, 123
Brimstone Museum, 141
Dakota Dinosaur Museum, 272
Dave's Down to Earth Rock Shop and Prehistoric Life Museum, 96–97
Desert Caballeros Western Museum, 20
Franklin Mineral Museum, 226
Geological Museum, 397
Ghost Town Hall of Fame, 204
John Hutching's Museum of Natural History, 357
John Wesley Powell Memorial Museum, 16
Klondike Gold Rush National Historical Park, 11
Living Rock Studios, 297–98
Mac's Museum, 201–2
Meteorite Museum, 235
Mr. and Mrs. Dan Midgley Museum, 291–92

National Mining Hall of Fame and Museum, 51
Nylander Museum, 143
Paterson Museum/Rogers Mill, 230
Petersen Rock Gardens, 302
Pioneer Auto Show, 331
Pipestone County Historical Museum, 182
Reed Gold Mine State Historic Site, 269–70
Smith Soil Monolith Collection, 375
Sweetwater County Historical Museum, 396
Twenty-Mule Team Museum, 41–42
University of Arizona Mineral Museum, 20

HEALTH & MEDICINE

Adams Center for the History of Otolaryngology—Head and Neck Surgery, 364
Bair Drug and Hardware Co. Living Museum, 378
Bakken, The: A Library and Museum of Electricity in Life, 181
Belhaven Memorial Museum, 266
Blindiana/Tactual Museum/Museum on the History of Blindness, 164
Center for the History of Foot Care and Foot Wear (The Shoe Museum), 314
Clara Barton National Historic Site, 152–53
Corner Drug Store, 190
Country Doctor Museum, 265
Damien Museum and Archives, 87
Dittrick Museum of Medical History, 278–79
Dr. John Harris Dental Museum, 275–76
Dr. Kate Museum, 392–93
Dr. Samuel D. Harris National Museum of Dentistry, 150
Dr. William D. Hutchings Office and Hospital, 108
Eichold-Heustis Medical Museum of the South, 5
Feet First, 94
Floyd County Historical Society Museum, 112
Fordyce Bathhouse Visitor Center, 25
Fort Crawford Medical Museum, 391
Glore Psychiatric Museum, 196–97
Hangar 9/Edward H. White II Memorial Museum, 354
Homeopathy Works, 381
Indiana Medical History Museum, 107
International Museum of Surgical Science and Hall of Immortals, 95
John Gorrie State Museum, 68
John R. Trautman Carville Museum, 136

Julia C. Bullette Red Light Museum, 218
Kam Wah Chung and Company Museum, 299
Kenneth W. Berger Hearing Aid Museum and
    Archives, 281–82
Macaulay Museum of Dental History, 324–25
McDowell House and Apothecary Shop, 130
Medical Museum, 17
Museum of Anesthesiology, 99
Museum of Menstruation (MUM), 153
Museum of Nursing History, 315–16
Museum of Ophthalmology, 33
Museum of Questionable Medical Devices, 181
Museum of the American Printing House for
    the Blind, 133
Museum of the Berkeley Springs, 382
Mütter Museum, College of Physicians of
    Philadelphia, 316
National Museum of Civil War Medicine, 152
New Orleans Historic Voodoo Museum, 139
New Orleans Pharmacy Museum, 139
Oldest Store Museum, 75
Porter Thermometer Museum (Dick Porter—
    Thermometer Man), 161
Sioux Empire Medical Museum, 331
Still National Osteopathic Museum, 194–95
Trash Museum/Hackensack Meadowlands
    Development Commission Environment
    Center, 226–27
University of Nebraska Medical Center Library,
    212
W. H. Tupper General Merchandise Museum &
    Louisiana Telephone Pioneer Museum,
    137
Wilhelm Reich Museum, 145–46

INDUSTRY

Alexander and Baldwin Sugar Museum, 86
American Cotton Museum, 349
American Guitar Museum, 263
American Hop Museum, 379–80
American Labor Museum/Botto House
    National Landmark, 226
American Maple Museum, 255
American Museum of Brewing History and
    Arts, 131
American Precision Museum, 362
American Sanitary Plumbing Museum, 165
Arizona Mining and Mineral Museum, 16

Auburn-Cord-Duesenberg Museum, 103–4
Ball Corporation Museum, 109
Baltimore Museum of Industry, 149–50
Barnum Museum, 55
Bauxite Museum, 22
Big Brutus, 126–27
Boott Cotton Mills Museum, 160
Brimstone Museum, 141
Bryant's Museum (Bryant's Stoves and Music,
    Inc.), 147
Camp Seven Museum, 372
Candy Americana Museum, 311
Catfish Capitol Museum, 184
Charles River Museum of Industry, 164
Computer Museum, 156
Cornish Pumping Engine and Mining Museum,
    171
Cowboys Then and Now Museum, 303
Crane Museum, 157
Crown Gardens and Archives/Bedspread
    Museum, 81–82
Culinary Archives and Museum at Johnson and
    Wales University, 323
Danbury Scott-Fanton Museum/Charles Ives
    House, 56–57
Degenhart Paperweight and Glass Museum,
    276–77
Dells Mill Water-Powered Museum, 386
Dr. Pepper Bottling, 346–47
Elberton Granite Museum and Exhibit, 82
Experimental Breeder Reactor #1, 89
Fall River Historical Society, 158
Fieldcrest Cannon Textile Exhibition, 267
First Century Museum (the Hormel Museum),
    177
General Petroleum Museum, 376
George Meany Memorial Archives, 154
Goodyear World of Rubber, 275
Greentown Glass Museum, 106
Harley-Davidson Motorcycle Plant and
    Museum (Rodney C. Gott Museum), 320
Hawaiian Railway Society, 87
Hays Antique Truck Museum, 30
Herbert H. Dow Historical Museum, 172
Herschell Carrousel Factory Museum, 259
Hitchcock Museum (John Tarrant Kenney
    Hitchcock Museum), 59
Hoover Historical Center, 284
Howard Steamboat Museum, 107

Ice House Museum, 111
Idaho's World Potato Exposition, 89–90
Indian Motocycle Museum and Hall of Fame, 163
Jasper County Historical Society Museum/Maytag Exhibit, 117
Jim Beam American Outpost, 129–30
John Lewis Mining and Labor Museum, 115
Jones Museum of Glass and Ceramics, 146–47
Kansas Barbed Wire Museum, 123–24
Kentucky Coal Mining Museum, 129
Kona Historical Society Museum, 85
Labor Hall of Fame, 66
Labor Museum and Learning Center of Michigan, 170
Lancaster Newspapers Newseum, 311
Lee Way Motor Freight Museum, 295
Le Sueur Museum, 180
Liquid Paper Museum, 238
Lock Museum of America, 59
Lock Ridge Furnace Museum, 305
Luhr Jensen Fishing Tackle Museum, 298–99
Lumberman's Museum, 145
Maine Maritime Museum, 142
Makoti Threshers Museum, 273
Marland Station Wall of Memories, 294
Martin Guitar Company, 312–13
Mary Kay Museum, 345–46
Mattatuck Museum, 60
McIlhenny Co., 135
Michigan Iron Industry Museum, 173
Mifflinburg Buggy Museum, 312
Minnesota Museum of Mining, 177
Mulberry Phosphate Museum, 73
Museum at the Fashion Institute of Technology, The, 248–49
Museum of Ancient Brick, 336
Museum of Ceramics, 280–81
Museum of Independent Telephony, 120
Museum of Nursing History, 315–16
National Bottle Museum, 253
National Corvette Museum, 129
National Heisey Glass Museum, 283
National Mining Hall of Fame and Museum, 51
National Plastics Center and Museum, 159
New England Maple Museum, 361
North Central Washington Museum, 380
Olde Fan Museum, 346
Original American Kazoo Company Factory and Museum, 256
Oscar Getz Museum of Whiskey History, 128

Oyster Museum, 365
Paterson Museum/Rogers Mill, 230
Penn-Brad Oil Museum, 307
Red Hook Brewery, 222–23
Remington Firearms Museum and Country Store, 257
Rice Museum, 325
R. J. Reynolds Tobacco, 270
Robert C. Williams American Museum of Papermaking, 79
RV/MH Heritage Foundation/Hall of Fame/Museum/Library, 105
Ryther Printing Museum, 124
Salt Museum, 258
Sandwich Glass Museum, 162–63
Saylor Cement Museum, 305
Select Sires Bull Hall of Fame, 284–85
Shovel Museum/Arnold B. Tofias Archives, 161
Slater Mill Historic Site, 323
Sloane-Stanley Museum/Kent Furnace, 58
Smith's Sewing Machine Museum, 343
Springfield Armory National Historic Site, 163
Studebaker National Museum, 110
Tamiment Institute Library/Wagner Labor Archives, 250
Telephone Museum, 79
Thomas Newcomen Library and Museum in Steam Technology and Industrial History/James R. Muldowney Printing Museum, 309
Thorniley Collection of Type, 377
Three Mile Island Visitors Center, 312
Turtle Mountain Heritage Center, 271
Vermont Marble Exhibit, 361
Watch and Clock Museum of the National Association of Watch and Clock Collectors (NAWCC), 307
Winchester Mystery House/Winchester Products Museum/Winchester Historic Firearms Museum, 33–34
Windham Textile and History Museum, 60
World o' Tools Museum, 341
Ybor City State Museum, 76
Youngstown Historical Center of Industry and Labor, 287

INVENTIONS

Alabama Historical Radio Society/Don Kresge Memorial Museum, 2
American Clock and Watch Museum, 56
American Precision Museum, 362

Bakken, The: A Library and Museum of
Electricity in Life, 181
Dr. Samuel D. Harris National Museum of
Dentistry, 150
Elwood Haynes Museum, 108
Farnsworth TV Pioneer Museum (Jefferson
County Historical Society), 92
Floyd County Historical Society Museum, 112
Gabe Self-Cleaning House/Business Building
Authority, 299–300
Garibaldi and Meucci Museum of the Order
Sons of Italy in America, 252
Goodyear World of Rubber, 275
Herbert H. Dow Historical Museum, 172
High Plains Museum, 123
John Gorrie State Museum, 68
Johnson Victrola Museum, 62–63
Joseph Priestley House, 313
Kansas Barbed Wire Museum, 123–24
Kenneth W. Berger Hearing Aid Museum and
Archives, 281–82
Liquid Paper Museum, 238
Lock Museum of America, 59
Mount Vernon Museum of Incandescent
Lighting, 151
Museum of American Heritage, 32
Museum of Jurassic Technology, 36
Museum of Questionable Medical Devices, 181
Museum of the Alphabet, 270
National Museum of Roller Skating, 210–11
National Plastics Center and Museum, 159
Parks Telephone Museum, 100
Patent Model Museum, 24–25
Pink Palace Museum, 337
Plainsman Museum, 208
Remington Firearms Museum and Country
Store, 257
Ryther Printing Museum, 124
Shaker Museum, 146
Stanley Museum, 144
Telephone Museum, 79
Thomas A. Edison Memorial Tower and
Museum, 227
Thomas Newcomen Library and Museum in
Steam Technology and Industrial History/
James R. Muldowney Printing Museum,
309
Time Museum, 100
U.S. Army Communications-Electronics
Museum, 225–26
U.S. Patent and Trademark Museum, 365

Vacuum Cleaner Museum, 301
Watch and Clock Museum of the National
Association of Watch and Clock Collectors
(NAWCC), 307
Whoop-n-Holler Museum, 371
Wright Brothers National Memorial, 268

KID-FRIENDLY
Academy of Model Aeronautics/National
Model Aviation Museum, 108–9
American Computer Museum, 201
American International Rattlesnake Museum,
234
Antique Boat Museum, 254
Aurora Fossil Museum, 265
Aviation Hall of Fame and Museum of New
Jersey, 231
Babe Ruth Birthplace and Baseball Center, 149
Baltimore Museum of Industry, 149–50
Barbie Hall of Fame, 31
Boys Town Hall of History, 208
Brookhaven National Laboratory (BNL)
Science Museum, 263
Burlingame Museum of Pez Memorabilia, 31
Call of the Wild, 170
Canal Museum, 308
Carole and Barry Kaye Museum of Miniatures,
38–39
Center for Puppetry Arts, 79
Circus World Museum, 386
Colorado Railroad Museum, 50
Computer Museum, 156
Crossroads of America, 221
Dakota Dinosaur Museum, 272
Denver Museum of Miniatures, Dolls and
Toys, 48
Doyle's Unami Farms/Corn Maze, 228–29
Dr. Samuel D. Harris National Museum of
Dentistry, 150
Earth Science Museum at Brigham Young
University, 358
Fairbanks Museum and Planetarium, 361–62
Feet First, 94
Furniture Discovery Center and the Furniture
Hall of Fame, 267
Grand Mound Interpretive Center, 179
Hall of Flame Museum of Firefighting, 17
Herreshoff Marine Museum/America's Cup
Hall of Fame, 321–22
Hertzberg Circus Collection and Museum, 354
Higgins Armory Museum, 166

Indian Motocycle Museum and Hall of Fame, 163
International Checker Hall of Fame, 188
International Kite Museum, 344
John James Audubon Museum and Nature Center, 131
Juliette Gordon Low Girl Scout National Center, 83
Kentucky Coal Mining Museum, 129
Kit Carson County Carousel, 46
Lawrence L. Lee Scouting Museum and Max I. Silber Library, 222
Louis P. Klein Broom and Brush Museum, 93–94
Maine Maritime Museum, 142
Marine Museum at Fall River, 158
Merry-Go-Round Museum, 285
Motorsports Hall of Fame of America, 174
Mount Vernon Museum of Incandescent Lighting, 151
Museum of American Heritage, 32
National Farm Toy Museum, 114
National Plastics Center and Museum, 159
National Scouting Museum, 133
Neil Armstrong Air and Space Museum, 286
New England Carousel Museum, 56
Northeast Historic Film, 143
Octagon House/America's First Kindergarten, 392
Owls Head Transportation Museum, 144–45
Pella Historical Village Museum, 117
Percussive Arts Society Museum, 294–95
Plymouth Historical Museum, 174
Prehistoric Gardens, 300
Rhode Island Fisherman and Whale Museum, 322
Seashore Trolley Museum, 144
Slater Mill Historic Site, 323
Studebaker National Museum, 110
Super Museum, 98
Teddy Bear Museum of Naples ("Frannie's"), 73
Thornton W. Burgess Museum, 163
Three Mile Island Visitors Center, 312
Tiny Town, 25
Toy and Miniature Museum of Kansas City, 194
Trash Museum/Hackensack Meadowlands Development Commission Environment Center, 226–27
Uncle Remus Museum, 82
Vermont Raptor Center, 362–63
White Pine Camp, 260
Wyandot Popcorn Museum, 283

LAW & DISORDER
American Police Center and Museum, 94
American Police Hall of Fame and Museum, 72
Billie Sol Estes Museum, 347
Billy the Kid Museum, 236
Bonnie and Clyde Festival, 136–37
Boys Town Hall of History, 208
Buford Pusser Home and Museum, 334
Carbo's Smoky Mountain Police Museum, 340
Cleveland Police Historical Society, Inc., and Museum, 278
Colorado Territorial Prison Museum, 46–47
Conspiracy Museum, The, 345
Dalton Defenders Museum, 121
Dalton Gang Hideout, 125
Fall River Historical Society, 158
Hideout, The, 387
Jesse James Farm and Museum, 194
Jesse James Wax Museum, 198–99
John Dillinger Historical Wax Museum, 109
Judiciary History Center, 88
Levi Coffin House State Historic Site, 106
Loud Cry Museum, 355
Matt's Museum, 137
Mercantile Money Museum, 197
National Civil Rights Museum, 337
National Voting Rights Museum and Institute, 6–7
New Jersey State Police Museum and Learning Center, 232
Northfield Historical Museum, 182
Old Idaho Penitentiary/History of Electricity in Idaho Museum, 90
Old Jail Art Center, 342
Old Jail Museum, 104–5
Patee House Museum/Jesse James House Museum, 197
Peace Museum, 95
Pinal County Historical Museum, 14–15
Scopes Museum/Rhea County Courthouse, 335
South Carolina Criminal Justice Hall of Fame, 325
Squirrel Cage Jail (Pottawattomie County Jail), 113
Thompson-Hickman Memorial Museum, 205
U.S. Border Patrol Museum, 347
World's Only Ku Klux Klan Museum, 326
Wyoming Frontier Prison Museum, 397

LOGGING, MINING, & FISHING

American Maple Museum, 255
Arizona Mining and Mineral Museum, 16
Arkansas Oil and Brine Museum, 26
Barnegat Bay Decoy and Baymen's Museum, 231–32
Bauxite Museum, 22
Beaver Island Historical Society/Mormon Print Shop Museum and Marine Museum, 175
Big Brutus, 126–27
Boise Basin Museum, 91
Brimstone Museum, 141
Caddo–Pine Island Oil and Historical Society Museum, 140
Camp Seven Museum, 372
Castle Rock Exhibit Hall, 371
Catfish Capitol Museum, 184
Central Nevada Museum, 217–18
Civilian Conservation Corps Museum/Higgins Lake Nursery, 174–75
Cold Spring Harbor Whaling Museum, 262
Cornish Pumping Engine and Mining Museum, 171
Cottage Grove Museum, 298
Dahlonega Courthouse Gold Museum, 81
Dave's Down to Earth Rock Shop and Prehistoric Life Museum, 96–97
Elberton Granite Museum and Exhibit, 82
Eureka Sentinel Museum, 214
Fisher Museum of Forestry, 162
Forest Capital State Cultural Museum, 74–75
Fourth Ward School Museum, 218
Franklin Mineral Museum, 226
Ghost Town Hall of Fame, 204
Hokenson Brothers Fishery, 387
Hot Springs County Historical Museum and Cultural Center, 398
John Lewis Mining and Labor Museum, 115
Kentucky Coal Mining Museum, 129
Klondike Gold Rush National Historical Park, 11
Koochiching County Historical Museum/ Bronko Nagurski Museum, 179–80
Lowell Thomas Museum, 53–54
Lumberman's Museum, 145
Maine Maritime Museum, 142
Marias Museum of History and Art, 204–5
Michigan Iron Industry Museum, 173
Minnesota Museum of Mining, 177
Montana Historical Society Museum, 202–3
Mulberry Phosphate Museum, 73

National Fish Culture Hall of Fame and Museum, 332
National Mining Hall of Fame and Museum, 51
National Museum of Coal Mining, 102
New England Maple Museum, 361
Otto Cupler Torpedo Company's Nitroglycerin Museum, 318
Pemaquid Point Lighthouse and Fisherman's Museum, 145
Penn-Brad Oil Museum, 307
Petrified Wood Park and Museum, 330
Reed Gold Mine State Historic Site, 269–70
Rollo Jamison Museum/ Mining Museum, 391
Salt Museum, 258
Searchlight Historical Museum, 217
Sweetwater County Historical Museum, 396
Thompson-Hickman Memorial Museum, 205
Tintic Mining Museum, 356–57
Twenty-Mule Team Museum, 41–42
University of Alaska Fairbanks Museum, 9
Vermont Marble Exhibit, 361
Western SkiSport Museum, 29
Yankee Fork Gold Dredge, 90–91

MEDIA & COMMUNICATIONS

American Advertising Museum, 301
American Radio Relay League/Museum of Amateur Radio, 58
Bair Drug and Hardware Co. Living Museum, 378
Cle Elum Historical Telephone Museum, 371
Curt Teich Postcard Exhibit and Archives, 101
Dr. Kate Museum, 392–93
Eureka Sentinel Museum, 214
Farnsworth TV Pioneer Museum (Jefferson County Historical Society), 92
Folger Shakespeare Library, 65
French Cable Station Museum, 161–62
H. H. Bennett Studio Foundation Museum, 392
Karpeles Manuscript Library Museum, 71
Lancaster Newspapers Newseum, 311
Lum 'n' Abner Museum and Jot 'Em Down Store, 26
Macculloch Hall Historical Museum, 228
Minnesota Museum of Mining, 177
Museum of American Political Life, 60
Museum of Independent Telephony, 120
Museum of Postal History (Delphos, OH), 279–80
Museum of Postal History (NYC), 249

Museum of the American Printing House for the Blind, 133
National Liars Hall of Fame, 209
Navajo Code Talkers Room, 236
Original Pony Express Home Station No. 1 Museum, 124–25
Paper House, 162
Parks Telephone Museum, 100
Patee House Museum/Jesse James House Museum, 197
Rosenbach Museum and Library, 316
Ryther Printing Museum, 124
Sinclair Lewis Boyhood Home, 182–83
Telephone Museum, 79
Thomas Newcomen Library and Museum in Steam Technology and Industrial History/James R. Muldowney Printing Museum, 309
Thorniley Collection of Type, 377
U.S. Army Communications-Electronics Museum, 225–26
U.S. Army Signal Corps Museum, 82–83
Vintage Telephone Equipment, 377–78
W. H. Tupper General Merchandise Museum & Louisiana Telephone Pioneer Museum, 137
Wolfsonian, The (formerly Collection of Decorative and Propaganda Arts), 72–73
Words and Pictures Museum of Fine Sequential Art, 160

MILITARY

Air Heritage Museum and Aircraft Restoration Facility, 305–6
Alaska Aviation Heritage Museum, 8
Bataan Memorial Military Museum & Library, 241
Bennington Museum, 359
Blaine County Museum, 202
Bob Burns Museum, 27
Champlin Fighter Aircraft Museum, 16
City of Las Vegas Museum and Rough Riders Memorial Collection, 237
Clara Barton National Historic Site, 152–53
Colorado Ski Museum–Ski Hall of Fame, 53
Columbia River Exhibition of History, Science, and Technology, 376
Corner Drug Store, 190
Cornish Pumping Engine and Mining Museum, 171
Cut and Thrust Edged Weapons Museum/Co-op Gallery, 310
Dennison Railroad Depot Museum, 280
Fort Delaware, 63
Fred E. Weisbrod Aircraft Museum/International B-24 Museum, 52
Frontier Relics Museum, 14
General Lewis B. Hershey Museum, 103
Great Plains Black Museum, 211–12
Higgins Armory Museum, 166
Historical Electronics Museum, 153
International Mother's Day Shrine, 382–83
Japanese Cultural Center of Hawaii, 88
John F. Kennedy Special Warfare Museum, 266
Matt's Museum, 137
Monroe County Historical Museum, 173
National Atomic Museum, 235
National Cryptologic Museum, 152
National Knife Museum, 335
National Museum of Civil War Medicine, 152
Navajo Code Talkers Room, 236
New Bern Civil War Museum, 268
Parris Island Museum, 326
Paterson Museum/Rogers Mill, 230
Phelps County Historical Museum, 210
Pig War Museum, 373
Presidents Cottage Museum, 384
Remington Firearms Museum and Country Store, 257
Skenesborough Museum/Whitehall Urban Cultural Park Visitor Center, 260–61
Springfield Armory National Historic Site, 163
Titan Missile Museum, 15
Trianon Museum and Art Gallery, 48
UDT-SEAL Museum, 70
U.S. Army Chemical Corps Museum, 3–4
U.S. Army Communications-Electronics Museum, 225–26
U.S. Army Engineer Museum, 191–92
U.S. Army Signal Corps Museum, 82–83
Western SkiSport Museum, 29
Wheels Through Time Museum, 99
William Breman Jewish Heritage Museum, 80
Wright Museum of American Enterprise, 223

MONEY & STAMPS

Cardinal Spellman Philatelic Museum, 165
Crane Museum, 157
Curt Teich Postcard Exhibit and Archives, 101
Genoa Courthouse Museum, 214–15
Higgins Foundation/National Bank Note Museum and Library, 117
Mercantile Money Museum, 197

Money Museum, 368
Museum of American Financial History, 249
Museum of Postal History (Delphos, OH),
    279–80
Museum of Postal History (NYC), 249
Museum of the American Numismatic
    Association, 47
Post Mark Collectors Club Museum, 276
Treasures of the Sea Exhibit, 63
Western SkiSport Museum, 29

MOVIES, TV, THEATER, & RADIO

Alabama Historical Radio Society/Don Kresge
    Memorial Museum, 2
American Costume Museum, 189
American Radio Relay League/Museum of
    Amateur Radio, 58
Ava Gardner Museum, 269
Birthplace of John Wayne, 119
Bob Burns Museum, 27
Cheryl Ladd Room, 329–30
Cowboys Then and Now Museum, 303
Degenhart Paperweight and Glass Museum,
    276–77
El Paisano Hotel, 350
Eureka Sentinel Museum, 214
Fairmount Historical Museum/James Dean
    Exhibit, 105
Farnsworth TV Pioneer Museum (Jefferson
    County Historical Society), 92
Folger Shakespeare Library, 65
Gene Autry Oklahoma Museum, 293
Geronimo Springs Museum, 242–43
Goulding's Museum, 358
Hello Gorgeous!!, 32
Hollywood High School Museum, 37
Hollywood Studio Museum, 37
Joe Franklin's Office, 248
Judy Garland Historical Center in the Central
    School Heritage and Arts Center, 178
Liberace Museum, 215
Lingerie Museum, 38
Lum 'n' Abner Museum and Jot 'Em Down
    Store, 26
Lunchbox Museum, 6
Magic Lantern Castle Museum, 354
Mario Lanza Museum, 315
Museum of Radio and Technology, 383
National Farm Toy Museum, 114
Northeast Historic Film, 143
Rex Allen Arizona Cowboy Museum, 21

Roy Rogers–Dale Evans Museum, 43
Science-Fantasy Preserves, 38
Searchlight Historical Museum, 217
Super Museum, 98
Tom Mix Museum, 291
Vent Haven Museum, 131
Virginia City Radio Museum, 218–19
William S. Hart Museum, 40
Wyandot Popcorn Museum, 283

MUSIC & DANCE

American Guitar Museum, 263
Band Museum, 25
Bily Clock Museum/Antonin Dvořák Exhibit,
    118
Bing Crosby Library, 378
Black Archives of Mid-America, 193
Black History Museum, 367
Bob Burns Museum, 27
Bob Wills Museum, 355
Brewer's Bell Museum, 344
Bryant's Museum (Bryant's Stoves and Music,
    Inc.), 147
Danbury Scott-Fanton Museum/Charles Ives
    House, 56–57
Delta Blues Museum, 185–86
Eubie Blake National Museum, 150–51
Eunice Museum, The, 136
Exotic World Burlesque Museum and Hall of
    Fame, 42
Folger Shakespeare Library, 65
Gene Autry Oklahoma Museum, 293
George E. Case Collection of Antique
    Keyboards, 327
Geronimo Springs Museum, 242–43
Gertrude Pridgett "Ma" Rainey House, 81
Graceland Too, 187
Great Plains Black Museum, 211–12
Hammond Museum of Bells, 24
Hank Williams, Sr., Boyhood Home and
    Museum, 4
Hello Gorgeous!!, 32
Hollywood High School Museum, 37
Hotel Turkey, 355
House of Cash, 336
Institute of Jazz Studies, 229
International Bluegrass Music Museum, 133–34
Jimmie Rodgers Museum, 187
Joe Franklin's Office, 248
John Dillinger Historical Wax Museum, 109
Johnny Mercer Museum, 79

Johnson Victrola Museum, 62–63
Koshare Indian Kiva Museum, 50–51
Lawrence Welk Museum, 43
Lee Conklin Antique Organ Museum, 170
Lefty Frizzell Country Music Museum (Pioneer Village), 344
Lenoir Museum, 339
Liberace Museum, 215
Louisiana Country Music Museum, 138
Ludwig and Christina Welk Homestead/Lawrence Welk Birthplace, 274
Marcella Sembrich Opera Museum, 253–54
Mario Lanza Museum, 315
Martin Guitar Company, 312–13
Miles Musical Museum, 24
Mummers Museum (New Year's Shooters and Mummers Museum), 315
Museum of Radio and Technology, 383
Museum of the Gulf Coast, 352–53
Music House, 167
Musical Museum, 255
Musical Wonder House, 147
National Oldtime Fiddlers Hall of Fame, 92
Nordica Homestead Museum, 143
Old U.S. Mint: New Orleans Jazz Collection and Carnival Exhibit, 139–40
Old West Museum, 329
Original American Kazoo Company Factory and Museum, 256
Patsy Cline at the Kurtz Cultural Center, 369
Percussive Arts Society Museum, 294–95
Pink Palace Museum, 337
Rose Museum at Carnegie Hall, 249–50
Scott Joplin House State Historic Site, 198
Shrine to Music Museum, 333
Sincerely Elvis, 338
Smitty's Juke Box Museum, 351–52
Stephen C. Foster Memorial, 318
Stephen Foster State Folk Culture Center, 76
Streitwieser Foundation Trumpet Museum, 318
Surf Ballroom, 113
Tabor Opera House, 51
Ted Lewis Museum, 278
Templeton Music Museum and Archives, 188
Tomb of Mystery Museum, 4
Totem Pole Park, 292
W. C. Handy Home, Museum, and Library, 3
Windmill Museum/Tex Ritter Museum, 351

NATURE & OUTDOORS

American Maple Museum, 255
American Museum of Fly Fishing, 360–61
Arizona-Sonora Desert Museum, 20
Bailey-Mathews Shell Museum, 75
Bakken, The: A Library and Museum of Electricity in Life, 181
Barnegat Bay Decoy and Baymen's Museum, 231–32
Birds of Vermont Museum, 360
Call of the Wild, 170
Castle Rock Exhibit Hall, 371
Civilian Conservation Corps Museum/Higgins Lake Nursery, 174–75
Connecticut River Museum, 57
Dakota Dinosaur Museum, 272
Devil's Millhopper State Geological Site, 70–71
Dorflinger Glass Museum, 319–20
Earth Science Museum at Brigham Young University, 358
Eva Parker Woods Cottage, 85–86
Fairbanks Museum and Planetarium, 361–62
Fisher Museum of Forestry, 162
Fly Fishing Museum, 298
Fred Bear Museum, 71
Frost Entomological Museum, 319
Hayden Prairie, 112
Historic Bartram's Garden, 315
Hoh Rain Forest Visitors Center, 372
International Bioregional Old Route 66 Visitors Center and Preservation Foundation, 15
International Fly Fishing Center, 203
International Wolf Center, 177–78
John Hutching's Museum of Natural History, 357
John James Audubon Museum and Nature Center, 131
John May Museum Center, 47
Lawrence L. Lee Scouting Museum and Max I. Silber Library, 222
Lightning Field, The, 239
Limberlost State Historic Site, 106
Lotusland, 34–35
Luhr Jensen Fishing Tackle Museum, 298–99
Martin and Osa Johnson Safari Museum, 121
Mister Ed's Elephant Museum, 313
Museum of the Berkeley Springs, 382
Museum of Western Colorado, 50
National Buffalo Museum, 273

National Fish Culture Hall of Fame and
Museum, 332
National Scouting Museum, 133
No Man's Land Historical Museum, 293
Noyes Museum of Art, 229
Nylander Museum, 143
Ocean City Life-Saving Station Museum, 153–54
Of Sea and Shore Museum, 375
Oyster Museum, 365
Paul Jensen Arctic Museum, 299
Peary-MacMillan Arctic Museum, 142–43
Petrified Wood Park and Museum, 330
Pratt Museum, 9–10
Prehistoric Gardens, 300
Rhode Island Fisherman and Whale Museum,
322
Smith Soil Monolith Collection, 375
Smokejumper and Aerial Fire Depot, 203–4
Smokey Bear State Historical Park, 235
Sweetwater County Historical Museum, 396
Thornton W. Burgess Museum, 163
Trash Museum/Hackensack Meadowlands
Development Commission Environment
Center, 226–27
Vermont Raptor Center, 362–63
Wave Hill, 245
Wendell Gilley Museum, 147
White Pine Camp, 260

POLITICS & GOVERNMENT
American Bicentennial Museum, 2
American Labor Museum/ Botto House
National Landmark, 226
Billie Sol Estes Museum, 347
Blaine County Historical Museum, 91
Bread and Puppet Museum, 360
Center for Political and Governmental History,
135–36
Civilian Conservation Corps Museum/Higgins
Lake Nursery, 174–75
Clear Lake Historical Museum, 387
Conspiracy Museum, The, 345
Dan Quayle Center and Museum, 107
Eugene V. Debs Home, 110
Floyd County Historical Society Museum, 112
Forbes Magazine Galleries, 247–48
Gallery of Also-Rans, 125–26
Garibaldi and Meucci Museum of the Order
Sons of Italy in America, 252

George and Lurleen Wallace Center for the
Study of Southern Politics, 6
George Meany Memorial Archives, 154
Great Plains Black Museum, 211–12
Homesteads Tower Museum, 335
House of the Temple Library/Museum, 66
Jim Bowie Museum, 140
John Lewis Mining and Labor Museum, 115
Karpeles Manuscript Library Museum, 71
Labor Hall of Fame, 66
Labor Museum and Learning Center of
Michigan, 170
Levi Coffin House State Historic Site, 106
Museum of American Political Life, 60
Museum of the American Presidency, 45
National Civil Rights Museum, 337
National Cryptologic Museum, 152
National Gallery of Caricature and Cartoon Art,
66–67
National Voting Rights Museum and Institute,
6–7
Peace Museum, 95
Presidents Cottage Museum, 384
Prudence Crandall Museum, 56
Ronald Reagan Presidential Library and
Museum, 41
Sequoyah Birthplace Museum, 341
Tamiment Institute Library/Wagner Labor
Archives, 250
Titan Missile Museum, 15
Valley Park Shortline Railroad/Agriculture/
Historic Museum (C. B. "Buddie" Newman
Museum), 189
Winston Churchill Memorial and Library in the
United States, 192
Wolfsonian, The (formerly Collection of
Decorative and Propaganda Arts), 72–73
Youngstown Historical Center of Industry and
Labor, 287

RELIGION & PHILOSOPHY
African Art Museum of the S.M.A. Fathers, 231
American Museum of Asmat Art/Bishop
Sowada Gallery, 183
A. R. Mitchell Memorial Museum of Western
Art, 53
Ave Maria Grotto, 1–2
Bailey House Museum (Maui Historical Soci-
ety Museum), 87

Beaver Island Historical Society/Mormon Print Shop Museum and Marine Museum, 175
Bob Jones University Art Gallery and Museum, 326
Creation Evidences Museum, 348
Damien Museum and Archives, 87
Don Brown Rosary Collection, 379
Eldridge Street Synagogue, 247
Emy-Lou Biedenharn Foundation, 138
First National Church of the Exquisite Panic, 247
Fruitlands Museums, 158–59
Garden of Eden and Cabin Home, 124
Gold Pyramid House, 101
Harmony Museum, 309–10
House of the Temple Library/Museum, 66
Indian Temple Mound Museum, 70
Jacques Marchais Museum of Tibetan Art, 252
James L. Kelso Bible Lands Museum, 317
John G. Neihardt Center, 208
Judaica Museum, 244–45
Koreshan State Historic Site, 69–70
Living Rock Studios, 297–98
Loud Cry Museum, 355
L. Ron Hubbard Life Exhibition, 37–38
Mardi Gras Museum, 185
Marietta Johnson Museum, 2–3
Mennonite Heritage Museum, 122–23
Mount Angel Abbey Museum, 302
Museum at Lower Shaker Village, 221
Museum of Western Jesuit Missions, 192
Museum of Woodcarving, 391–92
National Jewish American Sports Hall of Fame/B'nai B'rith Klutznick National Jewish Museum, 67
Navajo Tribal Museum, 21
New Orleans Historic Voodoo Museum, 139
Oneida Nation Museum, 390
Palestinian Gardens, 187
Paradise Garden, 83
Parker Ranch Visitor Center and Museum, 85
Prabhupada's Palace of Gold, 383
Prayer Museum, 186
Saint Anne Shrine, 158
Shaker Museum, 146
Sylvia Plotkin Judaica Museum of Greater Phoenix, 17
Teutopolis Monastery Museum, 100–1
Touro Synagogue, 322
24-Hour Church of Elvis, 301
Uinta County Historical Museum, 395

U.S. Army Communications-Electronics Museum, 225–26
William Breman Jewish Heritage Museum, 80
Winston Churchill Memorial and Library in the United States, 192
World Methodist Museum, 268

RIVERS, LAKES, & OCEANS

Antique Boat Museum, 254
Bailey-Mathews Shell Museum, 75
Baltimore Public Works Museum, 150
Barnegat Bay Decoy and Baymen's Museum, 231–32
Boulder City/Hoover Dam Museum, 213
Caddo–Pine Island Oil and Historical Society Museum, 140
Campus Martius: The Museum of the Northwest Territory/Ohio River Museum, 282
Canal Museum, 308
Carpenter Museum of Antique Outboard Motors, 222
Cold Spring Harbor Whaling Museum, 262
Connecticut River Museum, 57
East Martello Museum and Gallery, 71–72
Eva Parker Woods Cottage, 85–86
Fall River Historical Society, 158
Gary J. Hebert Memorial Lockhouse, 141
Heritage *Hjemkomst* Interpretive Center, 181–82
Herreshoff Marine Museum/America's Cup Hall of Fame, 321–22
Hokenson Brothers Fishery, 387
Holland Museum (formerly the Netherlands Museum), 171
Howard Steamboat Museum, 107
Inland Seas Maritime Museum (formerly the Great Lakes Museum), 285–86
Kalmar Nyckel Foundation and Shipyard, 64
Keokuk River Museum/*George* M. *Verity*, 115
Mac's Museum, 201–2
Maine Maritime Museum, 142
Makah Cultural and Research Center, 374–75
Marine Museum at Fall River, 158
Marsh's Free Museum, 374
McLarty Treasure Museum, 72
Memory Lane Museum at Seattle Goodwill, 376–77
Motorsports Hall of Fame of America, 174
Museum of Man in the Sea, 74
Museum of the Gulf Coast, 352–53

Museum of Yachting, 322
National Fish Culture Hall of Fame and
    Museum, 332
Ocean City Life-Saving Station Museum, 153–54
Of Sea and Shore Museum, 375
Old Coast Guard Station Museum, 368
Oyster Museum, 365
Paterson Museum/Rogers Mill, 230
Peary-MacMillan Arctic Museum, 142–43
Pemaquid Point Lighthouse and Fisherman's
    Museum, 145
Rhode Island Fisherman and Whale Museum,
    322
Shore Village Museum (The Lighthouse
    Museum), 146
Skenesborough Museum/Whitehall Urban
    Cultural Park Visitor Center, 260–61
Steamship Bertrand Display, 116
Titanic Museum, 163–64
Treasures of the Sea Exhibit, 63
UDT-SEAL Museum, 70

SCIENCE & TECHNOLOGY

Alabama Historical Radio Society/Don Kresge
    Memorial Museum, 2
American Clock and Watch Museum, 56
American Computer Museum, 201
American Museum of Science and Energy, 340
American Precision Museum, 362
Arkansas Oil and Brine Museum, 26
Ashfall Fossil Beds State Park, 212
Aurora Fossil Museum, 265
Aviation Hall of Fame and Museum of New
    Jersey, 231
Bakken, The: A Library and Museum of
    Electricity in Life, 181
Baltimore Public Works Museum, Inc., 150
Belhaven Memorial Museum, 266
Big Brutus, 126–27
Blindiana/Tactual Museum/Museum on the
    History of Blindness, 164
Boulder City/Hoover Dam Museum, 213
Brookhaven National Laboratory (BNL)
    Science Museum, 263
Canal Museum, 308
Charles River Museum of Industry, 164
Cle Elum Historical Telephone Museum, 371
Cleveland Police Historical Society, Inc., and
    Museum, 278
Columbia River Exhibition of History, Science,
    and Technology, 376

Computer Museum, 156
Computer Museum of America, 44
Creation Evidences Museum, 348
Dittrick Museum of Medical History, 278–79
Eichold-Heustis Medical Museum of the
    South, 5
Elwood Haynes Museum, 108
Experimental Breeder Reactor #1, 89
Farnsworth TV Pioneer Museum (Jefferson
    County Historical Society), 92
French Cable Station Museum, 161–62
Frost Entomological Museum, 319
Gary J. Hebert Memorial Lockhouse, 141
Great Plains Black Museum, 211–12
Herbert H. Dow Historical Museum, 172
Historical Electronics Museum, 153
Indiana Medical History Museum, 107
John Gorrie State Museum, 68
Joseph Priestley House, 313
Lock Ridge Furnace Museum, 305
Los Alamos Historical Museum, 237
Magic Lantern Castle Museum, 354
Mattatuck Museum, 60
Meteorite Museum, 235
Michigan Museum of Surveying, 172
Midwest Old Threshers Heritage Museum and
    Museum of Repertoire Americana, 116
Mount Vernon Museum of Incandescent
    Lighting, 151
Mulberry Phosphate Museum, 73
Musée Mécanique, 32
Museum of American Heritage, 32
Museum of Holography, 95
Museum of Independent Telephony, 120
Museum of Jurassic Technology, 36
Museum of Man in the Sea, 74
Museum of Ophthalmology, 33
Museum of Questionable Medical Devices, 181
Museum of the Alphabet, 270
National Atomic Museum, 235
National Cryptologic Museum, 152
National Lighter Museum, 294
National Plastics Center and Museum, 159
Old Clock Museum, 351
Old Idaho Penitentiary/History of Electricity in
    Idaho Museum, 90
Outagamie Museum and Houdini Historical
    Center, 385
Parks Telephone Museum, 100
Porter Thermometer Museum (Dick Porter—
    Thermometer Man), 161

Real World Computer Museum, 306–7
Robert C. Williams American Museum of
	Papermaking, 79
Ryther Printing Museum, 124
Saylor Cement Museum, 305
Science-Fantasy Preserves, 38
Scopes Museum/Rhea County Courthouse, 335
Seashore Trolley Museum, 144
Slater Mill Historic Site, 323
Telephone Museum, 79
Teton Flood Museum, 92
Thomas A. Edison Memorial Tower and
	Museum, 227
Thomas Newcomen Library and Museum in
	Steam Technology and Industrial
	History/James R. Muldowney Printing
	Museum, 309
Three Mile Island Visitors Center, 312
Time Museum, 100
Trash Museum/Hackensack Meadowlands
	Development Commission Environment
	Center, 226–27
U.S. Army Communications-Electronics
	Museum, 225–26
U.S. Patent and Trademark Museum, 365
University of Arizona Mineral Museum, 20
Vacuum Cleaner Museum, 301
Watch and Clock Museum of the National
	Association of Watch and Clock Collectors
	(NAWCC), 307
Wilhelm Reich Museum, 145–46
Winchester Center Kerosene Lamp Museum, 61

SPORTS
Academy of Model Aeronautics/National
	Model Aviation Museum, 108–9
Aiken Thoroughbred Racing Hall of Fame and
	Museum, 324
American Museum of Fly Fishing, 360–61
American Saddlebred Horse Museum, 195
American Saddle Horse Museum, 132
Antique Boat Museum, 254
Babe Didrikson Zaharias Museum, 343
Babe Ruth Birthplace and Baseball Center, 149
Bailey House Museum (Maui Historical
	Society Museum), 87
Barnegat Bay Decoy and Baymen's Museum,
	231–32
Bob Feller Hometown Exhibit, 119
Bowling Hall of Fame and Museum, 197
Burgwardt Bicycle Museum, 259

California Surf Museum, 44
Carrie M. McLain Memorial Museum, 10
Cheyenne Frontier Days Old West Museum, 394
Clear Lake Historical Museum, 387
Colorado Ski Museum–Ski Hall of Fame, 53
Dalton Defenders Museum, 121
Dog Mushing Museum, 9
Don Garlits Museum of Drag Racing and
	International Drag Racing Hall of Fame,
	73–74
Fly Fishing Museum, 298
Fred Bear Museum, 71
Garst Museum (Darke County Historical
	Society Museum), 281
George F. Boyer Museum and National
	Marbles Hall of Fame, 232
Golf House/USGA Museum and Library, 225
Great Plains Black Museum, 211–12
Herreshoff Marine Museum/America's Cup
	Hall of Fame, 321–22
International Checker Hall of Fame, 188
International Fly Fishing Center, 203
International Tennis Hall of Fame and
	Museum, 322
Jack Dempsey Museum, 51–52
Koochiching County Historical Museum/
	Bronko Nagurski Museum, 179–80
Lacrosse Hall of Fame Museum, 151
Luhr Jensen Fishing Tackle Museum, 298–99
Marias Museum of History and Art, 204–5
Motorcycle Heritage Museum, 286
Motorsports Hall of Fame of America, 174
Museum of Family Camping, 220–21
Museum of Man in the Sea, 74
Museum of the Gulf Coast, 352–53
Museum of Yachting, 322
National Balloon Museum, 114
National Bird Dog Museum and Field Trial Hall
	of Fame, 336
National Farm Toy Museum, 114
National Jewish American Sports Hall of
	Fame/B'nai B'rith Klutznick National
	Jewish Museum, 67
National Jousting Hall of Fame, 366
National Museum of Roller Skating, 210–11
National Soaring Museum, 256
National Sprint Car Hall of Fame and Museum,
	115
National Wrestling Hall of Fame and Museum,
	296
Negro Leagues Baseball Museum, 193–94

New England Ski Museum, 221–22

NMPA Stock Car Hall of Fame/Joe Weatherly Museum, 325

Ocean City Life-Saving Station Museum, 153–54

Paul W. Bryant Museum, 7

Pendleton Round-up Hall of Fame, 300

Remington Firearms Museum and Country Store, 257

Richard Petty Museum, 269

Roger Maris Museum, 272

Saint Charles Archery Museum, 377

Santa Cruz Surfing Museum, 35

Skenesborough Museum/Whitehall Urban Cultural Park Visitor Center, 260–61

South Dakota Amateur Baseball Hall of Fame, 330

Trapshooting Hall of Fame and Museum, 285

U.S. Bicycling Hall of Fame, 230–31

U.S. Chess Hall of Fame and Museum, 67

U.S. Hockey Hall of Fame, 178

U.S. National Ski Hall of Fame and Ski Museum, 171

U.S. Slo-Pitch Softball Association Hall of Fame Museum, 367

Water Ski Museum–Hall of Fame, 76

Weightlifting Hall of Fame, 320

Western SkiSport Museum, 29

Wheels Through Time Museum, 99

World Figure Skating Museum and Hall of Fame, 47

TOYS, GAMES, DOLLS, & MINIATURES

Academy of Model Aeronautics/National Model Aviation Museum, 108–9

American Museum of Magic, 172

Ave Maria Grotto, 1–2

Barbara Barbe Doll Museum, 276

Barbie Hall of Fame, 31

Bauer Toy Museum, 348

Bird's Eye View Museum of Miniatures, 110

Burlingame Museum of Pez Memorabilia, 31

Carole and Barry Kaye Museum of Miniatures, 38–39

Center for Puppetry Arts, 79

Colorado Railroad Museum, 50

Crossroads of America, 221

Denver Museum of Miniatures, Dolls and Toys, 48

Dougherty House–Victorian Wedding Museum, 282

Fairbanks Museum and Planetarium, 361–62

Fly Fishing Museum, 298

Forbes Magazine Galleries, 247–48

Furniture Discovery Center and the Furniture Hall of Fame, 267

George F. Boyer Museum and National Marbles Hall of Fame, 232

Indian Motocycle Museum and Hall of Fame, 163

Inland Seas Maritime Museum (formerly the Great Lakes Museum), 285–86

International Kite Museum, 344

Kemerer Museum of Decorative Arts, 306

Louis P. Klein Broom and Brush Museum, 93–94

Marvin's Marvelous Mechanical Museum, 169

Musée Mécanique, 32

Museum of Miniature Houses and Other Collections, 104

National Farm Toy Museum, 114

National Video Game and Coin-Op Museum, 198

New England Carousel Museum, 56

Old West Museum, 329

Patent Model Museum, 24–25

Plymouth Historical Museum, 174

Rockwell Museum, 254–55

Teddy Bear Museum of Naples ("Frannie's"), 73

Tiny Town, 25

Toy and Miniature Museum of Kansas City, 194

Treasures of the Sea Exhibit, 63

U.S. Chess Hall of Fame and Museum, 67

Van Horn's Antique Truck Museum and Circus Room Display, 115–16

Victorian Doll Museum and Chili Doll Hospital, 258–59

World Famous Fantastic Museum (OR), 303

World Famous Fantastic Museum (WA), 380

World Kite Museum and Hall of Fame, 374

TRAVEL & LEISURE

Academy of Model Aeronautics/National Model Aviation Museum, 108–9

American Airlines C. R. Smith Museum, 347–48

American Diner Museum, 323

American Hop Museum, 379–80

American Museum of Fly Fishing, 360–61

Antique Boat Museum, 254

Atlantic City Historical Museum, 224–25

Barnum Museum, 55

Beer Can House, 349

Bridgehampton Historical Museum, 261
Burgwardt Bicycle Museum, 259
California Route 66 Museum, 42
California Surf Museum, 44
Camp Washington-Carver, 382
Campus Martius: The Museum of the Northwest
    Territory/Ohio River Museum, 282
Canal Museum, 308
Carpenter Museum of Antique Outboard
    Motors, 222
Coney Island Museum and Sideshows-by-the-
    Seashore, 245–46
Curt Teich Postcard Exhibit and Archives, 101
Dennison Railroad Depot Museum, 280
Devil's Rope Museum and Route 66 Museum,
    351
Dixie Truckers Home and Route 66 Hall of
    Fame, 97–98
Fly Fishing Museum, 298
Fordyce Bathhouse Visitor Center, 25
General Petroleum Museum, 376
George F. Boyer Museum and National
    Marbles Hall of Fame, 232
Germaine Cazenave Wells Mardi Gras
    Museum, 138–39
Golf House/USGA Museum and Library, 225
Green-Wood Cemetery, 246
Greyhound Bus Origin Center, 178–79
Harley-Davidson Motorcycle Plant and
    Museum (Rodney C. Gott Museum), 320
Harvey House Museum, 122
Hertzberg Circus Collection and Museum, 354
H. H. Bennett Studio Foundation Museum, 392
Howard Steamboat Museum, 107
International Bioregional Old Route 66 Visitors
    Center and Preservation Foundation, 15
International Checker Hall of Fame, 188
International Fly Fishing Center, 203
International Kite Museum, 344
International Tennis Hall of Fame and
    Museum, 322
International Towing and Recovery Hall of
    Fame and Museum, 335
International UFO Museum and Research
    Center, 240
Julia C. Bullette Red Light Museum, 218
Kentucky Avenue Museum, 225
Lawrence L. Lee Scouting Museum and Max I.
    Silber Library, 222

Liberty Belle Antique Slot Machine Collection,
    217
Lightner Museum, 75
Little A'Le'Inn/Area 51 Research Center, 216
Lucy the Margate Elephant, 227
Luhr Jensen Fishing Tackle Museum, 298–99
Lunchbox Museum, 6
Mardi Gras Museum, 185
Marine Museum at Fall River, 158
Marland Station Wall of Memories, 294
Martin and Osa Johnson Safari Museum, 121
Marvin's Marvelous Mechanical Museum, 169
McDonald's Museum, 95–96
Miles Musical Museum, 24
Motorcycle Heritage Museum, 286
Mummers Museum (New Year's Shooters and
    Mummers Museum), 315
Musée Mécanique, 32
Museum of Beverage Containers and
    Advertising, 338
Museum of Family Camping, 220–21
Museum of the Berkeley Springs, 382
Museum of Yachting, 322
National Balloon Museum, 114
National Museum of Roller Skating, 210–11
National Road/Zane Grey Museum, 284
National Soaring Museum, 256
New England Carousel Museum, 56
Ocean City Life-Saving Station Museum,
    153–54
Oklahoma Route 66 Museum, 290–91
Old U.S. Mint: New Orleans Jazz Collection and
    Carnival Exhibit, 139–40
Overland Trail Museum, 52–53
Petrified Wood Park and Museum, 330
Pioneer Auto Show, 331
Presidents Cottage Museum, 384
Red Hook Brewery, 222–23
RV/MH Heritage Foundation/Hall of
    Fame/Museum/Library, 105
Saint Charles Archery Museum, 377
Santa Cruz Surfing Museum, 35
Seashore Trolley Museum, 144
Seaside Museum and Historical Society, 302–3
Shady Dell RV Park and Campground, 13
Smitty's Juke Box Museum, 351–52
Space Murals Museum, 238–39
Streitwieser Foundation Trumpet Museum, 318
Super Museum, 98

UFO Enigma Museum, 240
UFO Museum, 301
United States Bicycling Hall of Fame, 230–31
U.S. Slo-Pitch Softball Association Hall of
    Fame Museum, 367
Warren L. Fuller Breweriana Collection, 186
Water Ski Museum–Hall of Fame, 76
White Pine Camp, 260
World Famous Fantastic Museum (OR), 303
World Famous Fantastic Museum (WA), 380
World Kite Museum and Hall of Fame, 374

WHEELS & RAIL
Auburn-Cord-Duesenberg Museum, 103–4
Brimstone Museum, 141
Bryant's Museum (Bryant's Stoves and Music,
    Inc.), 147
Burgwardt Bicycle Museum, 259
California Route 66 Museum, 42
Carhenge, 207
Casey Jones Museum, 189–90
Chevyland U.S.A., 210
Colorado Railroad Museum, 50
Crossroads of America, 221
Curt Teich Postcard Exhibit and Archives, 101
Deere & Co. Administrative Center, 98
Dennison Railroad Depot Museum, 280
Devil's Rope Museum and Route 66 Museum,
    351
Dixie Truckers Home and Route 66 Hall of
    Fame, 97–98
Elwood Haynes Museum, 108
Floyd County Historical Society Museum, 112
Garst Museum (Darke County Historical
    Society Museum), 281
Geographical Center Pioneer Village and
    Museum, 274
Greyhound Bus Origin Center, 178–79
Harley-Davidson Motorcycle Plant and
    Museum (Rodney C. Gott Museum), 320
Hartung's License Plate and Automotive
    Museum, 97
Harvey House Museum, 122
Hawaiian Railway Society, 87
Hays Antique Truck Museum, 30
High Plains Museum, 123
Hinckley Fire Museum, 179
Indian Motocycle Museum and Hall of Fame,
    163

International Towing and Recovery Hall of
    Fame and Museum, 335
Labor Museum and Learning Center of
    Michigan, 170
Lee Way Motor Freight Museum, 295
Marland Station Wall of Memories, 294
Max Nordeen's Wheels Museum, 102
Midwest Old Threshers Heritage Museum
    and Museum of Repertoire Americana,
    116
Mifflinburg Buggy Museum, 312
Minnesota Museum of Mining, 177
Motorcycle Heritage Museum, 286
Motorsports Hall of Fame of America, 174
Muscle Car Ranch, 289–90
Museum of Alaska Transportation and Industry,
    11–12
National Corvette Museum, 129
National Motorcycle Museum and Hall of
    Fame, 332
National Road/Zane Grey Museum, 284
National Sprint Car Hall of Fame and Museum,
    115
NMPA Stock Car Hall of Fame/Joe Weatherly
    Museum, 325
Oklahoma Route 66 Museum, 290–91
Old West Museum, 329
Owls Head Transportation Museum, 144–45
Pioneer Auto Show, 331
Plymouth Historical Museum, 174
Richard Petty Museum, 269
RV/MH Heritage Foundation/Hall of
    Fame/Museum/Library, 105
Seashore Trolley Museum, 144
Shady Dell RV Park and Campground, 13
Southeast Museum, 254
Stanley Museum, 144
Studebaker National Museum, 110
United States Bicycling Hall of Fame, 230–31
Valley Park Shortline Railroad/Agriculture/
    Historic Museum (C. B. "Buddie" Newman
    Museum), 189
Van Horn's Antique Truck Museum and Circus
    Room Display, 115–16
Walter P. Chrysler Boyhood Home and
    Museum, 122
Warther Museum, 280
Wheels Through Time Museum, 99
Whoop-n-Holler Museum, 371

Little Museums Fans!

We'd love to get your input. Send us your special finds and not-to-be-missed nearby attractions, tell us about your favorite little spots (domestic and global) and what you think about ours, and please do send in any corrections or changes to the listings inside. We invite you to stop by our website and check out our updates and new discoveries online.

Website: http://www.littlemuseums.com

E-mail: authors@littlemuseums.com

Snail Mail: Little Museums
Ink Projects
511 Avenue of the Americas
Rm. 296
NY, NY 10011